Cost Accounting:
A Decision Emphasis

Fourth Edition

Germain B. Böer
Vanderbilt University

William L. Ferrara
Stetson University

Debra C. Jeter
Vanderbilt University

Lamont F. Steedle
Towson State University

Charles J. Pineno
Clarion University

2001

DAME
Thomson Learning™

Australia • Canada • Denmark • Japan • Mexico • New Zealand • Philippines
Puerto Rico • Singapore • South Africa • Spain • United Kingdom • United States

Cost Accounting: A Decision Emphasis—Fourth Edition, by Germain Böer, William L. Ferrara, Debra C. Jeter, Lamont F. Steedle, and Charles J. Pineno

Desktop Publishing: Sheryl New

Graphic Artists: Sheryl New

Cover Design: Andrea P. Leggett

Cover Photos: © Corel Professional Photos and WordPerfect. Images may have been combined and/or modified to produce final cover art.

Printer: Braun-Brumfield, Inc. / Sheridan Books, Inc.

Printed in the United States of America

4 5 6 7 04 03 02 01

For more information contact Thomson Learning Custom Publishing, 5101 Madison Road, Cincinnati, Ohio, 45227, 1-800-355-9983 or find us on the Internet at http://www.custom.thomsonlearning.com

For permission to use material from this text or product, contact us by:
- telephone: 1-800-730-2214
- fax: 1-800-730-2215
- web: http://www.thomsonrights.com

Library of Congress Cataloging-in-Publication Data: 00-131995

ISBN 0-87393-912-3

This text is printed on acid-free paper.

PREFACE

We have continued to make changes in the text to address issues faced by modern day managers. This edition includes a new opening chapter that introduces students to problems faced by todays managers; Chapter 12 is a completely new chapter that covers the use of contribution accounting in managing a modern business, and Chapter 15 has been completely rewritten to clearly focus on the relevant issues.

We have maintained the integration of modern manufacturing concepts, computer data bases, and management decision making so the student studies these issues in a coherent context. Businesses large and small use data bases to capture and store operating data, and this book recognizes this reality by bringing these concepts into the world of cost and management accounting. Throughout the first seven chapters we demonstrate how management accounting systems function in a world of databases. We introduce this information in a natural manner that is consistent with the way accountants use computers.

The concept of just in time manufacturing appears throughout the book, and students learn to think about, evaluate and compare these systems to the traditional cost accounting systems still used by many companies. We also refer to real companies throughout the text. For example, we use Compaq Computers in our discussion of cost-volume-profit analysis, Caterpillar, Inc., in our coding discussion, and Joslin Sign Company in our discussion of job order costing. We also use real cases whenever possible in the problems at the end of each chapter.

Throughout the early sections we make a clear distinction between information managers use for decision making and information they must provide to external stakeholders. Product costs, for instance, used for management decisions differ from the ones used for external reporting. We emphasize this difference in Chapter 7 with several examples.

The book has eighteen chapters. The first chapters deal with fundamentals like cost accounting for operations, planning and control of manufacturing costs, marketing and the planning and control of profits, and capital budgeting and cash flows. The remaining chapters cover special integrative issues like by-products and joint products, divisional performance and transfer pricing, environmental costs, and a closing chapter on management accounting and the future.

This text should serve students well who have already completed an introduction to management accounting. However, it should also work in a two semester sequence where students have not previously had an introduction to management accounting.

For the students who already have a foundation in introductory managerial accounting, a variety of ways to sequence the contents of the book exist. We have presented the information in a manner that leaves the instructor free to exercise his or her discretion and preferences in organizing the contents of the course. The authors wish to express their appreciation to the Institute of Certified Management Accountants (U.S.), The Society of Management Accountants of Canada, The American Institute of CPA's and the Canadian Institute of Chartered Accountants for their permission to use problems based upon their respective professional examinations.

TABLE OF CONTENTS

TABLE OF CONTENTS IN DETAIL

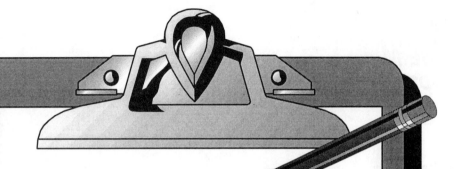

Learning Objectives

After reading this chapter, the student should have an understanding of:

✔ The management accounting approach.

✔ Management accounting at different organizational levels.

✔ Responsibility accounting.

✔ Planning and control decisions.

✔ Standards of ethical conduct.

THE MANAGEMENT ACCOUNTING APPROACH

Modern cost accounting provides essential information to all levels of management for their decision making. In today's business world, the study of current cost accounting concepts and techniques yields insights into both the manager's role and the management account-ant's role in an organization. Today's management accountant spends far more time on strategic planning, internal control and computer-based operations and much less time on traditional accounting functions than in the past. Corporations considered on the leading edge of management accounting practices include such names as **Abbott Laboratories, Boeing, Caterpillar, Hewlett-Packard** and **U.S. West**.

The manager who faces a decision armed with a complete set of information and analyses has a distinct advantage over an equally talented but less fully equipped decision maker. The purpose of management accounting is to provide managers with complete and detailed analyses subject to certain cost-benefit constraints. Whether a manager faces a routine, daily "rubber stamp" decision or one that involves the implementation of a breathtakingly innovative idea, well organized information helps the manager do what is best for the company. Because of the vast range of possibilities, management accountants face an exciting but challenging task. No set of rigid rules or principles exists to lead them through this process; instead, management accounting information should be organized in whatever manner is clearest, most understandable, and most appropriate to the problem at hand.

According to the Institute of Management Accountants (IMA), in the promulgated statement "Definition of Management Accounting," management accounting is defined as:

Management accounting is the process of identification, measurement, accumulation, analysis, preparation, interpretation, and communication of financial information used by management to plan, evaluate, and control within an organization and to assure appropriate use of and accountability for its resources. Management accounting also comprises the preparation of financial reports for non-management groups such as shareholders, creditors, regulatory agencies, and tax authorities.

▸ *THE CHANGING WORLD OF MANAGEMENT ACCOUNTING* ◂

Management accounting is a constantly evolving field that adapts, assimilates, and shifts into new shapes as managers face problems that require the use of data for planning, managing, and controlling operations. What is now called management accounting began life under the label "cost accounting" at some point in the distant past, and split off from cost accounting some time in the 1950's when management accounting textbooks first appeared. To help get some idea of where we are now, we review some of the concepts related to management accounting that are changing.

▸ *Shift from "Costing" Emphasis to "Decision Making" Emphasis*

In the early days cost accounting was very different than today. Consider the following quote from a 1919 cost accounting book describing the procedures accountants should use to prepare cost sheets (sheets on which the product costs were summarized):[1]

The procedure in handling cost sheets may be summarized as:

1. Preparing the cost sheets.
2. Posting the information as shown by the detailed material, labor, overhead, and production reports.
3. Compiling and proving the costs; that is, adding the departmental material, labor, and overhead costs and transferring the results to the summary of costs so as to show the job, order, or article cost.
4. Checking and comparing the costs so that discrepancies may be eliminated and true costs established.
5. Disposing of the cost sheets, which would include transferring the costs to:
   a. The production reports
   b. Stock records
   c. Plant asset records
   d. Other summaries

This book was focused exclusively on procedures that accountants follow to track and report costs. The student who completed this book could tell a company what forms to use, how to file them, and how to extract data from them for reports, but he or she would have little conceptual framework for thinking about how managers, or anyone else, would use the information. One writer described the difference between cost accounting and management accounting in these words:

"...cost accounting texts dealt entirely with numbers, while management accounting recognizes that human beings use the numbers."[2]

---

[1] *Cost Accounting*, by Nicholson, J. L. and J. R. D. Rohrbach, 1919, New York, NY: The Ronald Press Company.
[2] "Reminiscences About Management Accounting" by R. N. Anthony, *Journal of Management Accounting Research*, Fall 1989, pp. 1-20.

Not surprisingly, the contents of cost accounting books changed over the years. The number of chapters devoted to inventory valuation (costing of inventory) declined from 73% in the 1945-50 period to 46% by the 1970's; chapters devoted to cost control remained the same during this period; and chapters devoted to management decision-making increased from 6% in the early period to 33% in the 1970's.[3] In essence, we could argue that the current text is devoted almost 100% to management decision-making in one form or another, and the tools that help make those decisions.

> Managers make decisions and monitor subordinates who make decisions. Some of the knowledge used to make decisions comes from the accounting system. Likewise, accounting numbers such as costs, revenues, and profits are used to evaluate the performance of managers and their subordinates. Therefore, many managers use accounting data to some extent for operational decision making and performance evaluation.[4]

As the textbooks changed, so did the accounting profession. The professional organization that counts management accountants as its primary membership, the Institute of Management Accountants, has also evolved over time. Founded in 1919 as the National Association of Cost Accountants (NACA) with 37 members, the organization was started to provide a forum for industrial accountants to share experiences and to attack problems they faced that were unique to internal accountants. For example, during World War I the U.S. government purchased materials from companies using "cost plus" contracts, but there was much confusion about how cost should be computed under these contracts. This was one of the first issues tackled by the new organization.

The organization grew, matured, and broadened its focus from just cost accounting to issues related to management control. The development of computerized accounting systems starting in the 1950's enabled accountants to provide a much broader range of services to company managers, and the organization recognized this in 1957 when it dropped the word "Cost" from its name and became the National Association of Accountants (NAA). As the role of the internal accountant grew to encompass more duties such as financial analysis and financial management, the organization changed its name again in 1991 to the Institute of Management Accountants (IMA).

A recent study of more than three hundred veteran practitioners by the IMA found that the nature of work performed by management accountants has changed significantly over time. Approximately four-fifths of the practitioners participating in the study spend more time analyzing information and participating in decision-making than five years earlier. They also spend more time on activities such as strategic planning, internal consulting, process improvement, and performance evaluation than previously.

---

[3] "Cost and Management Accounting: Yesterday and Today," by C. T. Horngren, *Journal of Management Accounting Research,* Fall 1989, pp. 21-32.
[4] *Accounting for Decision Making and Control* by J. L. Zimmerman, Second Edition, 1997, Chicago, IL: Irwin.

▸ Shift to Increasing Emphasis on Services

The U.S. economy has experienced enormous growth in the service sector since the time when the early cost accounting books were written. The following graph contrasts the manufacturing and non-manufacturing sectors in terms of employment from 1948 to 1998. As this graph shows, the number of workers in manufacturing has remained almost steady for this period while the number in other types of employment has grown significantly.

A look at Gross Domestic Product (GDP) provides further evidence of this shift to services; the following chart presents GDP (adjusted for price level changes) generated by services and durable goods plus nondurable goods for 1929 through 1998, with the GDP for durable goods plus nondurable goods used as a proxy for the GDP for the manufacturing sector. A calculation of the fraction of total GDP produced by the service portion of the economy shows that it has grown from 29% in 1929 to over 40% in 1998.

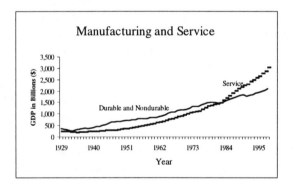

In this text we strive to introduce and illustrate concepts that are equally applicable to service enterprises and manufacturing or merchandising concerns. Although the term "management accounting" is still sometimes used interchangeably with "cost accounting," management accounting deals with far more than cost calculations. Among the other issues arising in the business world and addressed in this text are ethical issues, quality control, and environmental concerns. Management accountants play a role not only in tracking costs, but also in planning and controlling the business as a whole. For example, there has been a dramatic transformation of the workplace. Shop floor teams or work groups have been granted increased control over their own actions compared to a worker in a traditional assembly line. This increased control is known as worker empowerment. Companies that empower their work groups raise a number of questions that require the use of accounting to constrain the range of acceptable managerial behavior or action. Management accounting in the social constitution of work groups and work place transformation can make a significant contribution to the ultimate success of such changes.

► NEW CONCEPTS IN MANAGEMENT ACCOUNTING ◄

The field of management accounting boasts its share of "buzz" words and popular or "new" concepts. In this section, we include a brief introduction to a few such terms and concepts, as well as some examples.

Thomas Johnson and Robert Kaplan published *Relevance Lost: The Rise and Fall of Management Accounting* in 1987, considered by some to be a landmark criticism of traditional product cost accounting techniques. Johnson and Kaplan questioned the usefulness of traditional product cost data for management decision-making, centering their criticism on the use of "outmoded cost allocation techniques that fail to reflect current production methods and cost patterns."[5] Possible alternatives for adjusting to the conditions described by Johnson and Kaplan have since emerged in accounting literature, including two basic concepts. The first, originated by Kaplan himself, is referred to as **activity-based cost management (ABCM)**. ABCM attempts to overcome the problems associated with traditional absorption cost accounting through an improved system of product costs based on their utilization of underlying activities associated with the manufacturing process. The second alternative builds on the **just-in-time inventory management** and **pull-through manufacturing methodologies** developed by the Japanese. This alternative, called the **Theory of Constraints (TOC)**, denies the relevance of product costs as a basis for decision-making in most modern production environments.

A fundamental problem in business today is that the quality of information received and the timeliness with which it is received do not lead to optimal business performance. Metrics drive business behavior and ultimate success or failure.

At the end of the sales quarter, employees in manufacturing companies get to watch the "post quarter game." The game is played by white-shirted middle managers who run around with spreadsheets trying to determine what went wrong again with the numbers. Why did the quarter turn out the way it did?

Who ordered all that inventory? Will we ever use it? If we could use the inventory, is it an asset? How much would it cost us to hold that asset? If we can't use it, how much is it worth tomorrow? Faulty metrics may generate the wrong answers. Most measures used by business managers today are based on "antiquated financial methods."[6]

---

[5] "Activity-Based Costing and the Theory of Constraints: Using Time Horizons to Resolve Two Alternative Concepts of Product Cost," by Ralph B. Fritzsch, *Journal of Applied Business Research*, Winter 1997/1998, vol. 14, issue 1, pp. 83-89.
[6] "Real-Time Performance," by Ann Grackin, *Manufacturing Systems*, April 1998, Vol. 16, issue 4, page 100.

Efforts are underway by members of the financial community, including the application of the Theory of Constraints and Activity-Based Cost Management described below, to introduce new financial concepts and systems to solve these problems. As discussed in the following sections, however, none of these techniques is appropriate for every situation.

▸ Activity-Based Cost Management

Activity-based cost management (ABCM) is a method used to compute the cost of a unit of output that requires the identification of multiple output measures, sometimes called **cost drivers**, for each of various activities involved in the production process. Activities may include such processes as setups, issuance of purchase orders, or completion of quality inspections. Once a company has determined the cost, output measures, and capacity of each activity, a process map may be constructed to show the relationship of each activity to other activities and to the products.

In contrast, traditional product costing calculates product cost on a volume-based measure such as the number of direct labor hours. Under traditional costing (sometimes called *full absorption costing*), the cost per unit of product increases (decreases) as the production level declines (rises). Cooper and Kaplan proposed ABCM as an alternative to traditional costing in 1992 in an article in which they demonstrated an aspect of activity-based costing that made use of the *practical capacity* of activities.[7] Arguing that many resource demands are not proportional to the volume of production or sale, they suggested an alternative system that estimates the cost of resources used to produce outputs. In essence the weighting system is more sophisticated, more complex, and potentially more accurate in some instances.

▸ Theory of Constraints and Throughput Analysis

The **Theory of Constraints (TOC),** largely attributed to the efforts of Eliyahi Goldratt, is a systems approach rooted in the assumption that every organization has at least one *constraining factor* that inhibits the organization's ability to meet its objectives. TOC focuses on profit maximization by assuring that the limiting factor is used to maximum efficiency. The key to profit maximization is to concentrate on producing and selling those products that provide the highest throughput per unit of constraining factor.

Throughput is the total production volume through a facility during a specified time period. It may also be thought of as the rate at which a system generates money through sales after considering material costs, commissions, and distribution cost. Throughput examines the entire process, which involves money, investment, and controls simultaneously, rather than cost management in isolation. To work effectively, the data should be in the hands of the most appropriate individual who impacts performance, not individual managers removed from daily decision-making at the enterprise level. For example, shop-floor operators may know best how to utilize the constraint, which orders generate the largest margin, etc. In its ideal form, TOC creates a powerful link between day-to-day

---

[7] "Activity-Based Systems: Measuring the Cost of Resource Usage," by Robin Cooper and Robert Kaplan, *Accounting Horizons*, September 1992, Vol. 6, issue 3, pp. 1-13.

processes—from the plant-floor operator to the executive—and the performance of the firm.[8] For service organizations and for firms with highly skilled employees, the constraint may be the time of a few key employees.

TOC has broad applications in diverse organizational settings.

TOC challenges managers to rethink some of their fundamental assumptions about how to achieve the goals of their organizations, about what they consider productive actions, and about the real purpose of cost management.[9]

The use of TOC as a management philosophy is a dynamic process, as the limiting or constraining factor is likely to shift over time. Once the constraining factor has been identified, for example, management examines whether the constraining factor can be increased. If so, some other factor may become the constraint, and the analysis must be revised based upon the new facts. Management should also continue to monitor operating expenses for labor and administration, as well as investments in inventory and productive assets.[10]

Actual small business illustration of applying TOC to improve profitability:

Daufel Enterprises is a small business that produces hand-tied fishing flies. A fishing fly consists of feathers, furs, and synthetics placed on a hook and seamed with thread. The fly tier constructs these flies to represent aquatic organisms upon which fish feed.

Two issues that conflict in the fly-tying industry are quality and speed. The faster a tier can construct a fly, the higher the profit. On the other hand, if speed is the sole focus, quality suffers.

If the Daufel brothers (who have been cited as tying some of the best patterns in the business)[11] do not personally tie the flies, their quality will suffer. Thus, in their business, the brothers' time is the constraining factor. To perform the constraint analysis, the brothers had to monitor their own time spent working on each type of fly. They knew intuitively that the Thorax Dun required more time than the others to tie. They also knew it had the lower contribution margin, so they were not surprised when the results indicated it had the lowest throughput per labor hour. However, they were surprised by other results of the throughput analysis, which ultimately suggested switching much of their effort to the Woolly Bugger, which had the next to lowest contribution margin but the second highest throughput per hour.[12]

---

[8] "Real-Time Performance," by Ann Grackin, *Manufacturing Systems*, Vol. 16, issue 4, page 100, April 1998.

[9] "IMA Issues Two New SMAs," *Strategic Finance*, by Terri Funk and Anthony Gambin, June 1999, vol. 80, issue 12, page 89.

[10] "An Application of the Theory of Constraints," by J. Gregory Bushong and John C. Talbott, *The CPA Journal*, April 1999, vol. 69, issue 4, pages 53-55.

[11] *Patterns, Hatches, Tactics, and Trout*, by Charles Meck, 1995: Vivid Publishing.

[12] "An Application of the Theory of Constraints," by J. Gregory Bushong and John C. Talbott, *The CPA Journal*, vol. 69, issue 4, pages 53-55.

▸ *Different Costs for Different Purposes*

TOC and ABCM may be argued to represent conflicting viewpoints of product cost. Faced with this conflict, the normal reaction is to ask which way is the right way. The Institute of Management Accountants (at that time the National Association of Accountants) asked this same question in its Global Solutions II seminar in May 1990.

One answer to this question is that different costs are appropriate for different uses. Given the mostly fixed nature of short-run decision costs and the generally variable nature of these costs in the long run, it follows that the product costing techniques whose assumptions about cost most closely match each situation will produce better results than methods whose assumptions are different. Since the type of costs found in short-term decision situations differ from the type in long-run decisions, different costing techniques may be appropriate in each situation. By assuming that production costs are largely fixed, Eliyahu Goldratt's Theory of Constraints appears to be most applicable for short-term decision situations.

As most of Goldratt's works are mainly concerned with production scheduling and operations, the criticism of traditional costing techniques to make short-term decisions appears justified. In contrast, the "proportionality assumption" implied in ABCM demands that most costs be treated as variable, making this method most applicable to decisions involving long-term costs (for example, in such strategic planning areas as new product introduction, new manufacturing process design, and the development of a long-term marketing strategy).[13] Although each method may be best applied either to short-term or long-term decisions, neither is particularly well-suited to the middle range of decision types involving a mix of fixed and variable elements. One possible solution, proposed by Robert Koehler, is the use of **direct costing** (described in a later chapter of this text) for continuous product costing and for financial reporting, in addition to TOC and ABCM where appropriate.[14]

▸ *Outsourcing*

One of the trends in management accounting and decision making is an increasing emphasis on outsourcing, or using external suppliers for certain products or services. The outsourcing trend is continuing to grow, in part because many businesses are dramatically changing the way in which they operate. Thus, it becomes increasingly important for management accountants to know how best to assess the desirability of the outsourcing alternative. Cash flow analyses are common here, as in many other decisions discussed throughout this text.

The desire to concentrate on core competencies in an effort to meet company objectives is one of the reasons businesses may adopt some form of outsourcing. Increasing focus on specialization provides an additional impetus for outsourcing. Staffing and outsourcing firms are among those providing outsourcing services. Accounting firms are also getting involved—not only by providing

---

[13] *Ibid.*

[14] "It's Time to Stop Overselling Activity-Based Concepts," by Robert Koehler, *Management Accounting*, September 1992, pp. 26-35.

the services themselves, but also by entering into engagements that help a business in analyzing both the need for outsourcing and how it can be most effectively implemented.[15]

Outsourcing is not without its critics. Perceived savings from an outsourcing agreement are achieved at a price. Outsourcing can lead to the risk of process inflexibility and an over-dependence on the supplier. In order for an outsourcing agreement to be successful, the organization must be prepared to spend management time—a significant commitment that is not always understood up front.[16]

One of Britain's most fashionable business strategies, outsourcing, was questioned recently by Bob Aylott, principal consultant at **KPMG Management Consulting**, who described many proponents of outsourcing as "fashion victims" and urged managers to pause and think before signing up to a process that could prove to be a big mistake. On a superficial level, outsourcing appears to be the most commercially viable choice, as cost benefits can be achieved through, for example, avoiding recruitment costs, eliminating capital requirements and sharing risks.

But what is the reality? Can external suppliers deliver 'control' more effectively? Not always. Control can come at a hidden price. For example, initial restructuring costs will be discounted over the life of the deal at an opportunity cost rate. Furthermore, the client can be required to pay an additional 'penalty' if the contract is terminated prematurely. Similarly, the organization must be able to absorb easily the changes that the supplier will inevitably bring to the client during the course of the outsourcing agreement. The supplier's main objective (cost), and the fact that the supplier is not involved with the 'politics' of the client organization, mean that the client must work to ensure that changes made are *with* the organization, not *to* it.[17]

Another example of outsourcing is **JP Morgan Investment Management's** decision to outsource its operations to **Bank of New York** (BNY), a decision that could prove a landmark move in fund management.[18] Although the strategic thinking behind the deal seems sound, the real test of success will not be clear until 2001 or 2002 when the full outsourcing should be complete and running. The outsourcing is scheduled to be carried out in stages, with the London business moving first, in the middle of the year 2000, after the Y2K ordeal has been hurdled, and the U.S. to follow in 2001.

The fund manager will be freed to concentrate on generating returns for its clients. If all goes as planned, it will place the Bank of New York ahead of the competition. The rest will be struggling to catch up. But there is a big if. First, there is little precedent for such a deal. **Mercury Asset Management** managed to sell its back office to the **Royal Bank of Scotland** in 1995. The **WM Company** won the outsourced business of **Scottish Widows** in 1996. But there has been nothing of this scale and complexity.

Second BNY will have to build from scratch the system to accommodate JP Morgan. Tom Perna, BNY's custody head, concedes they are heading into uncharted waters. The industry will watch this space very closely for any evidence of indigestion or disharmony between the two parties.[19]

---

[15] "Turning to Outsourcing," by Howard Wolosky, *The Practical Accountant,* Nov. 1997, vol. 30, issue 11, pp. 65-68.
[16] "Victims of Outsourcing 'Fashion' Fail to Count the Costs," *Management Accounting,* London, April 1998, vol. 75, issue 4, p. 10.
[17] *Ibid.*
[18] "JP Morgan's Evolutionary Leap of Faith," by Julian Marshall, *Global Investor,* May 1999, issue 122, page 3.
[19] *Ibid.*

▸ TYPES AND NATURE OF ACCOUNTING ◂

A distinction is often made between financial accounting and management accounting. Financial accounting focuses on reporting to external parties such as stockholders, government regulators and other interested parties. The financial statements prepared are based on generally accepted accounting principles. On the other hand, management accounting measures and reports financial and nonfinancial information that provides managers with the basis for making decisions to meet the organizations' goals and objectives. Since executive compensation is often directly affected by the financial results, managers rely on both financial accounting and management accounting.

Within management accounting, cost accounting measures and reports financial and nonfinancial information that relates to the acquiring and processing of resources by an organization to produce products and/or services. Other areas within management accounting include expectations and goals for the future (budgeting and forecasting), decision making (such as whether to make or buy a product), and how best to influence the behavior of personnel. Although the Institute of Management Accountants provides statements on management accounting practices, management accounting is not as restrictive as financial accounting with its generally accepted accounting principles (GAAP). Management accounting tends to be far more detailed and wide-ranging than financial accounting. The primary goal of management accounting is to provide the information internal decision-makers need to carry out their responsibilities within the organization successfully.

▸ TYPE AND SIZE OF ORGANIZATION ◂

This text emphasizes profit seeking organizations; however, many of the concepts and practices also apply to not-for-profit organizations. If profit seeking organizations are to earn reasonable profits, their managers must know and understand the financial effects of their decisions and plans. In addition, they must monitor any deviations in actual performance from planned performance. Managers of all organizations from the smallest to the largest follow variations of these practices to accomplish their goals. We illustrate these activities with budget and standard cost systems in later chapters. Specific techniques and procedures vary with the type and size of the organization; however, the basic principles of management accounting apply for all organizations.

The need for a formal accounting system increases in direct proportion to the number of operating units and management personnel in the organization. Consider, as an analogy, the case of human transportation. When they walk, individuals need no control devices. They know the route they want to follow, and their visual and auditory senses tell them whether they are on the route. However, as soon as they switch to automobiles, they need instruments. Their senses cannot gauge their speed accurately enough to keep within established limits, nor can they tell how much gas is in the tank, how much air pressure in the tires, or the rate at which the battery is charging or discharging. Flying requires more skill and more instruments to keep abreast of actual conditions and approaching difficulties. The larger and faster the airplane, the greater the need for more and better instruments; and as the plane increases in size, eventually more than one person will be required to handle it. So management hires a crew and provides it with specialized instruments. Then managers must develop a communications system to coordinate the functions of the crew.

A one-person business has little need for control data because the owner knows what has been accomplished and what is being done. However, this individual owner can still use management accounting information. For example, the owner needs information from his or her cash budget to predict the month when large cash outflows or large cash inflows will occur. This budget helps determine when a bank loan will be necessary and when the company will generate enough cash to pay off the loan. Small size does not mean a company has no use for management accounting.

At the other extreme, the multi-plant company or multi-unit organization is like the multi-engine airplane. Every crew member must know the current status and possible future problems of the mechanisms for which he or she is responsible, and other members of the flight crew must receive this data so they can evaluate its impact on the flight plan and estimated time of arrival. Just as a drop in oil line pressure reduces the total power of an airplane, a drop in efficient use of material in one operation reduces total company profits. Military planes use different controls and instruments from passenger airplanes, and firms making electronic products use different management accounting systems from those making school lockers. Different organizations facing different economic environments require different management accounting systems.

Successful organizations continuously adapt to changes in their environment and, in some cases, proactively change their environment. Today, organizations grow, merge, acquire other organizations, sell off part of their organization, and change leadership. Management accounting should help organizations recognize the need for initiating change, make these changes, and suggest the appropriate response to environmental changes as they inevitably occur.

At the company level, management accounting must be adaptable to both centralized and decentralized organizational structures to support, coordinate, and provide relevant information for decision-making activities. Although the relationship between organizational structure and management accounting information is as old as business itself, the *formal* and *systematic* consideration of this relationship may have begun when Alfred Sloan introduced responsibility accounting and profit centers at **General Motors**.

► PLANNING AND CONTROL DECISIONS ◄

Planning is implicit in the concept of control. **Planning** is deciding on an organization's objectives and goals, predicting results under alternative ways of achieving those goals, and deciding how best to attain the desired goals. **Control**, on the other hand, is taking actions that implement the planning decisions and deciding on specific *performance evaluation* techniques and the related feedback review that will help in *future* decision making. To be optimally successful, managers at all levels must know their objectives and goals; and the organization must have in place a coordinated team of employees to implement planning and control decisions.

Managers choose objectives and goals for the firm, and then build an organization to implement these objectives by selecting from among alternative methods and procedures as well as alternative combinations of physical and human resources. *Management accountants* do not necessarily choose the goals, methods, etc., but they make recommendations and place price tags on various alternatives. After making its choices, the firm has a plan of action, and the management accountant again plays an important role as the individual responsible for accumulating data and communicating information about deviations from the plan of action.

▶ STANDARDS OF ETHICAL CONDUCT FOR MANAGEMENT ACCOUNTANTS ◀

Accountants consistently rank high in public opinion surveys on ethics' qualities exhibited by members of various professions. Professional accounting organizations and educational institutions play an important role in promoting high ethical standards. For example, the Institute of Management Accountants (IMA) issued a "Standards of Ethical Conduct for Management Accountants" in 1997. Exhibit 1-1 presents the IMA's guidance on issues relating to competence, confidentiality, integrity, and objectivity. Exhibit 1-2 provides practitioners with a possible course of action when conflicts arise. The IMA provides its members with an ethics hotline service. Members can call professional counselors at the IMA to discuss and seek help with their ethical dilemmas.[20]

▶ EMPHASIS ON CASH FLOW ◀

The role of cash flow analysis (both past and future) is crucial in decision making by managers, and thus in the concepts presented in this text. The measurement of the time value of money involves the basic concepts of future value and present value of a dollar. Cash management involves the planning and control of cash to meet the day-to-day cash needs of an organization efficiently and to invest temporarily idle cash to earn a return. The statement of cash flows provides useful information to help with cash management.

▶ RESPONSIBILITY ACCOUNTING ◀

Responsibility accounting systems emphasize the human element and its effects on operations. Responsibility accounting stresses management's control of activities within the segment of the organization for which a manager is responsible. Responsibility accounting links to the delegation of authority by assigning managers responsibility for those costs and revenues they control with their decisions. Accounting information is collected and classified on the basis of the responsibility structure of the organization. This information is, in part, the same information collected for planning and external financial reporting, but is reclassified to meet responsibility accounting needs. At **Diebold, Inc.** responsibility accounting is called empowerment accounting. Increasing numbers of companies are devising internal accounting systems that show personnel how costs are generated and how they can control them.

---

[20] Details of the IMA guidance on ethical issues, including its ethics hotline, are available on its Web site (www.imanet.org).

Practitioners of management accounting and financial management have an obligation to the public, their profession, the organization they serve, and themselves to maintain the highest standards of ethical conduct. In recognition of this obligation, the Institute of Management Accountants has promulgated the following standards of ethical conduct for practitioners of management accounting and financial management. Adherence to these standards, both domestically and internationally, is integral to achieving the Objectives of Management Accounting. Practitioners of management accounting and financial management shall not commit acts contrary to these standards, nor shall they condone the commission of such acts by others within their organizations.

Competence. Practitioners of management accounting and financial management have a responsibility to:

- Maintain an appropriate level of professional competence by ongoing development of their knowledge and skills.
- Perform their professional duties in accordance with relevant laws, regulations, and technical standards.
- Prepare complete and clear reports and recommendations after appropriate analysis of relevant and reliable information.

Confidentiality. Practitioners of management accounting and financial management have a responsibility to:

- Refrain from disclosing confidential information acquired in the course of their work except when authorized, unless legally obligated to do so.
- Inform subordinates as appropriate regarding the confidentiality of information acquired in the course of their work and monitor their activities to assure the maintenance of that confidentiality.
- Refrain from using or appearing to use confidential information acquired in the course of their work for unethical or illegal advantage either personally or through third parties.

Integrity. Practitioners of management accounting and financial management have a responsibility to:

- Avoid actual or apparent conflicts of interest and advise all appropriate parties of any potential conflict.
- Refrain from engaging in any activity that would prejudice their ability to carry out their duties ethically.
- Refuse any gift, favor, or hospitality that would influence or would appear to influence their actions.
- Refrain from either actively or passively subverting the attainment of the organization's legitimate and ethical objectives.
- Recognize and communicate professional limitations or other constraints that would preclude responsible judgment or successful performance of an activity.
- Communicate unfavorable as well as favorable information and professional judgments or opinions.
- Refrain from engaging in or supporting any activity that would discredit the profession.

Objectivity. Practitioners of management accounting and financial management have a responsibility to:

- Communicate information fairly and objectively.
- Disclose fully all relevant information that could reasonably be expected to influence an intended user's understanding of the reports, comments, and recommendations presented.

Source: Institute of Management Accountants, "Standards of Ethical Conduct for Practitioners of Management Accounting and Financial Management," *Management Accounting*, July 1997, p. 21.

Exhibit 1-1 *Standards of Ethical Conduct for Practitioners of Management Accounting and Financial Management*

In applying the standards of ethical conduct, practitioners of management accounting, and financial management may encounter problems in identifying unethical behavior or in resolving an ethical conflict. When faced with significant ethical issues, practitioners of management accounting and financial management should follow the established policies of the organization bearing on the resolution of such conflict. If these policies do not resolve the ethical conflict, such practitioner should consider the following courses of action:

- Discuss such problems with the immediate superior except when it appears that the superior is involved, in which case the problem should be presented initially to the next higher managerial level. If a satisfactory resolution cannot be achieved when the problem is initially presented, submit the issues to the next higher managerial level.

  If the immediate superior is the chief executive officer, or equivalent, the acceptable reviewing authority may be a group such as the audit committee, executive committee, board of directors, board of trustees, or owners. Contact with levels above the immediate superior should be initiated only with the superior's knowledge, assuming the superior is not involved. Except where legally prescribed, communication of such problems to authorities or individuals not employed or engaged by the organization is not considered appropriate.

- Clarify relevant ethical issues by confidential discussion with an objective advisor (e.g., IMA Ethics Counseling Service) to obtain a better understanding of possible courses of action.

- Consult your own attorney as to legal obligations and rights concerning the ethical conflict.

- If the ethical conflict still exists after exhausting all levels of internal review, there may be no other recourse on significant matters than to resign from the organization and to submit an informative memorandum to an appropriate representative of the organization. After resignation, depending on the nature of the ethical conflict, it may also be appropriate to notify other parties.

Source: Institute of Management Accountants, "Standards of Ethical Conduct for Practitioners of Management Accounting and Financial Management," *Management Accounting*, July, 1997, page 21.

EXHIBIT 1-2   *Resolution of Ethical Conflict*

► SUMMARY ◄

Management accounting is a dynamic, ever changing profession that faces interesting challenges as companies merge, downsize, streamline, and re-engineer for the global economy. The detailed cost analyses, flexible reporting systems, and adaptable tracking systems that management accountants create are more in demand now than ever. Managers must make timely decisions in today's world, and they need the help of the management accountant to make sure the decisions are the right ones. Computers enable accountants to develop analyses quickly of past data and projections of future data. The management accountant keeps one eye on the past as an anchor and the other on the future where the firm is headed.

► QUESTIONS ◄

1-1. What is the purpose of management accounting?

1-2. Define management accounting.

1-3. Is management accounting the same as cost accounting? Discuss.

1-4. What differences exist between financial accounting and management accounting? Is management accounting separate and distinct from financial accounting?

1-5. Explain how the size of an organization relates to the extent of applications of management accounting.

1-6. Define responsibility accounting. What is accomplished by using the responsibility approach?

1-7. Why is planning considered implicit in the concept of control?

1-8. Distinguish between planning, decision-making, and choosing between alternative courses of action.

1-9. Discuss confidentiality, objectivity, and independence as presented by the Standards of Ethical Conduct for Management Accountants. Contrast with the standards for CPAs.

1-10. Competence and proficiency in accounting are the prime qualifications of a management accountant. Discuss.

1-11. What courses of action should a management accountant consider to resolve ethical conflict?

1-12. Describe and contrast activity-based cost management with traditional costing.

1-13. What is the objective of theory of constraints?

1-14. Define the constraining factor of a manufacturing organization.

1-15. Why is it difficult to implement new concepts such as ABCM and TOC?

1-16. What concepts are more applicable for short-term decisions, long-term decisions?

1-17. What are the advantages and difficulties of outsourcing?

1-18. Why have organizations shifted their emphasis to cash?

1-19. Are the procedures in handling cost sheets stated in the chapter adequate for the contemporary management accountant?

1-20. Explain what is meant by a "decision-making" emphasis for management accountants.

1-21. Why has the U.S. economy experienced enormous growth in the service sector?

1-22. Are management accounting concepts applicable to service organizations? Explain.

Learning Objectives

After reading this chapter, the student should have an understanding of:

✔ The relationship among subsidiary ledgers, general ledgers, and computer databases.

✔ The classification systems companies use to capture information about costs and revenues.

✔ The definition of manufacturing costs and inventories relevant to management accounting.

✔ The principles of account code creation.

✔ The relationship between responsibility accounting and account codes.

MANAGEMENT ACCOUNTING SYSTEMS

Caterpillar, Inc., generated sales of over $10 billion for fiscal year 1993, and it employs over fifty thousand people. The company's products (over half of which are sold outside the U.S.) range from truck diesel engines selling for $30,000 to large tractors that sell for over $1 million. Clearly Caterpillar needs a good accounting system to track which products are selling to whom, which managers are most efficient, which products generate the most profit, which departments within a plant consume the most resources, etc.

If Caterpillar executives are to effectively manage thousands of employees scattered over the globe, they need a carefully designed accounting system to track and report relevant information. Even companies smaller than Caterpillar need a carefully designed accounting system to track and report relevant information. This chapter discusses issues accountants must consider to design an effective management accounting system that serves the needs of enterprise managers of large or small firms.

► THE STRUCTURE OF ACCOUNTING SYSTEMS ◄

Before computers gained widespread use in accounting, accountants recorded and summarized transactions in journals and ledgers by hand. Every movement of an asset into or out of a company generated an associated journal entry. Originally, all these journal entries were recorded in the general journal and posted or summarized in the general ledger. However, because of the volume of some types of transactions, accountants created special journals to hold the details of the transactions, and totals from these special journals were posted to the general ledger.

In addition, accountants created detailed ledgers, called subsidiary ledgers, to hold the details for certain general ledger accounts. Individual transactions were posted to the subsidiary ledgers, while summary totals were posted to control accounts in the general ledger. For example, accountants typically maintained a detailed subsidiary ledger for accounts receivable, in which each customer had an account. The total of this subsidiary ledger matched the total in the general ledger accounts receivable account. In a manufacturing firm, accountants also typically maintained a detailed subsidiary ledger for manufacturing costs to reduce the number of accounts in the general ledger. As with the receivables, the total of the individual manufacturing costs in the subsidiary ledger matched the balance in the control account in the general ledger.

In a computerized world, accountants maintain the same information; however they keep it in files or databases instead of in paper journals and ledgers and paper subsidiary ledgers. Thus, for example, a company will maintain a detailed file of transactions related to customer accounts or to manufacturing costs. Company personnel enter transactions into these detailed files as asset movements occur, and the computer system periodically (hourly or daily) makes summary postings to the general ledger accounts. In a computerized system the detail file often takes the place of both special journals and subsidiary ledgers.

► RELEVANT INFORMATION CLASSIFICATION ◄

For a manager at Caterpillar to manage effectively his or her operation, the accounting system must group transactions into meaningful categories; a single sales or a single expense amount for the entire company aggregates too much information to be useful to a manager. To provide useful information, accountants classify data as they record transactions, e.g., assets are classified as current assets or noncurrent assets, expenses as manufacturing, marketing or administrative, and revenues as sales or other income. Such classification lies at the heart of the accounting system.

► Manufacturing Costs

In a manufacturing firm, accountants typically classify manufacturing expenses into *direct materials*, *direct labor*, and *manufacturing overhead expenses*. Accountants call the materials used to make a product (e.g., the wood in a table, the steel in an automobile, and the plastic in a pen) *direct materials*. They call the labor expense for the workers who actually "touch" the product (workers who cut wood for a table, who place wheels on an automobile, and who insert the ink unit into the plastic barrel of a pen) *direct labor*. Any manufacturing costs not included in direct materials or direct labor cost (e.g., cost of electricity, rent, plant accountant salaries, and fork lift operator salaries) accountants call *manufacturing overhead*.

Accountants sometimes combine direct labor and manufacturing overhead into a single category called *processing costs*. In these systems, all manufacturing costs are either direct materials costs or processing costs. The *processing costs*, direct labor and manufacturing overhead, include all costs of turning materials into finished units.

► Manufacturing Inventories

Just as they use special classifications of expenses for manufacturing, accountants also define special inventory classifications in manufacturing. They distinguish among three categories of inventory: materials, work-in-process, and finished goods.

Materials. Materials consists of the stock of raw products on which no processing has occurred. Examples include steel for a Caterpillar plant or a Ford automotive assembly plant, wood for a furniture factory like Drexel, yarn for a cloth manufacturer like Milliken, and cotton for a textile plant. Accountants also include components purchased from outside suppliers in the materials category.

Work-in-process. Accountants call the accumulated cost of any incomplete products, work-in-process. For example, all the costs tied up in partially finished hydraulic excavators at Caterpillar, partially built Boeing passenger planes, or incomplete submarines at General Dynamics make up the work-in-process inventories for these companies.

Finished Goods. The costs of products ready to be shipped to a customer make up the cost of finished goods. The Caterpillar tractor awaiting shipment to a customer, the Nissan pickup parked in a holding lot at the plant, the baseball bats stored in the warehouse awaiting the start of the selling season; all these completed products fall into the category of finished goods.

► Additional Classifications / Segment Accounting

The above classifications touch on broad groupings used by accountants, but managers need much more detailed information to run the business effectively. A Caterpillar plant manager needs to know who authorized each plant expenditure, which customer generated the most sales for the plant, which plant department used the most factory supplies, etc. Segment accounting information provides this detail for managers.

Segment Accounting. Accountants use the term segment accounting to describe the process of tracking costs and revenues for individual segments of the firm. At Caterpillar, for instance, managers want to track costs at the plant, plant department, customer, product, and market territory levels. Each of these makes up a segment of the organization. The costs and revenues mentioned at the opening of this chapter refer to total revenues and costs for all Caterpillar operations, but the sales manager for the Southeastern U.S. needs information on costs and revenues for his territory, and the manager of the East Peoria plant needs information on costs charged to each department in that plant.

Two commonly used segments are product segments and organization (responsibility) segments. Accountants use product segments to collect revenue and expense information related to products. Caterpillar tracks total dollar sales generated by its D9 tractors, and it collects cost information related to the production and sales of these tractors as well. In addition, accountants collect information for organization, or responsibility, segments to relate costs and revenues to the managers who make decisions affecting those costs and revenues. Both these segments receive attention in the remainder of this chapter.

▸ *BASIC CODE STRUCTURE* ◂

Accountants capture the segment and other relevant information for each transaction through the use of account codes. Each code includes several fields with each field capturing information on a specific dimension of a transaction. These codes can be quite lengthy for a company like Caterpillar with complex operations around the world, or they can be short and simple for a company like the local auto repair shop. Consider the following example.

X	-	XXX	-	XX	-	XX
Class		Type		Location		Product

The first digit (field one) identifies an account from the following list of account classes.

Code	*Class of Account*
1	Asset accounts
2	Liability accounts
3	Equity accounts
4	Revenue accounts
5	Expense accounts

For expense transactions the second field describes the type of expense as illustrated by these marketing expenses.

Code	*Type of Expense*
101	General Salaries
103	Sales Personnel Salaries
120	Training Sales Personnel

The third field is very important for companies like Caterpillar, General Motors, IBM and other global companies with operations all over the world because it identifies the geographic location to which the transaction applies.

Code	Location
01	Houston
05	Los Angeles
07	Tokyo
09	London
10	Mexico City

The product code in the last field identifies the relevant product for the transaction. Notice how this system uses 99 to indicate that the transaction does not involve a specific product.

Code	Product
10	Hydraulic Excavators
11	Motor Graders
12	Track-Type Tractors
15	Scrapers
99	No product relevant

To illustrate a transaction's effect on all four fields, assume we wish to record the cost of training sales personnel to sell the Track-Type Tractors in Mexico City. The following eight digit code describes this transaction:

$$5 \quad 120 \quad 10 \quad 12$$

The first digit (5) indicates an expense, the second three (120) describe the type of expense (training sales personnel); the next two (10) reveal the expense was incurred in Mexico City, and the last two (12) show the company incurred the expense for Track-Type Tractors.

▸ CLASSIFICATION AND CODING OF GENERAL LEDGER ACCOUNTS ◂

The arrangement of general ledger accounts typically follows the order in which account balances appear in published financial statements. Usually the ledger begins with the balance sheet accounts and moves through the income statement accounts, and most companies use either a **block code** or a **group code** to classify accounts.

▸ Block Codes—An Example

Designers of block codes reserve a sequential block of numbers for each attribute. For example, Caterpillar might reserve the digits 1 through 19 for Cost of Goods Sold, digits 20 through 45 for Manufacturing Expenses, and digits 46 through 70 for Marketing and Selling Expenses. Designers choose the number of digits in a block code by considering the number of items to be coded and the need for future expansion.

Assume Caterpillar uses the following block code system for its accounts. It allocates blocks of codes from 1000 through 9999 for various assets, liabilities, revenue and expense accounts.

1000 - 1999	Assets	———————	Broad Category
1000 - 1049	Cash		
1050 - 1089	Accounts receivable		
1090 - 1099	Inventory	}	Accounts within
1100 - 1149	Plant and equipment		broad category
1150 - 1199	Investments		

2200 - 2379	Liabilities
2380 - 2399	Capital stock and retained earnings
3400 - 3415	Sales
4420 - 4999	Manufacturing expenses
5410 - 5999	Marketing and selling expenses
7490 - 9999	Administrative and other expenses

Caterpillar managers need sufficient details on cash for cash management purposes, so they establish the following cash accounts within the cash block code of 1000-1049. Accountants provide details within the blocks for other accounts in a similar fashion.

1001	Cash in Second National Bank, Peoria
1011	Payroll account Second National Bank, Peoria
1020	Petty cash
1031	Cash awaiting deposit
1041	Investments in short term paper

▸ Group Codes—An Example

In a group code (also called a hierarchical code) the interpretation of each succeeding symbol depends on the value of the preceding symbol or symbols. This code has several advantages: it captures more information than other codes for a given number of digits; users can easily memorize these codes; and, it fits the structure of data processing languages such as COBOL.

Assume Caterpillar decides to use a group code with twelve digits in four fields (account type, location, responsibility center, account details) instead of the block code illustrated earlier. The first field represents financial statement categories with the first digit identifying the specific category.

1XX-XXX-XXX-XXX	Current assets
2XX-XXX-XXX-XXX	Non-current assets
3XX-XXX-XXX-XXX	Current liabilities
4XX-XXX-XXX-XXX	Non-current liabilities and equity
5XX-XXX-XXX-XXX	Revenues
6XX-XXX-XXX-XXX	Expenses

To create additional expense categories, for example, accountants add codes in the first field as illustrated below.

600-XXX-XXX-XXX	Purchased materials—any kind
601-XXX-XXX-XXX	Purchased materials—steel
605-XXX-XXX-XXX	Purchased materials—steel castings

The second field identifies geographic location.

XXX-100-XXX-XXX	Peoria
XXX-200-XXX-XXX	Tokyo
XXX-300-XXX-XXX	São Paulo

The third field holds responsibility center, or segment, information.

XXX-XXX-005-XXX   Parent company activities
XXX-XXX-008-XXX   Manufacturing operations
XXX-XXX-009-XXX   Marketing operations

Interpretation of identifiers in the fourth field (account detail) varies with the unit originating the transaction as these two examples illustrate.

605-100-008-402
621-100-009-402

In the first transaction the 402 represents heat treating because it originated in manufacturing (code 008), but in the second transaction the 402 represents a salesperson because it originated in marketing (code 009).

▸ Cost/Expense* Classification Codes—An Example

Expense codes for manufacturing firms become quite complex as accountants devise systems to capture relevant cost information for various managers. Cost codes typically include these fields:

Cost classification
Cost center or department
Type of expense
Materials code
Responsible individual
Job number (if a job costing system)
Plant number
Product code (if a process costing system)

Assume accountants at Georgia Pacific, a wood products and paper company with 150 manufacturing facilities, decide to use a fifteen digit code to classify transactions in their accounts as shown below.

XX	XXXXXX	XXX	XXXX
Unit Number	Account Number	Responsibility Area	Product Identifier

The unit number identifies the company division or the location of the reporting unit (e.g., Alabama, Ontario, or Panama). The first three digits of the Account Number describe major cost groupings as illustrated below.

400XXX   Raw materials
500XXX   Administrative salaries
501XXX   Wages
530XXX   Advertising
540XXX   Freight charges

---

* In this text we use the terms cost and expense interchangeably.

The last three digits of the account number give additional details as these next two transactions illustrate.

400102   Outside purchases of raw materials of commodity code 02 (Silicone).

400201   Materials price variance on purchases of wood pulp (commodity code 01).

The responsibility area (or segment) code and the unit code allow managers to identify both the company division (building products—03) and the plant (Birmingham—380) responsible for the transaction. For instance, the complete transaction codes for the two previous transactions are:

03-400102-380-9999
03-400201-380-9999

Note the use of nines in the product identifier field. These nines indicate the transaction does not involve a specific product. Only in cases where the company uses a raw materials or other expense item for a specific product will a product number appear in this field. For example, a plant in Maine that uses certain chemicals exclusively to make tissue paper identifies those chemical costs with the product code for tissue paper.

In the case of marketing expenses, the product identification code provides valuable information to marketing executives. Consider these two examples.

03-530115-411-0030   Prime time TV advertising (530115) for the Florida division (03) for product 0030 which is the responsibility of the marketing manager whose code is 411.

03-530210-411-0030   Consumer cash rebates (530210) for the Florida division (03) for product 0030 which is the responsibility of the marketing manager whose code is 411.

As these two examples illustrate, the second three digits of the account field allow managers to track marketing expenditures by type of expense. For instance, if the company does a special marketing promotion for containerboard products in Chicago, accountants create a special code for that promotion to track expenditures related to it. Later managers can evaluate the promotion's profitability by relating promotion expenditures to the resulting sales.

▶ Classification and Coding of Materials—An Example**

The costs of raw materials and purchased parts for many manufacturing companies represents 60% to 85% of total manufacturing costs. Therefore, it is worthwhile for manufacturers to track the movement of materials carefully through their operations, and to have accountants develop codes to help accomplish this.

An excellent example of a materials code appeared in an Institute of Management Accountants (formerly National Association of Accountants) publication, and we provide an adaptation of that example below. The code is used by a manufacturing company for both purchased materials and finished products.

** National Association of Accountants, *Classification and Coding Techniques to Facilitate Accounting Operations.* N.A.A. Research Report 34, National Association of Accountants, April, 1959, pp. 35-37.

It has nine digits arranged into four fields, and the single digit first field identifies the major materials category.

Code Number	*Description*
0	Raw materials (e.g., steel, lumber)
3	Fasteners (e.g., bolts, screws)
6	Purchased parts
9	Manufactured parts and products

Additional fields provide identifying characteristics of the materials or products in each category. Examples for each of the four single digit codes follow.

In the raw materials category the second and third digits identify groups of materials that correspond to related inventory sub-accounts.

0	01	Hot rolled steel sheets
0	06	Cold rolled steel strip

The next three digits identify major dimensions such as metal gauge.

0	06	062	Cold rolled steel strip gauge .062
0	06	099	Cold rolled steel strip gauge .099
0	09	751	Hot rolled bars, 1" diameter

The final three digits identify specific items within a category or size. Numbers are assigned in sequence beginning with 001.

0	06	062	001	Cold rolled steel strip, gauge .062 straight edge
0	06	062	002	Cold rolled steel strip, gauge .062 rounded edge
0	06	062	003	Cold rolled steel strip, gauge .062 hardened steel

In the fastener code, the second digit identifies the type of fastener in the following way:

3	1x	Machine screws
3	2x	Tapping screws
3	3x	Wood screws

Digits three through six of the fastener code identify additional characteristics of the item such as fit, size, etc. For example,

3	31	955	Wood screw (3), oval head slotted long (1), nominal size 18 (9), 8 threads per inch (5), 1 1/2 inches long (5)

The final three digits of the materials code for fasteners identify the materials, the finish and the method of finishing. Consider this fastener example:

3	31	955	120	Wood screws (3), oval head slotted long (1), nominal size, 18 (9), 8 threads per inch (5), 1 1/2 inches long (5), steel brass finish C7 (120)

Codes for purchased parts, and manufactured parts are identical except for the first digit which designates whether an item is purchased or manufactured. When the first digit indicates an item fits either of these two categories, the next two digits identify the department which uses or produces the part or product. For example:

6 42   xxx xxx   Purchased part for a product assigned to department 42

9 42   xxx xxx   Manufactured part for a product assigned to department 42

Notice how the company uses the same number of digits it used to describe the fastener, but the numbers carry different meanings. The next three digits make up a catalogue number that is assigned in sequence for each department. For instance:

6 42   001   Purchased part for 2731 1/2 overhead door set, responsibility assigned to department 42

9 42   001   Manufactured part for 2731 1/2 overhead door set, responsibility assigned to department 42

When the company purchases parts from an outside company, it does not use the last three digits to provide descriptive information about the part. If the company manufactures the part, the last three digits provide descriptive information about the part, e.g.:

9 42   001 021   Manufactured part for 2731 1/2 overhead door set, responsibility assigned to Department 42, Brass

▸ *Other Relevant Codes*

Proctor & Gamble sells such products as Cheer, Spic & Span, Tide cleansing compounds, Crisco shortenings, Crest toothpastes, Ivory soaps, and Prell and Head and Shoulders shampoos, and it sells these products all over the world. Its annual sales exceed $29 billion, with more than half generated outside the U.S. Managers must track these sales by product, salesperson, and customer as well as other attributes.

Product Codes. Product codes can be short (a single digit), or they can be long like the following example.

Item	*Code Length (in digits)*
Part Number	19
Inventory Group	1
Product Group	2
Product Class	2
Commodity Code	4
Buyer Code	2
Planner Code	2

Manufacturing and inventory control personnel use the first two code segments (Part Number and Inventory Group) to manage materials flow; marketing managers use the next two for tracking product sales; and, purchasing uses the last three to track who is working with what commodity.

Salespersonnel Codes. Proctor & Gamble has over 90 thousand employees, and many of them work in sales. To track the revenue generated by each person involved in sales, accountants assign codes to each sales person.

Customer Identification Codes. Customer codes vary in length depending on how much information the company wants to collect about each customer. Some companies use the nine digit Dunn & Bradstreet number as an identifier, and others use the Department of Commerce place identifier number as part of their customer code.[1] This published set of codes provides unique identifiers for all named places in the United States as well as codes for state, county and zip code area.

▶ ACCOUNT CODES AND RESPONSIBILITY ACCOUNTING ◀

Account codes play a significant role in responsibility accounting systems. Companies that use responsibility accounting assign responsibility to a manager for every transaction entering the accounting system. That is, every transaction must bear the approval of a manager before accountants enter it in the system. Some manager must take responsibility for each materials purchase, each payroll check written, each issue of materials from a storeroom, and each outside purchase of supplies before accountants enter the transaction into the accounting system. In other words, every transaction has an owner, and the owner of a transaction is identified by the responsibility code for that transaction. This owner has full responsibility for his or her transactions, and no other manager can approve transactions for the manager unless they have been delegated the authority to do so.

▶ RESPONSIBILITY REPORTING SYSTEMS—MORE SPECIFICS ◀

Responsibility accounting systems produce reports at multiple levels in the organization. At the lowest level, the system generates reports that summarize the transactions that managers have directly approved. Thus, a production manager receives a summary at the end of the month of all the transactions he or she approved during the month, and a marketing manager receives a monthly report for all sales and cost transactions approved during the month.

However, the marketing manager receiving a report for the transactions he or she directly approved is responsible to a higher manager in the organization who is also interested in how well the marketing manager did last month. Consider the following example (a simplified one) for an organization with four sales people and two sales regions. This company uses the following code structure to capture data on sales and expense transactions.

XX	XXXX	XXX	XX
Account Class	Account Number	Responsibility Code	Product

The Account Class field indicates whether the transaction is an asset, liability, etc., and the account number represents the specific account to which the transaction applies. The next field captures the code for the individual with primary responsibility for the transaction who directly approves it, and the last field captures the product number. This company identifies the reporting relationships among managers and sales persons in its report generation software. With this code structure the company can produce reports for salespeople, region managers, and for the vice-president in charge of all marketing activities. Exhibit 2-1 on the next page illustrates these reports.

---

[1] U. S. Department of Commerce/ National Bureau of Standards, *Codes for Named Populated Places and Related Entities of the States of the United States.* FIPS PUB 55, (U. S. Department of Commerce, June 1, 1978).

```
1.  Salesperson Report
Salesperson:   Kathleen Smith
Sales  ....................................                              $  250,000
Expenses:
    Manufacturing Cost of Goods Sold ...........   $  180,000
    Customer Entertainment ....................       1,500
    Travel  .................................       2,200
    Salesperson Commissions .................       5,000          188,700
Amount Contributed to Cover Other
    Company Costs and Profit .................              $   61,300


2.  Western Region Manager Report
Amounts Contributed by Salespeople
    Kathleen Smith ...........................              $   61,300
    Michael Kruse ...........................                  85,240
        Total Amounts Contributed
           by Salespeople .......................             $  146,540
Expenses of Western Region
    Office Rental ...........................   $   5,400
    Utilities ...............................       1,500
    Salaries ................................      12,000
    Advertising in Territory ....................      25,000          43,900
Amount Contributed to Cover Other
    Company Costs and Profit .................              $  102,640


3.  Marketing Vice President Report
Amounts contributed by regions
    Western Region Contribution ...............              $  102,640
    Eastern Region Contribution .................                 160,250
        Total Amounts Contributed by Regions .....           $  262,890
Expenses of Marketing Vice President
    Company Advertising .....................   $  92,400
    Staff Salaries ...........................      45,000
    Special Promotions ......................      15,000
    Marketing Materials ......................      10,000         162,400
Amount Contributed to Cover Other
    Company Costs and Profit .................              $  100,490
```

Exhibit 2-1 *Responsibility Reports Aircraft Builders, Inc. for the Period Ended July, 20XX*

   Notice how each report (we show only one salesperson and one region report to simplify the example) shows the details for expenses specifically approved by each manager but only summary data (amount contributed) for the costs and revenues of individuals reporting to a specific manager. Exhibit 2-2 graphically depicts the relationships shown in the reports for Exhibit 2-1. Notice how reports at lower levels of responsibility tie into reports at higher levels in both Exhibits 2-1 and 2-2.

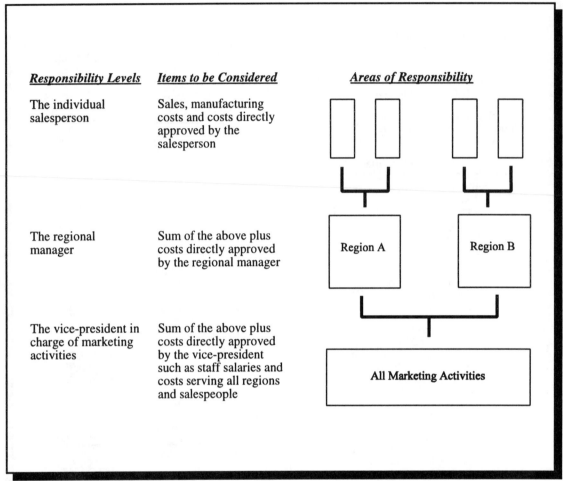

Responsibility Levels	Items to be Considered	Areas of Responsibility

The individual salesperson — Sales, manufacturing costs and costs directly approved by the salesperson

The regional manager — Sum of the above plus costs directly approved by the regional manager — Region A / Region B

The vice-president in charge of marketing activities — Sum of the above plus costs directly approved by the vice-president such as staff salaries and costs serving all regions and salespeople — All Marketing Activities

Exhibit 2-2

► USING ACCOUNT CODES TO SUMMARIZE DATA ◄

The following example illustrates how accountants use account codes to create various summaries of data. This example uses twelve transactions to demonstrate the power of account codes, but the reader should keep in mind that in a typical company the number of transactions will probably number in the thousands or millions per month.

This example uses a five field code to capture information about transactions.

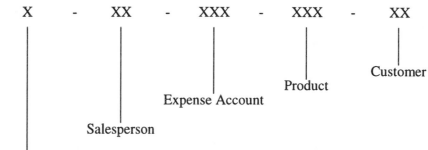

Type of Account (6 is expense and 7 is revenue)

In this system accountants fill a field with nines when it does not apply to a transaction, and they assign the expense account field a value of 700 for sales transactions. The value on the extreme right represents the dollar amount of the transaction.

7	40	700	105	32	91,000.00
6	60	108	999	99	259.85
6	60	132	999	99	68.93
7	40	700	109	32	6,100.00
6	70	343	999	99	21.89
6	10	132	103	99	45.62
7	50	700	102	34	7,000.00
7	70	700	106	27	16,800.00
7	50	700	110	34	9,800.00
6	70	260	999	99	546.23
7	70	700	108	27	42,000.00
6	10	260	103	99	25.28

To compute the total sales by customer for this set of transactions the accountant sorts the transactions on the customer field (fifth field) and takes a total for each customer, as follows:

7	70	700	108	27	42,000	
7	70	700	106	27	16,800	58,800
7	40	700	109	32	6,100	
7	40	700	105	32	91,000	97,100
7	50	700	102	34	7,000	
7	50	700	110	34	9,800	16,800
6	10	260	103	99	25.28	
6	70	260	999	99	546.23	
6	60	132	999	99	68.93	
6	60	108	999	99	259.85	
6	10	132	103	99	45.62	
6	70	343	999	99	21.89	

Customer 32 had the highest sales at $97,100, and customer 34 had the lowest level at $16,800. To measure the sales by sales person, the accountant sorts the transactions using sales person (second field) as the primary key and account type (first field) as the secondary key; then the accountant takes sales totals for each salesperson as follows:

6	10	132	103	99	45.62	
6	10	260	103	99	25.28	
7	40	700	109	32	6,100.00	
7	40	700	105	32	91,000.00	97,100.00
7	50	700	110	34	9,800.00	
7	50	700	102	34	7,000.00	16,800.00
6	60	132	999	99	68.93	
6	60	108	999	99	259.85	
7	70	700	108	27	42,000.00	
7	70	700	106	27	16,800.00	58,800.00
6	70	343	999	99	21.89	
6	70	260	999	99	546.23	

Salesperson 40 had the highest sales at $97,100, and salesperson 50 had the lowest sales of $16,800. Salespersons 10 and 60 had no sales for this period. The accountant follows the same process to compute the expenses related to each salesperson, or to each product.

A spreadsheet was used to perform the sorts and totals illustrated here; however, when transactions number in the thousands, or hundreds of thousands, a spreadsheet quickly reaches its limits. Fortunately, report writer software available for computers of all sizes makes it easy to generate reports that sort transactions and produce subtotals when the value of a field changes. A few simple commands to one of these report writers will produce subtotals and totals for any field specified by the accountant using the software. In addition, data base software allows a user to form queries that produce totals for various fields. For example, the following query will provide the total sales for customer 32.

SELECT SUM (AMOUNT) FOR CUSTOMER = 32

► SUMMARY ◄

In a manufacturing firm accountants classify inventory into the categories of materials, work-in-process, and finished goods. They further classify manufacturing expenses into direct materials, direct labor, and manufacturing overhead expenses. In addition, accountants create classification systems for capturing information about costs and revenues by product, by customer, by plant, etc., and they devise coding systems to collect this information on each transaction entering the system. Such systems allow accountants to summarize information for any field in the account code chosen and to prepare summary reports on relevant information for managers on a timely basis. These summary reports tie manager responsibility to the transactions they approve.

▸ QUESTIONS ◂

2-1. How do subsidiary ledgers and the general ledger relate to the structure of a computerized accounting system?

2-2. What are the common elements in the definition of direct materials and direct labor?

2-3. Give two examples of raw materials for an automobile assembly plant.

2-4. How does manufacturing overhead differ from direct materials?

2-5. Explain the difference between work-in-process and finished goods.

2-6. Describe segment accounting, and explain why it is important for large companies.

2-7. Explain the difference between product segments and organization, or responsibility, segments.

2-8. List the code fields a company with business operations around the globe might use to track costs and revenues.

2-9. Give an illustration of the codes for each of the four fields to record the expense for sales personnel in London who sell motor graders. Use the first example in the Basic Code Structure section of the chapter for the codes you need to answer this question.

2-10. Explain the difference between block codes and group codes.

2-11. What are the advantages of a group code over a block code?

2-12. How do managers use product code identifiers to collect information important for management decisions?

2-13. Explain how the accounting system tracks individual expenses so the accounting system can report to managers the expenses and revenues for which they are responsible.

2-14. Explain the relationship between the organization chart and the responsibility reports generated by the accounting system.

2-15. Explain the process accountants use to summarize the data captured by account codes.

2-16. What kind of information does the accountant include in a materials code?

► *EXERCISES* ◄

2-17. Responsibility Accounting for a Sales Territory.

    Melanie Rosenzweig manages the Eastern Sales Territory for the Salamander Corporation. She has fifteen salesmen working for her, and she has a small office staff. All expense accounts of the salesmen and all expenses of the Eastern Sales Territory must have her approval before they are paid. Sales for August were $250,000. The following list of expenses for August came to her office from the corporate headquarters:

Cost of goods sold	$ 190,000
Salesmen Salaries	35,000
Territory office rent	5,000
Salesmen expenses	3,000
Corporate accounting cost*	4,000
Corporate overhead**	2,000
Total	$ 239,000

    *   Corporate cost allocated to territories on the basis of total sales.
    ** Corporate cost allocated to territories on the basis of the
           number of employees in the territory

Required:

    Compute the amount that Melanie Rosenzweig contributed to cover other company costs and profit for August. Use only the expenses in her report that required her approval before they were paid.

2-18. Responsibility Accounting and Management Decisions.

    Three managers make all major decisions in your company about factors that affect expenses incurred by the company. Jay Marking handles all marketing activities and is responsible for all marketing costs. Drew Anderson handles manufacturing and has responsibility for all costs related to that activity. Finally, Mary Whitmire, company president, manages the company and has responsibility for administrative and support functions. The company does all manufacturing in its single plant in Gallatin, Tennessee, and all its employees work in this facility.

Required:

    Write the first name (Jay, Drew, or Mary) of the individual to charge with responsibility for each of the following expenses incurred by the company during the past month.

1. Raw materials used in manufacturing.
2. Advertising material purchased to promote sales.
3. Weekly payroll for the manufacturing operations.
4. Cost of paper used in data processing operations.
5. Cost of repairing a machine in the factory.
6. Cost of replacing several factory windows broken in a recent storm.
7. Cost of flying a salesman to call on a customer.

2-19. Account Codes and Transactions.

Use the codes in the Basic Code Structure section of this chapter to answer this question. Use 9's to fill any code field that does not apply to a specific transaction.

Required:

Prepare the four field code for each of the following transactions. The first transaction has been completed for you to illustrate the code you must prepare. Use your discretion and imagination when preparing codes not precisely covered by the "basic code structure" section of this chapter.

1. Expenditure for sales personnel salaries in Houston for people selling Scrapers.

5 103 01 15

2. Sales of Hydraulic Excavators in London.
3. Expenditure for General Salaries in Tokyo for workers who repair Track Type Tractors.
4. Expenditure for training sales personnel for individuals who sell Motor Graders.
5. Expenditure for General Salaries for office personnel in Mexico City.
6. Received spare parts in Los Angeles for Hydraulic Excavator repairs.
7. Sales of Motor Graders in Mexico City.

2-20. Account Codes and Responsibility Reporting.

Froeb Industries has two departments in its manufacturing plant: Stamping Department and Assembly Department. Each department has a manager, and they report to the plant manager who oversees the operation of the plant.

Accountants have devised a three field account code to capture data on costs incurred in the plant.

Field 1 Account Category (a 7 indicates an expense)
Field 2 Type of expense
Field 3 Responsibility code

Code numbers for the types of expenses
100 Materials
150 Supplies
200 Direct labor costs
300 Rent expense
400 General office expense
500 Utilities expense

Responsibility codes
10 Stamping Department
20 Assembly Department
50 Plant manager office

The accountant prepared the following list of transactions that occurred during the past month. The value in the field on the right of each transaction represents the dollar amount of the transaction.

7	100	10	$10,000
7	150	20	1,000
7	150	20	2,000
7	100	10	15,000
7	150	10	1,000
7	150	10	500
7	200	20	20,000
7	100	20	12,000
7	200	20	16,000
7	150	10	800
7	100	20	13,000
7	150	50	700
7	150	20	600
7	100	10	8,000
7	300	50	6,500
7	400	10	1,200
7	400	20	900
7	500	50	3,600
7	400	50	900

Required:

a. Prepare a cost report for the Stamping Department and for the Assembly Department that lists total amounts for each expense category.

b. Compute the total amount of materials costs used by both departments during the month.

c. Prepare a report for the plant manager in a format similar to the format for the Western Region Manager report in Exhibit 2-1. Remember that you will show only total expenses in this case instead of amounts contributed by salespeople.

d. Which field in the code structure used by Froeb Industries allows the company to collect cost information by responsible individual, and how might this help the company to control costs?

2-21. Account Codes and Inventory Values.

Chaney, Inc., collected the following list of data on asset balances from the different business locations it operates. The first field in the following codes indicates the type of asset (1 is inventory, 2 is receivables, and 3 is cash). The second field provides additional details; for example, if the first field is a 1, a 10 in the second field indicates raw materials inventory, a 20 indicates work-in-process inventory, and a 40 indicates finished goods inventory. The last field indicates the dollar amount for the element described by the first two fields.

1	10	$10,000
2	15	5,000
3	0	12,000
1	10	22,000
1	20	12,000

2	12	1,000
1	40	8,000
1	20	15,000
1	10	9,000
1	20	16,000
1	40	41,000

Required:

Determine the total amounts for each of raw materials, work-in-process, and finished goods inventories.

2-22. Responsibility Reporting System.

Malcolm Distributing sells products in an Eastern Territory and a Southern Territory. The company has two sales people in the Eastern Territory, and Michelle Roberts, one of the sales people, generated sales for the first six months of the year of $500,000. Cost of sales for the products she sold equaled $300,000; she earned commissions on these sales of $40,000; and, she spent $5,000 entertaining customers during the six month period.

Her boss, the manager of the Eastern Territory, incurred for the same six month period rent and utilities expenses of $15,000, salary expense of $20,000 for running the Eastern Territory office, and $60,000 of advertising for the Eastern Territory. Richard Tocknell, the other sales person in the Eastern Territory, was involved in activities which contributed $120,000 for the six months.

The vice president to whom the two territory managers report incurred $80,000 for company wide advertising and $60,000 for expenses of his office for the six months. The southern territory generated a six month contribution of $160,000.

Required:

a. Compute the amount Michelle Roberts generated to cover other company costs and profit.
b. Prepare reports for the Eastern Territory manager and the marketing vice president. Use a report format like that used in Exhibit 2-1.
c. How much would the total amount contributed by the marketing operations for the six months equal if Michelle spend $25,000 on entertaining customers instead of the amount she actually spent?

▶ PROBLEMS AND CASES ◀

2-23. Account Codes and Clothing Manufacturing.

A manufacturer of men's clothing has developed a code for men's suits as follows:

Number sold in units	Stock Number				Customer Number				Salesman
	size	cut	color	style	fabric	region	city	serial	
XXXX	36	R	3	21	24	1	3	6	4

Field descriptions for the code

1. Number sold: Units ordered. (4 character positions for digits)
2. Size: Men's suit size. (2 positions)

3.	Cut:	S small; R regular; L long; X extra long.(1 position)							
4.	Color:	1 blue; 2 brown; 3 grey; 4 black; 5 other. (1 position)							
5.	Style:	Manufacturer's style number keyed to pattern. (2 positions)							
6.	Fabric:	Manufacturer's fabric and price level code, first digit is price class, second digit is fabric code in price class. (2 positions)							
7.	Region:	1 northeast; 2 mid-Atlantic; 3 south; 4 north-central; 5 mid-west; 6 west. (1 position)							
8.	City:	Serialized within region. (1 position)							
9.	Customer:	Serialized within city. (1 position)							
10.	Salesman:	1 Herman; 2 Cy; 3 Al; 4 Irving; 5 Walter; 6 Jack; etc. (1 position)							

Excerpt from Transaction File for the Month

100	32	S	1	11	21	1	1	1	4
200	32	S	1	11	14	3	2	1	4
1,000	32	S	1	21	36	4	1	2	1
200	32	S	2	43	21	5	2	3	2
1,000	34	R	1	11	21	1	3	2	4
75	34	R	2	22	21	2	2	2	3
250	34	R	1	13	14	1	4	6	4
300	34	R	2	23	36	4	5	2	7
1,000	34	R	3	34	19	6	3	6	6
200	34	R	1	11	19	1	7	1	4
200	24	L	2	11	21	3	8	2	5
2,000	34	L	3	22	36	6	6	3	6
1,000	34	X	4	11	19	1	1	7	4
200	36	S	1	32	21	2	2	1	3
50	36	R	2	21	21	3	4	6	5
100	36	R	2	31	19	3	4	6	5
1,000	36	L	1	11	19	1	5	2	4
1,200	36	L	1	22	36	4	4	1	7
200	36	X	1	26	34	6	3	1	1
100	36	X	2	22	21	6	6	3	1
80	38	R	3	13	23	5	4	2	2
40	38	L	3	23	23	5	1	1	2
75	38	X	3	32	40	5	1	2	2
200	38	X	4	22	36	5	1	3	2

Adapted from a problem in Van Court Hare, Jr., *Systems Analysis: A Diagnostic Approach* Harcourt, Brace & World, Inc., 1967, pp. 103-104.

Required:

a. How many longs were sold on the west coast?
b. What is the most popular color this month?
c. What region had the greatest unit sales?
d. What do you think about the use of alphabetic and numeric codes in this code structure?

2-24. Responsibility Accounting and Expense Reporting.

Robert Wagner, Inc., rents the top four floors of a downtown Birmingham office building for its consulting operation. The company got a good deal on the rent when the president of the company negotiated the contract because office space was plentiful. The rental agreement calls for a single monthly payment of $20,000 per month for the duration of the five year lease. Although the president occupies a spacious corner office on the top floor, the square footage of floor space is roughly equal on each floor. Fortunately, each division of the consulting firm fits neatly on each floor so experts in each division are able to work together smoothly, and the division manager has an office near the workers. Each division manager receives a monthly statement of revenue and expenses for his or her division, and the president receives a similar report.

Required:

In which reports (Division Manager's and/or President's) would you include the $20,000 of rent expense each month?

2-25. Account Codes and Manufacturing Costs.

A manufacturing plant uses the following accounts to track expenses in its plant. Its code consists of only two fields (actually there are others, but plant personnel only work with these two).

Field	*Size*	*Meaning*
1	4	Expense description
2	3	Cost center name

Manufacturing Expense Accounts
1000 Indirect Labor
1100 Supervision
1300 Material handling

2000 Operating supplies
2200 Lubricants and cutting compounds
2300 Office supplies
2400 Drafting and engineering supplies
2600 Safety supplies

3000 Energy and utilities
3100 Electric power
3200 Electric lighting
3400 Gas

4000 Maintenance and repairs
4100 Maintenance labor
4200 Tool maintenance and repair
4300 Materials and outside contractors

Cost centers within plant
100 Heat Treatment
150 Plating Department
180 Axle Department

You received the following listing of transactions from the accounting system for transactions that occurred during the past month. The value on the right hand side of each transaction is the dollar amount of the transaction.

2400	180	$330
1100	100	950
1100	150	1,020
1100	180	1,000
1300	100	2,860
1300	150	1,850
1300	180	220
2200	150	120
4200	100	6,520
1100	100	950
1100	150	1,020
1100	180	1,210
1300	100	12,650
1300	150	1,370
1300	180	220
4300	100	48,550
4200	180	1,260
2300	100	130
2400	180	220
2300	180	60
1100	100	960
1100	150	980
1100	180	1,190
1300	100	13,650
1300	150	1,220
1300	180	900
2200	180	650
2300	100	130
1100	100	990
1100	150	1,020
1100	180	1,210
1300	100	1,200
1300	150	1,260
1300	180	250
3100	100	2,860
3100	150	15,320
3100	180	2,560
3400	100	25,640

Required:

a. Which cost center incurred the most expense during the period?
b. Which cost center used the most electric power?
c. Which expense account had the highest dollar amount charged to it during this period?

d. Prepare a cost report for the Axle Department that lists the expenses and the dollar amounts of the expenses incurred by this department. Does any expense in this report look unusual?

2-26. Account Codes and Product Profitability.

Chaney and Böer, Inc., has developed the following codes for tracking information about costs and revenues of their company. The company uses a nine field code for capturing information on transactions. The code fields are:

Field	Size	Meaning
1	1	Tells whether the item is expense (6) or revenue (7)
2	3	Identifies the Marketing administrative unit
3	2	Identifies the salesperson
4	3	Identifies the expense. This field receives a value of 700 if the transaction is a sale.
5	3	Identifies the product
6	2	Identifies the customer
7		Identifies the quantity sold if it is a sales transaction.
8		Dollar amount of transaction
9		Contribution margin on the sale for sales transactions

The codes used for the various fields are listed below:

Expense Class—Field 1
    6 Expense
    7 Revenue

Marketing Administration—Field 2
    201 Eastern Sales Director - Mr. Hans Stoll
    202 Western Sales Director - Mr. Roland Rust
    204 Market Research Administration - Mr. D. Scheffman

Sales people—Field 3
Eastern Sales Region
    30 Mr. Bruce Barry

Western Sales Region
    50 Mr. Joseph Blackburn
    70 Mr. Eric Johnson

Expense accounts—Field 4
   260 Customer Sales Meeting
   500 Price Concessions
   510 Special Promotions
   520 Quantity Discounts

Products—Field 5
   101 Beetlejuice
   102 Morgenstrudel
   103 Peanut Noodles
   105 Rolling Waters
   106 Eggalikes
   107 Walking Dogs
   108 Riding Kites
   109 Frackelburns
   110 Jimmy Crickets

Customers—Field 6
   10 Arrow Appliance, Inc.
   26 National Automotive
   31 Town & Country Sales

Transactions for the past month are listed below. Remember the far right column shows the margin for sales transactions. This field is blank for expense transactions, and the accounting system fills other fields with 9's when they do not apply to a particular transaction. The first number in each row is the number of the transaction, and the expense field has 700 when the transaction is a sales transaction.

1	7	201	30	700	106	26	50	$11,500	$3,500
2	6	201	30	500	106	26		900	
3	7	202	50	700	106	31	90	18,900	4,500
4	7	201	30	700	102	26	100	16,000	7,000
5	6	201	30	500	102	26		1,300	
6	7	201	30	700	108	26	60	51,600	15,600
7	6	201	30	500	108	26		5,700	
8	7	202	70	700	102	10	20	2,800	1,000
9	6	201	30	500	106	26		700	
10	7	202	70	700	103	10	80	8,800	4,000
11	7	201	30	700	102	26	70	11,200	4,900
12	6	201	30	500	102	26		400	
13	7	202	70	700	110	10	80	39,200	15,200
14	6	202	50	260	999	31		300	
15	7	202	50	700	105	31	90	80,100	35,100
16	7	202	50	700	101	31	30	2,700	300
17	7	202	70	700	106	10	90	18,900	4,500
18	7	202	50	700	102	31	50	7,000	2,500
19	7	202	70	700	106	10	80	16,800	4,000
20	7	202	50	700	110	31	100	49,000	19,000
21	7	202	50	700	102	31	80	11,200	4,000

22	7	202	70	700	110	10	80	39,200	15,200
23	7	202	70	700	109	10	10	5,900	3,900
24	7	202	70	700	101	10	70	6,300	700
25	7	201	30	700	101	26	80	8,800	2,400
26	7	202	70	700	107	10	80	11,200	8,000
27	7	202	70	700	109	10	70	41,300	27,300
28	7	202	50	700	101	31	50	4,500	500
29	7	202	70	700	109	10	60	35,400	23,400
30	7	202	50	700	110	31	70	34,300	13,300
31	7	201	30	700	106	26	70	16,100	4,900
32	6	201	30	500	106	26		1,100	
33	7	202	50	700	106	31	80	16,800	4,000
34	7	202	70	700	102	10	80	11,200	4,000
35	7	202	70	700	105	10	80	71,200	31,200
36	7	202	70	700	102	10	50	7,000	2,500
37	6	204	99	260	999	31		900	
38	7	202	50	700	106	31	90	18,900	4,500
39	6	202	70	520	999	10		1,600	
40	6	202	50	520	999	31		1,000	

Required:

a. What are the selling prices for Beetlejuice and Riding Kites?
b. Which customer generated the greatest contribution margin for the month?
c. Which customer would you consider dropping? Why?
d. Compute the unit manufacturing cost for Peanut Noodles and Rolling Waters. Which product generates the highest difference between unit selling price and unit manufacturing cost?
e. Of the following three products, which one contributed the most to company profits for the month?

Peanut Noodles
Rolling Waters
Walking Dogs

f. Which salesperson contributed the most to company profits for the month?
g. Which sales region contributed the most to company profits for the month?

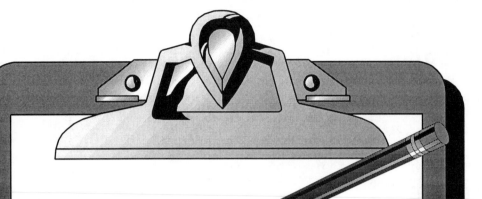

Learning Objectives

After reading this chapter, the student should have an understanding of:

✔ The basis of cost-volume-profit relationships including break-even analysis and the concept of contribution margin.

✔ The construction of break-even and profit-volume charts.

✔ Calculation of break-even points in units and dollars, including the use of contribution margin per unit and as a percentage in the calculation.

✔ The traditional vs. the contribution income statement.

✔ Relevant range, margin of safety and operating leverage vs. financial leverage.

✔ Extension of break-even analysis to determine the volume needed to achieve a desired operating income percentage (before and after taxes) and return on stockholders' equity.

$\mathcal{C}$OST-VOLUME-PROFIT ANALYSIS

Chapter 3

On June 15, Compaq announced a vastly expanded line of PCs — including 45 new models, for a total of 76 — as well as across-the-board price cuts of up to 32%.[1]

How did Eckhard Pfeiffer, CEO of Compaq, know he would make money at these new prices? What information told him Compaq could still earn a profit with a 32% drop in prices? We may not have instant answers to these questions, but we do know a tool that helps managers analyze data for decisions like these—cost-volume-profit analysis.

Whether producing computers, running a veterinary clinic, or manufacturing cowboy boots, managers can use cost-volume-profit analysis to calculate how much revenue to generate each day just to break even. Will Dr. Sally Johnson owner of Animal Medical Center increase or decrease her profits if she raises the price of vaccinating a cat? What happens to profits at Big West Boots if top management decides to slash advertising expense?

▶ USEFUL APPLICATIONS OF COST-VOLUME-PROFIT ANALYSIS ◀

Numerous applications of this important analytical tool exist for managers interested in maximizing their profits. Consider the following cases.

Case 1: Denice, office manager at Groner, Bryce, and Silvain, has been considering starting a small business to make and market hairbows. She will have to spend $20 per month to rent a bow making machine, and materials will cost $.60 per bow. She believes her bows will be extremely popular at a price of $1.00 each. But will she make any money?

Case 2: Shirts Galore operates a chain of shirt stores around the country. All shirts sold in the stores carry the same price regardless of the shirt style. Sales personnel receive a monthly base salary plus a sales commission on each shirt sold. The manager of the Clarksville store wants to increase the base monthly salaries and eliminate the sales commissions entirely. How would this change affect profits?

Case 3: Jim Garner, manager of the Franklin, Tennessee, location of Bryan Reeves Automotive urges Bryan to allow him to hire two more salespeople. Jim argues that, with two additional salespeople, he can increase sales by 15% each month. Bryan owns twelve auto dealerships throughout Tennessee, and he wonders how much the two salespeople will add to the Franklin operation's bottom line.

---

[1] Kirkpatrick, David "The Revolution At Compaq Computer" Fortune (December 14, 1992), p. 80.

Case 4: Managers at Eight by Ten, a photo dealer in Stillwater, Oklahoma, are arguing about the appropriate price for a new camera introduced last month by Minolta. Lonnie wants to charge $300 for the camera, which costs the store $200, but Nick argues that the store will fare better at a price of $250. Who is right?

Cost-volume-profit analysis does not provide magic answers to the questions raised in the above cases, but it does provide a useful starting point. Certainly, the manager who arms herself with the most complete set of analytical tools available stands a greater chance of success than one who relies on intuition alone. Decisions related to cost, volume, prices, and ultimately profits are extremely important. In this chapter we explore the interrelationships among these elements.

► COST-VOLUME-PROFIT ANALYSIS ◄

► Cost Behavior

To use cost-volume-profit analysis, managers must classify costs as variable or fixed. Variable costs vary in total directly with some activity or output, while fixed costs remain constant regardless of how much the output or activity varies. For example, if Dr. Johnson performs more surgeries, she uses more anesthesia, but the annual fire insurance premium on her building remains the same. The steel a manufacturer uses to make automobiles varies directly with the number of automobiles produced, but the depreciation on the plant remains constant regardless of the number of vehicles manufactured.

These two types of cost behavior patterns are depicted in the following graphs. The graph on the left depicts total variable costs while the one on the right graphs total fixed costs.

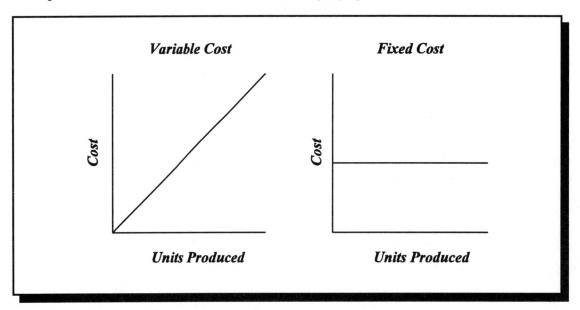

These graphs provide the foundation for the break-even chart discussed in the next section.

► Break-Even Graph

A firm operates at break-even when it earns exactly enough revenue to cover all its fixed and variable costs (with nothing left over for profit). Exhibit 3-1 presents break-even information in a convenient graph. This graph provides one means of analyzing cost-volume-profit relationships.

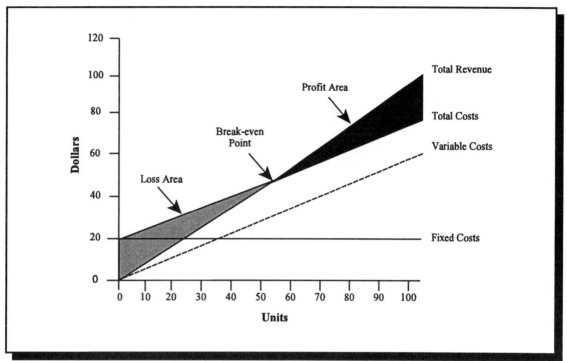

Exhibit 3-1 Denice's Hairbows Break-Even Graph

Exhibit 3-1 uses the facts introduced in Case 1 for Denice's Hairbows. The horizontal line at the $20 level represents monthly fixed costs for the bow making machine, a cost Denice recognizes as fixed because she must pay it whether she makes one bow or 5,000 bows each month. The dotted line that begins at the origin represents the total variable costs for the materials she purchases to make the bows. These costs increase in direct proportion to increases in output. The total cost line is the vertical summation of the variable and fixed cost lines.

The graph in Exhibit 3-1 shows what happens to total variable and total fixed costs. Although Exhibit 3-1 does not portray unit costs, unit variable cost remains constant while unit fixed cost varies inversely with volume. No matter how many hairbows Denice makes, the variable unit cost stays at $.60. However, as she makes more bows, the unit fixed cost declines because the fixed $20 cost is spread over more units. If she makes one bow in one month, its average fixed cost equals $20; if she makes 100 bows, the average fixed cost equals $.20. For most analyses managers do not use unit fixed costs; however, it is useful to recognize the distinction between unit variable and unit fixed costs.

The revenue line in Exhibit 3-1 equals unit selling price times the number of units sold, and the point at which it crosses the total cost line represents the break-even point. The shaded area to the left of the break-even point represents sales levels at which total costs exceed revenues, i.e., Denice loses money. To the right of the break-even point, the revenue line rises above the cost line, and Denice earns a profit.

▸ Algebraic Approach

Algebraically, Denice estimates the break-even point as follows, where x represents sales (in units) at the break-even point, VC_u represents unit variable costs, and SP_u represents the selling price of one unit:

$$
\begin{aligned}
\textit{Total Revenues} &= \textit{Total Costs} \\
&= \textit{Variable Costs + Fixed Costs} \\
SP_u(x) &= VC_u(x) + \textit{Fixed Costs}
\end{aligned}
$$

In Exhibit 3-1, we assume Denice sells her hairbows for $1 each, and her materials cost $.60 per bow (her variable cost). Therefore, the break-even point in units is:

$$
\begin{aligned}
\$1(x) &= \$.60(x) + \$20 \\
x - \$.60x &= \$20 \\
\$.40x &= \$20 \\
x &= (\$20 \div \$.40) \\
x &= 50 \textit{ hairbows}
\end{aligned}
$$

In dollars, she will break even at a sales volume of 50 units times a unit selling price of $1.00, or $50.

Similarly, if Denice wants to know how many hairbows she must sell to generate a particular amount of profit, she modifies the formula as follows, where x represents the needed level of sales in units:

$$
\begin{aligned}
\textit{Total Revenues} &= \textit{Total Costs + Profit} \\
SP_u(x) &= \textit{Variable Costs + Fixed Costs + Profit} \\
SP_u(x) &= (VC_u)(x) + \textit{Fixed Costs + Profit}
\end{aligned}
$$

To earn a profit of $50, Denice must sell:

$$
\begin{aligned}
SP_u(x) &= \$.60x + \$20 + \$50 \\
\$1x - \$.60x &= \$70 \\
.40x &= \$70 \\
x &= (\$70 \div \$.40) \\
&= 175 \textit{ hairbows}
\end{aligned}
$$

or, in dollars, 175 hairbows times $1, or $175.

▸ Contribution Margin

The contribution margin provides information closely related to break-even analysis. If a hairbow which sells for $1.00 has variable costs per unit of $.60, then each sale contributes $.40 toward fixed costs and profits. We refer to this $.40 as the contribution margin per unit. As a ratio or percentage, the contribution margin equals 100% minus the variable costs as a percentage of sales (60%), or 40% of sales. If Denice's Hairbows operates at a sales volume of $100, the contribution margin in total dollars is $100 - $60, or $40. See Exhibit 3-2, noting the three alternative presentations of contribution margin ($40, 40%, or $.40 a unit).

For a sales volume of $100:

	Total $	% Sales	Per Unit
Sales	$ 100	100%	$ 1.00
Variable Costs	60	60%	0.60
Contribution Margin	40	40%	$ 0.40
Fixed Costs	20		
Profit	$ 20		

At the break-even point:

	Total $	% Sales	Per Unit
Sales	$ 50	100%	$ 1.00
Variable Costs	30	60%	0.60
Contribution Margin	20	40%	$ 0.40
Fixed Costs	20		
Profit	$ 0		

Exhibit 3-2   *Denice's Hairbows Contribution Margin*

At the break-even point, the contribution margin exactly equals fixed costs. This is also illustrated in Exhibit 3-2 above.

Break-even problems may be solved quickly by using a contribution margin shortcut. Returning to the algebraic approach introduced in the preceding section, recall that sales at the break-even point may be computed as:

$$
\begin{aligned}
SP_u(x) &= VC_u(x) + Fixed\ Costs \\
SP_u(x) - VC_u(x) &= Fixed\ Costs \\
(SP_u - VC_u)(x) &= Fixed\ Costs
\end{aligned}
$$

By definition, SP_u - VC_u equals the contribution margin (CM_u). Thus, at the break-even point:

$$
\begin{aligned}
CM_u(x) &= Fixed\ Costs \\
x &= Fixed\ Costs \div CM_u \\
&= Break\text{-}even\ in\ Units
\end{aligned}
$$

For example, if Denice wanted to compute the break-even point, she could compute it as follows:

$$
\frac{Fixed\ Costs}{CM_u} = \frac{\$20}{\$.40}
$$
$$
= 50\ bows
$$

Similarly, to compute the sales needed to generate $100 profit, just add profit to the numerator as follows:

$$
x = \frac{Fixed\ Costs + Profit}{CM_u}
$$
$$
= \frac{\$20 + \$100}{\$.40}
$$
$$
= 300\ bows
$$

► Margin of Safety

Another measure related to the break-even chart is called the **margin of safety**. This measure indicates the dollar amount by which planned sales exceed the break-even point. For example, assume that Denice plans $100 of sales for her hairbow business. How much could her sales fall below the planned level without dropping into a loss?

Denice's margin of safety is $50, the amount by which the planned sales of $100 exceed the break-even sales of $50. Her margin of safety may also be expressed as a percentage of budgeted sales; the margin of safety percentage equals $50/$100, or 50%. Remember the margin of safety differs from profit. For example, if Denice had been operating at the break-even point of $50 and was able to increase her sales to $100, she would have a margin of safety of $50 but not a profit of $50. As seen in Exhibit 3-2, the profit is only $20. Don't forget that when sales increase, the total variable costs for Denice's materials increase also. Since variable costs increase by $30, the resulting profit is only $20.

► PROFIT VOLUME CHART ◄

Some accountants and managers criticize the break-even chart because of its emphasis on breaking even. If the managers of an already profitable company are considering price or cost changes, they are more interested in the profit effect of these changes than they are in the break-even point effect. For example, the following cost and revenue data relate to the Shirts Galore store in Clarksville (Case 2).

	Per Shirt	
Sales price	$	40

Variable expenses		
Invoice cost		18
Sales commission		7
Total variable expenses . . .	$	25
CM_u	$	15

Fixed expenses	*Per Year*	
Rent	$	80,000
Advertising		150,000
Salaries		70,000
Total fixed expenses . .	$	300,000

Current sales level	25,000	shirts

Each shirt has a contribution margin of $15 ($40 - $25). At a sales level of 25,000 shirts, this provides a total of $375,000 to cover fixed expenses and profit. Since fixed expenses total $300,000, The Clarksville store currently operates at a profit of $75,000.

Exhibit 3-3 illustrates a profit-volume chart for these data. This chart shows the break-even point, but it focuses attention on the profit effect of price, cost or volume changes. The Clarksville store has a break-even point, based on the current strategy, of 20,000 shirts ($300,000 Fixed Expenses ÷ $15 CM_u). On the profit-volume chart, the horizontal axis ($0 profit) represents the break-even line, and a profit line is drawn from a point on the vertical axis equal to the loss incurred at zero sales volume (fixed costs) to a point representing the profits obtained at any known volume (for example, 25,000 shirts and $75,000 profit). The slope of the profit line is determined by the contribution margin ratio (i.e., the higher the contribution margin ratio, the steeper the slope).

The profit line crosses the horizontal axis at the break-even volume of 20,000 shirts. The area to the left of the break-even point in this graph represents volume levels at which the contribution

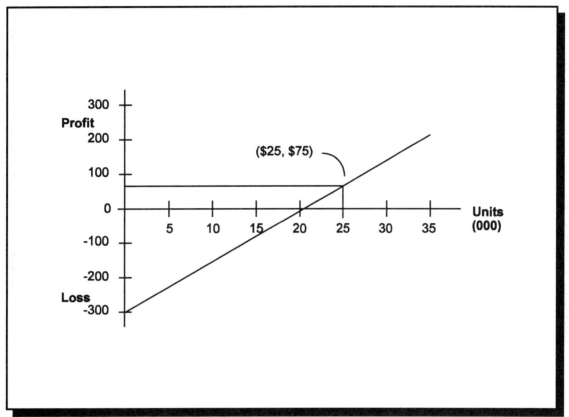

Exhibit 3-3 *Shirts Galore Clarksville Store Profit-Volume Chart*

margin does not cover fixed costs. To the right of the break-even point, the business earns a profit in an amount measured by the vertical distance between the horizontal axis and the profit line.

▸ Using the Profit Volume Chart

The manager of the Clarksville store wants to increase fixed sales salaries by $107,000 and eliminate sales commissions. Since the store already operates at a profit of $75,000, the manager is not particularly concerned about how this change affects the break-even point. If we assume that the current sales commissions provide no incentive whatsoever (rather an extravagant assumption), then sales would remain at the current level of 25,000 shirts. What would happen to profits at this level?

To help visualize the answer to this question, consider Exhibit 3-4. In this exhibit, a new profit line has been added, taking into account the proposed changes in fixed and variable costs. If the manager eliminates the $7 per shirt sales commission, the new contribution margin is $22 per shirt or 55% ($22/$40). In contrast, the original contribution margin was $15/$40 or 37.5%. The new profit line has a steeper slope due to the higher contribution margin ratio. Since fixed costs would be higher under the new plan, the new profit line crosses the vertical axis at a loss of $407,000, equal to the fixed costs when sales are zero.

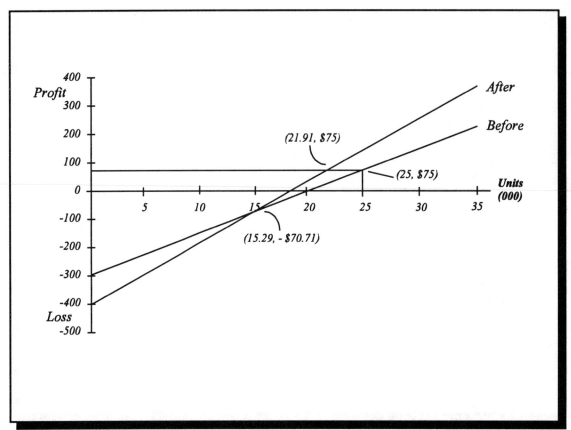

Exhibit 3-4 *Shirts Galore Clarksville Store Profit-Volume Chart*

In Exhibit 3-4, we see both the new profit line and the original profit line. At a sales volume of 25,000 shirts, the new strategy is clearly more profitable. We refer to the point at which the two profit lines cross as the point of indifference, and we can calculate it algebraically by setting total costs equal under both plans, as follows:

$$
\begin{aligned}
TC_1 &= TC_2 \\
VC_{u1}(x) + FC_1 &= VC_{u2}(x) + FC_2 \\
\$25x + \$300 &= \$18x + \$407 \\
\$7x &= \$107 \\
x &= 15{,}286 \text{ shirts}
\end{aligned}
$$

Thus, if we can assume the sales volume remains the same under either strategy, the new strategy would be more profitable at any sales level above 15,286 shirts. However, returning to the facts of the case, we must consider the validity of this assumption carefully. What happens if the commissions are, in fact, providing some degree of incentive to the sales staff? If the manager eliminates them, sales may drop. How far might sales drop below the current volume of 25,000 shirts before the new strategy results in lowered profits? A horizontal line on the profit chart in Exhibit 3-4 at a profit level of $75,000 reveals that a sales volume of 21,909 shirts under the new plan results in the same profit as a sales volume of 25,000 shirts under the old plan. Thus, managers prefer the new plan only if sales drop less than 3,091 shirts due to reduced incentives to the sales staff.

▸ TRADITIONAL VS. CONTRIBUTION INCOME STATEMENT ◂

The traditional income statement does not distinguish between fixed and variable costs. It does, however, distinguish between manufacturing or merchandising costs (cost of goods sold) and marketing and administrative costs. The contribution income statement, in contrast, emphasizes the distinction between variable and fixed costs by deducting all the variable costs (including variable cost of sales, as well as variable marketing and administrative expenses) first to arrive at the contribution margin before deducting any fixed costs. The two formats are illustrated in Exhibit 3-5 for the Bryan Reeves Automotive case introduced at the beginning of this chapter (Case 3).

Traditional		*Contribution*	
Sales	$ 500,000	Sales	$ 500,000
Cost of goods sold	280,000	Variable costs	340,000
Gross margin	$ 220,000	Contribution Margin	$ 160,000
Marketing and Admin. Exp.	120,000	Fixed Costs	60,000
Operating Income	$ 100,000	Operating Income	$ 100,000

Exhibit 3-5 *Bryan Reeves Automobile Dealership Conventional Income Statement Versus Contribution Income Statement*

While generally accepted accounting principles (GAAP) require the traditional format for financial statements prepared for outsiders, the contribution income statement format provides useful information for internal purposes. Suppose the current sales level for the Franklin dealership is $500,000, and operating income is currently $100,000. A traditional income statement proves of little help in addressing the effects of a 15% increase in sales with the addition of two new salespersons. Although we could easily compute the new sales level, we have no idea how much the expenses will change. Assume variable expenses are 68% of sales, and fixed expenses are $60,000. Variable expenses will increase (with volume), but fixed expenses will not.

The contribution income statement provides this breakdown. If we assume that the new salespersons are on straight commission (no fixed portion), then the new contribution income statement would appear as presented in Exhibit 3-6. If, on the other hand, the salespersons' compensation includes a fixed component, the contribution income statement could easily be adjusted for the increase in fixed costs.

	Current	*15% Increase*	*Projected*	*Percent*
Sales	$ 500,000	$ 75,000	$ 575,000	100%
Variable costs	340,000	51,000	391,000	68%
Contribution Margin	$ 160,000	$ 24,000	$ 184,000	32%
Fixed Costs	60,000		60,000	
Operating Income	$ 100,000		$ 124,000	

Exhibit 3-6 *Bryan Reeves Automobile Dealership Contribution Income Statement*

Finally, notice that the contribution margin does not appear anywhere on the traditional income statement. Yet this percentage provides information just as useful as any of the financial ratios usually computed for an income statement.

► LIMITATIONS OF COST-VOLUME-PROFIT ANALYSIS ◄

In Case 4 at the beginning of the chapter, Lonnie and Nick, managers of Eight by Ten, are arguing about the appropriate price for a new camera. Lonnie suggests $300, but Nick prefers $250. The camera costs the store $200. Both agree that they want the camera to generate a total profit, after deducting $1,500 of monthly advertising for the camera, of $3,000. How many cameras does the store need to sell to generate the $3,000?

With Lonnie's proposal, the CM_u is $300 - $200, or $100. Solving for a profit level of $3000:

$$x = \frac{\textit{Fixed Costs} + \textit{Profit}}{CM_u}$$
$$= \frac{\$1,500 + \$3,000}{\$100 \textit{ per camera}}$$
$$= 45 \textit{ cameras}$$

With Nick's proposal, the CM_u is $250 - $200, or $50.

Again, solving for a profit level of $3000:

$$x = \frac{\$1,500 + \$3,000}{\$50 \textit{ per camera}}$$
$$= 90 \textit{ cameras}$$

Cost-volume-profit analysis supplies the number of cameras needed under each proposal to generate $3,000 profit, but it doesn't remove a critical subjective element. Is Eight by Ten more likely to sell 90 cameras at the lower price of $250, or 45 cameras at $300? Unless Nick and Lonnie can agree on this question, the argument may continue.

► Relevant Range and Other Assumptions

We alluded to other limitations of cost-volume-profit analysis earlier in the chapter. The assumptions of linear revenues and linear total costs over some range of activity restrict the applications of this type of analysis. For example, a linear total cost relationship means that unit variable costs remain constant, and managers can use this assumption for cases in which production remains within the normal or relevant range of production activity. If production volume exceeds the normal range of production, unit costs may be different from the unit cost used in the analysis. The same holds true for activity levels below the normal range; unit costs may increase as output drops because of plant inefficiencies at low volume. When a firm operates outside the relevant range, selling prices and fixed costs may also change.

There are often different relevant ranges for different elements of both fixed and variable costs, as well as still another relevant range for sales price. One must recognize that all estimates of prices and cost must be made in the context of the specific volume levels and ranges under consideration. Cost-volume-profit analysis simplifies problems to make them fit the model. Yet this simplicity, through its isolation of one factor for analysis, is also one of the strengths of cost-volume-profit analysis. It allows an accountant or manager to focus his attention on the profit impact of price and cost changes; he can then use his judgment to adjust the results of the analysis for possible changes in competitor activity or in cost relationships. In some cases, he may wish to prepare a series of graphs or computations based on different assumptions.

The mix of products sold must also be considered. Cost-volume-profit analysis assumes that the mix of products sold by the company, or by one of its segments, remains constant throughout the relevant range of output. If the mix of products varies at different volume levels, the accountant must recognize that her analysis is faulty at the volumes at which the mix changes.

▸ OPERATING LEVERAGE VS. FINANCIAL LEVERAGE ◂

Managers sometimes refer to the contribution margin percentage or the contribution margin per unit as *operating* leverage. This margin measures the impact on profit of one dollar of sales if fixed costs remain stable. Financial leverage, on the other hand, refers to the impact on return on equity of substituting debt for equity.

With a contribution margin percentage of 40 percent, each dollar of sales increase or decrease yields a $0.40 leverage on profit if fixed costs remain stable. While high operating leverage is clearly a good thing with increasing sales volume, it can be devastating in a decreasing market, especially if fixed costs and break-even are relatively high.

Financial leverage is the ratio which converts return on long-term invested capital into return on stockholders' equity as shown below.

$$\text{Return on Long-Term Invested Capital} \times \text{Long-Term Financial Leverage} = \text{Return on Stockholders' Equity}$$

$$\frac{\text{Net Income}}{\text{Total Assets - Current Liabilities}} \times \frac{\text{Total Assets - Current Liabilities}}{\text{Stockholders' Equity}} = \frac{\text{Net Income}}{\text{Stockholders' Equity}}$$

$$\frac{\$115,000}{\$2,510,000 - 590,000} \times \frac{\$2,510,000 - \$590,000}{\$1,520,000} = \frac{\$115,000}{\$1,520,000}$$

$$5.99\% \times 1.263 = 7.57\%$$

Numerically speaking, financial leverage is 1.263, which means that financial leverage raises the return on long-term invested capital by 26.3 percent to yield a return on stockholders' equity of 7.57 percent. The 26.3 percent increase is a function of using debt rather than equity for financing. This can be shown by algebraically rearranging the long-term financial leverage as shown below. The difference between numerator and denominator in financial leverage is the long-term debt, which is 26.3 percent of stockholders' equity.

$$\text{Long-Term Financial Leverage} = \frac{\text{Total Assets - Current Liabilities}}{\text{Stockholders' Equity}} = \frac{\text{Total Assets - Current Liabilities}}{\text{Total Assets - Total Liabilities}} = \frac{\text{Stockholders' Equity + Long-Term Debt}}{\text{Stockholders' Equity}}$$

Like operating leverage, financial leverage works great during good times but can be devastating in a declining market, particularly if interest on debt (a financial fixed cost rather than an operating fixed cost) is relatively high. Hence, extremely high leverage of either form presents potential risk, with the riskiness influenced by fixed cost levels and by the stability or volatility of the marketplace.

▶ SOME EXTENSIONS OF COST-VOLUME-PROFIT ANALYSIS ◀

Tying cost-volume-profit analysis to ratio analysis provides some interesting extensions of break-even analysis. Consider the following data:

Selling price per unit	$ 10
Variable cost per unit	$ 6
Operating fixed costs	$ 470,000
Expected volume	185,000 units
Long-term liabilities	$ 400,000
Interest rate	10%
Stockholders' equity	$ 1,510,000
Income tax rate	40%

▶ Brief Review

As discussed earlier, we can compute the break-even point in terms of operating income as shown below.

$$\text{Unit Break-Even Calculation} = \frac{\text{Operating Fixed Costs}}{\text{Contribution Margin Per Unit}} = \frac{\$470,000}{\$4} = 117,500 \text{ units}$$

$$\text{Dollar Break-Even} = \frac{\text{Operating Fixed Costs}}{\text{Contribution Margin Percentage}} = \frac{\$470,000}{0.4} = \$1,175,000$$

▶ Level of Volume to Achieve Desired Operating Income Percentage

If a company wants to earn a 6% operating income percentage, we can modify the break-even calculations as follows:

$$\text{Level of Volume to Achieve Desired Operating Income Percentage} = \frac{\text{Fixed Operating Costs}}{\text{Contribution Margin Percentage} - \text{Desired Operating Income Percentage}} = \frac{\$470,000}{0.40 - 0.06} = \frac{\$470,000}{0.34} = \$1,382,353$$

A target operating income percentage of 6% reduces the profit margin percentage available to cover operating costs to 34 percent, and the following income statement shows these results in tabular form.

Sales	$ 1,382,353	100%
Variable Costs	829,412	60%
Contribution Margin . . .	$ 552,941	40%
Fixed Costs	470,000	34%
Operating Income	$ 82,941	6%

▸ Level of Volume to Achieve Desired Return on Stockholders' Equity

Just as managers can specify a target operating income percentage, they can also define a desired return on equity. Assume managers choose a 10 percent return as their goal and that company debt carries a rate of 10%. The basic calculations are as follows:

$$\begin{array}{l} \textit{Level of Volume to Achieve} \\ \textit{Desired Return on} \\ \textit{Stockholders' Equity} \end{array} = \dfrac{\begin{array}{ccc} \textit{Fixed Operating} & + & \textit{Interest} & + & \textit{Desired} \\ \textit{Costs} & & \textit{Costs} & & \textit{Return} \end{array}}{\textit{Contribution Margin Percentage}}$$

$$= \frac{\$470,000 \quad + \quad 0.10\,(\$400,000) \quad + \quad 0.10\,(\$1,510,000)}{0.40}$$

$$= \frac{\$470,000 \quad + \quad \$40,000 \quad + \quad \$151,000}{0.40}$$

$$= \frac{\$661,000}{0.40} = \$1,652,500$$

In this formulation, the contribution margin must cover fixed costs, interest and the desired rate of return on stockholders' equity. The following income statement verifies our results.

Sales	$1,652,500	100%
Variable Costs	991,500	60%
Contribution Margin .	$ 661,000	40%
Operating Fixed Costs	470,000	
Operating Income . . .	$ 191,000	
Interest Expense	40,000	
Net Income	$ 151,000	

$$\textit{Return of Stockholders' Equity} \ = \ \frac{\$151,000}{\$1,510,000} \ = \ 10\%$$

Taxes and the Desired Return. We next modify the above formulas to recognize the impact of income taxes (40% in our illustration). This formulation generates the required sales volume for a desired *after tax* operating income percentage or a desired *after tax* return on stockholders' equity. First, we must convert operating income percentages to before-tax percentages. For example, a 6% after-tax operating income percentage converts to a 10% before tax number as shown below:

$$\frac{\textit{after-tax percentage}}{\textit{(1-tax rate)}} = \begin{array}{c} \textit{pretax operating} \\ \textit{income percentage} \end{array}$$

$$\frac{0.06}{(1-.4)} = \frac{0.06}{.6} = 10\%$$

Similarly, a 10% after tax return on stockholders' equity converts to 16.67% as the following calculations show:

$$\frac{\textit{after-tax percentage}}{\textit{(1-tax rate)}} = \begin{array}{c} \textit{pretax return on} \\ \textit{stockholders' equity} \end{array}$$

$$\frac{0.10}{(1-.4)} = \frac{.10}{.6} = 16.67\%$$

The equations for these calculations are as follows:

$$\begin{array}{c}\textit{Level of Volume To}\\ \textit{Achieve Desired Operating}\\ \textit{Income (After Tax)}\end{array} = \frac{\textit{Fixed Operating Costs}}{\begin{array}{c}\textit{Contribution Margin Percentage - Desired}\\ \textit{Pretax Operating Income Percentage}\end{array}}$$

$$\begin{array}{c}\textit{Level of Volume To}\\ \textit{Achieve Desired}\\ \textit{Return on Stockholders'}\\ \textit{Equity (After Tax)}\end{array} = \frac{\begin{array}{c}\textit{Fixed Operating}\\ \textit{Costs}\end{array} + \begin{array}{c}\textit{Interest}\\ \textit{Costs}\end{array} + \begin{array}{c}\textit{Desired Pretax}\\ \textit{Return}\end{array}}{\textit{Contribution Margin Percentage}}$$

Clearly the sales volume must be higher than that in the preceding section because sales must cover taxes and still provide either a 6% operating income percentage or a 10% return on stockholders' equity (after tax).

► USEFULNESS IN DECISION-MAKING ◄

The break-even chart and the profit graph are most fruitfully employed as a means of presenting financial information in a graphical form. These graphs provide a readily understood picture of cost-volume-profit relationships for decision makers who are uncomfortable with numbers; or, even if the decision makers enjoy working with numerical analyses, the graphical presentation of data furnish a useful summary of the significant relationships.

For instance, if fixed costs are high, volume fluctuations usually result in wide fluctuations in profit. On the other hand, a business with low fixed costs generally experiences narrower swings in profit, as volume varies, than the firm with high fixed costs. Both these relationships can be concisely demonstrated by shifting the lines on the graph.

Do not assume that fixed costs are beyond the manager's control. No costs are truly fixed in the long-run, and some may even be altered in the short-run. Although reduction of fixed costs is one way to increase profits, remember also that low fixed costs do not necessarily indicate a good profit structure, for some of the most important approaches to enhanced profits require fixed cost increases to reduce variable costs or to increase revenues.

► SUMMARY ◄

Break-even or cost-volume-profit analysis provides managers with a useful technique for evaluating the relationships among cost, volume, and profit. These relationships, rather than knowledge of any specific break-even point, provide the real managerial value of this tool. When interpreting cost-volume-profit graphs or calculations, managers should keep in mind that linear relationships often do not hold at extremely high or extremely low levels of volume and that the mix of products sold can impact the results of these calculations. A particularly useful application of cost-volume-profit analysis is the contribution income statement, which presents information in a format readily adaptable by managers for profit analyses.

SEPARATING COSTS INTO FIXED AND VARIABLE COMPONENTS VIA THE HIGH-LOW METHOD

Accountants identify the fixed and variable components of a cost using the "high-low" method. Under this method, accountants determine the total costs for the minimum and maximum activity level of the usual operating range, and then use the following formulas:

$$\frac{Variable\ Cost\ Per}{Unit\ of\ Activity} = \frac{Change\ in\ Total\ Cost\ Between\ Minimum\ and\ Maximum\ Activity}{Change\ in\ Activity\ Units\ Between\ Minimum\ and\ Maximum\ Activity}$$

$$Fixed\ Cost^1 = \begin{array}{c} Total\ Cost \\ at\ Maximum \\ Activity \end{array} - \begin{array}{c} Variable\ Cost \\ at\ Maximum \\ Activity \end{array}$$

When they use this calculation, accountants assume that only the variable costs will change as activity changes.

The following example illustrates how accountants use these formulas to determine the variable and fixed components of marketing and administrative costs. The data represent total cost at high and low sales activity levels.

	Total Cost	Units of Sales
Maximum activity	$ 24,780	5,000
Minimum activity	18,570	3,200
Difference or change	$ 6,210	1,800

---

[1] Accountants can also estimate fixed costs by computing the total cost at an activity level of zero.

Since the fixed costs should normally be the same for both activity levels, the only costs that change are the variable costs:

$$Variable\ Cost\ per\ Unit\ of\ Activity\ =\ \frac{\$6,210}{1,800\ units}$$

$$=\ \$3.45\ per\ unit$$

$$Fixed\ Cost\ =\ \$24,780 - [(5,000)(\$3.45)]$$

$$=\ \$24,780 - \$17,250$$

$$=\ \$7,530$$

Note how the formulas approximate variable cost by calculating the average rate of cost change with respect to change in activity. This amount indicates how much total cost will change for each unit increase in the activity. Other methods of determining the fixed and variable components of cost will be discussed in the chapter on regression analysis.

▸ QUESTIONS ◂

3-1. Define the following: (a) break-even point, (b) break-even chart, (c) profit contribution percentage, (d) profit-volume chart, and (e) contribution per unit.

3-2. What is the relevant range as it relates to break-even analysis?

3-3. Why is relevant range only a guide which must be used with caution?

3-4. Define and distinguish between variable and fixed costs.

3-5. Discuss the limitations of break-even analysis which arise out of the assumptions underlying break-even analysis.

3-6. What are cost-volume-profit relationships?

3-7. Define the term margin of safety as it relates to break-even analysis.

3-8. Any change in the data used in the break-even calculations will have an effect on the margin of the safety. Discuss.

3-9. If the traditional income statement has the same operating income and net income after taxes as the contribution income statement, why bother going to the trouble of separating the fixed and variable costs? Discuss.

3-10. Contrast operating leverage with financial leverage.

3-11. Of what value is the distinction between fixed and variable costs for planning and decision-making purposes?

3-12. Of what value is the distinction between fixed and variable costs for control purposes?

▸ EXERCISES AND PROBLEMS ◂

3-13. Break-even Calculations.

The Best Company produces a single product to sell for $10 per unit. The company incurs $36,000 in fixed costs, and variable costs run $4 per unit.

Required:

a. Compute the contribution margin per unit.
b. Compute the break-even point in (1) units, and (2) sales dollars.
c. What would the total sales dollars have to be to produce a net income of $3,000?

3-14. Break-Even Calculations.

A company's budget shows sales of 300,000 units and revenues of $2,400,000. Variable costs are $1,200,000 and fixed costs are $900,000.

Required:

a. 1. What is the break-even point in units and dollars?
    2. What is the contribution margin percentage?
    3. Calculate the margin of safety.
    4. Construct a break-even chart and a profit-volume chart for the above data.

b. Assuming a 10 percent increase in sales prices and variable costs, recalculate, (1), (2) and (3) above.

c. Assuming a desired profit after tax (50% rate) of $100,000, what level of sales must be achieved to reach the $100,000 profit after tax?

d. Assuming a 10 percent reduction in variable costs and a 10 percent increase in fixed cost, recalculate (1), (2), and (3) above.

3-15. Approximating Cost-Volume-Profit Relationships.

A company does not have standard costs or budgets. For the past five years, sales and costs, respectively, were $46,000 and $37,000; $40,000 and $34,500; $54,000 and $40,000; $50,000 and $38,000; and $48,000 and $37,000. Projected sales and costs for the current year are $56,000 and $44,000. Fixed costs have been averaging $20,000 per year.

Required:

Analyze the company's projected operations for the current year and determine if the cost-volume-profit relationships of prior years are being maintained.

3-16. Projecting Profit and Break-Even Data.

A client has recently leased manufacturing facilities for production of a new product. Based on studies made by his staff, the following data have been made available to you:

Estimated annual sales 24,000   units

Estimated costs	*Amount*	*Per Unit*
Material	$ 96,000	$ 4.00
Direct labor	14,400	.60
Overhead	24,000	1.00
Administrative expense	28,800	1.20
Total	$ 163,200	$ 6.80

Selling expenses are expected to be 15 percent of sales and profit to be $1.02 per unit.

Required:

a. Compute the selling price per unit.
b. Project an income statement for the year.
c. Compute a break-even point expressed in dollars and in units, assuming that overhead and administration expenses are fixed but that other costs are fully variable.

3-17. Break-Even After Income Taxes.
The Wencam Company Ltd. produced and sold 55,000 units during 20x1. The following amounts were obtained from the financial statements for the year ended December 31, 20x1:

Sales	$ 2,475,000
Direct materials used ($)	467,500
Direct labor costs	805,750
Variable overhead incurred	269,500
Fixed overhead incurred	347,800
Selling and administrative costs:	
Fixed	187,200
Variable	129,500

     * The relevant range for fixed costs is 10,000 units to 85,000 units.

Expectations for 20x2:

1. Variable and fixed costs are expected to behave in the same manner as indicated above, but inflation is expected to increase costs in general by 12 percent.
2. The selling price is expected to be raised by 10 percent.
3. The company's 20x2 income tax rate is expected to be 35 percent.

Required:

How many units would the company be required to sell in 20x2 in order to earn net income after taxes of $211,250? Show all calculations.

(SMA adapted)

3-18. Break-Even After Taxes and Two Levels of Output.
The B.M. Company Limited had the following budgeted income statement based upon production and sales estimates of 20,000 units.

Sales		$ 400,000
Cost of goods sold:		
Direct Materials	$ 80,000	
Direct labor	60,000	
Variable Overhead	40,000	
Fixed Overhead	100,000	
Total cost of goods sold		$ 280,000
Gross profit		120,000
Selling and administrative costs:		
Variable	$ 30,000	
Fixed	40,000	
Total selling and administrative costs .		70,000
Net income before taxes		$ 50,000
Less : Income taxes (40%)		20,000
Budgeted net income after taxes		$ 30,000

(relevant range of 15,000 to 50,000 units)

Required:

a. How many units would the company have to produce and sell to attain a desired net income after taxes of $48,000? Show all calculations.

b. During 20x3 the company produced 25,000 units and sold 20,000 units. All costs and revenue behaved precisely as expected, but net income after taxes was $42,000 instead of the $30,000 budgeted. Why was the net income different from expected?

(SMA adapted)

3-19. Calculation of Prediction Error.

A company sets the price for its product at $300 per unit. Predicted variable costs are $175 per unit and fixed costs are expected to be $600,000 a year. Sales for the year are expected to be 8,000 units.

Required:

a. Determine the prediction error for net income if actual variable costs were $190 per unit. All other predictions are correct.

b. Assume all predictions were correct, except that 11,000 units could have been sold at the $300 price if enough had been available. However, only 8,000 units were produced and sold. Determine the cost of the prediction error.

(SMA adapted)

3-20. A "Target" Price and Profit.

The following data relate to the Howle Manufacturing Corporation for 20x2.

Sales (30,000 units)		$ 450,000
Returns, allowances, and discounts . .		13,500
Net Sales		$ 436,500
Cost of goods sold		306,000
Gross Profits		$ 130,500
. . . .		
Selling Expenses	$ 60,000	
Administrative expenses	30,000	90,000
Net income (before income taxes) . . .		$ 40,500

The budget committee has estimated the following changes in income and costs for 20x3:

30% increase in number of units sold.
20% increase in material unit cost.
15% increase in direct labor cost per unit.
10% increase in production overhead cost per unit.
14% increase in selling expenses.
7% increase in administrative expenses.

As inventory quantities remain fairly constant, the committee considered that, for budget purposes, any change in inventory valuation can be ignored. The composition of the cost of a unit of finished product during 20x2 for direct materials, direct labor, and manufacturing overhead, respectively, was in the ratio of 3 to 2 to 1. Production overhead and selling expenses are expected to be 50 percent fixed, and administrative expenses are normally 100 percent fixed. No changes in production methods or credit policies are contemplated for 20x3.

Required:

Compute the unit sales price (adjusted to the nearest full cent) at which the Howle Corporation must sell its only product in 20x3 in order to earn a budgeted income (before income taxes) of $60,000.

3-21. Evaluation of Cost-Volume-Profit Relationships.
Data for the year 20x7 are as follows:

> Sales, 150,000 units sold at $5 per unit.
> Variable costs, $3 per unit.
> Fixed costs, $200,000.
> Capital employed, $800,000.
> Federal income tax rate, 50 percent.

For the year 20x8, the following changes in cost-volume profit relationships are proposed:

a. Attempt to increase sales volume 15 percent via a 5 percent decrease in sales price.
b. Reduce variable costs 5 percent through the acquisition of new equipment which would add $20,000 to annual fixed costs and $100,000 to capital employed.

Required:

Determine which, if any, of the proposed changes would be financially justifiable. Assume that results for 20x8 would be the same as 20x7 without the proposed changes. Assume a minimum desired return of 6 percent after tax.

3-22. Calculate Break-Even, Margin of Safety and Decision-Making.
The Nova Company produces only one product Grassnipper. The company has received an order from a large retail chain store for 10,000 Grassnippers at $26 each. This sale will have no impact on the present sales (i.e., will not affect price or volume.)
The president noted from the income statement below that the unit cost of goods sold, based on 50,000 units, was $26.60; and although there would be virtually no marketing or administrative costs, she stated that the offer was $0.60 below cost.

Nova Company
Income Statement
Year Ended December 31, 20x4

Sales	$ 1,850,000
Cost of goods sold	1,330,000
Gross profit	$ 520,000
Marketing and administrative expense	250,000
Operating income	$ 270,000

Required:

a. What advice would you give the president on accepting the order if you have the following facts: (1) Nova will save $0.03 a unit because the chain will be putting on their own brand name labels; (2) of the total cost of goods sold, the variable amount is $1,006,400; and marketing and administrative variable cost is $146,000.

b. Based on the facts above:

1. Calculate the break-even point in units for 20x4.

2. Based on present sales level, calculate the margin of safety.

3. Another order is received for 5,000 units at $28. If the order is accepted, the chain's must be rejected due to available capacity. The president notes that the new order will bring a gross profit of $1.40 a unit ($28.00 - $26.60). Should she accept the new order over the chain's order?

3-23. A Problem in Decision-Making.

The Middle-Atlantic Territory of the Flick Company has produced results for the past three years which average as follows:

Sales		$1,380,000
Cost of goods sold-standard		975,000
Gross profit		$ 405,000
Operating expenses:		
Commissions—10% gross profit	$ 40,500	
Salaries	105,000	
Stationery	7,500	
Supplies	4,500	
Postage	1,500	
Travel	93,000	
Telephone	25,200	
Rent	6,900	
Depreciation	11,400	
Insurance	5,055	
Taxes—general	6,600	
Taxes—payroll	4,365	
Sales promotion	14,400	
Credit and collection	15,700	
Warehousing	7,200	
Delivery	18,300	
Home office expense	60,000	427,120
Net loss		$ (22,120)

Sales promotion and home office expenses are allocated to territories on the basis of sales revenues. Credit and collection expenses are allocated on the basis of customers, whereas warehousing costs are allocated on the basis of orders, and delivery costs are allocated on the basis of miles traveled.

The company recognizes some arbitrariness in its cost allocations to sales territories but feels that the allocations are necessary to portray adequately the income of each territory. To support bases of allocation, the company has found the following correlations to exist.

Sales promotion expenses	—	a variable rate of .2 percent of sales
Home office expenses	—	a variable rate of 1 percent of sales
Credit and collection expenses	—	a variable rate of $1.50 per customer per year
Warehousing expenses	—	a variable rate of $1.80 per order
Delivery expenses	—	a variable rate of $0.09 per mile traveled

During the past three years, the number of customers has averaged 500, number of orders has averaged 2,000, and miles traveled by delivery trucks in the territory has averaged 150,000. Payroll taxes usually average 3 percent total commissions and salaries.

The average sales breakdown is as follows:

| | Products | | |
	X	Y	Z
Units sold	80,000	60,000	100,000
Units selling price	$ 4.50	$ 4.50	$ 7.50
Total Sales	$ 360,000	$ 270,000	$ 750,000

Unit standard manufacturing costs for each product are as follows:

| | Products | | |
	X	Y	Z
Variable Costs	$ 1.50	$ 0.60	$ 3.60
Fixed Costs	$ 2.25	$ 3.15	$ .90
Total Unit Cost	$ 3.75	$ 3.75	$ 4.50

In terms of controls, the territory manager cannot influence the fixed portions of allocated costs, insurance, general taxes, and his own salary of $24,000.

Management is quite concerned about the profitability of this territory. They have tried every conceivable means of reducing costs to no avail. Now they are considering the following alternatives to improve income:

a. Abandon the territory.
b. Attempt to improve territory profit by a change in product mix via a heavier concentration on Product Y which contributes as much to fixed costs and profits as Product Z.
c. Operate as they are currently operating.

Complete abandonment of the territory would not result in a reduction of fixed manufacturing costs or the fixed costs of the home office or service departments. All other costs would be eliminated.

The heavier concentration on Product Y would not change the sales picture for Products X and Z nor the sales price of Product Y. A sales promotion program which will cost $30,000 annually is expected to increase unit sales of Product Y by 20,000. The extra production of Product Y will require overtime and thus a 10 percent increase in variable manufacturing costs and a $3,000 annual increase in fixed manufacturing costs. New customers should average 20, new orders would average 50, and miles traveled should remain stable.

Required:

a. If you were the accountant for the Flick Company, what would your calculations force you to recommend to management?
b. By how much would fixed costs of manufacturing, the home office, and service departments have to change for you to consider revising your recommendations?
c. What other income-improvement alternatives do you see in this type of situation?
d. How might capital employed in the territory enter into your recommendations?

3-24. Significance of the Profit Contribution Percentage, Factors Impacting on the Profit Contribution Percentage.
Assume the following:

> Present sales: $400,000 (100,000 units @ $4.00)
> Variable cost: $.72 per sales dollar ($2.88 per unit)
> Fixed cost: $80,000

  a. Find the effect on profit of:
   1. A decrease of 25 percent in sales volume.
   2. An increase of 25 percent in sales volume.
   3. An increase of 50 percent in sales volume.
  b. Same as (a) above except that variable costs equal $.60 per sales dollar.
  c. What is the effect (increase or decrease) of each of the following on the profit contribution percentage and the break-even point.
   1. An increase in sales price of 10 percent?
   2. A decrease in sales price of 10 percent?
   3. An increase of $.14 per unit in variable costs?
   4. A decrease of $.14 per unit in variable costs?
   5. An increase of 5 percent in total fixed costs?
   6. A decrease of 5 percent in total fixed costs?

3-25. Break-Even and Cost-Volume-Profit Analysis.
The Magic Silicon Manufacturing Company produces a product called Slipitey Slide on a line in one of its plants. The following data have been collected about this product on a per unit basis.

Sales price	$ 100
Variable costs:	
Material	45
Processing	10
Total variable costs	55
Contribution Margin	$ 45
Traceable monthly fixed cost .	$18,000

Required:

  a. Compute the monthly break-even sales in dollars.
  b. Compute the monthly contribution margin in dollars for sales of 1,000 units.
  c. If the company sells 500 units in one month, what unit sales price must the company charge to generate a contribution margin of $30,500?
  d. Assume the company normally sells 900 units per month. Compute the profit increase or decrease (indicate which) if the company drops the product from its product line.

3-26. Effect on Profits of One-Price Approach to Selling Automobiles.

The Sunday *New York Times* Business Section (October 11, 1992) contained a story ("Moving Out the Cars With a `No-Dicker Sticker,'" p. 12) about one price auto dealers and the profit effect of using a one price approach. The following questions use material from that story.

Required:

a. Robert Fisher of Reading, Pennsylvania, lowered his average contribution margin on automobiles from $1,100 to $700. Assume he sells 120 cars per month; how much must he cut monthly fixed expenses to make up for the reduced margin?

b. Use the information from question a to answer the following. How many additional units must Robert Fisher sell to make the same profit he made before the price change assuming his monthly fixed expenses remain the same as they were before the price change?

c. How much will Robert's monthly profit increase if he increases monthly sales to 207 units with the new price while reducing monthly fixed costs by $8,000?

d. "Mark Eddins instituted no-haggle selling in March at his Chevrolet-Mazda and Oldsmobile-Cadillac-Jeep/Eagle showrooms in Texas. Sales are up 50 percent at all franchises, he said." If Mark was selling 2,000 units per month at an average contribution margin of $1,200 before he switched to the no-haggle pricing approach, how much margin must each vehicle produce under the new system if Mark wants to earn the same monthly profit he generated before adopting the new pricing policy. Assume his fixed costs are the same after the change in pricing policy as they were before the change and that the 50% sales increase refers to unit sales.

e. Compute the break-even point in units for a dealer who incurs $66,000 per month in fixed costs and sells cars for $500 above dealer cost. The manufacturer whose cars he sells pays him a "holdback" of 3% of the suggested list price of the automobile for each car the dealer sells. Assume the average car the dealer sells has a suggested list price of $20,000.

f. Assume the dealer in question **e** currently has six salespersons working for him at an average annual compensation of $18,000 plus commissions of $500 per car sold. In addition each salesperson receives a benefit package that costs the dealer $2,400 per year. The average automobile sold costs the dealer (net of all discounts and factory refunds, including holdbacks) $17,500 and sells for $19,000. Compute the monthly profit impact of changing to a no-haggle price that drops the average price of the car to $18,400, that eliminates the entire sales force and replaces them with six customer service representatives who earn $15,000 per year plus annual benefits of $2,400, and that increases unit sales volume 30%. Before changing to the new system, the dealer sold 200 cars per month; under the new system the suggested list price remains at $20,000 per car.

3-27. Effects on Profits of Price Cuts.

Compaq announced a variety of price cuts on its machines in September of 1992, and the results were amazing. Sales soared, and the company could not produce products fast enough to meet customer demand. The following requirements are based on a story in the December 14, 1992 issue of *Fortune* that describes some of the events at Compaq.

Required:

a. Contribution margin before the price cuts was 34% of sales for a typical machine. How much will quarterly profit change if the company reduces prices by 20% and dollar sales double (assume quarterly sales before the price change were $500 million). Assume unit variable costs and company fixed costs remain constant as the price changes.

b. Assume that in addition to all the changes that occur in question a, Compaq also makes cuts in unit variable costs of 30%. By how much will profits change?

c. Third quarter sales at Compaq increased 50% over sales of the previous quarter to a level of $1.1 billion, and earnings from operations quadrupled from the previous quarter to $72 million. The contribution margin percentage for the quarter was only 28% in contrast to that of 34% for previous quarters. Compute your estimate of quarterly fixed costs for Compaq.

d. By studying and analyzing actual failures, Compaq engineers were able to reduce the burn-in time for new machines from 96 hours to 2 hours. Assume that each computer in the burn-in process requires two square feet of floor space in a manufacturing facility. How many square feet of manufacturing facility were made available by this change? Assume the company produces 5,000 units per day.

e. Use your answer to question d to answer this question. Compaq has a backlog of demand for its machines, so production space is at a premium. How much was the change above worth to the company if each square foot of production space generates a quarterly contribution margin of $2,000?

f. "Compaq has totally revamped how it prices its products. In the past, product designers totaled up the cost of all the features they wanted on a machine, figured out which sole supplier would provide each part at what price, and added on a margin like 40%. The total was the price to dealers who typically added another 15% markup.

"Now the process is reversed. Managers first establish what they want the street price to be based on competitive factors. Then they assume a dealer markup, subtract a Compaq gross margin—about 30% today—and instruct the departments of materials, engineering, manufacturing and marketing to resolve among themselves how to allocate the remaining costs to make the product." David Kirkpatrick "The Revolution At Compaq Computer," *Fortune* (December, 14, 1992), p. 86.

Assume you have assembled the following information about a new machine Compaq plans to introduce.

Components from Xeijang, Inc. . . . . $ 200
Components from Okie Electronics 150
Components from Compaq plant 450

Compute the price Compaq would have charged to its dealers under its old pricing system.

Assume a customer will pay $1,200 for this machine and that dealers still add 15% to their cost to arrive at the retail price. Compute the allowable cost for the components from the Compaq plant if the other components stay at the same cost as that shown above. Hint: The markup on cost is not the same as the markup on sales, e.g., a 15% markup on cost for an item costing $100 represents only about a 13% margin on sales.

$$\frac{.15}{1.15} = .13$$

Learning Objectives

After reading this chapter, the student should have an understanding of:

✔ The basic principles and problems of budgeting including terminology, purpose, scope, budget period, responsibility for and ultimate goal of budgeting.

✔ The difference between a flexible budget and a fixed or static budget.

✔ Moving or rolling budget.

✔ Return on invested capital as a part of the budgetary process, including alternative definitions of invested capital.

✔ The details of budget preparation including budgets for sales revenue, production, expenses, cash receipts and disbursements, income statement and balance sheet.

The CEO at Caterpillar, needs some idea of what sales will be next year to make sound decisions about how many tractors to produce, and the President of American Airlines must evaluate next year's air travel demand before selecting an offering of flight sche- dules for the airline. In both cases the executives use budget data to develop their final plans. When developed carefully and used appropriately, budgets can help any organization, whether profit-seeking or not-for-profit, to plan for and accomplish the firm's objectives.

This chapter discusses the development and use of budget systems. We introduce the case of Will Harper, an entrepreneurial student who needs additional funds for his college expenses and for his favorite foods and entertainment (burritos, concerts, etc.—essential items for a successful college career).

After presenting Will's case, we summarize the basic principles and problems of budgeting, including terminology, purpose, scope, budget period, responsibility for and ultimate goals of budgeting. In addition, we expand our discussion to include some terminology and techniques not illustrated by Will, but which should prove useful in more complex organizations.

▶ WILL HARPER ◀

▶ Student Entrepreneur

The jangle of the phone interrupted Will's concentration. He was still in the well-worn sweat shorts that he slept in every night. It was late September, and in a couple of months he would be switching to sweat pants. Already the nights were getting a little cooler. Today was Saturday, one day of the week when he could sleep in without worrying about being late for class. But he hadn't been sleeping. He had been sitting at his desk, sketching the outline for his business idea.

"Hello?"

"Will!" It was Marie's voice, usually sweet but edged today with irritation. "I thought you were going to call me."

"Huh?" He doodled the logo of Eastern State University as he talked. "Oh, yeah, right. I'm sorry. What time is it?"

"Nearly ten. I thought we were going out for breakfast."

"Do you still want to go?" he asked, half hoping she would say no. He wasn't really hungry at the moment.

"Do you?" returned Marie.

Will hesitated, unscrewing his fountain pen as he did so. An ink cartridge, a metal tip, a small plastic cap, a larger plastic cover, and, of course, the case. Pretty simple. These parts couldn't cost much.

"Well?" Marie prompted him.

"Huh?" For the life of him, Will couldn't remember what her question had been.

"Forget it!" Marie slammed the receiver.

As Will hung up the phone, he realized that Marie's irritation hadn't thwarted his enthusiasm for his project. What was it she had been asking anyway? Oh, yeah, it had to do with breakfast. Will's mother had always said Will would forget to eat if he had something on his mind.

Marie, on the other hand, never forgot to eat. He liked to tease her about consuming mammoth quantities of food, though she hardly weighed over a hundred pounds. He supposed he should call her back, but first . . .

He reached for the stack of graph paper on which he had been doodling and screwed his pen back together. Accounting paper would be more appropriate for what he had in mind, but the graph paper was handy.

▸ Will's Idea

The thing that had created so much tension between Will and Marie was his plan to make fountain pens to sell to students, school supporters, alumni, etc. Of course, the school's logo would be on each pen.

If he worked hard, maybe he could have the operation going by October. Will knew enough about business to know that November and December were critical months. He would promote the pens as smart, affordable Christmas gifts (only about $2.50 a pen) for students on a budget. Budget! That was what he needed, budgets for his new business.

▸ Sales Budget: The Starting Point

He remembered from his accounting class that a sales budget was the starting point for all the other plans or budgets. How many pens could he expect to sell? He chewed on his pen and estimated. More, certainly, in November and December, but some in October and some after Christmas. He decided to set up his sales plan for six months starting in October. Eastern State had an enrollment of approximately 30,000 students. If one of every ten bought a set of three pens, that would be 9,000 pens, and if alumni bought another 6,000 pens (there were a lot of alumni still in the community, after all), that would be a lot of pens! After some thought, he estimated 1,500 pens a month for the slower months and 4,500 each for November and December. See Exhibit 4-1.

Month	Volume	Unit Price	Revenue
October	1,500	$ 2.50	$ 3,750
November	4,500	2.50	11,250
December	4,500	2.50	11,250
January	1,500	2.50	3,750
February	1,500	2.50	3,750
March	1,500	2.50	3,750
Total	15,000	$ 2.50	$ 37,500

Exhibit 4-1 *Budgeted Sales Revenue for the Six Months Ended March 31, 200x*

▸ Production Budget

"Wow, if I plan to sell 4,500 pens in November, I better really get my production cranked up in October," Will surprised himself by speaking his thoughts out loud. He felt a sort of elation, as if by doing so, he had just cemented his idea, changing it from dream status to reality. Will figured that he needed at least half the estimated November sales in inventory at the end of October. This meant he must produce 3,750 pens in October to cover the expected 1,500 units of sales and to build an inventory of 2,250 by the end of October. In December, Will decided to lower production significantly in anticipation of only 1,500 pens sold per month after Christmas. He figured that 500 pens in ending inventory would easily take care of upcoming sales in succeeding months. See Exhibit 4-2.

	October	November	December	January	February	March	Total
Estimated Sales							
Volume	1,500	4,500	4,500	1,500	1,500	1,500	15,000
Add: Desired End.							
Inventory	2,250	2,250	500	500	500	500	500
Total Units Required	3,750	6,750	5,000	2,000	2,000	2,000	15,500
Minus: Beginning							
Inventory		2,250	2,250	500	500	500	
Production Required	3,750	4,500	2,750	1,500	1,500	1,500	15,500

Exhibit 4-2 *Production Requirements for the Six Months Ended March 31, 200x*

▸ Will's Resources

Of course, the real question of interest to Will was how much profit he could generate. But before he could even think about profits, he had to estimate the costs of producing the pens. He was not totally without resources. His grandfather had given him some common stock as a high school graduation gift. Unless he could earn more money by selling the stock and investing the proceeds in his business, he would be better off to stick with the return generated by the stock itself.

Somewhere Will had a copy of the company's annual report from last year, probably in a box in his closet. He pushed the sliding doors open, and a tennis racket tumbled off the top shelf, narrowly missing Will's head. He groaned as he started through a seemingly endless stack of papers.

Surprised, he emerged a few minutes later triumphantly bearing the annual report. Luckily it had been near the top. He recalled a conversation with his grandfather as he turned the pages.

"This may not be the most flamboyant investment around," Gramps had said. "It won't be one where you can brag about tripling your net worth in a matter of months. But year after year, it's been a steady, solid investment, averaging a good—"Gramps had gone on to specify a percentage, but here Will's memory failed him. He couldn't remember the amount.

Unsure how to read the annual report, Will considered phoning Gramps. Gramps had been quite an entrepreneur himself in his day, starting a laundry business from scratch and building it to a thriving profit earner, sought after by a number of investors. Gramps had finally sold for a tidy sum and retired to Florida. If Marie wasn't excited about Will's idea, Gramps would be. He reached for the phone.

But he hesitated with the phone at his ear. He would prefer to share his success with Gramps rather than his idea. Gramps would have his own ideas of how it should be done, probably good ones, but Will wanted to do it by himself. Slowly he returned the receiver to the wall and reached instead for a textbook.

▸ Return on Investment

Armed with a few formulas, Will estimated the return of the company he owned stock in for the past couple of years at an average of 12% per year on total assets, or 20% per year on stockholders' equity. The formulas Will used were:

$$\text{Return on Total Assets} = \frac{\text{Net Income}}{\text{Total Assets}}$$

$$\text{Return on Stockholders' Equity} = \text{Profit Margin} \times \text{Asset Turnover} \times \text{Financial Leverage}$$

$$= \frac{\text{Net Income}}{\text{Sales}} \times \frac{\text{Sales}}{\text{Total Assets}} \times \frac{\text{Total Assets}}{\text{Stockholders' Equity}}$$

If his fountain pen business was to be judged a success, then, Will figured he should earn better than 12% on any funds he got from selling his stocks. He was willing to consider borrowing from the bank, but either way he figured a better-than-12% return was a reasonable goal. How much would it cost him to make the pens?

▸ Costs of Making Pens

Materials, obviously, and labor, if he hired anyone to help him with the venture, not to mention the value of his own time, would make up the unit cost. He wouldn't include his time, he decided, but it would be something to think about in the end. After all, he could earn an hourly wage flipping hamburgers—he had done it in the past—but it wouldn't be half as much fun!

To estimate materials, he would have to make some phone calls. He spied the telephone directory poking out from under his bed. What was it doing there? Several phone calls later, Will had enough notes to begin estimating component costs, but what about labor? He reached for his jogging sweatshirt and pulled his stopwatch from the pocket. How fast could he assemble one of these pens? He unscrewed his pen, set his stopwatch, and began. Twenty-one seconds flat. Surely, with a little practice, he could do three a minute, maybe four.

But wait a second, he cautioned himself. He would be busy organizing the operation, selling the idea and the product . . . he would probably hire other students to assemble the pens. And if a couple of guys got together, they wouldn't always work steadily. Sometimes they might goof off a little. Heck, he would too! Being more realistic, he estimated that one worker could assemble 100 pens per hour. That was just under two pens a minute.

He started his third budget schedule. See Exhibit 4-3.

If he planned to produce 15,500 pens in the first six months (see Exhibit 4-2), he would be tying up over $17,000 in production costs alone, and that didn't include anything for advertising or travel to make contacts or selling labor, if he hired anyone to help sell. He needed several more budget schedules before he could project a profit (or loss) figure.

Variable costs:	Total per Unit
Direct Materials	
Cap	$ 0.10
Cover	0.10
Ink Cartridge (with metal tip)	0.65
Case (with logo)	0.25
Total Direct Materials	1.10
Direct Labor	0.10
Total direct materials and	
direct labor cost per unit	$ 1.20

Exhibit 4-3 *Budgeted Materials and Labor per Unit*

▸ Materials Costs

After the first six months, he would decide whether or not to stick with the business. In the meantime, he would assume a going concern; he remembered that assumption from accounting class. As he finished each month, he would need some components or direct materials inventory as well as finished pens inventory to start the next period. He estimated an ending inventory for each component (cap, cover, case, etc.) of 50% of the following month's planned production of pens. If he ended the first six months with a finished goods inventory of 500 pens, he would also need some components to begin the next period. See Exhibit 4-4.

	October	November	December	January	February	March	Total
Direct material requirements (Cap, cover, case, etc.)	1each/pen	1 per pen	1 per pen	1 per pen	1 per pen	1 per pen	1 per pen
Pens produced	3,750	4,500	2,750	1,500	1,500	1,500	15,500
Materials for production	3,750	4,500	2,750	1,500	1,500	1,500	15,500
Desired end inventory (units)	2,250	1,375	750	750	750	250	250
Materials needed	6,000	5,875	3,500	2,250	2,250	1,750	15,750
Less: Beginning inventory		2,250	1,375	750	750	750	
Purchases (in units)	6,000	3,625	2,125	1,500	1,500	1,000	15,750
times unit cost (see ex. 5-3)	$ 1.10	$ 1.10	$ 1.10	$ 1.10	$ 1.10	$ 1.10	$ 1.10
Cost of purchases	$ 6,600	$ 3,988	$ 2,338	$ 1,650	$ 1,650	$ 1,100	$ 17,325

Exhibit 4-4 *Direct Materials Requirements and Purchases for the Six Months Ended March 31, 200x*

▸ Flexible Budgeting

Long before the end of six months, Will figured he would be updating his budgets. If things looked promising, he might be expanding. If things weren't looking promising, he might be cutting back. He remembered another term from accounting class. It was amazing how concepts he'd never expected to remember, let alone use, had found a corner in his memory banks to take up residence. The term was flexible budgeting, which he remembered as meaning simply a budget which provides for adjustment to the actual conditions experienced, in contrast to a *fixed* or *static* budget, which does not. Another type of budget that Will remembered seeing or hearing about, and one which he thought sounded useful, involved dropping the past month (or quarter) from a budget and adding a new one, a sort of rolling budget. This type of budget was appropriately termed a moving budget.

► Labor Costs

He had already done some scribbling on labor costs, but he set it down now in an orderly fashion. He knew some students who would be glad to work for $10.00 an hour. That was better than they earned at McDonald's! Alternatively, he might pay them $0.10 per unit produced, a piece rate for labor. That would take the uncertainty out of how much goofing off to expect, and there would be an incentive for them to spend their time efficiently. Either way the budget would yield the same estimates, if the workers averaged 100 pens an hour. With production higher in the early months, he would bear higher direct labor costs in those months as well. See Exhibit 4-5.

	October	November	December	January	February	March	Total
Production Required	3,750.00	4,500.00	2,750.00	1,500.00	1,500.00	1,500.00	15,500.00
Requirements per unit (hr.)	0.01	0.01	0.01	0.01	0.01	0.01	0.01
Required Labor hours	37.50	45.00	27.50	15.00	15.00	15.00	155.00
Labor rate per hr.	$ 10.00	$ 10.00	$ 10.00	$ 10.00	$ 10.00	$ 10.00	$ 10.00
Direct Labor Cost	$ 375.00	$ 450.00	$ 275.00	$150.00	$150.00	$ 150.00	$ 1,550.00

Exhibit 4-5 *Direct Labor Requirements for the Six Months ended March 31, 200x*

► Overhead Costs

But what about overhead? He could operate out of his dorm room, he supposed, and store the pens in—his closet? His tennis racket was still laying on the floor. Will gave it a kick, shaking his head. He knew he could rent a storage unit for as little as $750 for six months, but that was a lot of money for a poor college student. Oh, well. He could figure it in now, and he could always come back later and trim costs if he had to. At least he would know what was or wasn't feasible. As for assembling the pens, they could get by using dorm rooms or lounges, at least in the beginning. This eliminated the need to estimate utilities and rent or depreciation on the production facilities, the sort of stuff typically included in manufacturing overhead.

► Marketing and Administrative Expenses

Next Will tackled a budget for selling and marketing the pens. As an afterthought, he added administrative expenses to the same budget. He smiled to think of himself as an administrator. Somehow he'd always imagined someone in that role who was a bit more—orderly. He picked up his tennis racket and positioned it carefully on the stack of sporting equipment so it wouldn't topple back out. Any day now, he promised himself, he was going to organize that closet.

Travel expenses. His old VW didn't use much gas, and he knew he couldn't really afford (or justify) a plane trip for this business; so travel expenses would be just gas and auto maintenance for local trips to the bookstore, to talk to someone in the alumni office, etc. Thirty-five bucks, let's say, essential for the initial contacts and another twelve to thirty-six a month, varying with how much selling he did. These estimates were pretty low, Will knew, but he was becoming concerned that his costs were piling up. To advertise in the school paper and the alumni magazine, he estimated $25 a month. He didn't want to scrimp on advertising because he figured it was vital to the success of the project, but luckily he knew these outlets to be quite reasonable.

Would he need to hire some of his friends to help him sell? The more he sold, the more profit he could hope for. A few hundred dollars for salespersons seemed wise, so he estimated $50 a month. Maybe a low hourly rate plus a small commission. Right in the middle of his marketing and administrative budget, the phone rang. It was Marie. His mind was still on his budget, and she hung up, more irritated than ever.

But the sound of the phone had given Will an idea. To keep travel down, he was thinking, he would do some of his work over the phone. He could use his dorm phone; so he just needed to include an estimate for long-distance calls to suppliers and out-of-town alumni, say $10 a month. Last he added $5 a month for office supplies. See Exhibit 4-6.

	October	November	December	January	February	March	Total
Variable:							
Travel expense	$ 12.00	$ 36.00	$ 36.00	$ 12.00	$ 12.00	$ 12.00	$ 120
Sales commissions	112.50	337.50	337.50	112.50	112.50	112.50	1,125
Total Variable	124.50	373.50	373.50	124.50	124.50	124.50	1,245
Fixed:							
Salespersons' salaries .	50.00	50.00	50.00	50.00	50.00	50.00	300
Advertising and promotion	25.00	25.00	25.00	25.00	25.00	25.00	150
Telephone	10.00	10.00	10.00	10.00	10.00	10.00	60
Office supplies	5.00	5.00	5.00	5.00	5.00	5.00	30
Travel expense	35.00						35
Total fixed	125.00	90.00	90.00	90.00	90.00	90.00	575
Total Variable and Fixed	$249.50	$ 463.50	$ 463.50	$ 214.50	$ 214.50	$ 214.50	$ 1,820

Exhibit 4-6 *Marketing and Administrative Expense Budget for the Six Months Ended March 31, 200x*

▸ Financing Costs

Now he was almost ready to put together a tentative budgeted income statement. Was he forgetting anything? Interest expense, he thought suddenly. If he relied on his grandfather's stocks, he wouldn't have any financing costs other than opportunity costs. But he might be better off to borrow from the bank and hang on to his stock. Interest rates were low right now. He would have to impress the lending officer to talk him or her into a loan, he knew, but look what a fine set of budgets he had come up with already! Once they were refined and typed neatly, he could handle a loan officer.

▸ CASH BUDGET ◂

As anxious as he was to see the bottom line on a budgeted income statement, he decided to do a cash budget first. This would give him some idea how much he might need to borrow, which in turn would help him estimate the effects of interest expense on profits. He also knew that a positive bottom line on an income statement—if he should end up in the black—wouldn't go far anyway if his cash flow fell apart on him. As a newcomer, he would need the business to start generating cash fairly quickly. He would need to estimate cash coming in and cash going out. Unfortunately, no cash would be flowing in until the pens were produced, sold, and cash was collected from the sale.

▶ Cash Receipts

For cash receipts, aside from borrowing, Will figured he had two sources: cash sales and collections on account. If he worked through the campus bookstore, he would probably not be able to make all sales for cash up front. Still, the advantages of using the bookstore as a vehicle for his operation outweighed the disadvantage of having to wait to collect. Will estimated 30% of his total sales to be cash sales, with the rest through the bookstore. If the bookstore would pay him with only a one-month delay, his collections on account would begin in November.

Thus, for October, he estimated cash receipts to be 30% of October sales of $3,750 or $1,125. In November, he would collect the remaining 70% of October sales ($2,625) as well as 30% of November sales ($3,375) for a total of $6,000. By December, cash receipts would be looking quite good.

▶ Cash Payments

What about cash payments or disbursements? From his recent phone calls with suppliers, it looked as if most required cash in advance. Again, as a newcomer, he didn't have much room to argue. His friends might be more lenient, but then again he knew they all enjoyed having cash for dates and such. Like Will himself.

In fact, to an extent, that's what motivated him to consider the project in the first place. It would be nice to be able to take Marie to a first-run movie occasionally or out for steaks instead of hamburgers. Surely he could make her see. He picked up the phone to dial.

When he hung up this time, Will was smiling. It was nearly lunch time, and a good juicy hamburger didn't sound bad after all. Marie wasn't complaining. He had just enough time to finish his cash budget and maybe budget an income statement too, if he hurried. He set the timer on his clock so he wouldn't forget Marie again and went back to work.

▶ Interpreting and Completing the Cash Budget

For the month of October, Will's budgeted outflows of cash exceeded his inflows by over $6,000 before financing, suggesting the need to borrow at least that amount. In fact he would need $6,600 for purchases of direct materials alone. Will added a financing section and entered a borrowing in October of $7,000 to allow a small cushion for any expenses he might have overlooked. See Exhibit 4-7.

By December, the inflows were substantially greater than the outflows, and Will figured he should be able to repay $5,000 on the loan by the end of that month. In January he planned to repay the remaining $2,000. If he borrowed the $7,000 at 10%, he would owe $175 of interest for the first three months, to be paid at the end of December. For January, though, his balance would drop to $2,000, cutting his monthly interest to $16.67. If he paid the loan off in full, along with interest of $16.67 for January, by the end of January, he would have no interest payments for February or March. He probably would need to pay estimated income tax installments somewhere along the line (he would have to check on this), but only if he showed a profit. He would wait and add estimated taxes, if necessary, after preparing a budgeted income statement.

	October	November	December	January	February	March	Total
Beginning cash balance ..		$ 775.5	$ 1,749.5	$ 4,623.5	$ 9,467.3	$11,077.8	
Add budgeted receipts:							
Cash sales (30%)	$1,125.0	3,375.0	3,375.0	1,125.0	1,125.0	1,125.0	$11,250.0
Collections on account ..		2,625.0	7,875.0	7,875.0	2,625.0	2,625.0	23,625.0
(collected in following month)							
Total budgeted receipts ...	1,125.0	6,000.0	11,250.0	9,000.0	3,750.0	3,750.0	34,875.0
Less budgeted disbursements:							
Purchases of direct materials	6,600.0	3,987.5	2,337.5	1,650.0	1,650.0	1,100.0	17,325.0
Direct labor	375.0	450.0	275.0	150.0	150.0	150.0	1,550.0
Storage unit rent	125.0	125.0	125.0	125.0	125.0	125.0	750.0
Marketing & administrative	249.5	463.5	463.5	214.5	214.5	214.5	1,820.0
Total budgeted disbursements	7,349.5	5,026.0	3,201.0	2,139.5	2,139.5	1,589.5	21,445.0
Cash increase(decrease) .	(6,224.5)	974.0	8,049.0	6,860.5	1,610.5	2,160.5	13,430.0
Financing:							
Borrowing	7,000.0						7,000.0
Repayments			(5,000.0)	(2,000.0)			(7,000.0)
Interest payments			(175.0)	(16.7)			(191.7)
Ending cash balance	$ 775.5	$ 1,749.5	$ 4,623.5	$ 9,467.3	$ 11,077.8	$ 13,238.3	$13,238.3

Exhibit 4-7 *The Cash Budget for the Six Months Ended March 31, 200x*

▸ BUDGETED INCOME STATEMENT ◂

Will's hand moved a little faster now as he scribbled, beginning with the month of October and anxious to see the bottom line on a budgeted income statement. He remembered to include interest expense for the month of October even though it wouldn't be paid until December. And, of course, income taxes! He groaned, and then he smiled instead. Tired of listening to his parents' generation grumble about taxes, he'd always vowed that if he ever made enough money to pay much in the way of taxes, he should be glad to be in that position. Forty percent of net income should be more than adequate. See Exhibit 4-8.

Bzzzz! Will reached for the alarm clock. His stomach was growling nearly as loudly as the clock. He was ready for a break.

After lunch, with a full stomach and a kiss from Marie still warming his lips, Will looked at his budgets again. Not bad. A total of $10,043 for the first six months, and debt free by the end of January if all went well.

▸ BUDGETED BALANCE SHEET ◂

There was at least one budget still missing. A budgeted balance sheet, that was it. Will picked up his pen and resumed work.

The cash budget provided an estimate for his cash balance at the end of each month; he estimated his accounts receivable balance as 70% of the current month sales. He obtained estimates for direct materials (caps, covers, cases, etc.) inventory in units at the end of each month from his Direct Materials Budget (Exhibit 4-4) and multiplied by a total components cost of $1.10 per unit (Exhibit 4-3). His finished pens inventory in units for each month came from his Production Budget (Exhibit 4-2), which he multiplied by $1.20 (materials and direct labor cost per unit from Exhibit 4-3).

For the first couple of months, he showed his loan balance as a liability of $7,000, as well as interest payable on the loan. By the end of December, he reduced the loan liability to $2,000 and

	October	November	December	January	February	March	Total
Sales	$ 3,750.0	$ 11,250.0	$ 11,250.0	$ 3,750.0	$ 3,750.0	$ 3,750.0	$ 37,500.0
Variable Costs:							
Manufacturing	1,800.0	5,400.0	5,400.0	1,800.0	1,800.0	1,800.0	18,000.0
Marketing and Administrative	124.5	373.5	373.5	124.5	124.5	124.5	1,245.0
Contribution Margin	1,825.5	5,476.5	5,476.5	1,825.5	1,825.5	1,825.5	18,255.0
Fixed Costs:							
Storage Unit Rent	125.0	125.0	125.0	125.0	125.0	125.0	750.0
Marketing and Administrative	125.0	90.0	90.0	90.0	90.0	90.0	575.0
Operating Income	1,575.5	5,261.5	5,261.5	1,610.5	1,610.5	1,610.5	16,930.0
Interest Expense	58.3	58.3	58.4	16.7	0.0	0.0	191.7
Income before Taxes	1,517.2	5,203.2	5,203.1	1,593.8	1,610.5	1,610.5	16,738.3
Federal Income Taxes	606.9	2,081.3	2,081.2	637.5	644.2	644.2	6,695.3
Net Income	$ 910.3	$ 3,121.9	$ 3,121.9	$ 956.3	$ 966.3	$ 966.3	$ 10,043.0

Exhibit 4-8 *Budgeted Income Statement for the Six Months Ended March 31, 200x*

eliminated interest payable, in anticipation of paying off $5,000 of principal and all interest through December. By the end of January, he hoped to pay off the remaining $2,000 with interest and be debt free. Well, not quite debt free, he remembered suddenly. He hadn't gone back to his cash budget yet to add income tax installments. If he'd made no payments to the I.R.S., he would owe income taxes at the end of each month. From the budgeted income statement (Exhibit 4-8), he obtained the amounts and added his income tax liability to the balance sheet. His owner's equity balance simply consisted of net income accumulated at the end of each month. After correcting a couple of errors in addition, Will was delighted to see his balance sheet balance.

▶ WILL'S BUDGETED RETURN ◀

He was still more delighted when he considered his return on investment. Dividing his net income for the first six months by his total assets at the end of the period, he arrived at an incredible return of 60% for the six month period. For a moment, he wondered if he had made a major miscalculation somewhere. Of course, by using his dorm room, he realized that he had managed to avoid one of the major expenses of a new business, the rent or depreciation on office and factory space. This had also kept his total asset base very low and had inflated his return somewhat. In view of this very favorable return, he wondered if he might be able to obtain more financing than he had originally projected.

Borrowing only $7,000 had been cutting it pretty close. If he borrowed more, say an additional $3,000, his total assets would be higher (depending on how rapidly he paid off the extra $3,000), as well as his interest, thus lowering his return, but he would feel more comfortable with a bit of a cash cushion for those unexpected expenses that might pop up. They had always had a habit of appearing in his personal budget when he was least prepared for them, and he suspected that running a business would be no different.

Will glanced at the clock. It was nearly 3:30. He reached his hand into the pocket of his jeans. If he remembered correctly, he still had a ten dollar bill after lunch. There it was—a ten and some

Assets

	October	November	December	January	February	March
Cash	$ 775.5	$ 1,749.5	$ 4,623.5	$ 9,467.3	$ 11,077.8	$ 13,238.3
Accounts Receivable	2,625.0	7,875.0	7,875.0	2,625.0	2,625.0	2,625.0
Materials	2,475.0	1,512.5	825.0	825.0	825.0	275.0
Finished Goods	2,700.0	2,700.0	600.0	600.0	600.0	600.0
Total Assets	$ 8,575.5	$ 13,837.0	$ 13,923.5	$ 13,517.3	$ 15,127.8	$ 16,738.3

Liabilities and Owners' Equity

	October	November	December	January	February	March
Income Taxes Payable	$ 606.9	$ 2,688.2	$ 4,769.4	$ 5,406.9	$ 6,051.1	$ 6,695.3
Loan payable	7,000.0	7,000.0	2,000.0			
Interest Payable	58.3	116.6				
Will Harper, Owner's Equity	910.3	4,032.2	7,154.1	8,110.4	9,076.7	10,043.0
Total Liabilities and Owner's Equity	$ 8,575.5	$ 13,837.0	$ 13,923.5	$ 13,517.3	$ 15,127.8	$ 16,738.3

Exhibit 4-9 *Budgeted Balance Sheet October 31, 199x through March 31, 200x*

change. He calculated quickly. If he and Marie took in a movie before five, they could get in for matinee prices and have money left over for one popcorn and one soda to share. Will was well accustomed to this kind of budgeting. Six months from now, if all went well, they should be able to afford an evening movie *and* snacks. Smiling, he reached for the phone.

► BUDGETING: SIMPLE TO COMPLEX ◄

In the case presented, Will Harper pulled together his knowledge of a variety of tools, some recalled from college classes and some developed to fit his needs, to plan the first six months of operations of a new business. With the aid of prior year budgets as examples and computer programs for speed, managers of far more complex operations go through the same basic process in planning and budgeting for upcoming periods. In larger organizations, more people are involved in generating the numbers and in preparing the schedules, but the process is essentially the same. In the following paragraphs, we discuss additional budget related issues.

► Terminology

Terminology varies, and some terms which are used interchangeably in one text or organization may have different meanings in another. For example, the terms *budget* and *forecast* are sometimes used synonymously. However, a rather general usage designates the coordinated plans of action for a period as the budget and uses the term forecast for a closeup estimate made during a budget period of the actual results expected to be realized. Alternatively, a forecast may be thought of as a manager's guess at what will happen in a future period, whereas a budget represents what a manager will try to make happen in a future period.

Sometimes the term budget, used in a more limited way, refers to expense items only. Companies which use budgets to plan and control manufacturing, marketing, and administrative expenses may state that they have a budget, or budgets. Such expense budgets are simply *parts* of a complete budgetary planning and control program. The companies which limit their budgeting to these areas do not have a budget as the term is used in its broadest sense.

The wide variation in the use of terms to designate the components of the overall program of budgetary planning and control can be extremely confusing. Thus in this and succeeding chapters we use the term *budget* to designate the total coordinated management plan for a stated period and the term *forecast* to designate estimates made during the budget period of the actual results expected. Units or parts of the budget will be preceded by identifying words such as *sales*, *expense*, and *cash*.

Companies use budgets to provide:

1. A realistic estimate of revenue and costs for a period and of the financial position at the close of a period, detailed by areas of management responsibility.
2. A coordinated plan of action designed to achieve the estimates reflected in the budget.
3. A comparison of actual results with those budgeted and an analysis and interpretation of deviations by areas of responsibility to indicate courses of corrective action and to lead to improvement in procedures in building future budgets.
4. A guide for management decisions in adjusting plans and objectives as conditions change.
5. A ready basis for making forecasts during the budget period to guide management in making day-to-day decisions.

► FLEXIBLE BUDGETING: AGAIN ◄

Since a predetermined series of related assumptions form the basis for a budget, managers should not regard a budget as an absolute requirement of performance where unfavorable deviations bring severe criticism and favorable deviations rounds of praise. To expect a sales manager to meet a sales budget which was based on expected good business conditions, even if there has been a sudden collapse of general business during the budget period, would be about as unrealistic as to expect a trucker to make a trip of 300 miles in five hours over secondary roads when the trip was originally planned for an interstate highway. The sales manager's budget should be revised to reflect the new business conditions. Thus, after it is developed as a plan of action, managers should *not* use a budget to evaluate *actual* performance under *actual* conditions in comparison with *budgeted* performance under *budgeted* conditions. The proper comparison is between *actual* performance under *actual* conditions and *budgeted* performance under *actual* conditions. As noted by Will in the case presented earlier, this is referred to as *flexible budgeting*, a process whereby budgets can be quickly revised to reflect budgeted results under actual conditions.

Because conditions do change, and sometimes very quickly, management needs the basic data to guide their current decisions. Without this data, the desired income and financial position will be achieved only by accident (not likely). The coordinated plans developed in building a flexible budget provide the basic data useful in making current decisions. The relationships which are established in the budget provide information on how current decisions in one phase of the business can and will affect other phases of the business. For example, if a company revises its sales estimate upward, management can use the basic budgetary relationships to revise production schedules, inventory quantities and estimates of revenue, expense, receipts and disbursements. With a good budgetary system, managers can readily access data for many decisions dependent on these revised schedules and estimates, and thus make each decision on the basis of the facts. In addition, a good manager considers and coordinates the effects of each decision on other phases of the business.

Some managers evaluate the success of a budget by the closeness of actual results to the budget. However, failure to achieve "on the nose" budgeting does not destroy the value of a budget or a budgetary system.

▸ The Budget Period

The period of time covered by a budget varies considerably between companies and even within a company for each of the individual budgets. There is no right length of time for any budget. Using too short a period makes budgeting excessively time-consuming, costly, and of little value for forward planning. If the period is too long, those who build the budgets will feel that there are so many unpredictable factors that it is useless to attempt to budget accurately.

To be useful some budgets must cover a period of six to twelve months. For example, a company will find it difficult to budget advertising expenditures on a monthly or even a quarterly basis. Managers must make space and time commitments at the start of the year, prepare copy and script, and maintain a continuing program of advertising planning for future years. Consequently, most companies develop advertising budgets for a twelve-month period.

A capital expenditure budget must give consideration to future resources required and the time required for their construction or acquisition. Therefore, it may cover a period of several years. In contrast, the inventory budget may be for a quarter, month, or week with plans adjusted as close-up forecasts are made.

Some companies prepare a complete set of budgets for each calendar or fiscal year. During the year, shorter-range forecasts are made by adjusting the annual budget figures. In the case presented earlier, Will recalled a useful type of budget known as a moving or rolling budget (i.e., budgets are prepared each quarter with each budget covering the next twelve month period by dropping the last quarter and adding the next quarter). On occasion the moving budget is prepared monthly (i.e., each month the past month is dropped and the twelfth future month is added). A moving cash budget can be a combination of quarterly, monthly, weekly, and daily reports.

Managers must adapt the budget period to the conditions peculiar to their industry, the purposes served by the budgets, and the requirements of the managers who use the budgets. Also, general economic or other conditions may cause a company to deviate from the customary budget periods to give management sharper, updated, and more informative data.

▸ Budget Committee

Although companies usually appoint a budget officer to administer the company's budget program, he or she has responsibility only for managing the budget process, not for the assumptions used in the budget or for the quality of the budget data. The budget committee has responsibility for these functions. Budget committee members are company executives who have no operating responsibilities for sales or production. A typical committee consists of the executive vice-president, controller, treasurer, and economist. Naturally in a smaller organization, where all these positions do not exist, this committee may include the president and chief accounting officer and possibly outside assistance.

The budget committee has the responsibility for assessing economic conditions expected during the budget period, estimating trends in price and wage levels, and reviewing other relevant data. These expectations provide the basic assumptions for the budget. The committee provides advice and consultation to managers as they prepare their individual budgets. After the budgets are reviewed by the budget staff for completeness and conformance to company guidelines, they go to the budget committee. The committee reviews each budget and, if they feel it needs changes, they recommend the changes to the person who developed the budget.[1] Finally, the committee submits a budget summary, along with interpretative comments and any recommended revisions, to company executives. Final acceptance rests with top management.

---

[1] A frequent cause of disagreement is related to budgetary slack (i.e., looseness in the budget). When budgets are used excessively as a pressure device managers try to include slack by overstating costs and understating revenues.

The budget committee also estimates possible long-term patterns of change in general economic conditions which will affect the demand for, or the cost of, products of the company. These estimates facilitate in the following ways:

1. Assist management in the development and evaluation of long-range plans.
2. Make possible a long-term projection of the cash and the working capital position.
3. Indicate resources required.
4. Evaluate financing requirements.
5. Indicate opportunities for the profitable investment of capital.
6. Provide management with the basis for making changes in organization structure and personnel to meet changing economic conditions.

▶ RETURN ON INVESTED CAPITAL ◀

▶ Bases of Measurement

One of the better bases of measuring business income for management purposes is the ratio of net income after tax to invested capital. It reflects the effectiveness of management for any business in which invested capital is significant. It would not be applicable for a business such as a law firm where personal ability is the determinant of income and invested capital is insignificant. Net income after tax as a percentage of sales is a ratio most frequently used in reports and analyses. However, the ratio of net income to sales gives no consideration to the amount of invested capital used to produce the sales and net income.

To meet the failure of the ratio of net income to sales to give recognition to investment, the return on invested capital is used. However, *invested capital* can be defined in at least three ways:

1. Stockholders' equity or capital invested by stockholders.
2. Total assets or capital invested by all suppliers of capital (equity + debt).
3. Total assets less current liabilities or capital invested by long-term suppliers of capital (equity + long-term debt).

The three definitions of invested capital may appear to be in conflict with one another, but that is not the case. They are interrelated via the notion of financial leverage. The interrelationship can be illustrated algebraically as indicated below.

$$\text{Return on Total Assets} = \frac{\text{Net Income After Tax}}{\text{Total Assets}}$$

$$\text{Return on Long-Term Invested Capital} = \text{Return on Total Assets} \times \text{Short-Term Financial Leverage}$$

$$= \frac{\text{Net Income After Tax}}{\text{Total Assets}} \times \frac{\text{Total Assets}}{\text{Total Assets} - \text{Current Liabilities}}$$

$$\text{Return on Stockholders' Equity} = \text{Return on Total Assets} \times \text{Short-Term Financial Leverage} \times \text{Long-Term Financial Leverage}$$

$$= \frac{\text{Net Income After Tax}}{\text{Total Assets}} \times \frac{\text{Total Assets}}{\text{Total Assets} - \text{Current Liabilities}} \times \frac{\text{Total Assets} - \text{Current Liabilities}}{\text{Stockholders' Equity}}$$

As we proceed in our discussions of budgeting, the specifics of these interrelationships will be made clearer. Their role in the budgeting process will also become more precisely identified. For now, however, we will concentrate on some issues relative to the definition of total assets.

► Defining Total Assets

The total asset figure employed by a company in the above equations is the sum of its assets as shown on its balance sheet.[2] Some companies refer to this as *investment* and refer to the ratio of net income after tax to investment as *return on investment*. This tends to be misleading for it may be interpreted as the return on the stockholders' investment.

Use of the total assets shown on the balance sheet means that each asset account is taken after deducting the applicable valuation accounts. Accounts receivable and property, plant and equipment are net of allowance for bad debts and accumulated depreciation, respectively. Inventories are at the balance sheet values, and a company using the LIFO basis of determining cost would probably have a lower asset total than one with the same quantities of the same materials costed on the FIFO basis.

Some companies use net asset values for all assets except property, plant and equipment. For the latter, they use original cost. Historically, two reasons are given for this. First, in periods of rising prices, original cost is closer to replacement cost than is depreciated value. This is hardly a solution to the problem. If managers desire to measure return against replacement values of the assets, they should state all assets at replacement values. The second reason is that cost provides a better basis for comparing units of the company, some of which may have new assets and others older and well-depreciated assets. This too is correcting only one phase of a problem. Older production facilities are generally less efficient and require more maintenance than new ones. The authors suspect that the more current justification for using original cost relates to implementing a cash flow orientation to ratio analysis.

Assets (as well as liabilities and stockholders' equity) used for calculating return on invested capital should be averaged insofar as possible. Year-end figures may be high or low because of management decision or because of seasonal influences of the industry. Within a company, a twelve-month moving average provides a very satisfactory basis of measurement and removes the pressure on units of the company to have low inventory or other asset accounts at the end of a year and to ignore asset values during the year. When comparisons are made with the returns of other companies, their assets should also be averaged if data are available.

► The Algebra of Return on Invested Capital

The best way to think about return on invested capital is in terms of return on stockholders' equity and the component parts of return on stockholders' equity. This is illustrated below by suggesting that return on stockholders' equity is a function of net income after tax as a percentage of sales, total asset turnover and financial leverage.

---

[2] Where a company has leased property it should include the discounted value of future lease payments among the property, plant and equipment and the long-term liabilities. Statement of Financial Accounting Standards #13 provides guidelines in this regard.

Return on Stockholders' Equity

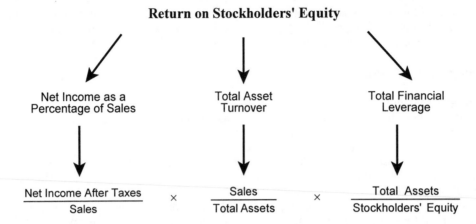

$$\frac{\text{Net Income After Taxes}}{\text{Sales}} \quad \times \quad \frac{\text{Sales}}{\text{Total Assets}} \quad \times \quad \frac{\text{Total Assets}}{\text{Stockholders' Equity}}$$

Net income after tax as a percentage of sales is easily understood as is total financial leverage if one remembers that total financial leverage is the product of short-term and long-term financial leverage. Total asset turnover is also easily understood if one thinks of it as *dollar of sales generated per each dollar invested in assets*—a capital intensity measure.

If there is a problem with the above, it is that top management is emphasized as opposed to operating management. In order to give operating management equal emphasis, non-operating or top management aspects of our three ratios should be differentiated from operating aspects. Pictorially this can be described as follows:

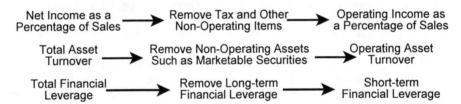

The net result of the above is a return on long-term operating capital which can be described as follows:

Return on Long-term Operating Capital

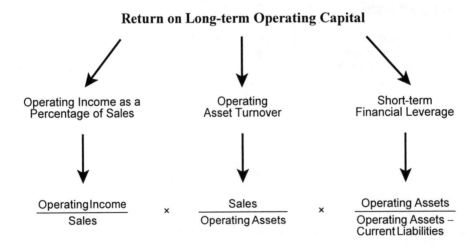

$$\frac{\text{Operating Income}}{\text{Sales}} \quad \times \quad \frac{\text{Sales}}{\text{Operating Assets}} \quad \times \quad \frac{\text{Operating Assets}}{\text{Operating Assets} - \text{Current Liabilities}}$$

If desired, the operating asset turnover and short-term financial leverage could be combined to produce a turnover of long-term operating capital.

The return on long-term operating capital emphasizes the financial evaluation of operating management since it is their responsibility to manage operating income, operating assets and short-term or operating debt. When the non-operating items and long-term debt are brought into the picture, our emphasis switches to the financial evaluation of top management.

▶ What is a Satisfactory Return on Invested Capital?

If results are to be planned, measured, and controlled, there should be some method of determining a satisfactory return on invested capital. Unfortunately, no formula has been developed which will do this. Judgment, based on comparisons with other companies and experience, is the only method of selecting return on invested capital objectives. The major factors to be considered are:

1. The best and the average returns of all companies.
2. The best and the average returns of similar industries.
3. The company position in the industry.
4. The competitive value of patents or secret processes of the company.
5. The possibility of new businesses entering the field and becoming significant competitors.

There is sufficient evidence in published corporate reports that the type of industry does not determine the return which may be expected in that industry. Companies with high, average, and low returns are found in every industry. The return achieved is the result of management, and no company should feel that its return is satisfactory and be lulled into complacency. However, there is evidence that companies which have a very small market share in an industry do not usually realize a high return. There is also evidence in some industries that the average return for the industry is low and only a very few companies are achieving a high return.

A company with patent protection on its products and processes or with secret processes should realize a higher return than its competitors who do not have these advantages. This higher return is the reward for developing or purchasing these advantages.

The possibility of new businesses entering the field and becoming significant competitors is determined primarily by industry rather than by individual company considerations. A fast growing industry or product line always seems to attract competitors.

Because of these varied influences a company with a broad product line should not expect to realize the same return on all products. Separate objectives need to be established for each line and for the total company.

The maximum average return over a period of three to five years should not be so high that it subsidizes inefficient competitors or invites new competition. As a rule of thumb, it would appear that a return on stockholders' equity should be three to five percentage points higher than the interest required on a company's long-term debt. For example, if a company pays an effective interest rate of 12 percent on its long-term debt, its return on stockholders' equity should be 15 to 18 percent to allow for the extra risk taken by stockholders.

As to how such a return should be attained, that is a matter of a particular firm's opportunities and constraints. All that is being developed here is a rule of thumb for return on stockholders' equity for the firm as a whole. How a particular firm stresses and combines the three factors (net income after tax as a percentage of sales, total asset turnover and financial leverage) which make up its return on stockholders' equity is truly a matter of its opportunities and constraints. The same is true with regard to how much each division, product or activity contributes to profitability. In any event, competitive conditions and attitudes concerning short-term vs. long-term profitability will be the determining factors.

► The Budgetary Process and Responsibility Reporting

Our illustration of budget building has been intentionally simple. More detailed breakdowns would illuminate more clearly the connection between budgeting and responsibility reporting. For example, a company may design systems to track sales and marketing expense by territories, by salespersons, or by customers and to monitor manufacturing costs by responsibility areas (e.g., cost centers or departments). We consider many of these important details in subsequent chapters. For now just remember that managers can use the budgetary process to measure and control the firm's overall financial performance, as well as divisional and departmental performance.

► SUMMARY ◄

The budgetary process formalizes the planning and control functions. Managers involved in the process must consider all aspects of the organization and must coordinate their efforts to bring the budgetary process to fruition. In a profit-oriented organization the budgetary process culminates in calculating the level of return on assets or stockholders' equity. If not sufficient, managers must review, challenge, and amend their plans to raise the projected level of return over time to maintain organizational continuity.

The case of Will Harper presented in the first part of the chapter summarizes the process undertaken in planning and budgeting for materials purchases, labor, overhead, marketing and administrative expenses, and financing needs in view of upcoming sales. Will's budgeting process culminates in computing the return projected for the first six months. Although happy with the projected return, Will recognizes the uncertainty inherent in projected numbers and considers modifying his financing plans to provide more of a cushion for contingencies.

▸ QUESTIONS ◂

4-1. Distinguish between budgets and forecasts.

4-2. How does budgeting provide a ready basis for making many day-to-day decisions?

4-3. When starting a budget program, why is it desirable to limit the amount of detail?

4-4. What is meant by the *budget period*? How long should it be?

4-5. What are the responsibilities of the budget committee? The chief budget officer?

4-6. What purpose(s) does a set of basic assumptions serve in budgeting?

4-7. Why is return on invested capital a more appropriate measure of management effectiveness than the percentage relationship between income and sales?

4-8. Why might the term *return on investment* be misleading when used as a synonym for *return on invested capital*?

4-9. Discuss the reasons for and problems involved in using the original cost of plant and equipment as part of the total invested capital?

4-10. How are return on invested capital, capital turnover, and percent profit on sales related?

4-11. With a capital turnover of 1.9 and a return on invested capital of 16 percent, what must be the net income as a percentage of sales?

4-12. With a return on invested capital of 14 percent and a percent profit on sales of 6 percent, what must be the capital turnover?

4-13. Is failure to meet a budget an indication of unsatisfactory performance?

4-14. Describe the budgetary process in detail.

4-15. Of what value is the distinction between costs which generate revenues and costs generated by revenues?

▸ EXERCISES AND PROBLEMS ◂

4-16. Budgetary Slack and Other Budget Concepts.
In recent years, budgets have become widely accepted as a key element in the organization's financial system. Budgets of some type are used in most organizations.

Required:

a. Briefly define *budget*. Identify and discuss the major purposes of budgets.
b. Discuss the effect of the budgeting process on the organization and its individual members. The following should provide guidance in preparing your answer.

1. Participation in preparing budgets.
2. Budgets as a pressure device.
3. Definition of budgetary slack.
4. Role of slack budgets.
5. Other considerations.

(SMA adapted)

4-17. Benefits of Budgeting.

You have recently been hired as the assistant controller of a small manufacturing company. Eager to demonstrate your knowledge, you have recommended to the controller that the company institute a budgeting program. The controller has responded as follows: "Budgeting is fine for large organizations operating in stable industries, but it is impractical for us to use a budget because of the uncertainty inherent in our business. Furthermore, a formal budget requires too much time to create and is outdated by the time it is completed."

Required:

Prepare a report to the controller supporting your contention that budgeting would be beneficial to the company.

4-18. Materials Usage Budget.

The Scotia Company produces two products: standard and custom. For 20x5, the company plans to produce 4,000 units of each product. These products require the raw material given below:

	Cost Per Unit	Standard	Custom
X	$ 2.00	2 units	
Y	2.50	1 unit	1 unit
Z	1.25		3 units

Required:

Prepare a materials usage budget for 20x5.

4-19. Direct Labor Budget.

Nova Company planned to produce 25,000 units of Gue and 29,000 units of Bic. Gue requires two hours of cutting and ¾ hour in finishing at direct labor rates of $6.00 and $10.50, respectively. Bic requires one hour in cutting and two hours in finishing at the same rates.

Required:

Prepare a direct labor budget for Nova Company.

4-20. Production Unit Budget.

Wright, Inc. manufactures pens. During 20x6, they predict a sales volume of 25,240,000 pens. At the present time, their finished goods inventory has 1,500,000 pens. Wright hopes to increase this inventory by 15 percent at the end of the year. Ignore work-in-process inventory.

Required:

Prepare a production budget in units.

4-21. Budget Disbursements for Payment of Purchases.

The Malden Company Limited produces units which sell for $50 each. Each unit requires four pounds of raw material at a cost of $4 per pound. Management policy is to have the following inventory levels on hand at the end of each month.

Finished goods = *15 percent of next month's budgeted sales*

Raw materials = *2,000 pounds* + *15 percent of next month's production requirements*

The company qualifies for a 1 percent discount by paying accounts in the month following purchases. Management has always followed the above inventory guidelines and has now budgeted the following sales:

January	$ 1,600,000
February	2,000,000
March	2,400,000
April	1,800,000

Required:

How much money should the company budget for disbursements in February for payment of purchases? Show all calculations.
(SMA adapted)

4-22. Analyzing Changes in Rate of Return.

The monthly balance sheets of a company show average total assets for a year of $100,000. Sales for the year were $160,000 and income after tax was $9,760. For the next year sales are budgeted at $186,000 and income after tax is budgeted at $11,532. The budgeted balance sheets show average total assets of $120,000.

Required:

If the budget amounts are realized, what will be the change in return on invested capital and what will be the reasons for the change?

4-23. Projecting Changes in Rate of Return.

For a year a company had sales of $600,000. Its variable costs were $300,000 and its fixed costs were $240,000. Its income tax rate was 50 percent. The invested capital was $500,000.

The president wishes to establish an objective of 1.5 percentage points improvement in return of capital employed.

Required:

What change would be required to achieve his objectives:
a. In sales volume with no change in the variable cost rate, fixed costs, or capital?
b. In fixed costs with no change in sales revenue, the variable cost rate, or capital?
c. In the variable cost rate with no change in fixed costs, sales revenue, or capital?
d. In invested capital with no change in costs or sales volume?

4-24. Costs of Budgeting Error.

The ABC Company Limited expected to be able to sell 10,000 units at $100 per unit, with variable costs of $38 per unit and fixed costs of $420,000. The company stocked the 10,000, but was able to sell only 9,000 units at $100 per unit, with the remainder being perishable and therefore of no value. The variable costs were actually $43 per unit.

Required:

What was the company's cost of its prediction error? Show all calculations.
(SMA adapted)

4-25. Budgeted Cash Disbursements and Cash Collections.

The following information concerning Stanley Limited has been made available to you, for the development of cash and other budgeted information for the months of July, August and September, 20x4:

a.   Balances at July 1 are expected to be as follows:

Cash	$ 5,500
Accounts receivable	437,000
Inventories	309,400
Accounts payable	133,055

b.   The budget is to be based on the following assumptions:
1.   Each month's sales are billed on the last day of the month.
2.   Customers are allowed a 3 percent discount if payment is made within ten days after the billing date. Receivables are booked at gross.
3.   Sixty percent of the billings are collected within the discount period, 25 percent are collected by the end of the month after the date of sale, 9 percent are collected by the end of the second month after the date of sale and 6 percent prove uncollectible.
4.   Fifty-four percent of all purchases of material and marketing, general and administrative expenses are paid in the month purchased or incurred. The remainder is paid in the following month.
5.   Each month's units of ending inventory are equal to 130 percent of the next month's units of sales.
6.   The cost of each unit of inventory is $20.
7.   Marketing, general and administrative expenses, of which $2,000 is depreciation, are equal to 15 percent of sales.

c.   Actual and projected sales are as follows:

20x4	*Sales*	*Units*
May	$ 354,000	11,800
June	363,000	12,100
July	357,000	11,900
August	342,000	11,400
September	360,000	12,000
October	366,000	12,200

Required:

Calculate the following:
a. Budgeted cash disbursements during the month of August, 20x4.
b. Budgeted cash collections during the month of July, 20x4.
c. Budgeted number of units of inventory to be purchased during the month of September, 20x4.
(SMA adapted)

4-26. **Projecting Cost of Goods Manufactured and Sold, and Income.**
The Softy Company, a producer of mattresses, has predicted total sales of 19,050 mattresses in 20x7. The company has three outlets for the product, the East Coast, the West Coast, and the Southern United States. The mattresses sell for $360, $400, and $430, respectively. The East Coast is expected to capture 40 percent of the sales with the other areas dividing the remainder equally.

In 20x6 it took 40 pounds of stuffing at $4.00 per pound and 20 yards of material at $3.00 per yard to make one mattress. Softy expects the cost of stuffing to go up 15 percent and the material to go up 8 percent. It takes 1½ hours of direct labor, which cost $13.00 per hour in 20x6, to make one mattress. Due to a new labor contract, labor costs per hour will rise 20 percent in 20x7. Because of improved machinery it will only take 1¼ hours to make one mattress in 20x7. Variable costs will be applied at a rate of $9.00 per direct labor hour and fixed overhead at $20 per unit. This is the same as in 20x6. Fixed overhead costs are expected to be $400,000 and the marketing and administrative costs to be $300,000.

At the end of 20x6, the inventory consisted of 620 finished mattresses, no work-in-process, 800 pounds of stuffing, and 600 yards of material. They plan to increase all of their inventories except work-in-process by 30 percent at the end of 20x7. Softy uses FIFO for inventory costing purposes.

Required:

a. Production budget in units.
b. Direct material requirements budget (in units).
c. Direct material purchase budget (in dollars).
d. Direct material usage budget.
e. Direct labor budget.
f. Variable manufacturing overhead budget.
g. Budgeted cost of goods manufactured statement.
h. Budgeted cost of goods sold statement.
i. Budgeted income statement.

4-27. **Budgeting Cash Receipts and Disbursements.**
The Arco Company budgeted the following data for the first quarter of 20x5.

	January	February	March
Sales Account—gross	$ 6,000,000	$ 6,600,000	$ 7,200,000
Cash sales	1,800,000	1,950,000	2,040,000
Accounts receivable written off	30,000	60,000	15,000

	December 31	January 31	February 28	March 31
Merchandise inventories	$ 1,050,000	$ 1,080,000	$ 1,095,000	$ 1,110,000
Accounts payable	1,200,000	1,290,000	1,305,000	1,320,000
Accounts receivable	1,500,000	1,560,000	1,575,000	1,590,000

Merchandise is marked up at 20 percent of the gross sales price. Cash discounts of 2 percent are normally given on 60 percent of the sales on account in the month of sale and 10 percent of the sales on account in the month after sale. Remaining sales discounts are not taken. There are no cash discounts on merchandise purchased. December sales on account are forecasted at $6,300,000.

Required:

Prepare schedules showing cash receipts from sales and cash disbursements on merchandise purchases for the months of January, February, and March.

4-28. Budgeting Cash Receipts and Disbursements.

The Barnes Company budgeted data for certain months in 20x5 and 20x6 as shown below. Merchandise is marked up at 20 percent of the gross sales price. All purchases of merchandise are on account with terms of 2/10, net/30. All purchase discounts are taken, and normally two-thirds of each month's purchases are paid during the month of purchase, whereas the other one-third is paid during the first month after purchase.

	December	January	February	March	April
Sales on account —gross ...	$ 4,500,000	$ 4,800,000	$ 5,100,000	$ 5,100,000	$ 4,800,000
Cash sales ...	600,000	630,000	660,000	660,000	630,000

Merchandise inventories at the beginning of each month are kept at 30 percent of that month's projected cost of goods sold. Even though all purchase discounts are taken: purchases, inventories, and cost of goods sold are all recorded gross.

Terms of sales on account are 1/10, net/30. Fifty percent of each month's sales on account are collected during that month, whereas 45 percent are collected in the succeeding month. The remainder is normally uncollectible. Only 50 percent of the collections in the month of sale in the following month are made early enough to receive cash discounts.

Required:

Prepare schedules showing cash receipts from sales and cash disbursements on merchandise purchases for the months of January, February, and March.

4-29. Projecting Net Income and Cash Flow.

The Rocky Gravel Company mines and processes rock and gravel. It started in business on January 1, 20x1, when it purchased the assets of another company. You have examined its financial statements at December 31, 20x1, and have been requested to assist in planning and projecting operations for 20x2. The company also wants to know the maximum amount by which notes payable to officers can be reduced at December 31, 20x2.

The adjusted trial balance follows:

The Rocky Gravel Company
Adjusted Trial Balance
December 31, 20x1

Cash	$ 51,000	
Accounts receivable	72,000	
Mining properties	180,000	
Accumulated depletion		$ 9,000
Equipment	450,000	
Accumulated depreciation		30,000
Goodwill	15,000	
Accumulated amortization		3,000
Accounts payable		36,000
Federal income		
tax payable		66,000
Notes payable officers		120,000
Capital stock		300,000
Premium on capital stock		102,000
Sales		900,000
Production costs		
(including depreciation		
and depletion)	552,000	
Administrative expense		
(including amortization		
and interest)	180,000	
Provision for Federal		
income taxes	66,000	
Total	$1,566,000	$1,566,000

You are able to develop the following information bearing on your assignment:
1. The total yards of material sold is expected to increase 10 percent in 20x2 and the average sales price per cubic yard will be increased from $4.50 to $4.80.
2. The estimated recoverable reserves of rock and gravel were 4,000,000 cubic yards when the properties were purchased. Thus, the rate of depletion per cubic yard has been set at $45.00 per 1,000 cubic yards ($180,000 ÷ 4,000).
3. Production costs include direct labor of $330,000 of which $30,000 was attributed to inefficiencies in the early stages of operation. The union contract calls for 5 percent increases in hourly rates effective January 1, 20x2. Production costs other than depreciation, depletion, and direct labor will increase 4 percent in 20x2.
4. Administrative expense, other than amortization and interest, will increase $24,000 in 20x2.

5. The company has contracted for additional movable equipment costing $300,000 to be in production on July 1, 20x2. The new equipment has a useful life of 20 years and will be depreciated on a straight-line basis.

6. The new equipment will be financed by a 40 percent down payment and a 6 percent three-year chattel mortgage. Interest and principal payments (one-sixth per installment) are due semi-annually on June 30 and December 31, beginning December 31, 20x2. The notes payable to officers are demand notes dated January 1, 20x1, on which 6 percent interest is provided for and was paid December 31, 20x1.

7. Accounts receivable will increase in proportion to sales. No bad debts are anticipated. Accounts payable will remain substantially the same.

8. Assume an income tax rate of 50 percent.

9. It is customary in the rock and gravel business not to place any value on stockpiles of processed material which are awaiting sale. Thus, all production costs are charged to the current period's revenues.

10. The company has decided to maintain a minimum cash balance of $60,000.

Required:

a. Prepare a budgeted income statement for 20x2.

b. Prepare a *cash flow* projection (cash budget) for 20x2 which will indicate the amount by which notes payable to officers can be reduced at December 31, 20x2.

c. Determine the budgeted return on capital employed.

Note: Round all amounts to the nearest $100. If the amount to be rounded is exactly $50, round to the next highest $100.

4-30. Budget Planning Case.

Machine Tools, Inc. manufactures custom machine tools for various metal working companies. Each machine produced must first go through a detailed design stage before entering the manufacturing process. This design process limits the number of machines the company can produce, but company managers would like to consider increasing the size of the engineering design group. Manufacturing activities do not constrain output because the company can subcontract the actual production of the machine to other manufacturers.

Customers pay for the machines in the following manner:

> 10% upon start of a job
> 40% upon completion of one-third of job
> 40% upon completion of two thirds of job
> 10% upon completion of job

Machine Tools, Inc., pays all material and other variable costs at the mid point in the completion of a job, and these costs amount to 50% of the selling price of the job. Jobs completed by the company can be classified as small or large. Small jobs require six months to complete, and large jobs require nine months to complete. Small jobs usually sell for $500,000 and large jobs sell for $1,500,000.

Each additional small job added to those in process requires one more design engineer, and if the company adds three design engineers it can add an additional large job to those already in process. Company managers estimate they need one engineering coordinator for each four engineers; adding one engineer above the four already covered by a coordinator requires the company to hire an additional coordinator. The company pays design engineers

$4,000 per month and engineering coordinators $3,000 per month. These amounts include all fringe benefits. These individuals will receive a 5% increase at the start of year 2. At the start of budget year 1 the company had 20 design engineers and five engineering coordinators at work, and these employees could handle all the jobs projected for the two year period. Any work level above the projected one will require additional engineers.

You have gathered the following data on past year activities and on anticipated future activities. Jobs booked refers to the number of jobs the company commits to deliver to customers, i.e., the number of jobs salesmen sell to customers.

	Past Year		Year 1		Year 2	
	Small	Large	Small	Large	Small	Large
January	1	0	1	1	1	1
February	0	0	1	0	2	0
March	2	1	2	0	2	1
April	0	0	1	1	1	0
May	0	0	1	0	2	1
June	1	0	3	0	3	0
July	1	1	0	1	1	1
August	0	0	1	0	2	1
September	0	0	2	0	1	0
October	1	1	1	0	3	0
November	0	0	1	1	1	0
December	2	0	0	0	1	1

Monthly cash expenses for the past year include:

Marketing	$ 10,000
Administration	120,000
Engineering & Manufacturing	
(excludes the cost of design engineers	
and engineering coordinators)	20,000

Marketing costs are expected to double for year 1 with another doubling for year 2, and administrative costs will rise approximately 1% per month for the two-year budget planning period. The company has a $2,000,000 loan outstanding at the beginning of year 1 on which it pays $500,000 per year plus interest at an annual rate of 24% on the unpaid balance. It pays both interest and principal in December of each year.

Company managers expect depreciation to remain at $20,000 per month for the two years, and the company accountant pays income taxes quarterly (35% of net income) starting in March of the first year.

Required:

1. Prepare monthly cash flow projections for the next two years.
2. What is the monthly cash flow impact of doubling the number of orders taken?

Learning Objectives

After reading this chapter, the student should have an understanding of:

✔ The relationship between responsibility accounting and cost centers, work cells, departments and flow lines.

✔ How to identify costs relevant for management decisions.

✔ The product costs relevant for output and product mix decisions.

✔ How bills of materials and product routings provide useful information to accountants.

✔ The essential elements of effective cost tracking systems.

✔ The impact of just-in-time manufacturing on accounting systems.

✔ The impact of just-in-time manufacturing systems on the cost accounting system.

COST ACCOUNTING SYSTEMS—PART I: RESPONSIBILITY ACCOUNTING, DECISION MAKING AND JIT

Chapter 5

How do managers maintain control over costs so they can make a profit? What costs should accountants include in product costs so managers can make profit maximizing decisions? Do different production systems like just-in-time impact the accounting system? How? These are just a few of the questions we will address in this first chapter on cost accounting systems.

We begin this chapter with a review of responsibility accounting and the organizational units related to it followed by a discussion of the cost information relevant for managerial decision making. As part of the discussion of costs for decision making, the chapter covers the development of relevant product costs for managerial decisions and the recording of costs related to production. Finally, we examine the impact of just-in-time manufacturing processes on the traditional accounting system and the types of information accountants collect for managers in such a system.

▶ RESPONSIBILITY ACCOUNTING ◀

As mentioned in Chapter 2, the managers who make decisions that impact costs are scattered throughout the organization, and they need to know how their decisions affect total company costs. Accountants have developed a means to implement this idea known as responsibility accounting. *Responsibility accounting* refers to an accounting system that ties every expense and revenue (even assets and liabilities) to the manager who determines its level, i.e., every expense and revenue account "belongs" to some manager who has authority to make charges to those accounts.

Since these managers are scattered throughout the company, accountants have developed a variety of organizational units to which they track costs. Some of these units are called *cost centers*, *departments*, *work cells*, or *lines*. A *cost center* is an organizational unit for which the accounting system accumulates costs; for example, a bag manufacturing company accumulates cost data for transactions originating in the cloth sewing center on the second floor of its Nashville plant. A *department* is similar to a cost center; however a department might include several cost centers. For example, each grinding machine in an air compressor manufacturing plant functions as a cost center, but all grinding machines are grouped together in the Grinding Department.

The concept of *work cells* is a recent development. A cell consists of a group of machines and people that can complete a whole sequence of operations on a product as opposed to a department that typically performs only one or two operations. These cells are frequently located along a *line* as shown in Exhibit 5-1. A line consists of a group of work cells, and it usually produces a single product or a single product line.

Companies create these different organizational units to assign cost responsibility and to provide logical units for collecting cost data. For instance, the managers of the air compressor plant established

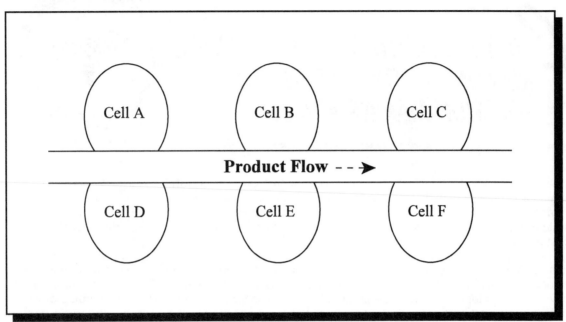

Exhibit 5-1

each grinding machine as a cost center because they need to monitor closely the costs traceable to each machine.

The machine operator approves any charges to his or her machine and, at the end of the month, receives a report on all charges made to that machine. In addition, the manager of the Grinding Department approves other expenses related to the entire department beyond those specific to the individual machines, and this manager receives a report at month-end on these expenses.

Thus, cost centers, departments, work cells, etc., enable accountants to record costs controlled by individual managers throughout the organization. This system creates gatekeepers throughout the company who watch over all transactions going into the accounts under their control.

The mechanics of such a system are relatively simple. The accountant devises an account code with a responsibility field and permits no transaction to enter the accounting system without a manager's responsibility code in this field.

The following code illustrates how accountants can track expenses to individual managers.

Account Class	Account Detail	Responsibility Code	Geographic Region

The first field, Account Class, indicates whether the transaction applies to an asset, liability, revenue, or expense. The second field identifies the kind of expense (labor, rent, materials, etc.); the third identifies the responsible individual; and, the last one specifies the geographic region in which the transaction originated. The third field provides information useful for the responsibility accounting system by identifying the person who approved the transaction so the accountant can periodically report costs and revenues to the managers of responsibility units.

The mechanics of establishing a responsibility accounting system are simple, but the organizational issues related to its implementation are complex. For instance, top executives must decide which manager should be in charge of each expense incurred by the company. This is no small task, and some companies must be reorganized before management can agree on who should have responsibility for rent expense, for example. But the payoffs are high; companies with successful responsibility accounting implementations can achieve significant improvements in profitability.

► COSTS FOR DECISION MAKING ◄

Basic economics suggests that managers who want to maximize profits should consider only those costs that a decision will change when they choose among possible alternatives. Accountants call these costs that change *incremental costs*. Thus, if a decision does not make a particular cost change, the manager should ignore the unchanging cost in his or her cost analysis for the decision. Consider the following example of an enterprising young man who decides to make some money at a local fair.

Jason Wilson rents a booth at the local fair for $1,000 for the duration of the week long event. He buys t-shirts from a supplier for $3 each and sells them for $10. Working by himself for ten hours per day, Jason can sell 1,000 shirts during the fair; however, if he hires a friend to work with him for the week for $1,200, he can increase sales to 1,500 shirts.

Decision: Should Jason hire the friend?
Relevant costs: (costs that change if Jason hires a friend)

Salary for friend	$1,200
Cost of added t-shirts (500 x $3)	1,500
Total cost increase	$2,700

Since hiring his friend will increase sales an additional $5,000 (500 shirts at $10 each) as compared to a cost increase of $2,700, it makes sense for Jason to hire his friend. In this example, Jason considered only the salary for his friend and the cost of the additional shirts he can sell because these are the only costs affected by the decision to hire his friend. He ignores the $1,000 rent for the booth because the decision to hire his friend has no impact on the cost of renting the booth. When Jason made the decision to rent a booth for the duration of the fair, his cost analysis included the $1,000 rent; but later decisions take this cost as a given because the decision to incur it has already been made.

► RELEVANT PRODUCT COSTS FOR PROFIT MAXIMIZING DECISIONS ◄

Just as Jason needed to know the cost increase associated with hiring his friend to sell t-shirts, managers of manufacturing firms need to know how much their costs will increase with the production of an additional unit of product.

If a manager is facing a decision to either increase the output of bicycles or the output of swing sets with both selling for the same price, the relevant question is "How much will total company cost increase when we make one more bicycle as compared to the cost increase for one more swing set?" The answer is easy for some companies since incremental product cost equals the cost of the materials used to make the product. For others it becomes more complex because labor cost varies with the number of units produced; and, in some cases accountants must perform detailed analyses of overhead costs to determine how much these costs vary with units of output. Chapter 3 refers to incremental costs per unit of output as variable costs.

Note the product cost we use here for profit maximizing decisions differs from the ones accountants use for external financial reporting (see Chapter 7 for a discussion of product cost for financial reporting). Financial reporting rules dictate inventory valuation procedures for external reports, while economic principles tell managers how to define product costs for profit maximizing decisions using the concept of incremental or variable cost per unit of output.

Consider a simple case in which incremental product cost includes only materials cost. The materials cost for a product usually comes from the *bill of materials*, a list of the materials and quantities needed to build a product. Adding materials prices to the list allows the accountant to extend price times quantity to compute incremental unit cost. Consider the example in Exhibit 5-2 for a heating element used in electric water heaters.

Direct Material	Unit	Qty.	Unit Price	Total
Wire, Gauge 22 C	Lb.	0.03	$ 8.00	$ 0.240
Pin, U-Term .75 x 2	Each	1.00	0.10	0.100
Ceramic bushing	Each	1.00	0.02	0.020
Bottom seal	Each	1.00	0.01	0.010
Tubing	Foot	4.20	0.16	0.672
Magnesium Oxide	Lb.	0.25	0.50	0.125
End seal	Each	1.00	0.02	0.020
Total incremental cost				$ 1.187

Exhibit 5-2 *Water Heater Element Bill of Materials*

If the company pays all workers a straight salary regardless of the number of units produced, then the incremental product cost per unit for this water heater element is $1.187. However, if the company pays workers by the hour, and sends them home when there is no work, then labor cost is a part of incremental product cost since it varies with the production of heater elements. Labor information is readily available in most manufacturing firms from the *product routing*. This routing lists the operations performed on the product, the sequence in which they are executed, the department in which they take place, the amount of labor time required for the operation, and, in many systems, the labor cost per hour in each department. The routing in Exhibit 5-3 for the heater element is illustrative.

Operation	Dept.	Labor Hours	Hourly Labor Cost	Total
Wind coil	20	0.008	$ 12.00	$ 0.096
Degrease	20	0.001	12.00	0.012
Automatic weld	50	0.012	11.00	0.132
Inspect and stretch	50	0.001	11.00	0.011
Hairpin bend	60	0.025	13.00	0.325
Squeeze press	60	0.025	13.00	0.325
Assemble flange	60	0.022	13.00	0.286
Second bend	60	0.010	13.00	0.130
Total incremental labor cost				$ 1.317

Exhibit 5-3 *Water Heater Element Product Routing*

Note how this routing indicates the department in which the operations take place, as well as the order in which they occur. Routing sheets like these are common in manufacturing operations; for complex products they can include thousands of steps and hundreds of departments.

Assuming that the company making these heater elements pays workers by the hour and sends them home when they are not needed, the incremental product cost includes the total of both the materials and the labor as follows:

> Direct materials cost (Exhibit 5-2) . . . . $ 1.187
> Direct labor cost (Exhibit 5-3) 1.317
> Incremental (Variable) Product Cost Per Unit . . . . $ 2.504

If the company also incurs incremental overhead expenses of $0.126 for each heater element produced, the incremental product cost per unit rises to $2.630 as shown below. Companies estimate overhead cost changes with increased output using methods such as scattergraphs or regression analysis to estimate the cost variation with output. Chapter 14 discusses these techniques.

> Direct material cost . . . . $ 1.187
> Direct Labor cost 1.317
> Manufacturing Overhead 0.126
> Incremental (Variable) Product Cost Per Unit . . . . $ 2.630

▸ Product Cost Sheets

Instead of showing only the incremental (variable) product cost in total, as above, some companies prepare a product cost sheet like the one in Exhibit 5-4, which identifies total cost increases in each department by type of cost.

This arrangement of product cost information allows managers to estimate easily the change or variability in total company cost caused by a change in output for a specific product. Managers use information like this when considering, for example, whether or not to purchase the work done in Department 20 from an outside supplier. The $.388 for this department provides an estimate of the amount of cost which purchase from an outside supplier replaces, so it is useful for make or buy decisions.

▸ Modifications in Incremental Product Costs

The arrangement of data in exhibit 5-4 also proves useful for those cases in which the assumptions used to estimate the incremental (variable) unit cost have changed. For example, suppose a firm is producing at capacity so any added output is possible only if employees work overtime. In this case managers must modify the cost numbers to take this new information into account. Consequently, the manager who must estimate the incremental cost of producing 100 more units will add $.6585 (.5 x $1.317) to the unit incremental cost to take into account the overtime pay needed for the additional units.

Consider another case. A customer orders 100 units at 4:00 in the afternoon to be delivered the next morning. The company can produce the units only if it has its employees work overtime, and it has to order additional material for the order for which the vendor charges a 20% premium because of such short notice. The manager dealing with the customer can refer to the product cost sheet to quickly compute the added labor ($.6585) and the added material cost $.2374 (20% x $1.187) for a new incremental unit cost of $3.5259.

	Dept. 20	Dept. 50	Dept. 60	Total
Direct Materials				
Wire, Gauge 22 C	0.240			$ 0.240
Pin, U-Term .75 x 2		0.100		0.100
Ceramic bushing			0.020	0.020
Bottom seal			0.010	0.010
Tubing		0.672		0.672
Magnesium Oxide		0.125		0.125
End seal			0.020	0.020
Total Materials Cost	0.240	0.897	0.050	1.187
Direct Labor				
Wind coil	0.096			0.096
Degrease	0.012			0.012
Automatic weld		0.132		0.132
Inspect and stretch		0.011		0.011
Hairpin bend			0.325	0.325
Squeeze press			0.325	0.325
Assemble flange			0.286	0.286
Second bend			0.130	0.130
Total Labor Cost	0.108	0.143	1.066	1.317
Variable Manufacturing Overhead				
Overhead Cost	0.040	0.030	0.056	0.126
Totals	0.388	1.070	1.172	$ 2.630

Exhibit 5-4 *Product Cost Sheet Electric Water Heater Element*

Cases like these arise all the time, so managers need an incremental (variable) product cost system that produces information in a format like Exhibit 5-4. This allows managers to readily adjust to cost or quantity changes. No accounting system can economically include incremental (variable) cost data for all possible cases a manager might face, so accountants create flexible systems that managers can easily adapt to the needs of a particular decision.

▶ Cost Tracking Systems

Accountants create cost tracking systems to enable managers to identify the dollar amount of cost incurred at any location in the firm. A good financial accounting system records the movement of assets into and out of the firm; a good cost accounting system expands this principle by recording asset moves across departmental or cost center boundaries as well. For accounting purposes, then, accountants treat each department within the firm as if it were a separate entity. Accountants record the movement of materials from the storeroom to a department on the manufacturing floor; they record its movement from one department to the next; and, finally, they record the movement of a finished unit from the factory to the warehouse. Whenever an asset crosses an internal boundary, the accounting system generates a transaction to record the movement.

In a manufacturing operation, costs typically flow from raw materials to work-in-process and from there to finished goods. The following sections illustrate the journal entries that record cost movement through raw materials and work-in-process, and Chapter 6 illustrates the journal entries to move costs into finished goods.

► Materials Cost Accounting

Materials make up the largest portion of manufacturing costs, and manufacturing companies devote significant resources to tracking and managing the flow of materials through the plant. The documents usually involved in materials purchasing and management are:

Purchase requisition —	An internal document that requests the purchasing department to order an item from an outside supplier.
Purchase order —	The document that authorizes a vendor to ship the specified goods to the company placing the order.
Receiving report —	The document workers in the receiving area complete to indicate how much and what kinds of materials have been received.
Materials requisition —	A form a worker completes to request materials from the materials storeroom.
Materials move ticket —	A document that indicates how much material was moved from one location in the plant to another location.

Computerized materials management systems dispense with most of these documents, except for the purchase order, but they still track the same information. For example, receiving personnel may use bar codes to identify the materials received and key the quantity received directly into the computer instead of writing it on a receiving report. Also, instead of completing a materials requisition document for materials, a worker may insert his name badge in a reader at the materials storeroom which captures his department and cost center, while the storeroom clerk enters the quantity of the items requested by the worker.

Three of these documents (receiving report, materials requisition, materials move ticket) generate journal entries, and these entries are illustrated below for each document.

> *Receiving report*
> Dr. Materials
>   Cr. Accounts Payable
>
> *Materials requisition*
> Dr. Work-in-Process Direct Materials (Department A)
>   Cr. Materials
>
> *Materials move ticket*
> Dr. Work-in-Process Direct Materials (Department B)
>   Cr. Work-in-Process Direct Materials (Department A)

► Labor Cost Accounting

The details of labor accounting depend on the type of cost system in place and the payment plan used for labor. For example, in a job order cost system (see Chapter 6 for a more detailed explanation of this system) workers record the time they spend on each job. Some companies have now automated this process by issuing name badges to workers with bar codes that allow a worker to enter into a computer system the start and stop times for each job. Hourly workers in many companies punch a time clock when they arrive and when they leave to record the number of hours worked, while salaried workers simply show up for work.

Regardless of the system used to capture labor time, the cost system must be able to assign labor costs to the appropriate job or location. A code that captures labor cost data by department or cost center (and job, if appropriate) helps to accomplish this task. For example, assume the Machining Department incurred $9,000 of direct labor cost for the past week and the Assembly Department incurred $6,600 for the same week. Accountants make the following entry to record these events.

```
Dr. Work-in-Process Direct Labor—Machining  . . . . . .    9,000
Dr. Work-in-Process Direct Labor—Assembly  . . . . . . .   6,600
     Cr. Wages Payable (and various withholdings)  . . . . . . . . . .          15,600
```

This entry records the direct labor for the two departments for the week and adds the cost to the work-in-process inventory.

▶ Overhead Cost Accounting

Tracking overhead costs is similar to tracking materials and labor costs; accountants identify the overhead costs with the individual approving the expense and with the department or cost center in which the expense occurred. For instance, the two departments for which labor cost was recorded in the above example would record the usage of disposable tooling (an overhead cost) with this entry:

```
Dr. Work-in-Process Manufacturing Overhead—Machining . . .    2,635
Dr. Work-in-Process Manufacturing Overhead—Assembly  . . .      575
     Cr. Materials (or Tools Inventory)  . . . . . . . . . . . . . . . . . . . . . . . . .         3,210
```

The managers of these departments receive a detailed report each month on the actual overhead they incurred during the month. See the example in Exhibit 6-6 in the next chapter for an illustration of one of these reports.

▶ ALTERNATIVE APPROACHES TO MANUFACTURING—JIT ◀

The discussion thus far has assumed that a manufacturing firm receives materials into a storeroom, issues it to departments, and tracks costs as they move from one department to another. Such traditional systems are common, but many organizations now use Just In Time production methods that provide greater economies and lower inventories than the system just described.

▶ What is Just In Time?

Just In Time (JIT) is a management philosophy that stresses a just in time use of materials, labor and facilities.[1] Some companies have dramatically reduced their inventories with this philosophy by eliminating factors, such as poor quality and machine breakdowns, that cause them to carry unnecessary inventory.

Poor quality requires a company to carry extra inventory to make sure some of the inventory on hand is usable, and machine breakdowns require extra inventory to allow the plant to keep operating

---

[1] Walleigh, Richard C., "What's Your Excuse for Not Using JIT?," *Harvard Business Review* (March-April, 1986):pp. 38-54.

while one of its machines is down for repair. On the other hand, matching the daily output of finished goods to the daily sales mix reduces inventory. Close cooperation with vendors gives additional impetus to inventory reductions by enabling vendors to deliver goods just as they are needed. Some companies have achieved inventory reductions of 90% by following the JIT philosophy.

Because JIT usually dramatically reduces inventory carrying costs, we devote the next section to a discussion of these costs.

► *Inventory Carrying Costs*

Accountants and operating managers often refer to the cost of keeping inventory on hand as "carrying cost." This cost includes shipping, storage, handling and financing, and most accountants express it as a percentage of inventory cost. Some carrying costs, such as warehousing, labor, depreciation of facilities, and insurance, remain constant with changes in inventory while others, like interest, obsolescence, and inbound freight, vary with the inventory level. Managers making short-term decisions may estimate an annual inventory carrying cost of 15% to 20% which includes only variable carrying costs (i.e., costs that vary with the level of inventory on hand), while those looking at long-term changes in the physical structures and procedures related to inventory may estimate a carrying cost of 35% to 40% which includes both fixed and variable carrying costs. For example, a company with $10 million in inventory and a short term, or variable, carrying cost of 20% will incur $2 million (20% x $10,000,000) each year in variable carrying costs.

► *Characteristics of a JIT Operation*

Simplification. Companies following the JIT philosophy work to simplify every process, product and piece of equipment. They standardize the electrical control systems for all machines on a flow line, use color codes to identify parts and components, and freeze production schedules to eliminate fluctuations in output.

Production managers work with product designers to simplify product design. This speeds up manufacturing and reduces the number of parts carried in inventory. Fewer parts in a product means fewer parts to purchase, store, track and count; it also means a reduction in potential errors, or opportunities to make something the wrong way. Similarly, each part inserted into an assembly provides an opportunity for incorrect assembly.

Fast Setups. Some companies have reduced the time to change dies on stamping machines from eight hours to twenty minutes. General Electric reduced die change time from 47 minutes to one minute forty seconds in one of its operations by standardizing die mountings on its presses, by building a two level die cart (one level holds the die removed, and the other holds the die to put in its place), and by training workers in the new die loading procedures.[2]

Fast setups allow a plant to produce in small quantities instead of in large batches. This reduces the need to carry large quantities of work in process inventory, increases quality (an incorrect machine adjustment results in only a small quantity of bad product), and allows the company to increase output without buying additional machines.

Demand Pull Versus Batch Push. Demand pull and batch push refer to the method used to move products through the production process. With a demand pull approach, a worker begins producing parts only when the next step in the process requests another part. In contrast, in a batch push process, workers stay busy by making parts in large batches; a mechanical device (like a fork

---

[2] Lesnet, Con E., "Facility found That Means of Implementing Quick Die Changes Were Readily At Hand," *Industrial Engineering* (November, 1983): pp. 50-54.

lift) removes the completed batches periodically and takes the parts to the next stage of the production process or to storage.

Under a demand pull system some workers may be periodically idle, but managers like the smooth production flow it produces and the high quality made possible by having workers within visual distance of one another. If a worker produces a defective product, the next worker in the line immediately notifies him or her and they fix the defect right away.

The following example contrasts the arrangement of operations in the two systems. The left diagram shows the arrangement of operations in a batch push environment, and the right one shows the sequential order for a demand pull system.

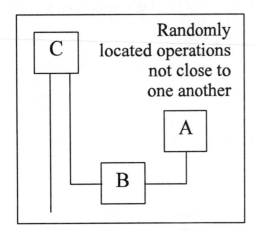

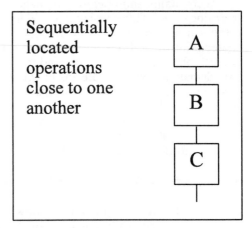

Note how the product moves from one non-sequential location to another in the layout on the left; in contrast, the one on the right moves the product in a straight line from operation A to operation C. This arrangement also affects the amount of inventory the plant must carry. For instance, because of the random location of the operations in the left diagram, each location must carry enough inventory to take care of unexpected delays in delivery of parts from previous operations, unexpected variations in machine and operator productivity, and unexpected machine breakdowns in machines.

Consider the impact on inventory carrying cost of the two systems as illustrated in Exhibits 5-5 and 5-6.

The batch push system must carry more inventory at each operation to cover materials movement variability, operator variability, and quality problems. A demand pull system needs only a small amount of work in process inventory, and this dramatically reduces inventory carrying cost. In a demand pull system workers move materials to the next operation when they finish their work; workers help one another to keep production moving smoothly; and, the line carries no inventory to cover quality problems because workers instantly detect and correct quality problems by inspecting their own work and the work of the person immediately upstream in the line.

Maintenance Strategy. Modern manufacturing firms use preventive maintenance procedures to keep their equipment running in near perfect condition. With this system, workers take "ownership" of the equipment they operate, maintaining it as carefully as if it belonged to them. Workers use checklists to make sure they follow the appropriate procedures when starting a machine,

Units needed to:	Operation A	Operation B	Operation C
Cover variability in materials movement	3,000	2,500	3,500
Cover variability in operator output	2,000	1,200	1,000
Cover quality problems	1,500	2,000	3,000
Total units for operation	6,500	5,700	7,500
Unit variable cost	$ 8	$ 15	$ 26
Total dollar investment	$ 52,000	$ 85,500	$ 195,000
Annual carrying cost at 25%	$ 13,000	$ 21,375	$ 48,750
Total annual carrying cost	$ 83,125		

Exhibit 5-5 *Inventory Carrying Cost for a Batch Push Approach*

Units needed to:	Operation A	Operation B	Operation C
Cover variability in materials movement	5	5	5
Cover variability in operator output	5	5	5
Cover quality problems	2	2	2
Total units for operation	12	12	12
Unit variable cost	$ 8	$ 15	$ 26
Total dollar investment	96	180	312
Annual carrying cost at 25%	$ 24	$ 45	$ 78
Total annual carrying cost	$ 147		

Exhibit 5-6 *Inventory Carrying Cost for a Demand Pull Approach*

and they do routine maintenance jobs like lubrication and inspection to keep the equipment operating in peak condition at all times. Companies are willing to incur the costs of preventive maintenance programs because they know the far greater expense of machine breakdowns.

To illustrate the magnitude of machine breakdown costs, consider this example. An automobile company was experiencing down time of 70 minutes per day on the trim and final assembly section of its assembly line.[3] Any stoppage in trim and final assembly shuts down the entire assembly line. Total cost of this down time consisted of the idle labor cost and the cost of lost production (a contribution margin of $2,000 per unit). Approximately 1,300 people worked on the production line at a variable cost of $11 per hour. Thus, the daily cost of idle labor was:

($11/hr./person)   x   (1.167 hr./day)   x   1,300 people   = $16,683

Assume the firm could sell all the vehicles it produced, and customers would buy a competitor's vehicle if they could not obtain one from this company. Consequently, any lost production caused

---

[3] Gallimore, Devin F. and Richard J. Penlesky, "A Framework for Developing Maintenance Strategies," *Production and Inventory Management Journal* (First Quarter, 1988), pp. 20-21.

lost sales. Each vehicle had a cycle time (time to complete one vehicle) for the assembly line of 1.4 minutes. Thus the cost of lost production per day was:

[($2,000 per unit)/(1.4 min. per unit)]   x   (70 min./day)   = $100,000

Total breakdown cost thus amounted to $116,683 per day, or about $29 million per year, and the largest component of this cost was the contribution margin lost from the units not produced.

The company made a one time investment of $110,000 and a commitment to spend an additional $260,000 annually to reduce the daily down time from 70 minutes to 5 minutes. A five minute daily down time carries an approximate annual cost of $2,084,000, as compared to the original annual cost of $29 million. Thus the one time investment paid for itself in approximately one day.

Because so many modern manufacturing firms use demand pull approaches to production, their production operations suffer almost complete shutdowns if a critical machine stops operating. Consequently, the managers of these firms concentrate on effective preventive maintenance programs that preclude machines from breaking down. The lost margins from a breakdown in such an environment, as the above example shows, are often too large for managers to take chances with unreliable machines.

► THE ACCOUNTING IMPACT OF JIT/TRANSACTION VOLUME ◄

Just In Time production systems have significantly improved the profits of manufacturing firms and they also substantially impact the accounting system. To illustrate this accounting impact, consider first the journal entry volume for a company using a traditional accounting approach compared to a just in time manufacturing process. It receives shipments four times daily from each of ten suppliers, makes forty journal entries a day to record the receipt of merchandise, and issues forty purchase orders daily to authorize these shipments. Such transaction volume can hopelessly backlog the work in an accounting office. In a JIT environment accountants must devise more efficient ways of handling these transactions.

To illustrate the accounting impact of JIT systems, we contrast two extreme cases. A comparison of the two extremes illustrates the accounting system impact of JIT production systems.

► Accounting Transactions in a Batch-Push System

Consider the three department example used on page 5-10 and assume materials flow to work-in-process storage after each department finishes working on the product. The following list of journal entries includes only those required to record the movement of materials from raw materials storage to finished goods for this batch-push process.

1. Requisition materials from materials area to department A.
2. Move materials from department A to work-in-process storage.
3. Move materials from work-in-process storage to department B.
4. Requisition added materials for department B.
5. Move materials from department B to work-in-process storage.
6. Move materials from work-in-process storage to department C.
7. Requisition added materials for department C.
8. Move finished units to finished goods inventory.

Of course, there are additional entries for labor and overhead items, and there may be several entries for each of the elements listed here. A company with two hundred cost centers and a batch push manufacturing system could easily generate several thousand transactions per month, and every transaction creates an opportunity for a mistake. When mistakes occur, accountants must devote effort to correcting the mistake; and, with thousands of transactions in a month, a company needs a large staff of accountants to handle the task of correcting mistakes. A demand pull system, in contrast, requires far fewer transactions and thus fewer mistakes, as illustrated in the next section.

▸ Accounting Transactions in a Demand-Pull System

To illustrate the reduction of entries in a demand pull system, consider the case of Nissan Motor Manufacturing, U.S.A. of Smyrna, Tennessee. Nissan purchases all of its vehicle seats from a Vintec plant located twenty miles from the Nissan plant. Nissan's computer sends a message to Vintec when a vehicle shell leaves the paint room in the Nissan plant; this message triggers the printing of a bar code label and a description of the seats needed on a printer in the Vintec plant. Workers at Vintec have four hours to complete the seats, load them on a truck, and deliver them to the Nissan plant floor where they will be installed in a vehicle. Nissan has no materials storage area for seats; they sit in racks near where they will be used by assembly workers.

Nissan issues one purchase order for the year to Vintec, it prepares no receiving reports for the seats received, and it pays Vintec each week by looking at the number of vehicles completed that week. Vintec sends no invoices or monthly statements to Nissan—it just receives a weekly electronic funds transfer for the seats used by Nissan. With this system, Nissan requires just one journal entry per week for the seats:

> Dr. Cost of Goods Sold
> Cr. Cash

Contrast this with the multiplicity of journal entries for the batch-push system. The Nissan system eliminates all entries for materials requisitions and materials movement, and, because Nissan transfers ownership of completed vehicles to its sales company immediately upon their completion, it can debit cost of sales instead of inventory for the seats received from Vintec.

Why does Nissan need so few journal entries for its system? First of all, it carries only about two hours of seat inventory; thus its managers can readily determine whether all the seats ordered actually arrived—they just look to see that every completed vehicle has seats. They do not need a receiving report to tell them the seats arrived. They eliminate materials requisitions by requiring Vintec to deliver the seats to the point at which workers will use them to build a vehicle. They remove the need for purchase orders by issuing as few as one per year to their sole source of supply.

The Nissan example of demand-pull manufacturing illustrates how this approach to manufacturing radically reduces the number of journal entries required for the cost system and how control of materials costs moves from the accounting system to the production system. Companies like Nissan also eliminate detailed labor reporting by paying workers a salary and avoiding the tracking of how many hours an employee works in each department. Such companies merely look to see if a worker showed up for work instead of creating an expensive system to count the number of hours the employee worked in each part of the plant.

▸ SUMMARY ◂

The cost system allows managers to estimate the amount that cost will change for a particular decision, and product cost systems help managers estimate the dollar amount total company cost increases with the production of an additional unit. The bill of materials and product routings help managers develop these estimates.

The responsibility accounting system relates cost and revenue accounts to specific managers to provide the managers with information on how their decisions impact costs and revenues. Accountants develop account codes that allow costs and revenues to be traced to individual managers, cost centers or departments.

To relate costs to these segments accountants record the movement of assets and costs among internal organization segments. But the journal entries to record these transactions vary with the production system in use. A JIT system requires far fewer entries to track asset and cost movement than a traditional batch-push system.

► QUESTIONS ◄

5-1. Explain the relationship between work cells and responsibility accounting.

5-2. How do managers use responsibility accounting to manage costs in work cells?

5-3. List three fields accountants will most likely use in a cost code for a factory that plans to track costs by cost center and by production line.

5-4. What is the distinguishing characteristic of a cost relevant to a decision a manager has to make? Give a specific example.

5-5. What is the relationship between incremental unit cost and variable unit cost?

5-6. What is a bill of materials, and what is a product routing? How does the accountant use them for developing product costs?

5-7. For what reason do accountants create cost tracking systems?

5-8. Name and describe the three documents typically involved in materials purchasing and materials management.

5-9. Describe the journal entries a company usually uses to record the receipt of materials, the movement of materials to work-in-process, and the movement of units from one department to another within the plant.

5-10. What is inventory carrying cost?

5-11. Name and describe two characteristics of a just in time manufacturing system.

5-12. How does JIT affect the cost accounting system?

5-13. List the journal entries required to move materials from materials storage for a traditional manufacturing system, and then list the journal entries required for the same materials movement under a JIT system.

► EXERCISES ◄

5-14. Relevant Costs for Decision Making.

Jason Wilson who operates a t-shirt concession at a local fair is considering opening a store in a local shopping center. He can rent space in the shopping center for $5,000 per month, and he estimates his utilities at $1,200 per month. If he rents the space, he can hire either two full time employees at $1,500 per month for each employee, or he can hire one full time employee for $1,500 and two part-time employees for $600 per month per employee.

Required:

a. Compute the monthly incremental cost of opening the store with two full-time employees.
b. Compute the monthly incremental cost of opening the store with one full-time and one part-time employee.
c. Jason opens the store with one full-time and one part-time employee, and it is very successful. It is so successful he is considering adding another full-time employee. Compute the monthly incremental cost of adding the full time employee if the employee costs the same as the present full-time employee. Why is your answer different from question a in this exercise?

5-15. Relevant Cost Computation.

You are the owner of a home with a two-car garage, and you are a bargain hunter who has made some excellent buys on automobiles. However, your home has a garage that will hold only two automobiles or one auto plus a boat.

The following data show the original cost and the current sales prices of your two autos and boat. There is a well developed market for used automobiles and boats in your city, so it is easy to sell or acquire automobiles or boats identical to yours at the market value given.

	Cost	*Market Value*
Lincoln Continental	$ 4,000	$ 9,000
Chevrolet	15,000	16,500
Speed King Boat	20,000	5,000

A hailstorm with baseball-size hail is rapidly approaching your home, and you have three minutes to decide what to leave outside in the hail. What will you do? Give a cost justification for your answer.

5-16. Responsibility Code Design.

Mason Lawn and Garden manufactures equipment for the nursery industry. They produce twenty different products among which are machines that mix soil and fill flower pots with the mixed soil, machines that plant seeds in trays of potting soil, and sophisticated, computer controlled machines that companies use to carefully control the fertilizer, soil, and herbicide mix for experimental growing operations. Mason makes these machines in its Tennessee plant in three departments: Metal Shaping, Metal Cutting, and Final Assembly. It sells the equipment throughout the world, and has divided the world into twelve regions with a sales manager in charge of each region.

a. List the code fields accountants might use to satisfy the reporting needs of a responsibility accounting system for Mason Lawn and Garden.

b. Prepare the numeric codes you recommend the company use for tracking sales by product.

▸ PROBLEMS AND CASES ◂

5-17. Incremental Product Costs and Bill of Materials.

Your production manager provided you with the following list of materials used to make a lawn mower, one of the products manufactured in your plant.

Quantity	Description
1	Four cycle engine
5	Bolts—1/4 x 2
5	Lock nuts—1/4 inch
5	Washers—1/4 inch
1	Throttle cable
4	Wheel assemblies
1	Blade—22 inch
1	Handle assembly
1	Deck housing

The company purchases the engines for $40 each, and it purchases the bolts for $15 per thousand, the lock nuts for $12 per thousand, and the washers for $10 per thousand. It gets the throttle cable for $5, the wheel assemblies for $500 per one hundred, and the blades for $600 per one hundred. The handle assemblies come from a plant in Mexico and cost $12,000 (this includes all duties and tariffs) per thousand plus freight of $1,000 per shipment. Each shipment brings 2,000 handle assemblies to the plant. Deck housings come from a local metal stamping company that also paints them for a price of $25 each.

Required:

a. Compute the incremental cost of making one lawn mower assuming the company incurs incremental labor cost of $12 for each mower made.

b. The company is considering making a 24 inch mower that would require a slightly larger engine, a bigger housing, and a larger blade. The bigger engine would cost $50, the housing $30, and the blade $650 per hundred. Compute the incremental cost of making this larger mower if labor cost remains the same as for the smaller mower.

c. Assume the company makes 20,000 mowers per year. A supplier offers to sell the 22 inch blades to the company for $500 per hundred if the company orders 10,000 blades twice during the year. This means the company would carry an inventory on average of 5,000 blades; the company has an annual inventory carrying cost of 25%. Should the company accept the supplier's offer? Give calculations to support your answer.

d. The government has just signed an agreement with Mexico that removes all import duties on shipments coming from Mexico. The duties go from 20% to zero, and the freight charge drops by one-half because U.S. truck lines are now allowed to operate in Mexico. Compute the impact these changes will have on the incremental cost of making the 22 inch mower.

5-18. Product Cost and Bill of Materials for a Hospital.
Memorial Hospital collected the following information about costs for one of the meals prepared in its food services department. Quantities and prices for ingredients used in noon meal #16 (200 portions) are shown below:

	Price	*Unit*	*Quantity*
Meat	$ 4.50	Pound	40 lbs.
Vegetable #1	2.50	Two-pound package	8 lbs.
Vegetable #2	3.50	Five-pound package	50 lbs.
Salad	1.25	Pound	20 lbs.
Dessert	3.00	Pound	20 lbs.
Coffee	25.00	Five-pound can	5 lbs.
Bread	25.00	Twenty-loaf carton	5 loaves

Additional incremental costs per batch of 200 meals prepared:

Electricity, steam, etc....................	$ 1.35
Supplies	.90
Maintenance expense	.25
Total cost per batch	$ 2.50

Two cooks spend four hours each to prepare a batch of this meal. These two cooks work overlapping shifts so one-half of each cook's shift is devoted to this meal. In addition, a cook's helper spends two hours helping prepare this meal, and another cook's helper spends one and one-half hours preparing the salad. Two cooks and two cook's helpers are on duty every day for full shifts to prepare the meals the hospital needs. Hourly wages for these individuals are:

Cook	$12
Cook's helper	8

Required:

a. Compute the incremental cost for making one batch (200 portions) of this meal.
b. Compute the weekly amount spent for the cooks and cook's helpers who prepare the salad.
c. How much does your answer to question b change if the hospital makes five fewer meals on Wednesday? Explain.
d. Compute the incremental cost of upgrading the meal if the dietician at the hospital decides to use a different meat that costs $7.50 per pound.

5-19. Incremental Product Cost and Product Routings.
The managers at the water heater element plant illustrated in Exhibit 5-3 are considering automating the operations in Department 20. If they automate these operations, monthly fixed cost will rise by $3,000, and the labor cost related to operations in this department will be eliminated.

Required:

a. Compute the change in the incremental unit cost for the product illustrated in Exhibit 5-4 if the company makes this change.

b. Assume the company normally produces 20,000 water heater elements per month. Is it worthwhile for the company to make this change in production operations? Provide numerical calculations to justify your answer.

c. Compute the number of water heater elements the company must produce each month to make this investment in automation worthwhile. Hint: Think of the notion of breaking even as you develop your answer to this question.

5-20. Incremental Product Cost for Hydraulic Motors.

The production department at Black Hydraulics has given you the following bill of materials for one of its motors that sells for $300. All parts with a number ending in 999 are purchased from outside suppliers, and the remainder are manufactured at the Black plant.

Part Number	Description	Qty.	Unit Price
RS018991999	RS,HS SEAL CARRIER	1	0.5552
HS018979	PLUG, COOLING SAE 12L14	1	0.8000
RS018011	BEARING, THRUST .062 WIDE	1	1.6600
RS018015	RING, WIRE SAE 1074 Rc40	1	0.2000
RS018058	SEAL, BACKUP 1.0346 SHAFT	1	3.3200
RS018053	SEAL, SHAFT 1.0346 SHAFT	1	3.5620
RS037003999	RS ROTOR SET 03	1	5.5352
HS018025	BOLT, HHCS 1.75 (Y,A)	6	0.2400
HS037009	ROLLER PIN .410x.3654	9	3.6200
RS013301999	RS HOUSING 02	1	34.5200
RS018016	CAPLUG, 10W-BLUE (7/8)	2	0.0400
RS011100999	RS SHAFT 01 [1" STRAIGHT]	1	30.5520
RS012000	RS WEAR PLATE [FINISH]	1	6.5844

Required:

a. Compute the incremental materials cost of making the hydraulic motor.

b. Compute the cost of components and materials purchased from outside suppliers for one motor.

c. Compute the number of motors the company must sell to generate a total contribution margin of $2,000. Assume materials are the only variable costs in this case.

d. How much will the contribution margin percentage on the motor change if Black finds a supplier who will sell the RS ROTOR SET 03 for $1.50?

e. Compute the number of motors the company must sell to cover the $45,000 of directly traceable monthly fixed costs of the motor if all parts now purchased from outside suppliers drop in price by 20%.

f. How many ROLLER PINS will the company need for a month in which it plans to produce 400 of these motors?

5-21. Cost Impact of Output Changes.

You have gathered the following information about manufacturing one of your products. The cost for a unit of product which the company uses for preparing tax returns and other external financial reports is $38.50. The incremental materials and power costs are:

Unit materials cost	$15
Unit power cost	4
Total incremental cost	$19

The company hires labor in multiples of four workers whenever it opens another production line, and each production line can produce up to 2,000 units per month. Typical production is 14,000 units per month with seven production lines, but the company can produce as many as 30,000 units in one month by opening additional production lines. Each worker costs $1,500 per month, and the company always hires workers for a minimum of one month.

Required:

a. Compute the incremental monthly cost to the company of increasing current monthly output from 14,000 units to 16,000 units. Try the same question with an increase from 12,500 to 13,500 units.
b. Compute the change in total monthly cost if company managers decide to reduce monthly output from 22,000 units to 8,000 units per month.
c. Compute the total inventory value the company reports in its external financial statements if it has 4,000 units on hand at the end of the month.
d. Compute the incremental cost of producing another 200 units if the company is already planning to produce 4,100 units in the month when you will produce the 200 units.

5-22. Product Costs for a Clinical Laboratory Test.

The clinical laboratory in your hospital has collected the following information about the blood chemistry test it performs in its laboratory. Each test requires the following materials:

Disposable syringe	$ .75
Supplies, glassware, etc.	.05
Cotton, alcohol, and bandage	.10
Forms for recording data	.20
Reagents (chemicals used in test)	.10

Laboratory technicians draw blood samples from patients in the hospital and deliver the samples to the laboratory where they are prepared for analysis on a large analyzer. The analyzer reads a bar code on each sample to identify the patient, and it prints a chart and a numerical analysis of the specimen. Every hour a technician delivers the test results to the nursing station for the area where the patient is staying in the hospital.

Required:

a. Compute the incremental cost of performing a blood chemistry test.
b. The hospital administrator asks you to estimate the incremental monthly cost of adding a second shift in the laboratory to do blood chemistry tests for another hospital that wants to close its second shift. Your laboratory will perform another 10,000 chemistry

tests each month on this second shift, and it will hire two technicians at a monthly cost of $2,200 per technician to do the added tests. Compute the incremental monthly cost of taking on the added tests.

5-23. Journal Entries for Cost Tracking.

Your manufacturing plant uses a materials storeroom, two production departments, and a finished goods storage area to handle materials flow through the plant. During the past week the following events occurred.

a. Purchased materials for $20,000.

b. Issued $2,000 of materials to Department 420.

c. Issued $6,000 of materials to Department 560.

d. Received the labor distribution for the week:

Department 420 labor cost $3,000
Department 560 labor cost $4,500

e. Moved product with a materials and labor cost of $12,000 from Department 420 to Department 560.

f. Moved completed units with materials and labor cost of $26,000 from Department 560 to finished goods storage.

Required:

Prepare the journal entries to record the above transactions:

5-24. Impact of JIT on Journal Entries.

Channel Manufacturing produced the following journal entries to record the movement of materials through its production operations last week. The company follows a traditional batch push approach to manufacturing. These entries represent only the entries related to the usage and movement of materials.

Dr. Materials 25,000
    Cr. Accounts Payable 25,000
      To record receipt of materials

Dr. Work-in-Process—Dept. 1201 8,000
    Cr. Materials 8,000
      To record issue of materials to Dept. 1201

Dr. Work-in-Process—Storage 12,000
    Cr. Work-in-Process—Dept 1201 12,000
      To record movement of partially completed work to storage

Dr. Work-in-Process—Dept. 1201 6,000
    Cr. Work-in-Process—Storage 6,000
      To record movement of partially completed units from storage to Dept. 1201 for additional work

Dr. Work-in-Process—Dept. 1201 4,000
    Cr. Materials 4,000
      To record issue of more materials to Dept. 1201

Dr. Work-in-Process—Storage   9,000
   Cr. Work-in-Process—Dept 1201   9,000
     To record movement of units that Dept. 1201 has finished to storage to
     await completion in another department

Dr. Work-in-Process—Dept. 1690   9,000
   Cr. Work-in-Process—Storage   9,000
     To record movement from storage to Dept. 1690 of parts completed by
     Dept. 1201

Dr. Work-in-Process—Storage   18,000
   Cr. Work-in-Process—Dept 1690   18,000
     To record movement of partially done units from Dept 1690 to storage

Dr. Work-in-Process—Dept. 1690   18,000
   Cr. Work-in-Process—Storage   18,000
     To record movement from storage to Dept. 1690 of partially finished
     products

Dr. Finished Goods   24,000
   Cr. Work-in-Process—Dept. 1690   24,000
     To record the completion of the units and their movement to Finished
     Goods storage area

Managers at Channel decided to switch to a JIT manufacturing system that reorganized the production facility into a continuous flow line in which work flows smoothly from one operation to another. Suppliers make deliveries twice daily to the point on the line where the materials will be used, so Channel no longer has a materials storeroom. In addition, the company builds all items directly to customer orders, so units go directly to a truck for delivery to a customer as the unit is finished.

The company knows precisely how much materials from each supplier goes into each finished unit, so it pays suppliers electronically each week by transferring to their accounts the amount due for the materials included in the units completed during the week. It records the sales transaction as soon as a unit is finished, and it records the cost of goods sold weekly.

Required:

a. Assume all the above transactions occurred during one week in which the company was using JIT. Give the smallest number of journal entries to record these transactions if all the units produced during the week were sold for $100,000, and all materials received during the week were manufactured into completed units.

b. Why were you able to make fewer journal entries under JIT than the company made under its traditional approach to manufacturing? Explain.

5-25. Carrying Cost Computation.

Managers at Melrose, Inc., want to evaluate the profit effect of modifying their manufacturing operations. These modifications will increase annual operating costs by $120,000, but they will reduce average inventory by $1,000,000. The company accountant computed a long term inventory carrying cost of 30%.

Required:

a. Prepare an analysis that shows the annual profit impact of the proposed changes.
b. Compute the amount by which inventory would have to drop to make reductions in carrying cost just equal the annual cost increase of $120,000.
c. What is the lowest inventory carrying cost percentage that will make the modifications worthwhile? Ignore question b when you answer this question.

5-26. Maintenance Cost Analysis.

Cool Aire has been experiencing problems in the final assembly of its air conditioner operations. The conveyor that carries the compressors to final assembly periodically stops, and this effectively shuts down the entire plant. Variable costs per unit approximate $100, and each unit sells for $160. Because it is now the peak period for sales, any unit not manufactured results in a unit not sold. Each unit has a cycle time of .6 minutes, i.e., one unit is produced every .6 minutes.

Down time averages 80 minutes per day, and the 200 workers receive $15 per hour in wages and benefits. Labor is a variable cost for this company.

Required:

a. Compute the daily cost of idle labor.
b. Compute the daily lost contribution margin because of the down time.
c. Assume the company spends a cash lump sum of $100,000 and an additional $120,000 per year to reduce daily down time to ten minutes. Compute the annual profit effect of this expenditure if the initial investment is written off over five years. Assume Cool Aire operates 250 days per year.

5-27. Cost Impact of Setup Time Reduction.

Max Stratton, plant manager for Stratton Enterprises, developed the following data on a machine used in one of his operations.

Setup time	6 Hours
Processing hours available per month	300
Monthly demand:	
Fitting	25,000
Housing	87,250
Batch size:	
Fitting	2,000
Housing	9,000
Incremental cost per unit:	
Fitting	$25
Housing	15

Required:

Use these data to answer the following questions.

a. Assume Stratton Enterprises does ten setups per month. How many productive hours does the company have available each month on its machine

b. Because of the long setup times Max keeps 5,000 units of the Fitting and 10,000 units of the Housing on hand on average to cover demand during changeovers. Compute the annual carrying cost if carrying cost amounts to 30%. Hint: compute the total incremental cost invested in inventory.

c.   Compute the change in carrying cost from your answer to question b if Max is able to reduce his setup time to ten minutes which allows him to carry only 500 units of the fitting and 800 units of the Housing.

5-28.   JIT Cost Analysis.

Prior to last year Stellar Manufacturing Company used a traditional approach to manufacturing its product. The company made labor cost vary with output, and it used a functional organization for manufacturing operations that grouped like operations together in departments on the factory floor. Maintenance operations were performed in a separate department, and purchasing operated as a separate operation as well.

You have the following information on one of the company's products, Big Slammer, produced under this functional factory organization.

Raw materials used to make one unit:
Steel . . . .   500 lbs.
Parts kit   1
Labor required to produce one unit:
25 hours

Steel costs $2 per pound, and Stellar purchases the parts kit for $550 per kit. Labor earns $15 per hour, and incremental overhead cost is $3 per labor hour; the $3 includes $1 for incremental maintenance cost. The rest of the incremental overhead cost consists of factory supplies that vary with the number of units produced. The company includes these costs in the labor overhead rate because labor hours also vary with the number of units produced. The fixed monthly costs of the different departments that produce the Big Slammer (these departments also produce other products for Stellar) amount to $150,000.

Late last year the company switched to a JIT approach and organized its manufacturing activities into a series of separate flow lines. Each line produces a single product, and each line does its own routine maintenance as well as its own purchasing. The line producing the Big Slammer now employs 20 workers who produce five units per day. During lulls in production the workers do routine maintenance on their equipment, and the small, full time maintenance staff does maintenance work too complex for the production workers. An additional person works full time for the line to handle purchasing and materials management. This person earns $2,000 per month. Assume employees work eight hour days five days per week and that each month has four weeks.

The supervisor for the line making the Big Slammer costs $2,500 per month. Total monthly fixed factory cost to support all lines amounts to $240,000 per month. Under the former system the company spent $20,000 monthly advertising the Big Slammer, but with the new system's faster delivery times it spends only $5,000 monthly advertising the product. The selling price for the product has not changed from the $6,000 the company received last year.

Required:

a.   Compute the incremental (variable) unit cost of the Big Slammer under both the traditional manufacturing system and under the JIT system. Explain why the numbers differ.

b.   Compute the fixed costs directly traceable to the Big Slammer under both the traditional system and under the JIT system. Explain why the fixed costs have changed.

c.   Compute the monthly break even sales for the Big Slammer under both the traditional and the JIT manufacturing systems.

5-29. Review of Incremental Costs.

Kathy Brown, president of the Movable Corporation, has asked for your help in performing a cost analysis so she can make some decisions. Her accountant has accumulated the following cost data for you on a wheel barrow manufactured in her plant:

Unit sales price		$ 25
Incremental unit cost		15

Monthly plant operating costs that do not vary
  with output:

Depreciation of building	$ 1,200
Lease payment - Machine #1	400
Maintenance - Machine #1	300
Personnel costs	11,500
Total monthly plant costs	$13,400

Normal monthly sales	1,000	units

The company produces the product in the company's only plant, and it produces the wheel barrow only during the day shift. The plant has sufficient capacity to produce an additional 200 units per month if demand for the product increases. If production goes above 1,200 units per month, the company must add a second shift with a consequent increase in monthly maintenance cost to $500 and an increase in personnel costs to $15,000.

Required:

a. Compute the incremental cost of increasing monthly production by 100 units if current monthly production is scheduled at 900 units.
b. A customer has offered to buy 300 wheel barrows per month at a price of $17 per unit. Prepare a cost analysis of this offer assuming that Kathy Brown will not add a second shift. Prepare a second analysis on the assumption that she will add a second shift to handle the added work.
c. Compute the incremental cost of increasing production from 1,000 units per month to a level of 1,400 units per month.

5-30. Review of Incremental Costs.

Claymore Corporation has accumulated the following cost information about one of its plants:

Monthly plant operating costs:

Lease payment	$18,000
Supervisory personnel	12,000
Maintenance contract	6,000
Total monthly operating costs	$36,000

Unit incremental cost of production		$ 10
Unit selling price		18

Normal monthly production in units	4,000

Since the plant is operating below its maximum capacity, the company president is considering an increase in production of 300 units per month. However, his son (a recent graduate of an outstanding Eastern business school) wants to shut down the plant because an analysis he prepared shows the company would be more profitable without the plant. A plant shutdown would require a lump sum payment of $50,000 to break the lease. Assume all future costs will be the same as those shown above.

Required:

a. What cost and what dollar amount of cost should the president consider in deciding whether to increase output? Explain.
b. What cost and dollar amount of cost should the president consider if he wants to consider closing the plant? Explain.
c. Determine which of the following possibilities is preferable, assuming that the corporation wants to maximize profits:
    1. Continue to produce 4,000 units per month.
    2. Increase production as advocated by the president.
    3. Shut down the plant.
d. Assume the company can eliminate all incremental unit costs and all maintenance costs if it closes down for two months. What is the monthly fixed cost while it is closed down? Explain.
e. The company is considering changing its production process and adding another product line. The modification in the production process would enable the company to reduce incremental labor cost for the present product by $2 per unit. The new product would use all the labor no longer needed by the old one plus it would require a fixed staff of people costing $3,000 per month. The new product has incremental materials cost of $3 per unit, sells for $6, will have monthly sales of 2,000 units and uses the same overhead facilities as the other product. Prepare an analysis to show the monthly profit impact of adding the new product.

5-31. **Incremental Costs and Shipping Schedule Change.**
    The credit manager for Sportswear, Ltd., is violently opposed to a plan proposed by the plant manager to start shipping seasonal goods to customers as they are produced (approximately 90 days before customers normally order the goods), with the company billing the customer 120 days later. The company currently gives 30 day terms, and ships the product from its warehouse as the customer orders it.
    The plant manager proposes to start this new system beginning with products manufactured in April for the fall season. Such a system, argues the credit manager, will increase bad debts, lengthen the average days in receivables, and increase the amount of company borrowings to finance the receivables.
    The plant manager argues that early shipment of merchandise will reduce average inventory by $500,000 which will enable the company to reduce its warehouse rental cost by $15,000 per year.
    The accounting department has developed the following information to help analyze the economic impact of this proposal:

Increase in accounts receivable	$1,000,000
Average bad debt expense	2% of receivables
Average cost of funds	12%
Inventory carrying cost	25% of inventory cost

Required:

Prepare an analysis of the estimated profit impact of this proposal.
Hint: Make sure to include only costs that change in your analysis.

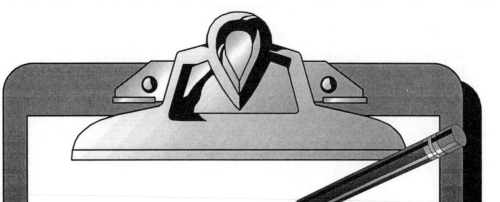

Learning Objectives

After reading this chapter, the student should have an understanding of:

✔   The basic elements of job order cost and process cost systems.

✔   How to use the reports generated by a job order cost system.

✔   The journal entries required to track the flow of costs in a job order cost system.

✔   The cost tracking and reporting used in project management systems.

✔   The cost tracking procedures for process cost systems and the reports used in such systems.

✔   The role of backflush accounting in process cost systems.

✔   The importance of fixed cost layers to management decision making.

Cost Accounting Systems—Part II Job Order and Process Costing

We continue the discussion of cost accounting systems begun in the last chapter by describing two typical approaches to cost collection: **Job Order** cost systems and **Process** cost systems. Job order systems focus cost collection efforts on jobs or projects being produced by a company while process systems focus cost collection efforts on cost centers or departments. Many companies use a blend of these two systems, but for discussion purposes we will treat them as separate systems.

As in the last chapter, we continue our focus on management's use of cost information via responsibility reporting and decision making. Our concentration is still on incremental or variable product costs per unit. Chapter 7 will consider issues like inventory valuation, accounting for scrap, and cost flow assumptions related to financial reporting for job order and process cost systems.

► JOB ORDER COST SYSTEMS ◄

Companies that use job order cost systems usually build "one of a kind" products like buildings, bridges, oil tankers, power plants, or signs. These products may take a few hours to produce or they may take years to complete. For example, a printing job may require two hours to complete, but the Trans Alaska Pipeline from Prudhoe to Valdez required over four years to build and the World Trade Center in New York City took ten years to complete. During the time these projects were under way, accountants had to record the costs incurred on each project in order to help project managers maintain cost control and complete their projects within time and cost budgets.

► The Basic Job Cost System

To illustrate the elements of a job order cost system we begin with the case of Joslin Sign Company, a Nashville company that designs and manufactures signs for businesses.[1] These signs range in price from $2,000 to $200,000, depending on the size and complexity of the sign. For example, a rectangular sign, lighted with internal fluorescent lights, with two plastic faces in three colors sells for about $3,000. If the customer wants neon lettering on the sign, the price increases significantly; and, if the customer wants an unusual shape for the sign, e.g., a sign in the shape of a banjo with neon strings, the price takes another dramatic jump.

---

[1] Joslin Sign Company actually exists, and it really does manufacture signs in Nashville.

► Production Processes

Four departments at Joslin typically work on the production of a sign: Drawing and Pattern, Wood Shop, Paint Room, and Final Assembly. Drawing and Pattern works with the customer to develop a drawing that represents the customer concept for the sign; it then transforms this drawing into a pattern that workers use to create the sign. The Wood Shop uses this pattern to create a wooden mold; it places a sheet of 1/4 inch plastic over the mold, heats it, and draws the soft plastic to the wooden mold with a vacuum to create the sign face.

Next, the plastic faces move to the Paint Room for painting with the colors the customer ordered. This department also paints any aluminum sheeting used on the outside of the sign. While Wood Shop and Painting work on their parts of the sign, workers in Final Assembly build a steel frame for the sign, install ballasts for the lights, and wire the sign for connection to the customer's electrical system.

If Joslin worked on only one sign at a time, the company would have no trouble keeping track of costs incurred to make a sign. However, the company might have ten to twenty signs under construction at one time; therefore, it needs a method for identifying costs with individual signs. The company accountant designed the following six field code to capture cost data on these signs.

Expense Account	Department	Responsible Person	Job Number	Part Number	Quantity

The code uses both a department and a responsible person field because Joslin wants to keep track of expense by individual function within some departments. For example, the Drawing and Pattern department manager wants to know how much time each pattern maker spends on each job. The Job Number field, of course, captures the number assigned to each job, so every transaction receives a code that identifies it with a specific job. Finally, because the company wants information on the specific parts used on each job, it includes a Part Number field in the code.

The Cost Reporting System for Jobs. With this code, accountants can easily produce reports for individual jobs, individual departments, or individuals within departments. The following example (Exhibit 6-1) shows an abbreviated report the manager of Final Assembly receives weekly; his report includes all the jobs he has in process, although this example shows only a single job.

The plant manager who has responsibility for all jobs in the plant receives a weekly report illustrated in Exhibit 6-2.

This weekly report provides a summary of all jobs underway in the plant by showing both those costs incurred to date in each department and the total budget for each job. For instance, expenditures on the Harpeth Valley Ford sign slightly exceed budget in the first two departments but remain under budget in the last two departments. To determine this job's progress in Final Assembly, the plant manager can estimate the remaining work needed and compare it to the remaining budgeted dollars to see if the job will remain within budget.

Report Interpretation. Although the Harpeth Valley Ford job is only slightly over budget in two departments, the Grinders Switch Eatery job is already in serious trouble. Overspending in the first two departments by $830 has already put this job so far over budget that it appears unlikely the company can even come close to budget on this job. Either the workers in the first two departments were very inefficient, or the initial quote overlooked some difficulties in producing this job. In either case, this report alerts the plant manager to the problem while the sign is still under construction

Week 2 of July

Job 342-Harpeth Valley Ford	Quantity		Amount
Labor Costs			
Week 2 of June	15	Hrs.	$ 225
Week 4 of June	35	"	525
Week 1 of July	60	"	900
Total actual to date	110	"	$ 1,650
Budgeted amount	250	"	3,750
Remaining budgeted amount for labor	140	"	$ 2,100
Materials			
Two inch angle iron	300	feet	$ 280
NO. 12 black strand wire	50	feet	25
Lamp 8-16 foot slimline	4		165
7500V 60MA Transformer	1		120
400WHPS Encased ballast	1		220
NO. 12 blue strand wire	50	feet	6
12060PBKM Transformer	1		350
SHT 26G 4X10	4		35
1/4" x 3/4" RH Bolt	49		4
Fastener 121.5HB	6		3
Fastener 14 HN	49		55
Total material charged to date			$ 1,263
Budgeted amount			2,500
Remaining budgeted amount for materials ...			$ 1,237
Summary			
Total charges to date for Final Assembly			$ 2,913
Total budget for Final Assembly			6,250
Remaining budgeted amount for			
Final Assembly			$ 3,337

*Joslin has no incremental (variable) overhead cost, so the sign costs include no overhead.

Exhibit 6-1 Joslin Sign Company Final Assembly Weekly Report*

instead of after it is complete. The manager might still have time to take some cost saving steps in the last two departments to overcome some of the problems in the first two.

Using Job Cost Information. In addition to monitoring ongoing expenditures on jobs, companies like Joslin Sign keep accurate records for individual jobs to improve the quality of estimates on future jobs. Once Joslin quotes a price for a sign, the company cannot demand more money from that particular customer. However, careful records on costs from past jobs help managers create better cost estimates for future jobs by making these data available to job estimators. For example, suppose a customer wants a rectangular sign 8 feet by 15 feet with four colors on two plastic faces. A review of past records shows the company built a sign 8 feet by 12 feet last year at a cost of $5,894. The job estimator uses this information to estimate the cost for making the larger sign; she takes the bill of materials for the old sign, adds the new features and new dimensions for the components, and multiplies quantities by current prices to arrive at a cost estimate. She then considers resource constraints, market conditions, and desired delivery date to develop a price quote for the sign.

	Drawing & Patterns	Wood Shop	Paint Room	Final Assembly	Total
Job 342—Harpeth Valley Ford					
Cost incurred to date	$ 1,500	$ 300	$ 100	$ 2,913	$ 4,813
Budgeted amount	1,420	280	650	6,250	8,600
Remaining budgeted amount	(80)	(20)	550	3,337	3,787
Job 350—Grinders Switch Eatery					
Cost incurred to date	$ 860	$ 920	$ 0	$ 35	$ 1,815
Budgeted amount	460	490	800	500	2,250
Remaining budgeted amount	(400)	(430)	800	465	435
Job 361—Paul's Steak and Grill					
Cost incurred to date	$ 200	$ 0	$ 0	$ 0	$ 200
Budgeted amount	400	150	650	340	1,540
Remaining budgeted amount	200	150	650	340	1,340

Exhibit 6-2 *Joslin Sign Company Weekly Report for Plant Manager*

Some companies gain a competitive advantage by using good job cost history files to generate bids for new projects faster than their competitors. Quickness of response to customer requests translates into higher prices and higher profits for firms using their cost systems to create value for customers.

▶ Journal Entries for Job Order Cost Systems

Job order cost systems capture material and labor costs through journal entries that record these costs by department and by job. For example, a journal entry to record the use of steel angle iron on a sign at Joslin Sign Company captures the movement of material cost to work-in-process inventory by identifying the Final Assembly department and the job (number 116) with the transaction as shown below.

> Dr. Work-in-process—Final Assembly, Job 116   500
>   Cr. Materials   500

Costs charged to each sign move from department to department as the sign moves through the shop, and the total costs for a sign accumulate in the Final Assembly department because it is the last department in the sequence. For example, the journal entry to record the movement of the Harpeth Valley Ford sign from Drawing & Patterns to Wood Shop is:

> Dr. Work-in-process—Wood Shop   1,500
>   Cr. Work-in-process—Drawing & Patterns   1,500

At the completion of a sign, accountants record the event with a journal entry that transfers the total cost accumulated for the sign from work-in-process inventory to finished goods inventory. Assume the Harpeth Valley Ford sign illustrated in Exhibit 6-1 was completed by Joslin at its budgeted cost of $6,250. The accountant makes this entry to record the completion of this sign:

> Dr. Finished goods—Harpeth Valley Ford   6,250
>   Cr. Work-in-process—Final Assembly   6,250

In summary, the journal entries for job cost systems track the movement of materials, labor, and manufacturing overhead costs (where appropriate) through work-in-process to finished goods.

▸ PROJECT MANAGEMENT AND JOB COSTING ◂

Even though Joslin Sign tracks costs for individual signs manufactured in its plant, some job cost systems (like those for the Alaska pipeline) are tied in more closely to the location where the product is being produced. These cost systems usually are imbedded in the project management system used to manage the overall project. Operations management courses typically cover the details of project management, but we will review a simple example here to illustrate how cost information relates to the project management system.

▸ Project Management and Critical Path Calculations

Consider first of all the basic approach to project management. Project managers typically break their projects into manageable pieces called tasks or activities. For example, a chemical plant that plans to replace a feed line pipe might break the project into the following pieces:

Erect scaffold
Purchase valves
Purchase pipe
Place new pipe
Place new valves
Weld pipe
Remove scaffold

The manager of this project then estimates the time required to perform each task and computes the amount of slack available for each task. Slack represents the amount of time a manager can delay a task without delaying completion of the total project. Project managers watch time carefully on their projects because they are usually under tight time limits, and some construction projects even pay a bonus to the contractor for timely completion of the project. The manager in our chemical plant example prepared the following time calculations for the feed line pipe change project.

Activity	Duration	Early Start	Early Finish	Late Start	Late Finish	Slack
Erect scaffold	2	1	2	19	20	18
Purchase valves	25	1	25	6	30	5
Purchase pipe	20	1	20	1	20	0
Place new pipe	4	21	24	21	24	0
Place new valves	4	26	29	31	34	5
Weld pipe	10	25	34	25	34	0
Remove scaffold	5	35	39	35	39	0

Exhibit 6-3 *Critical Path Calculation in Days*

To replace the pipes, the project manager must first purchase the pipes, put them in place, and then weld them together. This sequence of activities (plus removing the scaffold) has zero slack, so it makes up the critical path through this group of tasks, i.e., any slippage on any of these tasks delays the overall project. The 18 day slack for erecting the scaffold and the 5 days for purchasing the valves tells the manager how long he or she can delay these tasks without slowing down completion of the total project. Managers compute the slack as the difference between the earliest and the latest a task can start. They compute the late start time by deducting the time to complete the task from the date the task must be completed. For example, the scaffolding must be in place when the pipe arrives, and the pipe will arrive 20 days after the manager orders it. Thus, deducting the two days from the 20 means the scaffold construction must start at the beginning of day 19 so it is finished just as the pipes arrive at the end of day 20. The manager must have the valves in place by the end of day 34, so deducting the four days needed to install the valves provides a late start of day 31. Of course the earliest the manager could place them is on day 26 because it takes 25 days to get them to the site.

▸ Cost Tracking in Project Management Systems

Project managers must do more than just manage time—they must also keep an eye on the cost of a project. The primary difference between tracking costs for projects and for jobs like those at Joslin Sign lies in the additional details tracked on projects. In addition to tracking costs to each job, managers must also track costs to the individual tasks of each job. For example, a contractor who builds houses has developed the following account code for tracking costs on housing projects.

Expense Account	Responsible Person	Job Number	Part Number	Task Number	Quantity

This code allows the contractor to track costs for individual tasks, as well as for the total job.

▸ Illustration of Project Cost Management

We will use a housing contractor to illustrate cost reporting for project management because it allows us to use an example with few tasks, but remember that accountants use the same approach on projects with thousands of tasks (like the Alaska Pipeline or the World Trade Center). Most project managers prepare a chart of the tasks they must complete on a project to visualize the sequence of activities. Figure 1 shows the chart for one of the houses the contractor is building. Construction starts on March 1, 2002 and is supposed to finish on June 22, 2002.

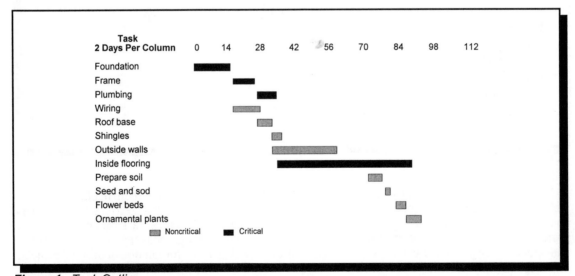

Figure 1   *Task Outline*

Notice how the bars represent sequential relationships: The framing activities cannot start until the foundation is complete, and the bar representing the framing task starts on the chart after the end of the bar representing foundation construction. Where bars overlap, they represent tasks that can proceed simultaneously. Also, the dark bars in this case represent the critical path tasks, and the gray ones represent the non critical tasks.

▸ Project Reporting Systems

The contractor receives periodic reports on the progress of this job, and Exhibit 6-4 illustrates the time report the manager in charge of constructing the house receives.

Task	Planned Length	Actual Length
Foundation	17	19
Frame	9	28
Plumbing	10	8
Wiring	10	10
Roof base	8	9
Shingles	5	5
Outside walls	29	20*
Inside flooring	42	3*
Prepare soil	5	0
Seed and sod	2	0
Flower beds	3	0
Ornamental plants	4	0

*Tasks partially completed

Exhibit 6-4 Report of Actual and Planned Times by Task (in days)

The manager can see from this report that some real problems occurred with the framing task. It took 19 more days than scheduled. However, the cost report in Exhibit 6-5 gives even more reason for alarm. Not only did the project exceed its time estimates for the first two tasks, but the costs exceeded their budgeted amounts also. In fact, unless the manager of this project can find some way to reduce the remaining costs, the total cost for completing the house will equal $169,862, a cost overrun of $15,318. The project manager can easily see at this point that this project is in trouble.

The reports for project management systems, then, differ from other job order cost systems in that they report costs by individual tasks as well as by job whereas the Joslin Sign system reports costs by job and by department. Although not illustrated here, project reporting systems can also generate reports as workers complete specific segments of the project instead of waiting until the end of the month. For example, the manager of this project could generate a report on costs and time when the foundation is complete or when the roof is complete. Such reports keep project managers up to date as various segments of the project reach completion.

We used relatively small projects to illustrate the basics of project cost management systems, but these basics apply to billion dollar projects just like they apply to these small projects. Only the number of tasks changes; a project like the Alaska Pipeline has thousands of tasks instead of the twelve used here for the house. However, the time and cost data collected for a massive project are the same as for our simple example.

Task	Original Estimate	Cost To Date	Cost Remaining	Revised * Estimate
Foundation	$ 11,920	$ 14,050	$ (2,130)	$ 14,050
Frame	20,880	31,510	(10,630)	31,510
Plumbing	21,680	16,560	5,120	21,680
Wiring	6,400	5,700	700	6,400
Roof base	6,592	7,500	(908)	7,500
Shingles	5,400	7,050	(1,650)	7,050
Outside walls	40,600	12,000	28,600	40,600
Inside flooring	30,240	2,000	28,240	30,240
Prepare soil	5,832	0	5,832	5,832
Seed and sod	400	0	400	400
Flower beds	600	0	600	600
Ornamental plants	4,000	0	4,000	4,000
	$ 154,544	$ 96,370	$ 58,174	$ 169,862

*The Revised Estimate column represents the larger of the Original Estimate column and the Cost to Date column.

Exhibit 6-5 *Project Cost Report for the Period March 1 Through April 30, 2002*

► PROCESS COST SYSTEMS ◄

In contrast to job order cost systems that focus cost collection efforts on individual jobs, process cost systems focus on individual departments or processes. Accountants use process cost systems for manufacturing operations that produce the same product continuously in one or more departments or processes. A Dow chemical plant, for example, collects costs for each distilling, mixing and heating process in one of its plants. An Exxon petroleum refinery collects costs for each cracking tower and related process that converts crude oil into gasoline. A Tecumseh plant that manufactures air conditioner compressors collects costs for each machining process, each cleaning process, and each assembly process through which the compressors pass. A process cost system, then, gathers costs by process because a process manufacturing company incurs its costs in individual processes.

Because the journal entries to record costs differ for demand pull and batch push systems, we discuss the cost systems for both manufacturing approaches in the next sections.

► Cost Flow—Demand Pull / Just-in-Time Systems

We illustrate a process cost system by considering a John Deere plant with two production flow lines, one for lawnmowers and another for utility vehicles. The plant uses a just-in-time system for managing production on the two lines. As suppliers deliver motors and handles to the lawn mower line, accountants charge the material costs directly to the line. Labor and manufacturing overhead costs work the same way—at payroll time, the accountants assign payroll costs to the lines where the employees work, and they also charge any manufacturing overhead expenses to the line where they originate.

Assume accountants use the following account code to capture cost information for the plant.

Expense Account	Department or Line	Responsible Individual

The second field (department or line) provides the critical information for the process cost system because it identifies the production line to which each cost transaction belongs. By sorting transactions on the second field, we obtain the total for the following journal entry.

Dr. Work-in-process—Direct materials, Lawnmowers   250
Dr. Work-in-process—Direct labor, Lawnmowers   2,100
Dr. Work-in-process—Overhead, Lawnmowers   25
    Cr. Accounts payable   275
    Cr. Wages payable (and withholding accounts)   2,100

Accountants make a similar entry for the utility vehicle manufacturing line.

Periodic Reports. At month end, the manager of the Lawnmower line receives a report (see Exhibit 6-6) on all costs approved by him during the month.

Monthly Report
Lawnmower Line—Centerville Plant
Line Manager: Jack Martin

Expense	Amount
Direct labor	$ 60,000
Mower handles	13,440
Mower housings	56,000
Mower wheels	22,400
Four cycle gasoline engines	1,341,479
Packing boxes	33,600
Packing materials	11,200
Gloves, aprons and cloths	560
General supplies	1,120
Gauges and tools	168
Gasoline	22
Fasteners	7,280
Labels	12,880
Problem solving team expenses	2,521
Total expenses for the month	$1,562,670

Exhibit 6-6 *Monthly Cost Report for Lawnmower Line*

This report shows Mr. Martin, the manager of the Lawnmower line, the total dollar amount of costs charged to his line during the month. The manager of the utility vehicle line receives a similar report for the expenses her line incurred for the same period.

Backflush Accounting. Accountants usually remove all the expenses charged to the line at the month-end closing of the books. They do this with a *backflush* entry. This entry flushes from work-in-process those costs charged to it during the month and moves them to finished goods inventory. If the Lawnmower line had no units in process at month end (a highly likely event since it only takes a few minutes to assemble a mower), accountants record the following backflush entry.

Dr. Finished goods   1,562,670
    Cr. Work-in-process—Lawnmower line   1,562,670

However, if the line still has, say 200, mowers in process at month-end, the accountant makes an allowance for this ending inventory by using a standard cost or an average cost based on last month's data. This standard or average cost provides a simple means for moving costs to finished goods. For example, assume the 200 mowers were on average one-half complete with an average cost for a complete mower of $325 from last month. Thus, the ending inventory would have a cost of (200 x 1/2 x $325) $32,500 assigned to it with the remaining cost of $1,530,170 flushed through to finished goods.

> Dr. Finished goods   1,530,170
> Cr. Work-in-process—Lawnmower line   1,530,170

Journal Entries for Demand Pull Systems—A Summary. To summarize, the journal entries for a demand pull system fall into two categories:

1. Charge direct materials, direct labor, and manufacturing overhead to the production lines as the costs occur during the period.
2. Remove costs from the line at the end of the period with a backflush entry.

▶ Cost Flow—Batch Push Systems / General

If the John Deere plant used a batch push approach with randomly located operations instead of the just-in-time system for managing production flow, accountants would use the same account codes. However, the system would include codes for numerous departments instead of just a lawnmower line and a utility vehicle line. The departmental managers would receive periodic cost reports similar to the one received by the lawnmower line manager, but with only the costs for their individual departments. However, the number of transactions required to move costs through the system would differ significantly from that for the JIT or demand pull system as explained in Chapter 6.

The JIT system has basically only two processes or departments (i.e., the entire flow line) to which accountants track costs, but under a batch push approach the John Deere plant would have, say, twenty departments with each department responsible for making only one part for the mowers or the utility vehicles. Thus there would be a tube cutting department, a tube bending department, a paint department, several assembly departments, a stamping department, and so forth. Every time a batch of product moves from one of these departments to work-in-process storage or to another department, the accounting system generates a journal entry.

▶ Cost Flow—Batch Push Systems / Journal Entries

The batch push system, in summary, requires many journal entries to record numerous inventory movements because of the lack of JIT and sequentially arranged lines. It requires at least the following entries:

1. Charge direct material, direct labor, and manufacturing overhead costs to departments.
2. Record movement of product parts from a department to work-in-process storage.
3. Record movement of parts from work-in-process storage to departments.
4. Record costs of parts moved from one department to another.
5. Record movement of finished units from work-in-process to finished goods.

► *THE RELEVANCE OF FIXED COSTS TO DECISION MAKING* ◄

At this point it might appear that fixed costs are irrelevant to management decisions because in this chapter and the previous one we omitted fixed costs (we considered only incremental or variable costs per unit) from consideration when computing product costs. However, nothing could be further from the truth. Fixed costs are relevant to decisions that change fixed costs. Before examining this issue in detail, consider how fixed costs arise in a firm.

► *Fixed Cost Layers*

One way to look at fixed costs is to explore the sequential way managers generate fixed costs. An initial management decision locks in a layer of fixed costs, and subsequent decisions place additional fixed cost layers on top of the existing ones. For example, when GM decided to locate its Saturn plant in Spring Hill, Tennessee, that decision locked in a base layer of fixed costs (property taxes, insurance costs, etc). Choosing to construct a plant with three separate buildings locked in another layer of fixed costs (depreciation of buildings, utility costs, etc); and, when they decided to use the lost foam method for casting parts, this decision set the level of another group of fixed costs (depreciation of equipment, depreciation of molds, costs of tooling, etc). These cost layers pile up, and the sum total of these fixed cost layers equals the total fixed costs of the firm. Figure 2 presents a graphical image of these cost layers.

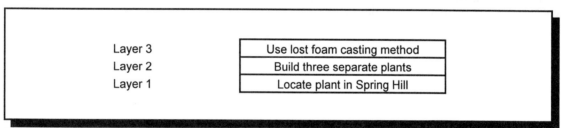

Layer 3	Use lost foam casting method
Layer 2	Build three separate plants
Layer 1	Locate plant in Spring Hill

Figure 2   *Fixed Cost Layers*

Regardless of the number of automobiles Saturn produces in one month, the costs fixed by those earlier decisions remain unchanged. So output fluctuations will not change the costs in one of these layers, but other management choices can impact these costs.

To change the fixed costs in any one of these layers, managers must reconsider the decision that originally created the fixed cost layer. Staying with this original decision keeps the cost at its existing level—only by identifying the original decision, reconsidering the issues addressed in that decision, and then choosing to change that decision can managers increase or decrease the amount of fixed cost in that layer.

For instance, if Saturn managers decide to reconsider their decision to use the lost foam method for casting parts, then all the fixed costs related to this operation become relevant for this decision. If Saturn managers consider whether to keep design engineers in Michigan or move them to Spring Hill, then the cost of facilities will change (decrease in Michigan and increase in Tennessee), and the fixed cost of salaries for design engineers may change. All these fixed costs become relevant for the decision to move the design engineers.

► Identification of Cost Layers for Decision Making

The account coding system can readily capture data that relates costs to various fixed cost layers. For instance, using a cost code with a location field allows managers to capture cost data by individual plant, by work cell within the plant, and by individual machine in a work cell. Whenever a manager wants to consider changing an operation in, or the configuration of, a work cell or cost center, he or she need only summarize the costs incurred at that location to identify the fixed costs his or her decisions might change. Consider the following case:

A Saturn manager decides to consider whether to move product designers from Michigan to Spring Hill, Tennessee. The manager gets the following listing of fixed monthly expenses incurred by the design group in Michigan.

Salaries	$ 2,345,000
Travel (to and from Spring Hill)	120,000
Rent, utilities, etc.	680,000
Equipment depreciation	110,000
Total monthly fixed costs	$ 3,255,000

She reviews these expenses with other managers to estimate how much they will change if designers are moved to Spring Hill. Her discussion with various managers provides the following set of fixed cost estimates if the designers move.

Salaries	$ 3,100,000
Travel (to and from Michigan)	21,000
Rent, utilities, etc.	450,000
Equipment depreciation	140,000
Total monthly fixed costs	$ 3,711,000

Since the new monthly fixed costs exceed the original monthly fixed costs, the manager decides not to move the designers.

Notice that the manager considered only the fixed costs that would change with the decision to move the designers. None of the costs in the bottom two layers were impacted by this decision, so they were omitted from the analysis.

► SUMMARY ◄

Accountants use two approaches to collecting and reporting cost information for responsibility reporting and decision making to manufacturing managers: job order costing, and process costing. Job order costing collects and reports incremental or variable product cost information with the job as the focus of cost collection efforts while the process cost system focuses on individual processes that create the product. Job order cost systems tend to be used by companies that produce one of a kind products while mass production companies use process costing. Process cost systems differ in complexity depending on whether the system is organized as batch push or demand pull. Finally, managers consider fixed costs in their decisions when they make decisions that change these costs.

▸ QUESTIONS ◂

6-1. How do job order and process cost systems differ?

6-2. What difference would an accountant expect to find between the account codes used by a pipeline construction company and those used by a chemical plant producing ethylene?

6-3. Why do managers collect cost data for individual jobs?

6-4. Explain how a manager can use cost information on past jobs to develop a price quote for a new job.

6-5. What is a critical path?

6-6. The manager of a construction project tells you he has plenty of slack in one of the tasks on his job. What does he mean?

6-7. How does cost tracking for project management differ from cost tracking for a job cost system like that used by Joslin Sign Company?

6-8. Describe the format and content of a project cost report the construction manager for a housing project receives weekly or monthly.

6-9. How do the cost reports for a department manager in a company using a job order cost system differ from those in a company using a process cost system?

6-10. Describe backflush accounting.

6-11. When do managers take fixed costs into account in their decisions?

6-12. Why is it important for managers to identify fixed cost layers in their company?

▸ EXERCISES ◂

6-13. Account Codes and Job Cost Systems.
   Chaney Construction has given you the following information about its account codes that it uses for construction projects. The company builds roads, manufacturing plants, office buildings, etc. The account code structure it uses is:

General Account	Responsibility Code	Job Number	Detail Account	Dollar Amount

The account codes are listed below.

General Accounts
   01   Purchases of services and materials
   02   Equipment rental
   03   Salaries and wages
   04   Other

Responsibility Codes
10	Jack Smith
20	Joe Roberts
30	Mike Stevens
40	Eldon Jones

Job Numbers
100	Highway project
400	Factory building
600	Motel project

Detail accounts
101	Outside engineering expense
102	Construction labor
103	Core drilling
104	Rock excavation
105	Rock fill
106	Fuel
107	Engineering salaries
109	Drinking water and ice
110	Concrete block purchase
111	Steel purchases
112	Cement purchases
113	Bulldozer
114	Soil compactor
115	Excavator

You produced the following list of transactions from the company data base for the past week.

02	10	100	114	$ 5,000
01	40	100	109	125
01	20	400	110	16,000
02	30	600	115	1,600
02	40	400	115	3,600
01	40	600	105	1,200
01	30	600	101	4,800
02	10	100	113	6,500
01	40	100	112	7,800
01	30	600	106	500
01	40	600	101	3,500
01	20	400	103	1,500
01	40	100	106	3,500
02	20	400	113	3,600
01	40	400	111	8,700
03	30	600	107	4,500
03	20	400	107	2,500
03	10	100	107	4,200
03	10	100	102	6,500
03	20	400	102	24,500
03	30	600	102	46,000

Required:

a. How much did the company expend on the highway project during this week?
b. Which job incurred the highest cost during the week?
c. How much expense is Eldon Jones responsible for this week?
d. For what type of equipment rental did the company incur the highest expense during this week?
e. How much did the company spend on construction labor this week?

6-14. Job Cost Reports.
Hathaway Manufacturing builds trucks for electrical utilities. The company purchases trucks direct from major manufacturers with cab and frame complete, but with no equipment over the back wheels. Hathaway then adds bucket lifts, tool boxes, and the metal framework needed to hold all this together to the basic truck to create the vehicle used by the utility to work on power poles.

Southern Utilities, Inc., has ordered a truck from Hathaway, and Hathaway managers prepared the following cost estimate for this truck:

Basic truck from Ford	$ 35,000
Bucket assembly	25,000
Steel framework	15,000
Steel sheeting	8,000
Hydraulic systems	20,000
Total materials	$103,000
Labor cost estimates	
Metal working	$ 20,000
Assembly	10,000
Painting	5,000
Total labor cost	$ 35,000

Hathaway has purchased at the budgeted amount the truck from Ford, the bucket assembly from a local supplier, and it has done two thirds of the work on the steel framework. In doing this the company spent $10,000 on labor in the Metal Working Department.

Required:

a. Prepare a report similar to the one in Exhibit 6-1 for company managers.
b. The plant manager estimates the company will have to spend another $30,000 on labor to finish the job and that an additional $30,000 will be spent on materials for the job. Compute the total estimated cost of the completed job.
c. Use the same information you used for questions a and b, and write a short report to the plant manager telling her whether you expect any cost problems with this job.

6-15.   Job Cost Reports for a Plant Manager.

You are the manager of a sign manufacturing plant that makes custom built signs for businesses. At the end of the week your accountant gave you the following report on the three signs currently under construction.

	Drawing & Patterns	Wood Shop	Paint Room	Final Assembly	Total
Job 496—Wimpy's Burger Barn					
Cost incurred to date	$ 2,000	$ 490	$ 2,500	$ 0	$ 4,990
Budgeted amount	2,250	450	950	1,285	4,935
Remaining budgeted amount . . .	$ 250	$ (40)	$ (1,550)	$ 1,285	$ (55)
Job 952—Joe's Bar and Grill					
Cost incurred to date	$ 1,560	$ 150	$ 0	$ 0	$ 1,710
Budgeted amount	600	150	1,200	825	2,775
Remaining budgeted amount . . .	$ (960)	$ 0	$ 1,200	$ 825	$ 1,065
Job 321—Midlife Insurance					
Cost incurred to date	$ 2,485	$ 750	$ 1,465	$ 2,325	$ 7,025
Budgeted amount	2,400	625	1,350	4,625	9,000
Remaining budgeted amount . . .	$ (85)	$(125)	$ (115)	$ 2,300	$ 1,975

Required:

a.   Review this report and determine if any of the jobs might create cost problems for you.
b.   How much will the Midlife Insurance job cost if all remaining work in the Final Assembly Department is done at the budgeted amount?
c.   Assume the Paint Room incurs $1,400 of expense to complete the sign for Joe's Bar and Grill: how much will this sign exceed its budgeted amount if all work in Final Assembly is done at the budgeted amount for that department?

6-16.   Job Cost Journal Entries.

Use the information in the report for Exercise 6-15 to answer this question.

Required:

a.   Prepare journal entries to record the labor and material costs charged to the Wimpy's Burger Barn sign in each of the first three departments. Assume one-half the costs in each department are labor, and the remainder are materials.
b.   Prepare the journal entries to move the costs of the Wimpy's Burger Barn sign from Drawing and Patterns to the Wood Shop.

6-17.   Critical Path Calculations.

You have the following tasks and estimated times (in days) for a project your company is considering.

Task	Estimated Time
A	2
B	1
C	3
D	3
E	3
F	1
G	8

You can start tasks A and B at the same time; task C must follow task A, and task E must follow task C. Task D must follow task B, and task F must follow task D. Both tasks E and F must be completed before task G can begin.

Required:

a. Use the above information to complete a schedule like the one in Exhibit 6-3.
b. Which tasks make up the critical path?
c. How much slack does task B have?
d. After starting the project you discover that it will take 15 days to finish task G instead of the original estimate of 8 days. How will this affect your completion of the project?

6-18. Project Time Reports.

Rudolph Martin does landscape design and installation for general contractors. He has provided you with the following list of tasks for one of his jobs, the landscaping of an office building in an industrial park.

Task Code	Task	Estimated Hours
A	Design landscape plan	20
B	Prepare soil	40
C	Install irrigation system	60
D	Plant trees	20
E	Install shrubs	30
F	Sod entire area	50

Rudolph has just finished planting the trees and he wonders whether he will meet his time target on this job. He gives you the following printout from his payroll system; this printout shows the hours each worker spent on each task. The task code on the printout corresponds to the codes used in the above list.

Employee	Task Code	Hours
Frank Jones	B	25
Robert Smith	C	15
Julie Brown	A	25
Julie Brown	D	12
Kate Roberts	C	25
Kate Roberts	D	10
Pete Zimmer	B	15
Pete Zimmer	C	25

Required:

a. How many hours does Rudolph expect this job to take given his experience to date?
b. If laying the sod and installing the shrubs requires the estimated number of hours, how many labor hours will the job take?
c. Which tasks appear to be taking longer than originally estimated?
d. What task should Rudolph try to estimate more carefully on his next job? Why?

6-19. Flexible Budget Reports for Flow Line.

The Centerville plant that manufactures lawnmowers (See Exhibit 6-6) established the following flexible budget amounts for its lawnmower line. The company produced 11,200 lawnmowers last month, and it provided the following flexible budget data.

Direct labor—all salaried at $60,000 per month

	Unit Cost			
Mower handles	$ 1.100			
Mower housings	5.000			
Mower wheels	1.950			
Four cycle gasoline engines	120.000			
Packing boxes	2.400			
Packing materials	0.600	plus	$ 125	per month
Gloves, aprons and cloths	0.050	plus	60	per month
General supplies	0.100	plus	50	per month
Gauges and tools	0.020			
Gasoline	0.001	plus	20	per month
Fasteners	0.650			
Labels	1.150			
Problem solving team expenses . . .	0.050	plus	1,800	per month

Required:

a. Prepare a flexible budget report that shows variances for each expense. Use data from Exhibit 6-6 as the actual expenses for the month. Hint: Multiply the unit cost by the number of units produced and add on the monthly amount, if any, to calculate the budget amount.

b. Which expense items appear to be the biggest problems?

c. If the company decides to increase production by 50% above the 11,200 unit level, how much does Jack Martin expect his total mower wheel cost to be for the month?

6-20. Backflush Entries.

Rustler Boot Company manufactures cowboy boots in its El Paso plant. It charges all materials, labor and overhead costs directly to the line where the boots are made and uses a backflush entry to remove the costs from the line at month end.

The company charged a total of $60,000 in costs to the Bubba boot line last month to make 3,000 pairs of boots. Use average unit cost from last month for your journal entries.

Required:

a. Prepare the backflush entry at month end for the current month if 3,000 pairs of Bubba boots were started and finished during the current month with a total cost of $60,800 charged to the line.

b. Prepare the entry if 3,000 pairs were started during the month, but only 2,900 pairs were completed with the remaining 100 pairs one-half complete at month end.

c. Prepare the same entry as required for question b, but assume the boots are three-fourths complete.

6-21. Cost Layers and Cost Analysis.

Arbuckle Auto Auctions purchased 100 acres of land on the outskirts of Chicago in 1955. Arbuckle uses the land to receive, store, and prepare autos for auction. Property taxes amount to $300,000 per year on the site, and maintenance of asphalt surfaces and the fences surrounding the property equal $50,000 per year.

The company also operates a facility on the property that cleans and waxes vehicles to get them ready for auction. The manager of this facility earns $45,000 per year, and the employees earn $5 per vehicle prepared for auction. This facility handles 25,000 vehicles per year with the six employees who work on auto preparation. Other monthly fixed costs for the vehicle preparation facility amount to $40,000 per month. The wax and cleaning compounds used to prepare vehicles amount to $1 per vehicle. Other annual fixed costs at the Chicago facility (excluding the vehicle preparation center) equal $500,000 per year.

Required:

a. Compute the total annual costs of operating the entire 100 acre facility with its present 25,000 unit annual volume.

b. Compute the total annual costs if the company handles 30,000 vehicles per year.

c. How much will the annual earnings of an employee in the vehicle preparation facility increase if the facility moves from a level of 25,000 per year to 30,000 vehicles per year?

d. Company managers are considering having an outside firm do the vehicle preparation instead of using its own employees. If the company does use the outside firm it will tear down the building now used for vehicle preparation and convert it into a parking lot. Compute the annual costs at the Chicago site the company will no longer incur if the vehicle preparation facility is torn down.

e. How much property tax cost did you include in your answer to question d? Why?

► PROBLEMS AND CASES ◄

6-22. Job Cost Reporting for Educational Seminars; Break-even Analysis.

"Why can't our accounting department give us decent reports on our seminars?" complained Leslie Boone as she looked at the computer printout she received from her university accounting department. "Every time I get one of these reports I have to decipher what it means." Leslie Boone is the Director of Seminar Programs for her university, and she manages the offering of two and three day seminars for managers who want to learn more about specific management topics like accounting and marketing.

Below is a copy of the report Leslie is complaining about. She also has provided you with a copy of the codes the accounting department uses to identify transactions affecting the seminars she runs for her university.

Management Programs
Manager: Leslie Boone
For the month ended May 31, 1995

Account	*Program*	*Amount*
160	A	$ 5,000
160	Q	8,000
110	A	2,800
160	F	5,500
110	Q	800
200	A	15,000
190	A	700
200	F	7,500
110	Q	400
200	A	20,000
200	F	10,000
200	Q	15,000
110	F	1,800
190	F	225
120	Q	1,800
120	A	4,200
130	A	3,600
130	Q	2,400
130	F	3,500

Account Code	*Description*
110	Copy work
120	Food services
130	Speaker fees
160	Promotional mailing
190	Supplies
200	Seminar revenue

Program Code	*Description*
A	Advanced Accounting
Q	Quality Management
F	Financial Markets

Required:

a. Compute the expenses incurred for each seminar Leslie offered during the past month.
b. Compute the revenue generated by each seminar.
c. Which seminar generated the most contribution margin?
d. What is the approximate cost per attendee for meals if Leslie charges $500 per seminar for each attendee?
e. The speakers at the seminars receive a fixed fee negotiated individually with each speaker, and the promotion for a seminar depends on the number of mail pieces sent to promote the seminar. Leslie is considering offering another seminar just like the Advanced Accounting seminar she offered this past month. Compute the estimated break-even attendance for this seminar if promotional mailing costs increase 20% above those for the one offered this past month. Assume speaker's fees will remain the same, and use the information from question d.
f. Using the same data from question e, how much contribution margin will the seminar generate if Leslie draws 100 people to the seminar?

6-23. Cost Estimate and Price Quote from Job Records.

Bobby Joslin received a call from a customer who wants a sign for his business, and Bobby promised to deliver a price quote to the customer in two days. The sign the customer wants is similar to the Hopkins Catfish Farm sign Bobby made for a customer last year, so Bobby asks his accountant to print a listing of the materials and labor costs incurred for the Hopkins sign. The listing below shows the materials and labor for this sign.

Hopkins Catfish Farm

Part Number	Part Description	Quantity	Price	Total
TRA12030P	Transformer	2	$ 200.00	$ 400
TRA09030P	Transformer	1	180.00	180
TRA075030	Transformer	1	350.00	350
GTOWRE	Electrical wire	50	0.20	10
SHT22G4X10	Plastic sheeting—22 gauge	17	3.50	60
SHT24G4X10	Plastic sheeting—24 gauge	5	6.00	30
FAS141SAB	Fasteners	20	0.50	10
POPRIVET316	Rivets	800	0.10	80
ALU2X2X14	Aluminum framing	8	100.00	800
IRN1.5316F	Angle iron	60	5.00	300
TRA15030P	Florescent lights	10	6.50	65
TRA12030P	Florescent lights	2	7.50	15
MAP633	Translucent paint	4	35.00	140
MAT42217	Red paint	1	80.00	80
MAT42202	Blue paint	4	65.00	260
XYLOL	Yellow paint	5	50.00	250
Total material costs				$ 3,030

Labor Costs

	Quantity	Hourly Wage	Total
Drawing & Patterns	50	$ 20.00	$ 1,000
Wood Shop	20	15.00	300
Paint Room	40	15.00	600
Final Assembly	140	15.00	2,100
Total labor costs			$ 4,000
Total cost of sign			$ 7,030

Since the current customer wants a bigger sign than the Hopkins sign, Bobby estimates that he will need 50% more electrical wire, aluminum framing, angle iron and fluorescent lights. He also thinks the sign will require 25 feet of the 22 gauge and 10 feet of the 24 gauge plastic sheeting as well as double the amount of paint used on the Hopkins sign. All the other materials should remain the same for the new sign.

Labor costs should remain the same except for a 20% increase in the Paint Room and a 10% increase in Final Assembly.

Required:

a. Estimate the materials and labor costs for the new sign.

b. In setting prices Bobby uses the rule of thumb that a sign should generate $100 of contribution margin for each day it spends in process in his shop, and he estimates this sign will require 35 days (seven weeks) to complete. Compute the selling price Bobby will use for this sign.

c. Because Bobby knows customers often wait until the last minute to order a sign, he modifies his pricing rule described in question b by increasing his quoted price as the customer requests faster delivery. He adds 10% to the price for a one week (five days) delivery time reduction, 20% for a two week reduction, and 50% for a three week reduction. Compute the price Bobby will quote to the customer for the new sign for each of these delivery time reductions.

d. Assume labor cost for this sign will increase 50% if Bobby takes one week off the delivery time, 80% if he takes two weeks off the delivery time, and 100% if he takes three weeks off the delivery time. Which delivery time will make the most money for Bobby? Use information from question c to answer this question. Show calculations to support your answer.

e. What business advantage does a company have over its competitors if it maintains detailed job cost information like that illustrated in this problem?

6-24. Critical Path Calculations; Budget Preparation.

"Boy oh boy! I don't know if we can ever get this budget done on time." Rob commented to Stephanie Wood, his boss. "We just can't seem to get our people to complete the process fast enough. Manufacturing is finished before sales, and sales complains that personnel gets finished before they have all the information about marketing plans. Our finance staff complains all the time about not having the information they need for the cash budget until the last minute. We need to do something about all this."

"Try using a project approach in which you list the budget steps, compute the time required for each step, and identify the critical path through these steps," suggested Stephanie. "You know, that just might help us," responded Rob.

Rob raced back to his office and compiled the following list of budget steps and the estimated number of days to complete each one.

Budget Task	Estimated Days
Historical analysis	10
Analyze past sales	5
Economic Forecast	10
Initial sales budget	5
Personnel requirement	7
Material requirements	6
Marketing budget	14
Manufacturing budget	5
Cash budget	5

"We can do our historical analysis and our analysis of past sales simultaneously, but we cannot do the economic forecast until we finish both these tasks," mused Rob. "Of course we need the initial sales budget before we can determine our personnel needs, our material needs and our marketing budget. We could finish the manufacturing budget while we are working on the marketing budget, so that only leaves the cash budget for completion after we finish these two budgets. I wonder if Stephanie is right that this analysis will allow us to beat our eleven week (55 days) budget preparation schedule from last year."

To help with his analysis, Bob prepared the following slack computations.

Task	Estimated Time	Early Start	Early Finish	Late Start	Late Finish	Slack
Historical analysis	10	1	10	1	10	0
Analyze past sales	5	1	5	6	10	5
Economic Forecast	10	11	20	11	20	0
Initial sales budget	5	21	25	21	25	0
Personnel requirement . . .	7	26	32	28	34	2
Material requirements . . .	6	26	31	29	34	3
Marketing budget	14	26	39	26	39	0
Manufacturing budget . . .	5	33	37	35	39	2
Cash budget	5	40	44	40	44	0

Required:

a. Name the steps in the budget process that make up the critical path.

b. How many working days will it take to complete this budget, and how does it compare to the time it took the company to prepare the budget last year?

c. Stephanie is still not happy with the time Rob developed, so she asks him to see how long it will take to complete the budget process if both the personnel requirements and the material requirements budgets are reduced by four days. Compute the change in the total time to complete the budget with these new times for these two tasks. How much did it change the total time for completing the budget? Why?

d. If Rob can speed up the historical analysis by two days, how much will total time for completing the budget change? Why?

6-25. Cost Layers, Cost Changes, and Conversion to JIT; General Review.

Bert Smith, plant manager for the Magnum Co., has been studying the process his company uses to manufacture the three products it makes in its Nashville plant, the company's only plant. He has heard about JIT, and he wants to consider using it in the plant. However, he is concerned about the economics of JIT at the plant because it would cause him to convert his work force from an hourly basis to a salary basis.

Bert called you into his office to discuss the issue with you, and he had a series of questions he wanted you to help him answer. You quickly realized that you could not answer his questions without a significant amount of analysis, so you requested a meeting three days from now at which time you will present the results of your analyses. Bert pulled together a set of information for you based on the present operation, and he gave you the financial statements for the latest year.

Magnum Co. Financial Statements
Balance Sheet
December 31, 20x1

Assets

Cash	$ 100,000
Receivables	450,000
Inventories	2,525,000
Net Plant Assets	4,120,000
Other Assets	500,000
	$ 7,695,000

Liabilities and Equity

Payables	$ 1,250,000
Long Term Debt	4,000,000
Stock	1,000,000
Retained Earnings	1,445,000
	$ 7,695,000

Income Statement
For The Year Ended December 31

Sales	$ 9,300,000
Variable Cost of Sales	2,900,000
Variable Margin	6,400,000
Fixed Operating Expenses	
Administrative	$ 750,000
Manufacturing	2,450,000
Marketing	700,000
Depreciation	500,000
Other	800,000
Inventory Carrying Costs	1,010,000
Total Fixed Expenses	$ 6,210,000
Net Profit Before Taxes	$ 190,000
Taxes	66,500
Net Income	$ 123,500

The following data provide the unit variable (incremental) costs for the three products manufactured by Magnum, their selling price, and the quantity sold during the past year.

Products	Incremental Unit Cost	Unit Selling Price	Quantity Sold
Grinder		$70	30,000
Material	$20		
Labor	2		
Overhead	8		
	$30		
Chopper		50	60,000
Material	$ 5		
Labor	1		
Overhead	4		
	$10		
Blender		60	70,000
Material	$15		
Labor	3		
Overhead	2		
	$20		

The diagram on the next page shows the production process for the current system and for the JIT system. With the current system, the Grinder and the Chopper begin production in the Machining department. Then workers send the parts for the Grinder to the Grinding department which works only on Grinders, and they send the parts for the Chopper to the Chopper department which works only on Choppers. Workers start building the Blender in the Blender department, and this department handles no other products. Finally, all three products move through the Finishing department for final assembly and packaging.

The numbers printed just below the box for each department represent the amount of annual fixed cost traceable to that department.

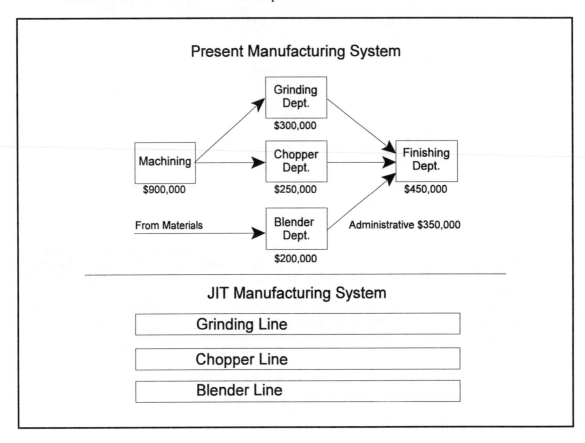

Of the $700,000 spent on marketing last year, $250,000 was devoted to advertising the company and its products. The advertising expenditure was divided in the following manner:

Name recognition for the company	$ 60,000
Grinder advertising	40,000
Chopper advertising	50,000
Blender advertising	70,000
Advertising that features all three	
products simultaneously	30,000
Total expenditure on advertising	$ 250,000

The company expects to make no changes in advertising expenditures if it shifts to a JIT production system.

6-26. JIT Changes

If the company changes to a JIT production system it will make the following modifications in its operations.

1. The production process will consist of three lines, and each line will work on only one product. All fixed costs of the departments formerly devoted to the individual products will move to the new JIT lines.

2. All workers will shift to a salaried classification (and become a fixed cost), and the company expects fixed labor cost for each line to be 10% less than the variable labor cost incurred for each product during the past year.

3. The Machining department will disappear with its equipment scattered among the three lines. The company expects to divide the annual fixed costs of Machining equally among the three lines.

4. The Finishing department will also disappear. Each new line will absorb part of the activities now handled by this department. Managers expect total annual fixed costs of the former Finishing department to drop by $150,000; of the remainder, they expect two-thirds to go to the Blender line, and the rest they will split evenly between Chopper and Grinding.

5. The unit incremental overhead for each product will drop to one-half the current level because of changes in the production process, but this change will cause fixed administrative costs for manufacturing to rise by $100,000 above their current level of $350,000 because of conversion of variable manufacturing overhead to fixed manufacturing overhead.

6. Inventory will drop by $1,525,000 because of the adoption of JIT, and you can assume that annual carrying charges amount to the same percentage of ending inventory as they did under the old system.

Required:

a. Compute the incremental (variable) unit cost for each product under the JIT production system. Why are they different from the original incremental unit costs?

b. You decide to prepare a new set of financial statements for the company assuming it is using JIT. To do this you plan to recast the financial statements from last year to show how they would look if the company had used JIT last year. Prepare financial statements using all the changes JIT will cause at Magnum.

c. What major differences do you see between the two sets of financial statements?

d. Compute annual break-even sales dollars for Magnum using both the current manufacturing system and the JIT system. Assume inventory levels will remain at the given levels for the foreseeable future. Why do you get different break-even points? Explain.

e. Compute the total annual fixed and variable costs identified directly with the Blender under both the current manufacturing system and the JIT system. Units sold for the Blender amount to 70,000. Why do the cost totals differ?

f. How much did the shift to a JIT production approach change the inventory turnover? Show calculations to support your answer.

g. Do you think Magnum uses a job order or a process cost system to track costs? Explain.

h. The manager of the Grinder line asks you to estimate the total costs that will be charged to his line if he produces 40,000 units next year. Be sure to include all costs charged to his manufacturing line, but omit any marketing costs outside of his area of responsibility.

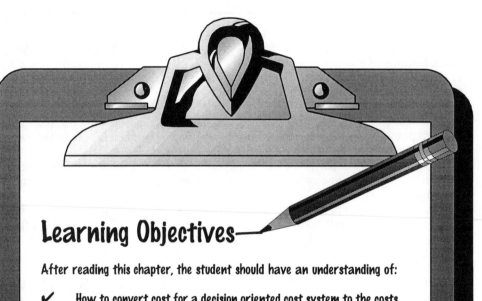

Learning Objectives

After reading this chapter, the student should have an understanding of:

✔ How to convert cost for a decision oriented cost system to the costs required for external reporting.

✔ Basic entries in actual cost systems and their quantification under both job order and process costing.

✔ Equivalent units and their critical role in process costing via both weighted average and FIFO cost.

✔ Process costing under single and multiple processes.

✔ Treatment of spoiled units under both job order and process costing.

Generally accepted accounting principles (GAAP) and tax authorities, e.g., the Internal Revenue Service (IRS), require companies to include an appropriate portion of all manufacturing costs in the inventory values in published financial statements and income tax reports. In addition, the Robinson Patman Act prohibits companies from selling products below their production cost. All these requirements impact the methods and practices accountants use to develop cost information for external reporting—the topic of this chapter.

The next section shows how accountants adjust data from an internal decision focused cost accounting system to comply with external reporting requirements. After illustrating the conversion from decision making data to external reporting data, we review the elements of cost accounting systems designed to produce external reporting data on a routine basis.

► COST INFORMATION FOR EXTERNAL FINANCIAL REPORTING ◄

Chapters 5 and 6 focused on management uses of cost information, while this chapter concentrates on information relevant to external stakeholders, like shareholders, bondholders, and the government. Financial reporting rules promulgated by the Securities and Exchange Commission, the Financial Accounting Standards Board, and the IRS govern the content of external reports, and the cost data accountants use for inventory valuation and cost of sales computations must comply with these rules.

► The Matching Principle

The matching principle plays an important role in financial reporting rules; this principle requires accountants to match costs against revenues in a manner that fairly presents the results of operations for the reporting period. Conceptually, this means that products accumulate costs as they move through the manufacturing process, and these costs build up and remain a part of the product cost held in inventory until the company sells it. Keep in mind that accountants attach only manufacturing costs to the product for financial reporting; selling and administrative costs are excluded from product costs for financial reporting purposes.

This process sounds easy, but accountants sometimes find it difficult to determine how much production cost to attach to each unit that passes through a plant. They can readily measure materials costs and usually have little trouble calculating labor cost (as illustrated in Chapter 5 for the water heater element), but allocating or applying manufacturing overhead to individual products can create problems.

For example, the Fleetguard plant in Cookeville, Tennessee, makes over one hundred different kinds of oil and air filters. How does an accountant apply equipment depreciation for a metal stamping machine to the LA-670 oil filter or the AC-35 air filter? Both products use parts stamped on the same stamping machine. Any method Fleetguard accountants use to apply manufacturing overhead to these filters is somewhat arbitrary because accountants have no precise method for identifying manufacturing overhead expenses with individual products. Consequently, accountants must rely on approximation methods to assign overhead to manufactured products. Exhibit 7-1 illustrates one such method.

The Single Product Case

Total heater elements produced during year	50,000
Manufacturing overhead costs for the year	$ 60,000
Overhead costs per unit ($60,000 ÷ 50,000)	$ 1.20
Beginning inventory units	None
Cost of Goods Sold (40,000 units)	
Materials cost (40,000 x $1.187)	$ 47,480
Labor cost (40,000 x $1.317)	52,680
Overhead assigned to cost of goods sold	
(40,000 x $1.20)	48,000
Total Cost of Goods Sold	$ 148,160
Ending Inventory Valuation (10,000 units)	
Materials cost (10,000 x $1.187)	$ 11,870
Labor cost (10,000 x $1.317)	13,170
Overhead assigned to ending inventory	
(10,000 x $1.20)	12,000
Total ending inventory value	$ 37,040

Exhibit 7-1 *Allocation of Manufacturing Overhead to Cost of Sales and Ending Inventory*

► Assigning Manufacturing Overhead to Inventory—The Single Product Case

Exhibit 7-1 demonstrates how accountants can add manufacturing overhead to materials and labor cost for a water heater element to compute a product cost suitable for financial reporting. The accountant combines a portion of actual overhead cost for the period with the materials and labor cost traceable to the product to compute cost of goods sold. The bill of materials and the product routings provide the materials and labor cost, but the accountant must make an allocation of manufacturing overhead to determine the total amount of cost to match with sales for the year.

In Exhibit 7-1 we assume no beginning inventories and no ending work in process, so the accountant need only apportion the actual manufacturing overhead incurred for the year between the cost of goods sold and the new units added to inventory. The company incurred $60,000 of overhead for the year to produce 50,000 heater elements for an average manufacturing overhead of $1.20 per unit. Since the company sold 40,000 heater elements during the year, the accountant adds $48,000 ($1.20 x 40,000) of overhead to cost of sales for the period. This overhead plus the materials ($47,480) and the labor ($52,680) provide a total cost of sales of $148,160.

In a similar fashion, the ending inventory of 10,000 units has an overhead amount of $12,000 ($1.20 x 10,000) allocated to it to represent the amount of overhead assigned to the units still on hand. When these units are sold, this amount of overhead, along with the materials and labor costs, will be charged to cost of goods sold to match these production costs with the revenues they generate.

Instead of assuming no beginning inventories, suppose the company started the year with 5,000 units at a cost of $19,480 and the company sold a total of 45,000 units; assume further that the company uses the first-in-first-out (FIFO) costing method for inventory. Under these conditions, the cost of sales for the 45,000 units would appear as follows using both the data above and from Exhibit 7-1.

Cost of Sales

Inventory costs from last year (5,000 units) . . . . $ 19,480
Cost of goods sold for current year
    production from Exhibit 7-1 (40,000 units)   148,160
         Total . . . . $ 167,640

The ending inventory cost remains the same because under FIFO it includes only costs incurred during the current year, while last period's costs in the form of beginning inventory (the "first" costs), along with a portion of current period costs, are charged to cost of sales.

▸ Assigning Manufacturing Overhead to Inventory—The Case of Multiple Products

Assigning overhead to the heater element in the previous example was easy because the company manufactured only one product. However, if the company fabricated several products (the company on which our multiple product example is based actually makes about 75 products in its plant), the accountant would be unable to compute a sensible overhead cost per unit by dividing total units produced into the overhead cost since units of product in the multiple product case do not all contain the same amount of overhead cost. In cases where companies produce multiple products, accountants usually choose a surrogate or approximate measure like labor hours or materials costs to assign overhead to products.

Labor Hour Overhead Rates. Many companies use labor hours as the base for applying manufacturing overhead to units produced. The popularity of labor hours as an overhead allocation measure may be explained as follows: The longer a product remains in the production process, the more it benefits from the manufacturing overhead services provided by the company. In a multiple product firm, different products require different amounts of time. Therefore, products that take longer to complete should carry more of the manufacturing overhead burden. Since labor time provides an approximation of the time a product spends in manufacturing, labor hours provide a reasonable base for assigning manufacturing overhead to products. Other overhead allocation bases accountants may use are direct labor dollars, materials costs, machine hours, and specific factors such as product weight. We illustrate the use of labor hours for overhead allocation in Exhibit 7-2 for the multiple product case.

Overhead Rate Calculation. To keep the calculations simple, we assume the company produces only two products, a heater element and a thermostat, and that it uses the FIFO inventory method. Since both products use the same overhead facilities, the company accountant must apportion manufacturing overhead between cost of sales and inventory for both products instead of just one product so cost data conform to external reporting rules. The accountant does this by dividing the actual direct labor hours worked for the year into the actual total overhead cost for the year of $240,000 to compute an overhead rate per labor hour of $6.00. (Notice we changed the amount of manufacturing overhead costs for this example from that used in Exhibit 7-1.)

Next, the accountant multiplies the $6.00 per hour overhead rate by the labor hours expended on units sold for each of the two products to derive the overhead amounts of $85,500 and $132,300 for the respective products. Once the accountant has made the overhead allocation to units sold, he or she can sum the three cost elements to compute total cost of sales for the year. The overhead in ending inventory is computed just as in Exhibit 7-1 except that we now have two products instead of only one, and we use the overhead rate of $6.00 per labor hour expended on inventory. The labor hours included in cost of goods sold and ending inventory are determined using the labor hour per unit calculations of Exhibit 7-2.

The Multiple Products Case

Total direct labor hours worked during year   40,000
   (heater Element 15,450 and Thermostat 24,550)
Manufacturing overhead costs for the year . . . . $ 240,000
Overhead costs per labor hour ($240,000 ÷ 40,000) . . . . $ 6.00

	Heater Elements	Thermostats
Beginning inventory	None	None
Units produced during year	5,150	12,275
Labor hours worked during the year	15,450	24,550
Labor hours per unit	3	2

Cost of Goods Sold	Heater Elements	Thermostats
Units sold	4,750	11,025
Direct labor hours in cost of sales	14,250	22,050
Materials cost	$ 47,480	$115,000
Labor cost	52,680	105,600
Overhead assigned to cost of goods sold .	85,500	132,300
Total Cost of Goods Sold	$ 185,660	$352,900

Ending Inventory Valuation		
Units in ending inventory	400	1,250
Direct labor hours in ending inventory	1,200	2,500
Materials cost	$ 11,870	26,000
Labor cost	13,170	18,000
Overhead assigned to ending inventory . . .	7,200	15,000
Total ending inventory value	$ 32,240	$ 59,000

Exhibit 7-2 *Allocation of Manufacturing Overhead to Cost of Sales and Ending Inventory*

Overhead Rate Impact of Different Methods. Notice that the direct labor hour method gives a different ending inventory value for the heater element from the unit of product method of Exhibit 7-1. Such differences commonly occur as accountants try alternative methods or different bases for allocating overhead to inventories. In all cases the accountant must exercise careful judgement to make sure the method chosen for assigning overhead to inventories appropriately matches costs and revenues. Matching costs and revenues is the most important factor to consider when choosing an overhead allocation method for developing external financial report numbers.

These examples (Exhibits 7-1 and 7-2) use a FIFO cost flow assumption. With the last-in-first-out (LIFO) costing method, the accountant works with ending inventory using the dollar costs of beginning inventory (except for increases in inventory) while the last, or most recent, costs are included in cost of goods sold (except for decreases in beginning inventory).

The discussion to this point has assumed a firm uses its cost system primarily for decision making and calculates costs for external reporting as needed at the end of each period using the techniques illustrated above. However, many companies operate their cost systems primarily for external reporting and prepare special analyses to develop data for decision making, which is the topic of the next section.

► EXTERNAL REPORTING COST SYSTEMS ◄

The preceding section concentrated on converting cost accounting data developed for management decisions into data useful for external reporting. Now we turn our attention to cost accounting systems designed primarily to serve external reporting needs.

A cost system operated primarily to produce data for external reporting operates similarly to the systems illustrated in the previous two chapters. The primary difference between a decision focused cost system and a financial reporting focused cost system lies in the way the systems handle overhead costs. While accountants record materials and labor costs identically in both systems, manufacturing overhead receives much more attention in a financial reporting focused cost system.

► Basic Journal Entries for Actual Cost Systems

Exhibit 7-3 depicts the flow of costs through a system with an external financial reporting focus. Notice the materials and labor costs flow through the accounts as in the last two chapters, but the overhead costs follow a different pattern. A decision focused cost system concentrates on who has responsibility for individual overhead expenses, but an external reporting focused cost system concentrates on making sure the overhead costs properly attach to the products moving through the plant. In order to do this, accountants must rely on advance estimates or forecasts of manufacturing overhead to apply manufacturing overhead to products as they move through the plant.

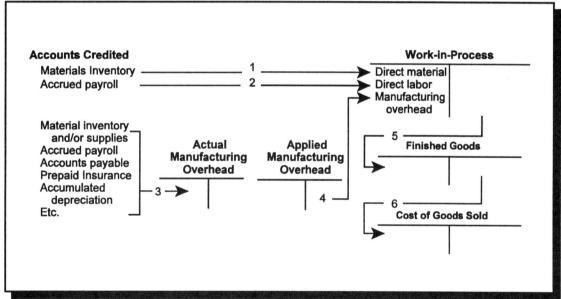

Exhibit 7-3 *Actual Cost System Process or Job Order Basic Journal Entries*

The journal entries for Exhibit 7-3 are as follows:

1. Dr. Work-in-process
        Cr. Materials inventory
    To record direct materials usage

2. Dr. Work-in-process
        Cr. Accrued payroll
    To record direct labor

3. Dr. Actual manufacturing overhead
        Cr. Supplies, accrued payroll, etc.
    To record actual manufacturing overhead

4. Dr. Work-in process
        Cr. Applied manufacturing overhead
    To record manufacturing overhead applied to production

5. Dr. Finished goods
        Cr. Work-in-process
    To transfer completed units to finished goods

6. Dr. Cost of goods sold
        Cr. Finished goods
    To record cost of units sold

► Manufacturing Overhead Cost Entries

As Exhibit 7-3 illustrates, accountants record all manufacturing overhead as it is incurred by debiting Actual Manufacturing Overhead and crediting a variety of appropriate accounts. However, when accountants apply manufacturing overhead to the products moving through the plant, they debit Work-in-Process and credit Applied Manufacturing Overhead. To make this journal entry, accountants must rely on a predetermined overhead rate based on labor hours, labor cost, materials cost, or some other overhead base. They develop this rate by estimating at the beginning of the year the amount of manufacturing overhead cost expected for the year, say, $460,000, and the estimated number of direct labor hours for the year, say, 100,000 hours. Dividing the 100,000 labor hours into the estimated manufacturing overhead cost of $460,000 produces a predetermined manufacturing overhead rate of $4.60 per labor hour.

Suppose an accountant wants to apply manufacturing overhead to work-in-process at month-end for a plant that worked 10,000 direct labor hours during the month. The accountant makes the following entry for 10,000 hours at $4.60 per hour.

Dr. Work-in-Process 46,000
    Cr. Applied Manufacturing Overhead 46,000

At the end of the period accountants close the Actual Manufacturing Overhead account to the Applied Manufacturing Overhead account. Because the accountant uses estimates of future manufacturing overhead costs and future labor hours to compute the overhead rate, the amount of manufacturing overhead costs actually incurred and the amounts applied to work-in-process virtually always differ. If the accountant applies more manufacturing overhead than the amount actually incurred, the excess is called over-applied overhead; if the accountant applies less overhead cost than actually incurred, this shortage is called under-applied overhead. The next chapter discusses this issue in detail.

► Journal Entries for Job Order Cost Systems

To illustrate the application of overhead to products in a job order costing system, we use the Harpeth Valley Autos sign that Joslin Sign Company was manufacturing in Chapter 6. Assume Joslin incurred $8,000 of materials and $4,000 of labor cost (500 labor hours) to complete the sign. Joslin records these events with the following journal entries.

```
Dr. Work-in-process . . . . . . . . . . . . . . . . . . . . . . . . . . . .   8,000
    Cr. Materials Inventory . . . . . . . . . . . . . . . . . . . . . . . . . . . .          8,000
        To record direct materials usage

Dr. Work-in-process . . . . . . . . . . . . . . . . . . . . . . . . . . . .   4,000
    Cr. Accrued Payroll . . . . . . . . . . . . . . . . . . . . . . . . . . . . .          4,000
        To record direct labor costs

Dr. Work-in-process . . . . . . . . . . . . . . . . . . . . . . . . . . . .   2,500
    Cr. Applied Manufacturing Overhead . . . . . . . . . . . . . . . . .          2,500
        To apply manufacturing overhead to the Harpeth Valley job
```

To produce the dollar amounts for the manufacturing overhead entry, the Joslin Sign Company accountants performed a series of calculations at the start of the year to develop a manufacturing overhead, or burden, rate for computing the amount of manufacturing overhead to apply to various jobs. Their calculations were developed as follows:

1. Company accountants estimated the total direct labor hours the company would use for the year at 100,000 hours.
2. The company estimated total manufacturing overhead for the coming year at $500,000.
3. Accountants divided the total manufacturing overhead of $500,000 by the estimated labor hours for the year of 100,000 to derive an overhead rate of $5 per labor hour.

Once accountants have this manufacturing overhead rate, they compute the manufacturing overhead to apply to a job by multiplying the number of hours worked on a job by the $5 rate. Thus, for the above journal entry, Joslin accountants multiplied the 500 hours worked on the Harpeth Valley Autos job by $5 to compute the $2,500 of manufacturing overhead allocated to the job. Accountants may apply manufacturing overhead expenses to jobs as jobs leave a department, or, more commonly, they allocate the overhead to the job when the company completes the job. At the completion of the sign, Joslin accountants make this journal entry:

```
Dr. Finished goods . . . . . . . . . . . . . . . . . . . . . . . . . . . .   14,500
    Cr. Work-in-process . . . . . . . . . . . . . . . . . . . . . . . . . . . . .          14,500
        To record the movement of the sign to finished goods
```

When Joslin delivers the sign to the customer, the total cost of the sign (materials, labor, and manufacturing overhead) is charged to cost of sales to match job costs with the revenue generated by the job. However, note that since the manufacturing overhead applied to the job is based on a predetermined rate of $5 per direct labor hour, the applied manufacturing overhead amount may differ from actual manufacturing overhead incurred. The entry to transfer the total cost (materials, labor, and applied manufacturing overhead) from finished goods inventory into cost of goods sold is:

Dr. Cost of goods sold	....	14,500
Cr. Finished goods	....	14,500

▶ PROCESS COST SYSTEMS FOR EXTERNAL REPORTING ◀

As mentioned in the last chapter, companies use process costing systems to collect costs by production processes instead of by jobs. The process through which a job passes becomes the focus of cost collection efforts. In a process cost system operated with a financial reporting focus, the costs of each process are assigned to the units that move through each process so the proper amount attaches to the units and moves from process to process and ultimately to finished goods and to cost of goods sold.

▶ Procedures for a Process Cost System: Some Illustrations

Process cost systems differ from one company to another because of unique company and product features. Some companies produce one product in one simple process (e.g., a company that puts galvanized coatings on sheet metal). Others, like oil refineries or chemical plants, produce multiple products in many complex processes. The illustrations in this section will relate to two hypothetical companies (e.g., a company with one process and another with two processes). These two companies allow us to cover the basic variations of process costing.

In the examples we illustrate the widely used weighted average method of product costing. At the end of our discussion we will describe how FIFO changes the calculations we use in our illustrations.

▶ Galvanizing, Inc.—A One Process Company

Assume No Beginning or Ending Inventories for Work-in Process. Galvanizing, Inc., produces galvanized buckets by purchasing metal buckets from a supplier and then dipping the buckets in a vat of molten metal. After the molten metal cools on the bucket, it produces a rustproof finish that prolongs the life of the bucket.

Galvanizing, Inc., showed the following results for a recent month. The company applies manufacturing overhead to work-in-process using an overhead rate of $2 per direct labor dollar.

Work-in-Process			
Cost to be accounted for:		Accounted for as follows:	
Direct material	$ 6,500	Completed and transfer-	
Direct labor	5,200	red 10,000 units	
Applied manufacturing		@ $2.21	$ 22,100
overhead	10,400		
	$ 22,100		$ 22,100

The costs put into process are used to compute unit costs and the cost of completed production. Since the company started and finished 10,000 buckets during the month and total costs were

$22,100, the unit cost is $2.21 per unit. The transfer to finished goods is $22,100, and accountants make the following journal entry to record the movement to finished goods.

> Dr. Finished Goods 22,100
> Cr. Work-in-process 22,100

Equivalent Units. One of the key figures in process costing is the calculation of *equivalent units*. In our illustration for Galvanizing, Inc., equivalent units equaled 10,000 units because all units were completed 100 percent from start to finish during the current period. However, a company will not usually have all units 100 percent complete when accountants prepare cost of production reports (e.g., at each month end), so accountants must develop an output measure called equivalent units, or equivalent production. This issue arises when a company has beginning or ending work-in-process inventories which are by definition less than 100 percent complete. Equivalent units refers to *the average number of finished units the work expended on work-in-process could have produced.* For example, a company with a month end work-in-process of 300 units one-half complete would have equivalent units of 150 units,. i.e., 300 units one-half complete equals 150 equivalent whole units. The concept of equivalent production is needed to calculate unit costs. Keep in mind that equivalent units do not represent tangible units, but rather a measure of work done.

Consider the following analogy. After a hard afternoon of practice a football player walks into the cafeteria and finds six apple pies of equal size on a table. He eats one-sixth of each pie; how many pies did he eat? If you answered the equivalent of one pie, you have already grasped the basis for understanding equivalent units. Now assume that there are 1,050 units in work-in-process, and each unit is one-third complete. These 1,050 units one-third complete are equivalent to 350 completed units (1,050 x 1/3).

Illustration Involving Beginning and Ending Inventories. The Galvanizing, Inc., example demonstrated how to compute the costs transferred to finished goods if there were no work-in-process inventories. In our next example, we illustrate what happens if the company has beginning and ending inventories of work-in-process. In the schedule below, we use the data from our last example except that we include a beginning inventory of 1,050 units one-third complete and an ending inventory of 2,100 units two-thirds complete. Accountants use an average percentage of completion (one-third or two-thirds, in our example) for work-in-process inventories because the stage of completion for individual items usually varies. We assume all costs are added uniformly throughout the process. This is an important assumption because if materials are added at the beginning of the process rather than uniformly, the computations will change considerably. We present an illustration where materials are added at the beginning of the process in a later section (Proctor, Inc.).

Work-in-Process		
Cost to be accounted for:		Accounted for as follows:
Beginning Inventory—		Transfer to finished goods—
1,050 units ⅓		10,000 units
complete .... $ 735		
Direct material 6,500		
Direct labor 5,200		Ending Inventory—2,100 units ⅔
Applied manufacturing		complete
overhead 10,400		
$ 22,835		

To compute the equivalent units of production for the month, we must include (1) completion of the unfinished portion of beginning inventory, (2) the partial completion of ending inventory, and (3) the total completion of units which were started and completed during the month.

Weighted Average Cost. The weighted average unit cost for a process results from the division of total costs charged to a process by the equivalent units, so the first step for this calculation is the computation of equivalent units. With the weighted average cost approach, accountants can ignore the degree of completion of beginning inventory (because beginning inventory is included in units transferred) and concentrate on the degree of completion of the finished units. For Galvanizing, Inc., this results in the following calculation.

	Equivalent Units	Cost
Transferred (completed)	10,000	
Ending inventory (2/3 of 2,100)	1,400	
Total	11,400	$ 22,835

Or, we can compute these same amounts this way.

	Equivalent Units	Cost
Transferred and completed:		
From beginning inventory		
(1/3 of 1,050)	350	$ 735
From this month's production		
(10,000 - 350)	9,650	
Ending inventory (2/3 of 2,100)	1,400	22,100
Total	11,400	$ 22,835

Accountants compute the weighted average unit cost by dividing the total costs for the month of $22,835 by 11,400 to arrive at a unit cost of $2.003. They use this weighted average unit cost to compute the costs transferred to finished goods and the cost of ending inventory. The total of these two amounts account for the total cost (debit) in the work-in-process account as follows.

Dr. Work-in-Process 22,835
    Cr. Various Accounts 22,835
        To charge work-in-process with costs of material, labor and overhead

This entry charges the $22,835 of cost to work-in-process, but from the above calculations we know that $20,030 (10,000 units x $2.003) of the cost was transferred out to finished goods, and the remainder of $2,805 remains in the process as the cost of ending inventory. These amounts are summarized below.

Transfer (10,000 units @ $2.003) . . . . $ 20,030
Ending inventory (2/3 of 2,100 units
    or 1,400 units @ $2.003) 2,805*
Total cost accounted for . . . . $ 22,835
* Rounded

The journal entry to move the costs from work-in-process to finished goods is as follows:

```
Dr. Finished goods ............................ 20,030
    Cr. Work-in-Process ................................ 20,030
```

► Proctor, Inc.,—A Two Process Company

Galvanizing, Inc., used only one process to produce galvanized buckets, but Proctor, Inc., uses two processes to manufacture special metal panels for the restaurant market. The first process stamps metal panels from coils of steel, and the second process applies several coats of special paints to the panels. This special paint withstands extreme heat and the constant cleaning required in restaurants without cracking or wearing off. Materials (steel sheeting) is added at the beginning of the Stamping Department, and materials (paints) are added continuously during the manufacturing process in the Painting Department. The company incurs labor and overhead costs ($2 per direct labor dollar) uniformly throughout both processes. Because the company incurs costs at different points in the production process for materials, labor, and overhead in these two departments, company accountants compute equivalent units and costs for each cost category separately.

Stamping Department

Cost to be accounted for:		Accounted for as follows:
Beginning Inventory 1,000 units:		
100% complete as to material	$ 1,104	Completed and transferred 10,000 units
20% complete as to labor	126	
20% complete as to overhead	252	
Direct material:		Ending Inventory 3,000 units
Material for 12,000 units started		100% complete as to material
into production	12,000	33⅓% complete as to labor
Direct labor	7,200	33⅓% complete as to manufacturing overhead
Applied manufacturing overhead	14,400	
	$ 35,082	

We follow the same process to compute the costs transferred from each department as used in Galvanizing, Inc., that is, we compute the equivalent units for the month and divide them into total costs for the month to arrive at a unit cost. The following four steps summarize these calculations:

1. Calculate equivalent units.
2. Determine production costs.
3. Calculate unit costs.
4. Calculate the cost of transfers and ending inventories.

Painting Department

Cost to be accounted for:		Accounted for as follows:
Beginning Inventory 2,000 units:		Transferred to finished goods 11,000 units
100% complete as to Process I ..	$ 6,060	
50% complete as to Process II:		Ending Inventory 1,000 units
Material	1,000	100% complete as to Process I
Labor	318	50% complete as to material
Overhead	636	50% complete as to labor
Transfer from Process I		50% complete as to manufacturing overhead
(10,000 units)	?*	
Direct materials	10,500	
Direct labor	3,500	
Applied manufacturing overhead	7,000	

* Value will depend on the costing method used. The dollar amount is not available until costs are calculated for Process I.

Calculations for the Stamping Department. The cost of production report on the next page for the Stamping Department illustrates these four steps using the weighted average method.

Calculations for the Painting Department. The same four-step process used for cost calculations in Stamping is followed for Painting. However, we add an additional column to the report for Painting to track the costs and units received from the Stamping Department. Notice how the first column in this report includes the $30,060 of cost transferred from Stamping to Painting (The Painting Department report is on the page following the Stamping Department).

Journal Entries. The journal entries to record these costs for the two departments are shown below:

Dr. Work-in-Process—Stamping	12,000	
Cr. Materials inventory		12,000
To record materials issues for Stamping		

Dr. Work-in-Process—Stamping	7,200	
Cr. Accrued payroll		7,200
To record direct labor for Stamping		

Dr. Work-in-Process—Stamping	14,400	
Cr. Applied manufacturing overhead		14,400
To record manufacturing overhead applied in Stamping		

Dr. Work-in-Process—Painting	30,060	
Cr. Work-in-Process—Stamping		30,060
To record transfer to Painting		

Dr. Work-in-Process—Painting	10,500	
Cr. Materials inventory		10,500
To record materials requisitions for Painting		

Dr. Work-in-Process—Painting	3,500	
Cr. Accrued payroll		3,500
To record direct labor for Painting		

Cost of Production Report

For the month of _____

Stamping Department

	Material	Labor	Manufacturing Overhead	Total
1. Equivalent units:				
Completed and transferred	10,000	10,000	10,000	
Ending inventory:				
100%	3,000			
33 1/3%		1,000	1,000	
Equivalent units	13,000	11,000	11,000	
2. Production cost:				
Beginning inventory	$ 1,104	$ 126	$ 252	$ 1,482
Added during month	12,000	7,200	14,400	33,600
Total costs	$13,104	$ 7,326	$14,652	$ 35,082
3. Unit costs (2÷1)	$ 1.008	$ 0.666	$ 1.332	$ 3.006

4. Total cost accounted for:
   Completed and transferred   10,000 units x $3.006 ..... $ 30,060
   Ending Inventory:
       Material: 3,000 units x 100% x $1.008 .... $ 3,024
       Labor: 3,000 units x 33 1/3% x $0.666   666
       Manufacturing overhead:
         3,000 units x 33 1/3 x $1.332   1,332   5,022
       Total costs .... $ 35,082

```
Dr. Work-in Process—Painting .................... 7,000
    Cr. Applied manufacturing overhead ................. 7,000
        To record manufacturing overhead applied in
        Painting

Dr. Finished goods ............................. 55,066
    Cr. Work-in Process—Painting ...................... 55,066
        To record transfer of completed units to finished
        goods
```

Posting the above entries provides the following work-in-process account balances:

Work-in-Process—Stamping

Beginning balance	1,482	Transferred to Process II:	30,080
Material	12,000		
Labor	7,200		
Applied manufacturing overhead	14,400	Ending Inventory	5,022
	35,082		35,082
Beginning balance next period	5,022		

Cost of Production Report

For the month of _____

Painting Department

	Stamping Dept. Material	Added Material	Labor	Manufacturing Overhead	Total
1. Equivalent units:					
Completed and transferred ..	11,000	11,000	11,000	11,000	
Ending inventory:					
100%	1,000				
50%		500	500	500	
Equivalent production ...	12,000	11,500	11,500	11,500	
2. Production cost:					
Beginning inventory	$ 6,060	$ 1,000	$ 318	$ 636	$ 8,014
Added during month	30,060	10,500	3,500	7,000	51,060
Total	$ 36,120	$ 11,500	$ 3,818	$ 7,636	$ 59,074
3. Unit costs (2÷1)	$ 3.010	$ 1.000	$ 0.332	$ 0.664	$ 5.006

4. Total cost accounted for:

Completed and transferred 11,000 units X $5.006		$ 55,066
Ending inventory:		
Material—Stamping Department:		
1,000 units x 100% x $3.010	$ 3,010	
Material—added: 1,000 units x 50% x $1.000	500	
Labor: 1,000 units x 50% x $0.332	166	
Manufacturing overhead:1,000 units x 50% x $.664	332	4,008
Total costs		$ 59,074

Work-in-Process—Painting

Beginning balance	8,014	Transferred to finished goods	55,066	
Material Process I	30,060			
Material added	10,500			
Labor	3,500			
Applied manufacturing overhead	7,000	Ending Inventory	4,008	
	59,074		59,074	
Beginning balance next period	4,008			

Accountants normally record cost of goods sold with a debit to the cost of goods sold account and a credit to finished goods inventory. Consequently, when Proctor, Inc., sells the 11,000 units in Finished Goods, it will debit cost of sales for $55,066. Make sure you can identify this number in the cost of production report for the Painting Department.

▸ FIFO Inventory Calculations

Because most firms use the weighted average method for computing costs for a financial reporting focused cost system we used this costing method throughout our illustrations of process costing. However, some companies do use the FIFO method of process costing, so we provide an example of the FIFO costing process using the case of Galvanizing, Inc.—a one process company. In the weighted average costing method, all units (beginning inventory and current month's production) are averaged into one unit cost whereas in the FIFO method each month's equivalent units are treated separately as shown below.

Units completed and transferred	10,000	
Add completed portion of ending inventory units (2/3 X 2,100)	1,400	
Total possible production this month	11,400	$ 22,835
Less completed portion of beginning inventory units(1/3 x 1,050)	350	735
Total equivalent production this month	11,050	$ 22,100

As this calculation shows, the total production for the month equals the equivalent units to: 1) finish the beginning inventory (1/3), start and finish 8,950 units (100%), and complete a portion of the ending inventory (2/3). We compute a unit cost of $2 by dividing equivalent units for the month (11,050) into costs incurred during the month ($22,100). Ending inventory is the equivalent number of complete units 1,400 (2,100 x 2/3) multiplied by the $2 unit cost for a total of $2,800. We calculate the transfer to finished goods as follows:

Beginning inventory (1,050 units) 1,050 units effectively 1/3 complete	$ 735
Costs necessary this period to complete beginning inventory (2/3 of 1,050 units or 700 @ $2 per unit)	1,400
Cost of 1,050 units completed	2,135
Remainder of transfer (8,950 units @ $2)	17,900
Total transfer (10,000 units)	$ 20,035

When the amount transferred ($20,035) is added to the amount in ending inventory ($2,800), the sum ($22,835) accounts for the total costs in beginning inventory $(735) plus current costs incurred of $22,100.

Note that under FIFO the costs of the beginning inventory occupied a significant place in the cost of production report. Accountants must compute separately the cost of completing the beginning inventory under FIFO because these costs are the first to be charged to cost of sales.

▸ Time of Adding the Factor of Production

In the preceding illustrations, we assumed direct materials were placed into production at either the beginning of the process or uniformly during production. If added at the beginning of production, materials are always considered to be 100 percent complete. If added uniformly during production, they are always subjected to a partial completion percentage. Companies can introduce materials into production at other points. For example, a company might add 100 percent of materials at any point in the production process, and, in such cases, materials are considered zero percent complete before they are added and 100 percent complete after they are added.

Some companies may use more than one type of materials and each type may be added to production at a different time. For example, materials A may be added uniformly throughout processing and materials B may be added 100 percent at the two-thirds stage in processing. In these cases accountants track each materials separately and compute a separate unit cost for each materials.

In the past, labor and manufacturing overhead were ordinarily added uniformly throughout production in each separate process. However, in some partly automated processes in today's plants, all labor might be added uniformly after the robots have completed their work. Under these circumstances, accountants must make allowances when calculating equivalent units and unit costs to make sure that adjustments are made for the different points in the process at which labor versus manufacturing overhead is added.

▶ Process Costing in Multiproduct Firms

Multi-product firms present special problems. Where individual products are manufactured in separate and distinct processes, accountants should incorporate service department costs into the manufacturing overhead rates for each process. If most products go through the same processes, accountants need to identify direct materials and direct labor costs with specific products and to develop a manufacturing overhead rate for each process that applies to the products being processed. Food canneries and shoe factories are good examples of manufacturing plants where different products follow some of the same processes.

The use of different size containers for one product in food canneries (as well as many other firms) makes it difficult to allocate costs to different sizes and varieties of the same product. Most firms solve this problem by calculating a unit cost for a *basic unit,* which in turn is used to compute costs of materials, labor, and overhead for all other units in terms of their relationship with the basic unit. For example, if a cannery produces three different size cans of peaches (i.e., No. 1, No. 303, and No. 2 1/2), accountants can compute the relationships between No. 1 and No. 303 cans and the *basic case* which, for our calculations, consists of No. 2 1/2 cans.

The following example illustrates how to convert different size cans into basic cases (24 cans in each) and how to use the unit cost for a basic case to calculate unit costs for the other size cases. Direct materials, direct labor, and manufacturing overhead are handled separately because cost relationships in multi product firms usually require such separations. Some firms calculate basic units using more than three cost groups. For example, a cannery might use raw product, sugar, salt, water, cans, cartons, other ingredients, labor by processes, and even various categories of manufacturing overhead.

In our present example, No 1. cans contain materials equal to 35 percent of the materials costs for No. 2 1/2 cans, 85 percent of the direct labor costs for No. 2 1/2 cans, and 90 percent of the manufacturing overhead costs for No. 2 1/2 cans. No. 303 cans involve 55 percent of the materials for No. 2 1/2 cans, 90 percent of the direct labor costs for No. 2 1/2 cans, and 95 percent of the manufacturing overhead costs for No. 2 1/2 cans. Companies usually use engineering studies to determine these conversion factors.

Production Data.

Direct Materials

Cases Produced (a)	Percent of No. 2½ Cases (b)	Basic Cases (a × b)
200 No. 1	35	70
300 No. 303	55	165
500 No. 2½	100	500
		735

Direct Labor

Cases Produced (a)	Percent of No. 2½ Cases (b)	Basic Cases (a × b)
200 No. 1	85	170
300 No. 303	90	270
500 No. 2½	100	500
		940

Manufacturing Overhead

	Percent of No. 2½ Cases (b)	Basic Cases (a × b)
Cases Produced (a)		
200 No. 1	90	180
300 No. 303	95	285
500 No. 2½	100	500
		955

Cost Data.

Cost Incurred

Direct materials	$ 4,410
Direct labor	2,115
Manufacturing overhead	2,895
	$ 9,420

Calculations.

Cost Per Basic Case (No. 2½ Case)

Direct materials ($4,410 ÷ 735)	$ 6.00
Direct labor ($2,115 ÷ 940)	2.25
Manufacturing overhead ($2,895 ÷ 965)	3.00
	$ 11.25

Cost Per No. 1 Case

Direct materials (35% of $6.00)	$ 2.10
Direct labor (85% of $2.25)	1.9125
Manufacturing overhead (90% of $3.00)	2.70
	$ 6.7125

Costs Per No. 303 Case

Direct materials (55% of $6.00)	$ 3.300
Direct labor (90% of $2.25)	2.025
Manufacturing overhead (95% of $3.00)	2.850
	$ 8.175

Proof of Calculations.

200 No. 1 cases @ $6.7125	$ 1,342.50
300 No. 303 cases @ $8.175	2,452.50
500 No. 2½ cases @ $11.25	5,625.00
Total costs incurred	$ 9,420.00

► Job Order vs. Process vs. Hybrid Systems

The procedures illustrated for job order and process systems in this chapter demonstrate the basics of these two systems, but in real life, there are many different hybrids of job order and process costing depending on the specifics of individual products and production processes. One often-mentioned hybrid is called "operation costing."

Under operation costing, the products use distinctive raw materials but go through the same processing. The manufacturing of clothing provides a typical illustration. In these cases, companies account for direct materials with a job order costing system, and they account for the combination of direct labor and manufacturing overhead (referred to as conversion cost) with a process costing approach.

Hybrid systems should present few problems to anyone truly conversant with the basics of job order and process costing. Creative application of these basics plus common sense are sufficient to develop an appropriate cost system.

► SUMMARY ◄

Companies can create cost systems that focus on decision making applications, or they can create cost systems that concentrate primarily on external financial reporting. Companies with decision oriented systems must adjust the numbers to comply with financial reporting rules when they prepare external financial statements. This requires them to allocate manufacturing overhead costs between cost of sales and ending inventory. This allocation enables accountants to match the costs associated with a product with the revenue the product generates.

Companies that create cost systems focused on external financial reporting apply overhead to production on an ongoing basis, so their costs are already in compliance with financial reporting rules. These companies develop an overhead absorption rate for allocating overhead costs to production as they produce products in contrast to a decision-focused system, where overhead is allocated to inventory and cost of sales at the end of the period.

SPOILAGE COSTS

► ACCOUNTING FOR SPOILAGE—JOB ORDER COST SYSTEMS ◄

Materials wasted or spoiled on a job usually entail no special journal entry. However, if spoilage becomes significant, then accountants and company managers may want to make separate journal entries to record the spoilage.

Accountants treat normal (expected) spoilage differently from abnormal (unexpected) spoilage. They consider normal spoilage a regular part of the product cost for financial reporting, but they create separate entries to record abnormal spoilage as an expense of the period in which the abnormal spoilage occurs.

Some modern manufacturing companies consider any amount of spoilage abnormal, and their accountants record and report the cost of this spoilage to highlight areas for possible improvement. For these companies, all spoilage is abnormal and subject to immediate reporting in the income statement. These companies have a "zero defect" philosophy.

Many companies use less stringent requirements and allow a small percentage for normal spoilage. For example, assume Joslin Sign Company uses a 1% allowance for spoilage on materials costs. Then any spoilage of $80 (1% of $8,000) or less on the Harpeth Valley Auto sign receives no special recognition. On the other hand, if a worker accidently connects a ballast to the wrong wires and burns out a $300 transformer, the accountant will recognize $220 of this amount as abnormal spoilage with the following journal entry.

Dr. Spoilage losses   220
    Cr. Work-in-Process   220

► SPOILAGE LOSSES—PROCESS COSTING ◄

Accountants distinguish between normal and abnormal spoilage in process costing just as they did in job order costing. Accountants treat normal spoilage as a part of the cost of good units produced, but they consider abnormal spoilage a loss of the period rather than as a part of the cost of goods produced. We use the following data to illustrate the accounting treatment of spoilage, assuming that spoilage is either all normal or all abnormal. Further assume managers identify spoilage at the end of processing when inspection takes place and that spoiled units have no market value.

Data for Illustration. Production costs for the period:

Direct materials	$ 12,000
Direct labor	15,000
Overhead	30,000
Total costs for the period	$ 57,000

Production data for the period:

Units put into process	13,000
Units transferred to finished goods	10,000
Spoiled units	1,000
Ending inventory (50% complete)	2,000
Beginning inventory	0

	Normal Spoilage	Abnormal Spoilage
1. Equivalent Units:		
Transferred	10,000	10,000
Spoiled	0	1,000
Ending inventory	1,000	1,000
Equivalent units	11,000	12,000
2. Total costs (from above table)	$ 57,000	$ 57,000
3. Unit cost (#2 / #1)	$ 5.1818	$ 4.7500
4. Cost of transfers and ending inventory		
Transferred	$ 51,818	$ 47,500
Spoiled	0	4,750
Ending inventory	5,182	4,750
Total costs	$ 57,000	$ 57,000

The zero for spoiled units in the normal spoilage column of the equivalent unit calculation indicates we consider the amount normal. This calculation method includes normal spoilage in the cost of good units produced. In the case of abnormal spoilage the calculation method treats spoilage costs as a loss of the period rather than as a part of the cost of good units produced.

Additional Considerations. In the above example, we made a number of simplifying assumptions to illustrate the problems of accounting for spoiled units. We assumed that spoilage was not detected until goods were complete, that spoilage was either wholly normal or abnormal, and that spoiled units had no market value. If accountants detect spoilage before completion, they must adjust the equivalent units calculation to take this into account. If some spoiled units are normal and others abnormal, the cost calculations should include normal spoilage in unit cost calculations of good units produced but report the abnormal spoilage as a loss on the income statement.

When spoiled units have a value (scrap value), accountants first offset this value against the *loss due to abnormal spoilage* which appears in the income statement; if there is no abnormal spoilage, accountants credit the scrap value against the costs of producing the good units. However, not all accountants agree on which part of the production costs to reduce. Should direct materials, direct labor, or manufacturing overhead be reduced? Some accountants resolve this problem by apportioning the scrap value among materials, labor, and manufacturing overhead based on the fraction of total cost each represents. However, most accountants avoid this method and use simpler methods which credit the salvage value of spoiled goods to only one cost element (manufacturing overhead is most often used) or even to miscellaneous income. They do this because it is practical and because the overall unit cost impact differs little from more refined methods.

In Chapters 8 and 9 where we discuss the use of standard costs we show another approach to handling the problem of spoilage. With standard costs, managers can more readily recognize the extent of spoilage beyond the normal amount. On the other hand, in those modern manufacturing companies that consider all spoilage abnormal, the standard costs make no allowances for spoilage.

PRODUCING AND SERVICE DEPARTMENTS

▸ Definition of Service and Producing Departments

Manufacturing firms generally classify departmental units into producing departments and service departments. Producing departments consist of those company segments in which workers actually make products. For example, managers call the department in printing plant that prints plane tickets a producing department because workers in that department make plane tickets. Likewise, managers call the area in which an automobile gets assembled a producing department.

On the other hand, managers call those areas that provide support to the producing departments service departments. These departments support the producing departments by providing services they need to operate. For example, the department in a metal stamping plant that does maintenance on the tools and dies used for making the metal stampings is called a service department. Other examples of service departments are personnel departments, material handling departments, power departments, and maintenance departments that maintain equipment used in producing departments. Workers in service departments do not directly touch the products the plant makes; they serve as helpers to the workers who actually touch the product the plant makes.

▸ Service Department Costs and Product Costs for Financial Reporting

Accountants who operate cost systems designed primarily for financial reporting must decide how to assign overhead costs for service departments to producing departments.

▸ Distributing Service Department Costs to Producing Departments

Since products only flow through the producing departments, accountants must devise reasonable methods for assigning service department overhead to the producing departments. Accountants assign service department costs to the producing departments on the basis of the

| | Power | Material Handling and Storeroom | Producing Departments | | | Total |
			Stamping	Finishing	Assembly	
Total payroll per department Including direct labor, indirect labor, and salaries	$ 52,000	$104,000	$208,000	$156,000	$104,000	$ 624,000
Percent of total	8⅓	16⅔	33⅓	25	16⅔	100%
Total square feet of floor space per department	3,000	3,000	6,000	6,000	6,000	24,000
Percent of total	12½	12½	25	25	25	100%
Total book value of equipment per department	$ 180,000	$ 90,000	$ 810,000	$ 630,000	$ 540,000	$ 2,250,000
Percent of total	8	4	36	28	24	100%
Total material and supplies requisitions per department	0	0	$ 105,000	$ 120,000	$ 75,000$	300,000
Percent of total	0	0	35	40	25	100%
Distribution percentages for power department based upon an engineering survey of potential and actual power usage in each department	0	10	30	30	30	100%

Exhibit 7-4 *Data on Basis for Distribution of Manufacturing Overhead Used in Exhibit 7-5*

services rendered to the producing departments. The two exhibits shown below illustrate the assignment of service department costs to producing departments for a manufacturing company.

▸ Distributing Overhead to Producing Departments When Service Departments Also Serve Other Service Departments

Typical service departments or operations are general plant, steam plant, electric generation and distribution, maintenance, and material transfer. General plant operations include general supervision and clerical services, staff departments, travel, telephone, and other costs applicable to the entire plant. We illustrate two of the popular methods for distributing these costs to the producing departments with the following data.

Departments	_Costs Distributed to Each Department_
Service 1	$ 10,000
Service 2	12,000
Service 3	8,000
Production 1	40,000
Production 2	50,000

Classification	Basis of Distribution (cost driver)	Power	Material Handling and Storeroom	Producing Departments			Total
				Stamping	Finishing	Assembly	
Salaries	Actual salaries per dept.	$ 5,000	$ 6,000	$ 6,000	$ 6,500	$ 5,400	$ 28,900
Indirect labor	Actual Indirect labor per dept.	8,000	20,000	8,200	9,400	4,300	49,900
Supplies	Actual requisitions per dept.	1,200	2,100	680	1,200	1,500	6,680
Employee benefit programs ..	Total payroll per dept.	200	400	800	600	400	2,400
Payroll taxes	Total payroll per dept.	425	850	1,700	1,275	850	5,100
Property taxes—buildings	Square feet per dept.	250	250	500	500	500	2,000
Insurance—buildings	Square feet per dept.	50	50	100	100	100	400
Depreciation—buildings	Square feet per dept.	625	625	1,250	1,250	1,250	5,000
Property taxes—equipment ..	Book value of equipment	96	48	432	336	288	1,200
Insurance—equipment	Book value of equipment	12	6	54	42	36	150
Depreciation—equipment	Actual equipment in each dept.	4,000	2,500	27,000	24,000	16,000	73,500
Total		$ 19,858	$32,829	$ 46,716	$ 45,203	$ 30,624	$ 175,230
Distribution of service department costs:							
Power		(19,858)	1.986	5,958	5,957	5,957	
Subtotal			$34,815	$ 52,674	$ 51,160	$ 36,581	$ 175,230
Material handling and storeroom			(34,815)	12,185	13,926	8,704	
Total manufacturing overhead per department				$ 64,859	$ 65,086	$ 45,285	$ 175,230
Measure of activity (direct labor hours)				20,000	10,000	7,000	
Manufacturing overhead rates:							
Total overhead per department/measure of activity				$3.24	$6.51	$6.47	

Exhibit 7-5 *Distribution of Manufacturing Overhead*

On the basis of an engineering survey it was determined that service departments render service as follows:

Service Department:	1	2	3
Producing 1	30%	45%	40%
Producing 2	50%	45%	40%
Service 1	0	10%	20%
Service 2	10%	0	0
Service 3	10%	0	0

The direct method. The *direct method* allocates the service department costs directly to the producing departments. The interaction between the service departments that relates the costs incurred in one service department because of the needs of another service department are ignored.

Direct Method

	S1	S2	S3	P1	P2	Total
Distributed Costs	$ 10,000	$ 12,000	$ 8,000	40,000	$50,000	$120,000

Service Department distribution:

	S1	S2	S3	P1	P2	Total
S1 (30/80, 50/80)	(10,000)			3,750	6,250	
S2 (45/90, 45/90)		(12,000)		6,000	6,000	
S3 (40/80, 40/80)			(8,000)	4,000	4,000	
Total				$53,750	$66,250	$120,000

The step method. The *step method* starts with the department that draws the least service from others and distributes it, disregarding the service which it uses.[1] Then the one which draws the least on the remaining ones is distributed, and so on, until all distributions have been made. In this case the costs are distributed in the order of S2, followed by S3 and then S1.

Step Method

	S1	S2	S3	P1	P2	Total
Distributed costs	$ 10,000	$ 12,000	$ 8,000	$40,000	$50,000	$120,000

Service department distribution:

	S1	S2	S3	P1	P2	Total
S2 (10%, 45% ,45%) ..	1,200	(12,000)		5,400	5,400	
Subtotal	$ 11,200		8,000			
S3 (20%, 40%, 40%) ..	1,600		(8,000)	3,200	3,200	
Subtotal	$ 12,800					
S1 (30/80, 50/80)	(12,800)			4,800	8,000	
Total				$53,400	$66,600	$120,000

Since accountants disregard the services used by those service departments distributed first, they must use the ratio of remaining percentages for the distribution. In this case, the 20 percent of S1 service to S2 and S3 is disregarded, leaving the total to be distributed based on the ratio of the remaining percentages. Thus, for the S1 distribution, the ratio is 30/80 and 50/80.

---

[1] In case of ties, the department with the greatest cost is distributed first.

► QUESTIONS ◄

7-1. Name two basic cost accounting systems and describe the conditions under which each should be used.

7-2. Describe the six basic entries in actual cost systems and specify how accountants accumulate the dollar amount of each entry under both job order and process costing.

7-3. Describe the difference between a cost system designed primarily for decision making and one designed primarily for financial reporting.

7-4. In a process cost system designed primarily for external reporting what information does the accountant use to compute the average unit cost used for matching unit cost with revenue? Where does this information come from or originate?

7-5. How are the dollar amounts of the following calculated under both job order and process costing for companies using cost systems primarily for financial reporting:

> Work-in-process inventory
> Finished goods inventory
> Transfer from work-in-process to finished goods
> Transfer from finished goods to cost of goods sold

7-6. How does conversion of decision making cost to cost for external reporting differ in single and multiple product firms?

7-7. Explain the matching principle, and explain its significance for product costing for external reporting.

7-8. What is equivalent production and why must it be recognized under process cost accounting?

7-9. What is meant by average cost as opposed to FIFO cost under a process cost system?

7-10. Why do companies often use labor hours to assign manufacturing overhead to units manufactured?

7-11. In a firm which manufactures one product in a variety of sizes, how might an accountant determine the labor, material and manufacturing overhead costs for the various sizes?

7-12. Discuss the following: "The essential difference between job order costing and process costing is the unit for which the company collects cost information. Under job order costing, the unit is the job, whereas under process costing the unit is the process."

7-13. Under what conditions might accountants use both process costs and job order cost in the same plant?

► EXERCISES ◄

7-14. Journal Entries and Sources of Data for Journal Entries.

Required:

a. Assume a job order cost system and refer to the following diagram:

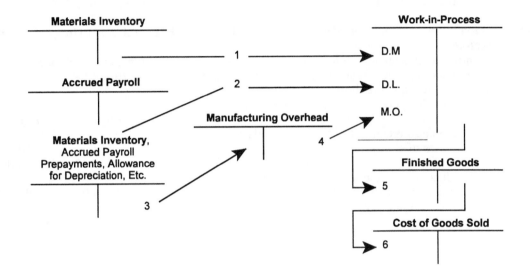

1. Prepare in journal form entries 1 to 6 (without dollar amounts).
2. Briefly describe the source of the data and the method of accumulating the data for each of the entries.

b. Assume a process cost system and answer questions (1) and (2) above under this assumption.

7-15. Conversion of Decision Making Cost to External Reporting Cost—Single Product Firm.

Hydraulics, Inc., a manufacturer of hydraulic motors produced 220,000 motors last year. The incremental cost per motor are:

Material . . . . $ 240
Labor   60

The company began the year with no inventory and completed the year with 20,000 motors on hand at year end. Manufacturing overhead for the year amounted to $110,000. Hydraulics, Inc., uses the FIFO inventory costing method for external reporting.

Required:

a. Compute the cost of goods sold the company will report in the financial statements it provides to external users.
b. Compute the dollar value of ending inventory the company will use in reports it provides to its bankers.
c. Assume the company sells the motors for $600 each and that costs other than manufacturing for the past year total $50 million. Prepare an income statement the company will use for external reporting if the tax rate is 40%.

7-16. Conversion of Decision Making Cost to Cost for External Reporting—Multiple Products.

Smith Candies manufactures two types of candies in its plant in Charleston. Information on these two products is shown below. Smith uses FIFO for reporting cost information to outside owners and creditors.

	Crunchies	Yummies
Beginning inventory (all finished goods 100 % complete)		
Cases of candy	15,000	10,000
Dollars (external reporting value)	$ 150,000	$ 50,000
Production information for the past year		
Number of cases produced	180,000	200,000
Incremental costs		
Material	$1,080,000	$ 600,000
Labor	360,000	150,000
Total labor hours worked	36,000	12,500
Ending inventory		
Cases of candy	10,000	15,000

Total manufacturing overhead for the year amounted to $291,000, and the estimated labor hours in ending inventory for the two products are:

Crunchies	2,000
Yummies	940

Required:

a. Compute the cost of sales the company will report in its external income statement for each product.
b. Compute the total ending inventory of finished goods reported in the balance sheet for each product.
c. Which product has the highest inventory turnover?
d. Explain how your calculation would differ for cost of sales and ending inventory if the company used LIFO instead of FIFO costing in its published financial statements. Present no calculations; just give an explanation.

7-17. Job Order Costs Including Journal Entries.

The M.G. Johns Manufacturing Company has a work-in-process inventory balance on January 1 of $134,000. This account was made up of the following items:

Job Order	Direct Material	Direct Labor	Manufacturing Overhead
1018	$ 15,000	$ 14,000	$ 7,000
1019	16,600	18,000	9,000
1020	25,000	19,600	9,800
	$ 56,600	$ 51,600	$ 25,800

A summary of January transactions follows:
1. Raw material purchases $68,200
2. Return of defective materials $4,500
3. Stores requisitions totaled $59,650
4. Stores requisitions were applicable to the following jobs:

No.1018	$ 21,000
No.1019	15,000
No.1021	13,500
No.1022	6,000
Indirect materials	4,150

5. Payroll for the month included:

	Gross Earnings	Withheld	Taxes Net
Direct labor	$ 80,600	$ 12,400	$ 68,200
Indirect labor	18,000	1,300	16,700
Factory salaries	25,000	5,800	19,200

6. Direct labor for the month was incurred for the following jobs. The applied manufacturing overhead rate is 50 Percent of direct labor cost.

No. 1018	$ 24,500
No. 1019	9,800
No. 1021	32,100
No. 1022	14,200

7. Other manufacturing costs incurred during January were:

Utilities	$ 2,300
Amortization of factory insurance	400
Depreciation of buildings and equipment	3,800

8. Jobs 1018 and 1019 were completed and sold for a total sales price of $225,000.

Required:

a. Prepare summary journal entries for January.
b. Post appropriate portions of these entries as well as the beginning inventory to a work-in-process T-account.
c. Post all transactions involving manufacturing overhead to appropriate T-accounts and discuss the disposition of any balance.

7-18. Job Order Costs and Spoilage.
Your company compiled the following data for Job No. 1689 which you completed last month:

	Department I	Department II
Direct materials	$4,850	$1,275
Direct labor	7,425	2,530
Other direct costs	0	495
Machine hours	450	680
Direct labor hours	3,700	800
Good units produced	1,200	1,150
Spoiled units	100	50

Manufacturing overhead is applied at $2.10 per direct labor hour in Department I and $4.50 per direct labor hour in Department II. Spoiled units are detected at the end of each process.

Required:

a. Calculate total unit costs for Department I assuming that 5 percent of good units produced are normally spoiled. Spoiled units have no salvage value.
b. Calculate total unit costs for Department II assuming that all spoilage is normal. Spoiled units can be sold as scrap for $2.00 per unit.
c. Prepare a journal entry to record the completion and transfer of Job No. 1689 to finished goods inventory.

7-19. Calculation of Equivalent Units.
Determine equivalent units assuming FIFO calculations in each of the following cases:

a. Beginning work-in-process 5,000 units 1/5 complete
Transfers to finished goods 12,000 units
Ending work-in-process 5,000 units 1/3 complete
b. Beginning work-in-process 5,000 units 1/5 complete
Units put into process 13,000 units
Ending work-ln-process 5,000 units 1/3 complete

7-20. Calculation of Equivalent Units, Unit Costs, Transfer, and Inventory.

The Ames Company had a beginning work-in-process of 8,000 units with the following characteristics:

Material (100% complete)	$16,000
Labor and manufacturing overhead (25% complete)	6,000

During the month 165,000 units were completed and transferred to finished goods and the ending inventory of work-in-process consisted of 4,000 units with the following characteristics:

Material (100% complete)

Labor and manufacturing overhead (75% complete)

Costs incurred during the month included $338,100 for material and $498,000 for labor and Manufacturing overhead.

Required:

Determine the following under both the weighted average cost method and the FIFO cost method.
a.   Equivalent units.
b.   Unit cost for materials.
c.   Unit cost for labor plus overhead.
d.   Dollar value of the transfer to finished goods.
e.   Dollar value of the ending work-in-process.

7-21. Calculate Equivalent Units, Unit Costs, Transfer, and Inventory.

The Ajax Company had the following summation of costs included in its work-in-process account.

Beginning inventory 1,000 units 3/4 complete as to materials, labor, and overhead	$ 7,575
Direct material	34,000
Direct labor	42,000
Applied manufacturing overhead 200% of direct labor	84,000
Total	$ 167,575

Units completed and transferred to finished goods were 22,000. Materials, labor, and manufacturing overhead are all added uniformly during production. Ending work-in-process consists of 4,000 units 50 percent complete.

Required:

Determine the following under both the weighted average cost method and the FIFO cost method.
a.   Equivalent units.
b.   Total unit cost.
c.   Dollar value of the transfer to finished goods.
d.   Dollar value of ending work-in-process.

7-22.   Converting Decision Costs to External Reporting Costs—Single Product.
Pet Care products produces a dry dog food in its San Diego plant. It began the year with 20,000 bags of dog food in inventory (external reporting value of $85,000), and it incurred the following incremental manufacturing costs during the year. The beginning inventory of finished goods that were 100% complete included 5,000 hours of labor time. Pet Care uses the FIFO costing method for costing inventory.

Incremental manufacturing costs for the year	
Material	$ 10,800,000
Labor	1,000,000
Incremental manufacturing overhead	500,000
Units produced during the year	4,000,000 bags
Fixed manufacturing overhead for the year	$ 5,170,000
Direct labor hours worked during the year	1,100,000

Using the bags of inventory on hand at year end and the number of bags produced during the year, the accountant for Pet Care computed an inventory turnover* for the year of 100 times. She also discovered that the labor time per unit for the ending inventory was the same as that for the beginning inventory.

*The company computed inventory turnover by dividing total units produced for the year by the number of units in ending inventory.

Required:

a.   Compute the number of units in ending inventory, and compute the number of labor hours included in the ending inventory.
b.   Compute the incremental cost of the units sold during the year. Use the average unit variable cost of the units produced to compute variable cost of sales.
c.   Compute the cost of goods sold reported in the income statement presented to external owners of the business.
d.   Explain why your answers to questions b and c differ.
e.   Compute cost of sales for the year and the value of ending inventory if the company uses the LIFO method of inventory valuation for external reporting. How do these amounts compare to the answer you computed for question b?

7-23. Correction of Errors Under Job Order Costing.

Required:

Journalize any necessary correcting entries for each of the following situations:
a. The overhead rate for Department I is $3 per direct labor hour. During May, 4,000 direct labor hours were expended in Department 1.
  1. Give the correcting entry if the accountant incorrectly uses a $2 an hour rate for journalizing the overhead application for May. Assume that the books have not been closed for May.
  2. Taking the data in (1) above, give the correcting entry if the books have been closed.
b. The overhead rate for Department I is $3 per direct labor hour. Job No. 18 had 200 direct labor hours applied to it. All these hours were applied with a $4 an hour manufacturing overhead rate to the job cost sheet. The journal entry for applied manufacturing overhead was properly recorded at the $3 rate:
  1. Give the correcting journal entry if the job is still in process.
  2. Give the correcting journal entry if the job is finished, not yet sold, and has been transferred to finished goods.
  3. Give the correcting journal entry if the job is finished, has been sold, and the books are not closed.
  4. Give the correcting journal entry if the job is finished, has been sold, and the books are closed.
  5. Give the correcting journal entry if the job is finished, half of it is sold, and the books are not closed.

7-24. Process Costing Cost of Production Report, Two Departments, Two Methods—Weighted Average and FIFO.

The Glueall Company produces a resin in two departments: X and Y. Materials are added at the beginning of the process. Conversion cost (labor and manufacturing overhead) is added uniformly throughout the process. The following information is available from June's production records:

	X	Y
Beginning work-in-process	15% complete 85,000 units	45% complete 62,500 units
Started in-process	215,000 units	
Transferred	245,000 units	297,500 units
Ending work-in-process	25% complete 55,000 units	75% complete 10,000 units

Costs:

Beginning work-in-process:	X	Y
From Preceding Department		$ 473,750
Materials	$ 40,500	97,750
Conversion (labor and overhead)	50,235	129,375
Added during the month:		
Materials	782,600	450,800
Conversion (labor and overhead)	969,240	1,417,600

Required:

Prepare a cost of production report using:
a. The average cost method.
b. The FIFO method.

7-25. Process Costing With Multiple Processes.
The Mousetrap Company produces a single line of traps. The bases are wood, and the mechanism is a metal spring and a two piece metal release which also holds the bait. Lumber is sawed to size for the bases. Wire is formed into springs. Releases are punched from brass plate. Punching time is the same for both parts of the release. Bases, springs, and the two parts of the release are assembled into finished traps which are packed at the assembly operation in boxes holding one dozen and placed in the finished stock warehouse. These boxes are packed in larger cartons at the time of shipment. On January 1 the in process and finished stock inventories were:

Cut bases (10,000 @ $0.036)	$ 360
Springs (12,000 @ $0.021)	252
Release—Part A (8,000 @ $0.012)	96
Release—Part B (11,000 @ $0.024)	264
Finished traps (63,000 @ $0.144)	9,072

For the month of January manufacturing costs were as follows:

Material:
Lumber used	$ 3,930
Wire used	708
Brass plate used-A	852
Brass plate used-B	2,025
Boxes used	3,150
Cartons used	1,317

Labor:
Base cutting	1,122
Spring forming	720
Release forming	819
Assembly	2,151
Shipping	810

Manufacturing overhead:

Base cutting	798
Spring forming	768
Release forming	1,638
Assembly	1,125
Shipping	249

January production was:

Cut bases	128,000
Springs	124,000
Release A	135,000
Release B	135,000
Traps assembled	126,000
Traps shipped	132,000

Required:

a. Calculate unit costs for each process assuming an average cost inventory flow.
b. Calculate:
    1. Cost of goods sold, and
    2. Ending inventory quantities and values.
c. Post opening inventory values and January transactions to T-accounts for work-in-process and finished goods. Compare the balances of the T-accounts with the ending inventories calculated in (b) above.

7-26. Job Order Costs With Multiple Processes.

A small manufacturer of molded plastic products uses a job order cost system. The productive operations are preforming, molding, inspecting and finishing, and packing and shipping. There are no jobs in-process at the beginning of the year. Actual costs for the month of January are shown as follows:

Direct Material Costs

Job	*Preforming*	*Packing & Shipping*
No. 1	$ 987	$ 38
No. 2	416	11
No. 3	1,410	63
No. 4	1,118	

Direct Labor Costs

Job	*Preforming*	*Molding*	*Inspecting & Finishing*	*Packing & Shipping*
No. 1	$ 50	$294	$ 118	$ 70
No. 2	28	110	30	30
No. 3	92	620	1,210	110
No. 4	76	418	96	

Actual Manufacturing Overhead Costs

Preforming	$ 150
Molding	2,220
Inspecting and finishing	1,400
Packing and shipping	225

Manufacturing overhead is applied to job orders using predetermined rates based on direct labor costs as follows:

Percent

Preforming	50
Molding	150
Inspecting and finishing	100
Packing and shipping	50

There is no count of production at preforming and all preformed material is molded immediately. Contracts with customers permit variations in the quantity shipped of plus or minus 5 percent of the quantity ordered. For January, data on orders, production, and shipments are as follows:

Unit Ordered, Produced, Shipped, Inspected and Finished

Order No.	Ordered	Molded	Good	Scrap	Packed	Shipped
1	10,000	11,000	9,900	1,100	9,900	9,900
2	5,000	5,400	5,100	300	5,100	5,100
3	40,000	42,000	40,880	1,120	10,000	10,000
4	25,000	26,000	25,100	900		

It was estimated that the Unit cost of order No. 3 would be $0.16.

Required:

a. Assume that all spoilage is normal.
   1. Calculate cost of goods sold for January.
   2. Calculate the January 31 inventory value for work-in-process.
   3. Calculate over- or underapplied manufacturing overhead for the month of January.
   4. Record January transactions in a T-account for work-in-process. Compare the balance of this T-account with the inventory value calculated in (2) above.
b. Discuss and describe how the above calculations would be affected if spoilage were partially or completely abnormal.

7-27. Prepare a Cost of Production Report.
   The Bost Company Ltd. operates a manufacturing process which requires the units to be processed through the cutting department from where they are then transferred to the assembly department where the units are completed. The company uses the weighted average method of accounting for costs in their process costing system.

Actual results for the month of July were:
a. The cutting department's production report for the month of July showed:
1. Work-in-process inventory--July 31 consisted of 4,000 units, 45 percent complete, with a cost of $12,840.
2. Units completed and transferred in July totaled 65,600 units with costs of $370,640.
b. The assembly department had the following results:
1. Work-in-process inventory--July 1 consisted of 15,750 units, 65 percent complete, with the following costs: transferred from cutting, $88,875; materials added, $11,818; and conversion cost (labor and manufacturing overhead), $263,025.
2. Work-in-process inventory--July 31 consisted of 17,280 units which were 55 percent complete.
3. Direct materials are added in the assembly department at the 60 percent stage; and during July, materials added to the process cost a total of $49,450.
4. Conversion costs for July totaled $2,072,060.
5. There was no spoilage in the assembly department.

Required:

Prepare a cost of production report in proper format for the assembly department for the month of July.
(SMA adapted)

7-28. Process Costing, Spoiled Units.
Wright Ltd., following process costing procedures, manufactures a single product in one department. On April 1, 20x1, the balances in the company's work in-process account, representing the costs of 5,000 units, were as follows:

Materials	$ 58,400
Conversion (labor and overhead)	88,000

During April, 20,000 units were placed in process; 19,000 units were completed and transferred to finished goods; 2,000 units were scrapped (of which normal spoilage was 1,200 units) at a point when all materials had been applied and 10 percent of the conversion work done; and 4,000 units remained in-process at month end. The closing work-in-process units were 100 percent complete as to materials and 50 percent complete as to conversion work. There was no inventory of finished goods April 1 and 50 percent of April's completed production was sold during the month.
Costs applied to production during the month were:

Materials	$ 491,600
Conversion (labor and overhead)	760,000

Required:

Prepare an appropriate schedule showing equivalent production, unit costs and cost disposition. The last item should show clearly a detailed breakdown of the total costs of $1,398,000 ($146,400 + $1,251,600) charged to the department in terms of ending work-in process, finished goods, cost of goods sold, etc.
(SMA adapted)

7-29. Process Costing Cost of Production Report, Spoiled Units.

The Advant Company Limited employs a process costing system using the weighted average method of accounting for costs. The first department in its process is the cutting department which has an inspection done at the 90 percent stage. Normal spoilage is assumed to be 10 percent of good units that pass the inspection point for the cutting department and is added to the cost of all units that pass the inspection. Actual results for the cutting department for the month of January were:

1. Work-in-process inventory--January 1 consisted of 24,000 units (60% complete) with total costs of $509,500 (materials of $289,500 and conversion costs of $220,000).
2. Work-in-process inventory--January 31 consisted of 12,000 units (95% complete).
3. Units completed and transferred to the next department in January totalled 78,000 units.
4. Total spoilage during the month was 10,500 units.
5. Materials added during the month totalled $921,550 (added at the beginning of the process).
6. Conversion costs during the month totalled $1,525,600 (added uniformly throughout the process).

Required:

Prepare a cost of production report in good format.

7-30. Process Costs With Two Processes.

Complete the missing items in the accounts below using an average cost inventory flow. Assume that materials are added 100 percent at the beginning of Process I and 100 percent at the 60 percent stage of Process II.

Work-in-Process

Beginning inventory (4,000) units:	
Materials (100% complete)	$ 6,200
Labor and overhead (50% complete)	4,650
Added: Material	38,000
Labor and overhead	43,000
Total	$ 91,850
Transferred to Process II:	
22,000 units	?
Ending inventory:	
Materials (7,600 units 100% complete)	
Labor and overhead	
(7,600 units 20% complete)	?
	91,850

Work-ln-Process II

Beginning inventory (12,000 units):	
Transfer (100% complete)	$ 45,000
Materials (only 50% of the units	
are past the 60% stage)	3,300
Labor and overhead (30% complete)	7,500

Transfer from Process I (22,000 units)	?
Material	$ 14,100
Labor and overhead	56,500

Transferred to finished goods:	?
(28,000 units)	
Ending inventory (6,000 units)	
Transfer(100% complete)	
Materials (70% of the units are past	
the 60% stage)	
Labor and overhead (50% complete)	?

7-31. Process Costs Including Defective Units.

You are engaged in an audit of the ABC Manufacturing Company's financial statements as of December 31, 20x6 and are in the process of verifying the pricing of the company's inventory of work-in-process and finished goods which is recorded on the company's books as follows:

Finished goods inventory	
(110,000 units)	$ 604,900
Work-in-process inventory—90,000	
units (50% complete)	830,480

The company follows the practice of pricing the above inventories at the lower of cost or market on a first-in, first-out basis. You learn that materials are added to the production line at the start of the process and that overhead is applied to the product at the rate of 75 percent based on direct labor dollars. You also learn that the market value of the finished goods inventory and the work-in-process inventory is greater than the amounts shown above with the exception of the defective units in the ending inventory of finished goods, the market value of which amounts to $1 per unit. A review of the company's cost records shows the following information:

	Units	*Materials*	*Labor*
Beginning Inventory			
January 1, 20x6			
(80% complete)	100,000	100,000	$ 160,000
Additional units started			
in 20x6	500,000		
Material costs incurred		550,000	
Labor costs incurred			997,500
Units completed in 20x6:			
Good units		500,000	
Defective units		10,000	
Finished goods inventory			
at December 81, 20x6			
includes 10,000 defective			
units.			

You also learn that defective units occur at the 60 percent level of completion. Assume that defective units are not a normal part of production and were units started and completed this year.

Required:

a. Schedules indicating:
  1. Equivalent production.
  2. Unit cost for materials, labor, and manufacturing overhead.
  3. Balance sheet valuation of finished goods, defective units, and work-in-process at December, 20x6.

  b. Journal entries (if any) to correctly state inventories of finished goods and work-in-process.

7-32. Process Costing With Spoilage.
   The Biltimar Company manufactures gewgaws in three steps or departments. The finishing department is the third and last step before the product is transferred to finished goods inventory. All material needed to complete the gewgaws is added at the beginning of the process in the finishing department and spoiled units, if any, occur only at this point. The company uses the FIFO cost method in its accounting system and has accumulated the following data for July for the finishing department:
   a. Production of gewgaws:

In-process, July 1 (labor and manufacturing overhead 3/4 complete)	10,000
Transferred from preceding departments during July	40,000
Finished and transferred to finished goods inventory, July	35,000
In-process, July 31 (labor and manufacturing overhead 1/2 complete)	10,000

   b. Cost of work-in-process inventory, July 1:

Costs from preceding departments	$ 38,000
Costs added in finished department prior to July 1:	
Materials	21,500
Labor	39,000
Manufacturing overhead	42,000
Total	$ 140,500

   c. Gewgaws transferred to the finishing department during July had costs of $140,000 assigned from preceding departments.

d. During July, the finishing department incurred the following production costs:

Materials	$ 70,000
Labor	162,500
Manufacturing overhead	130,000
Total	362,500

e. Normal spoilage at the beginning of the process is 10 percent of the units transferred in.

Required:

Calculate the following:
a. Cost of abnormal spoilage during July.
b. Cost of gewgaws transferred to finished goods inventory in July.
c. Cost of work-in-process inventory at July 31.
d. Prepare journal entries for the transfer and spoilage.
(AICPA adapted)

7-33. Process Costs With Two Processes and Spoilage.
   The King Process Company manufactures one product, processing it through two processes: No. 1 and No. 2. For each unit of Process No. 1 output, units of material X are put in at the start of processing. For each unit of Process No. 2 output three can of material Y are put in at the end of processing. Two pounds of Process No. 2 for each unit of finished goods started. Spoilage generally occurs in Process No. 1 when processing is approximately 50 percent complete. Assume that spoilage is normal. The company uses the FIFO basis for inventory valuation for Process No. 1 and finished goods, and average cost for inventory value for Process No. 2.
   a. Units transferred:

From Process No. 1 to Process No. 2 to finished goods	2,200 lbs.
From Process No. 2 to finished goods	900 gals.
From finished goods to cost of goods sold	600 gals.

   b. Units spoiled in Process No. 2—100 gallons.
   c. Materials unit costs: X—$1.51 per unit; Y—$2.00 per can.
   d. Direct labor and overhead: Process No. 1—$3,344; Process No. 2—$4,010.
   e. Spoiled units were sold for $100 which is to be considered miscellaneous income.
   f. Inventory data:

	Process No. 1 Beginning	Process No. 1 Ending	Process No. 2 Beginning	Process No. 2 Ending	Finished goods Beginning	Finished goods Ending
Units	200	300	200	300	200	500
Fraction complete	1/2	1/3	1/2	2/3		
Valuation						
Materials	$ 560		$ 0		$ 3,800	
Direct labor & overhead	108		390			
Process No. 1 costs			$2,200			

Required:

   Assuming separate accounts for each process and finished goods, prepare entries to record the transfer:
a. From Process No. 1 to Process No. 2.
b. From Process No. 2 to finished goods.
c. From finished goods to cost of goods sold.
d. Rework the entire problem assuming that spoilage is abnormal and is written off to spoilage expense.
Prepare schedules of computations to support entries.
(AICPA adapted)

7-34. Process Costs Involving Shrinkage.

Required:

a. Unit cost for materials.
b. Unit cost for conversion costs (labor + overhead).
c. Cost of the transfer to finished goods.
d. Cost of ending work-in-process.

Data for the problem:
a. Beginning work-in-process (570 gals.)—25% complete.

$$\begin{array}{ll}
\text{Material costs} \dots\dots\dots\dots\dots\dots & \$1,800 \\
\text{Labor and Overhead} \dots\dots\dots\dots & 600
\end{array}$$

b. Material placed in process (4,000 gals.)—$12,000.
c. Conversion costs ($15,800).
d. Transferred to finished goods (2,880 gals.).
e. Ending work-in-process (900 gals.)—1/2 complete.
f. Material is put in at the beginning of the process and during the process 20 percent of its weight is lost at a uniform rate.
g. The company uses the FIFO inventory method.
This type of problem is worked best by carrying all calculations through in original (before shrinkage) figures.

7-35. Comprehensive Review of External Reporting Values and Incremental Production Costs—Multiple Products.

An auto seat manufacturer makes three types of seats: Bucket, Chair, and Straight. You have collected the following information about production of these seats for the past year. The company uses the FIFO costing method for external reporting.

	Bucket	*Chair*	*Straight*
Beginning inventory			
Units	1,000	2,500	3,200
Labor hours in inventory	250	750	1,120
External report .... dollar value	$ 167,000	$ 458,500	$ 671,360
Incremental costs for the year			
Material	$ 7,500,000	$ 24,000,000	$ 57,600,000
Labor	250,000	900,000	2,240,000
Overhead	250,000	1,350,000	4,160,000
Production for the year	50,000	150,000	320,000
Labor hours worked for year	12,500	45,000	112,000
Inventory turnover	25	75	64
Total manufacturing costs for the year*	$102,487,500		

*This amount includes all incremental manufacturing costs for material, labor and overhead plus the fixed manufacturing overhead.

Required:

a. Compute the fixed manufacturing overhead cost incurred for the year.

b. Inventory turnover was computed by the company accountant using the units produced and the number of units on hand at year end. Compute the ending inventory in units for each product, and compute the number of labor hours in ending inventory assuming labor hours per unit in ending inventory is the same as the average labor hours per unit produced.

c. If the incremental cost per unit for beginning inventory is the same as the incremental cost per unit produced, what was the fixed overhead per labor hour the accountant used to compute the external cost value of the beginning inventory?

d. Compute the cost of goods sold and the ending inventory the company will report in its external financial statements.

e. Assume the company decides to use LIFO for costing inventory. Compute the cost of goods sold and the ending inventory it will report in its external financial statements.

f. Compute income statements for the company using both the FIFO and LIFO costing methods if the products sell for the following prices

Bucket	$300
Chair	350
Straight	380

and nonmanufacturing costs for the year amount to $50 million. Assume a 40% tax rate when preparing these two income statements.

g. Compute inventory turnovers for both the FIFO and the LIFO costing methods using an average of beginning and ending dollar investment in inventory. Why does your answer differ from the turnover values given in the problem?

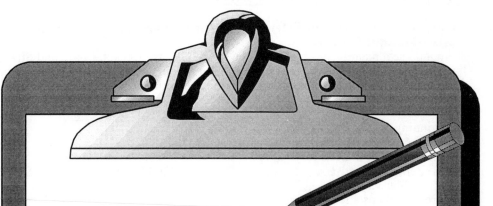

Learning Objectives

After reading this chapter, the student should have an understanding of:

✔   The development of standard costs including their purpose, benefits and the difference between physical standards and dollar standards.

✔   The difference between attainable and perfection standards.

✔   The determination of standards for direct material, direct labor, variable manufacturing overhead and fixed manufacturing overhead.

✔   The selection of an activity level for determining manufacturing overhead rates for inventory valuation for external reports.

✔   The use of normal volume vs. physical capacity and expected activity as the basis for determining manufacturing overhead rates for external reporting.

✔   Building standard costs for products.

✔   Using activity based costing to develop product costs.

STANDARD COST SYSTEMS: SETTING THE STANDARDS

Chapter 8

A standard, as defined by the Oxford English Dictionary, is *a definite level of excellence or a definite degree of quality, viewed as a prescribed object of endeavor or a measure of what is adequate for some purpose*. In management accounting we use the term standard to refer to a predetermined cost or price. The standard serves as a benchmark against which managers can compare actual costs or prices. We review two different approaches to standards: attainable standards, and perfection standards in this chapter. We also review and illustrate a cost system called activity based costing.

▸ Purpose and Benefits of Standards

Cost standards provide managers with a target against which they compare actual costs to identify costs that are out of control. Standards provide managers with a variety of benefits:

1. Control over costs through the identification of variances between actual and standard costs.
2. Informative income statements that identify excess costs as wastes and cost savings as gains.
3. Simplified cost accounting by valuing all inventories at standard.
4. Structured data for planning and special studies.
5. Other benefits including:

    a. The planning required to set up standards.
    b. Enhanced coordination and cooperation by and within all areas.
    c. Pursuit of both total and individual goals.

The first two benefits are obvious because clear identification of deviations from cost targets helps managers to control their operating costs. By attaching a standard cost to every item the company makes and sells, accountants can quickly determine unit costs for sales by just finding the standard cost for the item sold in a cost table. Also, the structure provided by a standard cost system enables accountants to determine quickly the cost data needed for special analyses of operations. For example, the product cost for the water heater element in Chapter 5 arranges data by cost element and by the location in which the cost is incurred so accountants and managers can quickly estimate the cost impact of a change in material or labor costs. Likewise, accountants specify in great detail the precise components of a product when they develop standards and standard costs for a product However, if a company keeps very detailed standards, the cost of maintaining the standard cost system may outweigh the benefits gained from the system. Accountants should always weigh the benefits of the system against its cost.

► Standards v. Standard Costs

Management accountants usually distinguish between standards and standard costs. Standards refer to the physical requirements of the product, such as how many pounds of material or hours of labor and processing time. Standard costs, on the other hand, represent the physical requirements of the products expressed in monetary terms. For instance, suppose a lawn mower manufacturer establishes a standard of eight feet of steel for the mower handle, and the company purchases the steel for $.20 per foot. The standard material for the handle is eight feet, and the standard cost of the handle is $1.60 (8 x $.20).

► Methods of Setting Standards

Companies usually establish standards by conducting a careful study of the quantities of material and units of labor needed to produce the product. Often the technical staffs of a plant such as industrial engineers, design engineers, and chemists have responsibility for setting standards. However, some companies use their production workers to study operations, analyze the work procedures, and to set the standards. In these companies workers use the standards to identify and correct operating problems immediately.

In cases where the technicians set the standards, they must be reviewed with, and approved by, the manager who will work with the standard. Unless the manager has input in setting a standard he or she may not work to attain that standard. After operating workers or technicians set the standards the accountants convert them into standard costs. In some operations which do not have technical personnel to set standards, managers use past experience modified by their judgment to set the standards. Sometimes accountants merely establish the standard costs based on past actual costs, but this has the disadvantage of building past inefficiencies into the cost standards.

► Types of Standards

Among the many approaches companies use to set standards, two common types are: (1) attainable standards, and (2) perfection standards. Companies use attainable standards for both cost control and for standard costs, while companies use perfection standards primarily for cost control alone. Also, some companies set perfection standards at a level that allows for zero waste, thus reminding workers and managers of how far the operations are from perfection.

► ATTAINABLE STANDARDS ◄

Attainable standards represent the cost the company should experience under efficient operation of existing facilities using specified materials. The attainable standard makes no allowance for inefficiencies which are expected during the period; inefficiencies arise from factors such as labor utilization, unbalanced volume, inadequate labor supply, inadequate supplies of standard materials, rearrangement of facilities, construction work, major maintenance programs, etc. The standards reflect the cost level expected for *efficient* operation in the period to which they apply. Managers set the standards at the beginning of an accounting period, usually a year, and use them to measure performance throughout the period.

However, some plants keep their standards for long periods of time. These companies make changes in standards only when they make major changes in production facilities or product specifications. Accountants call these standards *basic standards*. Some managers object to this type of standard because it creates a system in which deviations from standard are expected, so the cost variances generated by the accounting system have ambiguous meaning.

Still other plants change their standards often during an accounting period to reflect changes in production or product specifications. This constant use of current standards provides an excellent measurement of production efficiency but makes it difficult to compare operations at various times during the period. Also, cost reductions implemented during the period do not appear as favorable cost variances because of the immediate change in the standard for any operating improvement. This tends to dampen the enthusiasm of the organization because the members do not have the results of their efforts reflected during the remainder of the period as gains against the standards.

▸ Direct Materials Standards

Attainable direct materials standards are based on the type and quantity of material managers use to produce a finished product. In the first step chemists or engineers establish the bill of materials that shows the quantities of each material required for a standard lot or batch. They make allowances for normal material losses in initial processing to arrive at the quantity specified in the final bill of materials. Once they have finished developing the bill of materials, it must pass approval by several managers before the bill becomes part of the formal manufacturing system. These data are recorded in a permanent record (see Exhibit 8-1) which shows the required approvals of the standards. The manufacturing control system keeps all the records on bills of materials for all products, and engineers document any changes to a product (new material, change in product shape, or modification in product routing) with an *engineering change order*. Such a document describes the nature of the change, the effective date of implementation, and the product and materials impacted by the change.

The bill of materials is the starting point for the product cost standard. Materials handling personnel may make additional adjustments to the materials to allow for losses that occur outside of actual production. For example, a formula may call for 98 pounds of liquid; however, the material handling department knows that of every 100 pounds purchased two pounds will be lost through spillage. This means the company must purchase 1,000 pounds of liquid for every 980 pounds specified by the formula.

Purchasing personnel usually set the materials unit price standards. They set the prices at the average value expected for the coming year, or some other period if the company does not update standards annually. The company database contains a file of these prices for both purchasing and accounting personnel to use as needed. Accountants take the standard quantities from the bill of materials, adjust for any losses not accounted for in the bill of materials, and multiply them by the standard prices to arrive at the standard material cost for a product.

▸ Direct Labor Standards: Piecework Rates

Development of labor standards depends on how a company calculates employee earnings. If the company bases wage payments on straight piecework rates (i.e., workers are paid a fixed amount for each unit they produce), accountants use these rates as the direct labor standard cost, and unit standards are not required. If the piecework does not enable a worker to earn the minimum wage, the company must make a supplemental payment to bring the worker up to the legal minimum. In these cases, the extra amount appears as a labor cost variance in a manager's report.

▸ Direct Labor Standards: Hourly Rates

In companies that pay an hourly wage, managers use time and motion studies or an average computed from past experience to estimate the amount of time required to perform an operation. The standard times (minutes or hours) allow for things like breaks, worker fatigue, and idle time. Just as

Operation No. _____

Date Issued _____

Date Effective _____

Product _____

Cost Class: Formula ☐   Process Loss ☐   Defect Loss ☐   Scrap Loss ☐

Approval

Supervising Chemist	_____	Date	_____
Plant Controller	_____	Date	_____
Chief Industrial Engineer	_____	Date	_____
General Supervisor	_____	Date	_____
Superintendent	_____	Date	_____
Manager, Quality Control	_____	Date	_____

Exhibit 8-1 *Materials Specification for Standard Cost*

the accountant computed the standard dollar amount of material by multiplying the standard quantity by the standard price, he or she uses the same approach to compute the standard labor cost, i.e., multiply standard labor time by the standard labor rate per hour.

▶ Direct Labor Standards: Individual and Crew Standards

Instead of setting labor standards for an individual as discussed in the preceding paragraph, sometimes accountants set them for a group like a work crew. Accountants use a composite labor rate for the crew to develop the standard labor cost. For example, a fiberboard mill uses a crew to operate its forming machine. The machine tender earns $8.40, the pulp operator $7.60, the wet saw operator $7.20, and the three helpers $6.40 an hour. Summing the hourly wages for all these workers results in a composite rate of $42.40 per hour. The speed of the machine sets the time required to produce 1,000 square feet of fiberboard at 0.45 hours so the standard direct labor cost is $19.08 (.45 x $42.40) per 1,000 square feet.

► Direct Labor Standards: Standards for Quality Incentives

In addition to incentives based on quantity of production, some companies pay an additional bonus based on the quality of the production. This is particularly true in industries where defects that may have been caused in any stage of the production cycle cannot be detected before the final inspection of the goods. For example, acoustical fiberboard used to make acoustical tile is produced in large sheets that are cut, drilled, beveled and painted. Inspection takes place at the dry saw where workers number and record their clock number on each run, so inspectors at the dry saw can review the finished tile and assign defects to the board forming or finishing operations. Workers in the board forming and finishing operations receive bonuses if the percentage of defects charged to them is less than the incentive standard. In this case the standard labor cost of board forming and finishing includes the quality bonus expected for that operation.

► Manufacturing Overhead Standards: General

Accountants choose an approach for developing manufacturing overhead standards depending on whether they want to develop standards for a cost system focused on external reporting or on internal decision making. The external focused cost system concentrates on developing overhead rates like those discussed in Chapter 7, while the internal decision making cost system concentrates on estimating incremental variable overhead costs per unit of overhead (usually labor hours, machine hours, or some other readily available measure). Selection of the overhead unit is no easy task, and determining overhead standards is just as difficult.

Accountants find it much more challenging to develop manufacturing overhead standards than standards for direct materials and direct labor in part because manufacturing overhead is a "catch all" category for every manufacturing cost not included in direct material or direct labor. Overhead groups many factory costs together whose only similarity is that they are not direct material or direct labor. Physical standards exist for very few elements of manufacturing overhead in the same sense that physical standards exist for direct materials and direct labor.

Many companies divide overhead costs into fixed and variable cost categories to help estimate the cost impact of changes in output. A cost system designed for internal decision making must have this information in order to estimate the incremental cost of producing another unit of product. However, many accountants who design cost systems primarily for external reporting also make this distinction. The internal focused cost system uses the variable overhead costs for flexible budget calculations and for computing incremental product cost. The decision oriented system treats fixed costs as a lump sum amount that must be planned and controlled in total. In contrast, the external financial reporting focused cost system also develops an overhead rate for the fixed amounts.

The distinction between fixed and variable overhead is not always clear-cut. For example, the thread used in sewing shoe leather varies with the number of shoes manufactured, as do the screws, nuts, and bolts used in making wheelbarrows. However, are the costs incurred in the plant superintendent's office variable with output? Yes and no. Certain basic duties in the office must be done with or without output, and others are performed only when the rate of output requires them. Salaries of plant personnel do not vary with output, so they are a fixed cost. But what about the salary of a clerk or supervisor who is added because of increased output? The point here, as mentioned in Chapter 3, is that most fixed costs are fixed only for certain volume ranges (often called the *relevant range*[1], and at volumes above that range the cost jumps to a higher level while at volumes below that range, it drops to a lower level. Power costs, for instance, include both a fixed component, which remains stable regardless of output, and another component which varies with equipment usage. Chapter 14 includes extensive discussion of how accountants use data analysis to estimate the fixed and variable portions of overhead costs.

Accountants construct standard rates for manufacturing overhead as they did in earlier chapters; that is, accountants estimate the incremental overhead for decision making, and they estimate the fixed overhead rates for external reporting systems. The only differences in estimating for standard setting are:

1. Accountants use estimates of what manufacturing overhead costs should be rather than estimates what they will be.
2. For fixed overhead rates, accountants use of a level of activity different from the expected volume of activity as discussed in an earlier chapter.

▶ Manufacturing Overhead Standards for External Reporting: Selecting the Activity Level

The following discussion applies to the development of overhead rates for cost systems focused on external reporting requirements. Selecting the right activity level to compute the fixed overhead rate is critical in these systems. The activity level has significance only for the fixed element of overhead cost since variable overhead varies directly with the volume of activity. Accountants consider three different levels of activity when looking at the fixed overhead rate: expected (or budgeted) activity for the year; physical capacity of plant and equipment for the year (reduced by a percentage which represents normal down time); and an average of expected activity over a period of years, which is often called normal volume. The following example illustrates how accountants use each of these levels of activity to estimate a fixed overhead rate. The company in this example has a fixed manufacturing overhead of $960,000.

	Direct Labor	Standard Fixed Manufacturing Overhead	
Level of Activity	Hours	Costs	Rate
Expected Activity	100,000	$960,000	$ 9.60
Physical capacity	120,000	960,000	8.00
Average capacity	90,000	960,000	10.67

Which of the standard overhead rates for fixed overhead should the accountant use, $9.60, $8.00, or $10.67? The rate chosen affects the total unit cost and thus inventory values and cost of goods sold. Accountants debate the appropriateness of the three rates. Some accountants argue for the rate computed from the average activity, since most companies incur fixed overhead with the expectation that they will operate at the expected activity level of the plant in the foreseeable future. For example, managers commit to spend all costs associated with plant, property and equipment (depreciation, insurance, and taxes), so the company can meet expected sales for the next few years. These accountants argue against using physical capacity because managers purchase plant and equipment for their useful lives, not their physical lives. Based on this logic, a useful life calculation seems the most appropriate level of activity for applying the fixed portion of manufacturing overhead to inventory and cost of sales.

---

[1] As indicated in Chapter 3, the relevant range can be different for different fixed costs. Thus there are a whole series of relevant ranges, each one dependent upon the degree to which a cost is fixed.

▸ Manufacturing Overhead Standards: Determining Normal Volume

Choosing the appropriate normal volume for the fixed overhead rate requires accountants to consider a number of factors. For example, accountants must estimate the number of units they expect to sell, but this amount cannot exceed the actual production capacity of the plant. They must also consider cyclical patterns in the industry; that is, they must try to compute a normal volume that averages the highs of the cycle with the lows of the cycle.

Although an average for the total cycle has advantages, accountants are sometimes faced with the prospect of setting a normal volume for a new plant with no history of production. Also, a new plant will often operate below its potential capacity for several years as production increases to meet market demand. In this case, the accountant should use only a portion of the fixed costs to compute the fixed overhead rate. For example, for a plant operating at 65% of capacity the accountant might use 65% of the total fixed cost for computing the fixed overhead rate, and charge the remainder off as an operating expense of the period.

As this discussion illustrates, establishing a normal overhead volume requires the exercise of sound judgement by the accountants. Nonetheless, after establishing normal volumes, accountants convert them into units of production in each productive operation. Exhibit 8-2 illustrates this calculation for a fiberboard plant producing wallboard, roof insulation, and acoustical tile. Accountants make the conversion in reverse order of the flow of production. Managers increase standards for operations that generate scrap, trim, or other process losses, to arrive at their gross production, since accountants measure output in total units processed, whether good or bad. The production of one operation may set the production level of all processes which precede it. In the illustration, the Dry Saws gross production requires the Grinding, Forming, and Drying departments to produce enough so that the Dry Saws department can meet its production goal. Therefore, production of drying, forming, and grinding are all computed on the basis of the gross production going to the dry saws.

After accountants determine the activities of the production operations, they calculate the services needed from service departments at normal volume. Next the accountants estimate the total overhead expected for the normal volume and proceed to compute the overhead. We illustrate these calculations for the finishing and drying operations in Exhibit 8-2.

The normal volume for these two departments is:

Finishing	30,000	square feet
Drying	5,724	hours

Assume the costs the company *should* incur for these departments at normal volume are:

Department	_Variable_	_Fixed_
Finishing	$99,000	$54,000
Drying	34,344	21,465

| | | Normal Sales Volume | | | | | |
	Unit	½ Inch Wallboard	¾ Inch Roof Insulation	¾ Inch Acoustical Tile	Total	Percent of Capacity	Production Capacity
Sales	M sq. ft.	30,400	11,100	28,500	70,000		
Operation:							
522 Shipping	M sq. ft.	30,400	11,100	28,500	70,000		
521 Warehousing	M sq. ft.	30,400	11,100	28,500	70,000	70.0	100,000
422 Finishing:							
Finished production	M sq. ft.			28,500			
Scrap 5% of gross production							
Gross production	M sq. ft.			30,000	30,000	60.0	50,000
420 Preparation:							
Finished production	M sq. ft.	30,400	11,100		41,500		
Scrap 2% gross of production	M sq. ft.						
Gross production	M sq. ft.	31,020	11,327		42,347	84.7	50,000
222 Dry saws:							
Finished production	M sq. ft.	31,020	11,327	30,000	72,347		
Trim 2% of gross production							
Gross production		31,653	11,558	30,612	73,823	73.8	100,000
332 Drying:							
Hours per 1,000 sq. ft.		0.068	0.068	0.091			
Production	Hr.	2,152	786	2,786	5,724	79.5	7,200
331 Forming (same as dryer)	Hr.	2,152	786	2,786	5,724	79.5	7,200
220 Grinding:							
Lb. wood pulp per 1,000 sq. ft.		750	1,100	1,125			
Production	M lb.	23,740	12,714	34,438	70,892	70.9	100,000

Exhibit 8-2 *Normal Volume By Operations*

Then accountants calculate the standard manufacturing overhead rates like this:

	Overhead Expense	Normal Volume	Standard Overhead Rate
Finishing			
Variable overhead rate	$ 99,000	30,000	$ 3.30
Fixed overhead rate	54,000	30,000	1.80
Drying			
Variable overhead rate	34,344	5,724	6.00
Fixed overhead rate	21,465	5,724	3.75

▸ Spoilage Standards

Production personnel set standards for spoilage losses wherever they normally occur. For example, production managers may determine that workers usually lose one yard at the splice when they join two rolls of cloth, so they set this amount as the standard spoilage for this operation. In addition, breaks in the material occur as it runs over the machines, and production personnel estimate this spoilage amount by computing an average of past spoilage. Spoilage occurring after the first operation includes labor and overhead of prior operations in addition to the materials loss, and standard spoilage allowances must include these labor and overhead amounts.

▸ PERFECTION STANDARDS ◂

In contrast to an attainable standard, a perfection standard represents the cost which should result from perfect operation within existing product specifications and with existing equipment. In using these standards, managers assume materials always meet specification limits, no shrinkage or spillage occurs, scrap is zero, equipment always runs perfectly, and workers perform their jobs perfectly. These conditions result in minimum costs. Though difficult to attain, a manager may set these standards as a goal to strive for to become a world class operation. In JIT operations it is not unusual for machines to break down so infrequently that, for practical purposes, one can say they never fail. Here careful attention to quality by suppliers means that defects are just a few parts per million. As unrealistic as it may seem at first glance, perfection standards may make good sense for a world class manufacturer.

▸ Methods of Setting Perfection Standards

Like attainable standards, perfection standards are expressed in appropriate physical units such as work hours, square feet, pounds, gallons, etc. Since perfection standards represent perfect performance, accountants cannot set them based on average past experience. Instead, they use one of the following methods to develop the standard.

Theoretical Mathematical Calculations. This method represents the best basis for a perfection standard because it uses calculations unaffected by existing operations. Accountants get the data for their calculations from materials specifications, machine or equipment designers, design engineers, or from actual observation of the worker, machine, or equipment.

Supervised Tests. Many companies develop prototypes of their products before actually taking the product to production. They even set up prototype production lines in some cases to study the best way to build a product, and they run experiments on actual production lines before beginning full scale production of products. All this prototyping allows engineers to develop estimates of the best possible quantities appropriate for the new product. These estimates form the basis of the perfection standard.

Statistical Analysis. Accountants can use statistical data on past performance to set a standard by using the best performance ever attained as a representation of a perfect operation.

Perfection standards go through the same approval process as attainable standards, and accountants maintain the same records. The only difference between attainable standards and perfection standards is in the methods used to develop them.

▸ BUILDING STANDARD COSTS PER PRODUCT ◂

The standard cost per unit of finished product equals the sum of direct materials, direct labor, variable manufacturing overhead, and fixed manufacturing overhead. Sometimes companies measure output units in quantities such as a thousand square feet. The size of such units depends upon unit cost and usual sales quantities. For example, a manufacturer of picnic tables might build up a standard cost for external reporting for a table as follows:

Materials:
    30 Board feet of finished lumber @ $.60 per board foot . . . . $ 18.00
Labor:
    2 hours of direct labor @ $8.20 per hour 16.40
Variable manufacturing overhead:
    $6.00 per direct labor hour 12.00
Fixed manufacturing overhead:
    $3.20 per direct labor hour 6.40
Total cost per table $52.80

Exhibit 8-3 illustrates a more complicated example of developing a standard cost for external reporting. In this case, the company produces 3/4 inch acoustical tile, the same tile considered in Exhibit 8-2. Note how the company sets standards for warehousing and shipping in both exhibits.

▸ Shrinkage During Production

In some cases shrinkage occurs because of evaporation, spillage, or material adherence to containers. In other cases, like a textile mill, the yards of cloth produced at weaving shrink in washing, bleaching, or dyeing. If this loss is 5 percent, accountants reflect it in the standard product costs as shown in Table 1.

Table 1

	Square Yards	Rate	Cost
Cloth to dyeing	1,000	$ 1.600	$1,600
Dyeing costs			72
Total	1,000	1.672	1,672
Loss at 5%	50		
Dyeing production	950	$ 1.760	$1,672

In some processes, gains occur. For example, linseed oil takes on oxygen from the air when oxidized in the manufacture of a product. Here the weight of the oxidized oil exceeds that of the raw oil, and accountants include this increase in the standard unit cost of oxidized oil. In this case the standard cost of the processed oil is less than the raw material that entered the process!

▸ Spoilage During Production

In setting standard costs, accountants make allowances for spoilage at each operation. For example, in Exhibit 8-3 accountants reduce the units of fiberboard where spoilage occurs. They then divide total cost by the square feet after spoilage loss to create standard cost rates per 1,000 square foot. This provides standard costs by cost elements at every step in the production cycle.

	Quantity	Unit	Material Rate	Material Amount	Labor Rate	Labor Amount	Variable Manufacturing Overhead Rate	Variable Manufacturing Overhead Amount	Total Standard Variable Cost	Fixed Manufacturing Overhead Rate	Fixed Manufacturing Overhead Amount	Total Standard Cost
331 Forming:												
Chest stock—												
ground pulp	1,125	Lb.	0.0315	35.44	0.0156	17.55	0.006	6.75		0.0099	11.14	
Margose	2	Lb.	3.60	7.20								
Rekol	3	Lb.	6.90	20.70								
Labor and manufacturing overhead	0.091	Machine hrs.			31.20	2.84	210.00	19.11		270.00	24.57	
Total	1,000	Sq. ft.		63.34								
332 Drying	0.091	Machine hrs.					90.00	8.19		30.00	2.73	
333 Dry saws	0.091	Machine hrs.			24.00	2.19	6.00	0.55		6.00	0.55	
Total	980	Sq. ft.		63.34		22.58		34.60			38.99	
Trim loss	2%											
To finishing	1,000	Sq. ft.		64.63		23.04		35.31	122.98		39.79	162.77
442 Finishing:												
Paint	2	Gal.	11.70	23.40								
Labor and manufacturing overhead	1,000	Sq. ft.				5.25		2.55			2.10	
Total	1,000	Sq. ft.		88.03		28.29		37.86	154.18		41.89	196.07
Scrap loss	5%											
Packaged	950	Sq. ft.		88.03								
Packaged	1,000	Sq. ft.		92.66		29.78		39.85	162.29		44.09	206.38
Package material	1,000	Sq. ft.		6.30								
521 Warehousing	1,000	Sq. ft.				1.50		0.75			0.99	
Finished goods inventory	1,000	Sq. ft.		98.96		31.28		40.60	170.84		45.08	215.92
522 shipping	1,000	Sq. ft.				1.50		0.99			0.30	
Cost of sales	1,000	Sq. ft.		96.96		32.78		41.59	173.33		45.38	218.71

Exhibit 8-3 Product Standard Cost ¾-Inch 12-by-12-Inch Acoustical Tile

► ACTIVITY BASED COSTING ◄

We now describe activity based costing, a costing method that is enjoying a revival today. Activity based costing attempts to address the allocation of fixed overhead costs to products and processes by using more than one overhead allocation base to assign fixed overhead to products or processes. In our discussion we will focus on the product costing dimension and applications of activity based costing.

► Activity Based Product Costs

To illustrate the essentials of activity based costing, consider the following example. Nursery Machinery, Inc., manufactures equipment used in nurseries to fill flower pots, plant seeds in flower pots or seed trays, and it makes other equipment used by large nurseries to mechanize their operations. Mike Heard, one of the cost accountants at the company, attended a cost accounting conference and sent the following memo to his boss upon his return from the conference.

Memo Describing Activity Based Costing.

To: John Smith
From: Mike Heard
Subject: New Product Costing System

I have just returned from one of the most exciting conferences on cost accounting I have ever attended. Those fellows at Industrial Dynamics sure do know how to run a conference, and the ideas they presented were really on the cutting edge. I never realized before how inaccurate our product costs were; now I know how to compute accurate product costs that really show how much it costs us to make our products.

Speakers at the conference described a cost system called Activity Based Costing (ABC). This system takes all costs incurred in manufacturing a product plus those related costs in engineering, purchasing, and material handling and assigns them to the units produced. This gives an accurate unit cost that we can use for pricing and for deciding how much we really make on the products in our product line.

To illustrate this revolutionary costing system, I have taken one of our products, the Deluxe Pot Filler, and developed a new unit cost using Activity Based Costing.

Deluxe Pot Filler

Material Cost	$ 6,000
Labor cost 200 hours @$10	2,000
Welding operations 40 hours @ $40	1,600
Engineering design 40 hours @ $50	2,000
Material handling 5 hours @ $40	200
Purchasing 5 hours @ $20	100
Inventory storage 100 square feet @ $20/month	
divided by average of 10 units per month	200
Total Unit Cost	$12,100

Computation of Overhead Costs. As his memo illustrates, Mike is enthusiastic about this costing system called ABC. Our discussion of fixed overhead allocation to products in the last chapter focused on the development of a single overhead cost rate for costing products in a cost system focused on external reporting. In contrast, activity based costing uses multiple drivers (a driver is a factor like labor hours used to assign overhead to a product) to assign overhead to products. In the example for the Deluxe Pot Filler, Mike Heard used five different drivers to assign overhead to the product as compared to the single direct labor hour driver used in the past chapter.

To compute the overhead costs associated with the Deluxe Pot Filler, Mike made the following calculations.

It takes 20 hours of time in welding to complete this product, and the total costs of the welding operation were divided by the total welding hours used each month to get the hourly rate of $40.

Total monthly cost of Engineering, including all supplies and equipment costs for Engineering, were divided by the total engineering hours worked each month to get the engineering hourly rate. This rate was then multiplied by the average number of engineering hours each Deluxe Pot Filler requires to derive the engineering cost per unit of this product.

An analysis of the hours worked in Material Handling showed that 5 hours were used on average for each Deluxe Pot Filler manufactured.

Because of the electric motors used on this product, purchasing must spend a significant amount of time supporting the Deluxe, so Mike estimated the average monthly hours purchasing personnel devoted to the Deluxe which he divided by the average number of Deluxes produced each month to arrive at an average of five hours per unit. Dividing the total monthly purchasing cost by the total purchasing hours provided an estimate of $20 per purchasing hour.

▸ Activity Based Costing and Normal Volume

In this example, Mike Heard selected a volume number to divide into the total monthly costs of the departments he used for calculating the overhead for the Deluxe. He faced the same problem in choosing the appropriate volume measure for departments like purchasing or engineering design that accountants face when they attempt to set a normal production level for computing a single overhead rate. Instead of choosing a single normal volume for the overhead rate, accountants using activity based costing must choose a normal volume for each separate overhead factor they use in developing their activity based costing overhead rates. This can turn into a formidable job if the accountant wants to use, say, 200 different drivers.

▸ Activity Based Costing and Cost Accuracy

Advocates of activity based costing claim their calculation methods produce more accurate product costs than an overhead allocation system based on a single driver like direct labor hours. However, since the activity based costing system focuses on cost data for external reporting, it may not be important to have precise values for individual products because external reporting rules require proper matching of total manufacturing costs with sales. It is possible that an activity based costing system may just create more work for the accountant without adding to the value of the firm. However, many companies do appear to be using activity based costing in their operations, so many managers must find it worthwhile.

▸ SUMMARY ◂

This chapter examined the issues accountants must consider in setting cost standards for planning, control, and external financial reporting. Accountants must always remember to weigh the benefits of a standard cost system against the cost of developing and maintaining the system. A cost system with too many detailed standards may cost more than it adds to the value of the firm, but a more aggregate system may pay off handsomely for the company.

In particular this chapter dealt with setting standards, both attainable and perfection standards. We looked at some of the issues accountants must consider when setting standards for materials, labor and manufacturing overhead. We reviewed the setting of both variable and fixed overhead rates and noted the use of the fixed rate for use in developing product costs for external reporting. Accountants also have to deal with spoilage in setting standards, so we discussed some of the issues accountants face in factoring this cost into the standard cost. Finally, we reviewed the topic of activity based costing, a system for assigning overhead to products through the use of multiple overhead allocation bases called drivers.

▸ *QUESTIONS* ◂

8-1. What is the primary difference between a predetermined cost and a standard cost?

8-2. Of what value is the difference between *what costs are and what cost should be?*

8-3. Is it possible that an exemplary system of cost control may be effected through the use of physical standards rather than dollar standards? Explain.

8-4. Comment on the following: "Without clear statements of responsibility and the granting of authority necessary to fulfill responsibility, efforts designed to control costs will ultimately result in failure. Such statements of responsibility and granting of authority must exist for the enterprise as a whole as well as for each and every segment of the enterprise."

8-5. Comment on the following: "The setting of standards is basically an engineering function. Accountants enter into the setting of standards via the testing of standards and the conversion of physical standards into dollar standards. In those cases where accountants set standards on the basis of past actual costs, difficulties are bound to arise."

8-6. Define, distinguish, and discuss the merits and demerits of the following:
  a. Attainable standards.
  b. Perfection standards.

8-7. How is *make-up pay* built into cost standards covering piecework?

8-8. Would there be much incentive in an incentive system which has the level where incentive earnings start equal to a perfection standard? An attainable standard?

8-9. Define and distinguish between:
  a. Variable manufacturing overhead.
  b. Fixed manufacturing overhead.
  c. Direct manufacturing overhead.
  d. Indirect manufacturing overhead.

8-10. Discuss the following: "The fixed cost vs. variable cost distinction is an oversimplification of the economic facts of life. Students and even practitioners of accounting are often misled by this distinction in the sense that the ease with which people speak of fixed and variable costs leads to the false conclusion that fixed and variable costs represent two homogeneous pools of costs. We would all be better off if we spent more time emphasizing the fact that some costs are more or less fixed (or more or less variable) than other costs rather than the fact that costs can be classified into fixed and variable categories."

8-11. What is the *relevant range* and how does it relate to the fixity and variability of various costs?

8-12. Why is it reasonable to consider the use of two or more overhead rates based on the distinction between fixed and variable costs? How might one state a general limitation concerning the number of overhead rates based on varying rates of cost variability and cost fixity?

8-13. Define and distinguish between:
   a. Normal volume
   b. Expected activity
   c. Physical capacity
   d. Average capacity
   e. Expected capacity
   f. Practical capacity
   g. Normal capacity

8-14. Substantiate the following: "If variable costs vary directly with volume of activity, the level of activity used to establish the variable manufacturing overhead rate will not affect the rate."

8-15. Substantiate the following: "Only where costs do not vary directly with the volume of output will the level of activity used to establish the manufacturing overhead rate be of consequence."

8-16. How do the concepts of *physical life* and *useful life* affect the utility of expected activity, average activity, and physical capacity for purposes of developing manufacturing overhead rates?

8-17. Can perfection standards be used as the sole basis of effecting cost control or should they be used in conjunction with attainable standards? Should perfection standards normally be expressed as physical standards or dollar standards?

8-18. How is the allowance for shrinkage of materials reflected in standard costs? The allowance for spoilage?

8-19. How frequently should changes in standards be considered? What are the advantages and disadvantages of changes?

▶ EXERCISES AND PROBLEMS ◀

8-20. Calculating Standard Costs for Materials and Labor.
   A plastics molding company makes brown and white furniture rests. Operations are molding, inspecting, packing, and shipping.
   The standard cost of brown phenolic molding powder is $1.029 per pound and that of white urea molding powder is $1.47 per pound. Controlled tests indicate that the reported weight of powder used at molding operation is 2 percent less than the weight purchased. Specifications at molding are for the usage of 0.48 ounce of powder per furniture rest.
   Operators of the molding presses are paid incentives. Inspectors and packers are paid piecework rates and shippers are paid hourly rates. Labor costs are the same for brown and for white rests.
   The base hourly rate for molding-press operators is $6.30. The base for incentive pay (incentive efficiency level) is ten worker minutes per 100 and the expected efficiency level is eight worker minutes per 100. Gains from production above the incentive base are split 60 percent to the worker and 40 percent to the company.
   Inspectors and packers are paid $0.45 per 100 rests. The hourly rate in the shipping operation is $5.40 and the industrial engineers have set a shipping standard of three worker minutes per 100 rests.

Required:

   a. Calculate the standard materials cost per 100 pieces for both brown and white rests.
   b. Calculate the standard labor cost per 100 rests.

8-21. Building Standard Cost Per Product.

An ice cream manufacturer uses standard costs. The operations up to the hardening rooms are mixing, freezing, and packing.

The standard formula for a batch of mix is milk 600 pounds, cream 240 pounds, and sugar 360 pounds. Flavors are added at the freezing operation where 800 pounds of mix are used per 100 gallons of ice cream produced. Standards include 25 pounds of flavor per 100 gallons of chocolate ice cream and 19.9 pounds of flavor per 100 gallons of strawberry ice cream. Standard material usage prices per pound are milk $0.096, cream $0.24, sugar $0.165, chocolate flavor $0.72, and strawberry flavor $1.20. Package costs are $0.27 per gallon.

Standard labor rates are $0.0582 per pound of formula for mixing, $0.24 per gallon for freezing, and $0.45 per gallon packed for packing.

Standard manufacturing overhead rates as percentages of labor costs are mixing 100 percent, freezing 150 percent, and packing 50 percent.

Of the pounds mixed, 3 percent is lost before freezing. Of the gallons produced at freezing, 2 percent is lost in packing.

Required:

Calculate the total standard cost per 100 gallons of chocolate and strawberry ice cream transferred to the hardening room. (The identity of cost elements need not be retained through the production cycle.)

8-22. Calculating Standard Manufacturing Overhead Rates.

A company has built a new plant with a practical capacity of 1,200,000 units per year, assuming two shifts operating five days per week. Sales budgeted for the first year of operation are 400,000 units and estimated sales are 700,000 in the second year, 800,000 in the third year, 1,000,000 in the fourth year, and 900,000 in the fifth year. There are no major seasonal fluctuations in the industry and production facilities are balanced so that the entire plant can be considered as a unit. It is decided to use 70 percent of practical capacity as normal volume. Fixed overhead costs are budgeted at $500,000 for one shift operations for the first year and are estimated to be $756,000 per year for two shift operations in subsequent years. Variable overhead costs are budgeted at $0.25 per unit of production.

Required:
a. Calculate the standard manufacturing overhead rate for fixed and variable manufacturing overhead.
b. Discuss: Does the activity level selected to apply manufacturing overhead appear to be satisfactory?
c. In January of the second year 60,000 units are produced. With fixed manufacturing overhead of $756,000 per year (applicable uniformly to each month), how much would fixed manufacturing overhead be underapplied or overapplied?
d. What is the cause of the underapplication or overapplication and how might it be treated in the accounting records?

8-23. Calculating Standard Costs for Labor.

Required:

Determine standard labor costs per 100 units under each of the following conditions.

a. The base hourly rate is $9.00. According to a reliable time study, workers can be expected to produce 480 units of products during an eight hour day. Incentive pay starts when workers produce 400 units per day and 90 percent of the earnings above the incentive level is paid to the worker.

b. Add to situation (a) above that a quality incentive is also paid to workers. The expected rate of rejects is 24 per day and a bonus of $0.15 per unit is paid for all rejects under 40 per day. No quality bonus is to be paid any worker not producing at least 400 units per day.

c. A crew of workers operating a singe machine includes the following personnel:

> 1 leader @ $10.50 per hour
> 4 machine operators @ $7.50 per hour
> 2 helpers @ $6.30 per hour
> 1 materials mover @ $6.00 per hour
> 1 lubricator @ $5.70 per hour

Production is set by the speed of the machine which is normally set at 9,600 per day even though maximum speed is 12,000 per day.

8-24. Consideration of Shrinkage, Spoilage, and Weight Increase.

Required:

In each of the following cases, determine the cost per 100 units after consideration of shrinkage, spoilage, or weight increase.

a. Chemicals X and Y are mixed in the proportions of two pounds of X to one pound of Y in order to produce a prescription medicine. X has a standard cost of $0.30 per pound and Y has a standard cost of $0.24 per pound. Evaporation, spillage, and adherence to containers cause a shrinkage of 2 percent for both X and Y before they are put into the process. During processing, another 5 percent shrinkage occurs.

b. Reconsider situation (a) above as a case where instead of a shrinkage during processing, a weight increase of 5 percent occurs.

c. The Gym Suit Co. produces steel gray sweatshirts in large, medium, and small sizes. The fronts and backs of medium size sweatshirts are cut from bolts of material 100 yards long and 24 inches wide. Each bolt yields on the average 100 fronts and 100 backs of which 2 percent are improperly cut and are thus not usable. Another 2 percent are also not usable because of flaws in material. Each bolt of material costs $294.00. Laborers are paid a piece rate of $0.15 per front or back cut (excluding those improperly cut). Manufacturing overhead is applied at a standard rate of 200 percent of direct labor costs. One front and one back make a unit.

8-25. Consideration of Spoiled Units and Seconds.

The Ace Linen Company produces fitted bed sheets for cribs. These sheets are made of white, pink, or blue woven cotton which is produced in 100 yard bolts with 36 inch widths. Bolts of white woven cotton cost $48.00 per bolt and bolts of pink and blue woven cotton cost $52.80 per bolt.

Crib sheets are manufactured in two processes; that is, cutting and sewing. The sheets are cut in 60 inch lengths from each bolt in the cutting process. Then each 60 by 36 inch rectangular sheet is cut again at each corner so that a 5 square inch piece of cloth is removed from each corner. The corners are then sewn together so as to make each sheet fit naturally and comfortably over standard size crib mattress.

A diagram of a cut sheet is shown below. Dotted edges represent cut edges.

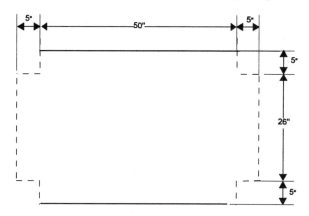

Of the sheets cut from each bolt, two are usually not useable because of either improper cutting or extensive material flaws. These unusable items are detected before the sewing process begins. Of every 100 sheets sewn, 80 are classified as perfects and 20 are classified as seconds. Cutting labor is based on a piece rate system of $0.16 per sheet cut and sewing labor costs are $7.20 per hour with a standard of 40 per hour. The total standard manufacturing overhead rate is 150 percent of direct labor costs. Sale price of seconds is $2.00 per sheet and sale price of perfects is $2.40 per sheet. No price differential exists for colored sheets.

Required:
a. Calculate standard costs per 100 blue, white, and pink sheets. Show total cost as well as labor, material, and manufacturing overhead per 100 sheets and do not segregate seconds and perfects in these calculations.
b. Reapportion costs of perfects and seconds so as to obtain an equal percentage mark-up on each.
c. Discuss the theoretical validity of the cost reapportionment.

8-26. Activity Based Costing and Product Cost.
    Use data from the example Mike Heard developed for the Deluxe Pot Filler in the chapter discussion to work this problem.
    Mike reworked his analysis of the overhead costs for the Deluxe one year later and found he needed to change some of his cost drivers and the unit costs for these drivers.
He developed the following schedule of new amounts.

	Driver Quantity		Driver Unit Cost
Welding operations	45	hours	$ 35
Engineering design	60	hours	50
Material handling	2,000	pounds	15
Purchasing	5	purchase orders	500
Inventory storage	600	square feet	100

Required:

a. Compute the new cost of the Deluxe Pot Filler assuming that materials and labor costs remain the same as in the original calculations.

b. Calculate the new product cost if managers work with their suppliers to reduce purchase orders, and the number of purchase orders per Deluxe drops to one.

c. One of the other accountants at Nursery Machinery, Inc., saw Mike's memo and responded, "I think this activity based costing will be to costly to implement in our company." State whether you agree or disagree with this accountant, and give solid reasons to support your position.

8-27. Building Standard Costs Per Product.

A new product of Elise Toiletries, Inc. is Lano-Lov Skin Lotion, to be sold in 4 ounce bottles at a suggested retail price of $4. Cost and production studies show the following costs:

Container

Item No.	Description	Cost	Comments
2147	4 oz. bottle	$22.00 per gross	Allow for waste and breakage—2%
315	Label	$13.20 per 1,000	Allow for waste and breakage—3%

Raw Materials

Item No.	Description	Cost	Quantity Used Per 125 Gallon Batch
4247	Compound 34A	$160 per 100 lb.	70.0 lb.
3126	Alcohol and glycerin	160 per 100 lb.	76.0 lb.
4136B	Perfume oil*		3.5 lb.

* Perfume oil is mixed by the company according to its secret formula.

Standard costs of a 90 pound batch of perfume oil are as follows:

Ingredients	$8,679.80
Direct labor (4.4 hours @ $9.12 per hour)	40.128
Manufacturing overhead ($30.00 per batch plus $7.80 per standard labor hour)	

Allowance for Lost Material

Overfilling, waste, and breakage—Allow 4% of standard material cost.

Direct Labor Per Gross

Compounding	0.12 hour @ $7.60
Filling and packing	1.00 hour @ $6.40

Manufacturing Overhead

Compounding . . . . $ 12.00 per standard labor hour
Filling and packing . . . . 6.00 per standard labor hour
                                             plus $3.60 per gross

Note: A gallon contains 128 ounces.

Required:

a. Prepare a standard cost sheet for one gross bottles of this product, arranging the data under the five subheadings listed above.

b. During the first week of production, 800 gross were produced. Actual direct labor costs for filling and packing were 780 hours—$5,054.40. Compute the standard direct labor costs for filling and packing, and analyze the difference between actual and standard into identifiable causes.

(AICPA adapted)

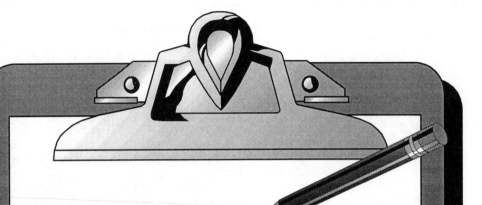

Learning Objectives

After reading this chapter, the student should have an understanding of:

✔ How to compute variances for prices paid and quantities used.

✔ How managers use variances to identify out of control expenses.

✔ How managers can use target costing to spot problems before a product enters production.

✔ How to collect data about competitors to perform cost benchmarking analyses.

✔ The basic accounting entries under standard cost systems.

✔ The disposition or treatment of variances in financial statements.

STANDARD COST SYSTEMS: MANAGEMENT REPORTS, ACCOUNTING PROCEDURES, AND TARGET COSTS

Managers use standard costs to help identify company segments in which costs are out of control, to identify problems with products as engineers design them, and to evaluate current operations against competitors. They use the differences between the standard cost and the actual cost, called a cost variance, to pinpoint specific costs or departments that need attention. The standards serve as a benchmark and help company managers to sift through the detailed information on company operations to focus on parts of the company that need special management attention.

In this chapter we discuss the computation of the cost variances, the manner in which these variances appear in management reports, and the journal entries accountants make to record the variances. We also consider how accountants can use target costs for cost management upstream from the production process, and we review the essentials of competitive benchmarking in the final section of the chapter. We first discuss the variances managers use to control operations and then the variances accountants compute for cost accounting systems with a focus on external reporting. In the chapter discussion we emphasize the use of variances, and we include detailed formulas for their computation in the Appendix to this chapter.

▸ THE BASIC STANDARD COST VARIANCES: A DECISION FOCUS ◂

Managers need answers to two questions from the cost variances:

1. Did we pay too much for a resource?
2. Did we use too much of a resource?

The answer to the first question comes from the price variance, a variance that reflects the difference between the actual price paid for materials, labor, or overhead and the standard cost for the item. To answer the second question, accountants compute the difference between the standard cost for the actual quantity used and the standard cost for the standard quantity to measure a usage variance. Consider the following example of these variances for lumber (1 x 12) a furniture company uses.

This company purchases 1 x 12 lumber in eight foot pieces to make tables, and accountants use a standard purchase price for the lumber of $2 per piece. The company purchased 500 pieces during the last month for a total cost of $1,200. Engineers established a standard quantity for each table of four pieces of lumber, and the company produced 100 tables last month. A check of the company records indicates the materials storeroom issued 410 pieces of lumber to production. The plant manager wants to know whether he paid too much for lumber and whether he used too much lumber to make tables last month. The following calculations answer his questions.

Did I pay too much for the lumber last month?

Standard cost for material purchased (500 pieces x $2)	$ 1,000
Actual cost of material purchased	1,200
Purchase Price variance (unfavorable)	$ (200)[1]

Did I use too much lumber last month?

Standard cost for standard quantity allowed for actual production ($2 x (100 tables x 4))	$ 800
Standard cost for actual quantity used (410 x $2)	820
Quantity variance (unfavorable)	$ (20)[2]

In this example, the answer to both the manger's questions is yes. The plant purchasing personnel paid $200 too much for the lumber purchased, and the operations used $20 too much lumber to make tables during the month.

▸ Variance Terminology

The previous example illustrated price and usage (quantity) variances for raw materials. Accountants compute similar variances for labor and overhead, but they use different terminology to describe these standard cost variances. They describe labor variances as:

Labor rate variance — the amount the actual total wages differ from the total standard wages.

Labor efficiency variance — the amount the total standard cost for the standard labor hours differs from the standard cost for the actual labor hours worked.

Accountants describe the overhead variances as:

Overhead spending variance — the amount actual overhead expenses differs from the standard overhead cost.

Overhead efficiency variance — the amount standard overhead cost differs from the overhead cost allowed for the overhead units (usually direct labor hours) actually used.

Accountants compute the labor variance and the material variance in the same way; only the names of the variances differ. The overhead variance differs slightly in its calculation because fixed costs must enter into the calculation, but this makes little difference to the basic calculation. Regardless of the complexity of the variance calculation, the resulting number still just helps a manager answer one of these two questions:

1. Did we pay too much for a resource?
2. Did we use too much of a resource?

---

[1] See the Appendix for another approach to computation of this variance.
[2] See the Appendix for an alternative computational method for this variance.

▸ Standard Cost Reports

We illustrate variance calculations and variance reporting for The Table Cutting Department of a furniture plant that makes a variety of products. The Table Cutting Department cuts lumber and shapes pieces of wood that are assembled into complete tables in a later department. The following data (Exhibit 9-1) list the standards company accountants have established for this department. As noted in earlier chapters, the reports for managers usually include only the costs they directly impact with their decisions. The standard cost variance reports follow this rule; consequently, all the items listed in the report for the Table Cutting Department manager apply to costs the manager of this department controls.

Standards

Material standards:	1 x 12	32 feet	@	.70 per foot
	2 x 4	30 feet	@	$0.40 per foot
Labor standards:		.5 hours	@	$5.00 per hour

Overhead standards:

	Variable Rate per Labor Hour	Fixed Amount per Month
Scrap	$ 0.05	$ 1,270
Indirect labor	0.10	850
Maintenance	1.50	1,200
Supplies	0.25	540
Supervision		2,940
	$ 1.90	$ 6,800

Actual Results

Units produced	1,650
Materials charged to department	
1 x 12 Lumber	$41,250
2 x 4 Lumber	$19,000
Labor costs	$ 4,455
Direct Labor Hours	860
Actual Overhead Expenses	
Scrap	$ 2,100
Indirect labor	1,400
Maintenance	7,590
Supplies	2,150
Supervision	2,940
	$16,180

Exhibit 9-1 *Cost Standards for Table Cutting and Actual Results for the Month*

Accountants use these data on standards and actual costs to generate the following report for Gene Kramer, the manager of the Table Cutting Department (Exhibit 9-2).

Supervisor: Gene Kramer
Period: July 20XX

Account	Budget	Actual	Variance
Materials usage variances			
Lumber 1 x 12	$ 36,960	$ 41,250	$ (4,290)
Lumber 2 x 4	19,800	19,000	800
Total Material Variance	$ 56,760	$ 60,250	$ (3,490)
Labor rate variance	$ 4,300	$ 4,455	$ (155)
Labor efficiency variance	4,125	4,300	(175)
Total Labor Variances			$ (330)
Overhead variances			
Overhead spending variances			
Scrap	$ 1,313	$ 2,100	$ (787)
Indirect labor	936	1,400	(464)
Maintenance	2,490	7,590	(5,100)
Supplies	755	2,150	(1,395)
Supervision	2,940	2,940	
Total spending	$ 8,434	$ 16,180	$ (7,746)
Overhead efficiency variance	$ 8,368	$ 8,434	(67)
Total Overhead Variance			$ (7,813)
Total Variances for Department			$ (11,633)

Exhibit 9-2 *Standard Cost Variance Report Table Cutting Department for the Month Ended July 31, 20XX*

Notice the report shows both a price and a quantity variance for each expense element in this report except for materials. Only the materials quantity variance appears in this report because the manager of the Table Cutting Department does not purchase his or her materials. The Purchasing Department buys all the materials the plant uses, and the manager of this department receives a report that shows the purchase price variances for each material he or she purchased during the period. This report shows an overhead spending variance for each overhead expense controlled by Mr. Kramer, but it shows the total overhead efficiency variance as a single number.

Exhibit 9-3 shows the detailed calculations for the variances included in the report for the Table Cutting Department. We suggest the reader rework the variances in the departmental report and compare the answers to the calculations in Exhibit 9-3. The Appendix shows formulas for these variance calculations.

▸ Report Summaries

This report for the Table Cutting Department is summarized in the report for the plant manager so he or she can identify departments with possible cost problems. Exhibit 9-4 shows the departmental report for the plant that includes the Table Cutting Department.

The plant manager can glance at the right column to identify which department has the worst cost problems. The Table Cutting Department immediately stands out, and the plant manager can see that the biggest problem in this department is overhead spending followed by material usage. A

Materials Variances	_1 x 12 Lumber_	_2 x 4 Lumber_
Standard cost calculations		
Total tables produced	1,650	1,650
Standard quantity per table (number of feet)	32	30
Standard cost per foot	$ 0.70	$ 0.40
Standard cost per table	22.40	12.00
Total standard cost for tables produced	$ 36,960	$19,800
Actual material charged to department	41,250	19,000
Variance for materials	$ (4,290)	$ 800

Labor Variances

1. Labor rate variance calculation	
Actual hours worked	860
Standard labor rate per hour	$ 5
Total standard cost for 860 hours	$ 4,300
Actual labor cost charged to Table Cutting	4,455
Labor Rate Variance	$ 155
2. Labor efficiency variance calculation	
Actual number of tables produced	1,650
Standard labor hours per table	0.50
Standard hours for units produced	825
Actual hours worked	860
Standard cost for standard hours (825 x $5)	$ 4,125
Standard cost for actual hours (860 x $5)	4,300
Labor Efficiency Variance	$ (175)

Overhead Variances

1. Overhead spending variance calculations	
Actual labor hours worked in Table Cutting	860
Variable overhead per labor hour for scrap	$ 0.05
Total standard variable overhead	43
Fixed scrap per month	1,270
Standard cost for scrap for the month	$ 1,313
Actual expense charged department for scrap	2,100
Scrap spending variance for the month	$ (787)

The remaining spending variances are computed in the same manner.

2. Overhead efficiency variance	
Actual number of tables produced	1,650
Standard labor hours per table	0.50
Standard hours for units produced	825
Actual hours worked	860
Standard cost for standard hours ((825 x $1.90) + $6,800)	$ 8,368
Standard cost for actual hours ((860 x $1.90) + $6,800)	8,434
Overhead Efficiency Variance	$ (67)

Exhibit 9-3 _Variance Calculations_

phone call to Mr. Kramer quickly reveals that maintenance was the primary cause of the overhead variances with an unfavorable spending variance of $5,100, and the 1 x 12 lumber caused all the problems with materials usage. The plant manager's report guided him or her to the problem department, and a phone call filled in the rest of the details on the problem.

Segment: Plant Manager   Period: July 2000

Department	Material Usage	Labor Rate	Labor Efficiency	Overhead Spending	Overhead Efficiency	Total
Stool cutting department	$ 280	$ (600)	$ (455)	$ 355	$ (315)	$ (735)
Bench cutting department	(1,200)	195	(195)	55	(74)	(1,219)
Table cutting department	(3,490)	(155)	(175)	(7,746)	(67)	(11,633)
Finishing department .	1,796	(443)	(4,125)	347	(900)	(3,325)
Maintenance department				120	(300)	(180)
Total	$ (2,614)	$ (1,003)	$ (4,950)	$ (6,869)	$ (1,655)	$ (17,091)

Exhibit 9-4 *Plant Manager Report Summary of Cost Variances for July*

A review of the bottom row of this report shows the plant manager which factor caused most cost variances during the month. In this case the labor efficiency was way down and the spending on overhead appears to be far too high. Managers should also investigate large and favorable variances for a couple of reasons: 1) Standards may be off. 2) A favorable purchase price variance, for example, could mean low material quality that will cause problems later on. We provide more examples of variance reports in later chapters for a variety of expenses.

▸ Interpretation of Specific Variances

Materials Variances. Companies use materials price variances to identify trends in materials prices. By computing a price variance, a company can immediately see how much its materials costs have risen above or dropped below its target. This enables managers to monitor closely the changes in one of the most significant costs of manufacturing. Materials constitute over 50% of manufacturing cost for the average manufacturing company.

Not only does it allow them to monitor changes in price, but the price variance also allows managers to monitor their suppliers, especially suppliers who are geographically dispersed. For example, a forest products company with operations in the Northwestern and Southeastern parts of the U.S. sorts price variances by supplier. This allows company managers to compare the price performance of suppliers in Arkansas to those in Oregon. It also pinpoints the suppliers providing the best prices, and managers can use this information to bargain with other suppliers.

The materials usage variance allows managers to pinpoint the location in the organization where material waste occurs. By identifying material quantity variances by responsibility center, the managers of a company can locate the source of excess material usage. This ability to identify the location of materials problems enables managers to correct problems before they hurt profits too much.

Labor Variances. Labor costs have declined to a relatively low level over the past 150 years. Labor costs are so small today in many manufacturing companies that some managers have dropped their labor cost variances. For example, Caterpillar no longer does detailed labor cost reporting, nor does Hewlett Packard. For these companies labor is a relatively small part of total expense, and the computation of labor variances in the past did little to improve profits. However, a firm with relatively high labor costs, like a construction company or a clothing manufacturer, will find these variances more worthwhile.

Many manufacturing firms, like Saturn, make production workers salaried employees, and this eliminates the hourly wage. In these cases, accountants do not compute a labor efficiency variance because all workers receive the same monthly salary regardless of the total hours worked. Accountants just compare total amounts paid to the workers to their total monthly salary to compute a labor rate variance.

Overhead Variances. As mentioned in the last chapter, overhead includes such a conglomeration of different items that accountants have a difficult time discussing what overhead expense really means. Overhead variances have this problem too. For overhead items with both fixed and variable components, accountants compute the variable portion and add it to the fixed amount to derive the total standard amount of overhead. They then compare this amount to the actual expense. For fixed expenses, accountants just compare total actual expenditures to the standard fixed amount. Thus, accountants compare actual expenses for items like administrative salaries to the standard fixed amount. Typically these expenses differ from the standard fixed amount only because of overtime pay or because a department has fewer (or more) than its full complement of employees.

Manufacturing overhead expenses are assigned to responsible managers who receive reports like the one illustrated earlier, so overhead cost problems can be quickly isolated and corrected.

▸ Cost Variances and Continuous Improvement

Management reports generated from standards in a continuously improving environment have less value than reports in a stable environment because of the sporadic nature with which improvements tend to occur. For example, suppose Mary Jane has a material standard of $6 for each unit produced on her line; Mary Jane makes improvements reflected in the attainable standard shown in the second column below. Because of some experimentation in making the improvements, her actual costs did not match the attainable standard, and the accounting system used the $6 standard to generate the variances in her report.

Week	Attainable Standard	Actual Cost	Variance From Standard
1	$ 5.75	$ 6.20	$ (0.20)
2	5.75	5.80	0.20
3	5.60	5.95	0.05
4	5.45	5.65	0.35

Since the company updates standards only quarterly, none of these improvements become part of the standards until the end of the next quarter. In the meantime, Mary must puzzle over just what the variances really mean. For instance, if she continuously updated her standards she would find the following variances in her performance report:

Week	Updated Standard	Actual Cost	Variance
1	$ 5.75	$ 6.20	$ (0.45)
2	5.75	5.80	(0.05)
3	5.60	5.95	(0.35)
4	5.45	5.65	(0.20)

In summary, managers in a plant pursuing continuous improvement will receive ambiguous signals from their traditional (not updated) standard cost variance reports. On the other hand, Mary Jane may not like the unfavorable variances revealed in the report with the updated standards. In fact, some companies actively pursuing JIT operations have dropped their variance reports altogether.

▶ STANDARD COST VARIANCES FOR EXTERNAL REPORTING COST SYSTEMS ◀

As noted early in this book, companies may develop cost systems primarily for internal decision making or primarily for external reporting. We now turn to a discussion of the standard cost variances unique to an external reporting focused cost accounting system. Both systems generate the same standard cost variances, except for the fixed overhead variance which does not appear in an internally focused system. Companies that use externally focused cost systems compute two variances for fixed overhead: a budget variance and a volume variance.

▶ Fixed Manufacturing Overhead: Budget Variance

The budget variance describes the difference between the standard fixed overhead expense and the actual expense incurred. For instance, a lunch box manufacturing company budgeted fixed overhead at $800,000 for the year, but it incurred $750,000 in actual fixed overhead expenses. Accountants call the difference of $50,000 between the standard amount of $800,000 and the actual of $750,000 the budget variance. In other words, the budget variance measures the amount the company over- or under-spent on fixed overhead for the year compared to its plans.

▶ Fixed Manufacturing Overhead: Volume Variance

As mentioned in an earlier chapter, whenever a manufacturing company sets a fixed overhead burden rate, it runs the risk that its estimate of projected production will differ from the actual production. These differences between predicted and actual production give rise to the volume variance.

Consider the following example. A company projected it would use 2,000 labor hours during the year and that it would incur $14,000 in fixed overhead. The company uses these amounts to compute a fixed overhead rate of $7 ($14,000 ÷ 2,000 hours) per labor hour. This company worked only 1,860 labor hours during the year (the accountants could not predict perfectly how many hours would be worked), but the actual hours are not as important in computing the volume variance as the standard hours for the company's actual level of output. For the 7,600 units produced, the standard labor time is 1/4 labor hour per unit, or 1900 labor hours.

Normal (or other denominator) level of activity	2,000	hours
Standard hours for actual level of output (7,600 x 1/4 hr. per unit) . .	1,900	hours
Idle hours, or unused capacity	100	hours
Fixed overhead rate	$ 7	
Volume variance	$ 700	Unfavorable

The volume variance comes about for one reason only: operating above or below the output level the accountants used to compute the fixed overhead rate. Whenever the company produces below this output level, accountants define the volume variance as unfavorable. The company must bear the same level of fixed costs, but they are spread over fewer units. On the other hand, if the company operates at a higher level of output, they are able to spread the same amount of fixed expenses over more units, and the volume variance is favorable.

Some companies complicate the calculation of overhead volume variances by adding an extra volume variance for "misused" or "overused" volume. If and only if this variance is considered important, you will need to consider the actual hours worked of 1860. We do not present this variance here because we believe it has little value for managers or accountants.

► BASIC JOURNAL ENTRIES IN STANDARD COST SYSTEMS ◄

Exhibit 9-5 illustrates the flow of costs in a standard cost system designed for external reporting. The four variance accounts on the right side of this exhibit make up the only difference between the accounts for actual and for standard cost systems. Typically accountants compute cost variances as transactions enter the system. For example, in some cases accounting personnel compute cost variances for materials by writing them directly on the face of the invoice before clerks enter the materials purchases into the system; the standard cost goes to the materials account, and the variance goes to the materials variance account.

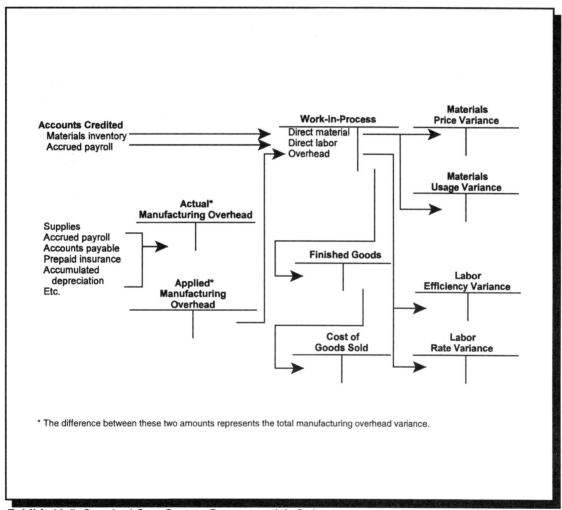

Exhibit 10-5 *Standard Cost System Process or Job Order*

▶ Actual Cost Systems vs. Standard Cost Systems

Accountants use actual costs to record materials used, direct labor accrued, and overhead incurred. They use standard costs to make transfers from work-in-process to finished goods and from finished goods to cost of goods sold. The work-in-process account contains material and labor variances which accountants remove from work-in-process by entries 1b, 1c, 2b, and 2c (see below). A variance account with a debit represents excess costs, whereas one with a credit balance represents cost savings. Study the following comparative journal entries to see how the two systems differ.

	Entry	Actual Cost System	Standard Cost System
1. a.	Record material usage	Dr. Work-in-process 　Cr. Materials inventory	Dr. Work-in-process 　Cr. Materials inventory
b.	Record materials price variance		Dr. or Cr. Materials price variance Dr. or Cr. Work-in-process
c.	Record materials usage variance		Dr. or Cr. Materials usage variance Dr. or Cr. Work-in-process
2. a.	Record accrual of direct labor	Dr. Work-in-process 　Cr. Accrued payroll	Dr. Work-in-process 　Cr. Accrued payroll
b.	Record labor rate variance		Dr. or Cr. Labor rate variance Dr. or Cr. Work-in-process
c.	Record labor efficiency variance		Dr. or Cr. Labor efficiency 　variance Dr. or Cr. Work-in-process
3.	Record incurred manufacturing overhead	Dr. Accrual manufacturing 　overhead 　Cr. Supplies, etc.	Dr. Actual manufacturing 　overhead 　Cr. Supplies, etc.
4.	Record application of manufacturing overhead	Dr. Work-in-process 　Cr. Applied manufacturing 　overhead	Dr. Work-in-process 　Cr. Applied manufacturing 　overhead
5.	Record over- or underapplied manufacturing overhead	Dr. Applied manufacturing 　overhead 　Cr. Actual manufacturing 　overhead Dr. or Cr. Under- over applied 　manufacturing 　overhead	Dr. Applied manufacturing 　overhead 　Cr. Actual manufacturing 　overhead Dr. or Cr. Under- or overapplied 　manufacturing 　overhead
6.	Record completion of goods	Dr. Finished goods 　Cr. Work-in-process	Dr. Finished goods 　Cr. Work-in-process
7.	Record sale of goods	Dr. Cost of goods sold 　Cr. Finished goods	Dr. Cost of goods sold 　Cr. Finished goods

▶ PROCESS STANDARD COSTS ◀

We illustrate the use of standard costs in a process cost system designed for external reporting with the following example. The T-account reports transactions for a single month.

Ending inventory consists of 800 units three-fourths complete for all cost categories, and the standard cost per unit is as follows:

Materials:
    2 pounds At $1.50 per pound . . . . $ 3.00
Labor:
    1 hour at $6.00 per hour 6.00
Variable manufacturing overhead:
    1 hour at $1.95 per hour 1.95
Fixed manufacturing overhead:
    1 hour @ $1.05 per hour 1.05
                                                                      $12.00

Work-in-Process

Beginning inventory:			Transfer to finished goods:	
1,000 units ½ complete as to			2,500 units at a standard	
materials, labor, and overhead			cost of $12.00 per unit	$ 30,000
(at standard cost)	$ 6,000			
Materials put in-process:				
4,900 lbs. used @ $1.35				
per lb. (actual cost)	6,615			
Labor put in-process:				
2,500 actual hrs. @ $5.70				
per hr. (actual cost)	14,250			
Manufacturing overhead:				
2,600 standard hrs.				
applied at a standard				
rate of $3.00 per hr.	7,800	To balance	4,665	
Total	$34,665	Total	$ 34,665	

▸ Ending Work-in-Process and Cost Variances

The balance in the T-account includes both standard costs and cost variances, and we separate these to arrive at a standard cost for ending inventory.

Ending Work-in-Process:

$$800 \ (3/4) \ \$12.00 \quad = \quad \$7,200$$

Materials price variance:

$$(\$1.50 - \$1.35) \quad x \quad 4,900 \quad = \quad \$735 \ favorable$$

Labor rate variance:

$$(\$6.00 - \$5.70) \quad x \quad 2,500 \quad = \quad \$750 \ favorable$$

We must compute the equivalent units of production to determine the standard hours allowed for the work done during the month because standard hours allowed results from multiplying actual units completed by the standard hours per unit. We use the FIFO inventory costing method in this example.

Equivalent Production:

Ending inventory 800 units 3/4 complete	600
Transfer to finished goods	2,500
Total possible production	3,100
Less: Beginning inventory 1,000 units ½ complete	500
Equivalent production	2,600

Materials usage variance:

$$[(2,600 \times 2) - 4,900] \quad x \quad \$1.50 \quad = \quad \$450 \text{ favorable}$$

Labor efficiency variance:

$$[(2,600 \times 1) - 2,500] \quad x \quad \$6.00 \quad = \quad \$600 \text{ favorable}$$

We can verify our calculations by summing the total variances and the ending work-in-process inventory to see whether they agree with the dollar amount required to balance the work-in-process account. In this case all the variances were favorable, so we deduct them from the standard cost of the ending inventory to derive the balancing amount in the account.

Ending work-in-process		$7,200
Less: Favorable variances:		
Materials price	$735	
Labor rate	750	
Materials usage	450	
Labor efficiency	600	2,535
Value to balance the account		$4,665

▸ JOB ORDER STANDARD COSTS ◂

Job order standard costs should be familiar to the reader who covered our earlier chapter on job order costing; in that chapter we were using standard costs without specifically calling the costs standards. Our examples in the job order section of this text illustrated reports in which actual costs were compared to the budgeted dollar amounts for various jobs. These budgeted amounts for jobs are the standard costs of the jobs.

▸ Using Standard Costs in a Job Cost System

Once a company has established standard prices for materials and labor, the company charges these factors to jobs at the standard price. The price variances for materials appear in the reports for the purchasing personnel, and the labor cost variances appear in the departmental managers' reports. As noted earlier, managers may receive detailed reports by job segments, and the reports for each segment will include comparisons of standard costs and actual costs charged to the job segment.

▸ UPSTREAM COST STANDARDS: THE CASE OF TARGET COSTING ◂

Managers must focus on waste prevention during product design if they want to become truly world class manufacturers. Product designers lock in approximately 80% of manufacturing costs by the decisions they make in designing a new product, so managers must consider the impact of design decisions on the profitability of their operations.

Several company functions are directly impacted by design decisions. Purchasing personnel, for example, must negotiate with vendors to acquire the components and materials going into the product, process engineers must design the manufacturing processes to make the product, and marketing personnel must work to sell the product. Smooth and consistent communications among these groups is essential if a company wants to create a product that is easy to manufacture at a low cost and easy to sell because it matches customer needs. Xerox has designed a system that addresses these issues, and the sample report shown below illustrates some of the features of this system.[3]

Moto Mower is designing a lawn mower for which it has developed a target production cost of $96 based on an expected selling price of $120 and a margin of 20%. The company has a system that allows any manager affected by the introduction of this new machine to print a report on demand showing the current projected production cost as compared to the target cost. Jack Wilson, a purchasing manager, printed the report in Exhibit 9-6 on June 24, 20XX.

Part Number	Description	M/B	Supplier	Quote	Type	Target	Variance
127K01540	Housing	1	Moto Mower	25	1	18	(7)
035G52463	Handle—Upper	1	Moto Mower	4	2	3	(1)
035L52463	Handle—Lower	1	Moto Mower	3	2	3	0
253W59871	Wheels	3	Plastics, In	10	4	8	(2)
0897E8531	Engine	3	Big Horse	70	3	64	(6)

Exhibit 9-6 Projected Cost Versus Target Cost June 24, 20XX

The report shows projected cost for each part of the product along with other useful information. For example, the M/B column indicates whether Moto Mower makes or buys the part; a 1 indicates a manufactured part, and a 3 indicates a purchased part. The column labeled "Type" indicates the type of cost estimate or price quote. The higher the number, the more definite the value. For instance, a 1 for a manufactured part indicates a preliminary estimate made by a manufacturing engineer, whereas a 4 indicates the part has been completely specified with exact material and labor estimates. Numbers between these two extremes indicate other degrees of definiteness for the estimate. For a purchased part, a 1 indicates a preliminary quote from a supplier, while a 4 means the company has already signed a contract at the given price.

Thus, the manager who prints this report from the system sees not only current estimated production cost compared to target cost but also information indicating how much faith to place in the estimated production costs. In this example, the project does not look promising because the original estimated selling price for the product was only $120.

Notice how the managers used standards here for a product that exists only as a concept. The standard cost, called a target cost here, represents a goal for the designers to achieve similar to the way managers have used production standards in manufacturing for years as a goal for operations personnel to achieve. Thus, although prepared months, or even years, before a product enters production, the target cost provides a benchmark for company managers much like the standard costs used in operations.

---

[3] This system was described at the National Association of Accountants conference "Cost Accounting for the Nineties" held in September, 1987, in Chicago.

► EXTERNAL COST STANDARDS: COST BENCHMARKING ◄

Some companies use external standards to evaluate their performance. With this approach, managers compare their costs, both product and operating costs, to other firms in the industry. Managers typically use cost benchmarking for mature products with long life cycles because of the time it takes to collect information on competitors. Managers identify the best company in the industry, estimate its unit production costs, and then uses it as the target for cost management decisions. The following hypothetical case illustrates how accountants can develop cost benchmarking information.

Rover, Inc., has identified Markel Manufacturing as the premier firm in its industry and has gathered publicly available information on Markel operations. Markel's cost of sales for last year amounted to $45 million for sales of 45,000 units—20,000 units of Hygrade and 25,000 units of Lowstyle. The company advertises that its 200 employees contribute $9 million annually to the local economy, and one of Rover's accountants heard a Markel manager say in a speech to a local accounting organization that Markel's overhead rate is 200% of direct labor cost. Because Rover purchases castings from one of Markel's suppliers, they know Hygrade castings cost $100 and Lowstyle $75. Rover bought and disassembled the two products; its engineers estimated Hygrade uses 1.5 times the noncasting materials used by Lowstyle. By timing the reassembly of the two products, engineers estimated that total labor cost devoted to Hygrade is double the total labor cost of Lowstyle. With this information Rover prepares the following unit cost estimate for the two products. Company accountants have decided to compute only the variable labor and material costs for the two units and to assume that all overhead costs are fixed.

Estimating Competitor Production Costs

	Hygrade	Lowstyle	Total
Labor Costs (two to one)	$ 6,000,000	$ 3,000,000	$ 9,000,000
Overhead--200% x labor cost	12,000,000	6,000,000	18,000,000
Material cost			
Castings	2,000,000	1,875,000	3,875,000
Total identifiable costs			30,875,000
Cost of sales			45,000,000
Cost of noncasting materials			$ 14,125,000
Assignment of noncasting material			
cost to products			
Hygrade 60%, Lowstyle 40%	$ 8,475,000	$ 5,650,000	$ 14,125,000

Estimate of Material and Labor Costs

	Hygrade	Lowstyle
Material		
Castings	2,000,000	1,875,000
Noncasting material	8,475,000	5,650,000
Labor	6,000,000	3,000,000
Total Material and Labor	16,475,000	10,525,000
Units produced annually	20,000	25,000
Unit Material and Labor	$ 824	$ 421

Exhibit 9-7

In spite of its simplicity, this example captures the essence of cost benchmarking.[4] The accountant gathers all available information about a competitor and deduces from this information the estimated production costs. After estimating the production costs of the competitor ($824 and $421 here), the accountant compares them to the cost of producing similar products in his or her company to identify areas for operating improvements. If the competitor has lower production costs, benchmarking calculations allow a company to identify cost problems before they cause serious competitive problems, i.e., before the competitor takes advantage of its lower production costs to sell the product at a lower price than your company. On the other hand, if a competitive analysis shows your company with lower costs than the competitor, it might indicate you can take market share away from the competitor with lower prices for the product.

▶ Disposition of Variances: Standards Kept Up-to-Date

The disposition of cost variances has significance for external reporting because the matching principle requires accountants to match revenues with the costs that gave rise to the revenues. To illustrate, consider an extreme case where a company sets standards at such a level that, say, one-half its manufacturing costs appear as variances; clearly this company must adjust its accounts and the amount of the variances it reports in its external reports. The auditor would not allow a company to expense inordinately large amounts of its manufacturing costs just because it set standards at the wrong level. Instead, a portion would need to be allocated to balance sheet inventory accounts.

If a company sets its standards at a reasonable level and keeps them up to date, then the variances may be reported as gains or losses in the income statement because the standard costs represent reasonable estimates of the actual costs of the products manufactured and sold. The volume variance may represent an exception to this rule. For example, assume a company suddenly finds itself producing at 120% of capacity because of a sudden increase in demand. In this case, the company will generate a large favorable volume variance that would normally be offset against cost of sales. However, in this case the auditor may require the company to restate its standard costs to include a smaller amount of fixed costs in the ending inventory. In effect, the operation above capacity reduced the fixed costs per unit, and financial reporting rules require companies to recognize this event. When variances and/or inventory levels are large, an alternate approach is to allocate all variances between the income statement and the balance sheet.

▶ Disposition of Variances: Standards Not Kept Up-to-Date

If a company allows its standards to become outdated so they do not reflect current operations, the accountant must analyze the cost variances to determine which represent excess costs or savings and which simply represent a portion of actual costs. Some companies estimate the amount their standards are too low or too high and apply a percentage adjustment to the inventory and cost of sales to compensate for the outdated standards. The reason some companies do not keep their standards up-to-date is the cost of making such revisions. Because it may cost a company thousands of dollars to do a detailed study of all its labor and machine standards, some companies perform these studies less frequently than up-to-date standards would demand.

---

[4] For a more detailed discussion of this process see Lou F Jones, "Competitor Cost Analysis at Caterpillar," Management Accounting (October, 1988), pp. 32-39.

► SUMMARY ◄

In this chapter we reviewed the computation and reporting of variances for management control. These reports help managers to identify trouble spots in the company and to take quick remedial action to bring costs under control. Cost systems that focus on external reporting have fixed overhead variances that arise because accountants cannot predict future levels of output perfectly. Whenever the actual volume of output differs from the predicted output, the system generates a volume variance that accountants must properly charge to cost of sales and/or inventory accounts.

We also considered the application of standards to products in the conception phase by reviewing the concept of target costing for new products. This cost control method develops a cost estimate for product designers that challenges them to create a product the operations personnel can manufacture at the target cost. Finally, we considered how accountants must dispose of variances for external financial reporting.

VARIANCE CALCULATIONS

In the chapter we reported variances for the three major categories of cost: Materials, direct labor, and manufacturing overhead. Here we compute these variances using a unit cost approach whereas in the chapter we worked mostly with total costs. Both approaches give the same answer, but some accountants prefer the calculation approach used here.

▸ Materials Variances

The formulas for computing the two materials variances are:

Purchase price variance	=	*(Standard price - actual price)*	*x*	*Actual quantity*
Materials usage variance	=	*(Standard quantity - Actual quantity)*	*x*	*Standard price*

We illustrate these calculations with the following data.

Materials standards:

Purchase price standard per eight foot piece	2
Standard quantity per table produced (number of pieces)	4
Actual purchases 500 pieces @ $2.40 per eight foot piece	1,200
Finished tables produced	100
Actual material used in production	410 pieces

Price Variance Calculation:

Standard price per unit	$ 2.00
Actual price per unit	2.40
Unfavorable purchase price variance per unit	(0.40)
Number of units purchased	500
Total Purchase Price Variance (Unfavorable)	$ (200)

Material Usage Variance Calculation:

Standard quantity (100 tables x 4 pieces)	400
Actual quantity used	410
Unfavorable variance	(10)
Standard price per piece	$ 2.00
Total Materials Usage Variance	$ (20.00)

▶ Labor Variances

The formulas for computing the two labor variances are:

Labor rate variance	=	**(Standard rate - Actual rate)**	x	**Actual hours**
Labor efficiency variance	=	**(Standard hours - Actual hours)**	x	**Standard hourly rate**

We illustrate these calculations with the following data.

Labor Standards:

Standard wage rate per hour	$ 5.00
Standard quantity of labor per unit produced	0.50
Actual labor cost for 860 hours of work ($5.18 per hour)	$ 4,455.00
Actual number of tables produced during the month	1,650

Labor Rate Variance Calculation:

Standard hourly wage rate	$ 5.00
Actual hourly wage rate	5.18
Amount actual rate exceeds standard rate	(0.18)
Actual hours	860
Labor Rate Variance (Unfavorable)	$ (155)

Labor Efficiency Variance Calculation:

Standard hours (1,650 x .5)	825
Actual hours	860
Amount actual hours exceed standard hours	(35)
Standard hourly rate	5
Labor efficiency variance	$ (175)

▶ Overhead Variances—Decision Focused Cost System

The formulas for overhead variances for a decision focused system are:

Overhead spending variance	=	**((Variable overhead rate x actual hours) +Budgeted fixed overhead)**	-	**Actual overhead cost**
Overhead efficiency variance	=	**(Standard hours - Actual hours)**	x	**Variable overhead rate**

We illustrate these variance calculations below.

Overhead Standards

	Variable Rate per Labor Hour	Fixed Amount per Month
Scrap	$ 0.05	$ 1,270
Indirect labor	0.10	850
Maintenance	1.50	1,200
Supplies	0.25	540
Supervision		2,940
	$ 1.90	$ 6,800

Actual Results

Units produced	1,650
Direct Labor Hours	860

Actual Overhead Expenses

Scrap	$ 2,100
Indirect labor	1,400
Maintenance	7,590
Supplies	2,150
Supervision	2,940
	$16,180

Overhead Spending Variance Calculations

Budgeted overhead cost:

Variable overhead (860 x $1.90)	$1,634	
Budgeted fixed overhead	6,800	$ 8,434
Actual overhead cost		16,180
Overhead spending variance		$ (7,746)

Computation of Overhead Spending Variances for Individual Overhead Expenses

Scrap expenses

Budgeted overhead cost:

Variable overhead (860 x $.05)	$ 43	
Budgeted fixed overhead	1,270	$ 1,313
Actual overhead cost		2,100
Overhead spending variance		$ (787)

Indirect Labor Expenses

Budgeted overhead cost:

Variable overhead (860 x $.10)	$ 86	
Budgeted fixed overhead	850	$ 936
Actual overhead cost		1,400
Overhead spending variance		$ (464)

Maintenance Expenses
　　Budgeted overhead cost:
　　　　Variable overhead (860 x $1.50) . . . .　$1,290
　　　　Budgeted fixed overhead . . . .　 1,200　　　$ 2,490
　　Actual overhead cost . . . .　　　　　　　 7,590
　　Overhead spending variance . . . .　　　　　　$ (5,100)

Supplies Expense
　　Budgeted overhead cost:
　　　　Variable overhead (860 x $.25) . . . .　$ 215
　　　　Budgeted fixed overhead . . . .　　540　　　$　755
　　Actual overhead cost . . . .　　　　　　　 2,150
　　Overhead spending variance . . . .　　　　　　$ (1,395)

Supervision
　　Budgeted overhead cost:
　　　　Variable overhead (860 x $0) . . . .　$　 0
　　　　Budgeted fixed overhead . . . .　 2,940　　　$ 2,940
　　Actual overhead cost . . . .　　　　　　　 2,940
　　Overhead spending variance . . . .　　　　　　$　　 0

Overhead Efficiency Variance Calculations
　　Standard hours (1,650 units x .5) . . . .　　　　　　$　 825
　　Actual hours . . . .　　　　　　　 860
　　Amount actual hours exceed standard . . . .　　　　　　　 (35)
　　Variable overhead rate . . . .　　　　　　$　1.90
　　Overhead efficiency variance . . . .　　　　　　$　 (67)

► QUESTIONS ◄

9-1. How do variance reports help managers to improve the profits of their companies?

9-2. What is indicated by a debit balance in a variance account? A credit balance? A zero balance?

9-3. Name the eight usual variances of standard costing?

9-4. Discuss: "There is no conceptual difference between the direct materials price variance and the direct labor rate variance."

9-5. Discuss: "There is no conceptual difference between the direct materials usage variance and the direct labor efficiency variance."

9-6. Discuss the validity of an efficiency variance for fixed overhead.

9-7. Is it easier and less costly to record transfers to and from inventories under standard costing as opposed to actual costing? Discuss.

9-8. Is it easier and less costly to determine ending inventories under standard costing as opposed to actual costing? Discuss.

9-9. Is there any one point in the double entry process when each specific standard cost variance must be recognized? Discuss and include in your discussion the possibility of a best point for recognizing each specific variance.

9-10. Under process standard costs, is it necessary to calculate equivalent units in order to determine materials price and labor rate variances? Materials usage and labor efficiency variances.

9-11. Discuss: "To apply standard costs to job orders is a very costly procedure since standards must be developed for many more operations and sequences than under process standard costs."

9-12. How can target costs help managers to control costs if these costs apply to products that do not even exist yet?

9-13. What problems can a manager experience with standard cost variance reports if the manager continuously improves operations?

9-14. What disposition should be made of variances if the standards used for recording general ledger entries have been kept up-to-date?

9-15. What disposition should be made of a volume variance when normal volume is use as the activity level?

9-16. Only the budget variance for fixed manufacturing overhead differs when using varying volume levels to set up the fixed manufacturing overhead rate. Discuss.

► EXERCISES AND PROBLEMS ◄

9-17. Calculating Variances.

Assume the following data concerns one year:

Actual Manufacturing Costs		Standard Manufacturing Cost Allowed	
Materials		Materials	
(1,000 lbs. @ $6.00) . . .	$ 6,000	(1,100 lbs. @ $5.90)	$ 6,490
Labor		Labor	
(3,200 hrs. @ $6.00) . . .	19,200	(3,250 hrs. @ $6.30)	20,475
Variable overhead	4,100	Variable overhead	
		(3,250 hrs. @ $1.20)	3,900
Fixed overhead	4,200	Fixed overhead	
		(3,250 hrs. @ $1.20)	3,900
	$33,500		$34,765

Standard costs allowed were based upon actual production of 500 units with standard hours of 6.5 per unit and standard materials of 2.2 lbs. per unit. Actual purchases of materials were 1,200 lbs. @ $6.00 per lb.

Required:

a. Calculate price and efficiency variances for materials, labor, and variable overhead costs.
b. Calculate budget, efficiency, and volume variances for fixed overhead costs (hours of capacity for the year are 3,400).
c. Total up the nine variances to see if they equal the difference between actual and standard costs (34,765 - 33,500 = 1,265).
d. Discuss the efficacy of efficiency variances for fixed overhead.

9-18. Departmental cost variance report.

A furniture manufacturer provides you with the following information about cost standards and actual results for operations for the past month.

Cost Standards for Stool Cutting and Actual Results for the Month

Standards
Material standards: 4 feet @ $.70 per foot
Labor standards: .2 hours @ $6.50 per hour
Overhead standards:

	Variable Rate per Labor Hour	Fixed Amount per Month
Supervision	0.00	$ 890
Supplies	3.00	800
Maintenance	1.50	300
Depreciation	0.00	1,610
	$4.50	$ 3,600

Actual Results

Units produced	2,600
Materials charged to Stool Cutting Department .	$ 7,000
Labor costs	4,435
Direct Labor Hours	590
Actual Overhead Expenses	
Supervision	$ 890
Supplies	2,400
Maintenance	1,000
Depreciation	1,610
	$ 5,900

Required:

a. Prepare a departmental performance report for the manager of the Stool Cutting Department for the month just ended.

b. Which expenses appear to be out of control, and which expenses appear to be well under control. Give reasons for your answer.

9-19. Interpretation of cost variance report.

Shown below is a budget report for a department in your company.

Company Name: Another Megacrisis
Department: Metal Working
Period: July
Supervisor: Lay Turner

Account	Budget	Actual	Variance
Materials Variances			
Sheet Steel Number 12	$ 42,350	$ 44,150	$ (1,800)
Coiled Steel Number 9	19,200	19,000	200
Total Material Variance	61,550	63,150	$ (1,600)

Labor Variances

Labor rate variance	4,300	4,955	(655)
Labor efficiency variance	4,125	4,300	(175)
Total Labor Variance			$ (830)

Overhead Variances

Overhead spending	9,356	16,180	(6,824)
Overhead efficiency variance ..	8,367	9,356	(67)
Total Overhead Variances			$ (6,891)
Total Departmental Variances .			$ (9,321)

Required:

Answer the following questions using the above data.

a. Which material seems to be causing the greatest problems?
b. How many excess feet of Sheet Steel Number 12 were used if the standard cost of the steel is $50 per foot?
c. Is labor expense above or below the level managers want it to be, and what caused most of the $830 labor variance?

9-20. Process Costing Journal Entries and Variance Calculations.
The Liquid Refreshment Company produces one product called Upsy Cola which has a standard cost per 100 gallons as follows:

Materials:
30 gallons of X @ $1.20	=	$ 36.00
70 gallons of Y @ $0.15	=	10.50

Labor:
4 hours @ $6.00	=	24.00

Manufacturing overhead:
Variable 4 hours @ $4.50	=	18.00
Fixed 4 hours @ $3.00	=	12.00
		$100.50

Actual results for the year included the following:

Production completed:	950,000 gallons
Direct labor hours:	38,000 @ $6.30 per hour
Purchases:	350,000 gallons of X @ $1.26 per gallon
	750,000 gallons of Y @ $0.15 per gallon
Material usage:	310,000 gallons of X;700,000 gallons of Y
Variable manufacturing overhead:	$165,000
Fixed manufacturing overhead:	$165,000
Capacity:	50,000 direct labor hours

Inventory data for work-in-process:

Beginning: 75,000 gallons, 100 percent complete as to materials and 50 percent complete as to labor or overhead
Ending: 75,000 gallons, 100 percent complete as to materials and 60 percent complete as to labor and overhead

Assume no beginning inventory for materials or finished goods.

Required:

a. Calculate all variances from standard including two for variable overhead and two for fixed overhead. Identify whether variances are favorable or unfavorable.
b. Journalize all general ledger entries for the year. Support all dollar amounts with appropriate calculations.
c. Give three definitions of *capacity* and indicate what impact these definitions could have on the disposition of the volume variance.

9-21. Process Costing Journal Entries and Variance Calculations.
The Amidon Company produces a product with the following standard cost per unit.

Material (2 lbs. @ $15 =)	$ 30
Labor (5 hrs. @ $6 =)	30
Overhead (5 hrs. @ $12 =)	60
	$120

The overhead rate for the year was determined on the basis of the following data:

Fixed overhead	$ 750,000
Variable overhead	2,250,000
Expected output	50,000 units

Actual data for the year were as follows:
1. Purchased 100,000 pounds of material at $14.70 per pound.
2. Labor was obtained at a price of $6.30 per hour.
3. Production completed 37,500 units.
4. 190,000 labor hours.
5. 90,000 pounds of material used.
6. Fixed overhead—$750,000
7. Variable overhead—$1,767,000.

Inventory data:
      Beginning: 1,000 units, 50 percent complete as to material, labor and overhead.
         Ending: 4,000 units, 75 percent complete as to material, labor, and overhead.

Required:

a. Calculate seven variances from cost standards, identify each precisely, and identify whether the variances are favorable or unfavorable.
b. Journalize all general ledger entries for the year.
c. Considering the measure of capacity used, discuss how one might most logically dispose of the volume variance.

9-22. Computation of purchase price variances.

Maxwell, Inc., gave you a copy of the following standard prices that it uses for materials and supplies it purchases from a variety of vendors.

Material and Supplies	Standard Price Per Unit
KR275-625	$ 100
KB350-184	50
FMA015-12	75
FMR015081	40
FMB48S	120

The following purchases were made during the month.

Material Name	Vendor	Quantity	Dollar Amount
KB350-184	Hammersmiths	1,000	$ 50,000
FMA015-12	Georges Supply	500	38,500
FMB48S	Wendell Kriebel	350	47,000
KR275-625	Roger's Mill	900	85,000
KR275-625	Kent Jones, Inc.	600	62,000
FMA015-12	Georges Supply	800	59,000
FMR015081	Hammersmiths	1,200	48,000
KR275-625	Roger's Mill	500	75,555
KB350-184	Kent Jones, Inc.	900	46,000
KR275-625	Wendell Kriebel	200	28,000

Required:

a. Compute the price variances for each material for the past month.
b. Compute the total variances from each vendor. Which vendor generated most of the price variances?
c. Which vendor provides the best price for KR275-625?
d. How would you use this information if you were the manager of this company?

9-23. Continuous Improvement and Cost Variances.

The Galvanizing Department of Wash Tub, Inc., through some very clever activities on the part of its manager, was able to produce the same ($800) material usage variance (based on updated standards) each month for a four month period even though the material per unit declined for each of these months.

Information on this department follows:

	Month 1	Month 2	Month 3	Month 4
Units produced	500	600	550	620
Standard material cost/ unit (Updated Standard)	$ 20.00	$ 18.00	$ 16.20	$ 14.58

Because of normal delays in processing paper work, the standard cost for Month 2 was updated simultaneously with the process improvement, but no updates were made in Month 3. In Month 4 the standard was updated, but not all the information made it to the standards department on time, so only the information for Month 3 was incorporated into the standard.

Required:

a. Compute the actual material costs charged to Galvanizing in each of the four months.
b. Compute the variances actually reported to the Galvanizing manager assuming standards were actually updated as described above.
c. Write a memo to the president of Wash Tub, Inc., telling her whether the manager of Galvanizing is doing a good job.
d. How valuable are cost variances in a just in time operation?

9-24. Cost variances and responsibility accounting.
    George Smith stormed into his office and called his plant manager immediately. "What are you guys doing down there in the plant? Your costs are higher than ever, and you told me you were getting things under control." The report that got George so excited is reproduced below.

Plant: Wiggington West
Period: Month Ended June 30, 1990

	Budget	*Actual*	*Variance*
Material	$ 16,000	$ 24,000	$ (8,000)
Labor	32,000	33,500	(1,500)
Overhead	20,000	21,000	(1,000)

The accountant for the company gathered the following information from the company production planning system.

Standard material per unit of finished product	4 pounds
Standard labor time per unit of finished product	2 hours
Actual labor hours used during June	4,100 hours
Actual units produced during June	2,000 units

The accounting system yielded the following information about the standard costs used:

Standard material cost per pound	$ 2
Standard labor rate	8
Variable overhead per labor hour	2
Fixed overhead per month	12,000

Material is charged to production on a first in first out basis using actual cost. The actual cost of the material charged to production for June was $24,000, or $3 per pound. The plant manager has been arguing against this method for several years, but the accountant keeps saying the method is necessary to arrive at the true net income each month.

Required:

a. Use sound responsibility accounting concepts to compute the amount of material cost that should have been charged to the plant manager for the material he used in June.
b. How many pounds too much material did the plant use in June?
c. What dollar amount of the labor variance was due to using too many labor hours in the plant?
d. Based on your answers to the above questions and on any other information you want to use, compute the total variances you would show for the plant for June. Give a justification for your answer.

9-25.   Calculating Variances.

The Dearborn Company manufactures Product X in standard batches of 100 units. A standard cost system is in use. The standard costs for a batch are as follows:

Raw materials (60 lbs. @ $1.35 per lb.)	$ 81.00
Direct labor (36 hrs. @ $6.45 per hr.)	232.20
Overhead (36 hrs. @ $8.25 per hr.)	297.00
	$610.20

Production for April 20x6, amounted to 210 batches. The relevant statistics follow:

Normal output per month	24,000 units
Raw materials used	13,000 lb.
Cost of raw materials used	$ 18,330.00
Direct labor cost	$ 50,371.20
Overhead cost	$ 61,776.00
Average overhead rate per hour	$ 7.80

The management has noted that actual costs per batch deviate somewhat from standard costs per batch.

Required:

Prepare a statement which will contain a detailed explanation of the difference between actual and standard costs.
(AICPA adapted)

9-26.   Revising Standards Costs to Actual Costs.

The Johnson Co. began operations on January 1, 20x6. It manufactures a single product. The company installed a standard cost system, but will adjust all inventories to actual cost for financial statement purposes at the end of the year.

Under its cost system, raw material inventory is maintained at actual cost. Charges made to work-in-process are all made at standard prices. Variance accounts are used into which all variances are entered as they are identified.

One-half of the cost of raw material for each unit is put into production at the beginning of the process and the balance when the processing is about one-third complete.

Standard cost was based on 256,000 direct labor hours with a production of 1,600 units. The standard cost per unit was as follows:

Material (100 lbs. @ $6.00)	$ 600
Direct labor (160 hrs. @ $3.75)	600
Manufacturing overhead (based on labor hrs.—160 @ $0.75)....	120
Total standard cost per unit	$1,320

A summary of the transactions for the year ended December 31, 20x6, shows the following:

Material purchased (180,000 lb. @ $6.60)	$ 1,188,000.00
Direct labor (247,925 hrs. @ $3.90)	966,907.50
Manufacturing overhead	148,755.00
Material issued to production	177,600 lbs.

Units processed:

Units completed and sold	1,000
Units completed and still on hand	500
Units one-half complete	150
Units one-fourth complete	30

Required:

a. Record transactions for the year in T-accounts for raw materials inventory, work-in-process, finished goods, cost of goods sold, manufacturing overhead, and each identifiable variance.

b. Prepare journal entries necessary to adjust accounts to actual costs for material, labor, and manufacturing overhead. Give identifiable supporting calculations showing clearly the method of arriving at each adjustment.

9-27. Income Statement, Variances, Journal Entries.
  The Smith Company uses a standard cost system. The standards are based on a budget for operations at the rate of production anticipated for the current period. The company records in its general ledger, variations in material prices and usage, wage rates, and labor efficiency. Overhead accounts include separate accounts for variations in activity from the projected rate or operations, variations of actual expenses from amounts budgeted, and variations in the level of efficiency of production.
  Standard cost data are as follows:

Materials:

Material A	$3.60	per unit
Material B	7.80	per unit
Direct Labor	6.15	per hour

	Special Widgets		*Deluxe Widgets*	
Finished products (content per unit):				
Material A	12	units	12	units
Material B	6	units	8	units
Direct labor	14	hours	20	hours

The general ledger does not include a finished goods inventory account; costs are transferred directly from work-in-process to cost of sales at the time finished products are sold.

The budget and operating data for the month of August 20x7 are summarized as follows:

Budget:

Projected direct labor hours	9,000
Fixed manufacturing overhead	$ 13,500
Variable manufacturing overhead	$ 40,500
Selling expenses	12,000
Administrative expenses	22,500

Operating data:

Sales:

500 special widgets	$158,100
100 deluxe widgets	49,200

Purchases:

Material A(8,500 units)	$ 29,175
Material B (1,800 units)	16,905

Material requisitions:

	Material A		Material B	
Issues from stores:				
Standard quantity	8,400	units	3,200	units
Over standard	400	units	150	units
Returned to stores	75	units		
Direct labor hours:				
Standard			9,600	hrs.
Actual			10,000	hrs.

Wages paid:

500	hrs. @	$6.30	
8,000	hrs. @	6.00	
1,500	hrs. @	5.70	

Other costs and expenses:

Manufacturing overhead	$ 60,375
Selling	9,750
Administrative	$ 19,380

Required:

a. Prepare journal entries to record operations for the month of August 20x7. Show computations of the amounts used in each journal entry. Raw material purchases are recorded at standard.

b. Prepare an income statement for the month which includes variances as an adjustment to cost of goods sold.

9-28. Target Costs and Automobile Design; Breakeven Calculations.
Detroit Autos has developed the following details on a new vehicle it is creating.

Vehicle System	Responsible Engineer	Target Cost
Engine	Fred Smith	$ 1,500
Brake	Jack Barnes	800
Interior	Jane Burris	650
Body	Mike O'Brien	1,200
Transmission	Mary O'Doul	1,100
Total target cost		$ 5,250

The company sets its target costs as it starts to develop the concept for a new automobile. It estimates the selling price to the dealer for the new vehicle and deducts 30% from this price to arrive at its target cost.

Six months into the development of this new vehicle, the engineers developed cost estimates for their component systems; the accountant on the design team prepared the following report with their estimates.

Vehicle System	Responsible Engineer	Target Cost	Updated Estimate	Cost Variance
Engine	Fred Smith	$1,500	$2,200	-700
Brake	Jack Barnes	800	700	100
Interior	Jane Burns	650	500	150
Body	Mike O'Brien	1,200	1,400	-200
Transmission	Mary O'Doul	1,100	1,500	-400
Total target cost		$5,250	$6,300	($1,050)

Required:

a. Compute the expected selling price for the vehicle to dealers.
b. Which engineer will have the most difficulty meeting the cost target?
c. After reviewing this report, the lead engineer held discussions with purchasing personnel. The purchasing department reviewed possible sources and found a supplier who will supply the steel for the body at a price 20% less than used in the original target cost, and this steel makes up 80% of the body system cost. How much impact will this new information have on the updated cost estimate?
d. Ignore the information in question c to answer this question. The company estimated it would incur annual fixed costs to manufacture this vehicle of $1,200,000. Compute the number of vehicles required to break even under both the original estimate and under the updated estimate.
e. The company expected it could sell 200,000 units of this automobile per year. Consider your answer to question c and explain whether you think the company should continue with this project.

9-29. Target cost reports.

You received the following printout from your cost management system giving you information about projected costs for a computer printer your company is considering making. The M/B codes and the Type codes are the same as those used in the chapter discussion.

Product: Computer Printer

Part Number	Description	M/B	Supplier	Quote	Type	Target	Variance
0325GG160	Plastic Cover	1	Printex	$2	1	$3	$1
0325GH160	Plastic Housing	1	Printex	4	2	4	0
9456PP623	Print head	3	Micro, Inc.	15	1	16	1
9432PP252	Platen	3	Dynaco, Ind.	3	4	3	0
0854GG323	Wiring	1	Printex	6	1	5	(1)
9432PP585	Electronics	3	Micro, Inc.	35	2	27	(8)

Required:

a. How much is the expected cost of producing this printer?
b. What total dollar amount of the expected unit cost is purchased from outside suppliers?
c. Is the estimated cost a relatively firm estimate? Why?
d. Suppose all the numbers in the Type column were the number 4, how would your answer change from that for requirement c?

9-30. Competitive cost benchmarking.

Paul Chaney, plant manager for Jeter Industries, was reviewing his file of clippings on Globetrotter Industries to see if he had enough information to estimate the cost of producing transmissions in their Pittstown plant. Clippings from two local stories in the Pittstown paper follow.

July 7, 1989

Globetrotter announced another successful year at their Pittstown plant. The plant which employs 800 workers contributes $17,200,000 to the local economy each year through its payroll. In addition to making some of the finest automobile transmissions available today, Globetrotter has begun exploring the possibility of moving into snow mobile transmissions, Pete Grainger, manager of the plant told this reporter.

August 15, 1989

Globetrotter shipped over 160,000 transmissions for the year ended June 30, 1989, the company reported today. Globetrotter, one of the world's most advanced manufacturers of automobile transmissions, announced today another successful shipment of goods bound for Japan. This is the second shipment of transmissions to that country, and plant manager Grainger said the company hopes to develop more customers in Japan.

In May the company announced the installation of new heat treating facilities that consume about 80% of the power his heat treating facilities require. He also knows Pittstown uses sophisticated computer controlled milling machines for much of its metal work while Jeter still relies on standalone operator controlled machines.

A local steel casting facility with annual sales of $32,000,000 indicated in its annual report that half its sales go to Pittstown, and the hydraulic pump supplier for Pittstown announced in a recent press release that 20% of its $40,000,000 annual sales go to this plant. Because Pittstown tries to minimize the number of suppliers, these are the only two major suppliers from which it buys materials. In fact, you estimate that these two suppliers handle 90% of Pittstown purchases.

Paul received this information from the accounting reports for the last fiscal year at Jeter Industries.

Easyflow Transmission #4521

Material cost	$ 195
Heat treating	25
Labor cost (12 hrs.)	145
Total cost	$ 365

Required:

a. Compute the labor hours per transmission for the Globetrotter Pittstown plant.
b. Compute the Globetrotter labor cost and compare it to the Jeter labor cost. What does this comparison indicate?
c. Compare Globetrotter material cost to Jeter material cost. Which company has lower material cost?
d. Compute the estimated heat treating cost per transmission for Globetrotter.
e. Contrast Globetrotter and Jeter product costs, and tell Paul Chaney where you think the company should focus its cost management efforts.
f. A customer has approached Jeter Industries with a request for a lower price because Globetrotter has offered to sell them transmissions at a price of $380. Can Globetrotter make any profit at this price? Show computations to support your answer. Could Jeter make any profit at this price?

9-31. Process Standard Costs With Multiple Processes.

The King Process Company manufactures one product, processing it through two processes: No. 1 and No. 2 Standard costs per unit, are as follows:

Process No.1:	
Material X (2 lbs. @ $4.53)	$ 9.06
Labor (½ hr. @ $6.60)	3.30
Overhead (½ hr. @ $4.50)	2.25
Process No. 1 unit cost	$14.61
Process No. 2:	
Material (3 cans of Y @ $6.00)	$18.00
Labor (2 hrs. @ $6.90)	13.80
Overhead (2 hrs. @ $5.25)	10.50
Process No. 2 unit cost	$42.30
Total unit cost:	
2 parts Process No. 1	$29.22
1 part Process No. 2	42.30
Total	$71.52

For Process No. 1, Material X is put in at the start of processing. For Process No.2, Material Y is put in at the end of processing. Process No. 1 output is placed in process at the start of Process No. 2.

Data for March:

1. Units transferred:

   From Process No. 1 to Process No. 2, ...   2,200   lbs.
   From Process No. 2 to finished goods, ...   900   gals.
   From finished goods to cost of goods sold, . . .   600   gals.

2. Materials purchases:

   X, 6,000   lbs.   @ $4.47
   Y, 4,500   cans   @ $6.15

3. Materials used:

   X, 4,600 lbs.
   Y, 3,100 cans

4. Labor costs:

   Process No. 1 . . . .   1,100 @ $6.60
   Process No. 2 . . . .   2,050 @ $6.75

5. Actual manufacturing overhead:

   Process No. 1 . . . . $ 5,100
   Process No. 2 . . . . $ 10,500

6. Inventory data:

	Beginning	Ending
Process No. 1		
Units	200	300
Fraction complete	½	⅓
Process No. 2		
Units	200	300
Fraction complete	½	⅔
Finished Goods		
Units	700	1,000

Required:

a. Calculate all variances for which specific data are available.
b. Enter all transactions for the period in T-accounts for work-in-process No. 1 and work-in-process No.2. Enter actual costs as debits and standard costs as credits. Assume that materials price variances are entered at the point of purchase.
c. Check the variances which show up in the T-accounts with those calculated in (a) above.

(AICPA adapted)

9-32. The Complete Budgetary Process Including Standard Costs.

The Rapids Manufacturing Company had the following trial balance as of January 1, 20x6:

Rapids Manufacturing Company
Trial Balance
January 1, 20x6

Cash	$ 840,000	
Accounts receivable	1,320,000	
Raw material X (70,000 lbs.) .	420,000	
Raw material Y (80,000 gals.)	360,000	
Work-in-process	300,000	
Finished goods (25,200 units) .	1,020,600	
Prepaid insurance	17,400	
Property, plant, and equipment	4,500,000	
Accumulated depreciation		1,650,000
Accounts payable—materials .		840,000
Accrued expenses		390,000
Federal income taxed payable .		720,000
Notes payable—bank		2,400,000
Common stock		2,100,000
Retained earnings		678,000
Total	$8,778,000	$8,778,000

Sales for the coming year were estimated at 150,000 units at $60.00 per unit. The standard cost of each unit of output consisted of the following:

Standard Cost Per Unit

Material:
2 lb. of X @ $6.00	$12.00
2 gal. of Y @ $4.50	9.00

Labor:
1 hr. @ $7.50	7.50

Manufacturing overhead—variable:
1 hr. @ $5.40	5.40

Manufacturing overhead—fixed:
1 hr. @ $6.60	6.60
Total unit cost	$40.50

The company was highly dissatisfied with its inventory levels, except in the case of work-in-process. It was decided to cut all inventories 50 percent by the end of the year except for work-in-process which was to remain stable. Only December purchases of 30,000 pounds of X and 40,000 gallons of Y are to remain unpaid as of the year-end. All purchases are remain unpaid as of the year-end. All purchases are anticipated to be made at standard prices.

One-third (2,500 units) of November sales (7,500 units) and two-thirds (7,000 units) of December sales (10,500 units) are expected to be uncollected as of December 31. Of the accounts collected during each year, 80 percent are normally subject to a cash discount of 2 percent.

The estimated manufacturing overhead for the year is as follows:

Estimated Manufacturing Overhead

Variable:

Indirect labor	$345,000	
Supplies	219,600	
Power	177,360	
Total variable		$ 741,960

Fixed:

Salaries	$331,840	
Depreciation	450,000	
Insurance	54,000	
Property taxed	71,000	
Total fixed		906,840
Total manufacturing overhead . . .		$1,648,800

Selling and administration expenses are estimated as follows for the years activities:

Salaries	$ 735,000
Supplies	54,000
Sales promotion	570,000
Telephone	48,000
Depreciation	120,000
Insurance	12,000
Interest	75,000
Property taxes	27,000
Total	$1,641,000

Accrued expenses at the end of the year are estimated at $33,000 which will include unpaid payroll, supplies, power, etc. Depreciation is, of course, a no-cash item, and all insurance bills amounting to $69,000 will be prepaid.

No variances are expected in the prices of materials, labor, or overhead elements. However, direct labor inefficiency of 10 percent is expected because of the addition of inexperienced workers. This 10 percent variance and any overhead variances are to be treated as additions to cost of goods sold.

The minimum desired cash balance is $840,000. Amounts needed to achieve this minimum can be borrowed from the bank in multiples of $3,000. Amounts in excess of this minimum can be used to repay bank notes in multiples of $3,000. Ignore the possibility of interest expense (for the purpose of simplification).

Required:

a. A budgeted income statement for the year—assume a federal income tax rate of 50 percent.
b. A cash budget for the year, including any changes in bank notes.
c. A budgeted balance sheet as of December 31, 20x6.
d. Calculate the projected return on invested capital.

Note: Before attempting a solution to this problem, the student would be wise to calculate production required, materials required, materials purchases, labor required, and overhead required.

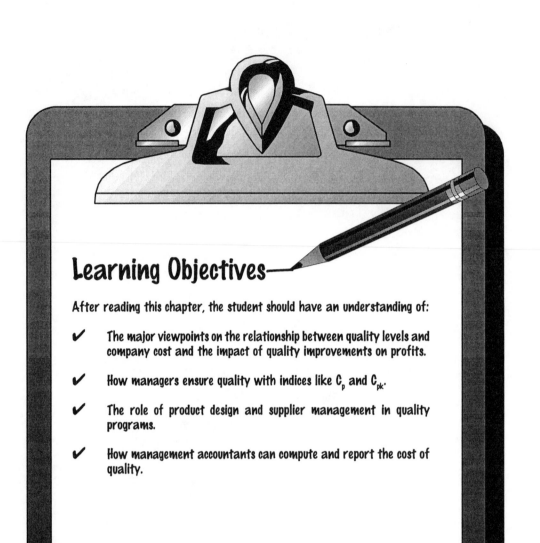

Learning Objectives

After reading this chapter, the student should have an understanding of:

✔ The major viewpoints on the relationship between quality levels and company cost and the impact of quality improvements on profits.

✔ How managers ensure quality with indices like C_p and C_{pk}.

✔ The role of product design and supplier management in quality programs.

✔ How management accountants can compute and report the cost of quality.

$\mathcal{C}$OST ACCOUNTING FOR QUALITY

Chapter
10

...3M cut waste in its production of double-sided industrial tape by 64%, slashed customer complaints by 90%, and boosted production by 57%—all in the past two years. Profits are way up, too.[1]

Modern managers expect their accountants to know how to analyze the impact of quality improvements on company profits, to report the results of quality programs, and to provide advice on measurement systems for quality initiatives. This chapter reviews the relationship between cost and quality, looks at analyses accountants can perform to help managers evaluate quality performance in an organization, and explores cost of quality systems. Although most of the discussion in this chapter will focus on manufacturing operations, organizations like hospitals, universities, banks, and hotels are reaping significant benefits from the application of quality principles to their operations as well.

► COST-QUALITY RELATIONSHIPS ◄

► Improving Quality Increases Cost

Discussants of the relationship of quality and cost may be grouped into three categories.[2] One group argues that quality improvements require total cost increases; this group assumes that quality improvements reflect differences in product attributes that require more expensive components or materials, added labor hours, or more expensive machinery to make the product. Individuals in this group, for example, argue that quality can improve only if the company hires better trained workers who cost more per hour than the existing workers, if it buys higher priced material to reduce scrap rates, or if it replaces its existing machinery with more expensive automated equipment at a major increase in plant asset investment.[3]

---

[1] "Top Products for Less than Top Dollar," *Business Week* (October, 25, 1991), p.66.
[2] Garvin, David A., "What Does 'Product Quality' Really Mean?" *Sloan Management Review* (Fall, 1984), pp. 35-38 covers these issues.
[3] Edmonds, Thomas P., Bori-yi Tsay and Wen-wei Lin, "Analyzing Quality Costs," *Management Accounting* (November, 1989), pp. 25-29. The authors of this article illustrate this point of view by arguing that companies should aim for an optimal level of quality because improving quality too much drives down profits.

▸ *Two Points of View on Cost Versus Quality*

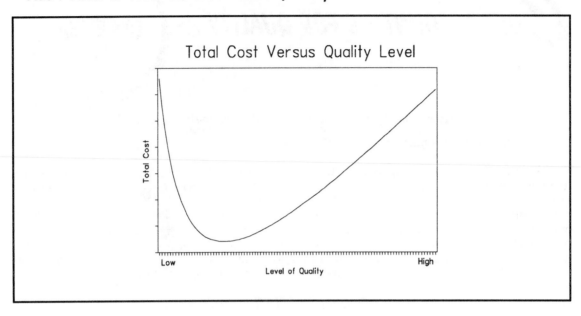

▸ *Improving Quality Reduces Cost*

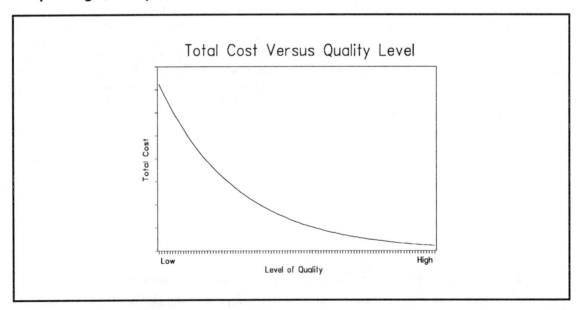

Another group, drawing on an operations perspective, argues that total costs decline as quality improves because the costs of improving quality are lower than the reductions in the cost of scrap, rework, and warranty expense. These individuals argue that the cost of training workers, for example, pales in significance to the reductions in total company cost brought about by eliminating rework and excess inventories. The two graphs above illustrate these two opposing views of quality-cost relationships.

▸ Improving Quality Increases and Then Reduces Cost

A third group argues that quality improvements may increase short-run costs but will lead to long run cost improvements. These managers base their argument on the following kind of reasoning: redesigning a product to make it easier to assemble reduces the number of workers needed for assembly while at the same time reducing assembly defects. Furthermore, consistently delivering a perfectly functioning component to each work station on an assembly line allows workers to spend all their time making good products, thereby continuously improving worker productivity and the company's profitability.

While the debate regarding the relationship between quality and cost has not been resolved, evidence is mounting in support of the last two groups of discussants. The rise in profits for companies like 3M in the quote which opens this chapter appears to be not a coincidence, but rather a direct result of improved quality.

Productivity improvements from high quality can be especially dramatic in non-manufacturing settings. Corning increased the productivity of its engineering group by reducing drawing errors from 35% to a low of .2%; this increase in quality allowed a smaller number of engineers to do more work than the previous group. USAA, an insurance and investment management company, expanded its owned and managed assets over a 22 year period from $200 million to $19 billion (a 95 fold increase) with only a five fold increase in its workforce. USAA ranks almost at the top in surveys of customer satisfaction with their insurance companies.[4]

▸ THE PROFIT IMPACT OF QUALITY ◂

It seems clear that quality impacts both company revenues and costs. But just what are some of the costs impacted by good or bad quality? How should an accountant prepare an analysis of the costs and revenues affected by quality? This section addresses these issues.

▸ Poor Quality and Costs

Poor quality can generate significant costs as the following data from a small chemical plant illustrate.

Annual Costs of Poor Quality at a Chemical Plant[5]

Type of Cost	Annual Amount
Rework	$ 48,804
Scrap	7,594
Retesting	7,100
Processing rejection forms	1,410
Customer complaints	280
Total Costs	$ 65,188

[4] Henkoff, Ronald, "Make Your Office More Productive," Fortune (February 25, 1991), p. 78.
[5] Juran, J. M. and Frank M. Gryna, Jr., *Quality Planning and Analysis: From Product Development through Use* (New York: McGraw-Hill Book Company), 1980, p. 17.

Juran and Gryna also report that a printing company spent $309,000 per year just correcting typographical errors, and that in another company workers spent a total of 75,834 hours per year searching for lost gauges.[6]

The potential for cost reduction from quality activities can be tremendous, as the following quote dramatizes.

> In IBM, there are currently over 400,000 employees; if each one removes defects from his or her work product that save just $1,000 per year, the company would save over $400 million. By contrast, it would take $2.66 billion of additional revenue to generate $400 million in profit.[7]

▸ Profit Improvement at Puryear

Consider the illustrative case of Puryear Lawn Products. Puryear operates a one hundred thousand square foot lawn furniture plant employing 100 employees. Before implementing a quality improvement program, the plant produced 1,000 units per day with a sales value of $30,000 and a material cost of $15,000. Annual warranty cost amounted to $500,000, and scrap and rework totaled $120,000 per year.

The accountant for the company believed that improved quality increases productivity and reduces long-term costs as suggested by the third group in the above section on cost-quality relationships. She estimated that daily output could be increased by 10% with no increase in employees, annual warranty costs could be lowered to $5,000, and yearly scrap and rework could be cut to only $6,000 with the implementation of a quality improvement program. Accordingly, she developed the following analysis to evaluate the quality impact on profits.

Puryear Lawn Products

1. Productivity improvements resulting from increased throughput

Annual sales increase (300 days x 10% x $30,000)	$ 900,000
Materials cost increase (300 days x 10% x $15,000)	450,000
Net profit increase from productivity growth*	450,000

2. Reduction in scrap and rework costs ($120,000-$6,000)   114,000

3. Reduction in warranty costs ($500,000 - $5,000)   495,000
   Annual profit improvement $ 1,059,000

   * Assuming a 6 day week and no increases in processing costs.

▸ Defect Level and Profits

To illustrate the profit impact of moving to zero errors, i.e., perfect quality, consider the following case in which a manager faces a choice between two approaches to quality. One alternative allows a 10% defect rate, while the other allows a zero defect rate. In this case, assume the reduction in defects occurs without added costs by implementing such measures as posting work

---

[6] *Ibid.*
[7] Kane, Edward J., "IBM's Quality Focus on the Business Process," *Quality Progress* (April, 1986), p. 28.

instructions near each work station, rearranging material flow, and giving workers the proper tools to do their work, measures which are virtually costless.

Zero Versus 10% Defect Rate

	10% Defects	Zero Defects
Annual Output	10,000	10,000
People Required	25	20
Storage Space Needed (square feet)	2,000	800
Machinery Investment	$ 55,000	$ 40,000
Software & Hardware	5,000	500
Inventory Investment	275,000	75,000
Annual Costs		
Personnel cost @ $30,000 per employee	$ 750,000	$ 600,000
Charge for Investment in Machinery 15%	8,250	6,000
Charge for Investment in Software & Hwd. 15%	750	75
Inventory Carrying Cost @ 20%	55,000	15,000
Total Annual Costs	$ 814,000	$ 621,075
Annual Cost Difference	$ 192,925	

With the higher defect rate the company must produce more units initially just to cover the defective ones; however, it will soon reach a steady state in which the inventory in rework status provides enough units to compensate for the defective ones. The higher defect rate alternative requires additional personnel to rebuild the defective units, to move the defective units to and from the rework area, and to store and count the inventory in rework status. This alternative also requires the company to purchase equipment like fork lift trucks and storage bins that increase investment, and it requires the company to purchase and maintain computer hardware and software to track all the defective units. Finally, all the additional inventory investment carries an annual cost. The net annual cost difference of $192,925 represents the additional cost the company incurs for producing with a 10% defective rate.

▸ Customer Satisfaction and Quality

Not only does poor quality affect company cost, it also impacts revenue. For example, every time a customer buys a bad product or service, that customer will tell other potential customers of the bad experience, and the result is reduced sales. The following example considers lost sales caused by poor products or services. In this example, managers have estimated the number of customers lost when one customer buys a bad product, an estimate that is admittedly subjective but nonetheless important.

Gulfstream, Inc., manufactures a line of healthy pet foods for the upscale pet food market. The company estimates that for every defective can of pet food it produces (a loose label, a can with a miscolored lid, or a can that fails to open properly for the customer), it loses the sale of five additional cans of pet food. Company managers have estimated the following schedule of unit sales for three months. The first row in the schedule shows the sales if Gulfstream produces perfect product, and the next two lines show the unit sales for two possible defect levels. Unit price amounts to $2 per can, and materials and packaging costs for each unit equal $.50.

	January	February	March	Total
Unit sales—perfect product	20,000	22,000	25,000	67,000
Unit sales—5% defective	15,000	16,500	18,750	50,250
Unit sales—10% defective	10,000	11,000	12,500	33,500

To help managers evaluate the profit impact of these unit sales, the accountant computes the contribution margin for the different defect levels. Since materials and packaging comprise the only variable costs for each can, the contribution margin of $1.50 per can multiplied by the number of cans gives the following schedule of product margins.

	January	February	March	Total
Margin—perfect product	$ 30,000	$ 33,000	$ 37,500	$ 100,500
Margin—5% defective	22,500	24,750	28,125	75,375
Margin—10% defective	15,000	16,500	18,750	50,250

This analysis reveals a $50,250 increase in contribution margin for the three months as the company moves from 10% defects to zero defects. While this analysis has not incorporated any additional costs associated with improved quality systems, it is clear that up to $50,250 can be spent to upgrade quality in these three months without impairing profits even in the short-run. Furthermore, this is before considering any extra costs caused by the poor quality; considering any extra costs associated with poor quality would make the analysis even more compelling for company managers. Analyses like these help managers to assess the profit consequences of alternative levels of quality.

▸ QUALITY MEASUREMENT ◂

Up to this point the discussion has described quality levels in percentage terms, but for the world class organization such measures are too coarse, i.e., not sufficiently demanding. Companies today use parts per million (ppm) to measure quality. In many manufacturing companies the goal is a defect rate of 50 parts per million, i.e., 50 mistakes for every one million opportunities to make a mistake. Motorola has a company goal to achieve a level of approximately 3 parts per million which is the statistical equivalent of 6 standard deviations or sigmas on both sides of the mean. Motorola refers to this as 6 sigma quality. A comparison of the percentage and the ppm measures in the following table helps demonstrate why companies use ppm instead of percentage measures of quality.

	Parts per
Percentage	*Million*
0.001%	10
0.010%	100
0.015%	150
0.100%	1,000
0.150%	1,500
1.000%	10,000
5.000%	50,000
10.000%	100,000

Notice that a 1% defect rate translates into 10,000 parts per million, and 10,000 sounds like a much larger number than 1%. In other words, a ppm measure is a much finer measure than the percentage measure. Companies that already have reached 1 or 2 ppm in their quality efforts are beginning to look at the feasibility of using parts per billion to push the frontier of quality measurement.

▸ Some Quality Measures

Some of the measures that accountants will encounter as they become increasingly involved in quality activities relate to process capabilities, and these are usually represented by indices like C_p or C_{pk}. The C_p index indicates the ability of a process to stay within the upper and lower limits specified by the product designer, and is computed by dividing the difference between the two limits by six standard deviations.

$$Cp = (Upper\ Specification - Lower\ Specification) \div (6\ x\ standard\ deviations)$$

For example, a builder tells a steel fabricator the length of a concrete steel reinforcing rod for a construction project must be 3 feet long plus or minus 1 inch. If the steel fabricator uses a machine that produces bars with a standard deviation in their length of .1 inch, the C_p index is 3.33. That is, the two inch difference between the lower and the upper length divided by six standard deviations equals a C_p of 3.33. The higher the C_p index, the greater the probability that the reinforcing rods will fall within the limits specified by the builder.

The C_p index assumes the average length of the rods produced by the cutting machine equals three feet; however, if the machine produces an average length of 3.2 feet, another measure, C_{pk}, provides a more suitable index of the ability of the cutting machine to produce acceptable rods for the construction job. The C_{pk} index starts with the C_p index and deducts a penalty because the average length of the rods is not three feet. In other words, C_{pk} is C_p - [(specified length - average length) / three standard deviations], or 2.66 = 3.33 - [(3.0 - 3.2) / (3 x .1)]. Always use the absolute value of the difference between the specified length and the average length when doing this calculation. As in the case of C_p, the higher the C_{pk} index, the greater the probability that the reinforcing rods will fall within the limits specified by the builder.

Both these indexes appear frequently in the quality literature, and accountants should develop an intuitive understanding of them to discuss quality issues with operating managers.

▸ Upstream Quality Management

Modern day organizations interested in high quality products and services have eliminated the "checking" activities (activities in which a quality inspector checks to see if the product is acceptable) from their quality departments and have passed these duties down to the workers who produce the product or service. Workers are responsible for inspecting their own work and the work of individuals who pass components to them. However, even with this dispersion of quality responsibility throughout the organization, the workers who create the product or service cannot build a good product from a poor design.

Product Design and Quality. Product design has a significant impact on quality and on the cost of fixing errors. For example, fixing errors during the product design stage costs much less than fixing them after the product reaches production. A software company estimates that it costs $5 to fix a program error during product design, $500 to correct the same error after the product is manufactured, and $1,000 to repair it after a customer buys the product.[8] Corning did a study and found the same

---

[8] Rice, Valerie and John McCreadie, "Credo at Small Companies: Quality Equals Simplicity," *Electronic Business* (October 16, 1989), p. 136.

phenomenon: ". . . at each step of the process, a drafting error became increasingly expensive to correct—$250 if it was caught before the toolmakers cut the tools, $20,000 if it was discovered before the assembly line started running, and as much as $100,000 if it was detected only after the pressings reached the consumer."[9] Progressive companies now devote as much time to quality control during product design activities as they do to quality control after a product reaches production.

Quality Outreach Programs. Not only do progressive companies move their quality efforts upstream of the production process, they also move them outward to their suppliers. For example, the Saturn Corporation in Spring Hill, Tennessee, does no inspection of incoming materials. Instead, they inspect their suppliers operations to see that parts meet specifications, and other auto companies like Honda and Chrysler follow the same process—they push inspection of incoming product to suppliers, and in some cases, to the suppliers of suppliers. Costs of eliminating poor quality continually decline as companies push the efforts further up the supplier chain because fewer and fewer companies have to devote resources to the elimination and correction of bad quality.

► COST OF QUALITY ◄

In spite of efforts to push quality control to suppliers, many companies continue to prepare reports on quality costs. The cost of quality refers to the cost of poor quality, including the costs of scrap, rework, etc. caused by inferior quality. Some companies have elaborate systems for reporting these costs and managers review the reports as they do other cost reports produced within the company.

Other organizations use cost of quality reports as a tool to seize management's attention by showing how much the company is wasting by not producing with higher quality. Precise measures for these costs are not too important, argues Lawrence Carr. He says that numbers that are "roughly right" are more useful than a complex accounting system which tries to be everything to everyone.[10] Regardless of the purpose for which a company uses cost of quality, it usually includes the following four cost categories.

1. **Internal Failure Costs.**

    As the name suggests, these costs occur before the product reaches the customer and include scrap, rework, yield losses, and downtime caused by poor quality.
2. **External Failure Costs.**

    External failure costs occur after the product reaches the customer. Included are the costs of staffing and maintaining a warranty department, the amounts paid to repair defective products, shipping costs, and so forth.
3. **Appraisal Costs.**

    The appraisal costs include all cost incurred by the organization to determine that materials and products meet standards. Most of these costs relate to inspection activities such as incoming material inspection, the cost of testing material on hand to see that it does not deteriorate, and the cost of test equipment maintained to support the inspection activities of the firm. Moving the inspection activities for incoming materials to the suppliers helps to reduce this cost.
4. **Prevention Costs.**

    This last category includes all the costs a company incurs to keep failure and appraisal costs to a minimum. It includes costs like quality planning, review of new products, training workers in quality procedures, quality data acquisition and analysis and quality reporting. Up to a point, the more a company spends on this cost, the less it will spend on the other categories of quality cost.

---

[9] Henkoff, *op. cit.*, p. 78.

[10] Carr, Lawrence P., "Applying Cost of Quality to a Service Business," *Sloan Management Review* (Summer, 1992), pp.72-77.

A typical Quality Cost Report might look like the one shown below.[11]

	Current Month
Prevention Costs:	
Quality training	$ 2,000
Reliability Engineering	10,000
Pilot studies	5,000
Systems development	8,000
Total prevention costs	$ 25,000
Appraisal Costs:	
Materials inspection	$ 6,000
Supplies inspection	3,000
Reliability testing	5,000
Laboratory	30,000
Total appraisal costs	$ 44,000
Internal failure costs:	
Scrap	$ 55,000
Repair labor	25,000
Rework labor	35,000
Downtime labor cost	40,000
Total internal failure cost	$ 155,000
External failure	
Warranty department costs	$ 65,000
Field repairs and replacements	45,000
Telephone system costs—800 numbers	15,000
Total external failure cost	$ 125,000
Total quality costs	$ 349,000

Individual quality costs can be major for some companies. For example, Business Week reported in 1982 that as much as 25% of the price of an automobile is caused by poor quality: scrap, rejected parts, inspection and repair and warranty costs.[12] Another example from the automobile industry is provided by Oscar Suris:[13]

> General Motors Corp.'s Saturn subsidiary, scrambling to fix a defect linked to 34 car fires, is recalling every one of the 352,767 vehicles it built before last April 15 in an action that could tarnish its hard-won reputation for superior quality.

> Repairs to the wiring system could cost Saturn as much as $8 million . . . .

These examples may sound extreme, but they illustrate the importance of quality costs in managing a complex organization. Most organizations in today's quality conscious environment

---

[11] Adapted from Roth, Harold P. and Wayne J. Morse, "Let's Help Measure and Report Quality Costs," *Management Accounting* (August, 1983), p. 53.
[12] "Quality: The U.S. Drives to Catch Up," Business Week, (November, 1, 1982) p. 66.
[13] Suris, Oscar, "Recall by Saturn Could Tarnish Its Reputation," The Wall Street Journal (August 11, 1993) p. A3.

should not experience quality costs like those described here, but one still hears stories of multi-million dollar product recalls caused by less than perfect quality.

► SUMMARY ◄

To stay competitive in the modern world, a company must strive for the highest quality in its products and services. The cost of poor quality is too high for a company to ignore its consequences. Dramatic cost reductions flow to the companies with successful quality programs, and stagnation and possible failure await those who ignore the call to build the very best products.

STATISTICAL PROCESS CONTROL CHARTS

Managers often use statistical process control charts to monitor process variability so that operators can make adjustments when a process goes out of control. They are based on the assumption that a certain amount of variation in a process is normal, and, so long as variation remains within the "normal" bounds, operators need make no adjustment. For example, workers would not adjust a machine which cuts concrete reinforcing rods so long as the rods produced by the machine stayed within the normal lengths usually produced by the machine. However, when the machine starts to produce rods longer than normal, a worker makes an adjustment to the machine. Stated another way, workers do not react to every change in the length of the reinforcing rod produced by the machine; they respond to changes in the process that indicate the machine has drifted to the production of rods that are too short or too long.

Statistical process control charts capture this information by having workers sample the output coming off the machine, record the measurements for each sample, and plot the mean and range of each sample on the chart. We illustrate this process with the following data on bale weight samples for a chemical plant that produces polyester fibers for a variety of applications.

Each day workers select one sample of three bales of fiber for weighing, and they plot the average weight and range of weights for each sample on a process control chart. The following data were collected during a two-week period.

Day	Sample Weights		
1	521	520	537
2	542	508	530
3	514	538	519
4	538	530	535
5	522	534	531

6	522	517	532
7	521	506	528
8	515	531	507
9	534	566	547
10	519	514	516

The average and the range for each sample appear to the right of the individual sample data in the following table.

Day	Sample Weights			Average	Range
1	521	520	537	526	17
2	542	508	530	527	34
3	514	538	519	524	24
4	538	530	535	534	8
5	522	534	531	529	12
6	522	517	532	524	15
7	521	506	528	518	22
8	515	531	507	518	24
9	534	566	547	549	32
10	519	514	516	516	5

The Average (X-bar) and Range charts plotted from these data appear below. Managers compute the average for each sample and then plot this average on the X-Bar chart. Notice the upper and lower control limit lines (labeled UCL and LCL) on these graphs. Operating managers establish these limits after carefully gathering data on process variability to determine its inherent variation. They set the limits a certain number of standard deviations (sigmas) from the process mean.

For example, in this case assume managers computed a mean of 525 and a standard deviation of 15 from past data; they set their control limits as two standard deviations from the mean. When setting the control limits, managers take into account factors such as the cost of correcting the process, the degree of control they want to exercise over the process, and the frequency with which they want a worker to adjust the process. Remember the standard deviation of a sample mean equals the process standard deviation divided by the square root of the sample size. In this case the control charts use a sigma of 8.66 (15 / 1.732, the square root of 3).

Notice how the mean bale weight for day nine of the month has exceeded the upper control limit. This tells the manager of this process to review the bale packing process to see if it is producing bales of the proper weight.

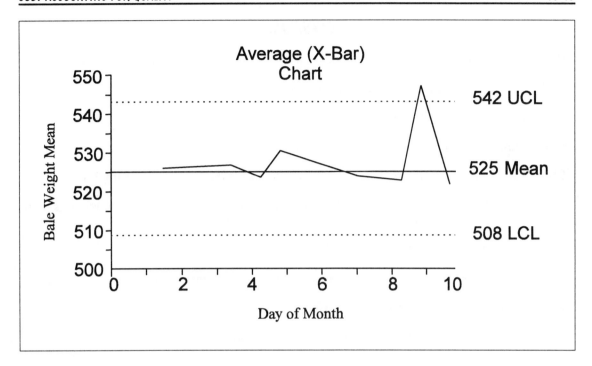

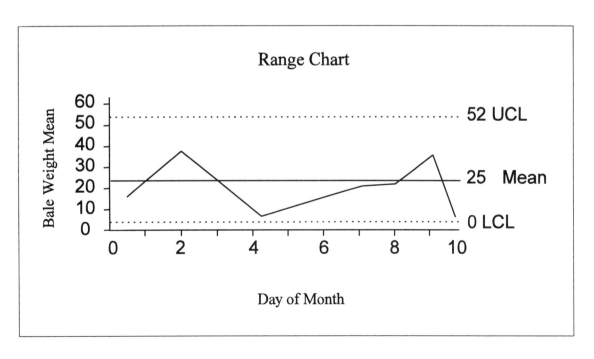

▸ QUESTIONS ◂

10-1. Describe the three schools of thought on the relation between quality and costs.

10-2. What specific kinds of costs does the level of quality affect?

10-3. If a company doubles its quality level what will this likely do to sales and costs?

10-4. Summarize the major arguments about the relationship between cost and quality.

10-5. How can an increase in quality cause costs to decrease? Give some examples.

10-6. If the defect rate for a company that produces lawn mowers goes up, what will this do to personnel costs, work-in-process inventory, and operating costs?

10-7. Explain the quality measurements C_p and C_{pk}.

10-8. Why do companies measure defects in parts per million instead of in percentage terms?

10-9. How do product design decisions affect the quality of manufactured products?

10-10. Name and describe the four categories of quality cost.

10-11. When a company increases its expenditures on prevention costs, what happens to the levels of other quality costs?

10-12. Describe a case of poor quality you encountered in the past. For the organization where you encountered the poor quality experience, estimate the change in its monthly profit if it could deliver perfect quality for every sales transaction.

▸ EXERCISES ◂

10-13. Cost of Quality Reporting.
   Frank Riney was reviewing the following list of expenses and wondering where he could use quality improvements to cut costs and bring his profits back into line with his budget. This list of expenses includes the expenses incurred at his plant for the past month.

Expense	Amount
Rework of defective parts	$ 35,000
Warranty expense	50,000
Freight on incoming material	130,000
Wages—quality inspectors	75,000
Wages—quality circle meetings	5,000
Scrap costs	85,000
Raw material used	11,890,000
Goods returned by customers	120,000
Wages—warranty department	35,000
Wages—incoming inspection of material	25,000
Direct labor	870,000
Depreciation—test equipment	12,000
Repairs on broken dies and tools	45,000
Indirect labor—idle time caused by machine breakdowns	20,000
Utilities expense	150,000
Engineering design expense	320,000
	$ 13,867,000

Required:

a. Compute the cost of internal failures.
b. Compute the cost of external failures.
c. If you were the manager of this plant and you could improve the quality of the products produced, which two costs would you choose as the first two for your quality efforts? Justify your answer.

10-14. Computing the Cost of Poor Quality.

A company produces 2,000,000 units of a product each year, and you have been asked by the president of the company to look into the costs affected by the quality of the products produced.

This company guarantees its products for one year from the date of purchase, and it pays all shipping costs for sending the defective unit to its Chicago repair center (approximately $5) and for sending the repaired unit back to the customer (another $5). This repair center works only on defective units covered by warranty, and you can assume all repairs are done perfectly. The company spends $450,000 each year for wages, rent, supplies, etc., for this repair center. The unit variable cost of each unit produced by the company at its Fort Wayne, Indiana, plant amounts to $40.

Required:

Use the above information to answer each of the following questions. Consider each question separately unless one question specifically refers to another.

a. Assume that one-half the defective units sent to the repair center must be replaced with new units because of defects too serious to repair. Compute the total quality costs the company incurs each year if it has a 10% defect rate.

b. Assume the defect rate changes to 5% and every defective unit can be repaired by the Chicago center. Compute the profit increase the company would experience if it reduced its defect rate to 800 parts per million, closed the Chicago center, and sent a new unit to any customer who had a problem during the warranty period with instructions to throw away the defective unit.

10-15. Cost Impact of Quality Improvements.

Quality impacts the production costs of manufacturing in many ways besides driving up inventory carrying costs. For example, one company estimates that it costs $5 to fix a defect during product design, $500 to fix the same defect after the product is manufactured, and $1,000 to fix it after a customer buys the product.[14] Assume this company produces 50,000 units per year with an error rate of 5,000 ppm.

a. Compute the annual cost the company incurs if management discovers the errors during product design.

b. Compute the annual cost if management discovers the errors after the product is in the hands of the customer.

c. Compute the annual amount the company can spend to improve its process so errors are discovered during product design instead of after they reach the customer without reducing profits below the level they are in question a.

10-16. Product Design and Quality Costs.

Use the information from problem 10-15 to answer this question.

a. Assume the company normally requires eighteen months to develop a new product with an error rate of 500 ppm after the product reaches the customer. Company managers would like to speed up by six months the release of a product now under development to take advantage of an emerging market for the product. They estimate the product will have a life of only 12 months as set out in the schedule below. The schedule also shows the units they predict they can sell each quarter, the selling price, and the unit variable cost.

	Units	Price	Cost
Quarter 1	10,000	$ 2,000	$ 1,000
Quarter 2	25,000	1,500	800
Quarter 3	40,000	1,200	600
Quarter 4	35,000	1,000	500

Managers can speed up product development by six months and release the product at the start of Quarter 1 if they spend $15,000,000 on development and production, or they can spend $10,000,000 on these costs and release the product at the start of quarter 3.

The development team working on the new product estimates it can get the product ready by the beginning of Quarter 1, but the error rate after the product reaches the customer will be an astonishing 100,000 ppm, 200 times the 500 ppm usual error rate.

---

[14] Rice, Valerie and John McCreadie "Credo at Small Companies: Quality Equals Simplicity," *Electronic Business* (October 16, 1989), p. 136.

Team members also say they can beat the normal error rate and introduce the product with a rate of only 200 ppm after the product reaches the customer if management allows them to bring out the product at the start of Quarter 3.

Should management speed up the introduction of the new product? Show calculations in good form to support your answer.

b. Explain why a company should consider improving the quality of the products it makes. In writing your answer consider the situation in question a, and explain what your answer to question a tells you about the issue of product quality.

10-17. Quality Costs and Customer Satisfaction.

Wanton Corporation produces a product that it sells directly to consumers. Company executives have been reading about quality and all the wonderful things it does, and they have asked you to prepare an analysis of the impact of alternative quality levels on the company's profits. You collected data on a popular product that you decided to use for a demonstration of the profit impact of quality.

You expect to sell 10,000 units in year 1, and you predict this quantity will grow at the rate of 30% each year if the company does everything right, i.e., every unit creates a satisfied customer. In other words, the market is growing at 30% per year, and your company will keep its market share if it does everything right. You decide to measure defects by counting the number of units produced and sold each year that result in a dissatisfied customer. In other words, even if the product was manufactured perfectly with no defects, a mistake made by a marketing person that causes an unhappy customer counts as a defect.

You estimate that each unsatisfied customer causes five potential customers to not buy your product. A slowdown in sales not only reduces total units sold, but it also affects the unit production costs. You know from discussions with manufacturing personnel that learning in the production process causes a reduction in the material used to produce each unit made. Thus, the unit cost in the second year is equal to the unit cost of the first year minus the number of units made in the second year times .0001. For example, with perfect quality during the second year the unit cost year is $10-(.0001 x 13,000), or 8.70. You plan to carry no inventory, i.e., you will produce exactly the number of units sold in each year. With a 5% error rate, the unit sales for the first year would be 7,500 units (10,000 - (500 x 5)).

You expect the company to sell 10,000 units in year 1 (if it has perfect quality) at a selling price of $20 and a unit variable cost (basically material cost) of $10. Selling prices expected for years two and three are $18 and $15 respectively.

Required:

Compute the annual contribution margin for each of the three years assuming the following defect levels:

a. Zero defects, i.e., every product sold is perfect.
b. The company produces with an error rate of 50,000 parts per million (5%).
c. Compute the total amount the company can spend to alter its organization to create a company that produces perfect product and not reduce total three year profits below those generated with an error rate of 50,000 parts per million. Ignore present value considerations in this calculation.

10-18. Computation of C_p and C_{pk} Measures.

Your company produces chemicals for use by dry cleaners, and it ships the chemicals in barrels with a specified weight of 500 pounds. Marketing and manufacturing personnel discussed at length the amount of variability a customer would accept in the weight of a barrel, and they decided that so long as each barrel was between 495 and 505 pounds customers would not complain. The standard deviation computed for the barrels shipped last month amounted to three pounds.

a. Compute the C_p index for the barrel weight.

b. Assume that for the past month the average weight of barrels shipped has been 498 pounds. Compute the C_{pk} index for the process.

c. Why do the two indexes differ?

▶ PROBLEMS AND CASES ◀

10-19. Inventory Level and Quality Level.

A consulting firm developed the following schedule depicting the relationships between product quality and various resources used within manufacturing operations. The two columns on the right show an index of how much labor and inventory a company must have on hand for various levels of quality. With perfect quality the index is 100.

For example, at a quality level that produces 10% defects a company must have 130% as much labor as one that produces at a rate of 100 defects per million, and it must carry 150% as much inventory as one that produces 100 defects per million.

Fraction Defective	Labor Index	Inventory Index
.1	130	150
8.00%	126	145
6.00%	121	139
4.00%	115	132
2.00%	108	124
1.00%	102	112
0.10%	101	102
0.01%	100	100

Your boss saw this table and asked you to estimate the value of increasing quality at your company. Your company currently spends $2,600,000 per year on wages, and it carries $15,000,000 in inventory. It also generates ten percent defectives with present operations and has an annual inventory carrying cost estimated at 20%.

Required:

a. Compute the annual profit effect of reducing the defective rate from 10% to 6% if the company incurs an additional annual cost of $50,000 to reduce the fraction defective.

b. Compute the annual labor cost if the company produces product with a defect rate of one hundred parts per million.

c. Compute the total annual cost reduction from current levels if the company can produce with a 1% defect rate.

d. Discuss the types of costs a company incurs as a result of poor quality.

10-20. Customer Service Costs; Elimination of a Department.

Durabond, Inc., believes in taking care of customer complaints quickly and efficiently, so it has created both a Customer Service facility and a Repair facility. The company has a Customer Service staff of six people who operate a telephone center that works with customer warranty problems. The center occupies space the company rents for $3,000 per month, and each worker earns a monthly salary (including fringes) of $2,500. Equipment rental at the center costs another $5,000 each month. The other department, the Repair facility, that rebuilds defective units costs $15,000 per month for salaries, rent, and utilities. The average variable cost of repairing a unit amounts to $1.50.

The company president believes the amount spent on this center is worthwhile because it allows the company to listen to customer complaints, to advise the customer on how to send the defective product back to the company, and to explain why the company cannot fix problems that occur outside the warranty period. In addition, the center prepares detailed reports on the number of customers handled each day, their questions and complaints, and the efficiency with which center personnel handle the customers. "We are in the business of making money, and a satisfied customer is the basis of our profitability" says the company president.

You gathered the following data on defects for the past six months to help you analyze whether the company really is following the most profitable approach to customer complaints.

March	2,250
April	3,150
May	2,465
June	2,350
July	3,100
August	3,220
Total	16,535
Average	2,756

Unit variable manufacturing cost for the product is $12, and average shipping cost to and from a customer is $1 each way. The company reimburses each customer for the cost of returning a defective unit to the company.

Required:

a. Compute the total monthly cost of running the Customer Service center. Exclude shipping costs from this calculation.

b. Compute the average shipping cost per month.

c. The marketing manager wants to change to a system of sending a new product to a customer whenever a problem occurs; the customer would keep the defective product instead of shipping it to the company for repair. Under this system, the Customer Service operation would be abolished, and the repair center would be closed down. Prepare an analysis to see if this alternative makes sense.

10-21. Statistical Process Control Charts.

Operators at a plant that produces hydraulic pumps collected the following data on seal groove depth. Use these data to plot Average and Range charts. The company uses a mean depth of .067 for plotting sample means with an upper control limit of .0677 and a lower control limit of .0663. It uses a mean range of .0012 with an upper control limit of .0024 and a lower control limit of 0.

Sample#	Sample Values in Thousandths				
1	67	67	68	67	67
2	68	68	68	68	68
3	69	68	68	68	69
4	68	68	68	68	67
5	67	67	66	67	67
6	67	67	67	67	67
7	67	68	66	68	67
8	69	68	68	68	68
9	66	67	67	66	67
10	67	67	68	67	67
11	68	67	67	68	68
12	66	67	67	66	67
13	67	67	66	67	68
14	67	67	68	67	66

Required:
a. Create a process control chart for the average groove depth.
b. Create a process control chart for the range of each sample.
c. Identify any samples that fall outside the control limits.
d. Describe any significant trends you see in the graphs.

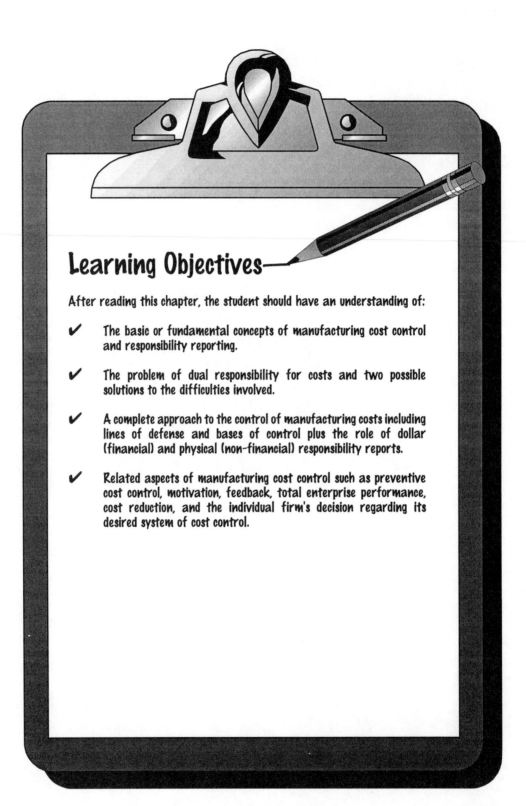

Learning Objectives

After reading this chapter, the student should have an understanding of:

✔   The basic or fundamental concepts of manufacturing cost control and responsibility reporting.

✔   The problem of dual responsibility for costs and two possible solutions to the difficulties involved.

✔   A complete approach to the control of manufacturing costs including lines of defense and bases of control plus the role of dollar (financial) and physical (non-financial) responsibility reports.

✔   Related aspects of manufacturing cost control such as preventive cost control, motivation, feedback, total enterprise performance, cost reduction, and the individual firm's decision regarding its desired system of cost control.

THE STRUCTURE OF MANUFACTURING COST CONTROL

All organizations strive to produce products or services at minimum cost consistent with the quality, specifications, and other representations made to customers. To do this, costs must be controlled. One approach to cost control is to take measures to ensure that actual costs conform to standard or expected costs.[1] Although the manufacturing function is emphasized in this chapter, the concepts and principles of cost control outlined apply to other functions in business firms and even to non-business organizations.

Industrial and design engineers often develop standard costs, basing the standards upon scientific studies.[2] However, in other cases, supervisors and management and staff personnel develop standard costs from records of past performance with (or sometimes without) modification. In still other cases, no pretense of using standards is made, but managers attempt to control costs through comparisons of past actual and present actual costs. In all cases, managers make efforts to keep actual costs in line with expectations.

▶ FUNDAMENTAL CONCEPTS ◀

▶ Cost Control and the Accounting Function

Before delving into the details of cost control for any organization, and in our case the manufacturing firm, note that cost control is an operating function, not an accounting function. The concept of responsibility reporting introduced in Chapters 2 and 6 will be expanded over the next few pages. Operating personnel such as the worker, the supervisor, and the plant superintendent control costs. The managerial accountant provides operating personnel with information necessary to implement cost control. The managerial accountant, as will be seen, can prepare a whole series of useful reports, but no report in and of itself controls costs. The action stimulated by the report controls costs. The person to whom the report is rendered takes this action; thus we may say that cost control lies in people and the actions that people take, not the reports rendered to people.

▶ Cost Control and Responsibility Reporting

To be effective, cost control must revolve about a system of responsibility reporting. Areas of responsibility within the organization must be identified. Areas of responsibility are the organizational units within a firm which are subject to the direction of an individual (sometimes a

---

[1] A new view of cost control seems to be emerging that focuses on upstream cost management. Also see "The New Cost/Management Accounting: More Questions than Answers," *Management Accounting*, October 1990 by William L. Ferrara.

[2] The standards referred to here are up-to-date standards, which may or may not be reflected in the double entry records.

committee or team). The individual in charge has been delegated the specific responsibility to accomplish an objective(s), and with that responsibility goes the authority necessary to accomplish the assigned objective(s).

Within a single area of responsibility, two or more subunits of responsibility may exist as part of the responsibility framework. For example, the president of a firm has a responsibility area which embraces the total firm, but he also has as subordinates three vice-presidents whose respective responsibility areas are production, marketing, and finance. In addition, the vice-presidents usually have subject to them other areas of responsibility such as plants, sales divisions, and the controller's office. The ultimate refinement in responsibility areas is the individual worker or, in some instances, a group of workers within a work center.

After the areas of responsibility are identified, costs must be accumulated in accordance with the areas specified. This is the essence of responsibility reporting (i.e., the accumulation of costs according to areas of responsibility in order that variances or deviations from standard or estimated costs can be identified with the person or group responsible). Cost reports prepared along responsibility lines are in effect report cards informing managers how well they have managed their costs or their costs and revenues.

► Controllable vs. Noncontrollable Costs

Often the literature on cost control distinguishes between controllable and noncontrollable costs. It makes sense to charge to an area of responsibility only those costs which are subject to the control of the person responsible for that area. Costs which are not subject to the control of a person or group should not be charged to that person or group. For example, departmental supervisors should not be charged with any part of the plant superintendent's salary. They should be charged only with materials, direct labor, and supplies. These are the costs a supervisor can control or influence.

If supervisors or workers were charged with costs outside their sphere of influence, they would most likely react with resentment and hostility. Charging people for costs they cannot control is like sending a bill to the wrong person and then sending a collection agent to collect the bill. Any worker or supervisor can spell out the factors of production over which he or she has control and knows that performance evaluations should be based on those factors.

► Costs Controllable by Me (or Us) vs. Costs Controllable by Others

The term noncontrollable costs is a misnomer. All costs are controllable by a person or a group at some point in time. For purposes of better understanding, it would be best to discard the distinction between controllable and noncontrollable costs. A more appropriate distinction for control purposes would be between costs controllable by me (or us) and costs controllable by others.

This new cost distinction is much more than nomenclature since it spells out the fact that all costs are controllable, and for responsibility reporting purposes the problem is a matter of determining who is responsible in order that costs can be accumulated by areas of responsibility. Within an individual firm there is a responsibility slot for each and every cost element.

► Fixed vs. Variable Costs and Control

In some instances, particularly at lower levels of an organization, we find substantial agreement between the fixed vs. variable cost dichotomy and the controllable by me (or us) vs. the controllable by others cost dichotomy. For example, a worker may exert influence over only variable costs such as direct labor used, materials used, and some elements of supplies and indirect materials used. A plant superintendent, on the other hand, is usually in a position to influence many fixed costs such as salaries of plant personnel and depreciation of plant equipment.

The fixed vs. variable dichotomy is not synonymous with the cost groupings for responsibility reporting. For responsibility reporting purposes, the relevant cost grouping relates to control and not to the fixity or variability of costs. However, within the group of costs subject to the control of an individual or group, it is useful to at least keep in mind (perhaps to use as subcategories) the distinction between fixed and variable costs because control procedures for fixed and variable costs differ significantly. Dividing variances from standards into price and quantity variances for individual costs provides managers with a cost control tool. To the extent that standard or expected costs are on target, such variances should be eliminated or minimized.

In contrast, the control over fixed costs occurs only when commitments are made (or not made), allowed to continue, or changed. Depreciation, for example, is controllable at the point of deciding to acquire property, plant and equipment. After a decision is made, the only remaining possibility for control is a subsequent decision. Such a subsequent decision may be to dispose of unnecessary equipment or to replace when new and better equipment and facilities become available. Other fixed costs are subject to control in the same manner as depreciation, that is, at the point of initial commitment and at the point when changes in commitments become possible. Examples include such costs as insurance and salaries.

▸ An Example of Responsibility Reporting Cost Distinctions

As an example of responsibility reporting distinctions, take the case of an individual department subject to the control of a supervisor. Consider the following costs incurred in the department:

1. Direct materials.
2. Direct labor.
3. Indirect labor.
4. Idle time.
5. Supplies.
6. Stationery.
7. Insurance on departmental equipment.
8. Federal and state taxes on departmental payroll.
9. Vacation and holiday pay for departmental employees.
10. Depreciation on departmental equipment.
11. Depreciation and insurance on the factory buildings which can be distributed to departments on the basis of floor space occupied.
12. Salary of the supervisor and his or her clerical staff.

For which of these costs does the supervisor have responsibility for and which do others have responsibility? Clearly the supervisor exerts influence over items 1 through 6. As for items 7 through 12, they may or may not be subject to the supervisor's influence.

Usually an insurance committee made up of upper level management personnel controls decisions related to insurance on buildings and equipment. Thus the supervisor would not be able to influence these costs. Since acquisitions of factory equipment and buildings are in most instances the responsibility of a top management committee, the depreciation on such items should not be charged to lower-level management personnel for responsibility reporting purposes. However, if a supervisor belongs to the committee which authorizes equipment expenditures or if he or she can recommend such acquisitions to the committee, the supervisor can influence the acquisitions and can justifiably be charged for depreciation on the acquisitions.

External forces (governmental units) set federal and state payroll taxes. Thus, some questions arise as to whether an individual company has any control over these taxes. However, with a bit of stretching (not really too much), one can conclude that upper level management could influence payroll taxes by its decision to remain in business or close shop and through its participation in various pressure groups which can (at least to some extent) influence labor legislation.

Labor-management negotiations determine union contracts and hence often establish vacation and holiday pay. Supervisors usually have no part in such negotiations and are thus not in a position to influence vacation and holiday pay. The management negotiators and those who instruct the management negotiators should be charged with responsibility for vacation and holiday pay.

An alternative view on controllability by supervisors concerning federal and state payroll taxes plus vacation and holiday pay is possible. For instance, there are some who believe that the person who does the hiring, which could be the supervisor, should be held responsible for the entire compensation package including all fringe benefits.

On the basis of recommendations made by a salary committee, management often sets salaries of supervisors and their staff. In such cases, supervisors have no influence. However, if the supervisors are able to recommend salary figures for their staff, they may exert influence over staff salaries and should be charged for them.

▸ A Conflict? — Cost Reporting for Control vs. Cost Reporting for Income Measurement

In the preceding section, we have emphasized the importance of charging a supervisor only with cost factors he or she can control. In earlier chapters on external financial reporting, in contrast, we demonstrated how all manufacturing overhead costs incurred in and for a particular department were used in calculating that department's overhead rate. These overhead rates are used to compute inventory valuations for the balance sheet and the cost of goods sold for the income statement. Hence we can illustrate a department report of costs taking two distinctly different forms.

First, a departmental cost report incurred in and for a department is shown as Exhibit 11-1.

Department A	Budget	Actual	Variance
Direct materials	$ 10,500	$ 10,200	$ (300) *
Direct labor	18,400	18,800	400
Indirect labor	2,800	2,900	100
Idle time	500	550	50
Supplies	340	325	(15)
Stationery	110	106	(4)
Salaries—department head	1,200	1,200	0
Salaries—staff	800	750	(50)
Depreciation—equipment	4,800	4,800	0
Depreciation—building	2,200	2,200	0
Payroll taxes	810	870	60
Insurance	220	220	0
Total	$ 42,680	$ 42,921	$ 241
* Favorable			

Exhibit 11-1   Departmental Cost Report

This exhibit illustrates some of the differences between actual and budgeted costs, but it is of limited value for responsibility reporting purposes. For responsibility reporting purposes, a supervisor should be charged only with cost factors he or she can control. For these purposes, the report should take the form shown in Exhibit 11-2. Note the inclusion of some fixed as well as variable costs in this exhibit.

Department A	Budget	Actual	Variance
Direct materials	$ 10,500	$ 10,200	$ (300)
Direct labor	18,400	18,800	400
Indirect labor	2,800	2,900	100
Idle time	500	550	50
Supplies	340	325	(15)
Stationery	110	106	(4)
Salaries—staff	800	750	(50)
Depreciation—equipment	4,800	4,800	0
Total—supervisor's responsibility	$ 38,250	$ 38,431	$ 181

Exhibit 11-2   *Department Costs Subject to Supervisor's Control*

Exhibits 11-1 and 11-2 illustrate the very significant difference between accounting for external reporting and accounting for responsibilities. External reporting requires consideration of all costs incurred in and for a department. However, responsibility reporting requires consideration only of those costs under the supervisor's control.

An interesting and perhaps useful combination of Exhibits 11-1 and 11-2 is Exhibit 11-3. Note the distinction between costs the supervisor is responsible for and costs others are responsible for. This distinction implements the cost classifications required for control purposes, and it also shows a complete list of all costs incurred in and for a department. This complete list informs the supervisor of two useful facts:

1. The supervisor's own cost performance in terms of costs he or she is responsible for.
2. The costs which the company must incur in order to support the supervisor's activities even though the supervisor is not responsible for such costs.

Obviously cost reports to supervisors should include the costs they are responsible for, and if costs they are not responsible for are included in the report, they must be separated from costs they are responsible for. However, another reason for including costs beyond those the supervisor is responsible for follows. Without the inclusion of these other costs in the report, the supervisor will perhaps not realize the size and extent of the useful and necessary organization behind him or her which is costly to operate. This point suggests the value of including (but distinguishing) costs a supervisor is not responsible for in the report covering the supervisor's cost responsibility. Thus a report which fits the concepts appropriate to income measurement can be converted into a very useful report for control purposes as long as the cost distinctions appropriate for control purposes are implemented in the report.

Department A	Budget	Actual	Variance
Direct materials	$ 10,500	$ 10,200	$ (300)
Direct labor	18,400	18,800	400
Manufacturing Overhead—			
Supervisor's responsibility:			
Indirect labor	2,800	2,900	100
Idle time	500	550	50
Supplies	340	325	(15)
Stationery	110	106	(4)
Salaries—staff	800	750	(50)
Depreciation—equipment	4,800	4,800	0
Total—supervisor's			
responsibility	$ 38,250	$ 38,431	$ 181
Manufacturing overhead—			
Other's responsibility:			
Salaries—department head . .	1,200	1,200	0
Depreciation—building	2,200	2,200	0
Payroll taxes	810	870	60
Insurance	220	220	0
Total department costs	$ 42,680	$ 42,921	$ 241

Exhibit 11-3   *Departmental cost Report Including Cost-Control Distinctions*

▸ Review and Résumé

Within a manufacturing plant there are three levels of responsibility reporting. They are the worker level, the department level, and the total plant level. A fourth level might be the vice-president in charge of all manufacturing activities, such as individual plants and staff departments serving all plants. For each of these levels, the problem is simply a matter of tracing to the individual in charge of each level the costs for which he or she is responsible (see Exhibit 11-5).

The labor, materials, and supplies that workers are responsible for can be traced to them. However, there is some question concerning whether or not it is worthwhile tracing costs to such small responsibility units. One solution is to combine a series of smaller areas into a larger responsibility area such as a work group, or work center, or department.

In making decisions related to the type of responsibility reporting, managers must consider the responsibility reporting as well as the *size* of the responsibility area. With smaller areas of responsibility such as the individual worker, managers may forego the formal reporting process in favor of an informal process such as visual or other sensory observation by a foreman or supervisor. When the cost of responsibility reporting more closely approximates the benefits involved (e.g., when the responsibility units are larger or when they have a history of cost control difficulty), the formal reporting process can be instituted. In many instances management may retain some aspects of the formal reporting process at the worker level—the usual case in point being a direct labor performance report by individual workers, as shown in Exhibit 11-4.

When the costs controllable by individual workers are added up, the department head or supervisor is responsible for the total. In addition, certain costs directly applicable to the supervisor's function must be included as well. These costs do not pertain to any individual worker, as the supervisor cannot or does not delegate these direct responsibilities. Thus the costs included within the supervisor's responsibility are those costs controllable directly and those controllable indirectly through his or her subordinates. This same analogy applies to the sum total of costs controllable by various supervisors to which must be added the cost of the plant superintendent's office to obtain the

Preforming Department			April 29, 20_____
Employee	Actual Producing Hours	Standard Hours of Output	Percent Performance
John Ames	8	10	125.0
Joseph Bart	6	7	116.7
Richard Arnold	5	4	80.0
Thomas Sohn	7	8	114.3
Albert Armstrong	8	8	100.0
Total	234	249	106.4

Exhibit 11-4   *Daily Labor Performance Report By Employee*

sum total of costs applicable to the plant superintendent's responsibility area. This analogy can also be applied to costs subject to the control of the vice-president in charge of all production activities.

The above is summarized diagrammatically in Exhibit 11-5. In addition, Exhibits 11-6 through 11-8 illustrate the concepts discussed here in terms of specific reports. The complete formal responsibility reporting system normally starts with the individual supervisor as indicated in Exhibit 11-6. For purposes of better understanding, the reader should trace the cost totals in Exhibit 11-6 to Exhibit 11-7 and the totals in Exhibit 11-7 to Exhibit 11-8. Note that actual costs appear in these reports only as variances from the budget as shown under the columns over or (under) budget for the current month and year-to-date. This is a common alternative to the format of Exhibits 11-1, 11-2, and 11-3.

▸ THE PROBLEM OF DUAL RESPONSIBILITY ◂

Difficulties arise the moment one begins to consider costs which can be influenced by an individual when such costs are traceable to another responsibility area. The problem usually shows up in the form of service department costs which can be influenced by both service department personnel and by personnel of the departments using the services. Consider as an example the inspection department. In this department costs are incurred which are controllable by the chief inspector and his or her subordinates. These costs are also controllable, or more properly, they can be influenced by the performance of producing department personnel in the sense that the level of performance in the producing departments may create difficulties in the inspection department. The maintenance department provides another example. The costs incurred in the maintenance department can be influenced by the head of maintenance and his or her subordinates as well as by those who ask for and receive the services of the maintenance department.

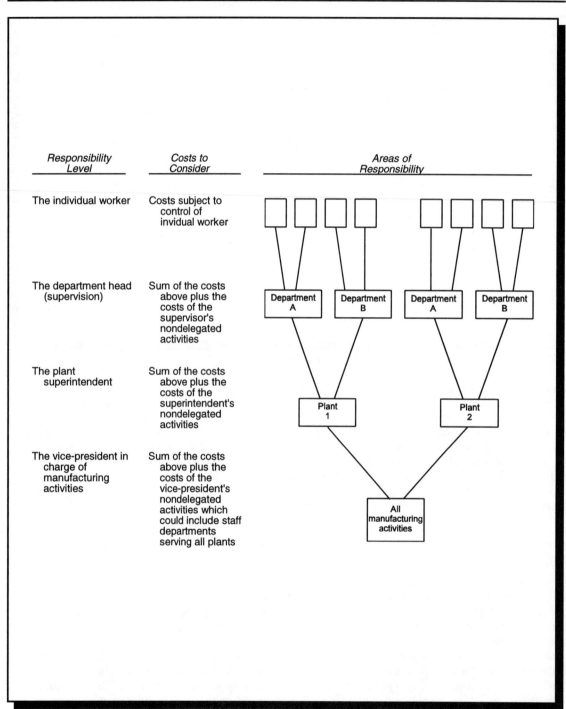

Responsibility Level	Costs to Consider	Areas of Responsibility

The individual worker — Costs subject to control of invidual worker

The department head (supervision) — Sum of the costs above plus the costs of the supervisor's nondelegated activities

The plant superintendent — Sum of the costs above plus the costs of the superintendent's nondelegated activities

The vice-president in charge of manufacturing activities — Sum of the costs above plus the costs of the vice-president's nondelegated activities which could include staff departments serving all plants

Exhibit 11-5   *Responsibility Areas and Costs in Manufacturing*

Exhibit 11-6 *Department Head Cost Report Performing**

Budget	Budget		Over (under)	
	Current Month	Year-to-Date	Current Month	Year-to-Date
Direct materials	322.9	1,411.0	(5.5)	(8.6)
Direct labor	153.6	693.8	8.1	5.4
Direct overhead—department head responsibility:				
Indirect labor	88.6	364.6	(5.3)	(5.2)
Idle time	19.6	79.4	(0.8)	(1.1)
Overtime	16.7	71.6	3.3	1.9
Small tools	15.4	62.3	(1.1)	(0.8)
Sundry supplies	61.4	210.6	(4.3)	(4.9)
Stationery	4.6	16.3	0.2	0.4
Total department head's responsibility . .	682.8	2,909.6	(5.4)	(12.9)

Exhibit 11-7 *Plant Superintendent Cost Report Plant 1**

Department				
Plant superintendent's office	6.5	24.1	(0.1)	0.2
Preforming	682.8	2,909.6	(5.4)	(12.9)
Molding	491.9	2,215.8	(3.2)	(5.7)
Inspection	53.6	198.6	0.8	1.2
Finishing	128.7	549.9	(2.1)	(2.4)
Maintenance	47.5	173.6	(3.4)	(2.3)
Receiving and shipping	28.1	73.4	0.6	1.2
Mold and toolmaking	69.2	249.6	0.7	(0.7)
Total superintendent's responsibility . . .	1,508.3	6,394.6	(12.1)	(21.4)

Exhibit 11-8 *Vice-President of Manufacturing Cost Report**

Vice-president's office	8.4	31.5	0.2	0.8
Plant I	1,508.3	6,394.6	(12.1)	(21.4)
Plant II	1,057.7	4,378.3	(1.7)	3.9
Plant III	931.3	3,857.2	(4.6)	(12.2)
Personnel	6.8	24.3	(0.3)	(1.1)
Engineering	27.1	93.2	(0.2)	2.1
Total vice-president's responsibility	3,539.6	14,779.1	(18.7)	(27.9)

* All data in thousands of dollars

► Solution 1

Which manager should be charged with those costs involving dual responsibility? Both the service department and the consuming department should be held responsible, and there is an approach which can hold both departments responsible and yet avoid the very difficult allocation of costs. This approach involves leaving all the service department costs in the service department and using a physical measure of consumption for consuming departments. Thus the service department personnel will be held responsible for the costs which they can influence in terms of dollars, and the consuming departments will be held responsible in terms of such physical measures as number of maintenance hours, number of material handling hours, and units inspected and rejected. In some cases the physical measures may be subclassified, for example, into different categories of maintenance hours.

A slight modification of this approach recognizes that some service department costs are directly traceable to consuming departments. Materials for a special maintenance job are a good example of this situation. This modification retains all service department costs in the service department, but adds to the physical measure of consumption for the consuming department a traceable dollar cost. The head of the consuming department receives a dollar measure of performance for traceable costs and physical measures of performance for costs which are difficult, if not virtually impossible to trace to the consuming department.

In these cases of service and consuming departments, there is a feature that may bother some individuals; the same costs are counted in the service department and then counted again in the consuming department even though the method of measurement may be different (physical vs. dollar measures). Accountants do this for two reasons:

1. The costs involve dual responsibility.
2. Each of the responsible individuals or groups must be put in a position where they realize that their responsibility is recognized and its extent of fulfillment will be measured.

This approach to the problem of dual responsibility avoids a difficult task; that is, the determination of which costs and how much of each a consuming department is responsible for. Consuming departments are held responsible in terms of physical consumption data (perhaps traceable dollar data too, if they exist), whereas the service departments are held responsible in terms of dollars of cost. The physical consumption data can be used in terms of actual vs. standard just as dollar data can. Thus, by avoiding allocation and substituting physical consumption data, managers solve the problem of dual responsibility. Both departments are held responsible.

► Solution II

Accountants encounter two problems when they use physical consumption measures to evaluate the responsibility of a consuming department. They are:

1. It is difficult to add up to a total figure for cost performance when some measures are physical and others monetary.
2. Physical measures do not illustrate the impact on net income of variations from standard.

To offset these problems, some accountants attach a price per unit to the physical measures of activity to convert the physical data into dollar data. Such a conversion has two beneficial results that offset these two problems.

1. The measures of cost performance are homogeneous; that is, all are expressed in terms of dollars rather than partly in dollars and partly in physical terms. This facilitates the summation of total cost performance.
2. Dollars reveal directly the impact on net income of variations from standard, but physical consumption measures do not.

To make this system work, accountants use a price (to be considered a service department standard overhead rate) per hour or other unit of service. This does not make a profit center out of the service department; it just converts physical facts into a dollar amount which makes the responsibility data homogeneous.

A useful adaptation of the price per unit attached to physical measures of consumption follows. Accountants charge the consuming department for service rendered at a fixed price per unit applied to the physical consumption measure, and credit the service department for the same amount. If accountants base the price per unit on a standard cost set at normal activity, the credits to the service department should reduce the net service department costs to zero under normal conditions. With this in mind, perhaps the cost performance objective of the service department is a reduction of its net costs to zero. Such an objective, if based upon reasonable performance standards and factor prices, might yield a useful form of motivation on the part of the service department. For example, in the case of a maintenance department it would be beneficial to the maintenance department to sell maintenance, especially preventive maintenance, to consuming departments in order to make certain that net maintenance department costs are reduced to zero. An offset to the pressure to sell would be the consuming department's resistance to unneeded maintenance since it would be charged for any maintenance services via a physical measure multiplied by a price per unit. The pressure to sell and the resistance to unneeded services culminate in the best combination of maintenance services.

▶ A COMPLETE COST CONTROL MODEL ◀

As the above discussion illustrates, managers usually begin their review of cost control by analyzing variances between standard (or budgeted) and actual costs or between past and current costs. For example, the variances from standards could be analyzed as to their root causes which then would be eliminated. Thus, the process of cost control is a three-fold process: (1) accumulate variances, (2) analyze variances in order to determine root causes, and (3) eliminate root causes.

This threefold process seems logical until one realizes that variances can be measured in many ways, at different times during and after production, and by many different people in the organization. For example, the accountant can accumulate material usage variances in terms of dollars and/or in physical terms (pounds, inches, etc.). The accountant can also accumulate such variances in total for all material usage, by categories of material, and more importantly, by responsibility areas such as departments or work centers. However, is there a need to wait for the accountant to accumulate variances in order to start the cost-control process? Is it not possible for workers on the production line as well as supervisors to (at least tentatively) measure variances by visual and other forms of sensory observation?

Workers and supervisors should be aware of production standards, and they might eliminate the root causes of some variances long before such variances are reported by the accountant, that is, by on the spot action taken by workers and supervisors who observe variances as they are occurring. In some instances, variances can even be observed and eliminated before they occur. A good example of this is a case where a worker spots an impending bottleneck and reports it to a superior who initiates corrective action before the bottleneck materializes.

In summary, accounting reports of variances are just a part of the cost control process. In order to appreciate the totality of the cost control process in the plant and the role that accounting reports play in the process, one must look at the organization structure. The organization of a manufacturing plant is the structure around which the control of manufacturing costs revolve. Each level in the organization represents a line of defense against inefficiencies and waste or out-of-line performance.

▶ Lines of Defense and Bases of Control

Exhibit 11-9 is a simplified organization chart of a plant. There are five levels in the organization chart, starting from the president and proceeding down through the vice-president, the plant superintendent, supervisors and workers. Review each level separately and study its relationships to other levels to assess the contribution each level might make to the total task of cost control.

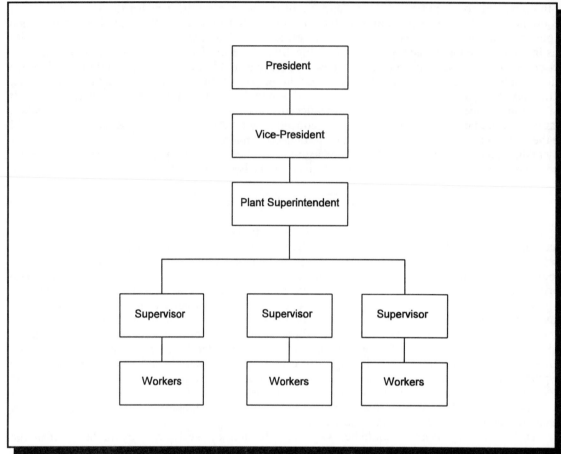

Exhibit 11-9   *The Manufacturing Organization—Each Level Represents A Line of Defense*

For each organization level to make a contribution to cost control, there must be bases or means of control available at each level. These are observation, physical data, dollar knowledge and dollar data, and various combinations of physical and dollar data. Some examples of dollar, physical, and combination measures of activity follows:

Dollar Measures:
    Total cost of sales
    Cost of sales classified by product, territory, etc.
    Cost of sales classified by category of cost--materials, labor, and manufacturing overhead
    Materials, labor, and manufacturing overhead classified by types of materials, labor, and manufacturing overhead
    Materials, labor, and manufacturing overhead classified by areas of responsibility
    Materials, labor, and manufacturing overhead classified by types within each area of responsibility

Physical Measures (Non-financial):
    Hours available for production
    Hours used for production
    Overtime hours
    Number of employees
    Average hours worked per week
    Units produced
    Units produced per hour
    Units produced per pound or yard of material
    Units rejected or classified as seconds
    Ratio of units rejected or classified as seconds to good units
    All the above physical measures classified by areas of responsibility

Combination Measures:
    Total cost per unit for each product
    Materials, labor, and manufacturing overhead cost per unit for each product
    Cost per unit for significant elements of materials, labor, and manufacturing overhead
    Cost per unit for significant elements of materials, labor, and manufacturing overhead classified by area of responsibility

▸ Appropriate Bases of Control

Not every organization level can use these bases of control; each level requires a different base of control. For example, physical data are the language of the shop, and thus they are appropriate for the lower levels of the organization. Dollar data, on the other hand, relate more to the language of the upper organization levels. This is not to say that physical data are not useful at upper organization levels or that dollar data are not useful at lower organization levels; some are just more appropriate or more important than others at various organizations levels.

At the worker level, the prime basis of control is observation. The worker can readily observe many facets of current production activity which are actually or potentially out of line. With the proper motivation, workers will take immediate action or report their observations to their superior and thus start in motion whatever activities are necessary to remove actual or potential sources of waste and/or inefficiencies. If the worker fails to observe actual or potential wastes, we might still be able to count upon the supervisor to observe waste. However, the supervisor is unable to observe everything under his or her jurisdiction, and thus must back up his or her limited observation time with reports concerning production activity. These reports are usually in terms of physical standards or objectives, such as ten units are to be produced per hour or each unit should contain one-half pound of material. Thus, if the workers fail to observe and the supervisor is unable to observe, the physical reports will bring to the attention of the supervisor sources of waste which must be eliminated.

In addition to physical reports, the supervisor should also have some knowledge of the prices of materials and labor. Such dollar knowledge will help the supervisor where a decision must be made about which source of waste to attack first. Dollar knowledge of materials and labor costs will help him or her make such a decision on the basis of the greatest cost savings. The supervisors in many plants are also the recipient of many dollar reports which are really the physical reports expressed in dollars and cents. Such dollar reports in conjunction with dollar knowledge help these supervisors to appreciate the impact of waste on net income and the fundamental importance of cost control.

As we travel up the organization ladder, observation becomes less important because there is too much to observe and the observing which is done must be done on a sample basis. Also, as we get farther away from the plant and the language of the plant, the reports that are prepared must be prepared in the language of the upper organization levels, that is, in terms of dollars and cents. Thus as we proceed to higher organization levels, observation and physical reports become less important and dollar reports become more important. At the top of the organization, the most important basis of cost control is an income statement with the standard cost variances spelled out very carefully. Such an income statement shows not only income that was earned but also what happened to the income that should have been earned.

▸ Lines of Defense and Bases of Control — A Résumé

Exhibit 11-10 illustrates how the various bases of cost control might fit into the organization structure. This illustration summarizes many of the preceding comments. Variances determined by observation, physical reports, and dollar reports all play a role in the cost control process. With the first line defense (i.e., workers) observation is most important. The fifth line of defense (i.e., the president) is aided by a report of income that shows what income was earned and what happened to that income that should have been earned. Physical data are more important at the more immediate lines of defense, and dollar data are more important at the more remote lines of defense. A final point to remember is that reports issued to more remote lines of defense are issued less frequently, and they are also more in summary form. More detailed and more frequent data are necessary for those individuals who are in a position to exercise on-the-spot control.

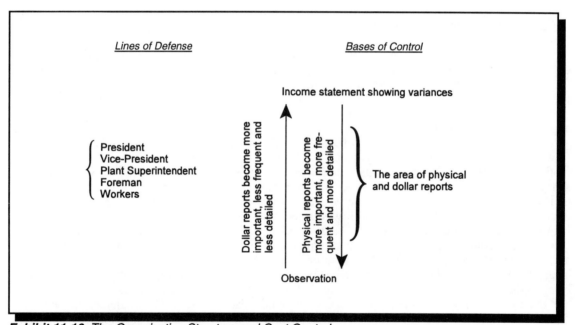

Exhibit 11-10 *The Organization Structure and Cost Control*

▸ The Formal Reporting Process — Why?

In many instances, observation by the worker or supervisor will result in the elimination of wastes which ultimately appear in physical and dollar reports even though these reports might be prepared on an hourly or daily basis. What then is the function of a physical or dollar report? Is it possible that some managements may judge physical and/or dollar reports to be unimportant since attentive workers and supervisors are all that is needed for sound cost control? These questions may seem harsh and difficult, but the answers to them should provide the reader with a better appreciation of the structure of cost control.

We used the term *lines of defense* at the beginning of this section to indicate that each level in the organization was a line of defense against waste and that some levels could actually be more important in cost control than other levels. Workers might be considered the first line of defense, supervisors the second line, and so forth. It is the function of the workers to observe actual or potential waste and to initiate through their superior whatever action is necessary to eliminate actual or potential waste. If the workers fail in performing their function, it is the function of the supervisor through his or her observation and reports to initiate whatever action is necessary to eliminate waste. However, in the case of reports, the supervisor should realize that the waste depicted in a report may already be eliminated, and thus before he or she initiates any action, workers should be asked, "What has gone wrong and what have you already done to correct the situation?" If the situation has already been corrected, no action is necessary; however, if the situation has not been corrected, the supervisor should then initiate action. This same question is asked over and over again in the organization upon receipt of a report. Thus, it should be quite clear that the function of a report, whether it be in physical or dollar terms, is to provide a means of judging how well assigned tasks have been accomplished and, furthermore, to provide each level in the organization (above the first) with the necessary information to ask questions of their subordinates concerning out-of-line conditions and what has already been done to correct such conditions. Without reports, a management will not be able to judge how effectively costs have been controlled, and furthermore, without reports management will not be able to ask those questions designed to find out whether remedial action is necessary.

Some managers may judge physical and dollar reports unimportant in cases where they trust their workers and supervisors. In addition, some managers may be very close to, or perhaps even a part of, the production operations and may feel reports are unnecessary. However, so long as people are fallible, there is a need for some minimal level of reports covering the performance of assigned tasks. This need is proportional to the size of the organization. It may also be influenced by the confidence that management has in its employees. One of the greatest tasks before any management is to decide on the content and the type of reports necessary to facilitate control of manufacturing costs.

▸ Cost Control

We now expand the model for cost control developed in the preceding sections to include preventive cost control. In essence, preventive cost control is a matter of having a sound, responsible, and motivated organization. Such an organization must have goals and the best available means to implement such goals. Three fundamental activities (or means) of preventive cost control are personnel administration, engineering, and production control.

In the case of personnel administration, there must be effective hiring and placement policies at all organizational levels. The right person for each job is the major goal here. Very closely related to this is the engineering function of determining expected performance. In other words, there must be a knowledge of the physical relation between the various types of inputs and outputs. This knowledge is preferably determined on the basis of engineering studies. Past results may also form the basis of expected performance. In whatever manner expected performance is determined, it should be made common knowledge or available to all levels in the organization. Production control activities are also essential to cost control. Proper production planning and control yield the appropriate quantities and qualities of inputs at the appropriate time.

With the idea of preventive cost control now established, we conclude that the control of manufacturing costs starts with preventive cost control, continues with variances accumulated by observation and/or in physical and dollar terms, and ends with whatever actions are taken to eliminate detected wastes. Preventive cost control attempts to stop waste before it starts. Observation by workers and supervisors helps stop waste before it starts or as soon as it is detected. Variance accumulations in physical terms are intended to detect wastes which evade observation. Variance accumulations in dollar terms occupy a residual position, but they illustrate in the best possible way (a way which is truly understandable to all) the impact of waste on net income.

Before concluding this chapter, consider five additional aspects of cost control: motivation, feedback, the total enterprise performance, cost reduction and cost control systems.

▶ ADDITIONAL ASPECTS OF COST CONTROL ◀

▶ Cost Control and Motivation

The importance of workers and other operating personnel striving to meet their cost goals makes motivation one of the most important phases of cost control. As mentioned earlier, cost control lies in people and the actions that people take, not the reports rendered to people. The managerial accountants can put together all the reports they desire, but if the people in the organization are not motivated, all reports could just as well be sent to the dead-letter office.

Motivation is more properly dealt with by behavioral scientists; therefore only a few general comments on motivation will be made here. Accounting reports can motivate via a report card effect; that is, the very fact that people realize their activities and accomplishments will be reported might automatically motivate them. In some instances this is true, but the report card idea is not sufficient since it takes more than pointing a finger to build up the necessary esprit de corps for motivation. In fact, the finger pointing technique sometimes has an adverse effect.

The essence of motivation would appear to be the recognition of the dignity of the individual and his or her fundamental importance to the enterprise. These ideas relate not only to all layers of management but also to the lowest person on the organization's totem pole. Without the cooperation of the worker, a system of cost control could be reduced to complete ineffectiveness. Avoid efforts to motivate through insincerity. We hear all too often that all you have to do is convince employees that they are important. Our suggestion here is never try to convince employees that they are important unless you are first aware of their fundamental importance to the firm. Honesty and sincerity are the building blocks of employee motivation, and these building blocks can be effectively buttressed by an occasional display of attention and appreciation via a kind word, a pat on the back and especially in these times, a sharing of profits. Top level managers should not be the only recipients of year-end bonuses.

▶ Cost Control and Feedback

We can think of the cost control process as a six step cycle: (1) plan, (2) organize, (3) motivate, (4) perform, (5) measure deviation from plans, and (6) make corrections to the plans or the performance or both if necessary.

Control is the process of making actual performance equal planned performance. Planning and organizing encompass the setting of goals (in our case, cost goals), deciding upon the means to attain such goals, and accumulating the resources (human and otherwise) necessary for the attainment of the goals.

Motivating involves the process of inducing human resources to use physical resources to attain targeted goals. Performance involves the accomplishment of the assigned task, and the measurement of deviations is intended to see how well the assigned task has been performed. Make corrections in the plans or in the means of attaining planned goals if some fault is found with the original plans and/or the means of attainment. Making corrections in performance is again a problem of motivation, for it takes more than the pointing of a finger to induce an individual into improved performance or the attainment of prescribed goals.

The Control Cycle

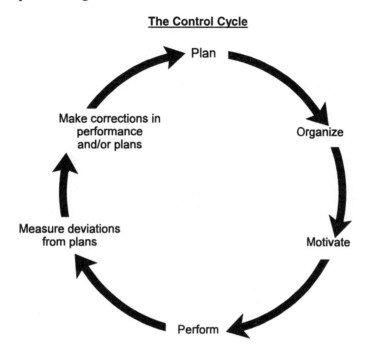

Once corrections are made, the control cycle repeats itself. The result is a new plan and/or revised performance standards. The new plan and/or the new performance standards provide the basis for a repetitive control cycle. This repetition is based upon the feedback concept, i.e., reporting to planners information concerning the measurement and correction of deviations so that plans and/or performance standards may be revised and implemented in succeeding cycles. The measurement and correction of deviations are an inherent part of each cycle, meaning that the cycle has inherent in it the means necessary to regenerate itself. This regeneration is the essence of the feedback concept.

The six steps in the control cycle can be arrayed against the phases of cost control as follows:

Steps in the Control Cycle	*Phases of Cost Control*
Plan	Preventive cost control
Organize	Preventive cost control
Motivate	Preventive cost control
Perform	Observation
Measure deviations from planned performance	Physical reports Dollar reports
Make corrections in performance and/or plans	Action taken upon the receipt of verbal and/or written reports

The important point here is that the process of cost control, like the control cycle, demands repetition on the basis of the feedback of information to the planners. This feedback of information concerning deviations and correction of deviations makes the process of cost control far more effective.

▸ Cost Performance vs. Total Performance of the Enterprise

Cost goals are hardly the only goals of an enterprise. Thus, it is important to consider total firm performance (or one of its parts) as opposed to cost performance. The gap between cost performance and total performance is filled by such things as revenue performance, human relations performance, public relations performance, and governmental relations performance.

Cost performance plus revenue performance equals profit performance. Profit performance includes rate of return on investment, total sales, sales by product lines or territories, as well as various expenses. Profit performance relates to how well the firm has achieved its cost and revenue goals. To achieve an appreciation of the total performance of the firm, we must add the nonfinancial goals, or qualitative goals, of the enterprise to the total of profit performance. Examples of these nonfinancial goals include relations with employees, unions, creditors, customers, local communities, society in general, and the various levels of government. These non-financial goals help us keep in mind the various stakeholders in the total performance of an organization. It is impossible to add all these facets of total performance into one single measure. However, to properly evaluate the performance of an individual, a segment of the firm, or the firm as a whole, there must be full realization of the totality of performance measurement.

Cost goals are just one of many groupings of goals within an enterprise. The individual worker, supervisor, and even upper level management should never be evaluated solely in terms of cost goals. It is the totality of performance that must be considered since we can easily find examples both where below-average cost performance is considered negligible when compared to employee relations performance and vice versa. Thus, this chapter on the structure of manufacturing cost control must be considered in its proper context; that is, the goals of a business enterprise are many, varied, and sometimes they are even in conflict. Controlling costs represents just one part of the total process of controlling performance.

▸ Cost Control /The Process of Continuous Improvement

In the preceding pages cost control has been the focal point of all discussions. Now we review cost control and its relation to cost reduction.

Through cost control actual costs are made to conform to standard or expected costs. However, it is critical that all standards be challenged on a continuing basis. Cost reduction refers to this challenging of existing cost standards to seek possible changes in equipment, materials, and even substitutions between various grades of materials and labor which could result in the same product or a very similar product at reduced costs. Alternatively, improved products may be produced at essentially the same cost, which could improve a product's competitive position or which could result in obtaining premium sales prices. A popular term for describing the continuous challenge of current standards is "continuous improvement."

Cost reduction is a must in all organizations (business or non-business), and it goes hand in hand with cost control. Cost control cannot be considered separate from cost reduction. Cost standards should never be accepted as unalterable, but should be regarded as goals to be met and improved upon on a continuing basis. Survival in our increasingly competitive world demands no less.

Everyone in the organization should be encouraged to use their ingenuity to reduce costs. Bonuses and profit sharing should encourage such ingenuity. Cost reduction, like cost control, is everyone's job. However, in larger organizations it would probably be wise to set up a special group whose task it would be to challenge existing standards. Such a group could be a part of the group charged with setting production standards.

▸ *The Individual Firm and Cost Control*

Within the individual firm, there are many ways to build a system to control costs. The major point is that every firm does make a decision, implicitly or explicitly, on the type of cost controls it will use. Such a decision cannot be avoided, and it should not be made haphazardly. In each case, management should make an informed and intelligent decision. Management must know which items can be controlled and the many bases of control (preventive cost control, observation, physical reports, and dollar reports) which can be used. Then management must select the basis or bases of control to be used in accordance with management desires concerning cost, benefit, and risk.

In each organization, management must consider the following questions when it makes its decision on its desired system of cost control:

Cost. How much does your system cost?

Benefit. How much benefit do you get from your system? Does the benefit exceed the cost?

Risk. Are you aware of the risk that your system of cost control entails concerning the possibilities for inefficiencies and waste? Are you willing to take the amount of risk currently involved, or do you wish to modify your risk by changing the bases of control underlying your cost control system?

▸ SUMMARY ◂

Cost control is an operating function, not an accounting function. People control costs; accounting reports do not. Nevertheless, the accounting function facilitates carrying out cost control measures.

Cost control and responsibility accounting go hand in hand. Costs should always be assigned to the individual or group able to influence them. In cases of dual responsibility, both responsibility areas must be involved; this may necessitate physical, as well as dollar, measures of performance.

The total or complete process of cost control involves lines of defense and bases of control. Lines of defense to facilitate cost control are the various organization levels. Bases of control are observation, physical data, dollar knowledge and dollar data, and various combinations of physical and dollar data. More important than any of the above is the development of a sound, responsible, and motivated organization.

SOME COMMENTS ON CONTROLLING MATERIALS PRICES AND LABOR RATES

In Chapter 9, controlling the usage of materials and labor were emphasized. In this appendix, the issues involved in controlling materials and prices and labor rates are addressed.

► CONTROLLING MATERIALS PRICES ◄

Price variances for materials have many dimensions different from usage variances. Usage can be determined with a fair degree of precision, but prices used in setting cost standards are the best estimates of prices that will exist in the period for which the standards are being set. Errors in the estimates or the inflationary process give rise to variances over which no one in the firm has control. Such variances relate more to external conditions than to internal conditions. For control purposes, managers should concentrate on those price variances which are related to internal conditions.

► Preventive Controls

The control of material prices starts with a sound and responsible organization which is properly motivated. Such an organization needs effective hiring, placement, and training policies. Beyond this, the preventive controls exercised over materials prices include determining the most economical quantities to buy, appropriate quality, the most economical methods of transportation, and the most reliable source of supply.

With specifications established, the purchasing department bears the responsibility to procure materials in accordance with the specifications at the best possible price. Since purchases must be coordinated with production schedules to ensure an adequate working inventory at all times, purchasing and production planning must work very closely in determining what quantities to purchase and when. When standard costs are used, the purchasing department sets standard materials prices for each period. These reflect the best possible estimate of the average price which will be paid for each material over the year or other period for which the standards will be used.

▸ The Control Process

Internal conditions which upset normal buying quantities and transportation methods make the control of material prices more challenging. Internal conditions prone to upset the control process include the acceptance of rush sales orders, failure of the plant to anticipate its needs, and abnormal spoilage by the plant. Any of these conditions may result in rush purchase orders in nonstandard quantities, which necessitate more expensive delivery methods.

The concept of lines of defense would fit the control process surrounding price variances with minor modifications. First managers must determine economical buying quantities, economical methods of transportation, the most reliable sources of supply and the price standards. Then the lines of defense would start with buyers, followed by a purchasing agent, followed by a plant superintendent, and then the president. Physical standards are impractical here, so dollar standards must be relied on.

A control procedure requires buyers to obtain clearance from the purchasing agent for acquisitions at off-standard prices. In addition, the buyers could be required to prepare memos on all orders involving off-standard prices.[3] The memos would contain an explanation, such as price change, rush order, excessive spoilage, or inability to use preferred transportation. Such memos should be periodically reviewed by the purchasing agent, who may also receive a dollar variance report monthly. This dollar variance report, which summarizes the memos prepared by buyers, could show data by classes of materials and causes of purchase price variances.

An important control procedure involves notifying divisions of the business, where possible, of the impact of their activities on materials' prices. For example, notify sales personnel of purchase price variances caused by accepting rush orders, and notify plant personnel of purchase price variances caused by abnormal spoilage or failure to anticipate needs.

The plant superintendent and the president in turn will receive summaries of materials price variances classified by responsibility centers and perhaps classes of materials. At each successive line of defense, the process involves determining the excusability of variances and recognizing any efforts already underway to eliminate controllable price variations (or the conditions underlying such variances). Errors in setting standards and unavoidable changes in suppliers' prices give rise to noncontrollable price variances.

Important tools in materials price control include the determination of economical quantities to buy, economical methods of transportation, and the dissemination of this information to all who can affect buying methods. This information, coupled with a need for clearing and explaining the causes of all price variances at the time an order is placed, would force managers to consider possible out-of-line conditions in a timely fashion. More remote lines of defense would serve to find out if price variations were justifiable, to determine if prior lines of defense appreciate the impact on income of off-standard prices, and to make sure that those who are able to affect price understand the inefficiencies and wastes that they can control.

▸ CONTROLLING LABOR RATES ◂

Labor rate variances are often of little consequence since determination is largely related to collective bargaining and community wage levels. However, at least two aspects of labor rate

---

[3] A useful modification of this approach could involve memos only for strategic materials or for those prices which are off standard by a stated percentage (e.g., 5%) or dollar amount (e.g., $1,000).

variances merit consideration for control purposes: the use of non-preferred workers and overtime. As an example of a non-preferred worker, consider the case where an $8-an-hour worker is used for a $6-an-hour job. With minor modifications, control of these two causes of labor rate variances can be worked into the line of defense framework. Lines of defense could extend from the supervisors through at least the plant superintendent. In such cases it would be the supervisor's job to keep production moving smoothly in order to avoid those rushes or bottlenecks which lead to the use of non-preferred workers or overtime work. In any case involving non-preferred workers, policy should require the supervisor to prepare a job change notice which details the causes and the workers involved. In cases where overtime work becomes necessary, the supervisor should be required to obtain approval for the overtime from his or her superior.

The use of non-preferred workers and overtime work may arise due to uneven production caused by unexpected bottlenecks, poor production scheduling, or the acceptance of rush orders. Unexpected bottlenecks, in turn, may arise from poor worker performance, delay in decision making by supervisors, poor scheduling, machine breakdowns and lack of materials. By explaining these out-of-line conditions in advance, the supervisor gives notice to higher lines of defense; all related parties thus become aware of their impact on wage rate variances. This awareness, coupled with the necessity to explain the reasons for the variances, provides information useful for eliminating unexcusable rate variances.

SOME COMMENTS ON CONTROLLING MANUFACTURING OVERHEAD

Manufacturing overhead is divided into fixed and variable components as indicated in earlier chapters. Some overhead costs are all fixed, others are all variable, while still others contain both fixed and variable components. Because of this behavior pattern of manufacturing overhead costs, the primary accounting basis of control is the manufacturing overhead budget.

► CURRENT CONTROL REQUIRED ◄

Until communicated, monthly budget reports simply reflect the degree of control attained. Control is made effective by informing all persons responsible for costs of the amounts budgeted for the scheduled production level and by providing them with sufficient information on a timely basis to determine whether they are keeping costs within these limits. In establishing these periodic review points, the cost of maintaining current control must be considered.

A useful combination of budget reports, standard cost variances, and current control techniques can be put together if manufacturing overhead costs are divided into four groups: (1) expenditures for factory buildings and equipment, (2) production department costs, (3) service department costs, and (4) other manufacturing costs. To put forth this combination effectively, we distinguish between operating and accounting bases of control. Accounting bases of control are flexible budget reports, standard cost variances, and special analyses of individual cost elements prepared on a daily or other periodic basis. Operating bases of control are simply all those other enterprise activities which are intended to make cost goals a reality. Operating bases of control encompass preventive controls and observation. These include hiring and placement policies, employee training programs, determination and dissemination of operating instructions covering the use of equipment and facilities, preparation of a budget, dissemination of budgetary information to all those having budgetary responsibility, a program for capital expenditure justification, and a program for preventive maintenance and observation.

▸ Expenditures for Factory Buildings and Equipment

In the case of expenditures for factory buildings and equipment, the operating basis of control is the program of pre-expenditure justification utilized by the company. This expenditure justification program, as good or as bad as it might be, is basic to the control of a large portion of manufacturing overhead. Those who exercise the power of decision over capital expenditures must realize that their decision can affect the cost and expense pattern of the company for many years to come. After the decision to spend is made, the time to control expenditures for factory buildings and equipment has to a large extent passed. In later chapters the process through which capital expenditures are evaluated will be considered in detail.

▸ Production Department Costs

Within production departments, costs must be further divided into three categories for control purposes. The categories are: (1) readiness to serve costs, (2) costs of operating equipment and facilities, and (3) other production department costs. Operating bases of control are different for each of these three categories. Readiness to serve costs are controllable by the committee or person who approves these costs, which include costs of supervision and other indirect labor costs as well as minor equipment expenditures. Observation by supervisors can establish the continuing need for and efficiency of such personnel. Minor equipment expenditures can be controlled on the basis of a capital expenditure justification program, which would establish the need for such minor equipment (replacement or expansion), after which observation by supervisors and plant superintendents could be used to check if the equipment was being used in accordance with instructions. Observation also serves to establish whether the equipment was needed in the first place simply by observing whether the equipment is being used in the manner and to the extent initially believed necessary.

Operating bases of controlling the costs of operating equipment and facilities relate to operating procedures established for use of the equipment. These instructions are determined by engineers or the vendor of the equipment. Test checks by engineers, maintenance staff, and departmental supervisors on how instructions are followed yield a fundamentally important basis of control. The cost covered here includes all costs incurred to operate the equipment and facilities. Examples are power for lighting fixtures, power or fuel for air conditioning or heating fixtures, power for all machinery and equipment used in the process of manufacturing and operating supplies such as cutting oils and lubrication supplies.

Supervisors control supplies by signing requisitions and by observing actual use. Control of the three categories of production department costs rests primarily on the use of operating bases of control. This means essentially the determination and dissemination of operating instructions and observation to test whether subordinates carry out instructions.

The flexible budget, which is the second level of accounting control, cannot ordinarily be used to test check operating controls in the same manner as regular recurring or rotating sample comparisons. This is true since flexible budgets covering the costs controllable within a responsibility center are ordinarily related to one overall output measure, such as direct labor dollars, direct labor hours, or machine hours. Intensive study of individual items may require analyses in output measures differing from those used in the flexible budget. For example, labor hours might be the basis of flexible budget computations, but cutting oils might be better tested in terms of machine hours. Another reason why flexible budgets cannot serve the function of regular recurring or rotating sample comparisons is that flexible budget reports are usually prepared on a monthly basis, whereas the comparisons could be necessary on a daily or weekly basis. Nonetheless, flexible budget reports provide an excellent approach to detecting those out-of-line conditions not detected by operating controls and the first level of accounting controls.

The third and last level of accounting control for production department overhead costs involves the standard cost variances for manufacturing overhead. Manufacturing overhead costs are primarily controlled by operating bases of control (including expenditure justification programs), determination and dissemination of operating instructions, and observation. Accounting controls are designed to detect all inefficiencies and waste, but their importance relates to the out-of-line conditions not previously corrected by the operating bases of control. Perhaps most important of all, the accounting bases of control illustrate the impact on net income of inefficiencies and waste.

▶ Service Department and Other Manufacturing Overhead Costs

The approach thus far discussed for production departments may be readily adapted to control costs of and other elements of manufacturing overhead such as costs associated with the offices of a plant superintendent and a manufacturing vice-president. Service departments include industrial engineering, the controller's staff, production planning, maintenance, storeroom, and material handling.

▸ QUESTIONS ◂

11-1. Distinguish among cost control, cost reduction, and continuous improvement.

11-2. Discuss: "Efficient organization and operation requires both cost control and cost reduction."

11-3. What is the role of accounting and accounting reports in the process of cost control?

11-4. Why is it essential to include responsibility accounting and areas of responsibility within the framework of cost control?

11-5. Define and distinguish among:

    a. Controllable costs
    b. Noncontrollable costs
    c. Costs controllable by me (or us)
    d. Costs controllable by others
    e. Fixed costs
    f. Variable costs

11-6. At what levels of the organization might fixed costs and costs controllable by others be synonymous?

11-7. Discuss: "The conflict between costs required for income measurement and costs required for control is one of the most difficult accounting conflicts to resolve unless one concentrates their attention on the very old accounting dictate 'different costs are required for different purposes.'"

11-8. What useful purpose can be served by including costs controllable by others in a responsibility accounting report?

11-9. How might the cost of responsibility accounting reports affect the extent to which a formal responsibility accounting system might be instituted?

11-10. What is missing when the costs subject to a supervisor's control are considered to be the sum total of the costs subject to the control of individual workers under the supervisor?

11-11. How might one solve the following problems concerning responsibility for costs:

    a. The need for reports covering the performance of each of three workers who operate a machine as a crew rather than as individuals.
    b. The need for determining the extent to which each and every element of maintenance cost should be charged to the maintenance department supervisor and the supervisors of each department using maintenance service.

11-12. Is there any necessary relationship between lines of defense and bases of control?

11-13. Discuss: "Since we can rely on the observation of workers and supervisors to detect deviations from standards, there is no need to prepare a whole series of formalized accounting reports. Long before the reports are prepared, observation can result in the correction of deviations."

11-14. What question should be asked upon the receipt of a responsibility accounting report?

11-15. Define preventive cost control.

11-16. Relate the steps in the control cycle to the phases of cost control.

11-17. Discuss: "Without motivation on the part of workers, middle management control activities and upper level management control activities are bound to be frustrated."

11-18. Discuss: "Controlling costs is just one phase of the total process of controlling performance."

11-19. Is it possible for an individual firm to avoid a decision on the type of cost control system to implement in its organization?

11-20. How might cost variations be eliminated before they occur?

11-21. Discuss how one might draw a distinction between physical and dollar reports in terms of reports more related to control as such vs. reports related to reviewing the results of control.

11-22. Discuss how one might draw a distinction between detail and summary reports in terms of reports more related to control as such vs. reports related to reviewing the results of control.

11-23. Define and distinguish between a fixed or static budget and a flexible budget. What type would you recommend, and why?

11-24. How is the distinction between operating and accounting controls related to preventive control, observation, physical and dollar reports?

11-25. What are the accounting bases of controlling manufacturing overhead costs, and what is the position of each within the framework of cost control?

11-26. On the Essence of Cost Control.
The question in the mind of management when it reviews the accounting reports appropriate for cost control is: "What are the causes of these variations and what has already been done to correct the situation?" rather than, "What are the causes of these variations, and how quickly can we determine what they are in order that they might be eliminated?"

Required:

Evaluate the efficacy of the above comments in terms of the materials presented in Chapter 9.

11-27. On the Essence of Cost Control.

The essence of cost control is an accounting report of variations between actual and standard. These reports may be prepared in physical terms or in terms of dollars. In any event, these reports are the signal that waste and inefficiencies have occurred. To control these wastes and inefficiencies is a prime goal of management. Thus, the variances must be analyzed in terms of root causes which must then be eliminated.

Required:

Evaluate the above paragraph in terms of the materials presented in Chapter 9.

11-28. On the Essence of Cost Control.

Cost control activities can eliminate only the continuation of out-of-line performance. This is true since no one can alter or undo what has already occurred. With this in mind, one must admit that cost control reports cannot be used to control events, but they can be used as the basis for "praise, criticism, or suggestions for change, all designed to improve future performance." A subtle way in which cost control reports might influence performance is via a *report card effect* since advance knowledge that cost control reports will be issued tends to provide a stimulus to better performance on the part of the person to be judged.

Required:

Evaluate the above paragraph in terms of the materials presented in Chapter 9.

11-29. Cost Reports and Motivation.

Required:

Discuss the following comment: "I am well aware of the fact that my supervisors are not in a position to influence those costs. However, I am still going to charge them for those costs. My goal is to have them become interested in those costs so that they might work themselves into a position to influence those costs. This to me is an ideal way of using cost reports as a motivational factor within our operations."

► EXERCISES ◄

11-30. Determining Cost Responsibility.

The following is a simplified organization chart showing the lines of responsibility for the Contex Company:

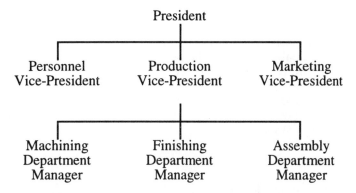

Prepare a schedule like the one shown below. Determine whether each given item is controllable by the officers shown on the chart. Give answers as "Yes" or "No."

	Controllable Costs			
	By Manager of Machining Department	*By Vice-President— Production*	*By Vice-President— Marketing*	*By President*
Production—direct materials				
Salary of marketing vice-president				
Direct labor—assembly				
Supplies—finishing				
Repairs and maintenance—machining				
Salary of manager—machining				
Depreciation—machinery				
Insurance—plant and equipment				
Property taxes				
Advertising and promotion				

11-31. Identify Costs Controllable by a Manager.

The manager of Department One is responsible for costs incurred by his department. As a manager, he is responsible for the purchase of supplies, maintenance and repair costs, and labor costs. Following are costs identifiable with his department:

Department supplies	$ 3,000
Manager's salary	2,000
Direct labor	10,000
Indirect material	1,600
Repairs and maintenance	1,100
Depreciation on equipment	2,000
Heat, light and power	700
Department travel	600
Inspection costs	800
Rework time	900

Required:

a. Identify the costs which are most likely controllable by the manager.

b. Under certain circumstances some costs may seem to be non-controllable by the manager, but in fact, they are controllable. Give an example from the costs listed above and explain how the cost you select may be controllable.

11-32. Identify Costs Controllable by a Vice-President and/or by a Manager.

The following data are taken from the records of a specific cost center which is controlled by a manager. Furthermore, a plant vice-president supervises the manager.

Raw materials and supplies	$ 20,000
Depreciation on equipment	1,000
Repair and maintenance costs	1,200
Direct labor	30,000
Heat, light and power	2,000
Salary of the manager	24,000
Rent for floor space	400
Rework time	1,000
Salary of vice-president	40,000
Property taxes	2,300
Plant security costs	1,200

Required:

Which of the above costs are most likely controllable by the manager? Which are most likely controllable by the plant vice-president?

11-33. Constructing a Series of Performance Reports.

Review Exercise 8-21. Assume that production workers in each operation report to a separate supervisor, each supervisor reports to a plant superintendent, and the plant superintendent reports directly to the president. Also, assume that all materials are purchased by the purchasing agent who reports directly to the president.

Wage rates have been set by a labor contract which has five years to run.

Required:

a. Identify the organization levels involved in the control of:
   1. materials usage
   2. labor efficiency
   3. materials prices
   4. labor rates
b. Identify the control problems involved in:
   1. materials usage
   2. labor efficiency
   3. materials prices
   4. labor rates
c. Discuss the series of reports that might be used in the process of controlling:
   1. materials usage
   2. labor efficiency
   3. materials prices
   4. labor rates
   Keep in mind the level for which each report is being prepared and the frequency of issuance for each report.

11-34. Constructing a Series of Performance Reports.
Review Exercise 8-25. Assume that there is a supervisor in charge of the cutting operations and a supervisor in charge of the sewing operations. These supervisors report to a plant superintendent who reports directly to the president of the company. All materials are purchased by the purchasing agent who reports directly to the president. A labor contract covers wage rates.

Required:

a. Identify the organization levels involved in the control of:
   1. materials usage
   2. labor efficiency
   3. materials prices
   4. labor rates
b. Identify the control problems involved in:
   1. materials usage
   2. labor efficiency
   3. materials prices
   4. labor rates
c. Discuss the series of reports that might be used in the process of controlling:
   1. materials usage
   2. labor efficiency
   3. materials prices
   4. labor rates
   Keep in mind the level for which each report is being prepared and the frequency of issuance for each report.

11-35. **On Performance Measurement.**

The stamping operation of a wheelbarrow manufacturing plant contains six stamping machines which are designed to stamp wheelbarrow trays out of pieces of sheet steel. Each machine requires one operator and three helpers are required to help handle the six machines.

Each machine is capable of stamping each of the four different trays that are made. For each different tray, a special die is used and different sizes and thicknesses of steel are required.

The machines are operated by electricity, and supplies used in the department are primarily lubricating oils.

The worker in charge of the stamping operation is called an assistant supervisor who reports to the general supervisor of the tray department.

Required:

Make a list of the various ways in which performance can be measured considering:

a. The machine operator
b. The assistant supervisor
c. The general supervisor
d. The plant superintendent

11-36. **On the Role of Performance Reports and Those Who Prepare Performance Reports.**

The following quotations are taken from Chris Argyris, Human Problems with Budgets, *Harvard Business Review*, vol. 31, pp. 97-110, Jan-Feb. 1953. This may be considered an old article but it leads to questions which are still pertinent today.

"Our interviewers suggested that the budget people perceive their role as being 'the watchdog of the company.'"

"In other words, the success of the finance people derives from finding errors, weaknesses, and faults that exist in the plant."

"Since the budget people are always looking for faults, they begin to develop a philosophy of life in which their symbol for success is not the error discovered but the very thought of the discovery of a possible new error."

"And so it went. In this cost conscious plant, six people on the supervisory level spent many hours trying to place the blame on someone else."

"At the close of a particularly violent budget meeting in which a top executive had flayed his subordinates needlessly, he ended by saying, `Now fellows, I'm sorry I got hot. But it's these budget figures — well, you know, I worry about them.' The subordinates all nodded their heads to indicate that they understood. They left the meeting room thinking, `Those damn budgets again. They get the boss all upset.'"

Required:

a. Point out and discuss erroneous attitudes concerning the role of performance reports.
b. Identify erroneous attitudes concerning the role of the preparer of a performance report, and discuss how these erroneous attitudes can easily frustrate a program of cost control.

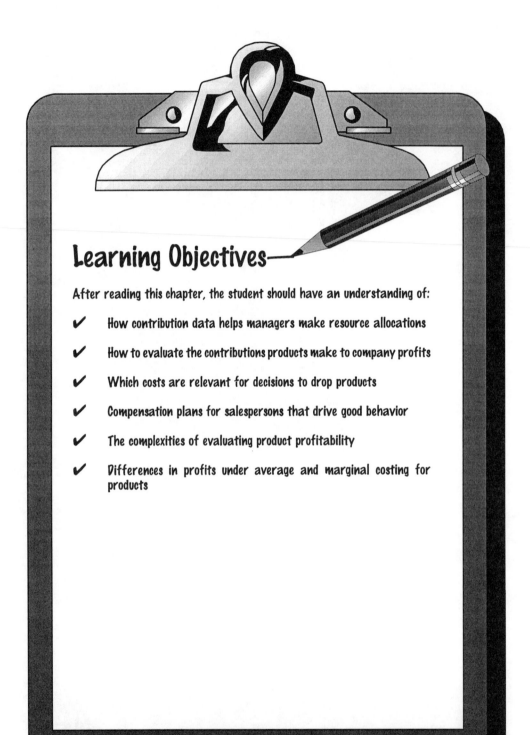

Learning Objectives

After reading this chapter, the student should have an understanding of:

- ✔ How contribution data helps managers make resource allocations

- ✔ How to evaluate the contributions products make to company profits

- ✔ Which costs are relevant for decisions to drop products

- ✔ Compensation plans for salespersons that drive good behavior

- ✔ The complexities of evaluating product profitability

- ✔ Differences in profits under average and marginal costing for products

CONTRIBUTION ACCOUNTING

Managers strive to allocate the resources at their command to their most productive use by moving resources from low value uses to high value uses. For example, mana-gers may shift advertising from one product to another, reassign personnel from one sales region to another, or move equipment from one product line to another if they think this new assignment will generate higher profits. An accounting tool that helps managers make the best resource allocation is contribution accounting, the topic of this chapter. Account-ants use the term *contribution* to describe the dollar amount that a product (or any other revenue generating company segment) *contributes* to company profits after all costs traceable to the product are deducted from the product revenue.

▸ BASIC CONCEPTS OF CONTRIBUTION ACCOUNTING ◂

We begin this discussion by looking at product and market segments although managers may use many other segments for contribution analyses such as distribution channel, customer, salesperson, mode of shipment, etc. Focusing on products and markets allows us to illustrate the basic concepts of contribution accounting without undue complexity.

In analyzing the profitability of products and markets, managers search out and evaluate alternative resource allocations that enable them to locate the most profitable combination of company resources. Consider the profit planning process managers typically use. Usually they start with a review of the present profit structure of current products and markets. Then they estimate the consequences of changing production and sales programs, product mix, sales volumes, product prices, etc. Within the framework of the profit plan managers can also evaluate the profit impact of manipulating the levels of programmed expenditures such as research, advertising and sales promotion.

▸ Relevant Concepts for Product and Market Segments

Accounting Entity. Each product or market segment is an accounting entity for which accountants collect cost and revenue data. For example, company accountants collect data on sales for each product the company sells, and they gather costs directly related to those products as well. These products may be grouped into lines using factors such as product composition (steel or plastic), end use (consumer or industrial user), or brand name. Markets can be classified according to geographic region, class of customer (end user or distributor), distribution channel (retail, wholesale, jobber), and so forth. In making their analyses managers may look at the total sales for a product, total sales in a specific region, or total sales for a particular customer. The decision a manager faces dictates the level of detail used in the contribution analysis. When considering customer profitability, managers consider revenue and costs by customer, and they may even look at individual transactions to evaluate the desirability of doing business with a customer.

Traceable and Joint Costs. When preparing a contribution report, accountants must distinguish between traceable and joint costs for the segment. Consider the product contribution report shown below.

Table 12-1
Contribution Report for Two Products

	Total	*Bicycles*	*Swings*
Sales	$ 390,000	$ 230,000	$ 160,000
Variable costs	130,000	60,000	70,000
Contribution Margin	260,000	170,000	90,000
Fixed costs traceable to products:			
Advertising	30,000	10,000	20,000
Product Contribution	230,000	$ 160,000	$ 70,000
Joint Fixed Costs			
Sales Promotion	30,000		
Production costs	10,000		
Total Joint Fixed Costs	40,000		
Contribution from both products	$ 190,000		

In this report all costs *traceable* to a product appear in the column for that product. For example, the variable costs in the column for the Bicycles are directly traceable to the Bicycles and will disappear if the company drops the Bicycles product. In contrast, the Sales Promotion and the Production costs are *joint* costs that support activities related to both products. If the company drops either of the products it will still spend the same money on promotion and production; neither cost supports a single product. Each cost *jointly* supports both products.

Traceable Cost: A cost directly identified with a product, market, salesperson, customer, etc. These costs typically go away when managers eliminate the object with which they are identified.

Joint Cost: A cost that supports multiple products, markets, salespersons, customers, etc. Because these costs support multiple activities the elimination of any one of the activities does not impact the level of this cost.

Managers use these two cost definitions to identify the costs changed by a specific decision. For example, if company managers are considering whether to drop the Bicycles, managers will not worry about the impact on the joint fixed production costs because they know these costs will continue in their present form. However, the variable and fixed costs traceable to the Bicycles will definitely be impacted by the decision to drop the Bicycles from the product line; the company will not spend money on materials or on advertising for a product it no longer sells.

A cost can be either a traceable or a joint cost depending on the perspective of the decision maker. In the schedule in Table 12-1 the promotion and production costs are joint with respect to the two products, but they are traceable to the two products in total. If these two products make up the toy line of the company, then managers who consider dropping the toy line treat these costs of $40,000 as traceable costs of the toy line. Managers must be careful to specify the decision under consideration to correctly identify joint and traceable costs for that specific decision.

Joint Revenues. Just as managers must consider the implications of joint costs, they must also consider joint revenues. Assume, for instance, that a tire company has found that when replacing tires, owners tended to buy the same brand put on the cars at the factory. Company accountants at the tire company can easily measure the dollar sales of tires to both the auto manufacturer and to the tire retailers. However, when evaluating these markets, managers must recognize that sales in one market affect the other. If managers conclude that sales to auto manufacturers are unprofitable and the company should concentrate on the replacement market, they will find that dropping the auto manufacturers leads to a drop in sales in the retail market. Just because accountants can analyze sales for individual products does not mean that customers look at the products in isolation.

Example: An owner of a hamburger store prepared the following analysis of hamburger and drink sales.

Table 12-2
Joint Revenues

	Total	Hamburgers	Drinks
Sales	$ 100,000	$ 80,000	$ 20,000
Variable costs	51,000	50,000	1,000
Contribution Margin	49,000	$ 30,000	$ 19,000
Fixed Costs	35,000		
Profit	$ 14,000		

The owner reviewed the data and concluded that since the Drinks were so profitable he would drop the Hamburgers (thereby reducing fixed costs by $10,000) and work a little harder to double drink sales to make almost the same profit he now makes. Two weeks after implementing the change, the company was out of business. Customers came to the store to buy hamburgers, and they bought drinks as part of their meal. Without the hamburgers customers were not interested in buying drinks. The revenues from the drinks and the hamburgers were joint revenues, and the owner made a mistake when he considered them as independent elements.

Direct and Indirect Costs. Accountants normally use the terms *direct costs* and *traceable costs* interchangeably when preparing contribution information. Thus the fixed costs traceable to a product or sales territory may be called "direct" or "traceable" costs. *Indirect costs* and *joint costs* are also related. An indirect cost is any cost not directly related to the object under consideration; for example, when looking at the direct and indirect costs of making a bicycle, accountants consider the material cost of the bicycle a *direct* cost of making the bicycle, but they consider the salary of the plant manager an indirect cost. Perhaps the best way to illustrate this concept is with the following story.[1]

A bakery distributed its products through route salesmen each of whom loaded a truck with an assortment of products in the morning and spent the day calling on customers in an assigned territory. Believing that some items were more profitable than others, management asked for an analysis of product costs and sales. The company accountant allocated all manufacturing and indirect marketing costs (driver salary, fuel cost, truck maintenance, etc.) to products to obtain a net profit for each product. The resulting figures indicated the company was selling some of the products at a loss, and management discontinued these products. However, when it dropped the products, the company's over-all profit declined. Dropping the products caused both the product revenue and the direct costs of the products to disappear. However, all the indirect costs of the discontinued products remained in place. The salary for the route salesman did not change; the amount of fuel consumed on the route stayed the same; and, the truck maintenance remained unchanged.

► Time Period Influences on Contribution Information

Managers set the time period they use for profit planning activities by considering the time frame required to carry out plans. Long-range planning emphasizes strategy, the research to develop products, and the sales promotion and advertising to develop new markets. This form of planning and decision making looks years ahead. In contrast, short-range planning focuses on specific operating plans for the coming month, quarter or year and on individual problems and opportunities as they arise.

Activity and Capacity Costs. *Activity* and *capacity* costs are related to the time periods managers consider in making profit analyses. *Activity costs* originate in and are controlled with current activity. Accountants often call these costs variable costs because they tend to vary proportionately with the volume of activity. However, for some variable costs the unit rate changes at some volumes. For example, materials prices may vary as the quantities purchased increases, and labor costs may rise because of overtime and shift premiums as output increases. Managers must watch for these changes because the incremental cost for an additional order when a plant is operating at high volumes may exceed the incremental revenue from that order.

Capacity costs arise because a going business must have physical facilities and an organization ready to support its operations. Because buildings, equipment, and experienced personnel have long acquisition lead times and long useful lives, companies acquire them in advance and keep them available regardless of the current level of activity. The cost of having the physical and personnel capacity available is called *capacity cost*.

Capacity costs tend to persist for long periods of time unless the company changes the type of products or the factors it uses to produce its products. The level of capacity costs can be changed at any time by decisions to enlarge, reduce, or change the composition of present capacity. External variables like salary levels, insurance rates, and tax rates also can affect the level of capacity costs. Capacity costs and fixed costs differ in that fixed costs refer to how a cost behaves as output changes, but capacity costs refer to the kind of management decision that generated the cost.

Committed and Programmed Capacity Costs. *Committed capacity costs* arise from investments in long lived commitments for physical facilities and services. For instance, depreciation, property taxes, and rental payments for long term leases make up typical committed

---

[1] Adapted from McFarland, Walter B., *Concepts for Management Accounting*, National Association of Accountants, 1966, p. 46.

capacity costs. Once managers commit to these costs they cannot reverse their decision without significant financial consequences. General Motors would incur significant costs if it decided to shut its Saturn plant because of its physical plant investment and the long term commitments it has made to personnel. Neither could be abrogated without major losses.

Programmed capacity costs, on the other hand, arise in functions staffed with salaried personnel and in purchased services such as advertising. Company managers plan these costs from period to period based on the expected level of activity, and the costs can be changed on relatively short notice with few penalties.

Contribution reports sometimes recognize these two types of capacity costs by using the following format.

Table 12-3
Contribution Schedule With Capacity Costs

	Total	Western Division	Eastern Division
Sales	$ 350,000	$ 100,000	$ 250,000
Variable costs	140,000	40,000	100,000
Contribution to capacity costs	210,000	60,000	150,000
Programmed capacity costs	115,000	30,000	85,000
Contribution to committed capacity costs	95,000	30,000	65,000
Committed capacity costs	25,000	5,000	20,000
Contribution to profits	$ 70,000	$ 25,000	$ 45,000

This format allows managers to focus attention on the variables impacted by different decisions. The items in the top three rows, for instance, respond to decisions that impact sales volume, sales price, or purchase price; any variation in one of these immediately impacts the contribution to capacity costs. Very short term decisions, such as product mix decisions, can also impact this contribution.

Next, management decisions that cover a longer term, say, one month, come into play on the row reporting programmed capacity costs. Managers can change these within weeks or months, so the management decisions influencing contribution to committed capacity costs cover a longer period than those influencing the items in the top three rows.

Finally, the committed capacity costs appear last in the report because they are very difficult to change and require a much longer time frame for managers to increase or decrease them. This report format presents information to management in increasing levels of unchangeability. The easiest to change items appear at the top of the statement, and the most difficult to change appear near the bottom. This arrangement allows managers to quickly focus their attention on the data that fits the time period they want to consider in their decision.

► MEASURING SEGMENT PROFITABILITY WITH CONTRIBUTION INFORMATION ◄

In addition to providing a good analytical tool, contribution reporting provides managers with a method for implementing responsibility accounting concepts in revenue generating segments of the organization. Managers can review contribution by product, salesperson, customer, distribution channel, or product line. The form in which managers review the data depends on the decision facing them. When evaluating which customers to keep, managers need contribution data by customer; when assessing the value of different products, managers need contribution by product and product line; and, when choosing which market region to expand, managers need contribution by region. Thus the accountant must be prepared to develop contribution information in many different formats.

► Contribution Hierarchies

All these contribution reports form a hierarchy of reports that fit together. The following reports illustrate this for a firm that has three divisions: Foods, Chemicals, and Fertilizers. The Food Division has three product lines, Bouillon, Baked Goods, and Sea food, and the Bouillon product line is sold through three different channels: Institutional, Home, and Vending Machine. The first contribution schedule in Table 12-4 shows contribution for the three divisions and profit for the total company.

Table 12-4
Division Contribution

	Company Total	Divisions		
		Foods	Chemicals	Fertilizers
Sales	$5,350,000	$850,000	$2,000,000	$2,500,000
Total Variable	2,620,00	395,000	1,000,000	1,225,000
Contribution Margin	2,730,00	455,000	1,000,000	1,275,000
Division Direct Fixed Cost	1,235,00	285,000	430,000	520,000
Division Contribution	$1,495,000	$170,000	$ 570,000	$ 755,000
Company Fixed Costs				
Administration	$ 250,000			
Marketing	185,000			
Research & Development	150,000			
Corporate Costs	85,000			
Total Corporate	$ 670,000			
Before Tax Net Income	$ 825,000			

With this arrangement of data managers can explore the profit consequences of moving resources from one division to another. For example, managers can assess the impact of moving $100,000 of division fixed cost from Chemicals to Fertilizers. If this causes the contribution of Chemicals to remain the same (sales could drop by $200,000) but improves that of Fertilizer by

$30,000 (sales increase $254,902), the company profits improve by $30,000. Analyses like these are easy with a contribution format for data.

If managers want to assess product lines in the Food Division, they can examine the contribution schedule shown in Table 12-5. This schedule shows the details for each product line sold by the Food Division. Notice how the total division contribution in this schedule matches that reported in Table 12-4. Again, managers can evaluate the impact of moving resources from one product line to another by considering the impact on the product line contribution. Changes in the total product line contribution measure the profit impact of the change in resource allocation.

Table 12-5
Division Contribution By Product Line–Foods Division

	Division Total	Product Lines		
		Bouillon	Baked Goods	Sea Foods
Net Sales	$850,000	$255,000	$170,000	$425,000
Total Variable	395,000	110,000	141,000	144,000
Contribution Margin	$455,000	$145,000	$ 29,000	$281,000
Product Line Direct Fixed Costs				
Production	$ 70,000	$35,000	$ 14,000	$ 21,000
Marketing	30,000	10,500	4,500	15,000
Total Product Line Fixed Cost	100,000	45,500	18,500	36,000
Product Line Contribution	$355,000	$99,500	$ 10,500	$245,000
Foods Division Fixed Costs	185,000			
Foods Division Contribution	$170,000			

A manager who is interested in which distribution channel for the Bouillon product line generates the most contribution can review the data in Table 12-6. Analyses like these enable managers to choose the distribution channel that generates the most contribution from sales of its products. They also allow managers to evaluate the profit impact of changes in resource allocations among distribution channels. Notice how the Bouillon product line contribution of $99,500 shown in Table 12-5 matches the total contribution reported in Table 12-6.

By arranging contribution schedules in a hierarchy like this, managers can review division, product line, or distribution channel profitability, select which segment to eliminate, or change the resource allocation among business segments.

Table 12-6
Product Line Contribution by Distribution Channel–Bouillon

	Product Line Total	Distribution Channel		
		Institutional	Home	Vending Machines
Sales	$255,000	$63,750	$89,250	$102,000
Total Variable Costs	110,000	44,000	21,225	44,775
Contribution Margin	145,000	19,750	68,025	57,225
Direct Fixed Costs of Distribution Channel				
Production	25,000	8,750	7,500	8,750
Marketing	6,500	2,925	1,625	1,950
Total Fixed Cost	31,500	11,675	9,125	10,700
Channel Contribution	$113,500	$ 8,075	$58,900	$ 46,525
Bouillon Product Line Fixed Costs				
Administration	$ 10,000			
Marketing	4,000			
Total	14,000			
Bouillon Product Line Contribution	$ 99,500			

Costs and Contribution Segments. In any contribution hierarchy, costs become traceable to different segments at different points in the hierarchy. Generally, the higher one moves up the hierarchy, the greater the number of costs traceable to that part of the hierarchy. This relationship of costs to product segments is as follows:[2]

Table 12-7
Relation of Costs to Product Segments

Type of Segment	Traceable (Direct) Costs	Joint (Indirect) Costs
Unit of product	Variable with units	All other costs
Product in the line	Above plus fixed to product	All other costs
Product line	Above plus fixed to line	All other costs
Plant	Above plus fixed to plant	All other costs
Division	Above plus fixed to division	All other costs
Company	All costs	None

[2] Raymond P. Marple "Management Accounting Is Coming of Age," *Management Accounting* (July, 1967), p. 7.

Traceable segment costs are the ones managers increase or decrease with decisions that change segment output, segment capacity, or segment marketing activities. These costs exist because the segment exists—if the segment disappears, the costs disappear. Since all costs would disappear if the company ceased to exist, all costs are direct costs of the company as a whole. As one considers smaller and smaller segments, more company costs become indirect or common costs. In other words, the smaller the segment under consideration by a manager, the smaller in number and value the costs impacted by that manager's decisions.

Managers can use a similar sequence of segments for developing information about the marketing side of the organization:

Table 12-8
Relation of Costs to Marketing Segments

Type of Segment	Traceable (direct) Costs	Joint (Indirect) Costs
Sales transaction	Variable product and selling costs	All other costs
Customer	Above plus fixed to customer	All other costs
Salesperson	Above plus fixed to salesperson	All other costs
Territory	Above plus fixed to territory	All other costs
Sales district	Above plus fixed to district	All other costs
Company	All costs	None

Tables 12-7 and 12-8 show two possible sequences managers can use for applying costs against revenues to measure stage by stage the contribution each segment makes to total company profits. The segment contribution in a sense is its contribution to company net profit.

▶ CONTRIBUTION ACCOUNTING AND THE COMPENSATION OF SALES PERSONNEL ◀

Contribution data can also help managers choose salesperson compensation plans. Consider the following data in Table 12-9 for a company with two salespeople who sell supplies to the garment industry. Both salespeople receive a commission of 4% of sales for everything they sell, and the company reimburses them for all costs they incur in making sales to their customers.

As this table shows both salespeople generate the same dollar amount of contribution margin, but Mary contributes the most to company profits. Not only does Joe sell a less profitable product mix (his contribution margin percentage is 17 points less than Mary's), but he also spends more ($4,000 versus $2,800) on customers than she does. The problem with the compensation system this company uses is that it rewards sales personnel for increasing sales instead of rewarding them for increasing profits. The reward structure is wrong.

A system that pays sales personnel a percentage of the contribution they generate encourages them to increase company profits while increasing their earnings. Suppose the company illustrated in Table 12-9 paid sales personnel 9% of the contribution they generated before compensation. This would result in the following set of payments to the two salespeople.

Table 12-9
Compensation of Salespeople

	Joe	Mary
Sales	$ 100,000	$ 70,000
Variable cost of units sold	59,500	29,500
Contribution margin	40,500	40,500
Contribution margin percentage	41%	58%
Expenses traceable to salesperson		
Travel and entertainment	2,000	1,000
Rush order costs	3,000	500
Total costs	5,000	1,500
Contribution before commissions	35,500	39,000
Commissions (4% of sales)	4,000	2,800
Net contribution to company	$ 31,500	$ 36,200

	Joe	Mary
Contribution before commissions	$ 35,500	$ 39,000
Commissions (9% of contribution)	3,195	3,510
Net contribution to company	$ 32,305	$ 35,490

Under this approach, Mary, who generates the greatest contribution for the company, gets the most pay. Such a system rewards those who add to company profits and penalizes those who do not. It aligns the financial goals of sales personnel with the financial goals of the company.

A firm can also use such a system to police the amount that sales personnel spend on wooing customers. Consider the case here; every time Joe spends $100 on a customer, his compensation will drop by $9 because of the $100 reduction in the contribution caused by the additional spending. Instead of hiring a large staff to watch carefully over expense reports, a company may tell its sales staff : "Spend all you want entertaining customers, but remember that your compensation drops by $9 every time you spend another $100 on a customer."

▸ DATABASE STRUCTURES AND CONTRIBUTION ACCOUNTING ◂

In order to capture data for contribution analyses accountants must design a code structure that allows managers to extract contribution data for a variety of company segments like product, customer, etc. Consider the contribution hierarchy for a company with three divisions illustrated in Tables 12-4, 12-5 and 12-6 . This company needs the following fields in its transaction code to capture the data presented in the contribution schedules:

Division
Product number
Distribution channel

To capture data for contribution analyses by product or market segment as listed in the last two tables, accountants need the following fields in the transaction code used to capture data on costs and revenues.

Field Name	*Description*
PDTNUM	Product Number
EXP	Expense code
PDTLIN	Product Line Number
PLANT	Plant Number
DIV	Division Identifier
CUSTNO	Customer Number
SPER	Salesperson Number
STER	Sales Territory Number
SDIS	Sales District Number
REVXP	Sales or Expense Identifier
AMOUNT	Dollar amount

With these eleven fields, company managers can extract from the company database the data required for any contribution analysis by product or market segment. Consider the following examples of information and the SQL codes that pull the data from the company database.

1. A manager wants to know the sales and costs related to product number 21.

   SQL code for revenues
   SELECT SUM(AMOUNT) FROM TRANSACT WHERE PDT=21 AND REVXP=R;
   SQL code for expenses
   SELECT SUM(AMOUNT) FROM TRANSACT WHERE PDT=21 AND REVXP=X;

These two commands provide the total revenue and expenses that are traceable to product 21, and combining them provides the manager with the total contribution for this product.

2. A manager wants the contribution for all products made at plant 15.

   SQL code for revenues
   SELECT SUM(AMOUNT) FROM TRANSACT WHERE PLANT=15 AND REVXP=R;
   SQL code for expenses
   SELECT SUM(AMOUNT) FROM TRANSACT WHERE PLANT=15 AND REVXP=X;

3. A manager wants all variable costs related to the sales of product 43. All variable costs begin with the number 3 in this system.

   SQL code for variable costs
   SELECT SUM(AMOUNT) FROM TRANSACT WHERE PDT=43 AND ACCT=3*;

This command will sum all variable costs related to product 43, and the manager can paste the result into a spreadsheet to complete the contribution schedule. Many commercial databases provide report writers to speed up this process, but in this book we present only the SQL codes to help the student become familiar with structure of the language.

► SPECIAL ANALYSES WITH CONTRIBUTION ACCOUNTING ◄

In this section we consider special analyses an accountant or manager can perform using contribution accounting. First we examine pricing analyses, then advertising and promotion expenditure evaluation, and finally we review the analyses that support product mix and product elimination decisions.

► Product Pricing Analyses

The contribution format helps managers evaluate tradeoffs between different pricing plans, different promotion plans, and interaction of prices and promotion. Consider the following example for a company that sells Garden Tractors and Lawn Mowers.

Table 12-10
Pricing Analyses

	Total	*Tractors*	*Mowers*
Sales	$ 145,000	$ 65,000	$ 80,000
Variable costs	95,000	40,000	55,000
Contribution Margin	50,000		
		25,000	25,000
Fixed Costs Traceable to Products	25,000	10,000	15,000
Individual Product Contribution	25,000	$ 15,000	$ 10,000
Common Fixed Costs	5,000		
Contribution from both products	$ 20,000		

Managers can assess the impact of price and volume changes by manipulating the prices and volumes of either product. For example, a manager wonders what would happen to total contribution if Tractor prices increased by 5% and volume dropped by 10%. She makes the changes and prints the results shown in Table 12-11. These results show that the price change would increase profits by $425, a relatively small amount since the total contribution was $20,000 before making the price change.

Next the manager asks what contribution will be if she drops Tractor prices by 5% for a 15% increase in volume while simultaneously increasing Mower prices 10% with a 20% drop in volume. This provides the contribution schedule in Table 12-12, and this analysis shows that the combined changes result in a greater contribution than the original analysis. Managers can study the contribution impact of different prices and volumes to choose the best price for a product. Of course, the manager must base all analyses like this on knowledge of customer reactions to price changes.

Table 12-11
Prices Increase 5% and Volume Drops 10%

	Total	Tractors	Mowers
Sales	$ 141,425	$ 61,425	$ 80,000
Variable costs	91,000	36,000	55,000
Contribution Margin	50,425	25,425	25,000
Fixed Costs Traceable to Products	25,000	10,000	15,000
Individual Product Contribution	25,425	$ 15,425	$ 10,000
Common Fixed Costs	5,000		
Contribution from both products	$ 20,425		

Note: The values for Tractors were computed as follows:
Sales = ($65,000 x 1.05) x .90 = $61,425
Variable costs = $40,000 x .90 = $36,000

Table 12-12
Price Changes for Both Tractor and Mower

	Total	Tractors	Mowers
Sales	$ 141,413	$ 71,013	$ 70,400
Variable costs	90,000	46,000	44,000
Contribution Margin	51,413	25,013	26,400
Fixed Costs Traceable to Products	25,000	10,000	15,000
Individual Product Contribution	26,413	$ 15,013	$ 11,400
Common Fixed Costs	5,000		
Contribution from both products	$ 21,413		

Note: The values for Tractors were computed as follows:
Sales = ($65,000 x .95) x 1.15 = $71,013
Variable costs = $40,000 x 1.15 = $46,000

Note: The values for Mowers were computed as follows:
Sales = ($80,000 x 1.10) x .80 = $70,400
Variable costs = $55,000 x .80 = $44,000

► Contribution Analyses for Advertising and Promotion Decisions

The same contribution format used for evaluating the profit impact of alternative prices and unit volumes also works for assessing the impact of different levels of promotional expenditures. Suppose, for instance, that the manager using the data in Table 12-10 wants to consider the impact of changes in advertising expenditures. She starts with the same data in Table 12-10 and then estimates the effect of different advertising expenditures on sales volume; she estimates that an increase of $5,000 in advertising for the Tractors will increase their sales by 10%, and she plans to take this amount of advertising away from the Mowers which will cause their volume to drop by 15%. Does this increase or decrease the total contribution from the two products? Table 12-13 shows the results of these changes.

Table 12-13
Shift Advertising Dollars from Mowers to Tractors

	Total	Tractors	Mowers
Sales	$ 139,500	$ 71,500	$ 68,000
Variable costs	90,750	44,000	46,750
Contribution Margin	48,750	27,500	21,250
Fixed Costs Traceable to Products	25,000	15,000	10,000
Individual Product Contribution	23,750	$ 12,500	$ 11,250
Common Fixed Costs	5,000		
Contribution from both products	$ 18,750		

Note: The values for Tractors were computed as follows:
Sales = $65,000 x 1.10 = $71,500
Variable costs = $40,000 x 1.10 x = $44,000

Note: The values for Mowers were computed as follows:
Sales = $80,000 x .85 = $68,000
Variable costs = $55,000 x .85 = $46,750

Although the other analyses showed that changing prices increased total contribution, this analysis indicates that shifting advertising from Mowers to Tractors does not increase the contribution. In other words, shifting advertising from Mowers to Tractors moves the advertising from a high value use to a low value use. The manager in this case would do better to keep the $5,000 of advertising expenditures with the Mowers.

▸ Product Profitability, Product Mix, and Optimal Resource Use

Managers can also use contribution data to evaluate product profitability, to determine the best mix of products, and to evaluate resource use. Actually, all these decisions are related, and Table 12-14 provides data on two products that illustrate these decisions.

This company manufactures large, heavy pumps customers use to pump water from deep coal mines or to pump gravel from a flooded gravel pit to trucks or rail cars. These pumps are approximately twenty feet across and six feet deep, and are very large.

The schedule shows the contribution for the two products for the past month. The plant manager asks, "Which product is the most profitable?" The answer to this question is not a simple one. For instance, the Coal Mine Pump has a 44% contribution margin while the Gravel Pit Pump has a 38% margin; however, the Gravel Pit Pump generates a total contribution of $13,000, an amount over twice the $6,000 from the Coal Mine Pump. Which is the correct measure of product profitability?

Actually, neither number provides the answer to the question. The contribution schedule tells managers how much monthly profits will drop if they eliminate either product, but it cannot tell them which product is the most valuable. To answer this question managers must consider how the two products fit the company strategy, how they complement other products, and what customers will do if they cannot buy one of the products from the company. The question about product profitability

Table 12-14
Product Profitability Analyses

	Coal Mine Pumps	Gravel Pit Pumps
Revenue	$25,000	$55,000
Material Cost	10,000	25,000
Labor Cost	4,000	9,000
Total Variable Cost	14,000	34,000
Contribution Margin	$11,000	$21,000
Contribution Margin Percentage	44%	38%
Traceable Fixed Costs	5,000	8,000
Product Contribution	$ 6,000	$13,000

is too vague. Does it mean the manager wants to know which product to eliminate? If so, the contribution schedule gives an answer to that question. Does it mean which product the company should push? The answer to that question relates to the impact of changing the level of resources devoted to advertising and promotion of a product (covered in an earlier section).

Another possible interpretation is that the manager wants to know how to allocate a scarce, or bottleneck, resource to the two products. If this is the case, the manager needs to know what happens to product contribution if more or less of a resource is assigned to that product. Suppose company managers are concerned about the possible scarcity of labor time, machine time or storage space in the plant. Table 12-15 shows the amount of each of these resources devoted to each product.

In this schedule we show how much of each bottleneck resource a product uses, and how much contribution margin it generates for each unit of the resource. The Coal Mine pump generates $220 for every machine hour it uses, and the Gravel Pit pump produces $300 for every machine hour it consumes. If machine hours are very scarce, then assigning a machine hour to the Gravel Pit Pump adds $300 to profits as compared to only $220 if that same hour is used on a Coal Mine Pump. The contribution margin per unit of the constraining resource tells managers which product should receive the resource to generate the greatest value for the company.

A list of contribution margin per resource unit enables managers to assign resources to their most valuable use whenever the resource becomes very scarce. For example, if a machine breaks down and managers must decide which product gets priority at the remaining machines, the products with the highest margin per machine hour get priority because they add the most to profits. The same reasoning applies to the other resources.

In the case where many constraints limit production, companies use linear programming models to compute the optimal combination of products to make. We use just one resource here to illustrate the concept.

In conclusion, when evaluating the desirability of different products, managers must consider company strategy, customer needs, and the resource constraints facing the company to decide which product gets priority in decision making. There is no simple answer to the question "Which product is the most profitable?"

Table 12-15
Resource Constraints and Product Profitability

	Coal Mine Pumps	Gravel Pit Pumps
Revenue	$25,000	$55,000
Material Cost	10,000	25,000
Labor Cost	4,000	9,000
Total Variable Cost	14000	34,000
Contribution Margin	$11,000	$21,000
Contribution Margin Percentage	44%	38%
Traceable Fixed Costs	5,000	8000
Product Contribution	$6,000	$13,000
Constraining Resources Used		
Machining hours	50	70
Labor hours	100	250
Total days in plant	20	60
Margin Per Constrained Resource		
Machining hours	$ 220	$ 300
Labor hours	110	84
Total time in plant	550	350

▸ Using a Contribution Approach to Budgeting

Some companies use a contribution approach to budgeting to encourage managers to increase company profits. With this approach managers begin the process by choosing a profit target. Then, they add common company fixed costs to this amount to arrive at the total contribution required from the marketing function. Marketing managers use this contribution goal to assign contribution targets to sales territories and individual sales personnel. Consider the following set of data for a company that manufactures equipment for the restaurant industry.

Profit Target	$ 50,000
Common Company Fixed Costs	
Manufacturing	120,000
Administrative	200,000
Total Common Fixed Costs	320,000
Contribution Goal for Marketing	$ 370,000

The company wants to make $50,000 of profit during the next quarter, so managers add the fixed costs of all nonmarketing activities to this profit target to get the total contribution that revenue generating activities must produce.

The marketing manager then uses this amount to determine the contribution targets for the two territories she manages. If her quarterly administrative costs amount to $30,000, then the two sales territories must generate a total of $400,000 in contribution to meet this target ($400,000-$30,000 equals the marketing contribution of $370,000). After many discussions with her territory managers, the marketing manager finally arrives at a contribution target for the West Territory of $250,000 and a target of $150,000 for the East Territory. Each territory manager follows a similar approach to assigning the contribution targets to their sales personnel. For example, the East Territory manager adds the direct fixed costs of his territory ($20,000) to the territory contribution target of $150,000 to compute the total contribution his sales people must generate, $170,000.

Although this discussion sounds very mechanical, this process usually proceeds with numerous meetings to discuss the appropriate contribution targets at each level in the organization. In every meeting managers are forced to deal with the fundamental economics of pricing, promotion, and unit sales volume for their company segment, and initial goals get modified as the discussions move toward final budget approval. A combination of this budgeting approach with a contribution based compensation plan provides managers with a powerful tool for managing company profits.

▶ FINANCIAL REPORTING AND CONTRIBUTION ACCOUNTING ◀

Contribution accounting has an impact on financial reporting because it provides different net income values than does absorption, or traditional, cost accounting. In absorption cost accounting a portion of fixed manufacturing costs is assigned to each unit sold whereas in a contribution approach no fixed cost is assigned to the units produced; only the unit variable costs are assigned to the units sold. This impacts net income only when inventory rises or falls from one period to the next. If inventory levels remain the same, both approaches to net income provide the same net income before tax. Table 12-16 illustrates these differences.

In this example the company has a single product with a variable cost of $10 and a selling price of $50. Total annual manufacturing costs amount to $240,000, and the annual production is normally 10,000 units for a unit fixed cost of $24. Additional administrative fixed costs amount to another $60,000 annually. We show data for three years of operation below. Notice that the net incomes are the same in the first year but differ widely in the next two years.

In the first year the company produces and sells the same number of units, so inventory levels do not change. However, in the second year the company builds inventory because it produces 10,000 units but it only sells 5,000 units. Under conventional, or absorption, costing $120,000 of fixed cost (5,000 units x $24 per unit of fixed cost) is pulled off the income statement and placed on the balance sheet as part of inventory cost. Consequently, absorption costing shows a net income for the second year that is $120,000 higher than the contribution accounting net income.

In year three the reverse happens. In this year the company still produces 10,000 units, but it sells all of these plus 5,000 units from inventory–the investment in inventory drops, and the absorption cost net income is lower by $120,000 (5,000 units x $24 per unit of fixed cost) because the fixed costs that were held on the balance sheet now move to the income statement. Net income under absorption costing fluctuates with the level of inventory, i.e., an increase in inventory causes the net income to rise, and a decrease in inventory causes the net income to fall.

This information is useful when looking at monthly or quarterly financial statements for a manufacturing firm; if the inventory for the firm rises and the firm is using absorption costing, the net income will have an upward bias relative to contribution accounting. Manufacturing firms that produce seasonal products and use absorption accounting often find that net income rises during periods of low sales (inventory is rising) and falls during periods of high sales (inventory is falling). Managers who receive a bonus based on net income can manipulate the net income generated by the absorption cost system by building inventory during bad months to boost net income.

Table 12-16
Absorption Accounting and Contribution Accounting

Year 1: Produce and sell 10,000 units

	Absorption Costing	Contribution Accounting
Sales	$500,000	$ 500,000
Cost of sales	340,000	100,000
Gross profit	160,000	400,000
Fixed costs	60,000	300,000
Profit	$100,000	$ 100,000

Year 2: Produce 10,000 units and sell 5,000 units

	Absorption Costing	Contribution Accounting
Sales	$250,000	$250,000
Cost of sales	170,000	50,000
Gross profit	80,000	200,000
Fixed costs	60,000	300,000
Profit	$ 20,000	$(100,000)

Year 3: Produce 10,000 units and sell 15,000 units

	Absorption Costing	Contribution Accounting
Sales	$750,000	$ 750,000
Cost of sales	510,000	150,000
Gross profit	240,000	600,000
Fixed costs	60,000	300,000
Profit	$180,000	$ 300,000

► CONCLUSION ◄

Contribution accounting allows managers to evaluate the profit impact of moving company resources from one use to another. Managers can evaluate the profit consequences of shifting resources from one division to another, from one product to another, or from one sales region to another. In every case managers are seeking the best allocation of company resources that will generate the highest possible profit. Contribution accounting helps with these decisions because it groups together revenues and expenses that are impacted by the same decisions. This allows managers to quickly perform analyses that show them the financial consequences of reassigning company resources. Companies can also use contribution accounting for management reporting to show managers their contribution to total company profits.

► QUESTIONS ◄

12-1. For what types of management decisions does contribution data provide relevant information to managers?

12-2. Give five examples of accounting segments for which managers might want contribution data.

12-3. Explain the difference between traceable and joint costs.

12-4. Give an example of products with joint revenues.

12-5. Define capacity costs. How do committed capacity costs differ from programmed capacity costs?

12-6. "All costs are traceable to the total company." Explain.

12-7. When a company has a scarce, or bottleneck resource, how does it decide which product receives priority in the use of this resource?

12-8. Why is the net income higher under absorption cost accounting than under contribution accounting when inventories increase?

12-9. Use the data in Table 15 to answer this question. To which product should managers assign an additional labor hour when labor hours are scarce?

12-10. Use the data in Table 10 to answer this question. If the price of Mowers increase by 10% and volume drops by 10%, how much must the fixed cost traceable to Mowers change in order to keep Mowers contribution at $10,000?

► EXERCISES ◄

12-11. **Contribution Statements.** Use the following information about two products produced by a company to develop a contribution schedule similar to that shown in Table 12-1. The data represent sales for the past month.

	Total	Tables	Chairs
Revenue	$ 85,000	$ 50,000	$ 35,000
Variable costs	35,000	20,000	15,000
Contribution margin	$ 50,000	$ 30,000	$ 20,000

You have gathered the following information about this company:

1. The company spends $10,000 monthly on advertising with $2,000 of that devoted to the Tables and $4,000 to the Chairs. The rest helps promote the company name.
2. Administrative costs equal $15,000 monthly, and administrators spend about one-half their time working on these two products and the rest on general company activities.

3. One machine with a monthly cost of $4,000 is devoted exclusively to packaging the Chairs, but all other equipment works on both products. Total monthly costs of machines and related activities, including the $4,000, equal $12,000.

Required:

a. Prepare a contribution schedule for this company showing contribution for the two products.
b. If company managers decided to drop one of these products, which one should they drop? Why?
c. Which products generates the greatest value for the advertising dollars devoted to it?
d. Which costs are joint costs with respect to the two products?

12-12. **Joint Revenues and Product Analysis.** You developed the following analysis of product contribution for your shop that specializes in ties and shirts.

	Total	Ties	Shirts
Revenue	$ 60,000	$ 25,000	$ 35,000
Variable costs	20,000	5,000	15,000
Contribution margin	40,000	20,000	20,000
Advertising and promotion	2,500	2,000	500
Product contribution	37,500	$ 18,000	$ 19,500
Rent and salaries	15,000		
Profit before taxes	$ 22,500		

Required:

a. Which product has the highest contribution margin percentage? Show calculations.
b. On average, customers spend about $5 on Ties for each $10 they spend on Shirts. Assume this holds true for any sales increases. How much will profit increase for a $1,000 increase in Shirt sales? Show calculations.
c. If the company stopped selling Shirts and started selling only Ties, would you expect company profits to increase or decrease? Why?
d. How can managers use the concept of joint revenues to make profit maximizing decisions?

12-13. Joint Costs and Decision Making. A restaurant manager in a hotel was reviewing the contribution schedule he received every morning for the for meals served in his restaurant the previous day.

	Total	Steak	Fish	Vegetarian	Desert
Revenue	$ 6,900	$ 2,000	$3,000	$ 700	$ 1,200
Variable costs	2,900	800	1,200	500	400
Contribution margin	4,000	$ 1,200	$ 1,800	$ 200	$ 800
Salaries--administrative	500				
Salaries--waiters	1,500				
Other costs	350				
Total	2,350				
Restaurant contribution	$ 1,650				

Required:

a. Which meal has the highest contribution margin percentage?

b. If sales of Steak meals doubled with all others remaining the same, how much would total contribution from the restaurant increase?

c. None of the salaries appear as traceable costs of the meals. Why did the accountant not include them as traceable costs of the meals?

d. Rework the schedule by dividing the total costs of $2,350 among the meals according to the dollar sales of meals (that is, Steak gets ($2,000 / $6,900) x $2,350 = $681). How much will total restaurant contribution to hotel profits change if the restaurant manager drops the Vegetarian meal? Give calculations and reasons to support your answer.

e. Which meal will add the most to hotel profits if meal sales increase by $1,000? Why?

12-14. Programmed and Committed Capacity Costs. The Alexander Corporation operates two divisions, the Northern Division, and the Southern Division. The contribution margins generated by these two divisions for the past month appear in the following table.

	Total	Northern	Southern
Revenue	$ 630,000	$ 280,000	$ 350,000
Variable costs	413,000	168,000	245,000
Contribution margin	217,000	112,000	105,000

The company accountant also compiled the following information about various fixed costs incurred by the two divisions.

	Total	Northern	Southern
Administrative personnel	$ 37,000	$ 15,000	$ 12,000
Depreciation	75,000	50,000	35,000
Plant maintenance	12,000	8,000	4,000
Advertising and promotion	40,000	25,000	15,000
Total expenses	$164,000	$ 98,000	$ 66,000

Required:

a. Prepare a contribution schedule like that in Table 12-3 using the above information.
b. Which division could more easily cut expenses if it ran into profit problems? Explain.
c. How does grouping capacity costs into the categories of Committed and Programmed help managers make decisions about operations?

12-15. Resource Shifting and Profit Maximization. You are the manager of the California territory of your company, and your accountant has prepared the following schedule for you showing the product contribution for three of your top product lines.

	Total	*Drives*	*Printers*	*Monitors*
Revenue	$765,000	$250,000	$325,000	$190,000
Variable costs	609,000	187,500	260,000	161,500
Contribution margin	156,000	62,500	65,000	28,500
Advertising	68,000	45,000	15,000	8,000
Product contribution	88,000	$ 17,500	$ 50,000	$ 20,500
Rent and salaries	15,000			
Profit before taxes	$ 73,000			

Required:

a. Which product line generates the most sales per dollar spent on advertising?
b. Assume you can shift $10,000 of advertising from Drives to Printers with a corresponding drop in Drive sales of $50,000 and an increase in Printers sales of $55,000. Compute the dollar amount profits increase or decrease because of this shift? Assume contribution margin percentages for the Drives and Printers remain the same.
c. Use the information in question b. Did moving advertising dollars from Drives to Printers move the advertising from a low value use to a high value use, or vice versa? Explain.
d. Would the contribution margin percentage for your territory increase or decrease with the change mentioned in question b? Show calculations.

▸ PROBLEMS AND CASES ◂

12-16. Recasting Income Statement to a Contribution Format.

"We can't keep supporting losing products like those in our wood line," said Mike McMahon, Director of Marketing for Brown, Inc. "Our monthly profit would increase almost $80,000 if we dropped this line. I don't see why Tom (Tom Abene, President of Brown, Inc.) makes us keep this product."

You work for the prestigious consulting firm of Britton, Corgan & Garber who have been hired to review the performance of the three product lines of Brown, Inc. You begin your review by interviewing Robert (Bucko) Layman, the young accountant who has responsibility for managing the accounting system.

Bucko explains that he is not very happy with the existing report developed by the previous accountant (Myron Goins) because it contains too many arbitrary cost allocations. For example, Bucko explains, only the "Fixed Division Expenses" in the fixed costs are traceable to any of the product divisions. None of the fixed manufacturing cost is traceable to any of the divisions.

"Of course," Bucko adds, "none of the expenses from the Selling & Administrative or any of the items listed in the statement below S&A are traceable to the product lines either. Our previous accountant just wanted to calculate a net income for each product line whether or not it made sense."

The financial statements these managers are discussing are shown below. All product transfers between the Wood Division and the Chemicals Division are made at market prices.

	Company Total	Plastics	Chemicals	Wood
Gross Customer Sales	$50,700,000	$1,200,000	$43,000,000	$6,500,000
Less: Returns	215,400	400	145,000	70,000
Allowances	190,000	0	130,000	60,000
Freight	728,000	8,000	550,000	170,000
Cash Discount	350,100	100	330,000	20,000
Total deductions	1,483,500	8,500	1,155,000	320,000
Net Customer Sales	49,216,500	1,191,500	41,845,000	6,180,000
Net Intercompany Sales				4,500,000
Net Sales	53,716,500	1,191,500	41,845,000	10,680,000
Cost of Sales:				
Materials Used	25,050,000	300,000	20,000,000	4,750,000
Supplies Used	3,255,000	35,000	2,300,000	920,000
Direct Labor & Fringes	4,400,000	100,000	3,200,000	1,100,000
Variable Overhead	1,440,500	60,500	970,000	410,000
	34,145,500	495,500	26,470,000	7,180,000
Net Contribution	19,571,000	696,000	15,375,000	3,500,000
Fixed Division Costs	6,160,000	60,000	4,000,000	2,100,000
Fixed Manufacturing	2,701,550	49,190	2,350,423	298,837
Total Fixed Overhead	8,861,550	112,290	6,350,423	2,398,837

Net Manufacturing Margin	10,709,450	583,710	9,024,577	1,101,163
Selling and Administrative Expense	4,300,000	72,727	3,727,273	500,000
Operating Inc (Loss)	6,409,450	510,983	5,297,304	601,163
Income Taxes	941,308	15,921	815,933	109,454
Net Earnings	$ 5,468,142	$ 495,062	$ 4,481,371	$ 491,709

Required:

a. Recast the income statements in a contribution format, and make any changes to the format that you think will improve the presentation of information in the statements.
b. Compute a breakeven sales amount for each of the product lines.
c. Which product line do you think is the most valuable? Why?

12-17. **Contribution Hierarchy and Profit Calculations.** The following organization chart shows the organization for a manufacturing firm that produces and sells a variety of products. The products are sold by salespeople who sell all the products. The company charges each salesperson with the variable production cost of each unit they sell, so all variable production costs are passed through to the marketing area. The numbers shown here are all budgeted numbers for the coming month. The numbers that appear in each organization block are the fixed costs traceable to that function. For example, the fixed costs for the V.P. of production are $15,000.

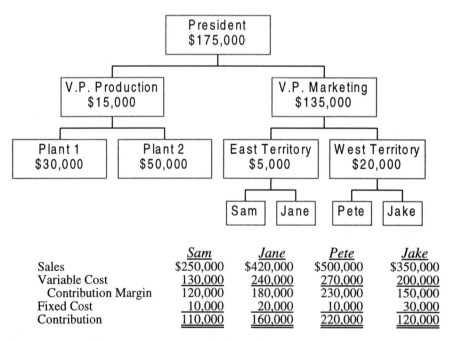

	Sam	Jane	Pete	Jake
Sales	$250,000	$420,000	$500,000	$350,000
Variable Cost	130,000	240,000	270,000	200,000
Contribution Margin	120,000	180,000	230,000	150,000
Fixed Cost	10,000	20,000	10,000	30,000
Contribution	110,000	160,000	220,000	120,000

The sales for each salesperson are shown in the table.

Required:

a. Compute the contribution for the East Territory.
b. Compute the contribution for the West Territory.
c. How much contribution does the marketing function generate for the company?
d. If fixed production costs rise by $5,000, how much must Jane increase her sales to keep company profits at the same level they are now?
e. How much are company profits?
f. If the company wants to add $10,000 in profits, how much must Sam increase his contribution to generate this amount of profit for the company? What will his sales be at this new level?

12-18. Pricing Analyses and Breakeven Analysis. Roberta is reviewing the following schedule of contribution for the three product lines she manages, and she asks you to prepare analyses to answer the following questions:

1. What is the breakeven dollar sales for my area of responsibility?
2. If I increase prices by 10% for the Toys, what is the new breakeven point for Toys?
3. How much will my total contribution for the quarter change if prices for toys increase 10% with a resultant drop in volume of 15%?
4. If I make the changes mentioned in question 3, how much can I spend on advertising Toys and still have the same contribution of $92,500 I had before the price change?
5. If I increase advertising for the Clothes by $20,000, what will my total dollar sales for all three products have to be to make the same product contribution of $259,500?

	Total	Toys	Clothes	Gifts
Revenue	$ 725,000	$ 325,000	$ 280,000	$ 120,000
Variable costs	397,500	187,500	130,000	80,000
Contribution margin	327,500	137,500	150,000	40,000
Margin percentage	45%	42%	54%	33%
Advertising	68,000	45,000	15,000	8,000
Product contribution	259,500	$ 92,500	$ 135,000	$ 32,000
Joint Costs				
Administrative costs	45,000			
Joint Advertising	85,000			
Total joint costs of product lines	130,000			
Contribution	$ 129,500			

Required:

Prepare answers to the questions your boss has asked.

12-19. Preparation of Contribution Schedules. Lustre Light, Inc. manufactures three lamps in its Nashville plant: (1) Table lamp, (2) Hanging lamp, and (3) Floor lamp. Workers begin work on each of the lamps in three separate departments that are devoted exclusively to the production of one of the lamps, i.e., the Table Department works only on the Table lamp, etc. The Finishing Department completes the finish on each lamp and puts it in a packing case for shipment; each lamp uses approximately the same amount of time in the Finishing Department.

The monthly fixed costs of production for each of these departments are:

Table Department	$15,000
Hanging Department	10,000
Floor Department	8,000
Finishing Department	20,000
Total	$53,000

The remaining plant costs amount to $50,000 per month. Because the plant was built with expansion in mind, each product uses about 20% of the current space in the plant. The remaining space is there for future expansion in business.

Planned monthly advertising costs for the three products in each of the two territories in which they are sold are:

	Southern Territory	Western Territory	Total
Table lamp	$ -0-	$1,000	$ 1,000
Hanging lamp	3,000	1,500	4,500
Floor lamp	4,000	5,000	9,000
Costs common to all lamps	9,000	2,000	11,000
Totals	$16,000	$9,500	$25,500

In addition to these marketing costs, the company spends $20,000 per month on image advertising that applies to the entire company. Each territory incurs monthly administrative costs of $3,000, and administrative activities in both territories benefit each product equally.

Company administrative costs amount to $75,000 each month.

Required: Do only the fixed cost section of the contribution reports when you answer this question.

a. Prepare contribution schedules for each territory.
b. Prepare a contribution schedule for the marketing function for the company.
c. Prepare an income statement for the entire company.
d. List and show the dollar amount of costs that are joint costs with respect to the three products.
e. List and show the dollar amount of costs that are joint costs with respect to the two territories.
f. Assume company managers drop the Table lamp, how much will company profits change if all other things remain the same?

12-20.   Resource Constraints and Product Profitability. White Water manufactures canoes and kayaks at its plant in the mountains of West Virginia. Robert Jones manages the plant that makes these two products, and he has asked you to prepare an analysis that will help him make decisions on product priorities in case one of the plastic cutting machines or one of the ovens used for curing the boats has a problem.

Each boat is produced by first cutting sheets of plastic to the correct size for a particular boat. Then workers place these sheets in a die made specifically for one of the boats where they are shaped. After assembling these pieces workers glue them together, paint them, and place them in ovens for curing.

Data on product contribution and company profits for the past quarter appear below.

	Total	Canoes	Kayaks
Revenue	$ 1,010,000	$ 350,000	$ 660,000
Variable costs	430,000	150,000	280,000
Contribution margin	580,000	200,000	380,000
Traceable costs	140,000	85,000	55,000
Product contribution	440,000	$ 115,000	$ 325,000
Other company costs	210,000		
Profit before taxes	$ 230,000		

In addition to these data, you have gathered the following information from the operations database related to resource use.

	Total	Canoes	Kayaks
Labor hours	4,800	1,500	3,300
Cutting machine hours	1,100	400	700
Die usage in hours	1,350	500	850
Oven usage in hours	950	300	650

Required:

a. If the company had to drop one product, which one would you choose to drop assuming all other things remained the same? Why?

b. Which product generates the most contribution margin per dollar of sales?

c. Write a policy for Robert Jones that tells him which product should receive priority if a critical resource becomes a bottleneck. Be sure to show calculations to support your answer.

12-21. **Joint Costs and Joint Revenues and Product Line Profitability.** Ron Marshal was reviewing the product line contribution margins for the product lines that he manages. He was concerned about the low margin percentage for one of his lines, the Ovens.

	Total	Grills	Ovens	Carts	Parts	Accessories
Revenue	$ 1,065,000	$ 550,000	$ 230,000	$ 95,000	$ 80,000	$ 110,000
Variable costs	600,000	300,000	180,000	50,000	20,000	50,000
Contribution margin		250,000	50,000	45,000	60,000	60,000
	465,000					
Margin percentage	44%	45%	22%	47%	75%	55%

Ron works for a company that manufactures a variety of products for people who like to cook outdoors. It sells grills in several styles in addition to the ovens, and it provides replacement parts for all its products. Typically, the company has found that part sales equal approximately nine percent of the sales of the three main products. Accessory sales (cooking utensils, aprons, hats, etc.) tend to vary directly with the Grill and Oven sales. Carts are sold exclusively to people who purchase Ovens. These carts are specially designed so a customer can place the oven on a cart and move it to a location where the customer wants to bake or broil food.

The accountant who prepared the above schedule for Ron also gave him this information in a separate memo.

We spent $157,000 on advertising for the period covered by this schedule. Of this total, $85,000 was spent to advertise all our product lines, and the rest was spent on specific product lines. The amounts are:

Grills	45,000
Ovens	15,000
Carts	6,000
Parts	1,000
Accessories	5,000

We also spent another $45,000 on administrative costs related to these product lines.

Required:

a. Prepare a contribution schedule that shows total product contribution, and total contribution from all the product lines.
b. List the costs and the dollar amounts that are joint costs with respect to the product lines.
c. Name the joint revenues present in this set of products.
d. How much will contribution for all these products change if Ron drops the Ovens? You may have to make a few assumptions to do this calculation, but managers often have to make considered judgements about the cost and revenue impacts of changes they make.

► CASE ◄

12-22. Contribution Reporting and Conventional Cost Reporting and Bonus Plans. You work for a company that has a stringent policy on bonuses: Each manager receives a bonus only if he or she meets the budget profit target for each quarter. Any manager who misses the target profit (even if it is by a small amount) receives no bonus for that quarter. However, the manager who does meet the profit target receives a lump sum of $10,000 plus 5% of the quarterly profit.

Ellen Green manages the dishwasher division that makes a single product. Ellen has responsibility for both production and sales in this division. The dishwasher her division makes sells for $400 per unit, and it has a unit variable cost of $200; production fixed costs for her division equal $1,500,000 annually, and remaining division costs equal $800,000 per year. Quarterly production can go as high as 6,000 units, although the company usually produces no more than 5,000 units in any one quarter. Because of her good forecasting system, Ellen usually carries about 100 units in inventory at any one time; however, at the end of Quarter 3 she had exactly zero units on hand because of a last minute order.

Ellen has always used a contribution reporting approach for running her operation, but the company allows her to use either contribution reporting or conventional cost (absorption cost) for reporting numbers to the corporate office. She can make this choice at any time, but she must stay with a system for two years once she makes the choice.

Budgeted unit sales and budgeted profits for the four quarters of the current year are:

	Quarter 1	Quarter 2	Quarter 3	Quarter 4	Total
Budgeted Unit Sales	3,500	4,000	3,000	4,500	15,000
Budgeted Profit	125,000	225,000	25,000	325,000	700,000

Ellen has met or exceeded her profit targets in the first three quarters, but she is worried about Quarter 4. Even though she has been pushing her salesmen to move washers, it looks like she will be about 100 units short on sales for Quarter 4; and, she was counting on that bonus to pay for a trip to Hawaii for her and her family for Christmas.

Required:

What should Ellen do? Give numerical calculations to support your recommendations.

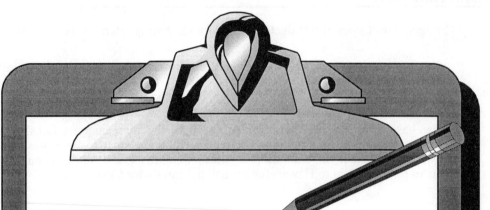

Learning Objectives

After reading this chapter, the student should have an understanding of:

✔   The essentials of budget variance analysis including comparisons of the master budget, the flexible budget and actual results.

✔   The sequential process of budget variance analysis involving increasing detail from levels 0 through 3.

✔   The analysis of sales variances including sales price and sales volume variances and the separation of the sales volume variance into sales quantity and sales mix variances.

✔   The calculation of sales variances via alternatives such as sales revenue per unit, profit contribution per unit and profit contribution percentages.

✔   A behavioral twist on the sales mix variance resulting from concentrating on actual rather than budgeted contribution margins.

✔   Differences in variance calculations resulting from using absorption costing rather than direct costing and where production and sales volume are different.

✔   Budget variance analysis and the control process.

PROFIT PLANNING, CONTROL AND FLEXIBLE BUDGETS

The master budget for the year represents the final outcome of the annual process. It is the guide to action as well as the basis for comparison with comprehensive, covering the entire area of planning, control, and uation. The following, with its many parts discussed in earlier chapters 4), are the major components which culminate in the master budget.

profit planning actual results. It is performance eval-(especially Chapter

Operating Budgets	_Financial Budgets_
Sales budget	Cash budget
Inventory budget	Balance sheet
Production budget	Statement of cash flows
Cost of goods sold	Working capital
Marketing expenses	Long and short range
Administrative expenses	
capital budgets*	
Others: Research and	
development, engineering, etc.	
Income Statement	

* To be discussed in Chapter 15

In this chapter, we will concentrate on the operating budgets comparing actual with budgeted results in terms of combining the variance analysis of standard costing with the variance analysis of marketing activities. We will also consider how these variances, as well as other measures of activity, aid in the process of cost and profit control.

We will introduce these concepts using an illustration for Carry-All, Inc., a leading manufacturer of canvas consumer products such as attaches, duffle bags, backpacks and tote bags. Carry-All sells its products exclusively through agreements with direct mail merchandisers, telemarketing firms, charitable organizations, college bookstores, professional sports franchise stadium shops, etc. Carry-All's marketing representatives earn commissions on all such sales arrangements.

The remainder of the chapter is organized into three parts. The first provides a comprehensive example of budget variance analysis and the analysis of sales variances. The next section extends the discussion to an illustration of sales mix variances in multi-product firms. The final section illustrates several practical applications in budget variance analysis and discusses its role in the control process.

▶ ESSENTIALS OF BUDGET VARIANCE ANALYSIS ◀

Carry-All markets two of its most popular products through college bookstores. These items, the traditional tote style book bag and a backpack style of book bag, are produced in college colors with university logos. Estimated market demand data extracted from the sales budget and selected cost figures from the production, marketing and administrative budgets are given below.

	Tote bag	*Backpack*
Selling price per unit	$ 25	$ 37
Unit sales volume	96,000	85,000
Budgeted sales dollars	$2,400,000	$3,145,000
Variable costs per unit:		
Manufacturing	$ 13.50	$ 18.60
Marketing—5% of sales	1.25	1.85
Fixed costs:		
Manufacturing		$ 600,000
Advertising and promotion		185,000
Marketing and administrative		625,000

▶ The Master Budget[1]

We use these data to prepare the master budget income statement in Exhibit 13-1. The concepts and procedures illustrated are also applicable to companies producing more than two products. Note that we use a direct costing income statement which does not unitize fixed costs, and does not allocate fixed costs to product lines. Also note that the master budget is based upon budgeted volume, budgeted prices and budgeted costs.

▶ Actual Results

Exhibit 13-2 portrays the actual income statement results for the year. First, we explain the profit variance between budgeted and actual results using the sequential approach proposed by Shank and Churchill.[2] This sequential approach uses progressively more detailed or complex analyses. The various levels of analysis are usually referred to as levels 0, 1, 2, and 3.

▶ Master Budget vs. Actual—Level 0

Level 0 is the very basic comparison of master budget and actual net income before tax as shown below. Even if the level 0 variance is immaterial, further analysis might still be advisable because of offsetting favorable and unfavorable variances at a lower level. For Carry-All, the large unfavorable variance indicates the company did not attain the budgeted income. To find out why, further analysis is required.

---

[1] Sometimes referred to as the fixed or static budget.
[2] Shank, John K. and Neil C. Churchill, "Variance Analysis: A Management Oriented Approach," *The Accounting Review*, Vol. LII, No. 4.

Level 0 Analysis

	Net Income Before Tax
Master budget	$ 980,750
Actual results	148,650
Variance	$ 832,100 U

Carry-All, Inc.
Year Ending December 31, 20__

	Total	Tote bag	Backpack
Unit sales	181,000	96,000	85,000
Selling price		$ 25	$ 37
Sales	$ 5,545,000	$ 2,400,000	$ 3,145,000
Variable costs:			
Manufacturing	2,877,000	1,296,000	1,581,000
Marketing (5% sales)	277,250	120,000	157,250
Total	$ 3,154,250	$ 1,416,000	$ 1,738,250
Profit contribution:			
Dollars	$ 2,390,750	$ 984,000	$ 1,406,750
Per unit	$ 13.209	$ 10.25	$ 16.55
Percentage	43.12%	41.00%	44.73%
Fixed costs:			
Manufacturing	$ 600,000		
Advertising and promotion	185,000		
Marketing and administrative	625,000		
Total	$ 1,410,000		
Net income before taxes	$ 980,750		

Exhibit 13-1 Master Budget Income Statement Budgeted Volume, Budgeted Prices, Budgeted Costs

▸ Master Budget vs. Actual—Level 1

Level 1 shows more detail than level 0. Instead of just portraying the bottom line difference, level 1 deals with the major income statement item (such as sales revenues and costs) which result in the bottom line difference. A simple level 1 analysis is shown below. We show more details in Exhibit 13-3, which we could have made even more detailed by including product line data.

Level 1 Analysis

	Actual Actual Volume Actual Prices Actual Costs	Master Budget Budgeted Volume Budgeted Prices Budgeted Costs	Variance
Sales	$ 4,767,000	$ 5,545,000	$ 778,000 U
Variable costs	3,193,350	3,154,250	39,100 U
Profit contribution	$ 1,573,650	$ 2,390,750	$ 817,100 U
Fixed costs	1,425,000	1,410,000	15,000 U
Net income before tax ...	$ 148,650	$ 980,750	$ 832,100 U

Carry-All, Inc.
Year Ending December 31, 20__

	Total	Tote bag	Backpack
Unit sales	180,000	93,000	87,000
Selling price		$ 26	$ 27
Sales	$ 4,767,000	2,418,000	2,349,000
Variable costs:			
Manufacturing	2,955,000	1,345,000	1,610,000
Marketing (5% sales)	238,350	120,900	117,450
Total	$ 3,193,350	$ 1,465,900	$1,727,450
Profit contribution:			
Dollars	$ 1,573,650	$ 952,100	$ 621,550
Per unit	$ 8.743	$ 10.238	$ 7.144
Percentage	33.01%	39.38%	26.46%
Fixed costs:			
Manufacturing	$ 592,000		
Advertising and promotion	195,000		
Marketing and administrative	638,000		
Total	$ 1,425,000		
Net income before taxes	$ 148,650		

Exhibit 13-2 *Actual Income Statement Actual Volume, Actual Prices, Actual Costs*

Carry-All, Inc.
Year Ending December 31, 20__

	Actual Actual Volume Actual Prices Actual Costs	Master Budget Budgeted Volume Budgeted Prices Budgeted Costs	Variance
Units	180,000	181,000	1,000 U
Sales	$ 4,767,000	$ 5,545,000	$ 778,000 U
Variable costs:			
Manufacturing	2,955,000	2,877,000	78,000 U
Marketing (5% sales)	238,350	277,250	38,900 F
Total	$ 3,193,350	$ 3,154,250	$ 39,100 U
Profit contribution:			
Dollars	$ 1,573,650	$ 2,390,750	$817,100 U
Per unit	$ 8.743	$ 13.209	$ 4.466 U
Percent	33.01%	43.12%	10.11%
Fixed costs:			
Manufacturing	$ 592,000	$ 600,000	$ 8,000 F
Advertising and promotion	195,000	185,000	10,000 U
Marketing and administrative	688,000	625,000	13,000 U
Total	$ 1,425,000	$ 1,410,000	$ 15,000 U
Net income before taxes	$ 148,650	$ 980,750	$ 832,100 U

Exhibit 13-3 *Master Budget vs. Actual Level 1 Analysis (expanded)*

▶ Master Budget vs. Actual—Level 2

Level 2 analysis uses the concept of flexible budgeting. In Chapter 10 we developed a flexible budget by using actual volume of output to develop a clear picture of cost performance and perform cost variance analysis. Here we use it to examine profit variances.

In a pictorial sense, we can portray the impact of flexible budgeting on the analysis of profit variances. Note, that the flexible budget allows us to separate the profit variance into its two parts (i.e., cost efficiency and sales efficiency).

As shown clearly above, the difference between actual results and the flexible budget is the difference between actual costs at actual volume and budgeted costs at actual volume. This difference measures cost efficiency. The difference between the flexible budget and the master budget relates to marketing issues (i.e., the difference between budgeted and actual volume and between budgeted and actual selling prices). An unfavorable sales efficiency variance does not automatically suggest that the marketing unit is responsible. It could be caused by a situation where marketing had secured enough orders to meet its sales budget but the production unit did not produce the quantities requested.

The details of our level 2 analysis are contained in Exhibits 13-4 and 13-5. Exhibit 13-4 shows a flexible budget income statement while Exhibit 13-5 shows the variances corresponding to the above pictorial representation. Before moving on to our level 3 analysis, we shall illustrate pictorially an alternate form of level 2.

▶ Master Budget vs. Actual—Level 2 Alternative Form

We can alternatively express level 2 analysis as shown below. The only difference between this form and the original one is that we use budgeted prices instead of actual prices in the flexible budget column. This change combines the sales price variance of marketing with the cost efficiency variances. Either version of the level 2 analysis is acceptable.

Level 2 Analysis   Alternate Form

Actual	*Flexible Budget*	*Master Budget*
Actual Volume	Actual Volume	Budgeted Volume
Actual Prices	Budgeted Prices	Budgeted Prices
Actual Costs	Budgeted Costs	Budgeted Costs

Cost Efficiency Variances ／ Sales Efficiency Variances*

Total Income (profit) Variance

*These will be subdivided later into sales quantity and mix variances.

Carry-All, Inc.
Year Ending December 31, 20__

	Total	*Tote bag*	*Backpack*
Unit sales	180,000	93,000	87,000
Selling price		$ 26	$ 27
Sales	$ 4,767,000	2,418,000	2,349,000
Variable costs:			
Manufacturing	2,873,700	1,255,500	1,618,200
Marketing (5% sales)	238,350	120,900	117,450
Total	$ 3,112,050	$ 1,376,400	$ 1,735,650
Profit contribution:			
Dollars	$ 1,654,950	$ 1,041,600	$ 613,350
Per unit	$ 9.194	$ 11.20	$ 7.05
Percentage	34.72%	43.08%	26.11%
Fixed costs:			
Manufacturing	$ 600,000		
Advertising and promotion	185,000		
Marketing and administrative	625,000		
Total	$ 1,410,000		
Net income before taxes	$ 244,950		

Exhibit 13-4   *Flexible Budget Income Statement Actual Volume, Actual Prices, Budgeted Costs*

Carry-All, Inc.
Year Ending December 31, 20__

	Actual Act. Volume Act. Prices Act. Costs	*Cost Efficiency Variances*	*Flexible Bud.* Act. Volume Act. Prices Bud. Costs	*Sales Efficiency Variances*	*Master Bud.* Bud. Volume Bud. Prices Bud. Costs
Units	180,000	—	180,000	1,000 U	181,000
Sales	$ 4,767,000	—	$ 4,767,000	$ (778,000) U	$ 5,545,000
Variable costs:					
Manufacturing	2,955,000	$ (81,300) U	2,873,700	3,300 F	2,877,000
Mktg (5% sales)	238,350	—	238,350	38,900 F	277,250
Total	$ 3,193,350	$ (81,300) U	$ 3,112,050	$ 42,200 F	$ 3,154,250
Profit cont:					
Dollars	$ 1,573,650	$ (81,300) U	$ 1,654,950	$ (735,800) U	$ 2,390,750
Per unit	$ 8.743	—	$ 9.194	—	$ 13.209
Percent	33.01%	—	34.72%	—	43.12%
Fixed costs:					
Manufacturing	$ 592,000	8,000 F	600,000	—	600,000
Adv. and prom.	195,000	(10,000) U	185,000	—	185,000
Mktg and adm.	638,000	`(13,000) U	625,000	—	625,000
Total	$ 1,425,000	$ (15,000) U	$ 1,410,000		$ 1,410,000
Net income before tax	$ 148,650	$ (96,300) U*	$ 244,950	$ (735,800) U*	$ 980,750

* Total variance: Actual vs. Master budget . . . . $ 832,100 U

Exhibit 13-5   *Variance Analysis with Flexible Budgeting Level 2 Analysis*

▸ Master Budget vs. Actual—Level 3 Cost Variances

Our final profit variance analyses provide more detail concerning cost and sales efficiency variances. In this section we will deal only with cost efficiency variances. The next section will deal with sales efficiency variances.

We describe the cost efficiency variance, $96,300 unfavorable, of Exhibit 13-5 in more detail in Exhibit 13-6 where we look at each of our two products. Even more detail than shown in Exhibit 13-6 could be provided. For example, the manufacturing cost variances could be presented in terms of the price and quantity variances of standard costing. Thus, the earlier material on standard costing is completely compatible with this type of budget variance analysis.

Carry-All, Inc.
Year Ending December 31, 20__

Variable manufacturing costs
Budgeted:
Tote bag: 93,000 units at $13.50	=	$ 1,255,500	
Backpack: 87,000 units at $18.60	=	1,618,200	
Total budgeted			$ 2,873,700

Actual:
Tote bag: 93,000 units at $14.462	=	$ 1,345,000	
Backpack: 87,000 units at $18.506	=	1,610,000	
Total actual			2,955,000
Variance*			$ (81,300) U

Variable marketing costs (sales commission)
Budgeted (5% of sales):
Tote bag: 5% of $2,418,000	=	$ 120,900	
Backpack: 5% of $2,349,000	=	117,450	
Total budgeted			$ 238,350
Actual (5% of sales)			238,350
Variance			$ 0

	Budgeted	Actual	Variance
Fixed costs:			
Manufacturing*	$ 600,000	$ 592,000	$ 8,000 F
Advertising and promotion**	185,000	195,000	(10,000) U
Marketing and administrative**	625,000	638,000	(13,000) U
Total fixed cost variance			$ (15,000) U
Grand total—cost efficiency variances ..			$ (15,000) U

* Obviously manufacturing variances could have been partitioned into the price, quantity, etc. variances of standard costing. To do so in this case we need more detail concerning actual manufacturing costs.
** Fixed advertising and promotion costs as well as fixed marketing and administrative costs could easily have been subdivided into more detailed categories.

Exhibit 13-6 *Cost Efficiency Variances Level 3 Analysis Budgeted Costs vs. Actual Costs at Actual Volume*

▸ *Master Budget vs. Actual—Level 3 Sales Variances*

Sales efficiency variances are analogous to the cost efficiency variances of standard variable costs. For sales efficiency, there is both a *sales price* and a *sales volume* variance as computed below. Note the similarity to the price and quantity variances of standard costing.

<u>*Level 3 Analysis—Sales Efficiency Variances*</u>
(Using Sales Revenue Per unit)

Sales price variance	(Budgeted price – Actual price) Actual Volume		
	(BP per unit – AP per unit) AV		
Tote bag sales price variance	(BP - AP) AV = (25 - 26) 93,000	=	$ 93,000 F
Backpack sales price variance	(BP - AP) AV = (37 - 27) 87,000	=	870,000 U

Sales volume variance	(Budgeted volume – Actual volume) Budgeted price		
	(BV – AV) BP per unit		
Tote bag sales volume variance . . .	(BV - AV) BP = (96,000 - 93,000) 25	=	$ 75,000 U
Backpack sales volume variance . .	(BV - AV) BP = (85,000 - 87,000) 37	=	74,000 F
Total sales efficiency variance			$778,000 U

As illustrated above, the sum of the price and volume variances for both products accounts for the $778,000 unfavorable sales efficiency variance *in sales dollars* shown in Exhibit 13-5. As in standard costing, the favorable or unfavorable nature of a variance is determined by examining the difference between budgeted and actual prices and budgeted and actual volumes.

▸ *Master Budget vs. Actual—Level 3 Sales Variances: Alternative Form*

Often accountants compute sales efficiency variances using profit contribution data rather than sales revenue data. When using profit contribution data, the total sales efficiency variance is accounted for *in profit contribution dollars* $735,800U as verified in Exhibit 13-5. The variances are calculated as illustrated below.

<u>*Level 3 Analysis—Sales Efficiency Variances*</u>
Alternative Form (Using Profit Contribution Per unit)

Sales price variance	(Budgeted contribution – Actual contribution*) Actual Volume		
	(BC per unit – AC per unit) AV		
Tote bag sales price variance	(BC - AC) AV = (10.25** - 11.20*) 93,000	=	$ 88,350 F
Backpack sales price variance . . .	(BC - AC) AV = (16.55** - 7.05*) 87,000	=	826,500 U
Sales volume variance	(Budgeted volume – Actual volume) Budgeted contribution		
	(BV – AV) BC per unit		
Tote bag sales volume variance . .	(BV - AV) BC = (96,000 - 93,000) 10.25**	=	$ 30,750 U
Backpack sales volume variance	(BV - AV) BC = (85,000 - 87,000) 16.55**	=	37,100 F
			$735,800 U

  * Actual contribution data are based on actual prices and budgeted variable cost per the flexible budget.
  ** Budgeted sales price   (budgeted variable manufacturing cost + sales commission) per the master budget.

The variances still have the same names as before (price and volume) even though we use profit contribution data. The dollar amount of the price variance will be the same if the variable costs are constant per unit. This is not the case in this example because of the variable marketing costs. In subsequent illustrations, we will use this alternate form.

▸ Summary

The various levels (0, 1, 2 and 3) of variance analysis for the profit budget provide a fairly succinct approach to tying together the essential ingredients of cost and sales variances. As indicated, the notion of flexible budgeting is critical in measuring these variances. In the next section of this chapter, we will delve a little more deeply into the sales efficiency variances by considering a special variance for sales mix.

▸ SALES EFFICIENCY VARIANCES INCLUDING SALES MIX ◂

▸ Sales Price Variance Does Not Change/Sales Volume Variance Does Change

In the typical multi-product company like Carry-All Inc., sales efficiency variances can be calculated as above or they can be adjusted to include a sales mix variance. Quite often in practice, the sales mix variance is included.

The sales price variance does not change when the sales mix variance is introduced. This can be readily seen by comparing the calculations below with those in the previous section. The variance which changes or is adjusted is the sales volume variance.

Level 3 Analysis—Sales Efficiency Variances
Using Profit Contribution Per Unit
With Sales Mix Variance

Sales price variance	(Budgeted contribution – Actual contribution) Actual Volume	
	(BC per unit – AC per unit) AV	
Tote bag sales price variance	(BC - AC) AV = (10.25 - 11.20) 93,000	= $ 88,350 F
Backpack sales price variance	(BC - AC) AV = (16.55 - 7.05) 87,000	= 826,500 U
Sales quantity variance	(Budgeted volume – Actual volume) Budgeted avg contribution	
	(BV – AV) B~AC per unit	
Tote bag sales quantity variance ...	(BV - AV) B~AC = (96,000 - 93,000) 13.209	= $ 39,627 U
Backpack sales quantity variance ..	(BV - AV) B~AC = (85,000 - 87,000) 13.209	= 26,418 F
Sales Mix Variance	(Budgeted vol–Actual vol) X (Budgeted contribution–Budgeted avg contribution)	
	(BV - AV) (BC per unit - B~AC per unit)	
Tote bag sales mix variance	(BV - AV) (BC - B~AC) = (96,000 - 93,000) (10.25 - 13.209)	= $ 8,877 F
Backpack sales mix variance	(BV - AV) (BC - B~AC) = (85,000 - 87,000) (16.55 - 13.209)	= 6,682 F
Total sales efficiency variance		$ 735,800 U

▸ Sales Volume Variance Splits Into Sales Quantity and Sales Mix

To be precise, the sales volume variance does not change. It is actually split into two variances (quantity and mix) as indicated below.

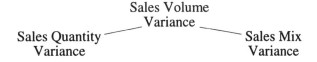

Sales Volume
Variance

Sales Quantity   Sales Mix
Variance   Variance

The split of the sales volume variance into quantity and mix variances is sometimes easier to visualize pictorially as above rather than algebraically as below. Nonetheless, with a little effort one should be able to visualize the algebraic combination of quantity and mix variances into the volume variance.

Sales volume variance . .   (Budgeted volume - Actual volume)   X   Budgeted contribution per unit
(BV - AV) BC per unit

Sales quantity variance . .   (Budgeted volume - Actual volume)   X   Budgeted average contribution for all products per unit
(BV - AV) B~AC per unit

Sales mix variance . . . . .   (Budgeted volume - Actual volume)   X   (Budgeted contribution per unit - Budgeted average contribution per unit)
(BV - AV) (BC per unit - B~AC per unit)

Sales volume variance	=	Sales quantity variance	=	Sales mix variance
(BV - AV) BC per unit	=	(BV - AV) B~AC per unit	=	(BV - AV) (BC per unit - B~AC per unit)

In essence the sales quantity variance holds the budgeted average contribution for all products constant and emphasizes the difference between budgeted and actual volume. The mix variance, on the other hand, concentrates on the *difference* between the budgeted contributions of individual products and the budgeted average contribution for all products when examining the differences between budgeted and actual volumes.

The idea is to have more volume of those products with a higher than average contribution and less of those with lower contributions. Thus a *favorable* mix variance occurs when high contribution products make up a disproportinately higher portion of the mix. The opposite case causes *unfavorable* mix variances.

When first encountered, the mix variance often appears difficult to comprehend, but careful examination of these examples will help interpret these variances. For practice, trace all numbers back to Exhibits 13-1, 13-2 and 13-4.

► ADDITIONAL ISSUES IN BUDGET VARIANCE ANALYSIS ◄

Previous examples measured sales volume in units. However, when sales volume is measured in dollars, some interesting changes can take place in the calculation of variances, especially the sales mix variance.

► Measuring Sales Volume—Dollars or Units

A comparison of sales efficiency variances for Carry-All, Inc. illustrates that dollar amounts of individual variances, as well as their favorable or unfavorable nature, can change when switching from units to dollars as a measure of sales volume. When sales volume was measured in units, contribution margins were on a per unit basis and sales efficiency variances were illustrated in the previous section. When sales volume measured in dollars, contribution margins are on a percentage basis and sales efficiency variances are shown below.

Level 3 Analysis—Sales Efficiency Variances
Using Profit Contribution Percent
With Sales Mix Variance

Sales price variance	(Budgeted contribution % - Actual contribution %) Actual $ volume				
	(BC % - AC%) Actual $ volume				
Tote bag sales price variance	(BC% - AC%) AV$	=	(41.00 - 43.08) 2,418,000	=	$ 50,294 F
Backpack sales price variance	(BC% - AC%) AV$	=	(44.73 - 26.11) 2,349,000	=	$ 437,384 U

Sales quantity variance	(Budgeted $ volume - Actual $ volume) Budgeted average contribution %				
	(BV$ - AV$) B~AC%				
Tote bag sales quantity variance	(BV$ - AV$) B~AC%	=	(2,400,000 - 2,418,000) 43.12	=	$ 7,762 F
Backpack sales quantity variance	(BV$ - AV$) B~AC%	=	(3,145,000 - 2,349,000) 43.12	=	$ 343,235 U

Sales mix variance	(Budgeted $ volume - Actual $ volume) Budgeted contribution % - Budgeted average contribution %)				
	(BVS - AV$) (BC% - B~AC%)				
	(BV$ - AV$) (BC% - B~AC%)				
Tote bag sales mix variance	(BV$ - AV$) (BC% - B~AC%)	= (2,400,000-2,418,000) (41.00-43.12)	=		382 U
Backpack sales mix variance	(BV$ - AV$) (BC% - B~AC%)	= (3,145,000-2,349,000) (44.73-43.12)	=		12,816 U
					$ 735,761 U*

* Rounding error $ 39

This example illustrates that individual variances can be calculated in a variety of ways. Right or wrong is not the issue, the issue is that each individual real life circumstance should be analyzed to determine which method of variance calculation is appropriate.

In this case, the specific issue is, "should sales volume be measured in dollars or units?" The specific answer to this question greatly depends upon whether or not the physical units of individual products are additive.

▸ The Mix Variance—A Behavioral Twist

Years ago we noticed that in a particular firm the sales mix variance was measured by using the difference between actual rather than budgeted contribution margins. In this instance a motivational or behavioral intent was the driving force. A mix variance measured in terms of actual contribution margins could entice marketing decision-makers to adjust their thinking about product mix in the direction of what is actually happening in the market place rather than what was projected to happen.

As shown below, this approach still accounts for the total sales efficiency variance even though the individual price, quantity and mix variances are different. In addition to the change in the mix variance calculation, note the changes in the price and quantity variance calculations.

Level 3 Analysis—Sales Efficiency Variances
Using Profit Contribution Per Unit
With Sales Mix Variance - A Behavioral Twist

Sales price variance	(Budgeted contribution - Actual contribution) Budgeted volume					
	(BC per unit - AC per unit) BV					
Tote bag sales price variance	(BC - AC) BV	=	(10.25 - 11.20) 96,000	=	$ 91,200	F
Backpack sales price variance	(BC - AC) BV	=	(16.55 - 7.05) 85,000	=	$ 807,500	U
	=					
Sales quantity variance	(Budgeted volume - Actual volume) Actual average contribution					
	(BV - AV) A~AC per unit					
Tote bag sales quantity variance	(BV - AV) A~AC	=	(96,000 - 93,000) 9.194	=	$ 27,582	U
Backpack sales quantity variance	(BV - AV) A~AC	=	(85,000 - 87,000) 9.194	=	$ 18,388	F
Sales mix variance	(Budgeted volume - Actual volume) X (Actual contribution - Actual average contribution)					
	(BV - AV) (AC per unit - A~AC per unit)					
Tote bag sales mix variance	(BV - AV) (AC - A~AC)	=	(96,000 - 93,000) (11.20-9.194)	=	6,018	U
Backpack sales mix variance	(BV - AV) (AC - A~AC)	=	(85,000 - 87,000) (7.05 - 9.194)	=	4,288	F
Total sales efficiency variance					$ 735,800	U

Just as with the previous issue of whether sales volume should be measured in dollars or units, right vs. wrong is not the issue. Accountants should always analyze the analytical and behavioral context of each individual real life circumstance to determine the appropriate method of variance calculation.

► Production Volume vs. Sales Volume

We assumed production and sales volume were equal in all preceding illustrations. This meant inventory levels were constant, since a difference between production and sales volume would change inventory levels. Now we must address the issue raised if production and sales volume are not equal.

We show below that the inclusion of inventory changes causes us to have two flexible budgets (i.e., one for sales and one for production). The difference between the two flexible budgets (which represents the change in inventory level) yields separate production and sales variances.

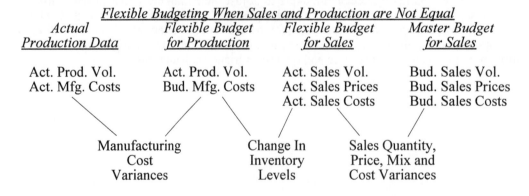

Flexible Budgeting When Sales and Production are Not Equal

Actual Production Data	*Flexible Budget for Production*	*Flexible Budget for Sales*	*Master Budget for Sales*
Act. Prod. Vol.	Act. Prod. Vol.	Act. Sales Vol.	Bud. Sales Vol.
Act. Mfg. Costs	Bud. Mfg. Costs	Act. Sales Prices	Bud. Sales Prices
		Act. Sales Costs	Bud. Sales Costs

Manufacturing Cost Variances   Change In Inventory Levels   Sales Quantity, Price, Mix and Cost Variances

▸ Absorption Costing vs. Direct Costing

In previous illustrations we used a direct cost approach and fixed manufacturing costs were not unitized. If absorption costing had been used, Exhibit 13-1 would look like Exhibit 13-7. We could revise the actual and flexible budget income statements of Exhibits 13-2 and 13-4 in a similar fashion.

Carry-All, Inc.
Year Ending December 31, 20__

	Total	*Tote bag*	*Backpack*
Unit sales	181,000	96,000	85,000
Selling price		$ 25	$ 37
Sales	$ 5,545,000	$ 2,400,000	$ 3,145,000
Costs of sales*	3,471,000	1,584,000	1,887,000
Gross profit:			
Dollars	$ 2,074,000	$ 816,000	$ 1,258,000
Per unit	$ 11.459	$ 8.50	$ 14.80
Percent	37.40%	34.00%	40.00%
Operating expenses:			
Advertising and promotion	$ 185,000		
Marketing and administrative:			
Variable	277,250		
Fixed	625,000		
Total	$ 1,087,250		
Net income before tax	$ 986,750 **		

* Cost of sales includes unitized fixed manufacturing costs of $3.00 per unit for tote bags and $3.60 per unit for backpacks. These rates are derived using the normal fixed overhead rate of $6 per labor hour and the standard production time of .5 hour for tote bags and .6 hour for backpacks.

** The $6,000 difference in income between Exhibits 15-1 and 15-7 is the result of absorption costing unitizing fixed manufacturing costs at a normal rate of $6 per labor hour for the 99,000 labor hours in the master budget (48,000 for tote bags and 51,000 for backpacks.) This totals $594,000 as opposed to the budgeted fixed manufacturing overhead of $600,000. The $6,000 is in essence a projected production volume variance.

Exhibit 13-7 *Master Budget Income Statement Absorption Costing Budgeted Volume, Budgeted Prices, Budgeted Costs*

With the three revised absorption costing income statements, variance calculations would proceed as before except that we use *gross profit* data instead of *profit contribution* data. Using gross profit data with the unitized fixed manufacturing cost allows us to calculate the production volume variance of absorption costing.

▸ Budget Variance Analysis and the Control Process

At this point, it should be obvious that the development of a profit plan and the measurement of variances from that plan as discussed in this chapter, is just part of an approach to attaining profit goals. To achieve profit goals, there must be a process of control (i.e., a process designed to make sure that profit goals become a reality).

Management accounting should facilitate the control process. However, there are many ways to do this. Top management has a special responsibility when it faces the decision concerning the type and extent of accounting data to use in its control process.

Accounting controls, especially those involving data expressed in financial terms, occupy a residual position. Foremost in importance is preventive control (i.e., the development of a sound, responsible and motivated organization). Of almost equal importance is observation. Physical data and reports are next in importance. Dollar data and reports, especially standard cost and flexible budget variances, occupy a residual position. In most instances the true role of standard cost and flexible budget variances is to detect variances which have evaded the more proximate bases of control such as observation and physical reports. Standard cost and flexible budget variances also have the role of quantifying the profit impact of operations not running at standard or budget.

Given the above, it makes great sense to concentrate on selected daily (sometimes hourly) and weekly reports in physical and even dollar terms. For example, the following daily and weekly reports can be very useful in monitoring direct materials and labor as well as sales activity on a very current basis:

1. Physical quantity of various direct materials used per physical quantity of output generated by various production departments and plants.
2. Physical quantity of various categories of direct labor used per physical quantity of output generated by various production departments and plants.
3. Spoilage (quality) reports by various products in various production departments and plants.
4. Physical and dollar quantity of various products sold by various sales personnel in various sales territories.
5. Purchases of materials at prices more than a designated percentage off standard with information on who approved such purchases.
6. Sales of products at prices and other terms more than a designated percentage off budget with information on who approved such sales.

On a weekly or monthly basis, similar reports can be prepared for other items relative to production, sales, and even administrative activities. For example:

1. Indirect labor hours and/or costs per physical quantity of output generated by various production departments and plants.
2. Indirect materials quantities and/or costs per physical quantity of output generated by various production departments and plants.
3. Energy costs and/or quantities per physical quantity of output generated by various production departments and plants.
4. Head counts of personnel in various service and administrative departments related to appropriate measures of activity.
5. Sales and marketing costs by salespeople and territory related to sales activities and results by salespeople and territory.
6. Data on product mixes being sold as well as inventory levels.
7. Data on cash, receivables and payables.
8. Various summations of daily and weekly reports.

These reports recognize the existence of key variables in every organization and in every segment of every organization. These key variables, when monitored in terms of some standard or budget expectation, should help management at all levels to control activities on a current basis. There should be few, if any, surprises with regard to off-standard or off-budget performance at the end of a month, quarter or year. The various daily and weekly reports should alert management to what is going on and to the potential size of the various standard cost and flexible budget variances before they are calculated at the end of a month, quarter or year.

Thus as indicated above, the role of standard cost and flexible budget variances is residual in nature. The recipient of such variance data should think of the following question, "What has gone wrong (or better than expected) and what has already been done to correct (or enhance continuation of) the situation?" There are prior lines of defense whose task it is to monitor activities and institute corrective action if needed. It is observation and that whole series of key variables monitored on a daily, weekly, etc. basis which is the heart of the control process.

A very useful analogy can be added here in order to summarize these thoughts on the control process. The control process needs a soul as well as a heart. Both are essential. That soul is preventative control which, as mentioned earlier, is the development of a sound, responsible and motivated organization.

▶ SUMMARY ◀

The master budget provides the plan or guide to action. Budget variance analysis serves as the basis for comparing that plan to actual results achieved. However, budget variance analysis should not be thought of as more than just a part of the control process. The totality of the control process involves preventive control as well as a whole series of monitoring and corrective activities which are on-going on a daily, weekly, etc. basis. The task confronted by every organization is to think through this total process in terms of its own specific circumstances. Then and only then can an organization decide on the specific variables to be monitored and the timing of the monitoring process for each variable chosen to be monitored.

▸ QUESTIONS ◂

13-1. Define the term master budget.

13-2. Generally speaking, the flexible budget method is accepted as a better approach for comparison to actual results, yet the comparison to the fixed or master budget is also important. Discuss.

13-3. Most variance analysis is involved with financial differences. Why are non-financial data also important?

13-4. Contrast the sequential approach to variance analysis using the various levels of analysis with responsibility accounting.

13-5. The sales efficiency variance can be further divided into price and volume variances. Briefly define both.

13-6. The volume variance can be further divided into quantity and mix variances. Briefly define both.

13-7. Describe the situation when an unfavorable sales efficiency variance could possibly be caused by the production department.

13-8. Discuss the behavioral implications of using actual profit contribution rather than budgeted profit contribution when calculating sales quantity and mix variances.

13-9. "There should be few, if any, surprises with regard to off-standard or off-budget performance at the end of a month, quarter or year." How can management avoid surprises?

13-10. List the various daily and weekly reports that the management accountant could produce to alert management of possible problems.

13-11. The level 0 analysis of the CPA Company's net income is as follows:

Master budget income ...	$ 1,356,860
Actual net income	1,196,390
Variance	$ 160,470 U

List the information required for each subsequent level of analysis (i.e., levels 1, 2, and 3).

► EXERCISES ◄

13-12. Sales Efficiency Variances, One Product.

The Big Division of Large Company produces only one product. Sales for the previous period amounted to $639,918. The beginning and ending inventory contained 1,375 and 1,200 units respectively, and 12,000 units were produced. Budgeted sales for the same period were 11,500 units at $55 per unit.

Required:

a. Calculate the sales efficiency variance.
b. Calculate the sale price variance and the sales volume variance.
c. State briefly the possible reason for the variances.

13-13. Sales and Cost Variances, One Product.

JK Enterprises sold 550,000 units during the first quarter ended March 31, 20x1. These sales represented a 10 percent increase over the number of units budgeted for the quarter. In spite of the sales increase, profits were below budget as shown in the condensed income statement presented below.

JK Enterprises
Income Statement
For the First Quarter Ended March 31, 20x1
($000 omitted)

	Budget	Actual
Sales	$ 2,500	$ 2,530
Variable expenses:		
Cost of goods sold	$ 1,475	$ 1,540
Selling	400	440
Total variable expenses	$ 1,875	$ 1,980
Contribution margin	$ 625	$ 550
Fixed expenses:		
Selling	$ 125	$ 150
Administration	275	300
Total fixed expenses	$ 400	$ 450
Income before taxes	$ 225	$ 100
Income taxes (40%)	90	40
Net income	$ 135	$ 60

The accounting department always prepares a brief analysis which explains the difference between budgeted net income and actual net income. The analysis, which has not yet been completed for the first quarter, is submitted to top management with the income statement.

Required:

Prepare an explanation of the $125,000 unfavorable variance between the first quarter budgeted and actual before tax income for JK Enterprises using a single amount for each of the following variations.

1. Sales price difference.
2. Variable unit cost difference.
3. Sales volume difference.
4. Fixed cost difference.
(CMA adapted)

13-14. Sales Efficiency Variances, Two Products.
  The sales of the Razzle Dazzle Company for the second quarter were as follows: Razzle 26,700 units, $868,818 and Dazzle 36,120 units, $966,210.
  The budgeted sales for the same period were Razzle 32,000 units at $30 per unit and Dazzle 32,000 units at $28 per unit.

Required:

a. Calculate the total sales efficiency variance.
b. Separate the sales efficiency variance, by product, into the sales price and sales volume variances.

13-15. Responsibility for Sales Efficiency Variances.
  Massachusetts Mugs, Inc. manufactures personalized coffee mugs. The following data pertains to the marketing effort for the period:

	Actual	*Budget*
Sales	120,000 mugs $ 360,000	130,000 mugs $ 396,500

Required:

a. Calculate the sales price and volume variances.
b. Further investigation into sales revealed that the marketing department reduced prices to increase volume. The latter proved successful as orders were booked for 140,000 mugs during the period. Production capacity was budgeted for 150,000 mugs but the production department was only able to produce 120,000 mugs. Under the circumstances discuss who is responsible for the variances.

13-16. Sales Efficiency Variances, Three Products.
  The Clean Sweep Company manufactures three products. The sales by product for the first quarter is shown in the following report:

Clean Sweep Company
Sales Report
For the First Quarter End, 20x6

Product:	*Actual* Units	Price	Total	*Budget* Units	Price	Total
Pans	12,250 at	$ 6.50	$ 79,625	15,000	$ 6.00	$ 90,000
Brooms .	13,170 at	8.50	111,945	15,000	9.00	135,000
Handles .	32,000 at	3.80	121,600	30,000	4.00	120,000
			$ 313,170			$ 345,000

Required:

Calculate the sales price and volume variances by product.

13-17. Prepare Statements for Each Level of Analysis.

North Pole Enterprises manufactures wrought iron stands for Christmas trees. Analysis of their accounts show the following actual results for 20x4:

Sales—13,500 units	$ 357,480
Cost of goods sold	$ 266,070
Gross profit	$ 91,410
Marketing and administrative expenses	80,351
Net income	$ 11,059
Fixed costs and expenses:	
Manufacturing costs	$ 44,400
Marketing and administrative expenses	62,477

Budgeted sales for 20x4 were 14,000 units for $374,500. Variable manufacturing standard cost was $16.30 per unit and variable marketing and administrative expenses were budgeted at 5 percent of sales. Assume budgeted and actual fixed costs are equal.

Required:

Prepare statements illustrating the variances between budget and actual for North Pole Enterprises using the sequential approach (i.e., prepare an analysis for the first three levels illustrated in the chapter).

13-18. Prepare Statements for Three Levels of Analysis.

The Gridiron Manufacturing Company produces two products and had the following actual results:

Gridiron Manufacturing Company
Income Statement
For the Period Ending May 31, 20x2

	Total	Footballs	Helmets
Unit sales	27,000	13,950	13,050
Selling price	$ 26	$ 27	
Sales	$ 715,050	362,700	352,350
Variable costs:			
Manufacturing	443,250	201,750	241,500
Marketing and administrative	35,752	18,135	17,617
Contribution margin	$ 236,048	$ 142,815	$ 93,233
Fixed costs:			
Manufacturing	$ 88,800		
Marketing and administrative	124,950		
Net income	$ 22,298		

The company expected to sell 14,400 footballs and 12,750 helmets at $25 and $37, respectively. The variable manufacturing costs per unit were budgeted at $13.50 for balls and $18.60 for helmets. Fixed manufacturing expenses were budgeted at $90,000. The total budget for marketing and administrative expenses was $163,088 which included variable expenses calculated at 5 percent of sales.

Required:

Prepare the first three levels of variance analysis as outlined in the chapter.

► PROBLEMS AND CASES ◄

13-19. Sales Variances, Two Products.

The Bell Company manufactures and sells two models of typewriters, Quik Speed and Super Speed. The budgeted and actual results of operations appeared as follows for the past fiscal year:

	Budgeted Results Quik Speed			Actual Results Quik Speed		
	Units	Price	Total	Units	Price	Total
Sales	9,000	$200	$1,800,000	7,000	$200	$1,400,000
Variable costs	9,000	160	1,440,000	7,000	160	1,120,000
Contribution margin ...	9,000	40	$ 360,000	7,000	40	$ 280,000

	Super Speed			Super Speed		
	Units	Price	Total	Units	Price	Total
Sales	3,000	$300	$ 900,000	6,000	$300	$1,800,000
Variable costs	3,000	220	660,000	6,000	220	1,320,000
Contribution margin ...	3,000	$ 80	$ 240,000	6,000	$ 80	$ 480,000

	Total			Total		
	Units	Price	Total	Units	Price	Total
Sales	12,000	$225	$2,700,000	13,000	$246*	$3,200,000
Variable costs	12,000	175	2,100,000	13,000	188	2,440,000
Contribution margin ..	12,000	50	$ 600,000	13,000	$ 58	$ 760,000

* Averages rounded off to nearest dollar

Mr. Bell, the president, knew that he had met his target in terms of unit sales, costs, and contribution margins, but could not understand why an increase of 1,000 units in sales would create an increase of $160,000 in total contribution margin.

Required:

a. Explain and submit computations as to why actual total contribution margin differed from budgeted, using only:
   1. The sales volume variance.
   2. The sales quantity and mix variances.
b. Indicate and explain your preference for either the sales volume or the sales quantity and mix variance approach to account for the deviation from budgeted performance. (SMA adapted)

13-20. Calculate All Variances, Two Products.

Pizza To Your Door sells two sizes of pizza for delivery, regular (12-inch) and super (16-inch). The following budgeted per unit data refers to the two sizes:

	Regular	*Super*
Selling price	$ 6	$ 10
Variable costs:		
Cost of goods sold	3	4
Delivery commissions . . .	0.60	1

Total fixed costs were budgeted at $56,000 for the year. Sales revenue was budgeted as follows:

	Amount	*Pizzas*
Regular	$ 60,000	10,000
Super	100,000	10,000

Given below is the income statement for the year reflecting the actual data:

Sales revenue		148,150
Less: Variable costs:		
Cost of goods sold	67,000	
Delivery commissions . .	14,800	81,800
Contribution margin		$ 66,350
Less: Fixed costs:		56,600
Income before taxes		$ 9,750
Actual pizzas sold	13,000 regular at $5.85	
	7,000 super at $10.30	

The general manager noticed that 20,000 pizzas were sold as budgeted but the income before taxes was lower than budgeted by $8,250.

Required:

Prepare a worksheet for the general manager showing all the variances. Through these variances explain why the budgeted income was not attained.

13-21. Various Sales Variances.

Handy Dandy Tool & Equipment Corporation master budget data for the year ending May 31, 20x3 is as follows:

	Total	*Dies*	*Tools*
Unit sales	15,900	8,400	7,500
Selling price		$ 24	$ 36
Variable costs:			
Manufacturing	$ 266,970	$ 120,120	$ 146,850
Marketing and administrative	28,455	12,180	16,275

Actual data for the year ended May 31, 20x3 is shown below:

	Total	*Dies*	*Tools*
Unit sales	15,800	8,100	7,700
Selling price		$ 26	$ 26
Variable costs:			
Manufacturing	$ 264,415	$ 123,120	$ 141,295
Marketing and administrative	25,280	12,960	12,320

Hint: It would be appropriate to prepare a flexible budget income statement in detail before any variance calculations are attempted.

Required:

Calculate the sales price and volume variances using the following methods:
1. Sales revenue per unit
2. Profit contribution per unit
3. Profit contribution per unit with sales mix variance
4. Profit contribution percentage with sales mix variance.

13-22. Flexible Budgeting Plus Sales Variances.
    Pro Sport Clothing Company income data are presented below. The budget portion is based on the static or master budget method.

Pro Sport Clothing Company
Income Statement
For the Quarter Ending June 30, 20x7

	Actual	*Master Budget*	*Variance*
Sales	$181,644	$ 182,200	$ 556 U
Cost of goods sold	151,844	149,600	2,244 U
Gross profit	29,800	32,600	2,800 U
Marketing and			
administrative expenses	30,082	29,110	972 U
Income (loss)	(282)	3,490	3,772 U

The following are the details of the accounts in the income statement shown above:

	Actual			*Budget*		
	Units	*Price*	*Total*	*Units*	*Price*	*Total*
Sales:						
Product:						
T-shirt	6,730 at	$10.80	$ 72,684	5,800	$ 11.00	$ 63,800
Golf shirt	5,100 at	11.50	58,650	5,200	12.00	62,400
Sweatshirt	3,870 at	13.00	50,310	4,000	14.00	56,000

Variable costs and expenses:

Manufacturing				
T-shirt	$ 5.90	$ 39,707	$ 6.00	$ 34,800
Golf shirt	6.60	33,660	6.50	33,800
Sweatshirt	7.10	27,477	7.00	28,000
Marketing and				
administrative	5% sales	9,082*	5% sales	9,110
Fixed costs and expenses:				
Manufacturing		51,000		53,000
Marketing and				
administrative		21,000		20,000

* Rounded

Required:

a. Prepare a level 2 flexible budget income statement variance analysis.
b. Separate the sales efficiency variance into price, quantity and mix variances, using the profit contribution per unit approach.

13-23. All Variances for the Income Statement.

The president of Madison Avenue Auto Parts was disappointed with this period's results. While reviewing the income statement shown below, she muttered, "We have never been this far off budget before and this in spite of the fact that cost of goods sold shows a fairly substantial favorable variance."

Madison Avenue Auto Parts
Income Statement

	Actual	Master Budget	Variance
Sales	$ 1,276,230	$ 1,484,000	$ 207,770 U
Cost of goods sold	858,520	990,700	132,180 F
Gross profit	$ 417,710	$ 493,300	75,590 U
Marketing and			
administrative expenses	317,605	313,880	3,725 U
Income before taxes	$ 100,105	$ 179,420	$ 79,315 U

Glancing at the income statement you immediately notice that it is based on a static or master budget. Through further investigation you were able to extract the following information.

Budgeted sales were 70,000 units at a standard variable cost of $11.50 per unit. The variable marketing and administrative expenses were budgeted at 7 percent of sales. Actual variable cost per unit for the 57,000 units sold was $11.75 and actual variable marketing and administrative expenses amounted to $91,605.

Required:

a. Prepare a level 2 flexible budget variance analysis for the income statement.

b. Prepare an analysis of sales efficiency variances into sales price and sales volume variances using:
1. Sales price per unit.
2. Contribution margin per unit.
3. Contribution margin percentage.

13-24. Sales and Cost Variances, Two Products.

Handler Company distributes two home-use power tools, a heavy duty 1/2" hand drill and a table saw. The tools are purchased from a manufacturer that attaches the Handler private label on the tools. The wholesale selling prices to hardware stores are $60 each for the drill and $120 each for the table saw.

The 20x2 budget and actual results are presented below. The budget was adopted in late 20x1 and was based upon Handler's estimated share of the market for the two tools.

During the first quarter of 20x2, Handler's management estimated that the total market for these tools would actually be 10 percent below its original estimates. In an attempt to prevent Handler's unit sales from declining as much as industry projections, management developed and implemented a marketing program. Included in the program were dealer discounts and increased direct advertising. The table saw line was emphasized in this program.

Handler Company
Income Statement
For the Year Ended December 31, 20x2
(000s omitted)

| | Hand Drill | | Table Saw | | Total | |
	Budget	*Actual*	*Budget*	*Actual*	*Budget*	*Actual*	*Variance*
Sales in units.	120	86	80	74	200	160	40
Revenue	$7,200	$5,074	$9,600	$8,510	$16,800	$13,584	($3,216)
Cost of goods sold	6,000	4,300	6,400	6,068	12,400	10,368	2,032
Gross margin	$1,200	$ 774	$3,200	$2,442	$ 4,400	$ 3,216	($1,184)

| | Total | | |
	Budget	*Actual*	*Variance*
Unallocated costs:			
Selling	$ 1,000	$ 1,000	
Advertising	1,000	1,060	(60)
Administrative	400	406	(6)
Income taxes (45%)	900	338	562
Total unallocated costs	$ 3,300	$ 2,804	$ 496
Net income	$ 1,100	$ 412	$ (688)

Required:

a. Analyze the unfavorable gross margin variance of $1,184,000 in terms of
1. sales price variance.
2. cost variance.
3. sales volume variance.
b. Discuss the apparent effect of Handler Company's special marketing program (i.e., dealer discounts and additional advertising) on 20x2 operating results. Support your comments with numerical data where appropriate.
(CMA adapted)

13-25. All Sales and Cost Variances for One Product.
  The president of the T.F. Jackson Company, which manufactures insulated picnic coolers, has just received the following budget data.

T.F. Jackson Company
Budget Performance Report
For the Year Ended December 31, 20x3

	Budget	*Actual*	*Difference*
Units	10,000	11,000	1,000 F
Sales	$ 250,000	$ 272,250	$ 22,250 F
Cost of goods sold:			
Material	60,000	65,340*	5,340 U
Labor	40,000	42,790**	2,790 U
Manufacturing overhead:			
Variable	50,000	54,120	4,120 U
Fixed	30,000	30,000	0
Total cost of goods sold	$ 180,000	$ 192,250	$ 12,250 U
Gross margin	$ 70,000	$ 80,000	10,000 F
Variable marketing expenses	20,000	29,850	9,850 U
Fixed marketing and			
administrative expenses	20,000	20,000	0
Net income	$ 30,000	$ 30,150	$ 150 F

*   Actual materials used 32,500 kg.
** Actual labor used 2,100 hours

Standard unit production costs are as follows:

Materials: 3kg. at $ 2 per kg	$	6
Labor: 1/5 hour at $ 20 per hour	$	4
Variable overhead:		
$25 per direct labor hour		5
Fixed overhead:		
$15 per direct labor hour		3
Standard unit production cost	$	18

The president was pleased with the marketing manager's performance for the year as evidenced by her total favorable variance of $12,400 (22,250F - 9,850U). She decided to reward the marketing manager with a bonus to show her appreciation for a job well done. The president sent a memorandum to the production manager reprimanding him for his poor performance ($12,250 unfavorable variance) and blamed him for the company's lower than budgeted profit performance.

Required:

Was the president's evaluation of the marketing and production managers' performance correct? Fully explain your answer.

13-26. All Sales and Cost Variances for Two Products.

Ernest Company manufactures two products, SUBS and ADS, using similar inputs (materials X and Y) in varying degrees for each product. The products are manufactured in separate departments with the same standard labor rate in each department. The company uses a standard costing system recorded when the materials are issued to production.

Sales budgeted for 20x3: 60,000 units of SUBS at $180 per unit and 40,000 units of ADS at $275 per unit.

Actual sales for 20x3 were 63,500 units of SUBS for $11,112,500 and 35,600 units of ads for $9,968,000.

	SUBS	*ADS*
Standard costs per unit for 20x3 were:		
Direct material X ($5.20/kg.)	$ 36.40	$ 15.60
Direct material Y ($3.70/meter)	7.40	48.10
Direct labor ($18/hr.)	63.00	99.00
Variable overhead ($3 DLH)	10.50	16.50
Fixed overhead:*		
(SUBS $4/DLH)	14.00	
(ADS $6/DLH)		33.00
Total standard cost	$131.30	$212.20

* Based on activity levels of 60,000 units of SUBS and 40,000 units of ADS.

The records of the company were limited to the following information for 20x3:

1. Production totalled 65,000 units of SUBS and 38,000 units of ADS.
2. Direct material X: Purchase totalled 700,000 kilograms and cost $3,626,000. A total of 565,000 kilograms were issued to production.
3. Direct material Y: Purchases totalled 520,000 meters and cost $1,950,000. A total of 630,000 meters were issued to production (January 1, 20x3 inventory of Y was at an average cost of $3.60 per meter on a LIFO basis).
4. Direct labor: A total of 433,200 hours were worked with a total cost of $7,970,880.
5. Variable overhead for the company totalled $1,320,000.
6. Fixed overhead was $850,000 for the SUBS department and $1,320,000 for the ADS department.

Required:

a. Calculate and identify each variance which can be isolated for 20x3. Show all calculations.
b. What improvements would you recommend the company make in its recordkeeping and methods of isolating variances? Explain why each recommendation would be an improvement.
(SMA adapted)

13-27. **Analysis of Alternative Marketing Plans and Report on Variances with Actual Results.**
It is 4:30 p.m., December 29, 20x3, and you have just been requested by the Chairman of the Board of the Mason Products Company to submit a recommendation for the company's 20x4 pricing strategy by 9:30 a.m. tomorrow. You have already established new variable costs for the firms's three products as follows:

		Product	
	Anko	*Bipo*	*Coco*
Standard variable costs per unit:			
Material	$ 10	$ 8	$ 4
Labor	10	3	2
Overhead	10	6	4
Marketing	2	3	2

The sales manager has announced that he will be able to limit his variable selling costs to 10 percent of the selling price on Anko and Bipo and 5 percent on Coco. He has presented the following alternative plans to the board:

Plan		*Anko*	*Bipo*	*Coco*
I	Selling price	$ 40	$ 30	$ 18
	Estimated units sold	1,000	2,000	3,000
II	Selling price	$ 40	$ 40	$ 18
	Estimated units sold	1,000	1,000	3,000
III	Selling price	$ 50	$ 30	$ 18
	Estimated units sold	800	2,000	3,000
IV	Selling price	$ 35	$ 50	$ 25
	Estimated units sold	1,200	600	2,500
V	Selling price	$ 60	$ 30	$ 16
	Estimated units sold	600	2,000	4,500

The plant engineer has just completed a study which shows that the plant capacity is limited to 10,000 direct labor hours.

Required:

Part I:
a. Prepare a recommendation for the Chairman of the Board which will support the plan having the greatest profit contribution for 20x4. Direct labor cost per hour is $2.00.
b. Assuming the sales manager's demand data to be correct and the demand for each product to be independent of the other two, is there a "Plan VI" which you can suggest will provide greater profit contribution than any of the sales manager's plans?
c. To what extent would you expect to include fixed costs and assets employed (investment) in the evaluation of alternatives such as in this case?

Part II:
It is now January 3, 20x5, the Mason Products Company books are closed. The statement of operations reveals the following results for 20x4.

	Product			
	Anko	Bipo	Coco	Total
Revenue (actual)	$37,000	$60,000	$60,000	$157,000
Variable marketing costs (at standard) . .	3,700	6,000	3,000	12,700
Net sales revenue	33,300	$54,000	$57,000	$144,300
Cost of sales variable (at standard)	32,000	20,000	36,000	88,000
Profit contribution	$ 1,300	$34,000	$21,000	$ 56,300

Prepare a statement explaining the variances between the company's performance and the plan adopted under Part I, assuming the optimum plan was chosen.

13-28. Report on Variances.
The Small Products Division of Giant Co. Ltd. manufactures two unrelated products, Dwarfs and Midgets. This division operates as a profit center and, because of the highly competitive markets for its products, bases its annual budget on market share percentages. The president of the company has just received the following selected data for this division for the year ended December 31, 20x1:

	Budget	Actual
Market size (units)		
Dwarfs	4,800	5,040
Midgets	8,000	8,400
	12,800	13,440
Units produced & sold		
Dwarfs	120	106
Midgets	200	230
Total market share	2.5%	2.5%

Income Statement	Budget		Actual	
Sales				
Dwarfs	$ 6,000		$ 5,406	
Midgets	13,000	$ 19,000	14,490	$ 19,986
Variable manufacturing				
Dwarfs	$ 3,300		$ 2,915	
Midgets	10,100	(13,400)	11,615	(14,530)
Variable marketing				
Dwarfs	$ 300		$ 159	
Midgets	500	(800)	920	(1,079)
Contribution margin		$ 4,800		$ 4,287
Fixed costs		(3,600)		(3,600)
Net income before taxes . . .		$ 1,200		$ 687

Upon initial review, the president has called you, the controller, into her office.

"What is Tiny Smith (manager of Small Products Division) doing? I knew the markets were expanding beyond our expectations and I told Tiny that, if he attained the target market share, he'd get a bonus. Of course, I assumed the profits would increase proportionately. Why didn't they? How can the profits be lower than budget when sales were higher? Was I too hasty in offering the bonus? I want a complete analysis. I also want an assessment of Tiny's performance in light of the expanding markets and my explicit instructions."

Required:

Prepare a response to the president.

Learning Objectives

After reading this chapter, the student should have an understanding of:

✔ The need for analyzing cost behavior.

✔ The relationship between analyzing cost behavior and cost prediction or forecasting.

✔ The relationship between analyzing cost behavior and an appropriate measure of activity (i.e., output or standard input).

✔ Methods for analyzing cost behavior (i.e., separating costs into fixed and variable components).

✔ High-low analysis, scatter chart analysis and regression analysis as applied to separating costs into fixed and variable components.

✔ The statistical properties of regression analysis such as the standard error, the variance, correlation, and their use in determining which is the best regression and how good the best regression is.

Also, the reader is given some basic precautions with regard to using regression analysis and some thoughts on confidence intervals and t-values for the fixed and variable components of regression analysis.

$\mathcal{P}$ROFIT PLANNING, CONTROL AND COST BEHAVIOR

Throughout this text we have emphasized and utilized the distinction between fixed and variable costs. However, only in the case of an appendix to Chapter 3 did we refer to methods for examining cost behavior, that is, methods for separating fixed and variable costs. In that that instance, the high-low technique was used. Now in this chapter, we must examine a wider variety of methods and many of their implications.

▸ SOME BASICS ◂

Too often discussions of separating costs into fixed and variable proceed so quickly that we tend to overlook the fundamental objective and a requisite to the achievement of that objective. The objective is to improve our ability to predict or forecast costs and a requisite for this is an appropriate measure of activity.

▸ Cost Prediction or Forecasting—The Objective

Even a cursory review of previous chapters indicates that profit planning and budgeting cannot be done without the separation of costs into fixed and variable components. Thus analysis of cost behavior is essential to being able to predict or forecast costs under the variety of volume levels considered in profit planning.

▸ An Appropriate Measure of Activity—A Requisite

When considering only units of final output, such as tote bag and backpack bookbags in Chapter 13, the issue of an appropriate measure of activity can easily be overlooked. Bookbags (in physical terms) are obvious appropriate measures of activity to think of in terms of forecasting or predicting total costs. For example, Exhibit 13-1 illustrates a profit plan including fixed costs totaling $1,410,000 and variable costs per unit for tote bag and backpack bookbags of $14.75 and $20.45, respectively. An equation to predict total costs in that case would be as follows:

$$\begin{array}{ccccc} \textit{Total} & = & \textit{Fixed} & + & \textit{Variable Cost} \quad \textit{Units of} \\ \textit{Costs} & & \textit{Costs} & & \textit{Per Unit} \quad \text{x} \quad \textit{Activity} \\ \\ & = & 1,410,000 & + & 14.75T \quad\quad 20.45B \end{array}$$

The amount of predicted total cost would depend on the volume of activity expected for tote bags and backpacks.

The appropriate measure of activity is much less obvious when it comes to individual production and service departments within a firm even though it is the sum of those individual departmental costs which produce the illustrative total cost function above. For example, in the finishing department of the Lonesome Pine Furniture Co., a manufacturer of high quality pine furniture, what measure of activity should be used? Should it be actual physical output *finished* (the number of various pieces of furniture) or should it be some measure of input such as direct labor hours or machine hours?

▸ An Appropriate Measure of Activity—Output or Standard Input

Actual physical output of the various pieces *finished* would initially seem to be an appropriate measure of activity. Then one realizes that the assorted items of furniture worked on could all be so different that their physical quantities are not additive. What is needed is a *common denominator* calculation which converts the many various products worked on into an additive total.

The appropriate basis for such a common denominator is a standard input measure such as direct labor hours, machine hours or product flow time. For example, assume the following number of tables, chairs and stools are expected to be worked on in the finishing department during the coming year and they each require the indicated number of standard direct labor hours per unit. Note the additivity of the total expected standard direct labor hours.

Products	Units Expected To Be Worked On	Standard Direct Labor Hours Per Unit	Total Standard Direct Labor Hours
Tables	50,000	2.0	100,000
Chairs	100,000	.5	50,000
Stools	125,000	.7	87,500
Total			237,500

The standard input measure is in essence an output measure restated in terms of a common denominator. Now for purposes of forecasting costs in individual producing and service departments, we have an equation similar to the following:

$$\text{Total Costs} = \text{Fixed Costs} + \begin{array}{c}\text{Variable Costs Per}\\\text{Standard Direct}\\\text{Labor Hour}\end{array} \times \begin{array}{c}\text{Standard Direct}\\\text{Labor Hours for}\\\text{Expected Activity*}\end{array}$$

Standard direct labor hours for expected activity are often referred to as standard hours allowed.

Standard direct labor hours are a logical choice in the finishing department of Lonesome Pine because the tasks are labor intensive. In other departments, the unit of activity could be standard machine hours, standard product flow time or even standard materials costs. The specific functions or tasks of an individual department plus statistical analysis will determine the specific unit of activity to be used.

In those cases where standard costs are not available, expected rather than standard inputs are used as a measure of activity when predicting costs. This is not as good as it should be since expected as opposed to standard inputs do not yield as precise a measure of output.[1]

► *METHODS FOR SEPARATING FIXED AND VARIABLE COSTS* ◄

Methods for separating costs into fixed and variable components can be loosely classified as: (1) inspection of accounts, (2) engineering studies, and (3) mathematical and statistical analyses. This classification is considered loose because engineering studies are mathematically and statistically oriented. Nonetheless, the three categories will be found useful.

► *Inspection of Accounts*

The chart of accounts in each department and plant or other division of a firm can be analyzed in terms of which cost items are obviously fixed (such as rents and salaries) and which items are obviously variable (such as direct materials and sales commissions).

The other or not so obvious items (such as most, if not all categories of overhead) can then be subjected to the mathematical and statistical techniques to be discussed below. *The other or not so obvious items are typically referred to as mixed costs or even semi-variable or semi-fixed costs.*

The inspection of accounts can be a very cost efficient technique for identifying the obvious fixed and variable costs. On occasion, this technique is extended to the not so obvious items. In such cases, the individual or group reviewing the accounts distributes the accounts into fixed and variable categories based on a subjective estimate of whether the accounts are primarily fixed or primarily variable. Certainly the subjectivity involved in extending this technique is bothersome even though it is cost efficient.

► *Engineering Studies*

Engineering studies, like the inspection of accounts, are very helpful when it comes to the obvious fixed and variable costs. Such studies are usually based on the work measurement techniques used to determine the physical standards for labor and materials discussed in Chapter 8. However, for *mixed costs*, the mathematical and statistical techniques discussed below are necessary.

► *Mathematical and Statistical Analysis*

All of the mathematical and statistical analyses to be discussed here are designed to deal with costs which are not obviously fixed or variable. Costs such as direct materials, direct labor,[2] sales commissions, rents and salaries are assumed to be properly classified by engineering studies or

---

[1] Expected inputs such as expected direct labor hours, can be appealing because they appear to measure departmental effort in an overall sense. However, when it is realized that expected inputs include off-standard performance such as the labor efficiency variance, expected inputs are usually replaced with standard inputs.

[2] There is some question today as to whether labor is a fixed or variable cost. Variable union contract provisions, as well as legislation at local and federal levels, plus automation and robotics, have increasingly made labor costs more fixed in nature.

inspection of accounts. Mathematical and statistical analyses will thus deal only with those elements of manufacturing, marketing and administrative overhead which are called mixed costs.

In this category, we will examine three approaches to separating costs into fixed and variable elements. They are: (1) high-low analysis, (2) scatter chart analysis, and (3) regression analysis. Each of these approaches has the same objective (i.e., analyzing historical costs in order to use the analysis as a foundation for predicting future costs). In each instance, this objective will be formalized by quantifying the specific parameters in the equation for a straight line as indicated below.

$$
\begin{aligned}
\textit{Total Cost} \quad &= \quad \textit{a} \quad + \quad \textit{bX} \\[2mm]
&= \quad \begin{array}{c}\textit{Predicted}\\ \textit{Fixed}\\ \textit{Cost}\end{array} \quad + \quad \begin{array}{c}\textit{Predicted Variable}\\ \textit{Cost Per}\\ \textit{Unit of Activity}\end{array} \quad \textit{x} \quad \begin{array}{c}\textit{Units of}\\ \textit{Activity}\end{array}
\end{aligned}
$$

For illustrative purposes, all three approaches will be quantified using the data in Exhibit 14-1. Note that the data relates to a prior year's indirect materials costs (a mixed cost) and standard direct labor hours for the finishing department of the Lonesome Pine Furniture Co.'s manufacturing plant. This historical data is intended to help project next year's fixed, variable and total indirect materials cost.

Lonesome Pine Furniture Co.
Finishing Department
For the Year Ended September 30, 20__

Month	Standard Direct Labor Hours	Indirect Materials
October	40	$ 160
November	60	165
December	64	200
January	50	175
February	33	130
March	90	235
April	80	228
May	83	221
June	62	195
July	85	230
August	75	200
September	70	189

Exhibit 14-1 _Historical Data Indirect Materials Costs and Standard Direct Labor Hours_

High-Low Analysis. Basically, the high-low approach ignores all data other than the high and low activity. In Exhibit 14-1, the high and low activity occur in March and February, respectively. These two points are then used with the following algebraic equations to determine an estimate of the fixed and variable components of indirect materials costs. Note that the equations assume that only variable costs will change, that is, the fixed costs will remain the same and the difference between high and low costs will be the variable costs.

$$\begin{matrix} \textit{Variable Indirect} \\ \textit{Materials Costs Per} \\ \textit{Standard Direct} \\ \textit{Labor Hour} \end{matrix} = \frac{\textit{Change in Indirect Materials Costs Between High and Low Standard Direct Labor Hours}}{\textit{Change in Standard Direct Labor Hours Between High and Low Standard Direct Labor Hours}}$$

$$= \frac{\$235 - 130}{90 - 33} = \frac{\$105}{57}$$

$$= \$1.842 \textit{ Per Standard Direct Labor Hour}$$

$$\begin{matrix} \textit{Fixed Indirect} \\ \textit{Materials Costs} \end{matrix} = \begin{matrix} \textit{Total Indirect materials} \\ \textit{Costs at High* Standard} \\ \textit{Direct Labor Hours} \end{matrix} - \begin{matrix} \textit{Variable Indirect materials} \\ \textit{Costs at High* Standard} \\ \textit{Direct Labor Hours} \end{matrix}$$

$$= \$235 - \$1.842\,(90) = \$69.22$$

*The low point would yield the same fixed cost estimate.

The net result of our high-low calculations is the following quantified straight line equation.

$$\textit{Total Indirect Materials Costs} = \$69.22 + \$1.842 \textit{ Per Standard Direct Labor Hour}$$

Now if someone wanted to budget next year's indirect materials costs for a volume level of 82 standard direct labor hours, the budget prediction would be:

$$\textit{Budgeted Indirect Materials Costs} = \$69.22 + \$1.842 \times 82$$
$$= \$69.22 + \$151.04 = \$220.26$$

Mathematically, the essence of the high-low technique is to ignore all observations other than the high and low activity and to assume a straight line relationship between the high and low activity. The slope of the straight line is the estimated unit variable cost while the estimated total fixed cost is the intercept or intersection of the straight line and the vertical (Y) axis. All of this is shown graphically in Exhibit 14-2. The reader should note that either the high or the low point should yield the same fixed cost estimate since both points are on the same straight line. Furthermore, the reader should note the conceptual flaw of high-low analysis (i.e., it concentrates on extreme values and ignores all other observations).

High-Low Analysis: Some Modifications. In order to offset the high-low concentration on extreme values, some might like to examine the historical data such as Exhibit 14-1 and eliminate observations considered to be extreme. Data to be eliminated could be the upper and lower 5 percent or 10 percent. Another approach might be to soften the extremes by averaging the upper and lower 10 percent or 25 percent of the observations before using the high-low analysis. These modifications are essentially subjective, which can be bothersome to users of the analysis.

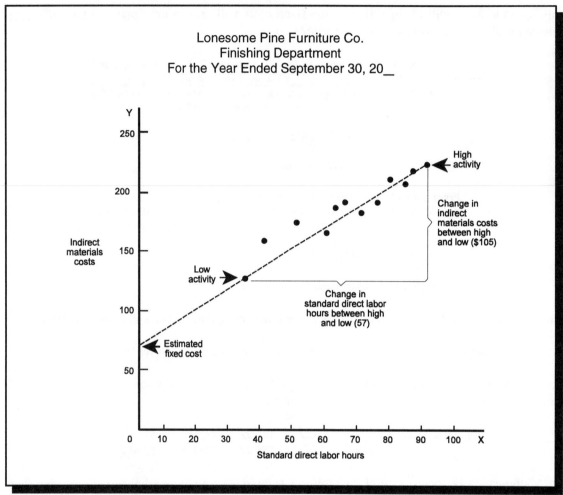

Exhibit 14-2   *Graphic Presentation of High-Low Analysis Indirect Materials Costs and Standard Direct Labor Hours*

Scatter-Chart Analysis. In essence scatter-chart analysis is an attempt to overcome the deficiency of high-low analysis (i.e., concentration on high and low activity while ignoring all other observations). The scatter-chart is a plotting of past observations such as those in Exhibit 14-1, which were plotted in Exhibit 14-2. This time, however, all observations will be considered rather than just the high and the low.[3]

---

[3] As will be discussed later, charting is also considered to be a useful precautionary first step in regression analysis. Charting yields a visual indication of the relationship between cost and activity which can be useful in judging which form of regression analysis to use.

The problem or conceptual flaw with scatter-chart analysis is that one tries to visually fit a straight line to all of the observations. Regardless of who does it, this "eye-balling" technique, is subjective and the straight line fit can differ depending on who does it. Furthermore, the same person could easily fit a different line to the same data each time a fit is attempted.

Exhibit 14-3 illustrates scatter-chart analysis. Note that the fit tries to have an equal number of observations above and below the line such that the fit represents an average of all the observations. In this particular case, the fit connects two of the twelve observations, one of which is the low activity point. However, a different person could easily fit a different straight line through the twelve observations.

Estimates of the variable and fixed components of indirect materials costs are derived from the straight line fit. The slope of the line determines the variable cost estimate and from this estimate an estimate of the fixed cost (or the Y intercept) can be made.

The estimates for the straight line fit of Exhibit 14-3 are included in Exhibit 14-3. Note that the slope of the line is determined by attaching a right angle (with sides parallel to the Y and X axes) to the line and using the two sides of the right angle to determine the slope. Also remember from basic geometry that any right angle similarly attached to our straight line will produce the same slope. In this particular case, the scatter-chart estimates are very close to the high-low estimates of fixed and variable costs. Obviously, this is not always true.

Regression Analysis.[4] Regression analysis is a technique which overcomes the limitations of both high-low and scatter-chart analysis. All observations are considered and the analysis is strictly analytical (i.e., not subjective).

To be precise, we shall consider in this section only *simple linear regression*. The objective is to statistically determine the straight line or linear relationship between two variables such as indirect materials costs and standard direct labor hours.

Our goal in simple linear regression is the same as under high-low and scatter-chart analysis. We wish to quantify the specific parameters in the equation for a straight line so that we might predict or budget future costs. In terms of our ongoing illustration, our budget equation is as follows:

Budgeted Indirect Materials Costs	=	*Budgeted Fixed Cost Component*	+	*Budgeted Variable Cost Component Per Standard Direct Labor Hour*	x	*Budgeted Standard Direct Labor Hours*

In statistical terms, the above equation is usually given as:

$$Y = a + bX$$ where

Y = *the dependent variable*

X = *the independent variable*

a = *the Y intercept*

b = *the slope*

---

[4] This discussion of regression analysis is predicated on the assumption that the reader is familiar with the technique of regression as it is covered in basic statistics courses.

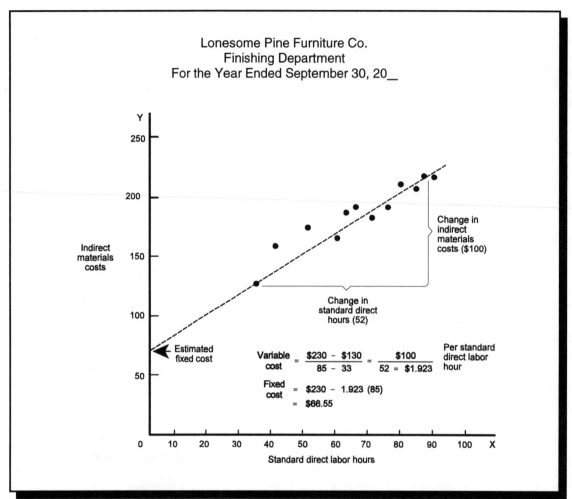

Exhibit 14-3   *Scatter-Chart Analysis Indirect Materials Costs and Standard Direct Labor Hours*

In order to quantify our equation, we take historical observations of Y and X such as those in Exhibit 14-1, for indirect materials costs and standard direct labor hours and solve what are known as the two normal equations of simple linear regression. These normal equations are designed to produce a *least squares prediction equation* (i.e., an equation for a straight line fit to a series of observations, where the sum of the squares of deviations of actual observations from the line is a minimum). The normal equations are:

$$\sum Y = na + b(\sum X)$$
$$\sum XY = a(\sum X) + b(\sum X^2)$$

The variables a, b, X and Y are as defined above while n is the number of observations in the sample being used to make estimates of "a" and "b."

Exhibit 14-4 takes the data of Exhibit 14-1 and provides a regression analysis of that data, including a solution of the two normal equations which have to be solved together because they are simultaneous. As the reader reviews Exhibit 14-4, he or she must remember that today's personal computers can handle the calculations involved in a few seconds using readily available statistical software. (See Appendix B for a discussion of regression analysis via the computer.) Either way, the net result of the regression is the quantified equation below.

$$\text{\textit{Budgeted Indirect Materials Costs}} = \$82.13 + \$1.695 \times \text{\textit{Budgeted Standard Direct Labor Hours}}$$

From a summary point of view it is easy to see that our three methods of mathematical and statistical analysis produce three different predictive equations (i.e., sets of a and b). These are indicated below:

Basic predictive equation .... $Y = a + bX$
High-low prediction .... $Y = 69.22 + 1.842X$
Scatter-chart prediction ..... $Y = 66.55 + 1.923X$
Regression prediction .... $Y = 82.13 + 1.196X$

In the particular case of budgeting for next year based upon the predictive equations determined from prior year data, our three methods would produce the following budgeted indirect materials costs for a budgeted volume level of 87 standard direct labor hours.[5]

High-low prediction .... $69.22 + 1.842(87) = \$ 229.47$
Scatter-chart prediction .... $66.55 + 1.923(87) = 233.85$
Regression prediction .... $82.13 + 1.695(87) = 229.60$

Since all of the budgeted amounts are very similar in this case, one could argue that the different methods may not produce results which are substantively different. Nonetheless, there is good reason to use regression analysis. Regression analysis is not subjective and it does include all observations. Regression analysis has also been made much simpler with the increasing use of personal computers. Above all, regression analysis has certain very useful statistical properties which will be discussed below.

---

[5] Common sense dictates that budget estimates for volume levels outside the range of observations used to set up predictive equations should be used with great caution.

Lonesome Pine Furniture Co.
Finishing Department
For the Year Ended September 30, 20__

Month	X	Y	XY	X^2
October	40	160	6,400	1,600
November	60	165	9,900	3,600
December	64	200	12,800	4,096
January	50	175	8,750	2,500
February	33	130	4,290	1,089
March	90	235	21,150	8,100
April	80	228	18,240	6,400
May	83	221	18,343	6,889
June	62	195	12,090	3,844
July	85	230	19,550	7,225
August	75	200	15,000	5,625
September	70	189	13,230	4,900
Total ($\sum$)	792	2,328	159,743	55,868

Regression equations:

$$\sum Y = na + b(\sum X) \text{ or } 2{,}328 = 12a + b792$$

$$\sum XY = a(\sum X) + b(\sum X)^2 \text{ or } 159{,}743 = 792a + b55{,}868$$

Solution:

$$159{,}743 = 792a + 55{,}868b$$

$$\frac{-66(2{,}328)}{6{,}095} = \frac{-66(12a) + -66(792b)}{3{,}596b}$$

$$\frac{6{,}095}{1{,}695} = \frac{3{,}596b}{b}$$

$$2{,}328 = 12a + 1{,}695(792)$$

$$2{,}328 = 12a + 1{,}342.44$$

$$985.56 = 12a$$

$$82.13 = a$$

Exhibit 14-4   *Regression Analysis of Indirect Materials Costs (Y) and Standard Direct Labor Hours (X)*

▶ STATISTICAL PROPERTIES OF REGRESSION ANALYSIS ◀

For our purposes, the main statistical properties of regression analysis relate to the *arithmetic mean* and the *standard deviation*. In basic statistics, when one wants to calculate an arithmetic mean of a series of observations, the observations are summed and divided by the number of observations. Related to the arithmetic mean is its standard deviation, which is a measure of the relationship between the arithmetic mean and the individual observations used to determine the arithmetic mean. In statistical terms, the standard deviation of the mean is the square root of the sum of the squares of the differences between the mean[6] and each observation divided by the number of observations.

Using statistical notation, the mean and the standard deviation are usually described as follows:

$$Mean \; = \; \mu \; = \; \frac{\Sigma Y}{n}$$

$$Standard \; deviation \; of \; the \; mean \; = \; \sigma \; = \; \sqrt{\frac{\Sigma (Y-\mu)^2}{n}}$$

One other basic statistical term is *variance*. The variance of statistics must be distinguished from the variances of standard costing and flexible budgeting. In statistics, the variance of the mean is the square of the standard deviation of the mean and is usually described as follows:

$$Variation \; of \; the \; mean \; = \; \sigma^2 \; = \; \sqrt{\frac{\Sigma (Y-\mu)^2}{n}}$$

Using the 12 observations of indirect materials costs in Exhibit 14-1, one can easily calculate estimates of the mean, variance and standard deviation of indirect materials costs. However, before this is done, the above equations must be adjusted because we are making estimates of *true* population parameters from a sample of 12 observations. The revised equations are indicated below and are calculated for indirect materials costs in Exhibit 14-5.

$$Estimated \; mean \; = \; \overline{Y} \; = \; \frac{\Sigma Y}{n}$$

$$Estimated \; standard \; deviation \; = \; s \; = \; \sqrt{\frac{\Sigma (Y-\overline{Y})^2}{n-1}}$$

$$Estimated \; variance \; = \; s^2 \; = \; \sqrt{\frac{\Sigma (Y-\overline{Y})^2}{n-1}}$$

Note in the above equations, the substitution of the estimated or sample mean ($\overline{Y}$), standard deviation (s) and variance (s^2) for the true population mean (μ), standard deviation (σ) and variance (σ^2) which are generally unknown. Also note the division by "n - 1" instead of "n." The minus "1" relates to the reduced degrees of freedom[7] resulting from the use of the estimated mean ($\overline{Y}$).

---

[6] In subsequent pages, the arithmetic mean will be referred to as the mean.
[7] See any basic statistics book for further explanation of degrees of freedom in these calculations.

Lonesome Pine Furniture Co.
Finishing Department
For the Year Ended September 30, 20__

Month	_Y_	$(Y - \bar{Y})^2$
October	160	1,156
November	165	841
December	200	36
January	175	361
February	130	4,096
March	235	1,681
April	228	1,156
May	221	729
June	195	1
July	230	1,296
August	200	36
September	189	25
Total ($\sum$)	2,328	11,414

$$\text{Estimated mean of } Y \quad = \quad \bar{Y} \quad = \quad \frac{2,328}{12} \quad = \quad 194$$

$$\text{Estimated standard deviation of } Y \quad = \quad s \quad = \quad \sqrt{\frac{11,414}{(12-1)}} \quad = \quad 32.2$$

$$\text{Estimated variance of } Y \quad = \quad s^2 \quad = \quad \frac{11,414}{(12-1)} \quad = \quad 1,037.6$$

Exhibit 14-5 *Calculation of Estimated Mean, Standard Deviation, and Variance of Indirect Materials Costs*

This introduction to the statistical properties of regression analysis began with a review of the mean and its standard deviation and variance. We feel this is necessary since the usefulness of *regression analysis is concerned with the percentage reduction in the variance of the mean.*

The regression equation, $(Y = a + bX)$, is in essence a *mean* value which relates a dependent variable Y with an independent variable X. *The idea is that the independent variable X will help yield a better predicted value for Y than the arithmetic mean of Y.* How much better the regression equation is relates to the variance of the regression equation vs. the variance of the mean.

▸ The Standard Deviation and Variance of Regression Analysis

The standard deviation and variance of the mean measures the dispersion of actual observations from the mean. The greater the dispersion, the less useful the mean as a predictor of future values of

Y, indirect materials costs in our case. Similarly, the standard deviation and variance of the regression equation measures the dispersion of actual observations from the predicted value of the regression equation. Note below the similarity between the standard deviation and variance of both the mean and the regression equation.

Estimated Standard Deviation and Variance

	Mean	*Regression Equation*[8]
Estimated standard deviation	$s = \sqrt{\dfrac{\Sigma\left(Y - \overline{Y}\right)^2}{n-1}}$	$s_e = \sqrt{\dfrac{\Sigma\left(Y - \hat{Y}\right)^2}{n-2}}$
Estimated variance	$s^2 = \dfrac{\Sigma(Y - \overline{Y})^2}{n-1}$	$s_e^2 = \dfrac{\Sigma(Y - \hat{Y})^2}{n-2}$

There are only three differences in the above equations:

1. The estimated standard deviation and variance of the mean are denoted s and s^2 while for the regression equation, they are denoted s_e and s_e^2. The symbol s_e is usually referred to as the standard error of the estimate.

2. The estimated or predicted value of the mean is denoted $\overline{Y}$ (Y bar) while for the regression equation $\hat{Y}$ (Y hat) is used.

3. Two degrees of freedom are subtracted for the regression equation whereas only one is subtracted for the mean. The two degrees of freedom deducted result from use of estimates for both "a" and "b" in calculating Y.

Calculations for s_e and s_e^2 using our indirect materials example are illustrated in Exhibit 14-6. Please note as indicated below the differences between the standard deviation and the variance of the mean and the regression equation as per Exhibits 14-5 and 14-6.

$$s = 32.2 \qquad s_e = 10.4$$
$$s^2 = 1,037.6 \qquad s_e^2 = 108.36$$

---

[8] An algebraic equivalent for the calculation of s_e which is often easier to use is:

$$s_e = \sqrt{\frac{\Sigma Y^2 - a(\Sigma Y) - b(\Sigma XY)}{n-2}}$$

Lonesome Pine Furniture Co.
Finishing Department
For the Year Ended September 30, 20___

Month	Standard Direct Labor Hrs. X	Indirect Materials Costs Y	$\hat{Y}$*	$(Y-\hat{Y})^2$
October	40	160	149.93	101.4
November	60	165	183.83	354.6
December	64	200	190.61	88.2
January	50	175	166.88	65.9
February	33	130	138.07	65.1
March	90	235	234.68	.1
April	80	228	217.73	105.4
May	83	221	222.81	3.3
June	62	195	187.22	60.5
July	85	230	226.20	14.4
August	75	200	209.25	85.7
September	70	189	200.78	139.0
				1,083.6

$$\text{Estimated standard deviation of regression equation} = s_e = \sqrt{\frac{1,083.6}{(12-2)}} = 10.41$$

$$\text{Estimated variance of regression equation} = s_e^2 = \sqrt{\frac{1,083.6}{(12-2)}} = 108.36$$

*The predicted values of Y using the regression equation, Y = 82.13 + 1.695 X, and the standard direct labor hours.

Exhibit 14-6   *Calculation of Standard Deviation (s_e) and Variance (s_e²) for Regression Equation of Indirect Materials Costs*

As indicated, both the standard deviation and the variance of the regression equation are considerably lower than similar measures for the mean. This in essence tells us that the regression equation is a better predictor of indirect materials costs (Y) than the mean. The regression equation, because it brings the variable X (standard direct labor hours) into the prediction process, makes the regression equation a better predictor than the mean. The basis for the regression equation being a better predictor than the mean in this case is simply the smaller variance or dispersion around the predicted value of Y. In the next section, the percentage reduction from s^2 to s_e^2 will be used to make judgments concerning how good a predictor one regression equation is vs. another regression equation.

▸ Correlation—The Reduction Between Variances

The strength of the relationship between the variables X and Y is measured by correlation. This strength, as alluded to above, is simply a matter of the percentage reduction in the variance of the mean compared to the variance of the regression equation. Note below how the percentage reduction in the variance is the basic measure of correlation, r^2, which is called the *coefficient of determination*. As indicated below, the introduction of the X variable made the regression equation a better predictor of indirect materials costs than the mean because it reduced the variance by 89.6 percent. Statisticians refer to this as explaining 89.6 percent of the variance.

$$r^2 = \frac{s^2 - s_e^2}{s^2} = 1 - \frac{s_e^2}{s^2}$$

$$= 1 - \frac{108.36}{1,037.6} = 1 - .104$$

$$= .896 \text{ or } 89.6\%$$

From the *coefficient of determination* or r^2 is determined the *coefficient of correlation* or r. Both r^2 and r measure the strength of the relationship between the variables X and Y. A strong relationship produces high values of r^2 and r whereas a weak relationship produces low values.

Generally, the value of r^2 varies between "0" and "+1".[9] A zero value for r^2 indicates that the variances of the mean and the regression equation are equal and that the regression equation is no better than the arithmetic mean as a predictor of Y.

A value of "+1" for r^2 indicates a variance of the regression equation of zero which means all observations of Y are on the regression line. Thus the regression equation should produce a perfect or errorless estimate of Y. As expected, higher r^2's are preferred to lower r^2's and the closer to "+1" the better.

The *coefficient of correlation* or r has basically the same meaning as r^2 but it should never be confused with r^2 since it will always have a higher value than r^2 except for the extremes of "0" and "1". The one difference between r and r^2 is that r can take on a value between "-1" and "+1". The minus or plus, which is determined by the sign of the estimated "b" in the regression equation, is an indication of whether the correlation between X and Y is negative and downward sloping or positive and upward sloping.

In summary, the *coefficient of determination* or r^2 tells us by how much the variable X improves our ability to predict variable Y. The measure of that improvement is the r^2 or percentage difference between the variance of the mean which ignores X and the variance of the regression equation which includes X. The *coefficient of correlation* or r simply tells us whether the correlation between X and Y is positive or negative.

---

[9] This comment ignores differences in degrees of freedom between s^2 and s_e^2.

▸ *Correlation—Comparing Regressions*

One of the most useful aspects of correlation is its application in comparing alternative regression equations. Assume the Lonesome Pine Furniture Co. also has available for its finishing department historical data on an alternative measure of activity, standard machine hours, as shown in Exhibit 14-7. The variable Y or indirect materials cost is the same, X_1 is now used for standard direct labor hours and X_2 is used for standard machine hours, the new measure of activity. We can determine a regression equation plus s_e^2, s_e, r^2, and r related to the new measure of activity, X_2, using a computerized regression package. These items compared to previous data for X_1 are shown below.

	Regression Using X_1	*Regression Using X_2*
Regression equation ...	$82.13 + 1.695X_1$	$66.5 + .729X_2$
S_e^2	108.36	146.89
S_e	10.41	12.12
r^2	.896	.858
r	.947	.926

Lonesome Pine Furniture Co.
Finishing Department
For the Year Ended September 30, 20__

Month	Indirect Materials Costs (Y)	Standard Direct Labor Hours (X_1)	Standard Machine Hours (X_2)
October	$ 160	40	125
November	165	60	145
December	200	64	185
January	175	50	120
February	130	33	108
March	235	90	220
April	228	80	225
May	221	83	202
June	195	62	180
July	230	85	207
August	200	75	212
September	189	70	170

Exhibit 14-7 *Data for Regression Analysis of Indirect Materials Costs (Y) and Two Alternative Measures of Activity: Standard Direct Labor Hours (X_1) and Standard Machine Hours (X_2)*

A comparison of the two regressions does indicate a difference in the regression equations which are to be used for predicting indirect materials costs. As to which regression equation is a better predictor we have to first look at the values for s_e^2 and s_e. These values tell us that there is more variability and thus greater potential for error in forecasting next year's indirect materials costs with machine hours rather than direct labor hours as our X variable. The variance, s_e^2, and the standard deviation, s_e, increase with the use of machine hours in the regression equation. In addition, the values for r^2 and r decrease with machine hours which is expected because of the greater variance with machine hours. Thus in this case, we would probably opt for the regression using direct labor hours.

In real life, our situation is not as easy as depicted above. Variances may not be as equally and substantively reduced as in this case of 89.6 percent and 85.8 percent. In real life, we may obtain a difference in variance reduction or r^2 of 74.7 percent vs. 54.3 percent or even 54.3 percent versus 23.2 percent. In such cases, we know which regression is better but we can have some difficulty feeling comfortable with the predictive power of the best regression.

► The Best Regression—How Good Is It?

There is no absolute answer to the question, "Is the best regression good enough?" All one can do is subjectively evaluate the statistical properties of the best or the two or three best regressions in terms of the objective of regression (i.e., cost prediction and the size of the possible error relative to cost prediction). For this purpose, the authors recommend subjective evaluation of the following:

1. The standard error (deviation) of the regression equation (s_e) relative to the regression equation.
2. The standard error (deviation) of each of the regression estimates ("a" and "b") relative to their respective regression estimates (i.e., s_a vs. a and s_b vs. b).[10]

As an illustration of subjective evaluation consider the two regressions for the Exhibit 14-7 data which produce the following comparisons:

	Regression Using X_1	_Regression Using X_2_
Regression equation	$82.13 + 1.695X_1$	$66.5 + .729X_2$
s_e	10.41	12.12
a	82.13	66.5
b	1.695	.729
s_a	11.84	15.89
s_b	.1736	.089

From basic statistics, we remember that if a distribution is normal, approximately 68 percent of that distribution will probably fall between +/- one standard deviation from the mean, 95 percent between +/- two standard deviations and 99 percent between +/- three standard deviations. This same idea can be used to subjectively judge the predictive ability of the best regression equations and each of their parts (i.e., "a" and "b").

---

[10] Determination of s_a and s_b will be discussed in Appendix A of this chapter.

Using the above data relative to each regression equation and assuming normality; 68 percent, 95 percent and 99 percent probability or confidence intervals for each of our regressions would be as follows using projections of 83 standard direct labor hours and 202 standard machine hours, respectively.

	Regression Using X_1			*Regression Using X_2*		
Budgeted indirect materials costs	82.13 + 1.695(83)	= 222.82		66.5 + .729(202)	= 213.76	
Confidence intervals						
68%	222.82 ± 10.41	= 212.41	233.23	213.76 ± 12.12	= 201.64	225.88
95%	222.82 ± 2(10.41)	= 202.00	243.64	213.76 ± 2(12.12)	= 189.52	238.00
99%	222.82 ± 3(10.41)	= 191.59	254.05	213.76 ± 3(12.12)	= 177.40	250.12

Many would probably not be too pleased about such confidence intervals as well as the budget estimates for indirect materials costs. The standard error (s_e) is 4.67 percent (10.41/222.82) and 5.67 percent (12.12/213.76) of the budget estimate for the two regression equations. This means (assuming normality) that an accounting variance as large as 4.67 percent or 5.67 percent of budget should be expected 68 percent of the time. These percentages double and triple when expanded to 95 percent and 99 percent confidence intervals. Similar comments could be made about the confidence intervals and percentages for forecasts of "a" and "b" as indicated below.

	Regression Using X_1			*Regression Using X_2*		
Budgeted fixed indirect materials costs (a)	82.13			66.50		
Confidence intervals						
68%	82.13 ± 11.84*	= 70.29	93.97	66.50 ± 15.89*	= 50.61	82.39
95%	82.13 ± 2(11.84)	= 58.45	105.81	66.50 ± 2(15.89)	= 34.72	98.28
99%	82.13 ± 3(11.84)	= 46.61	117.65	66.50 ± 3(15.89)	= 18.83	114.17

*See Appendix A for determining values of s_a.

	Regression Using X_1			*Regression Using X_2*		
Budgeted variable indirect materials costs (b)	1.695			.729		
Confidence intervals						
68%	1.695 ± (.1736)*	= 1.521	1.869	.729 ± (.089)*	= .640	.818
95%	1.695 ± 2(.1736)	= 1.348	2.042	.729 ± 2(.089)	= .551	.907
99%	1.695 ± 3(.1736)	= 1.174	2.216	.729 ± 3(.089)	= .462	.996

*See Appendix A for determining values of s_b.

With the above in mind, it may not be too difficult to understand the relative non-use[11] of regression analysis by practitioners when it comes to separating fixed and variable costs. Expected accounting variances as high as 4 to 5 percent of a total cost estimate, 14 to 23 percent of a fixed cost estimate

---

[11] See the staff research study, *Management Uses of Fixed and Variable Expense Analysis* published April 1, 1980, by the National Association of Accountants.

(11.84/82.13 and 15.89/66.50) and 10 to 12 percent of a variable cost estimate (.1736/1.695 and .089/.729) 68 percent of the time may just be too much to accept, especially when such accounting variances are related to r^2's of 89.6 percent and 85.8 percent. The cost of implementing a system of regression analysis may be too high relative to its supposed greater predictive ability when compared to alternative methods such as inspection of accounts and high-low analysis.

▸ SOME PRECAUTIONS ◂

To analyze cost behavior is not an easy task unless we are dealing with fairly obvious variable and fixed costs such as direct materials and salaries. Mixed costs which include practically all categories of overhead present the most difficulties. In this regard there are some useful precautions to take.

▸ Basic Precautions

There are some basic precautions which always must be kept in mind. These are:

1. **Historical data may not be a good predictor of the future.** For example, there may have been recent increases in labor rates or technological advances which have led to productivity improvements. Since historical data may not always be good predictors, we should always consider adjustments of such data for future expected circumstances which were not a part of past history.

2. **Seek out a common sense relationship between the cost being examined and the measure(s) of activity used.** Common sense should indicate a relationship between cost and activity measurements. It should be reasonable to expect that the activity drives the cost and does not merely correlate with it. When such a common sense relationship is lacking, even though a statistical relationship is present, great care should be exercised especially when the dollar amounts are significant.

3. **Consider subjective elimination of out of line data.** The elimination of nonrepresentative data points, or outliers, may be quite appropriate. For example, if monthly data are being used, the months covered by a labor strike or a partial plant shutdown should probably be eliminated.

4. **Consider adjustment of the data for inflation.** There is no doubt that when inflation is of consequence, all data should be deflated before attempts are made to separate fixed and variable costs.[12]

5. **Consider adjustment of the data for accounting techniques not consistent with separation of fixed and variable costs.** For example, if factory supplies are charged to expense when purchased rather than when used, some adjustment should be considered. Similarly, if property taxes are charged to expense when paid (often twice each year) rather than amortized equally over twelve months, some adjustment should be made. In both cases, the cost data points may need to be recalculated.

---

[12] See Hirschey and Pappas, *Managerial Economics*, 7th ed., 1993, Chapter 10, especially pp. 439-440 for a discussion of some of the issues involved.

6. **Regression is a statistical model subject to certain basic assumptions which cannot be violated.** These assumptions pertain to the linearity and independence of the variables and the variances and normality of the residuals. Results from regressions not having these properties must be reexamined, perhaps with the advice of an expert statistician.[13]

In all instances relative to these basic precautions, we should only be concerned with significant items. Among these, during the late 70's and throughout the 80's, has been the element of inflation. If inflation returns to such significant levels, there is no doubt that inflation adjustments will have to be considered.

▸ Other Precautions

Two other precautions which ought to be considered when mathematical and statistical analyses are used are *charting* and advanced techniques such as *multiple regression*. With today's computer software and the increasingly used personal computer, both are real possibilities. A chart (or graph) of the data is usually included in computer printouts of *simple linear regression* which was discussed earlier (see Appendix B). Such charts ought to be carefully examined to see if the data represents a reasonable *linear fit*. If not, non-linear or even multiple regression is a possibility. Similarly, learning or experience curves may also be appropriate. For these techniques which may someday become a part of accounting analyses, the reader is referred to advanced texts in statistics and management science.

▸ SUMMARY ◂

The distinction between fixed and variable costs is a very significant part of management accounting. To a large extent, this distinction is intended to facilitate prediction and analyses of cost behavior and ultimately profitability. Requisite to the separation of fixed and variable costs, is an appropriate measure of activity which should be a measure of output or standard input.

While there are many methods available for separating fixed and variable costs, the mathematical and statistical methods seem to be the most analytically defensible. In particular, regression analysis has much analytical power to commend it. Nonetheless, from a cost/benefit point of view, more simplistic analyses such as inspection of accounts and high-low analysis may be considered preferable. This is especially true when we recognize that historical data may not be a good predictor of the future.

What is perhaps most needed in this area is more research in real life settings concerning alternative methods of analyzing cost behavior. With the advent of personal computers and increasingly available software, it is truly feasible to test alternative methods which may include advanced techniques such as multiple regression.

---

[13] Many computerized regression packages routinely provide plots of residuals and test statistics, such as the Durbin-Watson statistic, that help determine if appropriate statistical properties are met. For a comprehensive review of these statistical assumptions, see Benston, George J., "Multiple Regression Analysis of Cost Behavior," *The Accounting Review*, October 1966, pp. 657-672.

SOME ADDITIONAL FEATURES OF REGRESSION ANALYSIS

▸ Determination of s_a and s_b

The regression coefficients "a" and "b" each have a standard error (deviation) applicable to them. As indicated in the body of the chapter, these are s_a and s_b. Each of these can be calculated as follows using data from Exhibits 14-4 and 14-6.

$$s_a = s_e \sqrt{\frac{1}{n} + \frac{\overline{X}^2}{\sum\left(X - \overline{X}\right)^2}} \quad or \quad s_e \sqrt{\frac{1}{n} + \frac{\overline{X}^2}{\sum X^2 - \overline{X}\sum X}}$$

$$= 10.41 \sqrt{\frac{1}{12} + \frac{4,356}{55,868 - 66(792)}} = 11.84$$

$$s_b = \frac{s_e}{\sqrt{\sum\left(X - \overline{X}\right)^2}} \quad or \quad \frac{s_e}{\sqrt{\sum X^2 - \overline{X}\sum X}}$$

$$= \frac{10.41}{\sqrt{55,868 - 66(792)}} = .1736$$

Today, these calculations of s_a and s_b are a normal part of the output of regression software.

▸ Confidence Intervals and t-values

Those who are statistically oriented tend to get involved with confidence intervals and *t-values* to test the degree of confidence they should have in the regression coefficients, "a" and "b," especially "b." The emphasis on "b" is related to the fact that "b" is an estimate of the variable cost and that "b" is the coefficient which by its existence signifies a relationship between activity and cost.

The *t-values* for "a" and "b" are calculated as follows using our previous data for standard direct labor hours.

$$t\text{-value for } a \; = \; \frac{a}{s_a} \; = \; \frac{82.13}{11.84} \; = \; 6.94$$

$$t\text{-value for } b \; = \; \frac{b}{s_b} \; = \; \frac{1.695}{.1736} \; = \; 9.76$$

These calculated t-values indicate the relationship between the mean values of "a" and "b" and their respective standard deviations, s_a and s_b. For example, the t-value of 9.76 for "b" indicates that a value of "0" for "b" is 9.76 standard deviations from the mean. Thus the odds of the b coefficient being "0" is remote at best. Similar comments about the t-value of 6.94 for "a" are also appropriate. The objective then of the calculated t-value is to get a feel for the odds that our coefficients could be zero. When the odds that each of our coefficients could be zero is remote, then we can have some confidence that there is both a fixed and a variable cost embedded in the data being analyzed. Those who are statistically oriented would say the coefficients are *statistically significant*.

The real question now becomes, "How much confidence should we have in our regression coefficients?" This question is usually resolved by using a table of t-values similar to the one attached to this appendix. The table of t-values is similar to a normal distribution table which cannot be used in this case because of the degrees of freedom involved (less than 30).

The t-values from the table help us determine confidence intervals for "a" and "b." For example, in the case of "b" a 95 percent confidence interval yields a t-value of 2.228 using 10 degrees of freedom[14] and $t_{.025}$ since our table is a one-tailed table. The t-value of 2.228 indicates that an observed value of "b" should be within 2.228 standard errors of "b" 95 percent of the time which is between 1.695 +/- 2.228(.1736). Since the table value of t (2.228), is lower than the calculated value of t (9.76), the odds that "b" could be "0" are truly remote. Thus whenever the table value of t for 95 percent is lower than the calculated value of t, there is only a remote chance (below 5 percent) that an observed value will be outside the confidence interval for 95 percent. Similar confidence intervals for 90 percent and 99 percent can also be constructed.[15]

---

[14] The ten degrees of freedom relate to the twelve observations used to determine the regression equation and the loss of two degrees of freedom resulting from use of estimates for "a" and "b".

[15] The table value of t for 90 percent and 99 percent confidence intervals is 1.812 and 3.169, respectively. Note that these values are taken from the t-table using ten degrees of freedom and $t_{.05}$ and $t_{.005}$ since the table is a one-tailed table.

Values of t

d.f.	$t_{.100}$	$t_{.050}$	$t_{.025}$	$t_{.010}$	$t_{.005}$
1	3.078	6.314	12.706	31.821	63.657
2	1.886	2.920	4.303	6.965	9.925
3	1.638	2.353	3.182	4.541	5.841
4	1.533	2.132	2.776	3.747	4.604
5	1.476	2.015	2.571	3.365	4.032
6	1.440	1.943	2.447	3.143	3.707
7	1.415	1.895	2.365	2.998	3.499
8	1.397	1.860	2.306	2.896	3.355
9	1.383	1.833	2.262	2.821	3.250
10	1.372	1.812	2.228	2.764	3.169
11	1.363	1.796	2.201	2.718	3.106
12	1.356	1.782	2.179	2.681	3.055
13	1.350	1.771	2.160	2.650	3.012
14	1.345	1.761	2.145	2.624	2.977
15	1.341	1.753	2.131	2.602	2.947
16	1.337	1.746	2.120	2.583	2.921
17	1.333	1.740	2.110	2.567	2.898
18	1.330	1.734	2.101	2.552	2.878
19	1.328	1.729	2.093	2.539	2.861
20	1.325	1.725	2.086	2.528	2.845
21	1.323	1.721	2.080	2.518	2.831
22	1.321	1.717	2.074	2.508	2.819
23	1.319	1.714	2.069	2.500	2.807
24	1.318	1.711	2.064	2.492	2.797
25	1.316	1.708	2.060	2.485	2.787
26	1.315	1.706	2.056	2.479	2.779
27	1.314	1.703	2.052	2.473	2.771
28	1.313	1.701	2.048	2.467	2.763
29	1.311	1.699	2.045	2.462	2.756
Inf.	1.282	1.645	1.960	2.326	2.576

The t-value describes the sampling distribution of deviations from a population value divided by the standard error. Probabilities indicated in the subordinate of t in the heading refer to a one-tailed area under the curve that lie beyond the point "t." Degrees of freedom are listed in the first column.

For example, in the distribution of the means of sample size n = 12, df = n - 2 = 12 - 2, then .05 of the area under the curve falls in the two tails of the curve outside the interval t = 2.228, which is taken from the $t_{.025}$ column of the table.

Source. The data of this table was extracted from Table III of Fisher and Yates, *Statistical Tables for Biological, Agricultural and Medical Research*, with permission of the publishers Oliver & Boyd Ltd., Edinburgh and London, 1974, p.46.

REGRESSION ANALYSIS VIA ELECTRONIC SPREADSHEETS

Solution of simple linear regression problems using the normal equations of least squares has changed markedly with the evolution of spreadsheet software like Lotus 1-2-3. The numerical computations illustrated in Exhibits 14-4, 14-5 and 14-6 are instead executed by spreadsheet regression functions in the blink of an eye. The accountant, however, still must do some very important organizational work.

When solving simple linear regression problems with spreadsheet software the accountant needs to enter and verify the sample data, identify the dependent (Y) and independent (X) variables, and indicate the location where the regression output is to be placed in the spreadsheet. Exhibit 14-8 illustrates how a spreadsheet would look if the plant accountant had used a spreadsheet software program like Lotus 4.0 for Windows 95 to derive the simple linear regression for indirect materials costs in the Finishing Department of Lonesome Pine Furniture Co.

▸ Regression Input

The sample data for the independent and dependent variable is recorded and verified, and placed in a specific column of the spreadsheet. (Note that this is the same data originally appearing in Exhibit 14-1.) The regression function, Range Analyze Regression in Lotus 1-2-3, is selected and executed.

The user is then asked to specify the location of the independent and dependent variables whereupon the appropriate columns are identified. The Compute option for the Y intercept is then selected so that the y-axis is calculated. Finally, the user is asked where the regression output is to be placed in the spreadsheet and the entire range or first cell is specified. The computer does the rest!

▶ Regression Output

The lower portion of the Lotus spreadsheet illustrated in Exhibit 14-8 shows the output provided in this example. Notice that the output may not be arranged in the order which one is accustomed to and may not be labeled in a familiar way.

REGRESSION ANALYSIS

Month	Standard Direct Labor Hours	Indirect Materials
October	40	160
November	60	165
December	64	200
January	50	175
February	33	130
March	90	235
April	80	228
May	83	221
June	62	195
July	85	230
August	75	200
September	70	189

Regression Output:

Constant	82.13404
R Squared	0.905086
X Coefficient(s)	1.694939
Std Err of Coef.	0.17357
Std Err of Y Est	10.4084
No. of Observations	12
Degrees of Freedom	10

Exhibit 14-8

Thus, it is critical that the user be conversant with basic regression concepts and terminology. An item-by-item review of the output of this example follows:

Constant is the estimate for a, the Y intercept or the estimate of the fixed cost component.

R Squared is the coefficient of determination (r^2).

X Coefficient (s) is the estimate for b, the slope or the estimate of the variable cost component per direct labor hour.

Std Err of Coef. is the standard error of the regression estimate of the coefficient (S_b).

Std Err of Y Est is the standard error (S_e) of the regression equation, which is the estimate of indirect materials cost (Y estimated).

No. of Observations is the sample size (n).

Degrees of Freedom are the degrees of freedom used to calculate the standard error (n-2).

▸ Using the Regression Output

From this output data, the knowledgeable user can perform all the cost prediction applications discussed in the chapter such as estimating indirect materials costs for a particular level of direct labor hours, comparing the predictability of this particular equation to alternative equations, or constructing confidence intervals for budgeted indirect materials costs. The reader should be aware that *using the computer to obtain the output* does not absolve the user from know how to *use the output to perform the necessary cost predictions.*

▶ QUESTIONS ◀

14-1.   What is the fundamental objective of, and the requisite for the separation of costs into fixed and variable components?

14-2.   Do you agree that profit planning and budgeting cannot be done without the analysis of cost behavior. If so why?

14-3.   Describe the equation to predict total costs and indicate the dependent element (variable).

14-4.   Discuss the appropriate measure of activity (volume) and the notion of a common denominator relative to analyzing cost behavior?

14-5.   What are three categories into which costs can be classified for purposes of analyzing cost behavior?

14-6.   List and describe the elements in the equation for a straight line.

14-7.   List and briefly explain three mathematical or statistical methods available to separate mixed costs into fixed and variable components.

14-8.   Explain the high-low method to separating mixed costs.

14-9.   The high-low method is said to deal only with extreme values. What approach might be taken to adjust for extreme values in the data?

14-10.   What is the main problem or conceptual flaw with the scattergraph approach to separating mixed costs?

14-11.   The simple regression equation is $Y = a + bx$. Explain each element in the equation.

14-12.   What are the main statistical properties of regression analysis?

14-13.   It is stated that regression analysis overcomes the limitations of both the high-low and scattergraph analysis, Explain why.

14-14.   To analyze cost behavior is not an easy task. List some precautions that should be taken when doing so.

14-15.   How can the strength of the relationship between variables be measured?

► EXERCISES ◄

14-16. Regression Terminology.

Explain the following as they relate to linear regression and correlation analysis: (also show equation where appropriate).

Required:

a. The method of least squares.
b. The slope of the simple linear model.
c. The variance (the random error) of the regression equation.
d. The coefficient of correlation between y and x.
e. The reduction in variance obtained by using the linear regression model.

14-17. Using the High-Low Method.

Consider the following information on the monthly repair cost for a delivery truck.

Miles Traveled	Monthly Repair Costs
3,000	$ 1,350
6,000	1,500
8,000	3,050
5,000	2,100

Required:

Approximate the variable and fixed cost components using the high-low method.

14-18. Using the Scattergraph Method.

Consider the following information on the monthly inspection cost for a production process.

	Hours Worked	Inspection Cost
January	20,000	$41,000
February	28,000	55,000
March	32,000	59,000
April	30,000	57,000
May	26,000	52,000
June	16,000	35,000

Required:

Approximate the variable and fixed cost components using the scattergraph method.

14-19. Using Simple Repression Analysis.

Consider the following information on the quarterly maintenance cost for a materials handling system.

	Hours Worked	Maintenance Cost
Quarter 1	19,500	$ 69,000
2	17,600	62,300
3	21,200	74,500
4	25,700	90,100

Required:

Approximate the variable and fixed cost components using the method of least squares.

14-20. Using High-Low and Scattergraph.

Carolina Textile Company had compiled the following data on their cafeteria costs for last year for the purpose of estimating costs for the coming year:

Month	Number of Meals	Cafeteria Costs
January	11,220	$ 44,020
February	9,800	40,100
March	16,110 *	61,200
April	9,600	38,800
May	10,300	40,870
June	8,800	34,700
July	4,650 **	21,120
August	8,700	36,334
September	9,820	38,760
October	10,900	43,620
November	10,100	40,100
December	9,680	38,648

* Carolina allowed a nearby firm to use the cafeteria while the firm was renovating its cafeteria.
** The production plant was shut down for summer vacation.

Required:

a. Separate cafeteria costs into fixed and variable elements using the:
  1. the high-low method
  2. the scattergraph method
b. Judging from the scattergraph approach, do you think the least squares method would be appropriate?

14-21. Using Three Methods for Separating Costs.

Mighty Metals, Inc. would like to adopt a method to determine the variable rate per machine hour in order to estimate its electricity costs for the months of May and June. The information provided below is actual data for the previous four months.

	Machine Hours Worked	Electricity Cost
January	1,200	$ 100
February	1,300	106
March	1,400	112
April	1,500	120

Estimated units to be produced:

May	1,067
June	1,134

Each unit requires 1.5 machine hours.

Required:

a. Compute the variable and fixed electricity cost components of total electricity cost using:
   1. The high-low method
   2. The scattergraph method
   3. The least squares method
b. For each method computed above, estimate the electricity cost for the months of May and June.
c. What method would you recommend and why?

14-22. Set Up a Least Squares Regression Equation and Explain the Variables.

During your examination of the 20x3 financial statements of Write-Well Co. Ltd. which manufactures and sells trivets, you wish to analyze selected aspects of the company's operations.

Labor hours and production supervision costs for the last four months of 20x3, which you believe to be representative for the year, were as follows:

Month	Labor Hours	Supervision Costs
September	2,500	$ 20,000
October	3,500	25,000
November	4,500	30,000
December	3,500	25,000
Total	14,000	$100,000

Required:

a.   What is the dependent variable?
b.   What is the independent variable?
c.   Set up the least squares normal equations and solve for the regression coefficients.
d.   What interpretation can you give to the coefficients?

14-23.   **Using Three Methods for Separating Costs.**
The information presented below are the hours used and the maintenance costs incurred for the production machinery of the Colonial Lantern Company. The company wants to know what the variable and fixed cost components are for the maintenance costs.

Month	Hours Used	Cost	Month	Hours Used	Cost
January	3,200	$1,590	July	3,740	$1,890
February	3,560	1,820	August	3,460	1,760
March	3,800	1,890	September	3,400	1,700
April	4,050	2,000	October	3,550	1,775
May	3,900	1,930	November	3,800	1,910
June	3,650	1,825	December	4,200	2,050

Required:

a.   Compute the variable and fixed maintenance cost components using:
   1.   The high-low method
   2.   The scattergraph method
   3.   The method of least squares
b.   Compare all three methods and give the reasons for using the method you feel is best.

14-24.   **Compute the Least Squares Regression Line Plus.**
Quick 'n Easy Printers wishes to estimate the relationship between the number of copies produced by an offset printing method and associated direct labor cost. Seven orders were randomly selected and the following information was obtained:

Order	Number of Copies	Total Direct Labor Costs
1	100	$ 2.80
2	8	3.00
3	150	3.40
4	50	2.40
5	20	1.80
6	200	4.00
7	175	3.80

The manager has calculated the following values:

$$\sum XY = 2{,}651, \quad \sum X^2 = 112{,}425, \quad \sum Y^2 = 67.84, \quad \sum Y = 21.2, \quad \sum X = 775$$

Required:

a. Compute the least squares regression line (to four decimal places).
b. The manager has just received a printing order for 125 copies. What is the predicted direct labor cost for this order?

14-25. Using the Least Squares Method to Separate Costs.

The XY Manufacturing Company makes a product called Z. Some of the manufacturing expenses are easily identified as fixed or directly variable with production. The cost accountant of the company is confronted with the problem of preparing a flexible budget for the coming year and wishes to determine the fixed and variable elements of the semi-variable manufacturing expenses.

The following details are provided for the first ten months of the past year:

Month	Units Produced	Semi-Variable Manufacturing Expenses
1	1,500	$ 800
2	2,000	1,000
3	3,000	1,350
4	2,500	1,250
5	3,000	1,300
6	2,500	1,200
7	3,500	1,400
8	3,000	1,250
9	2,500	1,150
10	1,500	800

Required:

a. Determine the fixed and variable elements of the semi- variable manufacturing expenses based on the first ten months of the past year by linear regression.
b. Was the use of linear regression by the XY Manufacturing Company appropriate in this case? Explain.

(SMA adapted)

► PROBLEMS AND CASES ◄

14-26. Compute the Cost of Production Using the Least Squares Method.

The Portland Plant of Standard Electronics produces a household appliance and the following annual data is given:

Year	Units Produced (in thousands)	Cost of Production (in thousands of dollars)
x1	11	$ 74
x2	13	78
x3	14	80
x4	15	81
x5	14	81
x6	16	85
x7	17	87

Required:

a. What is the estimated cost of production (to the nearest thousand dollars) for 20,000 units, using the method of least squares?

b. What would you calculate the limits of prediction to be for variable costs with probability of .95?

c. What is the estimated fixed cost of the plant's operations?

14-27. Analyzing the Regression Equation.

Amer Company is accumulating data to be used in preparing its annual profit plan for the coming year. The cost behavior pattern of the maintenance costs must be determined. The accounting staff has suggested that linear regression be employed to derive an equation in the form of $Y = a + bX$ for maintenance costs. Data regarding the maintenance hours and costs for the last year and the results of the regression analysis are as follows:

	Hours of Activity	Cost		Hours of Activity	Cost
January	480	$4,200	July	320	$3,030
February	320	3,000	August	520	4,470
March	400	3,600	September	490	4,260
April	300	2,820	October	470	4,050
May	500	4,350	November	350	3,300
June	310	2,960	December	340	3,160

Sum-Hours of activity	4,800
Sum-Cost	$ 43,200
Average (mean)-Hours of activity	400
Average (mean)-Cost	$ 3,600
a coefficient	684.65
b coefficient	7.2884
Standard error of the a coefficient	49.515
Standard error of the b coefficient	.12126
Standard error of the estimate	34.469
r	.99724
t-value of a-calculated	13.827
t-value of b-calculated	60.105

Required:

a. In the standard regression equation of $Y = a + bX$,
   1. Define the letter "b" in the equation
   2. Define the letter "Y" in the equation
   3. Define the letter "X" in the equation
b. If Amer Company decided to use the high-low method of analysis, what would the equation for the relationship between hours of activity and maintenance cost be?
c. Using the regression equation, calculate the budgeted cost for 420 maintenance hours in a month.
d. What is the coefficient of correlation for the regression equation for maintenance costs?
e. Calculate the total variance which can be explained by the regression equation.
f. What is the range of values for the variable maintenance cost such than Amer can be 95 percent confident of the true value of the variable maintenance cost.
(CMA adapted)

14-28. **Questions on Coefficient of Correlation and Confidence Levels.**
   A manufacturer of doodelbugs has determined that its average weekly labor costs function is as follows:

$$Y = -500 + 5.08X$$

where X is the number of machine hours. It has also been determined that:

$$\sum (Y - \hat{Y})^2 = 472,500$$
$$\sum (Y - \bar{Y})^2 = 617,661$$
$$n = 22$$
$$\bar{x} = 2,025$$

Required:

a. How does one interpret the coefficient of correlation? (Do not calculate.)

b. What is the coefficient of correlation in this particular problem?

c. What are the 95 percent confidence limits for the variable portion of the average weekly indirect labor costs if the number of machine hours are estimated to be 2,000 in a week?

(SMA adapted)

14-29. Decisions Using Regression Statistics.

The Garey Steel Corp. produces grinding balls for the mining industry. The balls are finished by rolling them between the surfaces of a large rotating grooved roll and two stationary alloy die segments which are subject to severe abrasion during the process. The average cost of die segments used last year was $4.23 per ton on a production volume of 197,600 tons of grinding balls.

The purchasing manager has been approached by a representative of an overseas supplier who claims that his company can supply die segments made from a superior new alloy for which average costs per ton of production has been established at $3.13. His company will guarantee a maximum cost of $3.60 per ton of production to Garey Steel Corp.

As an assistant controller, you have been assigned the task of providing information from which a decision regarding this new source can be made. Your first step was to do a regression analysis relating die segments costs per week to tons of balls produced per week based on production records from the past twenty-four weeks. The regression results are as follows :

Intercept (a)	6,711
Regression coefficient (b)	2.375
Coefficient of determination (r^2)	.82
Standard error of estimate (S_e)	1.412
Standard error of coefficient (S_b)	.791
t-value of b-calculated	3.003
Number of observations (n)	24

You have established from inputs by the sales and production departments that next year's production will be 175,000 units.

The plant manager is reluctant to replace the regular supplier with a potentially risky overseas supplier. He has specified that he will only buy the new die segments if it can be statistically shown, at a 90 percent level of confidence, that purchasing die segments from the current supplier will cost more than $3.60 per ton of production next year.

Required:

a. State which two statistics resulting from the regression analysis best describe the strength of the relationship between the cost of die segments and tons of grinding balls produced. Briefly explain the meaning of each of these two statistics.

b. How might you determine whether the new source of supply should be used.

(SMA adapted)

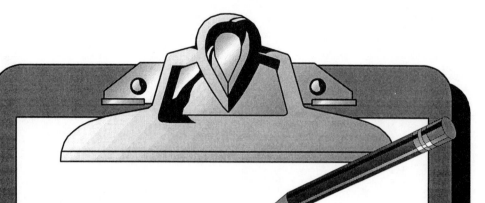

Learning Objectives

After reading this chapter, the student should have an understanding of:

✔   Basic methods for evaluating capital budgeting decisions,

✔   Decision criteria under cash flow accounting, such as net present value, internal rate of return on investment, payback and the profitability index.

✔   The impact working capital, salvage value and accelerated depreciation on cash flow analyses

✔   Cost of capital and the minimum required rate of return.

✔   Project riskiness and "what if?" or sensitivity analysis.

✔   Two specific capital budgeting decisions, equipment replacement and investing vs. financing decisions.

CAPITAL BUDGETING DECISIONS AND THE MANAGEMENT ACCOUNTANT

chapter 15

Without doubt, one of the most crucial decisions facing management is the capital budgeting decision. In the usual case, this decision involves a rather large commitment of funds with the hope of attaining objectives such as increased profitability, a greater share of the market, and even improved relations with employees, stockholders or the public-at-large.

Typical decisions relate to expansion via the addition of new products, plants, sales territories or the acquisition of entire companies. The significance of these decisions is immediately evident, since once the decisions are made, the company is committed to a pattern of activity and related expenditures for an extended period of time.

In this chapter, we will cover the basic methods for evaluating capital budgeting decisions and the criteria used will be examined. The theoretically preferred method (i.e., discounted cash flow analysis) will be applied to a few complex decisions, such as equipment replacement decisions and financing decisions.

► BASIC METHODS FOR EVALUATING CAPITAL BUDGETING DECISIONS ◄

► The Illustrative Setting

The basic methods for evaluating capital expenditures can be illustrated via the following new product decision being considered by Amex Hardware Company, a manufacturer of tools and related hardware items marketed through its nationwide system of local affiliate stores. Amex is deciding whether to produce and sell its own brand of replacement drill bits.

The Amex drill bits will be manufactured in an existing plant using a new state-of-the-art computer controlled robot capable of producing over 100 different sizes and types of bits. This equipment costs $300,000 with an estimated useful life of five years and no salvage value. The space in the plant to be used for producing the bits is currently used for warehousing. If the decision to produce and market drill bits is approved, Amex will have to rent warehouse space elsewhere at an annual cost of $25,000.

On the basis of estimates put forth by marketing, production and accounting personnel, the following revenue and cost data over the expected five year life of the robot were accumulated. The issue is, "Should Amex introduce the drill bits, given that it faces a 50 percent income tax rate and a corporate executive committee requirement of a 15 percent after tax return on investment?"

			Years		
Projected Data	*1*	*2*	*3*	*4*	*5*
Selling price per unit	$.26	$.26	$.27	$.24	$.23
Volume in units (millions)	4	6	7	5	4
Incremental costs:					
Variable manufacturing					
costs per unit					
(largely materials)	$.20	$.205	$.21	$.21	$.215
Variable marketing and					
administrative costs					
as a percent of sales	5.0%	5.0%	5.0%	5.0%	5.0%
Fixed costs (including					
$60,000 annual					
straight-line					
depreciation on the					
new equipment)	$110,000	$115,000	$120,000	$120,000	$120,000

▸ Incremental and Opportunity Costs

Included in the above projected data are all incremental costs whether they are manufacturing, marketing, or administrative, and whether fixed or variable. The only criterion for inclusion among the incremental costs is that the costs are expected to change because of the decision to introduce the new drill bit product line.

Of special interest at this time are the incremental fixed costs because included among them is a special form of incremental cost (i.e., an opportunity cost). In this case, the opportunity cost is the annual rental of $25,000 for warehouse space, which results from the decision to introduce the new product line.

Opportunity costs represent costs incurred because of opportunities lost or foregone if a particular course of action is taken. The cost of renting alternative warehouse space is an opportunity cost, since if the drill bits are produced, the former warehouse space will have to be replaced at an annual cost of $25,000.

An interesting feature of the $25,000 opportunity cost of warehousing is that it relates to the true cost of the space to be taken over by the production of drill bits. Some might erroneously want to state that the space cost is some share of plant depreciation. This is rejected on the basis that depreciation would be incurred with or without the new product line.

The true cost of the space relates only to the alternative uses of the space. In our case, the alternative use is for warehousing and if the alternative of using the space for warehousing is rejected, the extra warehousing costs thereby brought forth must be considered a cost of producing drill bits. In other cases, the opportunity cost of the space might not relate to warehousing; it might relate to annual rental income foregone if the space could be rented to another company. In all cases, the costs associated with uses[1] of space[2] should be considered in terms of alternative uses of the space. (It is highly doubtful that there will be no alternative uses for space in a well managed enterprise.) On the basis of the above data including the warehousing costs, projected income statements for each year of the five year life can be prepared as illustrated in Exhibit 15-1.

---

[1] The specific alternative to be used in determining opportunity costs is the most profitable alternative; that is, the alternative which will yield the greatest contribution or the greatest cost reduction.

[2] Another very interesting opportunity cost relates to alternative uses of time. The time involved could be executive time or the time of marketing personnel.

Amex Hardware Company
Proposed Drill Bit Product Line
Cash Flow Statements by Year (Add 000)

	Years				
	1	2	3	4	5
Sales	$1,040.0	$1,560.0	$1,890.0	$1,200.0	$920.0
Variable costs:					
Manufacturing	$800.0	$1,230.0	$1,470.0	$1,050.0	$860.0
Marketing and					
administrative	52.0	78.0	95.0*	60.0	46.0
Total variable costs ...	$852.0	$1,308.0	$1,565.0	$1,110.0	$906.0
Contribution margin	$188.0	$252.0	$325.0	$90.0	$14.0
Fixed Costs	110.0	115.0	120.0	120.0	120.0
Net income before tax ..	$78.0	$137.0	$205.0	$(30.0)	$(106.0)
Income tax (50%)	39.0	68.5	102.5	(15.0)	(53.0)
Net income after tax	$39.0	$128.5	$102.5	$(15.0)	$(53.0)

* Rounded to the nearest thousand.

Exhibit 15-1

▸ Cash flow Accounting

Cash flow concepts ignore all noncash adjustments that affect reported net income under accrual accounting rules. Only the receipt and disbursement of cash are considered relevant. Perhaps the most important accounting transaction ignored by the cash flow philosophy is depreciation since depreciation does not involve an outlay of cash. Cash outlays relative to plant and equipment are made at the time of purchase, however, rather than periodically as depreciation is recorded.

Other items relevant to cash flows inherent in accrual accounting include working capital items such as purchases on account, sales on account, accruals of various operating expenses and revenues, and other credit transactions involving receivables and payables. These items will be discussed later.

Assuming that the only non-cash transaction involved is depreciation, the calculation of the annual cash inflow will include the same incremental items considered under accrual techniques with the exception of depreciation. The calculation of annual cash inflow is as shown in Exhibit 15-2.

In the absence of accruals and deferrals, in essence the conversion of accrual accounting to cash flow accounting is simply the *adding back* of depreciation to the bottom line of the accrual income statement. A quick reaction to this method of calculating the annual cash inflows might be that an alternative method of calculation would be to skip both the *adding back* and the original deduction for depreciation. This however, would not work since the deduction of depreciation is necessary to determine the appropriate income tax to be paid.[3] Thus, the usual method for determining the expected annual cash inflows is to first deduct depreciation in order to properly calculate income taxes. Then the depreciation is added back in order to offset the earlier deduction of depreciation.

---

[3] When depreciation used for tax purposes differs from that used for financial reporting purposes, the depreciation for tax purposes is used in capital budgeting decisions.

Amex Hardware Company
Proposed Drill Bit Product Line
Cash Flow Statements by Year (Add 000)

| | Years | | | | |
	1	2	3	4	5
Sales	$1,040.0	$1,560.0	$ 1,890.0	$ 1,200.0	$ 920.0
Variable costs:					
Manufacturing	$ 800.0	$1,230.0	$ 1,470.0	$ 1,050.0	$ 860.0
Marketing and					
administrative	52.0	78.0	95.0*	60.0	46.0
Total variable costs ...	$ 852.0	$1,308.0	$ 1,565.0	$ 1,110.0	$ 906.0
Profit Contribution	$ 188.0	$ 252.0	$ 325.0	$ 90.0	$ 14.0
Fixed Costs:					
Cash items	50.0	55.0	60.0	60.0	60.0
Depreciation	60.0	60.0	60.0	60.0	60.0
Total fixed costs	$ 110.0	$ 115.0	$ 120.0	$ 120.0	$ 120.0
Net income before tax ..	$ 78.0	$ 137.0	$ 205.0	$ (30.0)	$ (106.0)
Income tax (50%)	39.0	68.5	102.5	(15.0)	(53.0)
Net income after tax	$ 39.0	$ 68.5	$ 102.5	$ (15.0)	$ (53.0)
Add depreciation	60.0	60.0	60.0	60.0	60.0
Cash flow after tax	$ 99.0	$ 128.5	$ 162.5	$ 45.0	$ 7.0

* Rounded to the nearest thousand.

Exhibit 15-2

The Projected Cash Flows. Exhibit 15-2 shows only the projected net cash inflows. Also to be considered is the cash outlay for the new robot of $300,000. These projections can then be summarized as shown below by years. Annual cash inflows are assumed to be received in their entirety at the end of each year. Also note that cash outflows are shown in parentheses.

Years	Cash Flows
0	$ (300,000)
1	99,000
2	128,500
3	162,500
4	45,000
5	7,000

As shown, the investment in the new robot is treated as a year 0 or *up front* cash outlay, which is expected to be recaptured by cash inflows in years 1 through 5. At this point, one not conversant with the cash flow technique might consider the above cash flow schedule to be in effect the solution to the problem since the total cash inflows exceeds the total cash outflow by $142,000. This conclusion is unwarranted since the required 15 percent after tax return has not been considered.

Net Present Value.. In the preceding section, mention was made of the erroneous adding of cash inflows and comparing the total to the initial cash outlay. The error in such an approach is that *one cannot add cash flows from different years since they are not really additive or comparable.* The lack of comparability relates to the fact that money to be received in the future is not as valuable as money in hand. Money in hand can be invested to earn income immediately while future monies cannot be invested until they are received.

In the present instance, the required 15 percent after tax return assumes that at least 15 percent should be earned on all investment proposals. Thus the difference between monies received in different years is considered to be 15 percent per year. For example, $100 received on January 1 can be invested at 15 percent and be worth $115 on January 1, a year later.

This 15 percent difference in the value of money is referred to as the time value of money. The time value of money can be calculated more easily and directly via the present value concept.

Present value tables, such as Table 1 in the appendix to this chapter, are prepared for the purpose of facilitating present value calculations. For instance, the following values (with the exception of the year 0 value which is always 1.000 for any discount rate) are obtained from the 15 percent column of Table 1.

Years	*Present Value of $1.00 @ 15%*
0	1.000
1	.870
2	.756
3	.658
4	.572
5	.497

The year 0 value of 1.000 indicates that a dollar in hand is worth $1.00. The year 1 value of .870 indicates that a dollar to be received in one year is worth only $.870 today if the time value of money is 15 percent, the year 2 value of .756 indicates that a dollar to be received in two years is worth only $.756 today if the time value of money is 15 percent, etc.

Verification of the $.870 value today of a dollar to be received in one year can be obtained by adding 15 percent to .870, i.e., .870 + .15(.870) = 1.0005 or $1.00.

Verification of the $.756 value today of a dollar to be received in two years can be obtained by adding 15 percent to .756 for one year and another 15 percent to the resultant value [.756 + .15(.756)] for another year. Thus $.756 invested for one year at 15 percent equals .756 + .15(.756) = .8694 or $.870 which when invested for the second year at 15 percent would equal $1.00 as shown above. Verification of the other values shown in Table 1 proceeds in a similar fashion.[4]

For our purposes, the present value factors of Table 1 are used to discount the cash flows, previously calculated, to their "here and now" or present value (i.e., their value at year 0 which is the beginning of year 1). This can be illustrated in tabular form as shown below. Note that the parentheses are used to indicate outflows and that the present value factors are used to multiply the cash flows in order to determine the discounted cash flows.

---

[4] Present value factors can also be verified by using the reciprocal of the compound interest or future value equation: $\frac{1}{(1 + i)^n}$ where i equals the rate of discount and n the number of years.

Year	Present Value Factors @ 15%	Cash Flows	Discounted Cash Flows
0	1.000	$ (300,000)	$ (300,000)
1	.870	99,000	86,130
2	.756	128,500	97,146
3	.658	162,500	106,925
4	.572	45,000	25,740
5	.497	7,000	3,479
	Net present value		$ 19,420

Since the *net present value* of the proposal to introduce the new product line is positive, the proposal is a "go" proposal. A positive net present value indicates that the proposal is expected to earn in excess of the required 15 percent rate. If the net present value were negative (the sum of the discounted inflows is less than the $300,000 year O outlay) the proposal would be no-go since a negative net present value indicates that the proposal is not expected to earn the required rate.

Internal Rate of Return on Investment. The internal rate of return on investment is determined by finding that rate of discount which makes the net present value of a project equal to zero (i.e., the discounted values of cash inflows and outflows are equal). In the preceding section, we found that the net present value of the drill bit project was positive, which indicated that the return was in excess of 15 percent. The method of determining the exact return is then simply a matter of discounting the cash flows at successively higher rates of discount until that rate which produces a *zero* net present value is found. For example, since the 15 percent rate is too low, let's try a test at a rate of 20 percent as follows:

Test 1

Year	Present Value Factors @ 20%	Cash Flows	Discounted Cash Flows
0	1.000	$ (300,000)	$ (300,000)
1	.833	99,000	82,467
2	.694	128,500	89,179
3	.579	162,500	94,088
4	.482	45,000	21,690
5	.402	7,000	2,814
	Net present value		$ (9,762)

The above test at 20 percent yields a negative net present value. Thus, the project is expected to earn a rate less than 20 percent. The next step is to try another test at a lower rate of discount, (e.g., 18%).

Test 2

Year	Present Value Factors @ 18%	Cash Flows	Discounted Cash Flows
0	1.000	$ (300,000)	$ (300,000)
1	.847	99,000	83,853
2	.718	128,500	92,263
3	.609	162,500	98,963
4	.516	45,000	23,220
5	.437	7,000	3,059
	Net present value		$ 1,358

At 18 percent the net present value is positive while at 20 percent it is negative. This indicates that the cash flow return on investment is between 18 percent and 20 percent. At this point, one could interpolate between the 18 percent and 20 percent columns of Table 1 to obtain a more exact approximation to the cash flow return on investment. For all practical purposes, however, it would be sufficient to conclude that the percentage is 18+% since the smaller net present value at 18 percent compared to 20 percent indicates that a more exact estimate would be slightly above 18 percent. When the cash flow return on investment is isolated as being between two adjacent columns in Table 1, visual approximation as indicated here is sufficient. Actually in most organizations today, personal computers handle all required discounting and can produce estimates as exacting as desired by evaluators of investment proposals.

Internal Rate of Return on Investment vs. Net Present Value. In the preceding pages, the two basic methods of evaluating an investment proposal via cash flow accounting have been explained. The net present value and the cash flow return on investment calculations both resulted in favorable appraisals of the proposed drill bit product line. A positive net present value calculated using the required 15 percent return indicated that the project would earn in excess of the 15 percent return. The cash flow return on investment was 18+% which exceeded the required return of 15 percent. If the net present value using 15 percent had been negative or if the cash flow return on investment had been less than 15 percent, the proposal should have been rejected.

▶ EXTENDING THE CASH FLOW METHOD ◀

▶ The Payback Period

The payback period has a number of variants. In its simplest sense, it is a measure of how quickly (in terms of years) an investment outlay will be recouped via the undiscounted cash inflows from an investment. The necessary calculations for the proposed drill bit line are put forth in tabular form below showing yearly cash flows and cumulative cash flows.

Year	Cash Flows	Cumulative Cash Flows
0	$ (300,000)	$ (300,000)
1	99,000	(201,000)
2	128,500	(72,500)
3	162,500	90,000
4	45,000	135,000
5	7,000	142,000

Thus the payback point is between two and three years. It is the point where cumulative cash flows turn positive. It is approximately 2.4 assuming cash flows are received evenly during year 3.

The essential criticism of the payback calculation is that it ignores the time value of money. As mentioned earlier, one should not add cash flows from different years until they are converted to their present value. Conversion to present value makes the cash flows additive since they are then reduced to their value at one point in time (i.e., year 0).

Cash flows could be discounted prior to their summation, a technique some call the discounted payback method. This will result in a longer payback time, but one which does take into account the time value of money. The discounted payback point is between three and four years for this example.

▶ The Profitability Index

The ratio of the discounted cash flows recovered to the cash outlay (\$319,420/300,000 = 1.065 in our example), is often referred to as the *profitability index*.[5] The profitability index measures what we can call in slang terms, "the biggest bang for the buck" in terms of present value. Thus in terms of the drill bit proposal, the ratio 1.065 indicates that for every dollar of present value invested, \$1.065 is returned in present value of cash inflows.

The ratio can be extremely useful when comparing alternative projects. For instance, in terms of maximizing dollars of present value, why should one invest in the present project which yields only \$1.065 in the terms of present value of inflows vs. the cash outlay for investment if there is another project available which will yield \$1.10 or \$1.20 or any higher amount?

▶ ADDITIONAL APPLICATIONS OF THE CASH FLOW METHOD ◀

Exhibit 15-3 presents a revised set of cash flows, which are explained below. These cash flows indicate that after incorporating working capital requirements, a positive salvage value, and tax allowances for accelerated depreciation and investment tax credits, the net present value of the decision to produce drill bits is \$50,042.

▶ Working Capital

In all previous analyses concerning the introduction of the drill bit line, the potential need of additional working capital was ignored. These illustrations assumed that the new robot was the only investment required. However, all capital budgeting decisions must consider the possibility of changes or increments in working capital. This is especially true with regard to new product introductions which will require additional investments in receivables and inventory (working capital components).

We assume in Exhibit 15-3 that incremental working capital is equal to 10 percent of sales. Due to the fact that proposed drill bit sales increase and then decrease, the amount of working capital first increases and then decreases. The net effect is that when working capital increases, there is a cash outlay; and when working capital decreases, there is a cash inflow. In Exhibit 15-3, the build-up of working capital occurs in years 1, 2 and 3, while the decrease or recapture of working capital occurs in years 4, 5 and 6. Year 6 reflects the fact that even though production is assumed to stop by the end of year 5, there are receivables still to be collected in year 6.

Investments in working capital can be devastating to all financial indicators. In fact, Exhibit 15-3 shows that if not all working capital is recaptured in year 6 (i.e., there are bad debts and/or unmarketable inventory), the new drill bit line may not be financially viable.

▶ Salvage Value of Equipment

We have also thus far assumed that the salvage value of the robot is zero at the end of its useful life. If the salvage value is expected to be other than zero (positive or negative), it must be included as a projected cash flow for year 5 which is the end of our project. A positive cash flow for the robot reflects the possibility that it will have a cash sales value, though for depreciation purposes we assume a salvage value of zero. A negative cash flow reflects the possibility that there will be disposal costs in excess of cash sales value.

---

[5] Some accountants call the profitability index the *net present value index*, and in the public and not for profit sector, it is called the *benefit/cost ratio*.

In order to draw the distinction between an estimated salvage or book value for depreciation purposes and the estimated cash sales value of equipment and other facilities at the end of a project's life, it is common to use the terminology of *terminal sales value*. Furthermore, the terminal sales value should be stated in after-tax terms since taxing authorities will usually tax the difference between book value and sales value.

Exhibit 15-3 introduces a cash sales value after tax of $100,000 for the robot at the end of year 5. As indicated, this positive inflow improves the financial viability of the project. Nonetheless, many would be cautious about such a proposal since its cumulative discounted cash flows do not turn positive until the end of the project. A yes or no decision on the drill bit line would ultimately depend on how comfortable one felt with the estimates of expected cash inflows for the sales value of the robot and the final recapture of working capital in year 6.

► Accelerated Depreciation Methods and Other Tax Allowances

The cash flow impact of accelerated depreciation is via taxes. With greater depreciation in early years, taxes payable are reduced in early years. The reduced early year taxes are exactly offset in later years when depreciation charges are reduced. However, the greater value of monies received earlier (early year tax savings or deferrals) increase the favorable nature of the calculations when compared to the original illustration. In Exhibit 15-2 straight line depreciation was used. The impact of accelerated depreciation is readily visible via an examination of Exhibit 15-3, which uses the sum-of-the-years digits method.

The investment tax credit was another feature of past income tax law that dramatically impacted an investment proposal in a favorable manner. Depending on modifications in tax law, the investment tax credit may exist again at some future time. Exhibit 15-3 shows the impact of a 10 percent investment credit. Thus, it is obvious that the investment tax credit as well as accelerated depreciation are deliberately designed by taxing authorities to make certain investments more attractive.

► COST OF CAPITAL ◄

► Determining the Minimum Required Rate of Return

Terminology in accounting is often not uniform or standardized. Thus, it is not uncommon to hear or see terms like "cost of capital," "minimum required rate of return" and "hurdle rate" used interchangeably. The authors, however, prefer to use each of the above terms with meanings similar to those used by the Society of Management Accountants of Canada (SMAC) in its Management Accounting Guideline No. 4.[6]

SMAC suggests that the specific discount rate to be used for a specific project can be illustrated with the following three- step procedure.

Step 1. Determine the firm's "cost of capital." Add an allowance for non-economic projects.
Step 2. Sum the above to determine the "minimum required rate of return." Add (or subtract) an adjustment for risk of the specific project.
Step 3. Sum the above to determine the "hurdle rate" for the specific project.

---

[6] Society of Management Accountants of Canada, Management Accounting Guideline No. 4, "Establishing the Discount Rate for Capital Expenditure Decisions" (1986), Hamilton, Ontario.

Amex Hardware Company
Proposed Drill Bit Product Line
Summary of Results
Using Accelerated (SYD) Depreciation,
the Investment Tax Credit, Working Capital,
an After Tax Terminal Sales Value of $100,000

Year	Present Value Factors @ 15%	Net Cash Flows	Discounted Cash Flows	Cumulative Net Present Value	Percentage Recovered
0	1.000	$ (300,000)	$ (300,000)	$ (300,000)	0%
0	1.000	30,000	30,000	(270,000)	10.0
1	.870	15,000	13,050	(256,950)	14.4
2	.756	86,500	65,394	(191,556)	36.2
3	.658	129,500	85,211	(106,345)	64.6
4	.572	104,000	59,488	(46,857)	84.4
5	.497	15,000	7,455	(39,402)	86.9
5	.497	100,000	49,700	10,298	103.4
6	.432	92,000	39,744	50,042	116.7

Determination of Working Capital Cash Flows and Total Cash Flows

Year	Sales	Working Capital @ 10% *	Incremental Working Capital	Regular Cash Flows **	Total Cash Flows
1	$ 1,040,000	$ 104,000	$ (104,000)	$119,000	$ 15,000
2	1,560,000	156,000	(52,000)	138,500	86,500
3	1,890,000	189,000	(33,000)	162,500	129,500
4	1,200,000	120,000	69,000	35,000	104,000
5	920,000	92,000	28,000	(13,000)	15,000
6	-	-	92,000	-	92,000

  * *The 10 percent of sales could be based upon current assets of 20 percent of sales less current liabilities of 10 percent of sales.*
 * * *Cash flows based upon accelerated (SYD) depreciation as follows:*

Year 1	100,000
Year 2	80,000
Year 3	60,000
Year 4	40,000
Year 5	20,000

Exhibit 15-3

The relationship between the above terms can now be seen more clearly. However, we should also consider the following definitions and additional explanatory comment.

Cost of Capital.—The weighted average cost of the combined sources of capital to the firm (i.e., debt plus equity).

Minimum Required Rate of Return.—The rate which must be earned or exceeded, on average, by all new projects if the value of the common shares of the firm is to be maintained.

Hurdle Rate.—The minimum required rate of return adjusted for any variance in the riskiness of a specific project from the average risk of the overall firm.

Determining the Cost of Capital. It may seem that the cost of capital would be nothing more than an expression of the current interest rate, but this is not true. There is no one current interest rate available in the money markets since interest rates are an attempt to measure risk as well as the time value of money. In addition, a company may not have to borrow funds for capital expenditures. Funds may be derived from the sale of preferred and/or common equity plus debt. Thus, when one considers measuring the cost of capital, it would be useful to consider the two sources of funds—debt plus equity.

The cost of debt funds could be considered as the interest rate to be paid reduced by the tax effect of being able to deduct interest for tax purposes. The cost of preferred equity could be considered the preferred dividend rate. Common equity funds are a little more difficult to deal with since there is no required dividend rate. For common equity funds, consider a rate three to five percentage points higher than the cost of preferred equity and debt. How much higher is a matter of judgment since we are dealing with a subjective estimate of the greater risk involved in being a common stockholder as opposed to a preferred stockholder or a holder of debt.

Assuming that each of the above elements of cost of capital is appropriate, would an individual company vary its cost of capital depending upon which element is to be used? Probably not because there is a relationship between a company's capital structure and the cost of its debt and equity capital. A company cannot issue more and more debt without affecting the cost of equity capital, and vice versa. With this in mind, one ordinarily comes to the conclusion that the cost of capital to be used in capital budgeting decisions is a weighted average of the cost of debt and equity capital designed to fit its desired capital structure.

The Allowance for Non-Economic Projects. Non-economic projects are projects which are not expected to provide measurable economic value. In a study of the Institute on Management Accountants (IMA) and SMAC, they are referred to as *must do* projects and are considered to be projects for which an economic evaluation is not feasible or not required.[7] The earlier mentioned SMAC report includes, in this category, projects related to safety or health of employees and those undertaken for compliance with governmental regulations and environmental protection.

The Allowance for Project Riskiness. This allowance amounts to an adjustment of the above calculations for a specific project when the riskiness of a specific project is significantly different than the average riskiness of the overall firm, which has already been built into the cost of capital. This is a very subjective item. For this reason, the authors suggest an approach in the next section.

▸ Riskiness and "What If?" or Sensitivity Analysis

Generally, risk is thought of in terms of variables for which one can construct or estimate probability distributions. However, for our purposes, we will consider riskiness in the sense of being unable to estimate variables with absolute certainty.[8] We must include every variable for which a measurement is given when trying to evaluate a capital budgeting decision. Thus, we must consider the uncertainty of the estimates of selling prices, sales volume or market shares, variable costs, fixed costs, useful lives of equipment and facilities, working capital, etc.

The problem of uncertainty or riskiness concerning the estimates of variables can be dealt with by considering the dollar size of various projects and the degree of knowledge and expertise concerning the implementation of various projects. Various categories of dollar size are relatively easy to comprehend. The same is not true for various categories of knowledge and expertise concerning implementation. Think about the decision to introduce the new replacement drill bit product line. Knowledge and expertise concerning implementation would involve whether or not we have related product lines (e.g., replacement saw blades, drills, other drill accessories, etc.) and how long and how successfully we have been involved with them. Inevitably, subjective judgments will have to be made about such knowledge and expertise, as with any project.

Our differential analytics become more and more costly as the project becomes more risky and uncertain. When there is little or no risk and uncertainty, a project could be analyzed simply in terms of its payback period (e.g., anticipated cash inflows must recover expected investment in two years or less). As risk and uncertainty increase, we go to single value best estimates of all variables and

---

[7] Arthur V. Corr, The Capital Expenditure Decision (1983), 5.
[8] See "Toward Probabilistic Profit Budgets," *Management Accounting* (October 1970), W. L. Ferrara and J. C. Haya.

then to high, medium and low estimates of typically critical variables such as selling price, volume, variable cost, inflation and even minimum required rate of return.

High, medium and low estimates can be accommodated in many cases by using the single value best estimates plus and minus 5 or 10 percent. Thus, in such cases, one would be asking, what would happen to Exhibit 15-3 if one or more critical variables increased (or decreased) by 5 or 10 percent? Finally, for projects where there is a great deal of risk and uncertainty, we expand the high, medium and low analysis of typically critical variables to a full scale "What if?" or sensitivity analysis of many variables. Given the risk and uncertainty in such cases, spreadsheets are utilized to enable accountants to ask and receive fast answers to their "What if?" questions.

As mentioned, the differential analytics along our continuum of risk and uncertainty are often accompanied by differential organizational approval levels. Projects involving lower dollar amounts and lower risk and uncertainty are approved at lower organizational levels with the reverse at higher organizational levels.

As a final thought in this area of risk and uncertainty, the reader should remember that accounting analyses are rarely, if ever, exact. In most instances analyses can only yield a *feel* for the financial dimensions of various projected activities and opportunities. The intuition and gut feel of a sharp person or group is generally critical when making decisions based on such analyses.

▸ SUMMARY ◂

Human nature is such that it always seeks to simplify or make routine the decision-making process. In the context of capital budgeting decisions, there may be an urge to come up with *one* best method of financial evaluation which embodies a single *best* criterion. The philosophy to be expressed here is that there is no single criterion even though there might be a *best* basic method (i.e., the cash flow method).

Each of the four cash flow criteria emphasizes a different dimension of the financial evaluation. Net present value emphasizes the scale of the project in year 0 dollars, internal rate of return on investment emphasizes the percentage return, profitability index emphasizes the "biggest bang for the buck" and payback emphasizes the project's break even point in years.

Arguing that one of the measures is superior to the others is in essence saying that it is best to concentrate on scale or percentage return or present value return per dollar invested or the break even point in years. Such an argument is spurious since it ignores the fact that each measure provides a useful view of the project that the other measures do not. In all cases, the authors recommend a full summarization of financial implications similar to that shown in Exhibit 15-3. Most firms today are fully capable of doing so with readily available computer software.

SPECIAL DECISION SITUATIONS

While most capital budgeting opportunities can be evaluated using the criteria discussed in the chapter, two special decision situations often arise that need special considerations. One is the *equipment replacement decision*, when old assets are disposed to make way for new ones. The other is the *investment vs. financing decision*, when the asset acquisition is combined with a financing opportunity.

► EQUIPMENT REPLACEMENT DECISIONS ◄

Assume that management of the Bag-A-Lot Supermarket is considering replacing the current bank of electronic cash registers with new optical scanning point-of-sale machines, a proposal to replace old machines with new equipment. **Assume the basic facts are as follows:**

Facts concerning new equipment
Cost (including installation)	$ 17,000
Useful life	5 years
Salvage value (expected terminal sales value)	$ 2,000
Annual cost savings before depreciation and tax:	
Reduction in variable operating cost per hour of	
$1.50 for 4,000 operating hours (double shift)	$ 6,000

Facts concerning old equipment
Book value	0
Salvage value (expected terminal sales value)	0
Useful life	5 more years
Tax rate	50%
Minimum after-tax return required by management	
(using annual tables)	10%

To simplify our presentation, we assume that the old equipment is fully depreciated (zero book value) and has no expected salvage or terminal sales value, but that nonetheless is still operative and has a remaining functional life of five more years. Thus, the old machines could be used for another five years or the new machines could be purchased and used for the same five-year period, since the new equipment has a useful life of five years.

Purchase of the new equipment must be justified in terms of the estimated cost savings during its five-year useful life. These cost savings must be converted into an annual after-tax cash inflow and then compared to the cost of the new machines in terms of discounted cash flows. In order to simplify our numerical illustrations, we only determine net present values and use straight line depreciation. The calculations are as shown below.

Derivation of annual after-tax cash inflow (cost savings)

Annual cost savings before depreciation and tax	$ 6,000
Less: Depreciation on new equipment	
(17,000 - 2,000) / 5	3,000
Taxable savings	$ 3,000
Tax at 50%	1,500
After tax savings	$ 1,500
Add: Noncash deduction - depreciation	3,000
Annual after-tax cash inflow	$ 4,500

Derivation of Net Present Value

Year	Cash Flow	Present Value Factor @ 10%	Present Value*	Cumulative Net Present Value
0	$ (17,000)	1.000	$ (17,000)	$ (17,000)
1	4,500	.909	4,090	(12,910)
2	4,500	.826	3,717	(9,193)
3	4,500	.751	3,380	(5,813)
4	4,500	.683	3,074	(2,739)
5	4,500	.621	2,794	55
5	2,000	.621	1,242	1,297

* All values rounded to nearest whole dollar.

Annual after-tax cash inflows are calculated using the assumption that variable operating costs are cash outlays. The reduction in these cash outlays is in effect a cash inflow. However, the cash inflow (savings) must be reduced to its after-tax amount. The after-tax amount must allow for the fact that depreciation on the new equipment is a deduction for tax purposes. Thus, after-tax savings are calculated using the depreciation deduction, but as discussed earlier, the depreciation must then be added to the after-tax savings to derive the annual after-tax cash inflow.

Note that year 5 inflows represent $4,500 for the after-tax savings and $2,000 for the expected salvage value of the new equipment. There is no taxable gain on the year 5 sale of the new equipment since the year 5 sales value and the book value are equal.

For this situation, all signals are GO. The net present value is positive considering savings only, and this is enhanced by the expected salvage value of the new equipment.

Derivation of Net Present Value

Years	Cash Flow	Present Value Factor @ 10%	Present Value*
0	$ (17,000)	1.000	$ (17,000)
1-5	4,500	3.791	17,060
5	2,000	.621	1,242
Net present value			$ 1,302

* All values rounded to nearest whole dollar.

▸ INVESTMENT VS. FINANCING DECISIONS ◂

Investment and financing decisions must be considered separately. Numerically, this point of view is illustrated by an uneconomical investment which can be made to look economical by combining the poor investment with a financing alternative.

Assume that a successful restaurant entrepreneur is considering acquiring facilities in a new shopping mall complex to operate her second Beef'n Brew franchise. She has determined the following set of facts related to a ten-year project time frame.

Investment in facilities	$ 330,000
Economic life of facilities	10 years
Salvage value of facilities at end of economic life	0
Net after-tax cash inflow	
Years 1 through 5	$ 70,000
Years 6 through 10	$ 50,000
Minimum required after-tax rate of return . .	15 %

A discounted cash flow evaluation of these facts is as follows:

Years	Cash Flows	Present Value Factor @ 15%	Present Value
0	$ (330,000)	1.000	$ (330,000)
1-5	70,000	3.352	234,640
6-10	50,000	1.667*	83,350
	Net present value		$ (12,010)

* The present value factor for years 6 through 10 is obtained by subtracting the year 5 factor from the year 10 factor in Table 2.

Assuming that the financial facts given above are the only items to be considered in this decision and that all relevant financial data has been presented, the above proposal must be rejected since it has a negative net present value.

Making a Bad Investment Look Good. Now let us see what happens if we improperly combine some financing data into this investment decision. Let us assume that mall ownership will allow the entrepreneur to pay for the facilities via a loan represented by three equal payments of $120,000; one a down payment and the others at the end of years 1 and 2. Our analysis might then proceed as follows:

Years	Cash Flow	Present Value Factor @ 15%	Present Value
0	$ (120,000)	1.000	$(120,000)
1	(120,000)	.870	(104,400)
2	(120,000)	.756	(90,720)
1-5	70,000	3.352	234,640
6-10	50,000	1.667	83,350
	Net present value		$ 2,870

Our investment proposal now looks acceptable since it can meet the 15 percent required rate of return. Intuitively, one automatically feels that something is wrong here since an unacceptable proposal has been changed to an acceptable one simply because the cash purchase of facilities is replaced by an installment purchase. In other words, the only change is a substitution of three $120,000 payments for one $330,000 payment.

The error illustrated here is simply a matter of combining an investment decision and a financing decision. *This should not be done.* Investment decisions and financing decisions must be kept separate or erroneous conclusions are apt to follow.

Properly Evaluating the Financing Decision. In the preceding illustration, mall ownership is offering the entrepreneur an opportunity to pay $300,000 in cash immediately or three payments of $120,000. The entrepreneur's decision concerning whether to pay $330,000 outright or three payments of $120,000, relates simply to the rate of interest implicit in the three payments of $120,000. The critical issue for the entrepreneur is to determine the rate of interest implicit in the loan proposal so that she may compare it with the rate of interest she would have to pay her regular lending sources, i.e. her borrowing opportunity rate. In this case, assume regular sources are represented by a line of credit with bankers offering to loan all necessary funds at 8 percent.

Using present value tables, one can quickly calculate the implicit interest rate of the mall ownership's installment plan to be approximately 9.4 percent as shown below. By subtracting the cash purchase flows from the installment purchase flows, one determines the difference which is the amount of the loan and payments on the loan. Then by determining the rate of discount which reduces the loan flows to zero, one determines the loan interest rate as indicated below.

Year	Cash Flows Installment Purchase	Cash Purchase	Difference or Amount of and Payments on Loan
0	$ 120,000	$ 330,000	$ (210,000)
1	120,000		120,000
2	120,000		120,000

Year	Amount of and Payments on Loan	8% Present Value Factor	Amount	10% Present Value Factor	Amount
0	$ (210,000)	1.000	$ (210,000)	1.000	$ (210,000)
1	120,000	.926	111,120	.909	109,080
2	120,000	.857	102,840	.826	99,120
	Total		$ 3,960		$ (1,800)

Which Decision is First.—Investment or Financing? Not many years ago, the norm was to make the investment decision first (assuming a cash purchase) and if the investment decision was positive, then go on to the financing decision. The logic behind the priority of the investment decision is based on the following thoughts:

"Why figure out how to acquire (finance) an asset before we determine if we should acquire (invest in) the asset. Given the many different ways to acquire (finance) an asset, we could waste much time trying to determine the best way to acquire (finance) an asset before we are sure the acquisition is profitable."

In recent years, however, a circumstance has arisen which may make it more reasonable to decide the financing decision before the investment decision. The particular circumstance is that a manufacturer may also be a source of financing and may use that financing to offer an installment purchase at an interest rate lower than the normal alternative costs of borrowing, as is the case of most automobile companies since the 1980's. A manufacturer who is also a financier can easily use its financing capability to offer such favorable financing terms (via an installment purchase) that sales are generated which might not otherwise be made. In essence, the manufacturer/financier may willingly incur a small loss on its financing activities in order to generate a more than offsetting profit on its manufacturing activities. Without the loss on financing, there might not be a sale. Today, computers, automobiles, copy equipment and many types of machinery are prime candidates for favorable financing terms via an installment purchase.

The lower-than-normal interest rate is literally the equivalent of a discount on the purchase price of an asset which should be considered in the investment decision. Such a discount could make an otherwise unattractive investment attractive. In this case, the financing decision should precede the investment decision in order to test for the existence of a discount on the asset's purchase price. The size of such a discount is equal to the difference between the cash purchase price and the lower present value of the installment payments discounted at the normal alternative cost of borrowing.

Given the above commentary, one should insist on the separation of investment and financing decisions. However, one cannot insist on the precedence of a favorable investment decision. In those instances where the manufacturer and the financier are one and the same organization, the financing decision should be considered first in order to test for the possibility of a discount on the purchase price of an asset via favorable financing terms.

► OTHER COMPLEX DECISIONS ◄

In a sense, the above "complex" decisions are not very complex. Greater complexity emerges with the tax implications of leasing and plant closing decisions. Mergers, acquisitions and joint ventures of a domestic and foreign nature can also be exceedingly complex because of their size, methods of financing, taxes, regulatory requirements and foreign exchange translation difficulties.

For these more complex decisions, the reader is referred to advanced texts on financial management as well as current periodical literature. What will be found in most instances is that exacting mathematical recipes for handling such decisions are not available. Common sense and painstaking study of each specific decision situation plus the basic concepts illustrated in the chapter are the primary tools for the analyst in these situations.

PRESENT VALUE TABLES

Table 1
Present Value of $1

Years Hence	1%	2%	4%	6%	8%	10%	12%	14%	15%	16%	18%	20%	22%	24%	25%	26%	28%	30%	35%	40%	45%	50%
1	0.990	0.980	0.962	0.943	0.926	0.909	0.893	0.877	0.870	0.862	0.847	0.833	0.820	0.806	0.800	0.794	0.781	0.769	0.741	0.714	0.690	0.667
2	0.980	0.961	0.925	0.890	0.857	0.826	0.797	0.769	0.756	0.743	0.718	0.694	0.672	0.650	0.640	0.630	0.610	0.592	0.549	0.510	0.476	0.444
3	0.971	0.942	0.889	0.840	0.794	0.751	0.712	0.675	0.658	0.641	0.609	0.579	0.551	0.524	0.512	0.500	0.477	0.455	0.406	0.364	0.328	0.296
4	0.961	0.924	0.855	0.792	0.735	0.683	0.636	0.592	0.572	0.552	0.516	0.482	0.451	0.423	0.410	0.397	0.373	0.350	0.301	0.260	0.226	0.198
5	0.951	0.906	0.822	0.747	0.681	0.621	0.567	0.519	0.497	0.476	0.437	0.402	0.370	0.341	0.328	0.315	0.291	0.269	0.223	0.186	0.156	0.132
6	0.942	0.888	0.790	0.705	0.630	0.564	0.507	0.456	0.432	0.410	0.370	0.335	0.303	0.275	0.262	0.250	0.227	0.207	0.165	0.133	0.108	0.088
7	0.933	0.871	0.760	0.665	0.583	0.513	0.452	0.400	0.376	0.354	0.314	0.279	0.249	0.222	0.210	0.198	0.178	0.159	0.122	0.095	0.051	0.059
8	0.923	0.853	0.731	0.627	0.540	0.467	0.404	0.351	0.327	0.305	0.266	0.233	0.204	0.179	0.168	0.157	0.139	0.123	0.091	0.068	0.035	0.039
9	0.914	0.837	0.703	0.592	0.500	0.424	0.361	0.308	0.284	0.263	0.225	0.194	0.167	0.144	0.134	0.125	0.108	0.094	0.067	0.048	0.035	0.026
10	0.905	0.820	0.676	0.558	0.463	0.386	0.322	0.270	0.247	0.227	0.191	0.162	0.137	0.116	0.107	0.099	0.085	0.073	0.050	0.035	0.024	0.017
11	0.896	0.804	0.650	0.527	0.429	0.350	0.287	0.237	0.215	0.195	0.162	0.135	0.112	0.094	0.086	0.079	0.066	0.056	0.037	0.025	0.017	0.012
12	0.887	0.788	0.625	0.497	0.397	0.319	0.257	0.208	0.187	0.168	0.137	0.112	0.092	0.076	0.069	0.062	0.052	0.043	0.027	0.018	0.012	0.008
13	0.879	0.773	0.601	0.469	0.368	0.290	0.229	0.182	0.163	0.145	0.116	0.093	0.075	0.061	0.055	0.050	0.040	0.033	0.020	0.013	0.008	0.005
14	0.870	0.758	0.577	0.442	0.340	0.263	0.205	0.160	0.141	0.125	0.099	0.078	0.062	0.049	0.044	0.039	0.032	0.025	0.015	0.009	0.006	0.003
15	0.861	0.743	0.555	0.417	0.315	0.239	0.183	0.140	0.123	0.108	0.084	0.065	0.051	0.040	0.035	0.031	0.025	0.020	0.011	0.006	0.004	0.002
16	0.853	0.728	0.534	0.394	0.292	0.218	0.163	0.123	0.107	0.093	0.071	0.054	0.042	0.032	0.028	0.025	0.019	0.015	0.008	0.005	0.003	0.002
17	0.844	0.714	0.513	0.371	0.270	0.198	0.146	0.108	0.093	0.080	0.060	0.045	0.034	0.026	0.023	0.020	0.015	0.012	0.006	0.003	0.002	0.001
18	0.836	0.700	0.494	0.350	0.250	0.180	0.130	0.095	0.081	0.069	0.051	0.038	0.028	0.021	0.018	0.016	0.012	0.009	0.005	0.002	0.001	0.001
19	0.828	0.686	0.475	0.331	0.232	0.164	0.116	0.083	0.070	0.060	0.043	0.031	0.023	0.017	0.014	0.012	0.009	0.007	0.003	0.002	0.001	
20	0.820	0.673	0.456	0.312	0.215	0.149	0.104	0.073	0.061	0.051	0.037	0.026	0.019	0.014	0.012	0.010	0.007	0.005	0.002	0.001	0.001	
21	0.811	0.660	0.439	0.294	0.199	0.135	0.093	0.064	0.053	0.044	0.031	0.022	0.015	0.011	0.009	0.008	0.006	0.004	0.002	0.001		
22	0.803	0.647	0.422	0.278	0.184	0.123	0.083	0.056	0.046	0.038	0.026	0.018	0.013	0.009	0.007	0.006	0.004	0.003	0.001	0.001		
23	0.795	0.634	0.406	0.262	0.170	0.112	0.074	0.049	0.040	0.033	0.022	0.015	0.010	0.007	0.006	0.005	0.003	0.002	0.001			
24	0.788	0.622	0.390	0.247	0.158	0.102	0.066	0.043	0.035	0.028	0.019	0.013	0.008	0.006	0.005	0.004	0.003	0.002	0.001			
25	0.780	0.610	0.375	0.233	0.146	0.092	0.059	0.038	0.030	0.024	0.016	0.010	0.007	0.005	0.004	0.003	0.002	0.001				
26	0.772	0.598	0.361	0.220	0.135	0.084	0.053	0.033	0.026	0.021	0.014	0.009	0.006	0.004	0.003	0.002	0.002	0.001				
27	0.764	0.586	0.347	0.207	0.125	0.076	0.047	0.029	0.023	0.018	0.011	0.007	0.005	0.003	0.002	0.002	0.001	0.001				
28	0.757	0.574	0.333	0.196	0.116	0.069	0.042	0.026	0.020	0.016	0.010	0.006	0.004	0.002	0.002	0.001	0.001					
29	0.749	0.563	0.321	0.185	0.107	0.063	0.037	0.022	0.017	0.014	0.008	0.005	0.003	0.002	0.002	0.001	0.001					
30	0.742	0.552	0.308	0.174	0.099	0.057	0.033	0.020	0.015	0.012	0.007	0.004	0.003	0.002	0.001	0.001	0.001					
40	0.672	0.453	0.208	0.097	0.046	0.022	0.011	0.005	0.004	0.003	0.001	0.001										
50	0.608	0.372	0.141	0.054	0.021	0.009	0.003	0.001	0.001	0.001												

Table 2
Present Value of $1 Received Annually for N Years

Years	1%	2%	4%	6%	8%	10%	12%	14%	15%	16%	18%	20%	22%	24%	25%	26%	28%	30%	35%	40%	45%	50%
1	0.990	0.980	0.962	0.943	0.926	0.909	0.893	0.877	0.870	0.862	0.847	0.833	0.820	0.806	0.800	0.794	0.781	0.769	0.741	0.714	0.690	0.667
2	1.970	1.942	1.886	1.833	1.783	1.736	1.690	1.647	1.626	1.605	1.566	1.528	1.492	1.457	1.440	1.424	1.392	1.361	1.289	1.224	1.165	1.111
3	2.941	2.884	2.775	2.673	2.577	2.487	2.402	2.322	2.283	2.246	2.174	2.106	2.042	1.981	1.952	1.923	1.868	1.816	1.696	1.589	1.493	1.407
4	3.902	3.808	3.630	3.465	3.312	3.170	3.037	2.914	2.855	2.798	2.690	2.589	2.494	2.404	2.362	2.320	2.241	2.166	1.997	1.849	1.720	1.605
5	4.853	4.713	4.452	4.212	3.993	3.791	3.605	3.433	3.352	3.274	3.127	2.991	2.864	2.745	2.689	2.635	2.532	2.436	2.220	2.035	1.876	1.737
6	5.795	5.601	5.242	4.917	4.623	4.355	4.111	3.889	3.784	3.685	3.498	3.326	3.167	3.020	2.951	2.885	2.759	2.643	2.385	2.168	1.983	1.824
7	6.728	6.472	6.002	5.582	5.206	4.868	4.564	4.288	4.160	4.039	3.812	3.605	3.416	3.242	3.161	3.083	2.937	2.802	2.508	2.263	2.057	1.883
8	7.652	7.325	6.733	6.210	5.747	5.335	4.968	4.639	4.487	4.344	4.078	3.837	3.619	3.421	3.329	3.241	3.076	2.925	2.598	2.331	2.109	1.922
9	8.566	8.162	7.435	6.802	6.247	5.759	5.328	4.946	4.772	4.607	4.303	4.031	3.786	3.566	3.463	3.366	3.184	3.019	2.665	2.379	2.144	1.948
10	9.471	8.983	8.111	7.360	6.710	6.145	5.650	5.216	5.019	4.833	4.494	4.192	3.923	3.682	3.571	3.465	3.269	3.092	2.715	2.414	2.168	1.965
11	10.368	9.787	8.760	7.887	7.139	6.495	5.938	5.453	5.234	5.029	4.656	4.327	4.035	3.776	3.656	3.543	3.335	3.147	2.752	2.438	2.185	1.977
12	11.255	10.575	9.385	8.384	7.536	6.814	6.194	5.660	5.421	5.197	4.793	4.439	4.127	3.851	3.725	3.606	3.387	3.190	2.779	2.456	2.196	1.985
13	12.134	11.348	9.986	8.853	7.904	7.103	6.424	5.842	5.583	5.342	4.910	4.533	4.203	3.912	3.780	3.656	3.427	3.223	2.799	2.469	2.204	1.990
14	13.004	12.106	10.563	9.295	8.244	7.367	6.628	6.002	5.724	5.468	5.008	4.611	4.265	3.962	3.824	3.695	3.459	3.249	2.814	2.478	2.210	1.993
15	13.865	12.849	11.118	9.712	8.559	7.606	6.811	6.142	5.847	5.575	5.092	4.675	4.315	4.001	3.859	3.726	3.483	3.268	2.825	2.484	2.214	1.995
16	14.718	13.578	11.652	10.106	8.851	7.824	6.974	6.265	5.954	5.668	5.162	4.730	4.357	4.033	3.887	3.751	3.503	3.283	2.834	2.489	2.216	1.997
17	15.562	14.292	12.166	10.477	9.122	8.022	7.120	6.373	6.047	5.749	5.222	4.775	4.391	4.059	3.910	3.771	3.518	3.295	2.840	2.492	2.218	1.998
18	16.398	14.992	12.659	10.828	9.372	8.201	7.250	6.467	6.128	5.818	5.273	4.812	4.419	4.080	3.928	3.786	3.529	3.304	2.844	2.494	2.219	1.999
19	17.226	15.678	13.134	11.158	9.604	8.365	7.366	6.550	6.198	5.877	5.316	4.843	4.442	4.097	3.942	3.799	3.539	3.311	2.848	2.496	2.220	1.999
20	18.046	16.351	13.590	11.470	9.818	8.514	7.469	6.623	6.259	5.929	5.353	4.870	4.460	4.110	3.954	3.808	3.546	3.316	2.850	2.497	2.221	1.999
21	18.857	17.011	14.029	11.764	10.017	8.649	7.562	6.687	6.312	5.973	5.384	4.891	4.476	4.121	3.963	3.816	3.551	3.320	2.852	2.498	2.221	2.000
22	19.660	17.658	14.451	12.042	10.201	8.772	7.645	6.743	6.359	6.011	5.410	4.909	4.488	4.130	3.970	3.822	3.556	3.323	2.853	2.498	2.222	2.000
23	20.456	18.292	14.857	12.303	10.371	8.883	7.718	6.792	6.399	6.044	5.432	4.925	4.499	4.137	3.976	3.827	3.559	3.325	2.854	2.499	2.222	2.000
24	21.243	18.914	15.247	12.550	10.529	8.985	7.784	6.835	6.434	6.073	5.451	4.937	4.507	4.143	3.981	3.831	3.562	3.327	2.855	2.499	2.222	2.000
25	22.023	19.523	15.622	12.783	10.675	9.077	7.843	6.873	6.464	6.097	5.467	4.948	4.514	4.147	3.985	3.834	3.564	3.329	2.856	2.499	2.222	2.000
26	22.795	20.121	15.983	13.003	10.810	9.161	7.896	6.906	6.491	6.118	5.480	4.956	4.520	4.151	3.988	3.837	3.566	3.330	2.856	2.500	2.222	2.000
27	23.560	20.707	16.330	13.211	10.935	9.237	7.943	6.935	6.514	6.136	5.492	4.964	4.524	4.154	3.990	3.839	3.567	3.331	2.856	2.500	2.222	2.000
28	24.316	21.281	16.663	13.406	11.051	9.307	7.984	6.961	6.534	6.152	5.502	4.970	4.528	4.157	3.992	3.840	3.568	3.331	2.857	2.500	2.222	2.000
29	25.066	21.844	16.984	13.591	11.158	9.370	8.022	6.983	6.551	6.166	5.510	4.975	4.531	4.159	3.994	3.841	3.569	3.332	2.857	2.500	2.222	2.000
30	25.808	22.396	17.292	13.765	11.258	9.427	8.055	7.003	6.566	6.177	5.517	4.979	4.534	4.160	3.995	3.842	3.569	3.332	2.857	2.500	2.222	2.000
40	32.835	27.355	19.793	15.046	11.925	9.779	8.244	7.105	6.642	6.233	5.548	4.997	4.544	4.166	3.999	3.846	3.571	3.333	2.857	2.500	2.222	2.000
50	39.196	31.424	21.482	15.762	12.233	9.915	8.304	7.133	6.661	6.246	5.554	4.999	4.545	4.167	4.000	3.846	3.571	3.333	2.857	2.500	2.222	2.000

▸ QUESTIONS ◂

15-1. Define the "capital budgeting decision."

15-2. Why is depreciation deducted under the accrual accounting method of evaluating capital expenditures and not under the cash flow accounting method?

15-3. Define the net present value. Define the internal rate of return. How are they related?

15-4. What is meant by the payback period?

15-5. How would required investments in working capital affect capital expenditure decisions under the discounted cash flow method?

15-6. What impact does the salvage value of equipment purchased have on the capital expenditure decision?

15-7. The three terms: cost of capital, minimum required rate of return and hurdle rate, are used interchangeably. However, they have different meanings. Define each term.

15-8. Why is difficult to determine the cost of capital rate?

15-9. All capital projects have an element of risk. Define risk and discuss how risk should and can be considered in the capital budgeting decision.

15-10. The investment decision and the financing decision should be considered separately: (1) explain what is meant by the financing decision, and (2) why must they be considered separately?

▸ EXERCISES ◂

15-11. Multiple Choice.
   Use the following data to answer questions 1 through 7. Joe's Fruit Cannery is considering the purchase of freeze-drying equipment for $84,000. The equipment has a five-year life and an expected salvage value of 4,000. Joe expects freeze-drying to create an increase in sales of 40,000 per year. Other relevant information consists of the facts that the federal income tax rate is 30%, the minimum desired rate of return is 24%, expenses other than depreciation are $10,000, depreciation is the only non-cash item and Joe uses straight line deprecation.

   1. What is the after tax net cash inflow per year for years 1-5?
      a. $26,400.
      b. $24,200.
      c. $10,400.
      d. $20,400.
      e. none of the above.

2. If the after tax net cash inflow is 29,000 per year what is the net present value of the investment closest to, *excluding* the year 5 cash inflow from salvage value?
    a. ($3,300).
    b. $9,810.
    c. ($1,236).
    d. $11,558.

3. If the after tax net cash inflow is $29,000 per year that is the net present value of the investment closest to, *including* the expected year 5 cash inflow from salvage value?
    a. ($3,300).
    b. $9,810.
    c. ($1,126).
    d. $11,558.

4. Assuming the same circumstances as in question 2 above, the internal rate of return (Cash Flow ROI) is *closest* to:
    a. 25%
    b. 24%
    c. 20%
    d. 18%
    e. 16%

5. Assuming the same circumstances as in question 3, the internal rate of return (Cash Flow ROI) is *closest* to:
    a. 25%
    b. 24%
    c. 20%
    d. 18%
    e. 16%

6. Assuming the same circumstances as in question 2, the *undiscounted* payback period of the investment is *closest* to:
    a. 3.4 years.
    b. 3.2 years.
    c. 3.0 years.
    d. 2.8 years.
    e. 2.6 years.

7. Assuming the same circumstances as in question 2, the *discounted* payback period of the investment is *closest* to:
    a. 3.4 years.
    b. 3.2 years.
    c. 3.0 years.
    d. 2.8 years.
    e. 2.6 years.

8. If a firm were to use sum-of-the-years'-digits depreciation instead of straight-line, for a particular project:
   a. The net present value would be higher, but the internal rate of return would be lower.
   b. The internal rate of return would be higher, but the net present value would be lower.
   c. There would be no difference in either net present value or internal rate of return.
   d. Total cash flows over the useful life of the project would be the same.

9. Hook, Inc. is planning to purchase a machine that will cost $50,000 and last 3 years. The machine will have no salvage value at the end of the third year. Hook's cost of capital is equal to 12%. The cash flow (net of taxes) in year one is $18,000 and the cash flow in year two (net of taxes) is $20,000. If the net present value on the project is a negative $3,746, what is the cash flow (net of taxes) for the third year *closest* to:
   a. $12,000
   b. $17,986
   c. $25,261
   d. $20,034

10. Galka Corp, is considering buying a machine that will cost $8,000. The machine will be depreciated on a straight-line basis over 10 years. (Assume 0 salvage value). The machine will generate additional net cash inflows before tax and depreciation of $3,680 per year. No other costs (except depreciation) will be incurred. The income tax rate is 50%. What is the accrual accounting (book-value) rate of return on the average increase in required investment?
   a. 8%
   b. 20%
   c. 36%
   d. 28%
   e. none of the above

15-12. Calculating Net Present Values and Internal Rate of Return on Investment.

Required:

a. Under each of the following circumstances, calculate the net present value of the cash flows, assuming a 25 percent cost of capital and ignoring taxes (use annual tables unless otherwise indicated).
   1. Cash inflows of $4,000 per year for ten years plus an immediate cash outlay of $20,000.
   2. Cash inflows of $3,000 per year for eight years plus an immediate cash outlay of $9,000, and cash outlays of $1,000 per year for the first three of the eight years.
   3. Cash inflows of 3,000 per month for five years plus an immediate cash outlay of $40,000, and monthly cash outlays of $300 for the five years.
   4. Cash inflows of $5,000 per year for three years and $4,000 per year for the succeeding two years. An immediate cash outlay of $10,000 plus a cash outlay of $3,000 per year for the first two years.
b. For each of the above situations, determine the rate of discount which will make the present value of cash inflows equal to the present value of cash outflows.

15-13. Calculate Net Present Value.

Compute the net present value of these individual cases at a discount rate of 10 percent.

		Future Period Inflows			
	Outlay	*1*	*2*	*3*	*4*
Moe	($ 4,000)	$ 2,500		$ 2,500	
Larry	($ 4,000)	$ 2,500			$ 2,500
Curly	($ 4,000)		$ 2,500	$ 2,300	

Required:

a. Which of the three investments is the most desirable?
b. Which is most desirable using a discount rate of 6 percent?

15-14. Calculate the Internal Rate of Return on Investments.

Compute the internal rate of return for each of the following independent investments.

		Future Period Inflows		
	Outlay	*1*	*2*	*3*
Groucho ...	($ 6,000)	$ 3,150		$ 3,570
Chico	($ 6,000)	$ 3,000	$ 3,560	
Harpo	($ 6,000)		$ 3,400	$ 3,380

Required:

If the investments are mutually exclusive or competing investments, which one would you choose?

15-15. Introducing a New Product.

S.P.B. Company is considering the introduction of a new type of flavored potato chip. An estimate of its net annual cash inflows can be derived from the following projections, plus annual depreciation of $60,000 over the new potato chip's expected five year life.

Selling price per unit	$ .26
Volume in units	5 million
Variable manufacturing costs per unit	$ .20
Variable marketing costs as a percentage of sales	5.0 %
Incremental fixed costs (cash items only)	$15,000

Elements of investment are expected to be purchase of equipment for $300,000 which has a useful life of five years, an expected salvage value of zero and a required investment in working capital equal to 20 percent of sales.

Required:

Given a 50 percent income tax rate and a 15 percent required after tax return on investment, should S.P.B. introduce the new potato chip?

15-16. Introducing A New Product.

S.P.B. Company is also considering the introduction of a new corn chip. An estimate of its net annual cash inflows can be derived from the following projections, plus depreciation of $70,000 for each year of the new corn chip's expected five year life.

	Future Period Inflows				
	1	*2*	*3*	*4*	*5*
Selling price per unit	$.26	$.26	$.27	$.24	$.23
Volume in units (millions)	5	7	7	4	3
Variable manufacturing costs per unit	$.20	$.205	$.21	$.21	$.21
Variable marketing cost as % of sales	4.0%	4.0%	4.0%	4.0%	4.0%
Incremental fixed costs (cash items only)	$70,000	$75,000	$70,000	$70,000	$70,000

Elements of investment are expected to be purchase of equipment for $350,000, which has a useful life of five years and an expected salvage value of zero.

Required:

a. Given a 40% tax rate and a 15% required after tax return on investment, should S.P.B. introduce the new product? Assume straight line depreciation.
b. Describe in words adjustments to your recommended solution based on accelerated depreciation, investment tax credits, cash flow patterns other than annual, working capital, and a salvage value other than zero.

15-17. Calculate Present Value of Cash Outflow.

Homebody Furniture Company purchased a delivery truck several years ago for $40,000. Its book value today $16,000. Homebody is considering the purchase of a new truck for $45,000. The before tax cash salvage value of the old truck at this time is $6,550.

Required:

Assume a 10 percent after tax minimum required return. If Homebody's tax rate is 45 percent, what is the present value of the net cash outflow for the new asset?

15-18. Equipment Replacement.

DeLand Enterprises is considering purchasing a new lathe for $9,000. It is estimated that it will have a useful life of ten years and a salvage value of $1,500.

Their old lathe, which cost $7,500 has been in use for five years of its estimated 15 year useful life. It is not expected to have any salvage value at the end of its useful life. At the present time, the lathe has a book value of $5,000 and can be sold for $4,500.

DeLand's after-tax required rate of return is 12 percent. The anticipated cost savings of the new lathe is $1,250 a year and the tax rate is 40 percent.

Required:

Using the net present value method, decide whether DeLand should purchase the new lathe.

15-19. Equipment Replacement.

Lucky's Limo Service is considering the purchase of a new stretch limo which will cost $42,500 and have an estimated salvage value of $5,000 at the end of its estimated useful life of five years. If Lucky purchases the new limo, it expects to have cost savings of $15,000 a year before depreciation and taxes. The savings represent a reduction in variable operating cost of $2 per hour for 7,500 operating hours.

The old limo to be replaced still has an estimated useful life of five years but has a zero book and cash value today. Lucky's required rate of return is 10 percent after taxes and the tax rate is 50 percent.

Required:

Based on the criterion of net present value, should Lucky's Limo Service purchase the new limo?

15-20. Equipment Replacement.

Assume Lucky's Limo Service (use the data in Problem 15-19 above) can get $7,500 cash for the old limo, which has a book value of $2,500. Assume the old limo has a zero cash salvage value today as well as at the end of year 5.

Required:

Calculate the net present value of the new proposal.

15-21 Capital Budgeting Installment Purchase.

City Charities Inc. must acquire a computer. The computer can be purchased outright at a cost of $130,000 or on installment at $40,000 per annum for five years. City Charities pays no income tax. All installment payments are made at the beginning of each year. Assume City Charities has the ability to borrow funds at 15 percent.

Required:

a. Should City Charities buy on the installment plan?
b. Would your answer change if the purchase price was $160,000?

▶ PROBLEMS AND CASES ◀

15-22. Lease or Own Merchandising Space.

The M Company, owner of an office building, is considering putting in certain concessions in the main lobby. An accounting study produces the following estimates on an average basis:

Salaries	$ 7,000
Licenses and payroll taxes	200
Cost of merchandise sold	40,000
Share of heat, light, etc	500
Pro rata building depreciation	1,000
Concession advertising	100
Share of company administrative expenses	400
Sales of merchandise	49,000

The investment in equipment, which would last ten years (no salvage value), would be $5,000.

As an alternative, a catering company has offered to lease the space for $750 per year, for ten years, and to put in and operate the same concessions at no cost to the M Company. Heat and light are to be furnished by the office building at no additional charge.

Required:

What is your advice to the M Company? Explain fully. Ignore taxes and assume alternative investment opportunities yielding 10 percent.

Hint: Think carefully about items in this problem which may be non-incremental. (AICPA adapted)

15-23. Calculate Break-Even and Net Present Value.

The Craddock Company is considering the purchase of a new machine costing $780,000. This machine has an expected useful life of five years and an expected salvage value of $30,000 at the end of five years, and it would be depreciated using the straight-line method. The machine is expected to reduce variable costs of production by 20 percent; however, it would require a machine operator costing $30,000 per year. The machine will increase the company's production capacity to 50,000 units per year (from the present capacity of 30,000 units).

The company's income statement for last year, when the company produced 30,000 units and sold 25,000 units, was:

Sales (25,000 units @ $38)		$ 950,000
Less: Cost of goods sold (20% fixed)		575,000
Gross profit		$ 375,000
Operating expenses:		
Variable selling and administrative	$ 250,000	
Fixed selling and administrative	100,000	350,000
Net income		$ 25,000

Ignore taxes.

Required:

a. Assuming that the unit sales price remains constant, what would be the company's breakeven point if it purchased the new machine?

b. Using the net present value method, determine whether or not the company should purchase the machine, assuming that sales demand is expected to be 50,000 units per year for the next five years and that the company's minimum desired rate of return is 10 percent.

c. Determine additional units of sale above 30,000 needed to break-even if the new machine is purchased. Use accrual and cash flow accounting.
(SMA adapted)

15-24. Investment in a Ballplayer.

The owners of a newly-franchised Class "AA" Baseball team are considering a deal with an older established team, whereby they can acquire the services of Peter Leduc, a great home run hitter and gate attraction, in exchange for Robert Blain (currently receiving an annual stipend of $15,000), plus $500,000 in cash. Leduc would be Blain's replacement as the center fielder.

The owner's accountants have assembled the following data:

Useful life of Leduc	5 years
Residual value of Leduc	$ 20,000
Useful life of Blain	5 years
Residual value of Blain	None
Current cash offer for Blain received from another Class "AA" team	$ 50,000
Applicable desired rate of return	10 %

Other information:

Year	Leduc's Salary	Additional Gate Receipts Because of Leduc	Additional Expenses of Handling Higher Volume
1	$ 60,000	$ 330,000	$ 33,000
2	70,000	300,000	30,000
3	80,000	200,000	20,000
4	80,000	100,000	10,000
5	72,000	40,000	4,000

Ignore taxes.

Required:

a. Based upon your analysis of the quantitative data given, recommend whether or not the team should acquire the services of Leduc.
b. List and explain the other factors that should be considered before making the decision. (SMA adapted)

15-25. Calculate Net Present Value, Working Capital Considered.

Taylor Knitting Company had the following income statement for the year ended December 31, 20x4 when the company produced and sold 18,000 sweaters:

Sales		$ 720,000
Cost of goods sold		576,000
Gross profit		$ 144,000
Operating expenses:		
Variable selling	$ 14,400	
Fixed selling	23,000	
Variable administrative	21,600	
Fixed administrative	43,800	102,800
Net income before taxes		$ 41,200

Cost of goods sold can broken down as follows:

Direct materials	35 %
Direct labor	42
Variable overhead (incurred in relationship to direct labor costs)	14
Fixed overhead (relevant range of 8,000 to 25,000)	9
	100 %

The company is considering the purchase of new knitting machines costing $150,000 with an expected useful life of five years and a salvage value of $25,000. The equipment would have a maximum capacity of 25,000 sweaters per year and is expected to reduce direct labor costs by 25 percent; however, it would require an additional supervisor at a cost of $40,000 per year. The machines would be depreciated over five years using the straight-line method of depreciation.

Production and sales for the next five years are expected to be:

> 20x5—18,000 sweaters
> 20x6—18,000 sweaters
> 20x7—20,000 sweaters
> 20x8—20,000 sweaters
> 20x9—20,000 sweaters

Ignore taxes.

Required:

a. Should the company purchase the equipment, assuming they have a minimum desired rate of return of 16 percent? Round amounts to the nearest dollar.

b. Assume working capital averages 10 percent of sales. Recalculate the investment decision above, assuming the additional working capital is necessary when sales increase.

c. What would be the company's breakeven point in units in 20x5 if they purchased the machine?

d. What would be the company's breakeven point in dollars in 20x5 if the 16 percent desired rate of return was to be covered. Assume the same circumstances as part a above.

15-26. Building a New Plant.
International Mining Corporation is considering building a new plant. Capacity would be 4.8 million tons a year of finished product. Management has made the following assumptions for the initial screening of the project.

1. Cost of the plant, $3,000,000,000.
2. The plant will take three years to build with the following rate of expenditures: year 0, $300 million; year 1, $600 million; year 2, $900 million; year 3, $1,200 million.
3. It will have a start up average production at one-third of maximum capacity during year 3 and two-third of maximum during year 4.
4. It will produce during the next eight years, 4 million tons each year.

5. Average selling price is expected to be $300 per ton, variable costs $100 per ton, and annual fixed cost (cash items) $100,000,000.
6. The plant cost of $3 billion will be depreciated over a ten year life using a zero salvage value and straight-line depreciation. Depreciation will start with the first year of operation (i.e., year 3).
7. Money is worth 10 percent after tax.
8. Income will be taxed at a rate of 50 percent.

Required:

In light of the above assumptions, would the project be considered economically viable by the end of year 12?

Additional Requirements:

1. How many years beyond year 12 would we have to operate at 4 million tons for the project to be worthwhile?
2. Would it be worthwhile to spend $100 million more in construction costs in year 1 in order to speed up construction by one year (i.e., complete construction by the end of year 2 with an outlay of $2,100 million in year 2 with an outlay of $2,100 million in year 2)? All revenue and cost projections would start one year earlier.
3. Using the original data, if money were worth 15 percent after tax, how many years beyond year 12 would we have to operate at 4 million tons for the project to be worthwhile? Hint: Continue calculations to year 50 and determine salvage (terminal) value needed to produce a positive net present value at the end of fifty years.
4. How might investments in added working capital impact this project? Answer only in terms of concepts involved.
5. How might the salvage (terminal) value of our plant enter into our calculations? No calculations are needed. Answer only in terms of the concepts involved.
6. What impact would accelerated depreciation used for tax purposes and an investment tax credit have on our calculations? No calculations are needed. Answer only in terms of the concepts involved.
7. Suppose one-half of the new plant's volume is not incremental volume (i.e., it is shifted from inefficient facilities which are being phased out). How would this assumption impact on the above calculations? No calculations are needed. Answer only in terms of the concepts involved.

15-27. A Complex Capital Budgeting Case.

O.K. Medical Systems Division is on the verge of making a commitment to produce and sell a revolutionary diagnostic device to hospitals and other medical facilities. About one year ago (January 20x2), a commitment was made to proceed with research and development activities which has resulted in five proto-type units which are currently being tested and refined - two in O.K.'s Research and Development Center and one in each of three research hospitals. For the next year (20x#), O.K. is planning to build and equip a new production facility which will have an annual capacity of 1,200 units. During 20x4, O.K. will continue to fine tune their new product and get their plant ready for production in 20x5.

At this time O.K.'s policy committee is reviewing financial and other economic data relative to the new product. The following actual and projected data are being used to determine whether or not O.K. should proceed with plans to build and equip the required new production facility which will in effect commit O.K. to produce and sell the new product.

1. Cash outflows are expected to be $25 million for 20x2, $50 million foot 20x3 (including $25 million for the new plant) and $30 million for 20x4.
2. All outflows for 20x2, 20x3 and 20x4 (other than the new plant costs) are for research and development.
3. The new plant will be depreciated using a ten year life, zero salvage value and straight-line depreciation.
4. Production costs (cash items only) are expected to be one third of the selling price of $150,000 per unit during 20x5, 30 percent in 20x6, 28 percent in 20x7, 25 percent in 20x8, and 23 percent in 20x9 and subsequent years.
5. Sales volume is expected to be 100 units in 20x5, 200 units in 20x6, 300 units in 20x7, 600 units in 20x8 and 1,000 units in 20x9 and the eleven subsequent years after which a technology superior product is expected.
6. Corporate headquarters has a policy of levying a charge of 20 percent of sales dollar volume to cover corporate marketing and administration activities.

Required:

a. In light of the above data should O.K. commit itself to the new plant and product?
b. Assume net income will be taxed at 50 percent and money is worth 10 percent after tax. How should O.K. react if the cost of money is 15 percent after tax? How many additional "what-ifs" should be investigated? Name five.
c. What would be the impact of an increase in working capital (inventory and receivables) equal to 10 percent of cash production costs? How about 20 percent?
d. What is your reaction to be necessity or reasonableness of a corporate overhead charge (e.g., the 20% of sales in this instance)? How about divisional overhead charge?
e. How would accelerated depreciation, the investment tax credit and expected salvage (terminal) value of our plant impact on our calculations and decisions?
f. How would anticipated inflation impact on the cash inflows and outflows considered above?

15-28. Additional Decisions Using Problem 15-27 Above.

O.K. Medical Systems must be fully aware of its customers' (hospitals and other medical facilities) economics as it continues to consider the production and sale of its revolutionary diagnostic device. Toward the end of 20x2, O.K.'s best estimates of its customers' economics were as follows:

Cost of equipment	$ 150,000	
Installation	50,000	
Annual personnel cost	60,000	per shift
Power, etc. per annum	25,000	per shift
Annual working days	240	days
Daily diagnostic	7	hours
Per patient time	1/2 hour	
Charge per patient	$ 75	

Required:

a. In light of the above data how many years of full capacity use would be required for one of O.K.'s customers to justify acquisition of the new diagnostic device? Assume money is worth 10 percent to O.K. customers which are non-taxable institutions.

b. How would the above analysis change if we were dealing with taxable institutions? Which variables would you like to "what if" in this case? Name three.

Learning Objectives

After reading this chapter, the student should have an understanding of:

✔ The basic issue in by-product and joint product accounting and the solution to the basic issue.

✔ Decision making relative to joint and by-products as related to products fixed in kind and proportion, products not fixed in kind or proportion, and products processed after separation.

✔ Allocation of joint product costs to by-products and joint products as they relate to measuring and motivating performance plus inventory valuation for financial reporting.

✔ By-product valuation when by-products have established market prices or are used as substitute materials or are treated as scrap.

✔ Joint product cost allocation based on physical quantities and sales values.

✔ Joint product cost allocation when there is processing after separation.

✔ The distinction between joint costs and common costs.

*A*CCOUNTING FOR BY-PRODUCTS AND JOINT PRODUCTS

chapter 16

Joint products arise in those cases where a single raw material produces two or more distinct products. These products are not distinguishable until after processing when a separation point is reached. Examples of joint products are the various cuts of meat derived in the meat packing industry from a head of beef and the various grades of fuel oil and gasoline derived in the petroleum-refining industry from a barrel of crude oil. A very interesting version of joint products are products such as clothing (shirts, skirts, etc.) which go through the same manufacturing processes but which are classified as firsts or seconds at the final inspection point.

Accountants further classify joint products according to the economic value of each joint product. They label products of lesser value by-products;[1] those of greater value retain the title joint product (sometimes prime, major or co-product). Thus, the only real difference between by-products and joint products is in relative values. For example, in the meat packing industry the various cuts of meat from one head of beef are called joint products, whereas the hides, fats and intestines are classified as by-products.

Another difference between by-products and joint products is that by-products are sold through different distribution channels than joint products. Joint products are usually sold through the same distribution channels to the same markets. As examples of this point, consider the differences in markets for various cuts of beef versus those for hides, fats and intestines.

The classification of different products into by-product and joint product categories is not absolute. The only real difference is one of relative values. An interesting example of a product which today is classified as a joint product, even though in the past it was classified as a by-product, is skim milk. The combination of *health consciousness, vitamin additives* and non-fat dairy products has turned skim milk into a product of greater relative value in the dairy industry.

With the above points in mind, the reader should recognize that in some instances only a management directive can solve the distinction between a joint product and a by-product. Furthermore, changes in consumer demands and preferences can change a product's classification from a by-product to a joint product or vice versa.

▸ Basic Issue in By-Product and Joint Product Accounting

Since by-products and joint products are produced simultaneously, accountants must determine how much cost is applicable to each product. In the meat packing industry, one knows how much a head of beef costs, but how much of that cost applies to the various cuts of meat, the hides, the fats and the intestines? The same difficulties arise in petroleum refining, dairying, and many other industries where all one knows for sure is the cost of a barrel of crude oil or the cost per hundredweight paid to

---

[1] If the value of a by-product is insignificant, such a by-product is considered scrap.

16-1

a dairy farmer for fresh milk. Thus the basic issue in by-product and joint product accounting is the allocation of costs to the many products which can be derived from a basic raw material.

▸ Solving the Basic Issue

The solution to the basic issue of allocating costs to by-products and joint products is easily resolved when one considers the *why* of cost allocation. In order to consider the *why* of cost allocation, one must consider three purposes for which cost data are accumulated. These purposes are: (1) decision making, (2) performance measurement and motivation, and (3) inventory values to be used in preparing financial statements. As we show in subsequent pages, these three purposes help resolve any problems relative to by-product and joint product accounting.

We illustrate these ideas for a mid-sized mineral processor, the Big River Rock Company. BRR's Stone City plant processes river stone, by extracting, washing and grading the stones into one inch (Grade X), half inch (Grade Y) and quarter inch (Grade Z) sizes. The specific examples in the following sections are based upon this basic situation.

▸ DECISION MAKING ◂

For *decision-making* purposes there is *no need to allocate* joint costs to the individual joint products. The decision to make and sell the various by-products and joint products depends solely upon total revenues and the total unallocated costs necessary to process all of the joint and by-products, which are inevitably produced together. Consider the following examples from the Big River Rock Company's Stone City Plant.

▸ Illustration #1—Products Fixed in Kind and Proportion

Assume the extraction and cleaning of river stone has avoidable costs of $100 per hundredweight and grading and processing costs are an additional $75. A hundredweight of stones usually yields ten pounds of Grade X, thirty pounds of Grade Y and sixty pounds of Grade Z. Assume the sales price of Grade X is $2 per pound, Grade Y is $3 per pound and Grade Z is $1 per pound.

Arranging the data in tabular form (Table 16-1) illustrates that it would not pay to extract and grade the stone since there is a loss of $5 per hundredweight under present market conditions. Note that there is no allocation of costs necessary to make this decision. The decision depends upon the total revenues of the joint products and the total unallocated costs involved.

▸ Illustration #2—Varying Products and Varying Proportions

Table 16-1 illustrates a situation where the kind and proportion of products derived from a basic material are fixed. In many instances the kind and proportion of products may vary. For example, a dairy plant can vary the amounts of various milks, cream, butter, cheese, and ice cream it produces. This case differs from our rock process case because of different processing costs for each combination of products.

Now let us assume the Big River Rock Company can change the proportion of grades extracted by choosing different locations from where to dredge for the stone. The location selected can result in any of the following combinations of product grades (Grade W is two inch size stone):

I.	20 lbs. of Grade X,	30 lbs. of Grade Y,	50 lbs. of Grade Z
II.	40 lbs. of Grade X,	20 lbs. of Grade Y,	40 lbs. of Grade Z
III.	40 lbs. of Grade Y,	40 lbs. of Grade Z,	20 lbs. of Grade W

Table 16-1

Revenues:
10 lbs. of Grade X	@	$2.00	$ 20.00
30 lbs. of Grade Y	@	3.00	90.00
60 lbs. of Grade Z	@	1.00	60.00
Total revenues			$170.00

Costs:
Extracting & cleaning	$100	
Grading & processing	75	175.00
Net loss		$ (5.00)

Grading and processing costs are $50 for combination I, $70 for combination II, and $90 for combination III. Sales prices are $3 per pound of Grade X, $4 per pound of Grade Y, $1 per pound of Grade Z and $3 per pound of Grade W.

Arranging the data in tabular form (Table 16-2) isolates the most useful combination to produce and sell without any allocations of cost. As determined by considering only total revenues and total costs, combination 1 is the most profitable. Of course we must recognize that the most profitable combination may change from period to period if costs and/or prices change.

Table 16-2

Combination	*I*	*II*	*III*
Revenues:			
Grade X @ $3 per lb	$ 60	$120	$ 0
Grade Y @ $4 per lb	120	80	160
Grade Z @ $1 per lb	50	40	40
Grade W @ $3 per lb ...	0	0	60
Total revenues	$230	$240	$260
Costs:			
Extracting & cleaning ...	$100	$100	$100
Grading & processing ...	50	70	90
Total costs	$150	$170	$190
Net income	$ 80	$ 70	$ 70

▸ Illustration #3—Processing After Separation of Joint Products

The preceding illustrations assume that processing ends at the point where joint products and by-products are separated. This need not be true, for in many cases a joint product or by-product is only a semifinished product which must or can be processed further after it is separated from its sister products, often referred to as a sell-or-process decision. Consider the following example.

Assume that Big River Rock Company can sell the quarter inch river stone in loose quantities (Grade Z) or in one pound boxes as aquarium gravel (product U). The location selected for digging can result in either of the following combinations of products:

I.	20 lbs. of Grade X,	30 lbs. of Grade Y,	50 lbs. of Grade Z
II.	40 lbs. of Grade X,	20 lbs. of Grade Y,	40 lbs. of Grade Z

Grading and processing costs are $50 for combination I and $70 for combination II. Processing and boxing Grade Z stone into aquarium gravel (product U) costs $0.50 per pound. Sales prices are $3 per pound of Grade X, $4 per pound of Grade Y, $1 per pound of Grade Z and $2 per pound of product U.

The decision whether to process a product further can be expressed algebraically in the form of a question [i.e., "Is the incremental revenue (IR) greater than the incremental cost (IC)?"]. If IR ≤ IC, then the decision maker would be indifferent or negative because additional revenue is equal to or less than the additional cost. Only when incremental revenue exceeds incremental cost will a manager process a product further.[2]

The first step in the solution of this problem is to consider whether Grade Z should be processed into product U. Since the incremental costs of processing Z into U are $0.50 per pound and the increased revenues derived from selling one pound of U rather than one pound of Z are $1 per pound ($2 - 1), there is no doubt about the profitability of processing Z into U. Each pound of U yields $0.50 more of profit than each pound of Z. Thus the combinations to consider include product U rather than product Z, as shown below:

III.	20 lbs. of Grade X,	30 lbs. of Grade Y,	50 lbs. of product U
IV.	40 lbs. of Grade X,	20 lbs. of Grade Y,	40 lbs. of product U

Table 16-3 shows that the most profitable combination is III. As usual there is no need to allocate costs in order to make the decision. The decision to process Z into U is based only on the increased revenues of $1 per pound which is greater than the increased processing costs of $0.50 per pound[3] and the decision to produce combination III is based on total costs and total revenues without any allocation to individual products.

► *OTHER USES OF COST DATA* ◄

The other two uses for accumulating cost data are measuring and motivating performance and inventory valuation for financial statements. In both cases, from a theoretical point of view, there would be no need to allocate joint materials costs if by-products and joint products were valued at their *net realizable value*, that is, sales price less the sum of: (1) marketing and administrative expenses incident to sale, (2) costs of packaging, handling, and transportation to customers, and (3) a provision for profit. Performance would be measured by comparing the net realizable value of all products produced with their total costs of production. Performance would be motivated by giving the producing departments credit for the net realizable value of their output. Inventories would be valued at net realizable value.

---

[2] If invested capital is affected by alternative product combinations and/or processing a product further, decisions would be made on a return on investment basis which could emphasize cash flows.
[3] We are assuming here that there are no negative effects of a long or short term nature from skipping the production of Grade Z. Such negative effects can be mitigated or overcome by introducing additional alternatives which allow for some production of Grade Z.

Table 16-3

Combination	III	IV
Revenues:		
Grade X @ $3 per lb	$ 60	$120
Grade Y @ $4 per lb	120	80
Product U @ $2 per lb	100	80
Total revenues	$280	$280
Costs:		
Extracting & cleaning	$100	$100
Grading & processing	50	70
Boxing gravel (Z into U)	25	20
Total costs	$175	$190
Net income	$105	$ 90

The net realizable value basis of valuing by-products and joint products removes the need for allocating cost between by-products and joint products. This makes a difficult (perhaps impossible) task unnecessary. However, not too many businessmen and regulators use or endorse the net realizable value basis of valuation except for by-products, since they inherently feel that joint products should not be valued in excess of cost and profitability should be determined by individual product. Thus they force upon themselves a need for allocating costs to individual joint products. The methods they use and the reasoning involved will be discussed in succeeding pages.

▶ BY-PRODUCTS ◀

By-products may be sold to customers in the form in which they are produced, processed further before being sold, or used as a material in other products. In a diversified company, their use as a material may be by a division other than the one which produces the by-products. This involves intercompany or transfer pricing, a case in which managers want to encourage the optimum utilization of by-products.

▶ General Principles of Valuation

The general principles for valuing by-products are:

1. The value should provide for competitive pricing of the products which use the by-product as a raw material.
2. An incentive should be provided: a) for the development of products which will utilize internally the by-products produced by a company and b) for finding sales outlets for any by-products which cannot be used internally by the company.
3. The established valuation procedure should emphasize long-term conditions and should minimize adjustments for temporary abnormal situations.

For purposes of determining values, by-products fall into three general classes:

1. Those which have an established market.
2. Those which do not have an established market and which are used as substitutes for other materials.
3. Those not readily marketable or usable as substitutes for other materials.

▸ By-Products With Established Markets

Some by-products have well developed markets with large numbers of buyers and sellers, so companies can purchase the by-products whenever they need them. The value of these by-products and the resultant credit given to the joint or prime product should be based on the established market prices. This policy applies if the by-products are used within the company or are sold to outside customers.

When by-products are both sold externally and used as a material in other company products, their value is usually set at the market price less the sum of: (1) marketing and administrative expenses incident to its sale, (2) the costs of packaging, handling, and transportation to customers, and (3) a provision for profit. The latter may be the percentage profit on sales earned by the prime product, the amount required to earn a stated return on invested capital, or an arbitrary rate of profit established by company policy. In essence, then, accountants value by-products with established markets at their *net realizable value*.

The company products which use a by-product valued on this basis are charged less than they would pay if they purchased it on the open market. This is fair to the joint products generating the by-product because they receive credit equal to the amount which would accrue if all the by-products were sold. It also provides an incentive to marketing to push sales of the final product since its profit is greater than if the by-product were purchased on the outside.

▸ By-Products Used as Substitute Materials

Accountants value by-products without an established market that are used as substitutes for other materials by using the value of the material which they replace. Because more or less of the by-product may be required than the material for which it is substituted and because other materials may have to be used with the by-product, accountants value the by-product by computing the difference between total manufacturing cost with the material to be replaced and total manufacturing cost with the by-product at zero value. From this amount accountants deduct the costs of transporting the by-product from the producer to the user of it as a substitute. The net amount is the maximum value attributed to the by-product. Company policy may call for this value to be reduced by some reasonable amount to encourage the user to make the substitution.

▸ By-Products With No Established Markets and Not Used as Substitute Materials

Some by-products have no established markets but can be sold either regularly or intermittently. For these the value is based on what the customer is willing to pay. Credit is given to the producer of the by-product only for quantities actually sold. Under these conditions the by-product, if held in inventory, is carried at no value, and no credits are given to the joint products when they are produced. When the by-product is sold, a credit to joint products is determined by deducting from by-product sales revenue the costs of selling, of preparing for sale, and of transporting the by-product. If the by-product must be processed further before it can be sold, accountants deduct the processing costs from the by-product sales revenue. If it is sold by a unit of a company other than the one which produces it, a provision for a profit to the seller is also deducted. Companies usually make the profit provision high relative to the profits realized by other products to encourage the seller to find markets for the by-product.

▸ By-Products Treated as Scrap

When by-products have an extremely low value, revenue from their sales is credited to miscellaneous income. That is, accountants treat the by-products as scrap (i.e., by-products with insignificant value).

▸ Summary—By-Product Costing

In each of the above cases (except when by-products are treated as scrap), accountants use the by-product's value to reduce the total costs of the remaining products. Pictorially this may be illustrated as shown below.

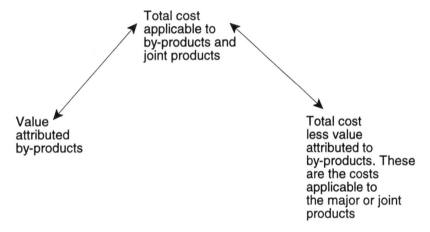

Note how the preceding discussion emphasized equity to the company segments producing the by-products and sales incentives for the units using the by-products. Equity and incentives provide a very useful motivational force within company units. This valuation can also be useful for valuing inventories on the balance sheet, since it is difficult to conceive of a more realistic value for an asset than its *net realizable value* or its value as a substitute material.

▸ JOINT PRODUCTS ◂

The basic issue in joint product costing is the allocation of common production costs to individual joint products. This is true even when by-products exist and the total cost applicable to by-products and joint products has been reduced by the value placed upon the by-products.

It is not generally accepted accounting procedure to value joint products at net realizable value even though such values are generally accepted for by-products. The generally accepted procedure is to find some method of allocating joint costs to joint products. Any procedure adopted will be arbitrary since there is no foolproof method of allocating common costs to joint products. Just consider how much of the cost of a barrel of crude oil should go to each of the 700 products a refinery can derive from a barrel of oil. The only thing we know with certainty is the cost of a barrel of crude oil and the physical quantities of the products a refinery derives from that barrel of crude.

The methods used to allocate costs to joint products are ordinarily based upon the relative proportions of either physical quantities or sales values, and these relative proportions are the basis of the allocations.

▸ Allocation Based on Physical Quantities

Consider again the example of the Big River Rock Company. Assume the extraction and cleaning of river stone costs $100 per hundredweight; that grading and processing costs are an additional $50; that a hundredweight of stones yields ten pounds of Grade X, thirty pounds of Grade Y and sixty pounds of Grade Z; and, that the sales price of Grade X is $2 per pound, Grade Y is $4 per pound and Grade Z is $1 per pound as shown below.

Grade	Weight (pounds)	Sales Price Per Pound	Sales Value
X	10	$ 2.00	$ 20.00
Y	30	4.00	120.00
Z	60	1.00	60.00
	100		$200.00

An allocation of costs based upon physical quantities uses the relative total weight of each product. For example, of the total weight of 100 pounds, 10 pounds or 10 percent applies to Grade X, and thus 10 percent of the extraction and other processing costs would be allocated to Grade X. Table 16-4 illustrates the complete allocation.

Table 16-4

Grade	Weight (pounds)	Relative Weights	Allocated Cost	Cost Per Pound
X	10	10%	$ 15	$ 1.50
Y	30	30	45	1.50
Z	60	60	90	1.50
	100	100%	$150	

Note how the physical quantity method generates an equal cost per unit of physical quantity, in this case $1.50 per pound. We could get the same result by dividing the total joint costs by the total units involved, i.e., $150/100 = $1.50 per pound.

In this illustration the physical quantities are pounds, but this is not always the case. Physical quantities can be gallons or liters, meters or linear feet, square feet, and even cubic feet. The products involved will determine the physical measure to use.

▸ Allocation Based on Sales Values

We use the same data on physical quantities to develop an allocation based upon sales values. For example, the total sales value of all products is $200, and the sales value of product X is $20 or

10 percent of the total sales value. Thus 10 percent of the materials and processing costs would be allocated to product X. Table 16-5 illustrates the complete allocation.

Table 16-5

Grade	Weight (pounds)	Sales Value	Relative Sales Value	Allocated Cost	Cost Per Pound
X	10	$ 20	10%	$ 15	$ 1.50
Y	30	120	60	90	3.00
Z	60	60	30	45	0.75
	100	$200	100%	$150	

A useful comparison of both methods of allocation can be made by comparing gross profit margins for each product under each method. This comparison is shown in Table 16-6.

Table 16-6

Allocation Based on Physical Quantities

Grade	Sales Price	Allocated Unit Cost	Gross Profit	Margin Percentage
X	$ 2.00	$ 1.50	0.50	25
Y	4.00	1.50	2.50	62½
Z	1.00	1.50	(0.50)	(50)

Allocation Based on Sales Values

Grade	Sales Price	Allocated Unit Cost	Gross Profit	Margin Percentage
X	$ 2.00	$ 1.50	0.50	25
Y	4.00	3.00	1.00	25
Z	1.00	0.75	0.25	25

Note that the allocation based upon physical quantities can yield differing gross profit percentages, whereas the allocation based upon sales values yields the same gross profit percentage for each product. In all cases, the sales value method yields the same gross profit percentage for all products, while the physical quantity method yields the same cost per unit for all products. Because of the equality of gross profit percentage the sales value method is considered preferable. The equality of profit percentage does not penalize any product's profit potential, and furthermore, the equality of profit percentage provides equal motivation to sell each of the joint products.[4]

▸ A Complication—Processing After Separation

If joint products are processed after they are separated, accountants face two problems with the sales value method of allocating joint costs:

◆ Should they use the sales values at point of separation or the sales values after additional processing?

◆ What if there is no sales value for a joint product at the point of separation?

Allocation When Sales Values Exist at Separation. Since the costs to be allocated to the joint products are the costs incurred before separation, it is usually considered appropriate to use sales values at the point of separation to allocate the joint costs. We illustrate this with a slightly different example from the Big River Rock Company.

Assume that the extraction and cleaning of river stone costs $100 per hundredweight; that grading and processing costs are an additional $60; that a hundredweight of stones yields fifteen pounds of Grade X, twenty pounds of Grade Y and sixty-five pounds of Grade Z; and, that the sales price of Grade X is $2 per pound, Grade Y is $4 per pound and Grade Z is $2 per pound. Assume that Grade Z stone will be boxed and sold as aquarium gravel (product U) at $3 per pound. The cost of packaging product U is $0.50 per pound. Table 16-7 illustrates the allocation based on sales value at *point of separation* which means we consider Grade Z sales value rather than product U.

Table 16-7

Grade	Weight (pounds)	Sales Value @ Separation	Relative Sales Value	Allocated Cost	Cost Per Pound
X	15	$ 30	12 1/2%	$ 20.00	$ 1.33
Y	20	80	33 1/3	53.33	2.67
Z	65	130	54 1/6	86.67	1.33
		$240	100%	$160.00	

The gross profit percentage provides a simple method of allocating joint costs according to relative sales value. This method yields the same gross profit percentage for all products, so one can determine the gross profit percentage and use it to reduce the unit sales value to the unit cost value.[5] For example, in the preceding case the total sales value is $240 and the total cost before separation is $160. The total gross profit is $80, or 33 1/3 percent of sales. With this figure, one can readily calculate the allocated cost per unit as follows:

---

[4] One can also support the sales value method because it will not violate the "lower of cost or market" inventory valuation rule. Note in Table 16-6 that the physical quantity method produces a unit cost greater than selling price for product Z.
[5] Similarly, as stated above, under the physical quantity method one can obtain the equal cost per unit by dividing total joint cost by total quantity.

	Grade		
	X	Y	Z
Unit sales value	$ 2.00	$ 4.00	$ 2.00
Less: Gross profit (33 1/3%)	0.67	1.33	0.67
Unit cost	$ 1.33	$ 2.67	$ 1.33

It should be obvious that the allocated cost can also be calculated by multiplying the sales value at separation by the cost percentage (e.g., allocated unit cost of X = $2.00 x 66 2/3% or $1.33).

Allocation When "No" Sales Values Exist at Separation. If there is no sales value for Grade Z at the point of separation (i.e., Grade Z stone has no value except as aquarium gravel,) the joint costs before separation cannot be allocated using sales values. We can approximate point of separation sales values, however, by using the gross profit percentage of total sales at completion of all products (including product U rather than Grade Z) and the total costs before and after separation. This percentage is determined by using the data shown in Tables 16-8 and 16-9 as follows:

Total sales value	$ 305.00
Total cost	192.50
Gross profit	$ 112.50

$$\text{Percent} \ = \ \frac{112.5}{305} \ = \ 36.88\%$$

Table 16-8

Grade	Weight (pounds)	Sales Price Per Pound	Total Sales Value
X	15	$ 2.00	$ 30.00
Y	20	4.00	80.00
U	65	3.00	195.00
			$ 305.00

Table 16-9

Joint costs:		
Materials	$100.00	
Processing	60.00	
Costs after separation:		
$0.50 per pound of U	32.50	
Total cost	$192.50	

We use the gross profit percentage of 36.88 percent to compute unit costs by deducting the gross margin from the individual sales prices as follows:

	Grade (product)		
	X	Y	U
Unit sales value	$ 2.000	$ 4.000	$ 3.000
Less: Gross profit (36.88%) . . .	0.738	1.475	1.106
Unit cost	$ 1.262	$ 2.525	$ 1.894

Since product U is Grade Z stone packaged at a cost of $0.50 per pound, the per pound joint cost applicable to Grade Z is $1.894 - $0.50 or $1.394. The joint costs of $160 are allocated to the three products as follows:

Grade	Weight (pounds)	Unit Cost	Total Joint Cost
X	15	$ 1.262	$ 18.93
Y	20	2.525	50.50
Z	65	1.394	90.61
			$ 160.04*

*$160.00 rounded

Accountants prefer to allocate joint costs on the basis of sales values at the point of separation if such sales values exist. If such sales values do not exist, the sales value at the point of final completion of the products should be used. Either way the method is essentially the same, that is, costs are allocated so they yield equal gross profit percentages on all products. Admittedly the method is arbitrary, but it does have the favorable features of not penalizing any product's profit potential and yielding an equal motivation to sell each of the joint products.[6]

► Summary—Joint Product Costing

As stated earlier, the problem of allocating joint costs to joint products is extremely difficult and perhaps impossible in theory. In such a case, any conceivable method of allocation is bound to contain elements of arbitrariness. The least arbitrary method seems to be the sales value method since it yields an equality of gross profit percentages. Essentially one might say that the sales value method is an attempt at equality or neutrality in arbitrariness designed to produce equal motivation to sell those products which are inevitably produced together.

The only way to eliminate the arbitrariness of joint cost allocations is to eliminate the allocation, and this can be done only if joint products are valued as by-products, that is, at their net realizable value. Such a valuation would be quite appropriate for balance sheet purposes, and it would also be

---

[6] Another method sometimes used to allocate the joint costs is to take the sales value of each joint product and subtract the cost to process further. This method is often referred to as the net realizable value method. The result is unequal gross profit percentages which could cause motivational problems.

	Sales Value	Cost After Separation	Net Sales Value	Relative Net Sales Value	Allocated Cost	Cost Per Lb.	Gross Profit Percent
X	$ 30.00		$ 30.00	11.01%	$ 17.62	$1.175	41.3 %
Y	80.00		80.00	29.36%	46.97	2.349	41.3 %
Z	195.00	$32.50	162.50	59.63%	95.41	1.468	34.4 %
	$305.00	$32.50	$272.50	100.00 %	$160.00		

quite useful for performance measurement and motivation. However, most accountants still prefer the arbitrariness of joint cost allocation to the difficulties and perhaps equal arbitrariness of estimating net realizable values.

▶ JOINT COSTS VS. COMMON COSTS ◀

As defined above, joint costs represent the costs of basic materials (processing costs too) from which two or more distinct products are inevitably produced. These costs are joint in the sense that they can be associated only with the sum total of the joint products produced. Any attempt to associate joint costs with the individual joint products is arbitrary since we know with certainty only the cost of the basic materials and the processing cost, and the physical quantities of joint products produced from the basic material.

In another sense, the term *joint costs* can be defined as costs which cannot be associated with segments of a firm on a nonarbitrary basis. Here we are no longer referring to two or more distinct products which inevitably emerge together from a basic material; we are referring to any and all costs which cannot be nonarbitrarily associated with segments of the firm. These costs could be materials, labor, manufacturing overhead, marketing expenses, and even administrative expenses. The segments involved could be individual products, product lines, orders, channels of distribution, departments, work centers, plants and sales districts.

The distinction between these two types of joint costs can be stated more succinctly as follows:

Group I - Those material and processing costs which produce two or more distinct products.

Group II - Those costs which cannot be non-arbitrarily assigned to a segment of a firm. The products (if any) involved need not be distinct products nor products which inevitably emerge together.

In the normal case, accountants use the term *joint costs* to describe Group I (which matches up very nicely with the definition of joint products) and they refer to Group II costs as *common costs*.

Exhibit 16-1 provides some more specific examples of common costs (Group II). Note in each case the difficulty of associating the common costs with the segments of the firm. Also, note how changing the segment changes whether the cost is a common cost or a traceable cost. A cost may be common to some segments but traceable to other segments of the firm. Note that costs are often traceable to large segments, but as these segments are subdivided many costs become common to the subdivisions.

We have discussed *common costs* in earlier chapters dealing with manufacturing overhead and profit planning. In Chapter 14, especially, we reviewed the analytical, behavioral and regulatory issues related to common costs. This chapter and Chapter 14 illustrate that both *versions* of joint costs involve the same issues. When making decisions, managers should concentrate on the total unallocated costs compared to the total revenues. When it comes to allocating joint or common costs, behavioral (motivational) and regulatory considerations should be given primary attention.

▶ SUMMARY ◀

At this point it should be relatively easy to understand why a chapter on by-products and joint products is included in the final section of this text. Essentially every facet of management accounting is involved in the accounting for by-products and joint products. Decision making, performance evaluation and motivation, plus inventory valuation are all significantly involved. The real task of the management accountant in these areas is to recognize and attempt to minimize the potential for conflict among these uses or purposes for accumulating cost data.

Cost Elements	*Common to*	*Traceable To*
Supervisor's salary	The many individual products or groups of products manufactured in the supervisor's department	The manufacturing function The supervisor's department
Real estate taxes on factory building	The many individual products or groups of products manufactured in the building	The manufacturing division The building Departments on the basis of square feet
Rent of district sales office	The many different orders taken, products sold, calls made, and other activities performed by salespersons nationally	The marketing function The sales district
Institutional advertising on a national telecast	The many different orders taken, products sold, calls made, and other activities performed by salespersons nationally	The marketing function The advertising division
Institutional advertising within a sales district	The many different orders taken, products sold, calls made, and other activities performed by salespersons within the sales district	The marketing function The advertising division The sales district
Corporate officers' salaries	The many different products, product lines, plants, and sales divisions of the company	The administrative function
Salesperson's travel expenses	The many orders taken, products sold, calls made, and other activities performed by the salesperson	The marketing function The sales district The salesperson and territory

Exhibit 16-1   *Illustrations of Common Costs*

► QUESTIONS ◄

16-1. Distinguish between by-products and joint products.

16-2. What is the basic issue in by-product and joint product costing, and how does its solution relate to "why" of cost allocation?

16-3. What are the general principles of valuation for by-products?

16-4. A by-product with an established market can also be used as a substitute material by the company producing it. When should it be sold, and when should it be used as a substitute material?

16-5. When a by-product has an established market, what items should be deducted from the market price to arrive at the by-product valuation?

16-6. When a by-product with no established market is used as a substitute material, how is its value determined?

16-7. A certain by-product is sold infrequently and at very low prices. When and how should a value be determined for the by-product and credited to the prime product? When answering this question first assume the by-product is treated as scrap and then as a by-product.

16-8. Can there be a difference in the gross margin percentages of individual joint products resulting from allocation of joint costs on the basis of physical quantities? Sales values?

16-9. How might one allocate joint costs when there is no sales value for one or more joint products at the point of separation of joint products?

16-10. How might one be able to avoid the allocation of costs to joint products when valuing joint products? Would this method be less arbitrary than cost allocation? Discuss.

16-11. Distinguish between joint costs and common costs, and discuss the reasons underlying why or why not common costs should be allocated to specific segments of a firm.

16-12. How can it be that an individual element of cost can be common and traceable at one and the same time?

► EXERCISES ◄

16-13. A Theory Question.

    a. Explain the basic difference in the method of accounting for joint products and by-products.
    b. State the conditions under which an item should be treated as a by-product rather than as a joint product.
    c. Explain the two principal methods of assignments joint costs to joint products.

16-14. Allocating Joint Costs Using Two Methods.

Three products are manufactured by the Mega Chemical Company from one raw material. To produce 24,000 units of AX-411, 18,000 units of BZ-902 and 18,000 units of CJ-555, 60,000 pounds of a raw chemical compound costing $198,000 are required. Processing costs are $22,000. Products AX-411, BZ-902, and CJ-555 sell for $5.60, $7.20 and $4.60, respectively.

Required:

Allocate the joint costs using:
a. The physical quantity method.
b. The sales value method.

16-15. Joint Costs and The Treatment of By-products and Scrap.

The Plastico Company is a manufacturer of a synthetic plastic. The initial mixing process yields two joint products, Plastex and Rubberoid, as well as a by-product, Goo-all. The manufacturing costs for the month of May were $60,000. There were 12,000 pounds of Plastex and 8,000 pounds of Rubberoid produced in May as well as 700 pounds of Goo-all. Plastex has a selling price of $4 per pound, Rubberoid has a selling price of $6 per pound and Goo-all is sold for $2 a pound.

Required:

a. Allocate costs under the physical quantity method:
   1. treating Goo-all as a main product.
   2. treating Goo-all as a by-product.
   3. treating Goo-all as scrap.
b. Allocate costs under the sales value method:
   1. treating Goo-all as a main product.
   2. treating Goo-all as a by-product.
   3. treating Goo-all as scrap.

16-16. Joint Costs and Decision Making.

Sunny Bright Apple Orchards can produce any of the following combinations of apple products from 1,000 pounds of apples:

a. 200 lbs. of Apple Butter, 300 lbs. of Apple Sauce, and 500 lbs. of Eating Apples.
b. 150 lbs. of Apple Butter, 200 lbs. of Apple Sauce, and 650 lbs. of Eating Apples.
c. 0 lbs. of Apple Butter, 200 lbs. of Apple Sauce, 400 lbs. of Eating Apples, and 400 lbs. of Candy Apples.

Selling prices are $.20 per pound of Apple Butter, $.25 per pound of Apple Sauce, $.275 per pound of Eating Apples, and $.26 per pound of Candy Apples. Basic growing and harvesting costs are $40.00 per 1,000 pounds, and processing costs are $60 for combination (a), $75 for combination (b), and $70 for combination (c).

Required:

a. Determine the most profitable combination of products to produce from the basic material.

   b. Would you produce the combination of products selected above if the resources (workers and machines) used per thousand weight could have been used to produce an alternative product or group of products which could bring forth net income of $150?

16-17. Joint Costs and Decision Making.
   State College Dairy can process 100 gallons of raw milk to yield any one of the following combinations of products:

   a. 60 gallons of skim milk, 20 gallons of 2% milk, and 20 gallons of whole milk.
   b. 30 gallons of skim milk, 30 gallons of 2% milk, and 40 gallons of whole milk.

   In addition, the company has the alternative of converting whole milk, after it is separated from its sister products, into an equal number of gallons of chocolate milk at a cost of $0.125 per gallon.
   Sales prices are $2.00 per gallon of skim milk, $1.875 per gallon of 2% milk, $2.125 per gallon of whole milk, and $2.30 per gallon of chocolate milk. Raw milk costs $80.00 per 100 gallons, and processing costs are $50 for combination (a) and $60 for combination (b).

   Required:

   a. Determine the most profitable combination of products to produce from the basic material.
   b. Would you produce the combination selected if chocolate milk could be sold for:
       1. $2.125?
       2. $2.25?
       3. $2.50?

16-18. Joint Costs and Decision Making.
   The Fido Dog Food Company can use 100 pounds of basic materials to produce any of the following combinations of dog feeds:

   a. 20 lbs. of Adult, 10 lbs. of Hi-Pro, and 65 lbs. of Puppy.
   b. 30 lbs. of Adult, 15 lbs. of Hi-Pro, and 55 lbs. of Puppy.
   c. 10 lbs. of Adult, 15 lbs. of Hi-Pro, and 72 lbs. of Puppy.
   d. 10 lbs. of Adult, 60 lbs. of Puppy, and 35 lbs. of Lo-Cal.

   Differences between weight of inputs and outputs in the above combinations are caused by shrinkage and expansion during production.
   In addition to the above combinations, the company has the alternative of converting Hi-Pro feed into Stress Diet feed, and Puppy feed into Liv-r Flav-r Puppy feed. The cost of converting Hi-Pro into Stress Diet is $0.30 per pound, and there is a normal shrinkage of 5 percent, based on original quantities, in the conversion process. The cost of converting Puppy into Liv-r Flav-r is $0.20 per pound, and there is a normal shrinkage of 10 percent, based on original quantities, in the conversion process.
   Sales prices are $1.50 per pound of Adult, $1.60 per pound of Hi-Pro, $1.45 per pound of Puppy, $1.55 per pound of Lo-Cal, $2.00 per pound of Stress Diet, and $1.75 per pound of Liv-r Flav-r. Basic materials cost $30 per 100 pounds, and processing costs are $60 for combination (a), $80 for combination (b), $85 for combination (c) and $90 for combination (d).

Required:

a. Determine the most profitable combination of products to produce from the basic material.

b. Would you produce the combination of products selected above if the resources (workers and machines) used per hundredweight could have been used to produce an alternative product or group of products which could bring forth net income of $80?

16-19. Joint Costs and a Decision on Processing Further.

The manager of the Parrot Division questions whether product EL-OA should be processed further.

Presently every batch of EL-O results in 3,750 units of EL-OA and 6,200 units of EL-OB. Total cost of each batch is $19,900 and EL-OA sells for $3.60 a unit and EL-OB sells for $4.10 a unit.

If EL-OA is processed further, additional costs would be $5,625 a batch and EL-OA would sell for $5.00 a unit. Further processing would also produce 300 units of a by-product BY-OA which could possibly be sold for $0.20 a unit.

Required:

a. Calculate the unit cost of EL-OA and EL-OB at split-off using sales values.

b. Should the Parrot Division continue to process EL-OA further?

16-20. Joint Products and Inventory Valuation.

Required:

Calculate costs per pound of each product produced under each of the following conditions. Use the sales value method.

a. Sweet Tooth Chocolate Company purchases their basic raw materials in 100-pound lots at $100 per lot. From each 100-pound lot, Sweet Tooth produces the following most profitable combination of products at a processing cost of $100:

Product	Weight (pounds)	Sales Price Per Pound
Mini Bars	60	$ 2.00
Standard Bars	30	2.50
Super Bars	10	3.00

b. Assume the same facts as above except that Standard Bars can be processed further by adding peanuts at a cost of $0.25 per pound of Standard Bars. Each pound of Standard Bars can be converted into one pound of Peanut Bars which have a sales price of $2.80 per pound.

c. Assume the same facts as in (a) and (b) except that there is no market and thus no market value for Standard Bars at the point of separation from its co-products.

16-21. Decision to Sell at Split-off or Continue Processing.

The Bella Perfume Company manufactures four types of perfume, Evening, Day, Cologne and Bath. Total joint processing costs to split-off were $390,400 in 20x1. An activity report showed the following information:

Product	Production (in grams)	Price Per Gram	Additional Processing Costs	Price Per Gram @ Split-off
Evening	2,000,000	$ .2300	$ 120,000	.20
Day	40,000	1.0000	24,000	.35
Cologne	10,000	.8000	—	.80
Bath	18,000	3.3333	4,000	$ 3.00

Required:

a. Calculate the gross margin at split-off for each product using the sales value method. Assume grams produced are the same at split-off and after additional processing. Also assume all products are joint products.

b. The Smell company is willing to purchase any amount of Bella's production at the split-off. Should Bella consider selling any or all of its production to The Smell Company?

16-22. Joint Costs, Calculating Gross Profits and Decision Making.

A pharmaceutical company manufactures two products, A and B, in a common process. The joint costs amount to $12,000 per batch of finished goods. Each batch amounts to 10,000 liters, of which 25 percent are Product A and 75 percent are Product B. The two products are processed further, but without any gain or loss in volume. The costs of additional processing are $0.30 per liter of Product A and $0.40 per liter of Product B. After the additional processing, the selling price of Product A is $2.10 per liter and the selling price of Product B is $1.60 per liter.

Required:

a. If the joint costs are to be allocated on the basis of the net realizable value of each product at the split-off point, what amount of joint costs will be allocated to each product? Net realizable value at split-off equals sales price after further processing minus further processing costs.

b. Prepare a schedule of gross margin by product and batch using the preceding allocation and assuming that 80 percent of Product A and 60 percent of Product B were sold, with no opening inventories of either product. Why are the gross margin percentages not equal for both products?

c. The company has discovered an additional process by which Product A can be transformed into Product AA which could be sold for $6 per liter. This additional processing would increase costs by $2.50 per liter. Assuming that there is no other changes in costs, should the company use the new process?

(SMA adapted)

16-23.   Joint Costs—Calculate Inventory Values.

The Stumper Company, which began operations at the beginning of 20x3, operates a process by which a raw material is converted into two major products called Marks and Colls. Raw materials costing $35 per kilogram are processed at a cost of $18 per kilogram and result in 50 percent of the output being Marks, 25 percent Colls, 15 percent a by-product called Salects, and 10 percent wastage. Marks are sold at $40 per kilogram, Colls are sold at $100 per kilogram (after being further processed at a cost of $24 per kilogram), Salects are sold at $10 per kilogram (with selling costs of $1 per kilogram), and the wastage is disposed of at a cost of $1.50 per kilogram.

During 20x3, the company fully processed a total of 26,000 kilograms of raw materials, disposed of all the wastage, and had the following sales revenues:

Marks	$ 448,000
Colls	553,000
Salects	37,500

Required:

Calculate the value of each of the ending inventories using the sales value method, assuming that the company treats the net realizable value of any by-product produced as a reduction in the cost of the joint-product process. Calculate to the nearest dollar and show all calculations.

(SMA adapted)

16-24.   Joint Cost Allocation and Decision Making.

The Alex Company has a production process whereby 120,000 pounds of raw materials are processed each month at a cost of $375,000 (including the cost of raw materials). The process results in the following outputs each month:

HYP—55,000 pounds per month
GYP—48,000 pounds per month
ROC—17,000 pounds per month

HYP can be sold immediately after processing for $26 per pound. GYP can be sold for $21 per pound, but only after further processing at a cost of $223,000 per month. ROC is presently sold for $1.50 per pound immediately after processing. ROC is considered a by-product of the process due to its low sales value compared to the other products.

The company is considering a new alternative for disposing of ROC whereby it would be sold for $43 per pound. This alternative would require the company to hire additional staff at a cost of $38,000 per month. The variable costs of further processing ROC would total $24.80 per pound. The equipment required can be leased at a cost of $67,000 per month. In addition, the company's accounting system would allocate $190,000 of existing fixed overhead to the new operation. Due to the higher sales value, the company would consider ROC to be another joint product if this alternative is followed.

Required:

a. Calculate the amount of joint cost to be allocated to each of the products under the company's present production methods, assuming the company allocates joint product costs on sales value.

b. How much would the company gain or lose if ROC is processed further, as proposed?

c. Explain how your answer to part (b) would change if the company allocated joint product costs based on physical volume or weight.

(SMA adapted)

16-25. Joint Cost Allocation and By-Product Income.

The Chemical Company produces two joint Products A and B from the same raw material. Also during the processing, a by-product X emerges which has a market value only if processed further.

The following information is available for the annual budget for the coming year:

> *Estimated sales:*
> | | | |
> |---|---|---|
> | Product | A .... | 240,000 lbs. @ $2.50 |
> | | B .... | 720,000 lbs. @ $1.50 |
> | By-product | X .... | Sell for $0.60 a pound |
>
> *Estimated costs:*
> Processing department
> | | |
> |---|---|
> | Materials .... | $ 312,000 |
> | Labor .... | 198,000 |
> | Overhead .... | 330,000 |
>
> *Costs after separation:*
> | | | |
> |---|---|---|
> | Product | A .... | $ 0.80 per pound |
> | | B .... | 0.45 per pound |
> | | X .... | 0.44 per pound |

Assume no beginning or ending inventories. Marketing and Administrative Expenses are 10 percent of sales. Of every 9 pounds of raw materials started in the processing department, only 8 pounds can be processed further for Products A and B. The remaining pound is of inferior quality and is set aside for Product X.

The director of marketing was concerned about measuring profit for each product and maintained that:

1. Sales of by-product X should be treated separately by assigning costs before and after separation from the processing department and allowing for marketing and administrative expenses but no profits.

2. A cost per pound should be established for Products A and B such that each product contributes the same profit percentage per sales dollar.

Required:

a. Calculate the "cost before separation" charged to the by-product.

b. Calculate the processing department's cost per pound of Product A and Product B.

(SMA adapted)

▸ PROBLEMS AND CASES ◂

16-26. **Joint Costs and Unit Cost Calculations.**

Suppose that one hog yields 300 pounds of ham, 200 pounds of chops, and 200 pounds of miscellaneous items. The sales value of ham is $1.20 per pound, of chops $1.40 per pound, and of miscellaneous items of $0.50 per pound. The hog costs $400 and processing costs are $20 per hog.

Suppose that one barrel of crude oil yields fifty gallons of gasoline, twenty-five gallons of fuel oil, and twenty-five gallons of kerosene. Sales value of gasoline is $0.96 per gallon, of fuel oil $0.64 per gallon, and of kerosene $0.72 per gallon. One barrel of crude oil costs $23 and processing costs are $5 per barrel.

Required:

a. Compute unit costs for the end products produced from the hog and from the barrel of crude oil. Use both the physical quantity method and sales value method.
b. Compute unit costs for the end products resulting from a barrel of crude oil from the following facts. Fuel oil can be converted into gasoline at the rate of six gallons for every nine gallons of fuel oil, and kerosene can be converted into gasoline at the rate of eight gallons of gasoline for every ten gallons of kerosene. Assume the same processing cost.
c. Describe the purposes for which these unit costs can and cannot be used (e.g., decision making, performance measurement, and inventory valuation).

16-27. **Valuing By-Products.**

The Fake Fruit Company produces four prime products and a by-product in one of its processes. Fake Fruit uses the by-product, Eggplant, as a substitute material in the formula for another of its products - watermelon. It can use all the by-product produced.

The materials formulas both without and with the Eggplant treated as a by-product are given in tabular from below. The costs of transferring the by-product to the watermelon operation are $0.03 per pound.

Materials Formulas Assuming Eggplant is Not a By-Product*

Apple	2,000	lbs.	0.145	$ 290
Banana	400	lbs.	0.300	120
Cherry	200	lbs.	0.350	70
Date	150	lbs.	0.400	60
Eggplant	1,000	lbs.	0.180	180
	3,750	lbs.		$ 720
Loss 4%	150	lbs.		
	3,600	lbs.	0.200	$ 720

Materials Formulas Assuming Eggplant is a By-Product*

Apple	2,000	lbs.
Banana	500	lbs.
Cherry	200	lbs.
Date	50	lbs.
By-Product (Eggplant)	1,000	lbs.
	3,750	lbs.
Loss 4%	150	lbs.
	3,600	lbs.

* Labor and manufacturing overhead costs are the same for each formula.

Required:

Assuming Eggplant is treated as a by-product, determine the credit per pound of Eggplant which should be given to the prime products, that is, the products which were produced in conjunction with the by-product.

16-28. Joint Costs: Calculate Gross Margin Using Probabilities.

Old Cracked Hill mines an ore that contains lead, silver and zinc. The first step after mining the ore is to extract the lead, silver and zinc. None of these raw metals has a market value at the split-off point, so they must be processed further if they are to be sold. Any raw metals that are not processed beyond split-off can be disposed of for zero additional cost. Production costs for 20x1 were:

	Fixed	*Variable*
Joint costs (before split-off)	$ 1,000,000	$ 2,000,000
Separable costs (after split-off):		
Lead	2,000,000	$13,000,000
Silver	1,000,000	7,000,000
Zinc	4,000,000	7,000,000

Production for 20x1 was 10,000 tons of lead, 2,000,000 ounces of silver and 12,000 tons of zinc. The production level and costs were expected to be unchanged for 20x2.

The company is uncertain about the prices that it will obtain for its products in 20x2. After a careful review of the market, management has established the following probability distribution for prices in the coming year.

Lead: Price per ton	$ 1,400	$ 1,150	$ 1,100	
Probability	.3	.2	.5	
Silver: Price per ounce	$ 50	$ 45	$ 38	$ 25
Probability	.1	.3	.5	.1
Zinc: Price per ton	$ 950	$ 750	$ 650	
Probability	.2	.4	.4	

Required:

Determine the expected value of the gross margin in 20x2 if operations are carried on in their most profitable form. Assume that sales equals production and that all fixed costs will continue unchanged for at least two years.
(SMA adapted)

16-29. Joint Products and Inventory Valuation.

During 20x1, the Juno Chemical Company started a new division whose operation consists of processing a mineral into commercial products: A, B, C, and D. However, product D is classified as a second or reject and is sold at a lower price.

The following information is available regarding the company's operations for 20x1:

Sales (including product D)	$ 24,480
Production costs	49,769
Marketing costs allocated to division	1,224
Normal profit goal	10% of sales

		Product			
	Total	*A*	*B*	*C*	*D*
Quantity (tons):					
Beginning inventory	0	0	0	0	0
Production	634	305	137	22	170
Sales	285	132	83	10	60
Ending inventory	349	173	54	12	110
Sales price per ton (constant throughout the period)		$ 100	$ 100	$ 100	$ 33

Required:

a. Compute the inventory values at December 31, 20x1, with all products treated as joint products. Use physical quantity and sales value methods.

b. Compute inventory values at December 31, 20x1, with product D treated as a by-product. Use physical quantity and sales value methods.

c. Recalculate, if necessary, the inventory values in (a) and (b) in accordance with the lower of cost or market rule.

(AICPA adapted)

16-30. Joint Costs Calculating Inventory Values and Decision-Making.

Robinson Company purchases unprocessed ore for $25 per ton and then processes the ore, at an additional cost of $40 per ton, to yield the following:

1. 20 percent of production results in "Repproc" which is further processed into "Super Repproc" at a cost of $75 per ton before sold for $190 per ton.

2. 75 percent of production results in "Dlog" which is sold for $95 per ton.

3. 5 percent of production results in a by-product which is sold for $27 per ton with marketing costs of $8 per ton.

The Robinson Company treats the net realizable value of the by-products as a reduction in the cost of producing the joint products. The company began the month without any inventories and processed a total of 2,600 tons of ore. At the end of the month, it had the following inventories:

"Super Repproc"   16   tons
"Dlog"   28   tons
"Repproc   0
1 ton of by-product

Required:

Using the "sales value" method of allocating joint costs, determine the value for each of the month end inventories
(SMA adapted)

16-31. By-Products and Joint Products.

The McLean Processing Company produces a chemical compound, Supergro, that is sold for $4.60 per gallon. The manufacturing process is divided into the following departments.

1. Mixing Department: The raw materials are measured and mixed in this department.
2. Cooking Department: The mixed materials are cooked for a specified period in this department. In the cooking process, there is a 10 percent evaporation loss in materials.
3. Cooling Department: After the cooked materials are cooled in this department under controlled conditions, the top 80 percent in the cooling tank is siphoned off and pumped to the Packing Department. The 20 percent residue, which contains impurities, is sold in bulk as a by-product, Groex, for $2.00 per gallon.
4. Packing Department: In this department special one gallon containers costing 60 cents each are filled with Supergro and shipped to customers.

The company's Research and Development Department recently discovered a new use for the by-product, if it is further processed in a new Boiling Department. The new by-product, Fasgro, would sell in bulk for $5.00 per gallon.

Under the new arrangement, the top 70 percent in the cooling tank would be siphoned off as Supergro. The residue would be pumped to the Boiling Department where 1/2 gallon of material, SK, would be added for each gallon of residue. In the Boiling Department process there would be a 40 percent evaporation loss. In processing Fasgro, the following additional costs would be incurred:

Material SK	$ 1.10	per gallon
Boiling Department:		
Variable processing costs	1.00	per gallon of input
Fixed processing costs	$ 2,000	per month

In recent months, because of heavy demand, the company has shipped Supergro and Groex on the same day that their processing was completed. Fasgro would probably be subject to the same heavy demand.

During the month of July 20x3, which was considered a typical month, the following materials were put into process in the Mixing Department:

Material FE	10,000 gallons @ $0.90 per gallon
Material QT	4,000 gallons @ $1.50 per gallon

July processing costs per gallon of departmental input were:

Mixing department	$ 0.40
Cooking department	0.50
Cooling department	0.30
Packing department	0.10

For accounting purposes the company assigns joint costs to its by-products equal to their net realizable value at point of separation. For the purpose of this problem, assume that net realizable value equals selling price.

Required:

Prepare a statement computing total manufacturing costs and profit for July that compares:

a. Actual results for July.
b. Estimated results if Fasgro had been the by-product.
(AICPA adapted)

16-32. Process Costing—Including By-Products and Joint Products.
    The Town Company is a manufacturer, producing two principal products known as XO and MO. Incidental to the production of these products, it produces a by-product known as Bypo. The company has three producing departments which it identifies as departments 101, 201, and 301. Raw materials A and B are started in process in department 101. Upon completion of processing in that department, one-fifth of the material is by-product and is transferred directly to inventory. One-third of the remaining output of department 101 goes to department 201 where it is made into XO and the other two-thirds goes to department 301 where it becomes MO. The processing of XO in department 201 results in a weight gain of material transferred into the department of 50 percent due to the addition of water at the start of processing. There is no gain or loss of weight in the other processes.
    The company considers the income from Bypo, after allowing 5 cents per pound for estimated marketing and delivery costs, to be a reduction of the cost of the two principal products. The company assigns department 101 costs to the two principal products in proportion to their net sales value at point of separation, computed by deducting costs to be incurred in subsequent processes from the sales value of the products.
    The following information concerns the operations during April 20x1.

	Inventories		
	March 31		*April 30*
	Quantity (pounds)	*Value*	*Quantity (pounds)*
Department 101	None	—	None
Department 201	800	$17,160	1,000
Department 301	200	2,340	360
Finished stock-XO	300	7,260	800
Finished stock-MO	1,200	18,550	700
Finished stock-Bypo	None	—	None

Inventories in process are estimated to be one-half complete in departments 201 and 301, both at the beginning and end of April.

	Costs	
	Materials Used	*Labor and Overhead*
Department 101	$134,000	$87,442
Department 201	—	31,950
Department 301	—	61,880

The materials used in department 101 weighed 18,000 pounds.

Sales	*Prices*
XO	$ 29.50 per lb.
MO	17.50 per lb.
Bypo	0.50 per lb.

Prices as of April 30 are unchanged from those in effect during the month.

Required:

a. Prepare a statement(s), fully supported by calculations, showing unit costs of each product, the dollar amount of transfers between departments, and the dollar amount of transfers to finished goods. Assume that the company uses fifo for inventory valuation.

b. Prepare a schedule of ending work in process and finished goods inventories supported by appropriate calculations.

(AICPA adapted)

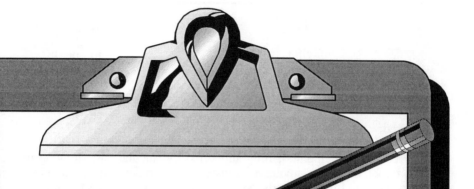

Learning Objectives

After reading this chapter, the student should have an understanding of:

✔ The objective of divisional performance measurement and decentralization.

✔ The distinction between responsibility reporting and information reporting plus the relationship of this distinction to controllable, traceable, and allocated items of cost and invested capital.

✔ The application of rate of return and residual income to divisional reporting.

✔ Controllable revenue and the manufacturing function which gives rise to the need for transfer pricing in divisional reporting.

✔ Available transfer prices when producing units to sell to external buyers.

✔ Available transfer prices when producing units to not sell to external buyers.

✔ Understanding how the opportunity to purchase from external sellers influences transfer pricing.

✔ A "market forces" framework for resolving goal congruence issues relative to intercompany transfer pricing.

✔ Useful alternatives to transfer pricing when management decides that the difficulties and problems inherent in setting transfer prices are not worth the effort.

DIVISIONAL PERFORMANCE AND TRANSFER PRICING

Chapter 17

With the trend toward large-scale organizations and decentralization of authority and responsibility within these organizations, there arises the issue of measuring performance of decentralized units or divisions. This issue of measuring divisional performance is an attempt to give life to the concept of an investment center as opposed to a cost center or a profit center.

In prior chapters we have considered both cost centers and profit centers from the responsibility reporting point of view. Cost centers, such as individual manufacturing departments, were defined as those areas of responsibility with which we associate costs controllable by the person in charge. Profit centers, such as a sales territory, were defined as those areas of responsibility with which we associate costs and revenues controllable by the person in charge. The final step in constructing areas of responsibility is the investment center. This is normally a major unit of a company, with which we associate elements of invested capital as well as costs and revenues controllable by the person in charge.

Basically, the investment center is an attempt to make the segments of the firm respond to a rate of return goal rather than just a cost goal (the cost center) or a profit goal (the profit center). Thus, in divisional performance and responsibility reporting we are concerned with the following algebraic expression:

$$Divisional\ Rate\ of\ Return\ =\ \frac{Controllable\ Revenues\ -\ Controllable\ Costs}{Controllable\ Invested\ Capital}$$

▸ PRELIMINARY OBSERVATIONS ◂

▸ Objective of Divisional Performance Measurement and Decentralization

In large scale organizations, top management has neither the time nor the intimate knowledge to be involved in detailed decision-making throughout the organization. The task of top management is to be involved in setting the broad guidelines under which each organizational unit operates and to set the overall standards of performance expected for each organizational unit.

Decentralization of authority and responsibility is designed to enhance decision-making and thus the performance of organizational units, while operating under the broad guidelines and standards set by top management. The key to decentralization is the authority and responsibility granted to the head of each decentralized unit or division. Decentralization of authority grants decision-making power to those who have the most detailed and intimate knowledge concerning decentralized divisions. Coupled with this is the decentralization of responsibility. Thus, those who have decision-making power can be held accountable for their decisions via an appropriate responsibility reporting system. Therefore the fundamental objective of decentralization is more informed and better decisions which will enhance the performance of each division and ultimately the entire organization. Systems for measuring divisional performance are designed to facilitate this objective.

Whether enhanced performance at the divisional level will enhance the performance of an entire organization is a matter of goal congruence. More will be said about this issue later.

▸ Responsibility Reporting vs. Information Reporting

At this point, the reader should recognize that there are good reasons for including more than controllable elements in reports measuring divisional performance. For example, in Chapter 13 the point was made that "costs controllable by others" could be added to a supervisor's responsibility report in order to show the supervisor the size and costliness of the organization necessary to support his or her activities. However, it was made quite clear that the two groupings of costs should remain separate and distinct in the responsibility report. Also, in Chapter 14 a series of behavioral and regulatory reasons were given for a full allocation of costs in product line profitability reports.

Now in the case of divisional performance, we are confronted with the same problem; that is, there are many who would like to add to divisional profit performance items that are "controllable by others." This insistence leads us into drawing a distinction between responsibility reporting and information reporting, as well as between controllable, traceable, and allocated items.

▸ Controllable vs. Traceable vs. Allocated Items

The key to the distinction between responsibility reporting and information reporting is the distinction between controllable, traceable and allocated items. Controllability refers to the ability of a manager *to significantly influence* an element of cost, revenue or invested capital. Traceability refers to the ability of accountants *to identify* elements of cost, revenue and invested capital with individual units of an organization in some reasonable or rational manner. Allocated items are those items which *cannot be identified* with individual units of an organization in some reasonable or rational manner. Allocated items are frequently referred to as items which are *arbitrarily assigned* to individual units of an organization.

As is almost obvious from the above terminology of *significantly influence* and *reasonable or rational manner*, not everyone will agree as to which specific items are controllable, traceable or allocated. Thus, in each individual organization, an agreement among affected parties will have to be reached and reviewed periodically relative to the specific items which are included in each category.

Perhaps the best way to illustrate with some specificity the distinction between controllable, traceable and allocated is through a series of reports as shown in Exhibits 17-1, 17-2 and 17-3.

Exhibit 17-1 is a profitability report for the Mid-West Sales Region of the Consumer Products Division of Goodwear Tires, Inc., a national tire manufacturer and retailer. The upper portion of the report, down to the "regional manager's operating profit," concentrates on those variable and fixed costs controllable by the regional manager. As is usual and reasonable in such reports, sales and variable costs are considered to be both traceable and controllable. Only fixed costs are thus involved in the distinction between controllable, traceable and allocated.[1]

---

[1] It could be argued that costs which are allocated via a percentage of sales are made variable by the management decision to allocate them as a percentage of sales. Such costs are really not variable - the method of allocation makes then appear variable and in essence treats them as variable. This result is very common for allocated items since accountants often resort to allocations based on a percentage of sales when there is no reasonable or rational manner to identify costs with segments of an organization.

Goodwear Tires, Inc.
Consumer Products Division
Mid-West Sales Region
Profitability Report

Sales		$1,500,000
Variable costs:		
Manufacturing—cost of goods sold	$ 690,000	
Marketing—commissions	79,500	
Total		769,500
Profit contribution		$ 730,500
Traceable fixed costs—controllable by regional manager:		
Manufacturing—cost of goods sold	$ 270,000	
Marketing:		
Advertising and promotion	50,000	
Salesperson and office salaries	64,000	
Depreciation	18,200	
Travel	30,000	
Stationery and postage	8,800	
Telephone and telegraph	13,400	
Total		454,400
Regional manager's operating profit		$ 276,100
Traceable fixed costs—controllable by others:		
Marketing:		
Manager's salary	$ 75,000	
Office rental	30,000	
Total		105,000
Regional operating profit		$ 171,100
Allocated costs:		
Marketing vice president's office (3% sales)	$ 45,000	
Division office (2% sales)	30,000	
Corporate office (2% sales)	30,000	
Total		105,000
Regional net profit before tax		$ 66,100

Exhibit 17-1

Note in Exhibit 17-1 that traceable fixed costs are divided into those which are controllable by the regional manager and those controllable by others. Also note that the allocated costs represent three layers of administration (i.e., marketing, divisional and corporate).

The responsibility reporting aspects of Exhibit 17-1 culminate with the "regional manager's operating profit." Similarly, the information reporting aspects of Exhibit 17-1 culminate in the "regional operating profit" and the "regional net profit before tax."

Hopefully it is clear that there is, or should be, no conflict between responsibility and information reporting. Responsibility reporting stresses the items to be used in evaluating a manager. Information reporting stresses the evaluation of an organization segment in terms of all traceable items. Information reporting also stresses certain behavioral and regulatory considerations via allocated items. In a sense, information reporting stresses the total economics of an organizational unit rather than the responsibility aspects.

Exhibit 17-2 is a profitability report for the vice president of marketing in charge of all the sales regions of the Consumer Products Division of Goodwear Tires. Note that at this higher organizational level traceable and controllable fixed costs are the same, a common occurrence. Also

Goodwear Tires, Inc.
Consumer Products Division
Vice President of Marketing Profitability Report
(Summation of All Regions in the Division)

Sales	$ 10,500,000	
Variable costs	5,200,000	
Profit contribution		$ 5,300,000
Traceable (controllable) fixed costs:		
Controllable by regional managers	$ 3,010,500	
Controllable by vice president of marketing	975,500	
Total		3,986,000
Marketing operating profit—		
vice president's responsibility		$ 1,314,000
Allocated costs:		
Division office (2% sales)	$ 210,000	
Corporate office (2% sales)	210,000	
Total		$ 420,000
Marketing net profit before tax		$ 894,000

Exhibit 17-2

Goodwear Tires, Inc.
Consumer Products Division
Division President Profitability Report
(Summation of all Divisional Marketing,
Manufacturing and Administrative Activities)

Sales	$ 10,500,000	
Variable cost:		
Manufacturing	$ 4,650,000	
Marketing	550,000	
Total		5,200,000
Profit contribution		$ 5,300,000
Traceable (controllable) fixed costs:		
Manufacturing	$ 2,036,000	
Marketing	1,950,000	
Division office	210,000	
Total		4,196,000
Division operating profit -		
division president's responsibility		$ 1,104,000
Allocated costs—corporate office(2% sales)		210,000
Division net profit before tax		$ 894,000

Exhibit 17-3

note that the allocated costs of the marketing vice president's office, which were not included among the traceable items in Exhibit 17-1, are now included among the traceable (controllable) fixed costs in Exhibit 17-2. Thus, the responsibility reporting aspects and the information reporting aspects in Exhibit 17-2 revolve around allocated division and corporate costs.

Exhibit 17-3 is a profitability report for the president of the Consumer Products Division, who is responsible for all the marketing, manufacturing and administrative activities of the division. At this higher organizational level, traceable and controllable fixed costs are again the same and yet another layer of allocated costs (i.e., the division layer) becomes a part of the traceable (controllable) costs.

Exhibits 17-1, 17-2 and 17-3 are intended to represent budgeted data. Even though marketing responsibility reports and aspects of marketing data have been stressed thus far, the impact of manufacturing should not be ignored. More will be said about manufacturing in succeeding pages.

▸ Divisional Rate of Return and Residual Income

The divisional report shown in Exhibit 17-3 only addresses divisional profitability in terms of costs and revenues related to the division. In order to address divisional rate of return or residual income, invested capital must be considered.

Interestingly, invested capital can be categorized in the same manner as costs. In addition, invested capital can be divided into controllable, traceable and allocated items. Thus, the divisional rate of return or residual income can be computed in terms of responsibility reporting and/or information reporting aspects. For illustrative purposes, let us assume that invested capital can be subdivided as follows for divisional reporting purposes. Note that since we are dealing with divisional data, traceable and controllable invested capital are considered to be the same. Also note that variable invested capital is based upon variable manufacturing cost.

Variable invested capital   –   20% of variable manufacturing cost or $930,000
Fixed invested capital:
    Controllable (traceable)   – $ 3,900,000
    Allocated corporate office   – $ 550,000

With the above data, one could easily calculate *two* divisional rates of return (i.e., one for responsibility reporting and another for information reporting) as follows:

$$\text{Responsibility Rate of Return} = \frac{\text{Division Operating Profit}}{\text{Variable + Controllable Invested Capital}} = \frac{1,104,000}{4,830,000} = 22.9\%$$

$$\text{Information Reporting Rate of Return} = \frac{\text{Division Net Profit Before Tax}}{\text{Variable + Controllable Allocated Invested Capital}} + \frac{894,000}{5,380,000} = 16.6\%$$

An alternative to the two different rates of return could be a division profitability report which embodies the residual income concept, as illustrated in Exhibit 17-4. Note that the three categories of invested capital [i.e., variable, traceable (controllable) fixed, and allocated], are included in their respective cost categories via a cost of capital measured at a before tax minimum desired rate of return of 15 percent. The authors admit to having a slight bias in favor of Exhibit 17-4 and the notion of residual income for divisional profitability reporting.

Goodwear Tires, Inc.
Consumer Products Division
Division President Profitability Report

Sales		$ 10,500,000
Variable cost:		
Manufacturing	$ 4,650,000	
Marketing	550,000	
Cost of variable capital		
(.15 x $930,000)	139,500	
Total		$ 5,339,500
Profit contribution		$ 5,160,500
Traceable (controllable) fixed costs:		
Manufacturing	$ 2,036,000	
Marketing	1,950,000	
Division office	210,000	
Cost of traceable (controllable)		
capital (.15 x $3,900,000)	585,000	
Total		4,781,000
Division residual income -		
division president's responsibility		$ 379,500
Allocated costs:		
Corporate office (2% sales)	$ 210,000	
Cost of allocated capital		
(.15 x $550,000)	82,500	
Total		$ 292,500
Division net residual income before tax		$ 87,000

Exhibit 17-4

▸ Controllable Revenue and the Manufacturing Function

What might appear to be the easiest aspect of divisional profit performance to deal with actually turns out to be the most difficult. The perils and pitfalls of attempting to quantify the amount of revenue subject to the control of a corporate division are lying-in-wait for the unwary enthusiast of divisional performance.

Actually, there would be no problem here if each division was totally *self-contained* (i.e., a separate and distinct entity which did not deal with any other division). In such a case, the revenues of the divisions could truly be said to be subject to the influence of divisional personnel. However, what happens when one division of a company uses or sells products or services produced by another division of the same company? What price shall the producing division charge the using division?

It should be obvious that the price charged would have an impact on the performance of both producing and using divisions, and thus the determination of this price - a transfer price - must be given serious consideration. It is our purpose in the next section to consider the basic issue in transfer pricing and some of the methods used to price intercompany transfers.

▸ Total Profit on a Product Line

When determining profit and return on invested capital by areas of responsibility within a company, it is impossible to tell from the periodic responsibility reports how much profit is realized on a product line on which there are intercompany transactions. For example, the profit on a line of products produced in one division would be in part both in that division and in another division producing a component used by the first division. Thus, using a transfer price other than cost can impede the objective of reflecting total operating results for a product line. Where product line profitability is needed for various management purposes and products are transferred at other than cost, product line profit reports can be generated via special analyses.

▶ METHODS OF DETERMINING TRANSFER PRICES ◀

In the general sense, a *transfer price* is a price charged by one unit of an organization for a product or service produced for another unit of the same organization. Our discussion will concentrate on decentralized units or divisions which are major units of a large organization, such as the Marathon Oil unit of USX Corporation. However, much of our discussion is applicable to a wide variety of small units of any organization in either the public or private sector. Among smaller units could easily be the maintenance department in a manufacturing plant as well as organization-wide service departments such as telephone and fax services, printing services, computer services and even a motor pool.[2]

▶ The Basic Issue in Transfer Pricing

The broad objective of transfer pricing is the same as the objective of divisional performance measurement and decentralization, i.e., more informed and better decisions by those who have the most detailed and intimate knowledge concerning decentralized divisions. More precisely, however, *the basic issue in or objective of transfer pricing is goal congruence*. The transfer price should motivate managers to work for the overall good of the total organization as they are   attempting to enhance the performance of their divisions.

In one sense, it would be entirely satisfactory for accounting purposes to make all intercompany transfers at cost. In fact, this would be very desirable, for it would make it unnecessary to determine profit on intercompany transactions and to eliminate it at the corporate level for tax and external reporting purposes. However, transfers at cost do not provide a measurement of the contribution to profit of each unit of the company. This measurement can be accomplished only when a transfer price other than cost is established for products and services as they move from one manager's area of responsibility to the next manager's area of responsibility, before the final products are sold to outside customers.

Where profit responsibility is placed below the level of the chief executive, transfer prices at other than cost are required to prepare performance reports for each area of profit responsibility. A division manager's profit report will be a measure of profit performance only if products of the division are *sold* to other divisions at prices which result in either a profit or loss. For example, assume that the industrial specialties division of a fiberboard company does not have a board-forming unit in their Harrisburg plant. They buy large blanks from the building products division's Atlanta plant and fabricate the specialties in Harrisburg. The transfer of the blank boards at cost would provide no measure of the profit performance of either unit. Furthermore, if the transfer was made at actual cost rather than standard cost, production inefficiencies or efficiencies in the building products division would be passed on to the industrial specialties division.

The objective of transfer pricing at other than cost is to permit each unit of a company to earn a profit commensurate with the functions it performs. It is not the intent that any unit should be

---

[2] The service department cost allocations to other service departments and producing departments as discussed in the body and appendix of Chapter 8 are cost based transfer prices. Much of the discussion in this chapter on standard cost based transfer prices is thus readily applicable to the discussion in Chapter 8.

guaranteed a profit. Under sound transfer prices, the possibility of incurring a loss will exist just as it does on sales to outside customers.

In subsequent pages, our discussion of transfer pricing methods will be subdivided in terms of whether producing units do or do not sell to external buyers. Our discussion of these methods will then close with some comments on whether or not the internal buyers can buy from external sellers.

▸ Producing Units Sell to External Buyers

List Prices. When the same product is sold to outside customers and to other units of the company, it is customary to use the same prices for external and intercompany sales. These prices are based on published price lists and give consideration to the volume purchased. Transfer prices are usually the same as would be charged to an outside customer for the same quantity on an order. However, company policy may call for transfer prices to be based on the lowest price quoted to outside customers to offset the presumption of the reduced sales effort required. Where stock items are sold, the lowest list price may be used regardless of the size of individual intercompany orders, both because of less sales effort and of the probability of annual volume exceeding the quantity at which a customer pays the lowest price.

The use of published list prices is a very defensible basis of transfer pricing. The internal buyer is paying prices which are just as low as those charged external customers and the internal seller is receiving the same profit that would be received if the same products were sold to outside customers. The internal buyer is also likely to be paying prices which are the same as, or lower than, what would be paid if the products were bought from competitors. Disagreements on transfer prices are eliminated or reduced to a very few which can be readily resolved. However, a discount from list prices may be justifiable as indicated below.

List Prices Minus a Discount. If one unit sells a product to external buyers and also to other units of the company, discounts from the list prices may be allowed to the internal buying units. Such discounts would give recognition to the costs and invested capital of each unit. For example, if a company had an export division which purchased its products from the other divisions, the transfer prices to the export division could be based on the list prices of the domestic divisions less a discount determined by a formula established as company policy.

Since such discounts should give recognition to costs and invested capital, some period must be selected for determination of these items. They may be based on an average of several prior years, on the budget for the year for which the discounts are to apply, or on an average of prior years and the budget.

For such discounts from list prices of the producing unit, the following factors should be considered:

1. Average cash discounts and freight allowed to outside customers of the producing unit.
2. Marketing expenses of the producing unit and other expenses that could be eliminated or reduced such as specific packaging, handling, etc.
3. Profit margin applicable to the marketing function of the producing unit expressed in terms of capital invested in marketing by the producing unit.

The sum of these three items expressed as a percentage of sales to outside customers at list prices is the total discount to be applied to the list prices of the producing unit. Note that items included in the discount are expenses which would not be incurred by the producing unit on sales to the using unit (Item 2) and a profit margin (Item 3) which the producing unit does not deserve since it does not perform the marketing function. Thus, the discount should be perceived as fair and equitable to both the producing unit and the using unit. The calculation of a transfer price by this method is shown below.

Profit margin (sales price less standard manufacturing cost plus cash discounts and freight allowed)	10%	
Less: Average marketing expenses	5%	
Margin after marketing expenses (a)	5%	
Percent invested capital in marketing (b)	20%*	
Profit margin applicable to marketing (a x b)		1%
Average cash discounts and freight allowed		2%
Average marketing expenses		5%
Total discount to buying unit		8%

* The other 80 percent of invested capital is assumed to be tied up in manufacturing and administrative activities.

▸ Producing Units Do Not Sell to External Buyers

Negotiated Prices. Products manufactured by one segment of a company for another (either for use as materials or component parts or for resale) are frequently not sold to outside customers. In such cases there are no list prices which can be used to establish a transfer price. The transfer price must either be set in negotiation between the managers of the buying and selling units or by the application of an established formula, usually based on a standard cost. The former may result in differences of opinion which must be resolved by higher authority. The latter requires that the formula be stated as company policy or there will be constant pressure for modification of the formula or some of its factors.

In the absence of list prices, negotiation could result in the most equitable transfer prices. They are prices which the seller is willing to accept and the buyer is willing to pay. Each manager will base the decision on the effect which the price will have on his or her profit and return on invested capital. It is, in effect, an attempt to obtain arm's-length pricing. *A very useful ingredient in such negotiations would be information on selling prices from external sources of supply, if they exist.*

The desirability of having the transfer prices negotiated must be appraised in the light of the amount of management time which will be consumed in the negotiations. This may include demands on the time of top management to resolve differences of opinion or to actually set the price if the two parties cannot agree on a price. *The latter has the effect of removing profit responsibility from the internal buyers and sellers and placing it with higher authority: a situation which should be avoided since it negates the notion of decentralized profit responsibility.*

Standard Cost Plus Profit—General Comments. When internally transferred products are not sold externally, the producing unit would not have list prices available to use in developing a discount formula (and thus a transfer price). If the buying unit sells the products to outside customers without further fabrication, the discount formula could be applied to the buying unit's customer price list. However, this would be a satisfactory method only if the customer prices were set by competitive market conditions. Otherwise the buying unit would be determining (without competitive constraints) what they will pay the producing unit when they set their sales prices.

An alternative approach, that works when the buying unit sells with or without further fabrication, is to use the standard cost of the producing unit plus a specified return on invested capital. This method can compute either a total standard cost per unit or a variable standard cost per unit plus a lump-sum fixed cost. As stated earlier, using standard costs avoids passing the efficiencies and inefficiencies of the producing division to the buying division.

Standard Cost Plus Profit—Total Cost Per Unit. The total standard cost per unit includes both variable and fixed manufacturing costs. Variable manufacturing costs (i.e., direct material, direct labor and variable manufacturing overhead costs) are based on the standard rates approved for the budget period. Fixed manufacturing overhead[3] per unit can be unitized on either budgeted or normal volume. The latter is preferable because it tends to level the transfer price over a period of years. However, when the production volume is determined primarily by the demands of the buying segment, there is justification for using the volume budgeted for the period. This places the effect of volume on unit costs and profits on the buying unit whose business determines the level at which the producing unit operates.

The profit factor is determined as a percentage return on the invested capital budgeted to manufacture the product at the budgeted or normal volume. The percentage is set by company policy. It may be the average return budgeted for the company, for the producing unit, or for the buying unit. Or, it may be an established rate to be used for all intercompany trading. Theoretically, the profit percentage should be the same as the residual income capital charge and the before-tax minimum required rate of return for capital budgeting. The calculation of a transfer price by this method is shown below.

Unit standard cost:		
Direct material		$ 1.00
Direct labor		.60
Variable manufacturing overhead		.40
Total variable cost per unit		$ 2.00
Fixed manufacturing overhead budgeted	$ 16,000	
Normal volume - 10,000 units (fixed cost per unit)		1.60
Total unit cost		$ 3.60
Invested capital:		
Variable [20% of variable manufacturing cost at		
normal volume (.2 x 2 x 10,000)]	$ 4,000	
Fixed	20,000	
Total invested capital	$ 24,000	
Desired return on invested capital - 15%	3,600	
Profit per unit to yield desired return at		
normal volume ($3,600 / 10,000)		.36
Transfer price		$ 3.96

One objection to this method is that the producing segment is guaranteed a profit at normal volume if it meets its unit standard costs and holds it fixed costs to budgeted amounts. It will incur gains or losses as volume exceeds or falls below normal, which is to some extent controlled by the buying segment. If budgeted volume were used, the producer could also have gains or losses as volume varied from the budgeted level, if policy did not provide for those to be passed on to the buyer.

This method does provide an incentive to the producer to meet or beat its standards and budgets, so that it will attain or exceed the desired return on invested capital. At the same time, profits of the buyer will not be affected by efficiencies or inefficiencies of the producer. Only to the extent that achieved efficiency is reflected in the standards for the next budget period will it be passed on to the buyer in that and future periods.

Where the total standard cost per unit plus profit method is used for setting transfer prices, there is usually a provision for adjustments for changes in material prices and wage and salary rates. The

---

[3] Some might argue that at least a portion of the budgeted administrative costs (perhaps marketing costs too) of the producing division should be included in the transfer price.

effect of these is passed on to the buying segment, which must then decide if its prices to customers should be changed accordingly.

Standard Cost Plus Profit—Variable Cost Per Unit Plus Lump-Sum Fixed Costs. Using a total standard cost per unit can be criticized because it unitizes fixed costs and treats them as if they are variable. This argument is the earlier discussed direct costing vs. absorption costing issue.

Accountants who prefer not to unitize fixed costs use the standard variable manufacturing cost per unit plus a lump-sum portion of the fixed manufacturing costs per year. This method is often referred to as a *two-part* transfer price. The lump-sum portion should be determined as a historical annual percentage of the normal or past average volume of the producing unit acquired by the buying unit.[4] This method is illustrated below using the same basic data as before, the desired return on variable capital as an addition to variable costs and the desired return on fixed capital as an addition to fixed costs.

Unit standard cost:		
Direct material		$ 1.00
Direct labor		.60
Variable manufacturing overhead		.40
Total variable manufacturing cost per unit		$ 2.00
Plus desired return on variable invested capital -		
15% x 20% of variable manufacturing cost		
(.15 x .2 x 2)		.06
Total variable charge per unit		$ 2.06
Fixed manufacturing overhead budgeted	$ 16,000	
Normal volume - 10,000 units		
Historical percentage acquired by buying unit	40 %	
Lump-sum portion of fixed manufacturing		
overhead (.4 x 16,000)	$ 6,400	
Plus desired return on fixed invested capital		
using same historical percentage acquired		
by buying unit (.15 x .40 x 20,000)	1,200	
Total fixed charge per year		$ 7,600

This method to determining a transfer price can give rise to much discussion in any classroom or industrial setting. Both the theory and the method of quantifying the theory behind this approach will definitely be a part of such discussions. Nonetheless, this method represents the only available approach to treating fixed costs as fixed costs.

▸ Opportunity to Purchase From External Sellers

Transfer prices established via list prices or a formula such as "standard cost plus profit" shouldn't present any difficulties as long as the list prices are based on actual market conditions and the formulas are reasonable. Negotiated transfer prices, however, can present difficulties if buying segments are captive customers of selling segments. The reason for such difficulties is that it is unlikely that a seller will give as much consideration to a customer that it cannot lose as to one that can take the business elsewhere. For this reason, many companies which have a policy of selling

---

[4] For additional related commentary on lump-sum apportionments of fixed costs, see Chapter 14 under "Product Line Income Statements - Additional Analytical Issues."

between units and measuring their profit, couple it with a statement permitting the buying unit to purchase the products outside the company if internal transfer prices are unsatisfactory to it.

The opportunity to purchase outside the company places the buying unit on an equal footing with the selling unit in negotiating prices. The seller must meet competitive outside offers or lose the business. The seller does not have a captive customer. The policy of permitting purchases from outside firms cannot be a tongue-in-cheek policy if it is to be effective. Top management must encourage the practice with praise for the buyer who secured lower prices and possible censure for the company unit which lost the business.

With the ability to purchase outside, the interest of a division manager may run counter to the interest of the overall organization. This is the goal congruence issue which has been mentioned in earlier chapters and again in this chapter. By purchasing externally a division may lower its costs, but the difference may not be enough to offset the lower profit contribution of the division which loses the internal sale. In such a case, top management may be sufficiently concerned that it may want to consider over-ruling an external purchase. This issue is discussed in the next section.

▸ RESPONSIBILITY REPORTING VS. EFFECTIVE DECISION-MAKING: A CASE OF GOAL CONGRUENCE ◂

The issue concerning the conflict between responsibility accounting and effective decision-making was well put many years ago by Howard C. Greer:[5]

> "If a manager is to be judged by the reported profitability of his division, pressure is on him to do two things:
>
> 1. Take whatever steps seem indicated to maximize the profits of his division, regardless of their effect on other divisions, or on the company as a whole.
> 2. Apply himself to manipulating the profit measurement procedures to his individual advantage, at the expense of other division heads less concerned or less influential.
>
> It may be properly said, of course, that the division manager should be broad enough in outlook to put company advantage ahead of division advantage, but if that is expected of him or her, it is unjust and ineffective to set up a measure of performance which has precisely the opposite bias."

Some might think that Greer overstated his case. However, there is much truth in Greer's commentary and thus it behooves us to consider the general nature of the problem posed by him.

With regard to Greer's second point on manipulating profit measurement procedures, divisions should be organized so that they are as self-contained as possible and the impact of transfer prices on divisional performance is minimized. Divisions conducting less than 10 percent of their business internally should not normally be too concerned with the issues discussed here. If the amount of internal business is 20 percent, 30 percent, or even higher, there could be a problem. Such problems should be minimized by the use of transfer prices based upon list prices and/or company-wide formulas. However, when the size of a specific transaction is perceived to be significant and there is an opportunity to purchase from external sellers at a lower price, Greer's first point could easily become a major difficulty.

---

[5] Howard C. Greer, "Divisional Profit Calculation—Notes on the Transfer Price Problem, "*N.A.A. Bulletin*, vol. 63, p. 6, July 1962.

As to Greer's first point, accountants must be aware of possible conflicts of interest between divisions and the company as a whole. What is a manager supposed to do when his or her own best interests are served by purchasing from a lower-priced external source but the company as a whole suffers profit-wise if the external purchase is made? Certainly the manager would at least be torn between two distinct loyalties—the division vs. the firm. To have him or her inconsiderate of either the division or the firm as a whole would be neither natural nor desirable. Thus, accountants should try to develop a framework within which a reasonable approach to settling the conflict of interest can be achieved. With this in mind, we offer a *market forces* framework which has both conceptual and pragmatic merit.

Our approach would first involve a negotiation of transfer prices on a periodic basis, for example every six months or every year. Negotiations more frequent than every six months run the risk of excessive use of executive time, whereas negotiations less often than every year run the risk of using transfer prices not in tune with the times. Attached to these negotiations would be an explicit statement that whenever an external market price is lower than the transfer price (and quality and delivery schedules are comparable), market forces would be allowed to run their course without interference from higher management. The essence of this approach is that divisional managers are encouraged to make their own decisions based upon their more intimate and detailed knowledge. Why should top management interfere when they have a lesser degree of knowledge? As stated earlier, top management interference would negate the notion of decentralized profit responsibility.

All that top management should require is proper notice of an impending decision to purchase externally in amounts exceeding a certain threshold. This would guarantee that top management would only interfere in cases of significance and it would also put pressure on divisional managers to settle their own disputes. In addition, top management should require a report from each division on a periodic basis (e.g., monthly or quarterly) concerning all external purchases made where an internal supplier is available. This report would also put pressure on divisional managers to settle their own differences in a reasonable manner.

▸ Market Forces at Work—General

In order to describe the expected consequences of reliance on market forces, the following general comments are offered. Market forces should yield satisfactory internal or external transactions as long as internal units are aware of these market forces and their incremental costs,[6] revenues and invested capital.

This awareness of incremental items and market forces should be considered in terms of at least a three-to-five year time frame. Thus, the illustrations below should be thought of in terms of their expected long-term consequences such as long-term profitability and keeping legitimate alternative sources of supply open and available for future needs.

▸ Market Forces at Work—Internal Purchase at Transfer Price

The brief example below illustrates the point. Assume variable and incremental costs are equivalent, there are no incremental items of invested capital and that quality and delivery terms are equal for internal and external transactions.

Units involved	1,000,000
Unit variable cost to produce	$ 2.65
Transfer price	$ 3.00
External market price	$ 3.25

---

[6] Incremental costs are referred to as *out-of-pocket costs* when costs are measured in terms of cash flow.

In this case, the internal buying unit would buy from the internal producing unit at the transfer price because it is lower than the external market price. An internal buying unit would not buy a comparable product externally at a $0.25 per unit premium. At a volume of one million units, the buying unit would lose $250,000 if it purchased externally. If the price differential were smaller, an occasional external purchase might be considered to develop and keep open alternative sources of supply. In some instances, it might even be appropriate to have an external supplier for some portion of a division's needs (if costs, quality and delivery terms are reasonable) in order to have an alternative source of supply.

Interestingly, in a situation such as this the producing unit might find it more advantageous to sell to an outsider at the higher external market price. To offset this, there should normally be a difference between transfer prices and external market prices which approximates the cost differential between selling to outsiders and selling internally. Major items in this cost differential are the costs of selling, transporting and marketing to outsiders. This is the basic reason for using list prices minus a discount to establish transfer prices.

▶ Market Forces at Work—Internal Purchase at External Market Price

In the situation below, note that the only difference from the previous case is a $0.50 per unit lower external market price. The internal buying unit should buy from the internal producing unit at the external market price; a legitimately lower external market price should force reduction of the transfer price to or near the external market price.

Units involved	1,000,000
Unit variable cost to produce	$ 2.65
Transfer price	$ 3.00
External market price	$ 2.75

If market forces coupled with common sense negotiations between buying and selling segments *are ignored*, the following scenario might prevail. Since the external market price is lower than the transfer price, the buying segment would gain by an external purchase. The amount of the gain is $0.25 per unit ($3.00 - $2.75) which at a volume of one million units would mean a total gain of $250,000 for the buying segment. However, the producing segment would suffer a loss of $0.35 per unit ($3.00 - $2.65) or $350,000 in total because of an external purchase. Thus, the company as a whole would suffer a $ 100,000 loss with the external purchase, calculated as follows:

Loss by the producing segment . .	$ 350,000
Gain by the buying segment	250,000
Net loss to the company	$ 100,000

Ignoring market forces yields a goal congruence problem since the external purchase produces a gain for the buying unit which is more than offset by the loss of the selling unit. Some would suggest that in such a case top management should overrule the external purchase and force an internal purchase at the external price. The position of the authors is that market forces and a *hands off* policy on the part of top management should produce essentially the same result without negative side effects. The goal congruence issue should disappear and top management would not destroy the essence of decentralization by overruling more informed decentralized decision-makers.

Assuming that internal buying and selling units are aware of the incremental effects of their decisions, market forces plus common sense negotiations should cause a reduction in the transfer price. This should effect an internal purchase at the external market price which would avoid the net loss to the company and still give a profit incentive to the buying segment as well as a cost reduction and control incentive to the producing segment.

Under these circumstances, the buying segment would retain its $250,000 gain and the producing segment would only lose $250,000 (their profit falls from $.35 to $.10 per unit). The company as a whole would produce at an incremental cost of $2.65 rather than purchase at the external market price of $2.75, thus avoiding a loss of $0.10 per unit or $100,000. The producing segment would suffer most, which ought to give the producing segment a cost reduction and control incentive.

The key to the prospects of the company as a whole is the difference between the unit variable cost to produce ($2.65) and the external market price ($2.75). It is to the company's advantage to let the market encourage an intercompany sale when the incremental cost is lower than the external market price per unit. The buying segment and the company as a whole are more profitable and the selling segment is given an appropriate incentive to *shape up*.

▸ Market Forces at Work—External or Internal Purchase at External Market Price

In the situation below, note that the only difference from the previous case is a $0.20 per unit increase in the unit variable cost. In this situation, market forces could easily produce a purchase outside the company.

Units involved	1,000,000
Unit variable cost to produce	$ 2.85
Transfer price	$ 3.00
External market price	$ 2.75

Again, since the external market price is lower than the transfer price, the buying segment would gain by an external purchase. The amount of the gain is $0.25 per unit ($3.00 - $2.75) which at a volume of one million units would mean a gain of $250,000 for the buying segment. However, the producing segment would suffer a loss of $0.15 per unit ($3.00 - $2.85) or $150,000 in total because of the external purchase. Thus, the company as a whole would benefit to the extent of $100,000 by an outside purchase, calculated as follows:

Gain by the buying segment	$ 250,000
Loss by the producing segment	150,000
Net gain to the company	$ 100,000

In this particular case, the solution is easily seen by looking at the difference between the unit variable cost to produce ($2.85) and the external market price ($2.75). Substituting an external purchase for an internal purchase would save $0.10 per unit and thus a total saving of $ 100,000 with a volume of one million units.

Solution by external purchase may cripple the internal producing unit and ultimately force it into liquidation. This should not be taken lightly since liquidation is a long-term decision having many side effects.[7] If the producing segment considers itself capable of reducing costs and making itself more competitive, market forces should produce an internal purchase at the external market price

---

[7] An external purchase in circumstances like these could ultimately put the company at the mercy of an external supplier who could subsequently raise prices. Caution must be exercised in order to protect the long term interests of the company. Multiple external suppliers might be appropriate unless a very cooperative long-term sole supplier relationship can be established.

even though the producing segment will suffer a loss in the short term. Again, internal units and the company as a whole are better off if market forces are allowed to prevail.

▸ Market Forces at Work—Some Conclusions

As indicated above, the issue of goal congruence should not be much of a problem if market forces are allowed to run their course. The essence of decentralization is preserved (i.e., those who are more informed are allowed and encouraged to make their own decisions). Profit and cost control incentives are encouraged while the overall good of the organization prevails.

However, the reader should recognize that there are circumstances where market and organizational forces may not work well enough to let them prevail. Top management may in such cases feel that they must intervene. Organizational factors which may force intervention are uncooperative personnel in decentralized units and decentralized units which are not sufficiently self-contained.

A market factor which may force intervention is competitive conditions, which are so intense today on a national and international scale that market forces in many lines of business must be monitored at the corporate level. This may run counter to the essence of decentralization, but that's the world as it is today. One need only think of the increasing impact of international cartels and national subsidization of industries such as copper, steel and automobiles during the 1980's to realize that market forces are more complex than ever.

▸ ALTERNATIVES TO TRANSFER PRICES ◂

Use of transfer prices gives life to the concept of an *investment center*. Without transfer prices, many of the responsibility centers within a company would remain *cost centers* or simple profit centers such as sales territories. There is nothing wrong with using cost and profit centers, but if such centers can be tied more closely to the major financial goals of the enterprise (i.e., a satisfactory return on invested capital), a company should do so. The use of investment centers provides an opportunity to restate the goals of cost and profit centers into forms which approximate more closely the return on invested capital concept.

Unfortunately, there are many difficulties involved in implementing intercompany transfer prices, particularly where goods transferred from one company segment to another are not also sold to outsiders or available from outsiders. When management finds that the difficulties and problems inherent in setting transfer prices are not worth the effort, they may decide to rely solely on the other measures of performance which are available. These other measures include many which were specifically mentioned in Chapter 13 under "Budget Variance Analysis and the Control Process."

Considering the other measures available, a lack of transfer prices and investment centers will not cause serious damage in many instances. The reports that result from transfer prices are just one of many available measures of performance. Profits and return on invested capital can be controlled without them in cases where the implementation of transfer prices is considered to be inappropriate and/or not worth the effort.

▸ SUMMARY ◂

Transfer prices are an absolute necessity if a company desires to measure rate of return or residual income by company units. However, the determination of transfer prices can be exceedingly difficult and in some cases impossible, without the use of top management's valuable time and discretion to resolve arguments. Thus, in some cases it may be desirable to forego using transfer prices and divisional rate of return or residual income and use other available measures of performance which will still enable management to control profits and return on invested capital.

▶ *QUESTIONS* ◀

17-1. What is meant by responsibility reporting and information reporting?

17-2. Distinguish between responsibility reporting and information reporting with specific reference to the elements of cost and invested capital relevant to each.

17-3. What purpose might be served by an information report?

17-4. In terms of responsibility reporting, distinguish between a cost center, a profit center, and an investment center.

17-5. In terms of information reporting, distinguish between a cost center, a profit center, and an investment center.

17-6. What difficulties are involved in determining the controllable revenues of a division if the division has no dealings of any kind with other company divisions?

17-7. If, regardless of the transfer price charged by one division to another, the net income of the company as a whole is not affected, why should management worry about transfer pricing?

17-8. What is the objective of transfer pricing at other than cost?

17-9. Why might a list price less a discount be more appropriate as a transfer price than a list price without a discount?

17-10. If an internal buying unit cannot buy from external sources because none exist or because management will not permit such a practice, is this a good reason to forgo a responsibility approach to divisional profit reporting? Discuss.

17-11. If an internal producing unit cannot sell to external sources because none exist or because management will not permit such a practice, is this a good reason to forgo a responsibility approach to divisional profit reporting? Discuss.

17-12. Can it be said that a combination of negotiation and ability to purchase and sell externally would most likely yield a transfer price based upon "list prices minus a discount?" Discuss.

17-13. What factors might have tendency to limit a manager's ability to manipulate the elements involved in divisional profit calculations?

17-14. What is meant by a potential conflict of interests between divisional responsibility reporting and effective decision-making?

17-15. Of what value is a comparison between unit variable or incremental cost to produce a product and unit purchase price of the same product from external sources of supply?

17-16. For what reasons might one consider transfer prices too difficult to deal with and thus substitute alternatives to transfer prices?

► EXERCISES ◄

17-17. Internal Reporting vs. External Reporting.
When transfers of product from one department to another are made in a manufacturing company, often the charge to the receiving department is made at a figure in excess of cost to the producing department.

Required:

a. Why is this practice followed? Explain.
b. In terms of external financial reporting, is there any need to eliminate the effect of these transfers in excess of cost? Discuss.

17-18. Responsibility Reporting vs. Information Reporting.
Rhoda Island, the manager of the Eastern Region of the Smaller Company received the following income statement for her region:

Eastern Region
Income Statement
For the Year Ending June 30, 20x1

Sales		$2,250,000
Cost of goods sold		1,440,000
Gross profit		$ 810,000
Operating expenses:		
Marketing	$ 620,850	
Administrative	190,000	810,850
Regional net loss		$ (850)

Rhoda Island was very discouraged with these results. She feels that because she is not in control of all expenses, a special report illustrating her profit responsibility should be prepared.

The following is a breakdown of the marketing expenses for the region:

Advertising and promotion	$ 75,000
Commissions (5% of sales)	112,500
Depreciation	27,300
Marketing vice president (allocated)	67,500
Rent	45,000
Sales manager's salary	112,500
Sales persons and office salaries	96,000
Stationery and postage	19,950
Telephone and communication	20,100
Travel	45,000
Total marketing expenses	$ 620,850

Note: Cost of goods sold is $1,120,000 variable and $320,000 fixed. All administrative expenses are allocated corporate costs.

Required:

a. Prepare a regional profit responsibility report for the Eastern Region of the Smaller Company.

b. Comment on Rhoda Island's performance using your answer to part (a) above.

17-19. Responsibility Reporting vs. Information Reporting.
The following is the income statement for the Western Region of the Bigger Company for the period ending June 30, 20x1.

Western Region
Income Statement
For the Year Ending June 30, 20x1

Sales		$ 15,750,000
Cost of goods sold		10,029,000
Gross profit		$ 5,721,000
Operating expenses:		
Marketing	$ 3,750,000	
Administrative	630,000	4,380,000
Regional net income		$ 1,341,000

Further analysis showed the following breakdown of costs and expenses:

	Manufacturing	Marketing	Division Office	Allocated Corporate Office
Variable . . .	$ 6,975,000	$ 825,000		
Fixed	3,054,000	2,925,000	$ 315,000	$ 315,000

Required:

Prepare a profitability report for the Western Region of the Bigger Company for Callie Fornia, the division president.

17-20. Calculating a Transfer Price.
The Comfort Fit Athletic, Inc. Manufacturing Division makes and sells fleece-lined sweatshirts externally. They also sell the sweatshirts to other company units for printing, sewing or embossing and resale as team and/or group souvenir merchandise.

Comfort Fit's policy is to establish transfer prices by setting discounts from list prices that allow the Manufacturing Division to earn the same percentage return on its capital employed in manufacturing on both trade and intracompany sales. Ten percent of the capital invested is related to the marketing function and there is little or no effort on intracompany sales.

The list price of the sweatshirt is $10, cash discount and freight allowances are 8 percent of list price and marketing expenses are 9 percent of list price. Manufacturing costs are $5.06 per sweatshirt.

Required:

Calculate the transfer price.

17-21.   Service Department Cost Allocation as a Transfer Price.

Redneck Industries has a highly automated tool shop. Fixed costs represent 75 percent of the costs to operate the shop, total budgeted costs per month amount to $275,000. Joe Bob Carter, the manager of Redneck's maintenance department was continually complaining that any work he had done in the tool shop was too expensive. He arbitrarily contracted out a large tooling job stating that "this job will only cost the department $22,670 by contracting it out, whereas the tool shop quoted a figure of approximately $30,000; on this basis my department will save over $7,000."

Required:

a.   Comment on Joe Bob's statement that the department will save over $7,000.
b.   Should the tooling department have matched the external price?

17-22.   Calculate a Transfer Price Using Various Methods.

The Halifax Company produces a line of frozen fish packs for sale to retail grocery stores. Halifax is decentralized into two main operating divisions, the fish preparation division and the fish packing and freezing division. Halifax Company wants to establish these divisions as a profit centers and consequently must arrive at a transfer price for the fillets "sold" by the preparation division to the packing and freezing division. The historical and projected cost data below were provided by the Halifax Company's managerial accountant.

	Actual Cost Per Fillet (last period)	Standard Cost Per Fillet
Direct material	$ 1.00	$ 1.95
Direct labor	2.00	.90
Overhead:		
Variable	.20	.30
Fixed	.15*	.30**
Total	$ 3.35	$ 3.45

Current market price per fillet	4.00
External sales and promotional expense per fillet	.10
Per-fillet profit factor for cost-plus techniques	.20
Per-unit fixed overhead for cost-plus techniques	.50

*   Based on 1,200 fillets actually prepared
** Based on 2,000 fillets normally prepared

Required:

a.   Using the information above, determine the price that will be assigned to a transfer of 1,200 fillets under reach of the following transfer pricing methods:

1.   Full actual cost per unit
2.   Standard cost per unit
3.   Standard cost plus profit per unit

   4. List price per unit
   5. List price minus per unit
   b. Which of these methods do you prefer and why? Is there a method not listed above which you might prefer? Why?

17-23. Impact of Negotiation and Ability to Buy and Sell Externally.
   The Frame-A-Home Company manufactures wooden picture frames which can be sold outright or used in the manufacture of framed artist prints. Picture frames and framed artwork are produced in two separate divisions. Picture frames can also be purchased from outside suppliers.

Required:

   a. If negotiation between the two divisions was required in order to establish a transfer price, what type of internal price (e.g., cost plus, list price, etc.) would be established if the frame division could sell externally and the artwork division could buy externally?
   b. How might this process of negotiation work if the external market price is $5.00 and the preliminary offer of the artwork division is $4.00?
   c. How might this process of negotiation work if the external market price is $5.00 and the preliminary offer of the frame division is $5.25? $5.00?
   d. How might this process of negotiation work if an external supplier offers a price of $5.00, the demand of the frame division is $5.50, and the unit variable cost of the frame division is $4.50? Should corporate headquarters dictate a price between $4.50 and $5.00 if the two parties could not agree?

▶ PROBLEMS AND CASES ◀

17-24. A Transfer Pricing Decision.
   The Industrial Specialties Division of The Fiberboard Company does not have a board-forming unit in their division. They buy large fiberboard blanks from the Building Products Division, which also sells the blanks to outsiders.
   Negotiations on transfer prices last year resulted in a transfer price of $47 per thousand square feet, which was $3 less than the external price. Total manufacturing costs per thousand square feet of fiberboard were $45. Sales to outsiders amounted to 1 billion square feet, which was 80 percent of total sales. Intra-company sales have usually averaged about 20 percent of total sales.
   No marketing costs were incurred on intracompany sales. Marketing costs related to fiberboard were $1,500,000, of which $500,000 were fixed. All administrative costs related to fiberboard were fixed and amounted to $200,000 last year. Of the manufacturing costs, an average of $3 per thousand square feet was represented by fixed costs.

Required:

   a. In negotiations for the current year, the Industrial Specialties Division is holding out for a transfer price of $46 based on an external supplier's offer of $46. What do you suggest?
   b. Would your suggestion in part (a) above change if the Building Products Division could replace intracompany sales with sales to outsiders at prices of $46 or above? Below $46?

c. If an external supplier offered a price of $43, what would you suggest? A price of $42? Below $42?

17-25. A Transfer Pricing Decision.

Company B has several product divisions. Each of these has its own manufacturing facilities and sells all or most of its output to outside customers. The company's policy is to encourage division managers to purchase within the company whenever possible. Division managers are allowed to negotiate a transfer price based on costs of production.

One of the company's divisions, Division X, buys all of its requirements of material from Division Y. This material is one of several products manufactured in Division Y. Until recently, Division Y was willing to supply this material to Division X at a transfer price of 80 cents a pound, just a few cents more than Division Y's estimated incremental cost. Division Y is now operating at capacity and is unable to meet all of its outside customers' demands for this product at a price of $1 a pound. The manager of Division Y has threatened to cut off supplies to Division X unless the manager of Division X will agree to pay the market price.

The manager of Division X is resisting this pressure. The division's budget for the current year was based on an estimated consumption of 1 million pounds of the material each month at a price of 80 cents. Since the division's budgeted income before taxes is only $250,000 a month, a price increase to $1 would bring the division very close to the breakeven point.

The company's central purchasing office has found an outside source of an equivalent substitute material at a price of 95 cents, but the manager of Division X sees no reason to go outside when a sister division can supply the material at an 80 cent cost. If cost was measured at Division Y's full manufacturing cost of 88 cents a pound, Division X would be giving Division Y a 12 cent profit on every pound at the $1 price.

Required:

a. Where should Division X obtain its materials, from Division Y or from the outside supplier? Support your answer.
b. Given the company's transfer pricing policy, is Division X likely to obtain its materials from the source that you have recommended in your answer to part (a) above? Explain.
c. In light of your answer to parts (a) and (b), what changes, if any, would you recommend in the transfer pricing policy? Give your reasons.
(SMA adapted)

17-26. Internal Purchase Price vs. External Price.

The National Paper Company has two divisions. Operating results for the year are shown below. The Bass Division usually sells 75 percent of it output to the Toss Division at the same price charged its regular customers, $20 per unit.

	Bass	*Toss*
Sales	$ 120,000	$ 400,000
Costs:		
Transferred from Bass		90,000
Other costs—variable	31,200	70,000
Other costs—fixed	50,000	160,000
Net income before taxes	$ 38,800	$ 80,000

Required:

If the Toss Division could purchase their total requirements from an outside supplier for $18.00 a unit, should Bass Division meet this price? Assume that Bass can sell no more than 25 percent of its production to outside customers. (Consider the situation from the overall company point of view.)

17-27.   Transfer Pricing: Sell Internally or Externally.
The Caplow Company is a multi-divisional company. Its managers have been delegated full profit responsibility and complete autonomy to accept or reject transfers from other divisions.

Division A produces a subassembly with a ready competitive market. This subassembly is currently used by Division B for a final product which is sold outside at $1,200 per unit. Division A charges Division B the market price of $700 per unit for the subassembly. Variable costs are $520 per unit and $600 per unit for Divisions A and B, respectively.

The manager of Division B feels that Division A should transfer the subassembly at a lower price than market because at market price Division B is unable to make profit.

Required:

a. Assuming transfers are made at the market price, compute Division B's profit contribution per unit and the total profit contribution per unit for the company.
b. Assume that Division A can sell all its production in the open market. Should Division A transfer goods to Division B? If so, at what price?
c. Assume Division A can sell only 500 units at $700 per unit (out of the 1,000 which it can produce every month)in the open market and that a 20 percent reduction in price is necessary to sell full capacity. Should transfers be made to Division B? If so, how many units should be transferred and at what price? Submit a schedule showing comparisons of profit contribution under the different available alternatives to support your decision.
(SMA adapted)

17-28.   Various Questions on Transfer Prices.
The Gerald Company has one product and two divisions. The Alpha Division produces a major subassembly which the Omega Division incorporates into the final product. There is a market for both the subassembly and the final product. Each of the divisions is a profit center and the subassembly has a transfer price based on the long-run average market price.

The controller has made the following *per unit* data available to each division manager:

Final product selling price	$ 450
Selling price for the intermediate product	300
Out-of-pocket cost for completion in the Omega division	225
Out-of-pocket cost in the Alpha division	180

Required:

a. Should transfer be made to Omega if there is no excess capacity in the Alpha division? Is the market price the correct transfer price? Give reasons.

b. Assume that Alpha Division's maximum capacity for this product is 1,000 units per month, and sales to the outside market are presently 800 units. Should 200 units be transferred to Omega division? At what relevant transfer price? Describe your reasoning with supporting calculations. Assume for a variety of reasons that Alpha will maintain the $300 selling price indefinitely; that is, Alpha is not considering cutting the price to outsiders regardless of the presence of idle capacity.

c. Suppose Alpha quoted a transfer price of $300. What would be the contribution to the firm as a whole if the transfer was made?

d. Suppose the manager of Alpha has the option of:
   1. Cutting the external price to $290 with the certainty that sales will rise to 1,000 units, or
   2. Maintaining the outside price of $300 for the 800 units and transferring the 200 units to Omega at some price that would produce the same income for Alpha as alternative (1).

What is the transfer price that would produce the same income for Alpha?

e. Name three bases for establishing transfer prices and state which basis you would recommend to the Gerald Company in the above situation?

(SMA adapted)

17-29. An Internal Transfer Pricing Decision.

The Fabricating Department of the Solid Foundation Corporation has been purchasing the steel reinforcement rods it uses in its concrete slabs from the Metals Department of Solid Foundation. The Fabricating Department purchases approximately 90 percent of the steel rod production of the Metals Department at $150 a ton. In the current year, the Metals Department expects to have steel rod sales of approximately 1,600 tons, of which 160 tons are to outside customers for $153 a ton with terms of 2/10, N/30. Approximately 60 percent of the outside sales are paid within ten days, and about 3 percent of the outside sales are never paid.

The Fabricating Department has been negotiating with several other suppliers for these rods and finds that it can purchase them from an outside supplier for $124 a ton. Unless the Metals Department reduces its price, Fabricating will use the outside supplier.

After doing some market research, the Metals Department feels that it can sell 90 percent of its present capacity to outside customers for $153 a ton @ 2/10, N/30, or 95 percent for $150 a ton @ 2/10, N/30. Under either of these two arrangements, the Fabricating Department will buy all their steel rods from outside suppliers.

Variable costs for the steel rods are $60 a ton and fixed costs are $63,000 a year. Marketing expenses are $4.50 a ton if sold to outside customers.

Required:

What results in the negotiations between the Fabricating and Metals Departments are likely in this case?

17-30. Transfer Pricing and Divisional Performance.

The Gun Division of the Gunny Company, operating at capacity, has been asked by the Electric Division of the Gunny Company to supply it with electrical fitting #3452. Gun sells this part to its regular customers for $22.50 each. Electric, which is operating at 50 percent capacity, is willing to pay $15 each for the fitting. Electric will put the fitting into a brake unit which it is manufacturing on essentially a cost basis for a commercial airplane manufacturer.

Gun has a variable cost of producing fitting #3452 of $12.75. The cost of the brake unit as being built by Electric is as follows:

Purchased parts-outside vendors	$ 67.50
Gun Division-fitting #3452	15.00
Other variable costs	42.00
Fixed overhead	24.00
	$ 148.50

Electric believes the price concession on the fitting is necessary to retain the brake job.

The Gunny Company uses return on investment and dollar profits in the measurement of division and division manager performance.

Required:

a. Assume that you are division controller of Gun. Would you recommend that Gun supply fitting #3452 to Electric? (Ignore any income tax issue.) Why or why not?

b. Would it be to the short-run economic advantage of the Gunny Company for the Gun Division to supply the Electric Division with fitting #3452 at $15 each? (Ignore income tax issues.) Explain your answer.

c. Discuss the organizational and managerial behavior difficulties, if any, inherent in this situation. As Gunny Company controller, what would you advise the company president to do in this situation?

(CMA adapted)

17-31. Transfer Price Decisions.

Nisvana Co. is a multi-division, fully decentralized organization in which each division is responsible for both profits and investment. Divisions and their managers are evaluated on return on investment (ROI); their managers are paid a bonus based on that measure.

Division A, presently operating at about 75 percent of capacity, wishes to produce a new assembly for a potential customer. This potential customer has agreed to purchase the new assembly at a price no greater than $29.15 per unit.

In order to meet the price stipulated by the customer, the cost of the new assembly, including an allowance for part PB4, has been carefully determined as follows:

Maximum selling price		$ 29.15
Less:		
Materials	$ 17.40	
Direct labor	4.60	
Variable overhead	2.30	
Fixed overhead	1.15	
	$ 25.45	
Profit allowance on assembly	.95	$ 26.40
Amount affordable for part PB4		$ 2.75

Division A has asked Division C to supply it with part PB4, a vital component of the new assembly, at the $2.75 price. Part PB4 is a stock item currently sold externally for $4.40.

Division C is presently operating at full capacity and refuses to sell the part to Division A at less than the market price. Division A has decided to take its case to corporate management. The cost structure for part PB4 is as follows:

Materials	$ 1.30
Labor	.90
Variable overhead	.50
Fixed overhead	1.00
	$ 3.70

Required:

a. How much would Nisvana Co. gain (lose) per unit if Division C were to sell to Division A?
b. What should the transfer price be in this situation?
c. Briefly discuss the key issues to be considered by top management in deciding whether to intervene in disputes over transfer prices.

(SMA adapted)

17-32. Transfer Pricing and Return on Investment.

The Wilson Company has several product divisions, each of which produces one product. Each of these divisions has its own manufacturing facilities and sells its output to both outside customers and other sister divisions. The company's policy dictates that purchases and sales must be internal wherever possible and that transfer prices are set at 112 percent of full manufacturing cost.

Division Red buys all of its requirements of material X from Division Blue. However, a close substitute for material X can be acquired from outside sources at a unit price of $115. Until recently, Division Red required one-half of Division Blue's output. Division Red has just expanded its capacity and will require 90 percent of Division Blue's output in the future.

Division Blue is presently operating at full capacity. The manager of Division Blue is very upset because Division Red's new demand requirements will cause his return on investment to drop below the company's required return of 12 percent based on invested capital at year end.

Division Red's product has a market price of $350. Last year, the invested capital base for Division Blue and Red was $500,000 and $900,000, respectively. Income statements for last year for the two divisions are as follows:

	Division Blue		Division Red	
Sales in units		12,000		6,000
Sales		$1,350,000		$2,100,000
Direct materials	$ 489,000		$ 930,000*	
Direct labor	240,000		300,000	
Manufacturing overhead:				
Variable	132,000		150,000	
Fixed	264,000	1,125,000	360,000	1,740,000
Gross profit		$ 225,000		$ 360,000
Marketing and administrative				
expenses (all fixed)		140,000		216,000
Net income		$ 85,000		$ 144,000

* Includes costs for units transferred from Division Blue.

Sales volume and costs for Division Blue are estimated to remain unchanged.

Division Red had just made an additional $600,000 investment to the $900,000 base investment to enable its capacity to expand to 10,800 units per year. Its materials, labor, and variable overhead cost per unit will remain the same as last year. Its total fixed manufacturing overhead is estimated at $600,000 and marketing and administrative expenses are estimated at $370,000 for the coming year.

Required:

a. Using the current transfer pricing policy and assuming that all output can be sold at last year's prices, calculate the estimated ROI for both Division Blue and Division Red for the current year.
b. Assume that the company's policy allows division managers to negotiate transfer prices.
   1. What is the minimum transfer price that Division Blue could accept and still earn a minimum ROI of 12 percent?
   2. What is the maximum transfer price that Division Red could accept and still earn a minimum ROI of 12 percent?
c. Briefly discuss the behavioral consequences of the following possible policies for the Wilson Company. Consider each policy independently.
   1. Purchases and sales must be internal wherever possible and transfer prices are set at 112 percent of full manufacturing cost.
   2. Transfer prices are set at 112 percent of the full manufacturing cost; division managers have total freedom regarding whom to buy from and sell to.
   3. Purchases and sales must be internal wherever possible, but division managers have total freedom to negotiate transfer prices.

(SMA adapted)

17-33. Transfer Pricing Policy.
   Elliot Swift and Co. is a multi-divisional paper company that manufactures a variety of containers for the food packing industry. The company is vertically integrated and each of its five divisions supply both internal company needs and the external market. The head office has set a policy requiring that all divisions must satisfy internal demands before external sales may be undertaken. Divisions that transfer (or buy) internally do so at a prescribed price at full cost plus 12 percent of cost. Since head office requires each designated profit center to return a minimum of 12 percent on sales before head office allocations, the transfer price of cost plus 12 percent was considered to be a fair one.
   Not all divisions were happy with the policies of Elliot Swift and Co. The Cardboard Fabricating Division (CFD) was particularly upset recently because the selling price for its products on the external market had risen rapidly in the past three months. The price increase induced CFD's sister divisions to expand their production to maximum capacity and demand all of CFD's production at the bargain price, forcing CFD to work at 100 percent capacity servicing internal demands.
   CFD's cost and demand structure for the current month was as follows:

$$\textit{Production capacity} \quad = \quad \textit{150,000 tons}$$
$$\textit{Market price} \quad = \quad \textit{\$240 per ton}$$

Cost per ton:

Materials	$ 60
Labor	40
Overhead*	50
Total cost	$ 150

* 60 percent of overhead is fixed.

CFD believes that its production costs and the current market price will remain stable, at least for the next month. CFD's sister divisions that purchase the fabricated cardboard add $150 in costs per ton ($20 of which is fixed) for processing the cardboard and sell their final products on the open market for $400 per equivalent ton.

CFD would like to take advantage of the high external market price, but because of company policy CFD has been forced to sell exclusively to its sister divisions. CFD believes that at least 60 percent of its production would be sold outside under current conditions.

Required:

a. For the next month, using the current transfer pricing policy set by head office, determine the income to CFD, its sister divisions and the firm as a whole.

b. Using calculations, explain briefly why CFD is unhappy with the current transfer pricing policy.

c. You have been hired by Elliot Swift and Co. as a management consultant to advise them on alterations of their transfer pricing policy. Provide them with a brief description of the defects of their system and recommendations to correct it.

d. Assume that head office decides to allow CFD to set its own transfer price and to sell externally if it wishes. Also, assume that negotiations between the divisions is impossible. Describe three options available to CFD.

(SMA adapted)

17-34. Service Department Cost Allocation as a Transfer Price.

The computer center of Second National Bank and Trust calculated its budgeted costs, which were based on unit usage by the branch offices, for the coming as follows:

Branch Office	Variable Costs	Fixed Costs	Total Costs	Unit Usage
North Branch .	$ 20,300	$ 162,400	$ 182,700	2,030
South Branch .	14,000	112,000	126,000	1,400
East Branch ...	12,300	98,400	110,700	1,230
West Branch ..	26,250	210,000	236,250	2,625
Mall Branch ..	30,250	242,000	272,250	3,025
Total	$ 103,100	$ 824,800	$ 927,900	10,310
Monthly	$ 8,592	$ 68,733	$ 7,325	859

With limited discussion, the manager of the computer center received agreement from all the branch offices of the above distribution. He stated "the agreement was not surprising because the investment and costs in the computer center were based on their requirements."

After the first month of operation, the computer center's actual costs were distributed as follows:

Branch Office	Total Costs	Unit Usage
North Branch	$ 13,888	143
South Branch	10,100	105
East Branch	10,257	106
West Branch	23,222	240
Mall Branch	20,320	210
Total	$ 77,787	804

The actual costs were $77,787 for 804 units of usage for an average cost per unit of $96.75.

The manager of the West Branch Office was very upset and she stated "our branch was charged $96.75 a unit for computer services and the budget rate was only $90 a unit. Also, you would think because of the large fixed cost in the computer center's budget and the fact that our office used more units than budgeted, that we would get a better rate. "In fact, she went on, "I think we should have been charged only $19,900 as follows:

Variable cost (240 units @ $10)	$ 2,400
Fixed cost budgeted (1/12 x $210,000	17,500
Total	$19,900

What is really happening is that we are paying for the under-usage of the service by the other branches and any inefficiencies of the center."

Required:

a. Comment on the statements made by the manager of the West Branch Office.
b. Discuss various ways that the computer center could charge out its services.
c. Illustrate the method you believe is best.

17-35. Evaluate Alternative Allocation Methods.

The Yacky Company Limited has three divisions: the Processing Division, the Wabit Division, and the Booster Division. Management has decided to shut down the Booster Division as it showed a net loss on last year's income statement (absorption costing). An examination of the income statement for the Booster Division and overall company operations reveals the following:

1. The direct material used by the Booster Division is called Aon and is received from the Processing Division. The Processing Division takes unrefined ore and puts it through a process which results in 45 percent output of Aon, 40 percent output of Bon (used by the Wabit Division) and 15 percent output of Con which is a by-product sold externally by the Processing Division each year. The Booster Division is charged 45 percent of the cost of purchasing and processing the unrefined ore.

2. Sales in the Booster Division last year consisted of 50,000 units with production of 30,000 units (inventories were depleted in anticipation of a shut-down).

3. The Wabit Division and the Booster Division share the same operating plant; therefore, depreciation on the building is allocated to the divisions based on the square footage

occupied. All other common general and administrative costs are allocated based on the actual sales revenue achieved by each division in the year.

4. Computer facilities (90% of all costs are fixed) are shared by the Wabit and the Booster Divisions with actual costs allocated based on the actual number of hours of computer time used. Last year, the Wabit Division cut back drastically on its use of computer time in order to increase divisional profitability.

Required:

Evaluate the company's cost allocation and performance evaluation methods and the company's decision to drop the Booster Division. Recommend an alternative where appropriate. (SMA adapted)

17-36. Service Departments and "Two Part" Transfer Prices.

Service department costs are incurred for the purpose of facilitating the operations of producing departments. Thus, the service department costs are, in reality, costs of the producing departments, and each producing department should bear the burden of their proportionate shares of service department costs.

In order to properly assign proportionate shares to each producing department, the costs of each service department should be segregated into fixed and variable portions. The fixed costs are incurred to be *ready to serve*, and thus they should be distributed on the basis of the average requirements (normal volume) of each producing department. The variable costs are incurred in order *actually to serve*, and thus they should be distributed on the basis of the actual service rendered.

An illustration of this method follows for a power service department (Service Department C):

Schedule of Horsepower Hours

	Producing Departments		Other Service Departments	
	A	*B*	*A*	*B*
Needed at normal volume	10,000	20,000	12,000	8,000
Used during the month	8,000	13,000	7,000	6,000

During the month of April, the expenses of operating the power service department amounted to $27,900; of the amount $7,500 were considered to be fixed costs. Assume budgeted and actual costs are equal.

**Proportion of Power Service Department Hours Needed
and Used by Other Departments**

	Normal Volume		Actual Usage	
	Amount	*Proportion*	*Amount*	*Proportion*
Producing departments:				
A	$10,000	10/50	$ 8,000	8/34
B	20,000	20/50	13,000	13/34

Other service
departments:

A	12,000	12/50	7,000	7/34
B	8,000	8/50	6,000	6/34
Total	$50,000	50/50	$34,000	34/34

Distribution of Power Service Departments Costs

	Producing Departments				Other Service Departments			
	A		*B*		*A*		*B*	
Fixed costs:*								
($7,500)	10/50	$1,500	20/50	$ 3,000	12/50	$1,800	8/50	$1,200
Variable costs:*								
($20,400)	8/34	4,800	13/34	7,800	7/34	4,200	6/34	3,600
Total		$6,300		$10,800		$6,000		$4,800

* Fixed costs per hour at normal volume are $.15 ($7,500/50,000) and variable costs per hour at actual volume are $.60 ($20,400/34,000).

Required:

Discuss the statements and illustration above in terms of its appropriateness for distributing service department costs.
(AICPA adapted)

17-37. Various Approaches to Charging Departments With Service Department Charges.
The Dartmouth Company charges its maintenance department costs to the other departments on an actual basis (i.e., it charges all its costs on an hourly average actual cost basis).

Some departments feel that the hourly budgeted average cost rate should be used. Others argue that the budgeted fixed cost dollars plus the hourly average variable actual cost rate should be used.

The maintenance budget is based on an estimated 12,500 hours per month required by the user departments. The maintenance department budgeted fixed costs to be $32,250 and variable costs of $69,000.

The total budgeted cost for budgetary purposes was allocated to the five departments, based on their estimated hours submitted to the maintenance department, as follows:

		Budgeted
Department	*Hours*	*Cost*
Ace	3,750	$ 30,375
Bass	4,250	34,452
Case	2,050	16,605
Debase	1,400	11,340
Efface	1,050	8,505
Total	12,500	$ 101,250

*$101,250 ÷ 12,500 hours = $8.10 an hour

The maintenance department actually worked 11,400 hours and accumulated cost of $94,620 for the month. The actual cost per hour and the following actual hours per department were used to determine departmental actual costs.

Department	Hours
Ace	4,800
Bass	3,150
Case	2,180
Debase	1,060
Efface	210
Total	11,400

Required:

a. The manager of Ace Department is disturbed with the large variance between actual cost charged, $39,840, and the budget of $30,375, shown on his report. He argues that because fixed costs do not vary, his charge should not increase proportionally with his increase in production. The manager feels the amount charged should be only the budgeted fixed cost dollars on the number of hours his department used. He calculates this amount to be $35,931 which he deems to be fairer amount. Discuss.

b. Discuss what method you would recommend to charge the user department with the maintenance costs.

1. The actual rate (i.e., actual costs - actual hours).
2. The budgeted rate (i.e. budgeted costs - budgeted hours).
3. Budgeted fixed cost dollars plus actual variable cost rate.
4. Budgeted fixed cost dollars plus budgeted variable cost rate.

Note: The charges to the user department will be different under methods (2) and (4) above.

Learning Objectives

After reading this chapter, the student should have an understanding of:

✔ Common types of environmental costs.

✔ The relationship between environmental costs and profits.

✔ The difference between a compliance and a prevention approach to environmental cost management.

✔ How reducing pollution can increase profits.

✔ The impact of pollution costs on capital expenditure analysis and break-even analysis.

✔ Some aspects of tracking pollution costs.

✔ External reporting aspects of environmental information.

The number of environmental regulations exceeds the number of tax regulations;[1] SEC requirements compel companies to report information on potential environmental costs to stockholders; and executives can serve jail time for environmental crimes.[2] Thus, managers cannot ignore the environment, and accountants must know how to develop financial analyses to support management decisions that affect the environment.

In this chapter we apply the tools and techniques described earlier in the book to specific cost and revenue problems related to pollution. For example, we examine the economics of pollution prevention, the tracking of pollution costs, the analysis of pollution cost prevention investments, and the external reporting requirements for pollution costs.

► ECONOMIC ASPECTS OF ENVIRONMENTAL COSTS ◄

We define environmental cost broadly to include the cost of any waste generated by a company to produce its main product. Our objective is to demonstrate cost and revenue analyses related to these costs rather than to provide a perfect definition of such costs. Accordingly, we include the costs of solid waste disposal, the sewer charges a company pays, and the legal fees it pays to obtain permits for waste discharge as part of the environmental costs of a company.

► Types of Environmental Costs

Environmental costs take a variety of forms, and we review some of them here. Companies already record most of these costs, but they usually do not specifically identify them as environmental costs. For example, waste disposal costs fall into the category of environmental costs although most companies include these in general operating costs. Also, the costly process of obtaining a permit to dispose of chemical waste at a plant may be scattered among legal expenses, outside contractor expenses, consulting expenses, accounting expenses, and several other cost categories. In this chapter we highlight these costs to illustrate how managers can evaluate the profit consequences of decisions that generate an environmental impact.

Routine pollution costs. Routine pollution costs include the costs of reducing existing pollution, cleaning up existing emissions, and paying penalties on the emissions not cleaned up. The Environmental Protection Agency estimated that U.S. firms spent over $100 billion on these activities in

---

[1] Carey, Bill, "Don't Understand the Laws? Hire An Attorney to Help," *The Tennessean*, Nashville, TN (December 12, 1993), p. E1.
[2] Cohen, Mark A., "Environmental Crime and Punishment: Legal/Economic Theory and Empirical Evidence on Enforcement of Federal Environmental Statutes," *The Journal of Criminal Law & Criminology* (Winter, 1992), pp. 1054-1108.

1990, and it forecast an increase to $200 billion by 1995.[3] The German chemical company, Bayer, spends as much annually on environmental costs as it does on labor.[4] Routine pollution costs can be more significant than labor costs.

Waste disposal Costs. Waste disposal costs consist of the fees a company pays to a firm that specializes in hauling away waste materials and scrap generated by a company's operations. Twenty five years ago these costs were minor. Waste disposal companies charged only $2.50 per ton to dump hazardous waste in a landfill in 1978 versus $200 per ton in 1988. Companies paid $50 per ton to burn waste in 1978 versus $200, or up to $2,000 for some types of extremely hazardous wastes, in 1987. In 1983 garbage companies charged $3 per ton to remove consumer trash, but in 1993 consumers can pay up to $130 per ton for the same service.[5]

Product costs. Environmental regulations also affect product costs. In fact, in some cases such regulations cause companies to phase out products, e.g., chlorofluorocarbons (CFC's), more commonly called freon. Many pesticides are heavily regulated and others such as DDT are banned outright in the U.S.

The automobile companies spend billions of dollars trying to comply with emissions requirements. For example, General Motors is spending $1.3 billion to comply with the California requirement that 10% of all cars sold in California have zero emissions.

Packaging costs. The amount a company expends to package its products can create significant costs for the company making the product and additional costs for the customers who must dispose of the packaging. Attention to packaging costs allowed Hyde Tool, a Massachusetts manufacturer of light tools, to reduce its purchases of packaging materials by eight tons per year. In the process it increased its own profits and reduced the disposal costs of its customers.

This brief discussion illustrates some of the environmental costs managers must manage. The next section reviews the relationship between environmental costs and profits.

► Environmental Cost Relationships [6]

Although, at first glance, one would think environmental costs always reduce profits, a closer examination reveals a different story. An expenditure on pollution control reduces company profits only if the expenditure creates no offsetting returns. A polluting firm can actually reduce its environmental costs in several ways:

♦   Use or reuse of recovered pollutants
♦   Sale of recovered pollutants, and
♦   Reduction of damage pollutants cause in the firm's production process

This relation between the expenditure on pollution abatement and the return from use or sale of the recovered pollutant is crucial in computing the profit effect of a given expenditure. The fact that virtually anything has a use at some price with some technology creates problems for analyses of pollution expenditures because future returns from pollution abatement expenditures are difficult to predict.

Nonetheless, a firm should evaluate alternative pollution abatement expenditures in terms of their profit impact. For example, in 1975, oil refineries were able to gain significantly greater benefits from expenditures to clean air than from expenditures to clean water. Floating roof tanks

[3] Environmental Protection Agency, *Environmental Investments: The Cost of a Clean Environment* (Washington, D.C.: EPA, 1990)
[4] *The Economist*, September 8, 1990, p.12.
[5] Buchholz, R.A., A.A. Marcus, and J. E. Post, *Managing Environmental Issues* (Englewood Cliffs, NJ: Prentice-Hall, 1992), pp.179-180.
[6] This discussion is adapted from Boothe, Joan Norris, *Cleaning Up: The Cost of Refinery Pollution Control* (New York: Council on Economic Priorities, 1975), pp. 33-50.

illustrate this. In a refinery, the sulfur recovered from hydrogen sulfide emissions and the hydrocarbons recovered by floating roof tanks provide valuable by-products from refinery pollution control efforts. A floating roof tank prevents evaporation and almost completely eliminates the release of hydrocarbons from storage tanks into the surrounding air. These roofs eliminate a source of air pollution, but, at 1975 price levels for petroleum products, they were a good investment because of the loss of product they also eliminated.

Carbon monoxide (CO) boilers provide another example; they enable a refinery to produce steam for power by burning wastes from fluid catalytic crackers. Refineries can flare the significant quantities of gases produced from crude oil processing thereby contributing to air pollution, or they can use the gases as a cheap source of fuel to reduce total production costs.

Identifying pollution costs is not always easy because they come in different forms. For example, accountants can divide pollution costs into two categories: costs of equipment, and costs of changing operating procedures and installing more meticulous housekeeping. As an illustration, a company can purchase equipment it will use strictly to control pollution with little relation to the production process, or it can spend money for environmentally motivated changes in the production process.

An engineer who chooses a cleaner, more expensive production process over a cheaper, dirtier alternative, does incur some expense for pollution control, even though the expenditure is not classified as a pollution abatement expenditure. For example, an engineer who chooses air cooling towers, which greatly reduce refinery water use and therefore water pollution, in preference to water cooling methods, causes the company to spend more on cooling towers. This added investment is appropriately called a pollution abatement cost even though the accounting system might not classify it as such.

Changing operating procedures to control pollution may or may not increase operating costs. Consider the case of sulfur oxides (SOx). A refinery can control SOx in a variety of ways. SOx forms when a refinery burns sulfur-laden fuel in furnaces and boilers. The SOx can be removed from the fuel before it is burned, or it can be captured after the fuel is burned. Either method requires an investment in capital equipment. Alternatively, a refinery may purchase low-sulfur fuel or natural gas to fire its furnaces and boilers, and these fuels cost more than the sulfur laden fuels. This approach to the elimination of SOx increases operating costs, and these operating costs vary directly with the output of the refinery. Thus a pollution prevention expenditure can either affect capital costs or it can impact operating costs. Managers should choose the method that has the least negative or the most positive impact on profits.

▸ Pollution and Profits

There is some disagreement about the relation between pollution and profits. Some managers believe that profits decline as pollution goes down because of the high cost of cleaning up effluent discharged by an operation. With this view, profits and pollution rise and fall together. In contrast, other managers, such as those at Hyde Tool, argue that pollution reduction increases profits. Hyde Tool reduced its purchases of water from 27 million gallons per year to 5 million gallons per year; this reduced the cost of water purchases by $29,000 per year and reduced its sewer charges by $43,000 per year.[7] Managers at this company argue that pollution reduction increases profits.

These two views are summarized in the following list of alternative actions related to a "compliance" versus a "prevention" approach to pollution:

Compliance	Prevention
End of pipe cleanup	Source reduction of pollution
Control = business cost	Prevention = business investment
Escalating compliance cost	Cost avoidance
Reactive orientation	Pro-active orientation

---

[7] DeVries, Douglas, "Yankee Thrift as Pollution Prevention at Hyde Manufacturing," *EPA Journal* (July-September, 1993), pp. 17-18.

Companies that follow a prevention approach to pollution attempt to take charge of their destiny by completely avoiding the regulatory environment. These companies actively manage their strategic development instead of allowing some environmental control agency to dictate the company's future.
The two graphs following demonstrate these two views of dealing with pollution.

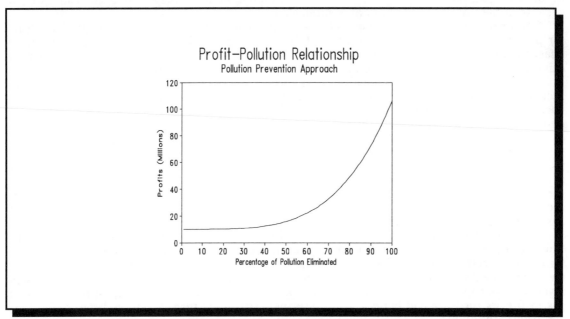

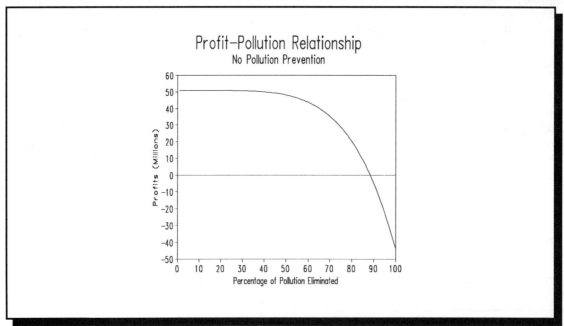

The bottom graph illustrates the prevailing view that reducing pollution causes profits to decline. This view assumes that pollution elimination means cleaning up pollutants after they have been produced. In contrast, the graph on the top represents the view of managers who assume that pollution can be prevented and that prevention of pollution not only costs less, but can even increase profits. Managers who follow this viewpoint use pollution prevention to increase profits, i.e., they make pollution prevention an integral part of their profit planning activities. This view is clearly articulated by Frank P. Popoff, CEO of Dow Chemical:[8]

"Success truly belongs, I believe, to those companies that not only comply with environmental standards, whether mandated or self-imposed, but do it more efficiently and effectively than others. If they conserve energy more effectively, for example, or if they deal with waste more efficiently through internal recycling or on-site disposal, they will ultimately reduce cost. I believe such companies will always have a competitive advantage . . ."

► Reducing Pollution Pays Dividends

An example of a company that increased profits by reducing pollution is Ciba-Geigy Limited. In its *Corporate Environmental Report 1992*,[9] Ciba-Geigy describes how it spent approximately $100 million at a Swiss facility to build a plant that provides on-site incineration to dispose of waste solvents. Ciba originally paid another company to do the incineration; now it does the incineration itself in a plant that generates 33% of the electricity and 90% of the steam for the Swiss facility. As a result, the plant buys 40,000 fewer barrels of oil each year with a resulting reduction in annual cash outflow of approximately $600,000.

In its Lampertheim facility in Germany, Ciba invested $4.8 million to reclaim sulfuric acid from one of its major processes. The sulfuric acid used in the original process led to the formation of waste water full of sulfuric acid, which went through a treatment plant before eventual discharge into the River Rhine. Ciba developed a new process that requires no sulfuric acid, thereby eliminating the purchase of 1.4 metric tons of sulfuric acid for each ton of good product produced. For an annual output of 20,000 tons, the savings amount to a yearly reduction in production costs of approximately $1.5 million.

Dow Chemical, another example, worked to develop a process for recycling and improving the control of a reactant used to make agricultural products in one of its California plants. Traditionally, the company had incinerated the reactant after a single use, but a team of engineers and researchers developed a process that reduced consumption of the reactant by 80% through recovery and reuse. This process eliminated 2.5 million pounds of waste per year and reduced annual costs by $8 million from their previous level. At one of Dow's Michigan facilities a waste reduction team developed a process modification that enabled the company to recover methanol it had been sending to a waste treatment plant. The team reduced methanol waste by 660,000 pounds per year saving the company $59,500 annually.[10]

Finally, Holderbank, a Swiss-based worldwide cement manufacturer, implemented a program to reduce its use of energy. Energy costs make up almost half the production costs for producing cement, and environmentalists are concerned about energy usage. Managers at Holderbank decided to review their production processes and to establish a plan to reduce energy usage. Since the company already used state of the art equipment, it concentrated on work procedures and work

[8] Avila, Joseph A. and Bradley W. Whitehead, "What is Environmental Strategy?" *The McKinsey Quarterly* (October, 1993), p. 55.
[9] *Corporate Environmental Report 1992*, Ciba-Geigy Limited, Basle, Switzerland, 1992.
[10] Schmidheiny, Stephan, *Changing Course* (Cambridge, MA: The MIT Press, 1992). pp. 265-269.

organization. The first year of operation with new work procedures and organization reduced energy costs almost $900,000.[11]

▸ A Cautionary Note

A review of the above examples could mislead a manager into believing that all pollution prevention increases profits. However, real life is not so simple. In cases in which companies focus on waste elimination and the conversion of waste into usable products, significant profit improvements do occur as pollution levels decline. In other cases requiring the development of completely new technologies or different manufacturing processes to eliminate emissions of gases or chemicals, the profit payoff may be negative. In these cases companies may spend far more on pollution prevention than the benefits they receive.

So, what should managers do? First they should study their operations carefully to see if they can benefit from a waste reduction program. Many companies can generate significant profit improvements from such programs, and managers should study this option carefully before deciding the company cannot benefit from waste reduction programs through pollution prevention. After exhausting all benefits from this program, managers should consider the development of new technologies or new processes. Such an approach allows a firm to reap the benefits of pollution prevention before tackling the expensive process of developing new production methods or new technologies.

▸ POLLUTION PREVENTION ANALYSIS ◂

In the previous section we reviewed examples of companies that increased profits by reducing pollution. Some companies argue that creating production processes that generate no pollution provides even greater benefits. If a company produces no pollution, it does not have to pay to eliminate the pollutants. Additionally, absence of pollution means a company does not have to worry about violating pollution regulations. However, managers should carefully review the economics of pollution prevention before adopting this approach.

▸ A Capital Project With No Pollution Prevention Practices

Consider the following examples. The first example illustrates the cash flows for a new plant that generates one pound of waste for each pound of good product. In this case the company pays a disposal company $.02 per pound to properly dispose of the waste. Exhibit 18-1 shows the initial investment, the estimated annual sales, and the annual cash operating costs for the plant over its predicted ten year life.

This plant requires $160 million to build, and it has annual operating costs of $25 million. Notice the environmental related cash outflows for the project: the company must make an initial investment of $700,000 to obtain a permit to discharge the waste the plant will produce and to build a storage facility for the waste before it is picked up by the waste disposal company. In addition, the firm will spend $1.13 million each year to cover costs like the fee paid to the waste disposal company, personnel hired to handle the waste, environmental engineering fees, and added insurance.

---

[11] *Ibid.*, pp. 274-277.

Proposed Plant Investment
No Pollution Prevention Practices Used

Initial Plant Investment	$ 160,000,000
Annual Fixed Cash Operating Expenses	25,000,000
Estimated Annual Production (tons)	15,000
Margin Per Ton Produced	$ 4,000

Environmental Costs
One Time Cash Outlays:

Permit Fees	$ 150,000
Legal Costs Related to Permit	50,000
Investment in Waste Storage Facilities	500,000
Total One Time Outlay	$ 700,000

Annual Outlays:

Disposal Company Fee	$ 600,000
Personnel Dedicated to Waste Disposal	400,000
Fees to Environmental Engineering Firm	80,000
Insurance Cost Related to Waste Disposal	50,000
Total Annual Cash Outlays	$ 1,130,000

Cash Flow Analysis

Initial Cash Outlay

Initial Plant Investment	$ 160,000,000
Environmental Outlays	700,000
Total Cash Outlay to Start Plant	$ 160,700,000

Annual Cash Flows

Annual Cash Margin Generated		$ 60,000,000
Annual Cash Outflows:		
Operating Cash Outflows	$ 25,000,000	
Environmental Related Cash Outflows	1,130,000	26,130,000
Net Annual Cash Inflow (Before Taxes)		$ 33,870,000

Present Value of Cash Inflows	$ 169,985,693
Initial Cash Outlay to Start Plant	160,700,000
Net Present Value	$ 9,285,693

Exhibit 18-1

▸ *Capital Project With Zero Pollution*

With all the factors incorporated in Exhibit 18-1, the planned investment has a before tax net present value (using a discount rate of 15%) of $9.3 million, a worthwhile investment for the company to make. However, if the company builds a plant with zero waste, the numbers look even better as Exhibit 18-2 shows.

In the second example, the company decides to spend $1 million to develop a production process that generates no waste; so the plant causes no damage to the environment. This means the company needs no waste discharge permit, no waste storage facility, and no payments to a waste disposal firm.

Proposed Plant Investment
Plant Generates No Pollution
Cash Flow Analysis

Annual Cash Flows
Annual Cash Margin Generated . . . . $ 60,000,000
Annual Cash Outflows:
    Operating Cash Outflows . . . . $ 25,000,000
    Environmental Related Cash Outflows   0   25,000,000
Net Annual Cash Inflow (Before Taxes) . . . . $ 35,000,000

Present Value of Cash Inflows . . . . $ 175,656,902
Initial Cash Outlay to Start Plant   161,000,000
Net Present Value . . . . $ 14,656,902

Exhibit 18-2

Because of the elimination of all these cash outflows related to waste, the company improves the net present value of its investment by almost 50% from $9.3 million to $14.7 million. In this case the pollution prevention investment could have cost slightly more than $5 million without a reduction of the original net present value. Pollution prevention can pay.

▸ Capital Project With 10% Pollution

Although these two extremes illustrate how pollution prevention can pay, the results would be less dramatic if the company only eliminated 90% of the waste. In that case, the firm still must obtain a permit for the discharge, so it incurs the same $700,000 for the permit as before. However, it spends less on the annual disposal fee, and it needs less expensive storage facilities. These changes (presented in Exhibit 18-3) yield only a $3 million improvement in net present value over the initial analysis.

Since the company must still incur significant costs for the permit, storage, and personnel even with a big drop in the quantity of pollutants it generates, a less than 100% reduction in pollutants does not bring about big reductions in pollution related expenditures. Reducing that last 10% of pollution provides significant benefits to the company, but even a one percent level of pollution requires all the initial $700,000 outlay. Consequently, companies that plan to use a pollution elimination strategy should carefully weigh the front end costs to make sure they can reap the benefits of total elimination. Getting rid of most of the pollution may not make enough difference to make a project profitable.

▸ Pay Now or Pay Later

Consider another case. A company is considering building an ethylene plant near a river, and the plant will last fifteen years. The company can spend $600 million to build the plant now with zero discharge into the river, or it can spend $550 million with discharges into the river. However, past experience has shown the company that plants making discharges into rivers generate no concern until population grows in the neighborhood of the plant, and this increased population demands cleaner water. In these cases, the company usually has to spend $200 million to retrofit the plant to clean up the water. In this example, assume the managers estimate that they would have to

**Proposed Plant Investment
90% of Pollution Eliminated**

Cash Flow Analysis

Annual Cash Flows

Annual Cash Margin Generated		$ 60,000,000
Annual Cash Outflows:		
Operating Cash Outflows	$ 25,000,000	
Environmental Related Cash Outflows*	530,000	25,530,000
Net Annual Cash Inflow (Before Taxes)		$ 34,470,000
Present Value of Cash Inflows		$172,996,955
Initial Cash Outlay to Start Plant		160,700,000
Net Present Value		$ 12,296,955
Original Net Present Value		9,285,693
Improvement in Net Present Value		$ 3,011,262
*Annual Outlays:		
Disposal Company Fee		$ 300,000
Personnel Dedicated to Waste Disposal		100,000
Fees to Environmental Engineering Firm		80,000
Insurance Cost Related to Waste Disposal		50,000
Total Annual Cash Outlays		$ 530,000

Exhibit 18-3

spend $200 million in 10 years for a water treatment plant to clean up the discharges from the ethylene plant. What should the managers do?

The following analysis illustrates how to evaluate the cash flow impact of these alternatives.

Project outlay with zero discharge	$ 600
Project outlay with discharge into river	550
Added cash outflow for zero discharge	$ 50
Present value of $200 million expended in	
10 years discounted at an annual rate of 12%	64
Long term present value impact of building	
the plant with discharges into the river	$ (14)

In this case the company's stockholders are better off if the company builds the ethylene plant with zero discharge because the present value of the $200 million spent ten years from now is greater than the added $50 million the company must spend now to produce zero discharge.

Evaluating possible environmental expenditures over the total life of a project allows managers to assess the financial impact on the firm of such expenditures. With the future cost of environmental expenditures continually rising, managers are wise to consider their impact when they build a plant instead of waiting until some regulation or, worse yet, some environmental disaster requires the company to expend hundreds of millions to clean up a problem.

► Break-Even Analysis of Pollution Expenditures

Many managers make pollution expenditures that are far less than $600 million, and for many of these smaller expenditures cost-volume-profit analysis provides a useful analytical tool. In the next few paragraphs we illustrate some of these applications.

Safety, Inc. Safety, Inc., manufactures safety screens and other devices for police cars and service vehicles. The small, family owned business generates sales of $60 million per year and produces an after tax (40% tax rate) profit of $2.4 million in most years. Variable costs equal 60% of sales, and annual fixed costs equal $20 million.

The company is evaluating a proposal to install equipment to recycle cleaning fluids and paints. The new equipment will increase annual fixed costs by $400,000, and will decrease variable costs from 60% of sales to 58% of sales. Should Safety, Inc., invest in the change? We will analyze the proposal assuming sales remain at $60 million.

Increase in contribution margin ((42% - 40%) x $60 million) . . $ 1.2   million
Increase in annual fixed costs 0.4
Before tax profit increase . . . . $ 0.8

This change to a cleaner production process clearly pays for itself because before tax profits increase by $800 thousand. But what does this change do for the company's break-even point? The annual break-even point under the existing system is $50 million ($20 million / .4). However, with the changed cost structure the new annual break-even point is $48.6 million ($20.4 million / .42), a drop of $1.4 million. In this example, the change to a cleaner production environment reduced the company break-even point and increased its profitability.

Brown Brothers Printing. Brown Brothers Printing uses large quantities of isopropyl alcohol in mixing the inks it uses to print paperboard cartons for its customers. The company is considering switching to a system that would completely eliminate the need for isopropyl alcohol in its ink solutions. To make this process change, company managers estimate annual company fixed costs will increase $180,000. Because the company only generates annual sales of $30 million, the president wonders how much sales will have to increase to cover this additional fixed cost if variable costs remain at 60% of sales.

Since the contribution margin is 40%, the company accountant quickly arrives at an answer of $450,000 ($180,000 / .40). The president thinks it would be easy to increase sales this amount, but he wants additional analyses. "How much would our contribution margin percentage have to increase to cover the added fixed costs?" asks the president. The accountant quickly sets up the following equation:

$$\$180,000 = Percentage\ change\ x\ \$30,000,000$$

Rearranging the terms provides this formulation of the equation.

$$Percentage\ Change\ =\ \frac{\$180,000}{\$30,000,000}$$
$$=\ .6\%$$

Since the variable costs need change less than 1% to cover the $180,000 increase in fixed cost, the accountant decides to prepare a comparative analysis of the annual cost of chemicals used to mix ink under the current and the proposed systems.

	Current System	New System
Isopropyl	$ 63,000	$ 0
Alkaless R	23,000	16,000
Hi-Tech Solution	65,000	15,000
Total costs	$ 151,000	$ 31,000

A comparison of the current annual cost of $151,000 with the changed system of $31,000 indicates the company would reduce variable costs by $120,000 per year, or a percentage of .40% ($120,000 / $30,000,000) of current sales. With the new contribution margin percentage (40.40%) the company need generate additional sales of only $445,545 ($180,000 / .4040) instead of the $450,000 ($180,000 / .4) required if the variable cost percentage remains constant. Because the president feels the company can easily increase sales by $1 million per year as indicated above, this analysis suggests the expenditure to change the production process is worthwhile.

As these two illustrations demonstrate, cost-volume-profit analysis can be a useful tool for evaluating expenditures on pollution prevention activities. We now turn our attention to the tracking of pollution expenditures.

▸ TRACKING POLLUTION COSTS ◂

Keeping track of pollution costs requires the same approach accountants use to accumulate data on any cost, i.e., the creation of a suitable coding system. To illustrate the structure of a code that enables a firm to capture environmental cost data, we describe the system at Ontario Hydro, a Canadian utility. Ontario Hydro has developed a data architecture for its management information system that allows it to collect data relevant for operating the company, and one of the variables management considers critical is information on environmental costs.[12]

▸ Data Structure

The data structure the company uses is illustrated on the next page.

Financial view. This data structure allows accountants to combine nonfinancial data such as quantities of materials or hours used, customer satisfaction measures, and project progress with financial data to give managers a relatively complete view of operations. The following comments consider three views of the data structure beginning with the dimension that includes the primary classification for both the financial and the operating information managers need.

Financial Account. This part of the data element represents the traditional general ledger accounts used for producing financial statements for external users.

Responsibility center. This segment of the code identifies the organizational entity responsible for the delivery of a product or service. Ontario Hydro uses this to identify cost centers, profit centers, and strategic business units as well as to designate subsidiary companies.

Service Unit. The company uses this field primarily to identify the originating and receiving units for internal transactions between divisions or cost centers. Transfer price information is collected in this field.

Resource Type. Accountants use this field to capture information on the types of resources used in performing work. For example, the field identifies the type of labor, kind of machine, or type of equipment used. The company also uses this field sometimes to further identify revenue streams by type of revenue such as revenue from large commercial users versus revenue generated by sales to governmental entities.

---

[12] Gosling, D.H., "Data Architecture: A Blueprint For Managing Your Business," *CMA Magazine* (October, 1993), pp. 17-23.

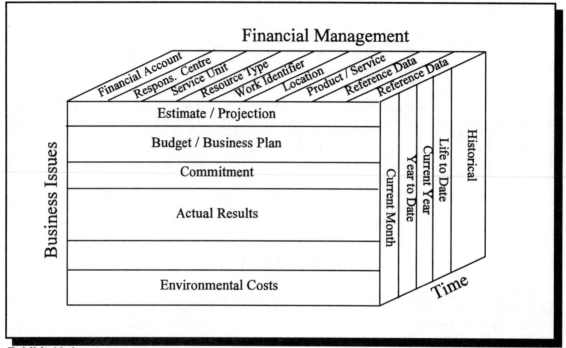

Exhibit 18-4

Work Identifier. The work identifier field enables the company to track information on individual projects such as construction projects, large maintenance projects, or power distribution expansion projects.

Location. This field identifies the geographic location of the element. Data collected by this field allows the company to track costs by individual building, individual work location, and individual city or province.

Product/service. Accountants use this field to identify the product or service involved in the transaction.

Business issues. The next view reflects business issues important to management. This view progresses from estimates and projections through actual results. In Exhibit 18-4 one slice of the actual results includes environmental cost data. Each transaction that affects environmental costs receives a code that identifies it as being a part of this slice of the information system. Ontario Hydro includes not only internal environmental costs but also data on externalities. Managers can review this data by location, by responsibility unit, or by individual expense item. This enables managers to review environmental cost from a number of perspectives.

Time dimension. The third dimension of the data reflects the traditional time slice of the information described by the other two dimensions. That is, managers can summarize information for any combination of data elements and views by date or time period.

Capturing environmental cost information, then, requires a code structure with the capability to track and record environmental cost as it is incurred. In addition, the Ontario Hydro system allows managers to input externalities not normally captured by the accounting system so these externalities are available to managers for analysis.

► EXTERNAL REPORTING OF ENVIRONMENTAL INFORMATION—THE SEC ◄

The SEC disclosure requirements have a significant impact on the reporting of environmental costs. Regulation S-K and SEC Releases govern how companies disclose the financial impact of environmentally related issues. These requirements govern how companies report liabilities for environmental cleanup and related remediation costs, and liabilities incurred to remain in compliance with increasingly stringent regulatory rules.

A cleanup liability arises whenever the U.S. Environmental Protection Agency (EPA) identifies a firm as liable for cleaning up a "superfund" site. Under the law governing these sites, a company can become a potentially responsible party if it currently owns or operates a site identified by the EPA, if it was a former owner of such a site, if it generated hazardous wastes that were dumped at the site, or if it transported hazardous substances to the site. The EPA can impose a penalty on a company that falls into any of these categories regardless of who is at fault. In fact, one company can be forced to pay the total cost of the cleanup even if many others were involved in creating the contamination. The company that pays for the cleanup is expected to seek compensation from the other companies involved. Thus the potential liability for superfund site cleanup can be very large.

The difficulty of estimating this liability varies from one case to another. For example, assume a company has been in operation for 50 years at five locations scattered throughout the U.S. and that it always disposed of any waste on the property where the waste was generated. The company can assess the significance of the waste buried at each location, its probability of falling under the superfund designation, and the estimated cost of cleaning up the site. Assume such an analysis produces the following table.

Estimated Liability for Superfund Cleanup

Location	Probability	Estimated Cost	Expected Value
Texas City, Texas	0.8	$ 50,000,000	$ 40,000,000
Phoenix, Arizona	0.5	30,000,000	15,000,000
Detroit, Michigan	0.7	40,000,000	28,000,000
Gary, Indiana	0.4	10,000,000	4,000,000
Newark, New Jersey	0.3	35,000,000	10,500,000
Total Estimated Liability			$ 97,500,000

Exhibit 18-5

If this company usually generates an annual profit of $35 million, this amount is material, and the company must report the estimated liability in its reports to the SEC. This may take the form of a paragraph in management's discussion of operations.

For the case in which the company does not control all its waste sites, the process of estimating liability becomes much more complex. Remember that sending one load of a hazardous waste to a site makes the company liable for the entire cleanup, even if the load was sent to the site twenty years ago and the company has had an exemplary environmental record for the past fifteen years. In such cases, the SEC requires companies to make a reasonable estimate of the possible future costs for reporting purposes. Obviously, in such cases, the definition of reasonable is much more subjective than usual.

▸ SUMMARY ◂

Environmental costs can represent significant amounts for companies operating today. The costs of cleaning up waste, the cost of building waste prevention processes, and the cost of developing environmentally friendly products can reach astronomical amounts. However, pollution prevention expenditures can add to profits for those firms that study the profit potential of waste and pollution elimination. Spending money to build a plant with zero waste can increase the net present value of the proposed expenditure as compared to a plant that does produce waste. The elimination of packaging for products can not only reduce the waste stream but can also increase profits because of lower expenditures on packaging materials. Accountants, then, should help managers evaluate the profit impact of pollution prevention expenditures to assure that companies make profit enhancing decisions when they consider pollution expenditures.

▸ QUESTIONS ◂

18-1. Name and define four types of environmental costs.

18-2. If your household paid $20 per month in 1993 for garbage pickup service, how much will you pay in 2003 if prices for home garbage pickup increase at the same rate as in the 1983-1993 period?

18-3. How might an oil refinery earn additional profits by reducing pollution?

18-4. "Increasing pollution always increases profits." State whether you agree or disagree, and provide examples to support your position.

18-5. How does a compliance approach to pollution control differ from a prevention approach?

18-6. What kind of financial advantages does a company gain from building a plant that generates zero pollution (at a relatively high cost) versus building one that pollutes (at a relatively low cost) which the company will retrofit later?

18-7. How can expenditures on pollution prevention impact the net present value of a project?

18-8. How can a company use its information system to capture data on environmental costs?

18-9. How does the "superfund" legislation impact the external financial statements for a company?

18-10. Why should executives concern themselves with the reporting of environmental costs to stockholders and other outsiders?

18-11. Describe a code structure for a firm that decides to capture information about environmental costs.

▸ EXERCISES ◂

18-12. Evaluation of Delayed Payment to Fix Pollution.
A chemical company can build a plant for $500 million now and retrofit it in 20 years for $200 million to clean up pollution, or it can spend $650 million now for a plant that produces no pollution. Ignore tax consequences and non financial considerations when answering this question.

Required:

a. If the company uses a discount rate of 12% for its capital investment projects, how much should the company spend to build its plant now, i.e., $500 million or $650 million?
b. At what discount rate would managers be indifferent between the two plants?

18-13. Water Recycling Evaluation.
A plant has been purchasing water from the local utility at a price of 6.5 cents per 100 gallons. The company pays a sewage charge based on the volume of water it pours in the sewerage system at 1 cent per 100 gallons. The company uses 150 million gallons of water annually with its present manufacturing system.

An engineer has suggested that the company spend $100,000 for some valves and pipes so the plant can recycle 80% of the water now flowing through the system. This would enable the company to purchase only 20% of the water volume it now uses.

Required:

a. Should the company invest the $100,000 for the pipes and valves? Give numerical calculations to support your answer.
b. If the price charged for water drops to one half the current price and the sewer charge doubles, should the company make the investment? Why? Provide numerical support for your answer.

18-14. Profit Impact of Water Reuse in Glue Mixing.

Ripley's Manufacturing builds wooden parts for overhead garage doors at its central Washington plant where it employs 100 people. The company processes 15 million board feet of lumber annually. The production processes involve drying, milling, joining, and gluing wood parts to form the door parts.

Managers are considering a new process for disposing of glue washdown waste water. Since Ripley uses water based glues in the production process, employees have suggested that the company simply use the waste water created from washing excess glue from the door parts to mix new batches of glue. To make this change, the company would have to spend $22,000 for containers and piping systems.

If Ripley makes the change it will reduce expenditures on permit fees by $1,000 per year, on sewer fees by $250 per month, on landfill disposal fees by $2,000 per year, and on pretreatment costs by $9,000 per year. Use a discount rate of 15% for present value calculations, a life of five years, and ignore tax effects in your calculations.

Required:

a. Should the company make the change? Provide numerical analyses to support your answer.
b. Compute the payback period for this investment.
c. Assume the company will write off this investment over five years. How much will annual before tax-profit change because of this investment?

► PROBLEMS AND CASES ◄

18-15. Water Recycling at a Citrus Plant.

Orange Growers, Inc., runs a packing house for processing citrus fruits like oranges, grapefruits, and tangerines for shipment to customers throughout the U.S. In the production process the fruit is first disinfected with a chlorinated water spray, and then washed with detergents and wetting agents to remove pesticides, residues, sooty mold, and dirt. Workers then apply a soluble red color additive to accentuate an orange color appearance to the actual yellow color of the fruit. Following this process they coat the fruit skin with an FDA food grade wax emulsion to lessen dehydration and prevent spoilage during shipment. Finally, workers add a fungicide to the fruit to retard spoilage.

All this processing of the fruit generates waste water that contains residuals of cleaning chemicals, wax and oil, sand, sooty mold, and fruit debris (leaves and twigs). On a typical day Orange Growers uses 15,000 gallons of water, and the local city waste water treatment plant has expressed concerns about the levels of the total Kjeldahl nitrogen (TKN), the chemical oxygen demand (COD), and the levels of oil, grease and copper in the water it receives from the plant. Orange Growers pays $5 per thousand gallons for water, and it expects this price to rise by 10% per year for the next five years.

An engineering firm suggested the company consider a system that consists of coagulation, flocculation, and primary sedimentation processes. In operation this system would use a 10,000 gallon clarifier (a settling tank), a septic tank, and a drain field. Construction of this system would cost $25,000, and would increase annual cash operating expenses by $8,000 per year. However, daily water purchases would drop to 1,000 gallons per day and sewer charges would decline to $600 per month from the current level of $750.

Required:

a. Compute the annual cash flows resulting from this project for the first five years. Assume the plant operates 300 days per year.

b. Compute the before tax net present value for this project using a discount rate of 15%. Assume a 10 year life for the new system.

c. Based on the calculations you performed for the first two parts of this question, do you think Orange Growers should invest in the new water system?

18-16. Evaluation of Alternative Pollution Levels.

Managers at Belmont, Inc., are considering building a plant that will produce no pollution. The company would have to spend $210 million to build the plant although it could build a plant with a normal level of pollution for only $200 million. With this polluting plant the company would incur a cost of five cents per pound to dispose of the waste generated by the plant. Other costs and investments related to the polluting plant are set out below.

Initial Plant Investment	$ 200,000,000
Annual Fixed Cash Operating Expenses	35,000,000
Estimated Annual Production (tons)	20,000
Margin Per Ton Produced	$ 4,000
Environmental Costs	
One Time Cash Outlays:	
Permit Fees	$ 150,000
Legal Costs Related to Permit	50,000
Investment in Waste Storage Facilities	200,000
Total One Time Outlay	$ 400,000
Annual Outlays:	
Disposal Company Fee	$ 2,000,000
Personnel Dedicated to Waste Disposal	320,000
Fees to Environmental Engineering Firm	50,000
Total Annual Cash Outlays	$ 2,370,000

Required:

a. Compute the net present value of this investment assuming the company builds the plant which generates a normal amount of pollution. Use a discount rate of 15%, a life of ten years, and ignore tax effects.

   b. Compute the net present value of the investment if the firm decides to build a plant that produces no pollution. Use a discount rate of 15%, and ignore taxes.

   c. Assume the firm reduces waste by 90%, reduces the annual cash outflow for personnel dedicated to waste disposal to $120,000, and reduces the annual fees to the engineering firm to $10,000. Compute the net present value of the investment for a discount rate of 15%. Ignore tax effects.

   d. Which alternative should the company choose from the two presented above? Why?

18-17. **Environmental Cost Analysis in a Jewelry Firm.**

   Watkins Jewelry manufactures men and women's jewelry that it sells under its own label and under the names of major retailers. Its plant in Southern Indiana employs 500 people, and annual sales exceed $60 million. The following income statement for the past year gives an idea of the cost structure of the firm. All amounts are in thousands.

Watkins, Inc.
Income Statement (in Thousands)
For the Year 20X5

Sales	$ 62,500
Variable production costs	29,500
Margin	$ 33,000
Operating Costs:	
Labor costs	$ 3,600
Plant costs	11,250
Marketing costs	8,500
Administrative costs	4,500
Total operating costs	$ 27,850
Before tax income	$ 5,150
Income taxes	1,854
Net Income	$ 3,296

   Although the jewelry designs are constantly changing, the metals Watkins uses for the jewelry remain the same. Workers stamp, fold or plate the metal using the specified designs for the jewelry. The plant produces two jewelry finishes—white and yellow. The white finishes include silver plating, rhodium finishes, and tin-based finishes. Watkins designers and manufacturing engineers have found silver the most desirable metal for the white finishes. However, because silver tarnishes when exposed to air, workers dip silver plated pieces in lacquer prior to finishing, packaging and shipment. Workers string the silver pieces on racks before passing them through a dip lacquering system. They then unstring the jewelry from the racks and strip the lacquer from the racks with ethyl acetate. The company now uses the ethyl acetate until it is exhausted and then hires a waste disposal firm to dispose of the material as a hazardous waste.

   The company president asked you to prepare an analysis of the purchase of an ethyl acetate recovery still that would allow Watkins to minimize the hazardous waste. This recovery still would allow the company to reuse the ethyl acetate several times before producing any hazardous waste. Your analysis indicates the variable costs for last year would have been only $26,450 if this recovery still had been in use and that Plant Costs would have been $13,285 instead of $11,250.

Required:

a. Compute the break-even point for the company assuming it continues with current operations, and compute the break-even point if Watkins installs the recovery still. Why do the two amounts differ?

b. Assume sales drop to $40 million. Which alternative (current system or use of recovery still) provides the higher net income?

c. Suppose sales increase by $10 million, which alternative will provide the higher net income for the company?

18-18. Pollution Prevention Investment at a Manufacturing Firm.[13]

Aluminum Fabricating, a subsidiary of Lighting, Inc., manufactures aluminum reflectors for track and recessed lighting products.

The company has a plant located in Massachusetts with 400,000 square feet of space in four buildings, and the plant generates annual sales of over $100 million. The Massachusetts plant employs 500 people, and 450 of these work in production jobs.

The manufacturing process involves six processes:

1. Workers cut sheet aluminum to form circles of varying diameters depending upon the product in which they will be used.
2. Next, the workers pass the parts to a Hydroform machine that presses the parts into a reflector shape. The reflectors acquire a thin oil coating in this step.
3. A worker loads the reflectors into baskets for processing in a vapor degreaser that washes, drains, rinses, and drains a second time to get the parts ready for the next step.
4. In step four workers buff the parts to give them a highly polished finish that reflects light.
5. In step five workers send the polished parts either to metal plating where they pass through a plating bath or to a painting process in which robots spray paint on the parts before they go into an oven for drying.
6. Finally, workers pack the reflectors for inventory storage or for shipment to customers.

This manufacturing process produces pollutants at two points: The vapor degreaser uses trichlorethylene (TCE), and the paint spray booth releases toxic air emissions that create breathing hazards for employees. The plant manager decided to attack both these pollution problems by replacing one degreaser with an aqueous solution model, by replacing the other with a combination degreaser/electrostatic powder coater unit (this uses a powder paint instead of a liquid paint), and by substituting a non petroleum-based oil for the petroleum oil now used in the Hydroform.

In 1990, the plant used 74 tons of TCE, and only 7 tons were removed and recycled by the plant. With the new equipment, the plant manager estimated that annual usage of TCE would drop to only 15 tons in 1991 and zero for the years after that. After considering several proposals from different equipment manufacturers, the plant manager selected one for detailed analysis. Total investment for this proposal is set forth below.

The manufacturer whose equipment the plant manager is considering prepared the following analyses as a part of the proposal. The salesperson for the firm said they always

[13] Adapted from "Lightolier, Inc., Fall River Division" published by the Massachusetts Office of Technical Assistance, Boston, MA 02202. (July, 1991).

provide these analyses for their customers. The company selling this machine will provide a maintenance contract that includes all parts and labor for $10,000 per year for the first five years and $12,000 per year for the last five years of the life of the machine. The salesperson did not include the cost of the maintenance contract in the analyses in the following three schedules.

Machine (including installation)	$ 117,250
Freight (estimated)	3,000
Waste water treatment	11,215
Rack/hanger cost (est.)	5,000
Total capital expenditures	136,465
Related expenses	14,900
Working capital	4,000
Total project expenditures	$ 155,365

Schedule I
In-Process Washing Machine
Incremental Impact on Operations - Net Profit

Period	Cost of Solvent	Solvent Disposal	Project Depreciation	Detergent Chemical Cost	Earnings Before Taxes	Net Profit
1990	$ 31,104	$ 3,120	$ 13,467	$ 10,500	$ 10,257	$ 6,257
1991	32,659	3,276	13,467	11,025	11,443	6,980
1992	34,292	3,440	13,467	11,576	12,689	7,740
1993	36,007	3,612	13,467	12,155	13,996	8,538
1994	37,907	3,792	13,467	12,763	15,370	9,375
1995	39,697	3,982	13,467	13,401	16,812	10,255
1996	41,682	4,181	13,467	14,071	18,325	11,179
1997	43,766	4,390	13,467	14,775	19,915	12,148
1998	45,955	4,610	13,467	15,513	21,584	13,166
1999	48,253	4,840	13,467	16,289	23,337	14,235
Total	$391,322	$ 39,243	$134,670	$132,068	$163,728	$99,873
Average	$ 39,122		$ 13,467		$ 16,373	$ 9,987

Note: The salesperson who prepared this analysis used a tax rate of 39% to compute the incremental net profit after taxes. For example, the tax on $10,257 at 39% is $4,000, so the net profit after taxes is $6,257 ($10,257 - $4,000). The salesperson also used a ten year life for the equipment to compute the straight line annual depreciation assuming no salvage value. The earnings increment before taxes consists of the current cost of solvent plus the cost of its disposal minus the new chemical cost plus depreciation. For example, in 1990, the company will spend $34,224 ($31,104 + $3,120) minus $23,967 ($13,467 + $10,500) to arrive at $10,257 as earnings before tax.

Schedule II
Incremental Impact on Operations - Capital Employed

Period	Beginning	Ending	Average	Average Capital Employed	Net Profit	Return on Capital Employed
1990	$ 136,465	$ 122,998	$ 129,732	$ 129,732	$ 6,257	4.8%
1991	122,998	109,531	116,265	116,265	6,980	6.0%
1992	109,531	96,064	102,798	102,798	7,740	7.5%
1993	96,064	82,597	89,331	89,331	8,538	9.6%
1994	82,597	69,130	75,864	75,864	9,375	12.4%
1995	69,130	55,663	62,397	62,397	10,255	16.4%
1996	55,663	42,196	48,930	48,930	11,179	22.8%
1997	42,196	28,729	35,463	35,463	12,148	34.3%
1998	28,729	15,262	21,996	21,996	13,166	59.9%
1999	15,262	1,795	8,529	8,529	14,235	166.9%
Total	$ 758,635	$ 623,965	$ 691,300	$ 691,305	$ 99,873	14.4%
Average	$ 75,864	$ 62,397	$ 69,130	$ 69,131	$ 9,987	14.4%

Schedule III
Incremental Impact on Operations - Cash Flow

Period	Net Profit	Depr.	Total Fund Provided	Capital Expenditures	Total Fund Applied	Net Cash Surplus/ Required	Cum. Cash Surp (Required)
1990	$ 6,257	$ 13,467	$ 19,724	$ 136,465	$ 136,465	($116,741)	($116,741)
1991	6,980	13,467	20,447		0	20,447	(96,294)
1992	7,740	13,467	21,207		0	21,207	(75,087)
1993	8,539	13,467	22,005		0	22,005	(53,082)
1994	49,375	13,467	22,842		0	22,842	(30,240)
1995	10,255	13,467	23,722		0	23,722	(6,518)
1996	11,179	13,467	24,646		0	24,646	18,128
1997	12,148	13,467	25,615		0	25,615	43,743
1998	13,166	13,467	26,633		0	26,633	70,376
1999	14,235	13,467	27,702		0	27,702	98,078
Total	$ 99,874	$ 134,670	$ 234,543	$ 136,465	$ 136,465		
Average	$ 19,975	$ 13,467	$ 46,909	$ 136,465			

The plant manager asked you to gather some additional information about the current costs of operating the existing equipment. You discovered the plant spends $20,000 per year for a maintenance contract for the 16 year old machine the plant now uses, and discussions with plant personnel indicated this will probably increase because the walls of the tanks in the current machine are badly corroded. Also you will spend at least $25,000 annually on parts for repairs to the current machine. The old equipment has a zero book value, and the scrap value of the equipment equals the cost of removing it.

Required:

a. The plant manager asks you to recalculate the numbers provided by the salesperson for the new piece of equipment. "Never trust anybody else's numbers" is the philosophy of the plant manager. Correct any mistakes, if any, you find in the schedules.

b. Prepare a schedule of annual cash flows you can use to evaluate the suitability of this project.

c. Compute the net present value of this project using a discount rate of 15%

d. Should the company make the investment if it uses a discount rate of 20%? Explain.

18-19. Environmental Expenditures at a Paper Company.[14]

Southern Paper operates a plant near Birmingham, Alabama, that employs 900 people in its research facility, corporate office, and operating plant. Its plant does coating, laminating and conversion for a variety of film, paper, and foil substrates that are used in electronics, graphic arts, publishing, engineering, and instant photography.

Southern produces the majority of colored, coated papers in two steps: First workers coat the paper with a pigmented base coat, consisting of a variety of solvents, nitrocellulose, clay, calcium carbonate, and, in approximately half the colored grades, a small amount of lead, chromium, and cadmium-based pigments. In this first step workers run the base-coated paper through a dryer that dries most of the solvent, and the remaining materials "set" on the paper. During the second step workers coat the paper with a top coat of solvent and nitrocellulose; they then dry the paper again and roll it on a reel where it awaits conversion.

Control systems collect the vaporized solvent from the first two dryers and send it to a carbon filter bed that absorbs the vapors. Another process distills the vapors and separates them into different types of solvents that are reused for mixing chemicals and for washing equipment. The distillation process produces residual solvents, coating pigments and other impurities that are loaded into drums. The company produces 2,220 drums of this waste per year; the company transports the barrels to an off site location and burns the waste.

Volatile organic compounds (VOCs) are emitted at three points in the current process, and these compounds create a health hazard for the employees and the surrounding community. Consequently, Southern management is evaluating plans to modify its plant to substitute a water based solution for solvents currently used. These aqueous based solutions consist of water, acrylic latex resin, and a small amount of ammonia and solvent, and the pigments are free of heavy metals. However, water based coatings have a shorter shelf life than the solvent based coatings (three months versus five years) because they are vulnerable to microbiological contamination. The mill expects that 100 drums of aqueous coating will spoil each year. The purchase price of a drum of aqueous coating is $456 and it costs Southern $180 to dispose of a drum of spoiled solution. Also, aqueous coatings can freeze in cold weather, so the mill will install a new steam heating system in the coating storage area that will cost $5,500 annually to operate.

The aqueous system will reduce emissions of VOCs from the coating process by 209 tons per year, and approximately 810 fewer drums of hazardous still bottoms will be generated. This will drop the annual cost of drum handling from $100,000 to $50,000 per year and drum storage to $2,000 per year from $10,000. Transportation of drums will also drop from $90,000 annually to $15,000. Other costs for the two systems are set out below.

[14] Adapted from *Total Cost Assessment: Accelerating Industrial Pollution Prevention through Innovative Project Financial Analysis* United States Environmental Protection Agency, Washington, D.C. May, 1992, pp. 90-124.

Investment for the Aqueous/Heavy Metal-Free Conversion

Initial investment
Purchased Equipment:

Process Equipment	$ 91,740
Waste Water Treatment System	163,000
Coater Upgrade	150,000
Steam Utility Connection	30,000

Engineering Services

Planning	110,500
Engineering	85,410
Total depreciable investment	$ 630,650
Startup Costs—Materials and Labor	23,159
Total initial outlay	$ 653,809

Annual operating costs for the two systems

	Present System	New System
Annual operating costs	$ 4,970,468	$ 4,829,594
Aqueous coating costs		
Spoilage (100 drums @ $456)		45,600
Disposal of spoiled drums		18,000
Annual operating costs of steam heat		5,500
Drum handling costs		
Drum handling	100,000	50,000
Drum storage	10,000	2,000
Transportation of drums	90,000	15,000
Total annual operating costs	$ 5,170,468	$ 4,965,694

Southern Paper uses the straight line method of depreciation and it pays a corporate income tax rate of 40%. For evaluating capital projects Southern uses a discount rate of 15%. Use a ten year life for this project when computing depreciation and cash flows.

Required:

a. Compute the change in annual waste management costs from the existing system to the new system.

b. Compute the net present value and the payback period for this project.

c. Assume Southern plans to reduce total annual waste management costs by one-tenth each year until they reach zero in year 11 and that its regulatory costs will also drop to zero by year 11. To bring about this reduction, Southern will spend an additional $50,000 per year for the ten year period. Compute the new net present value and the payback period for this new set of circumstances.

d. How much could Southern spend annually to bring about the cost reductions described in question c and still have the same net present value you computed for question b?

INDEX

THE SONG
OF THE DODO

Island Biogeography
in an Age of Extinctions

———

DAVID QUAMMEN

Maps by Kris Ellingsen

PIMLICO

PIMLICO

An imprint of Random House
20 Vauxhall Bridge Road,
London SW1V 2SA

Random House Australia (Pty) Limited
20 Alfred Street, Milsons Point, Sydney
New South Wales 2061, Australia

Random House New Zealand Limited
18 Poland Road, Glenfield, Auckland 10, New Zealand

Random House South Africa (Pty) Limited
Isle of Houghton, Corner of Boundary Road & Carse O'Gowrie,
Houghton 2198, South Africa

Random House UK Ltd Reg. No. 954009

First published in the United Kingdom by Hutchinson 1996
Pimlico edition 1997

9 10

Papers used by Random House UK Limited are natural,
recyclable products made from wood grown in sustainable forests.
The manufacturing processes conform to the environmental
regulations of the country of origin

Printed and bound in Great Britain by
Antony Rowe Ltd, Chippenham, Wiltshire

ISBN: 978-0-7126-7333-4